THE USE OF NUCLEAR WEAPONS AND THE PROTECTION OF THE ENVIRONMENT DURING INTERNATIONAL ARMED CONFLICT

In 1996, the International Court of Justice delivered an Advisory Opinion on the legality of the use of nuclear weapons in which the Court stated that 'while the existing international law relating to the protection and safeguarding of the environment does not specifically prohibit the use of nuclear weapons it indicates important environmental factors that are properly to be taken into account in the context of the implementation of the principles and rules of the law applicable in armed conflict.'

The present work analyses this conclusion, focusing on the question of whether or not the use of nuclear weapons during international armed conflict would violate existing norms of public international law relating to the protection and safeguarding of the environment. Although the use of weaponry during armed conflict is usually related to the protection of individuals, the rapidly emerging appreciation of, and the worldwide realisation of the intrinsic value of, the natural environment as an indispensable asset for the continuation of life, including human life, on this planet, both for present and future generations, warrants a thorough and extensive examination of the question of the (il)legality of the employment of nuclear weapons from the point of view of international environmental protection law.

The book consists of two parts. Part I discusses the historical development and the effects of nuclear weapons; Part II discusses the protection of the environment during international armed conflict under *ius in bello, ius ad bellum* and *ius pacis*. Only then is it possible to assess the legality of the use of nuclear weapons under this particular set of rules.

Studies in International Law: Volume 18

Studies in International Law

Volume 1: Between Light and Shadow: The World Bank, the International Monetary Fund and International Human Rights Law
Mac Darrow

Volume 2: Toxics and Transnational Law: International and European Regulation of Toxic Substances as Legal Symbolism
Marc Pallemaerts

Volume 3: The Chapter VII Powers of the United Nations Security Council
Erika de Wet

Volume 4: Enforcing International Law Norms Against Terrorism
Edited by Andrea Bianchi

Volume 5: The Permanent International Criminal Court
Edited by Dominic McGoldrick, Peter Rowe and Eric Donnelly

Volume 6: Regional Organisations and the Development of Collective Security
Ademola Abass

Volume 7: Islamic State Practices, International Law and the Threat from Terrorism: A Critique of the 'Clash of Civilizations' in the New World Order
Javaid Rehman

Volume 8: Predictablity and Flexibility in the Law of Maritime Delimitation
Yoshifumi Tanaka

Volume 9: Biotechnology and International Law
Edited by Francesco Francioni and Tullio Scovazzi

Volume 10: The Development of Human Rights Law by the Judges of the International Court of Justice
Shiv Bedi

Volume 11: The Environmental Accountability of the World Bank to Third Party Non-State Actors
Alix Gowlland-Gualtieri

Volume 12: Transnational Corporations and Human Rights
Edited by Olivier De Schutter

Volume 13: Biotechnologies and International Human Rights
Edited by Francesco Francioni

Volume 14: Human Security and International Law
Barbara von Tigerstrom

Volume 15: The Arms Trade and International Law
Zeray Yihdego

Volume 16: Africa: Mapping New Boundaries in International Law
Edited by Jeremy Levitt

Volume 17: Forced Migration, Human Rights and Security
Edited by Jane McAdam

The Use of Nuclear Weapons and the Protection of the Environment during International Armed Conflict

Erik Koppe

·HART·
PUBLISHING

OXFORD AND PORTLAND, OREGON
2008

Published in North America (US and Canada) by
Hart Publishing
c/o International Specialized Book Services
920 NE 58th Avenue, Suite 300
Portland, OR 97213-3786
USA
Tel: +1-503-287-3093 or toll-free: (1)-800-944-6190
Fax: +1 503 280 8832
E-mail: orders@isbs.com
Website: www.isbs.com

Hart Publishing, 16C Worcester Place, Oxford, OX1 2JW
Telephone: +44 (0)1865 517530 Fax: +44(0)1865 510710
E-mail: mail@hartpub.co.uk
Website: http://www.hartpub.co.uk

British Library Cataloguing in Publication Data
Data Available

ISBN: 978-1-84113- 745-2

Typeset by Hope Services Ltd, Abingdon
Printed and bound in Great Britain by
TJ International Ltd, Padstow, Cornwall

Acknowledgments

This book could not have been written without the help and support of a number of people. First of all, I would like to thank my *promotor* Prof Dr Wil D Verwey for putting his trust in me when he undertook to supervise me for this study; for remaining confident in a positive outcome; and for making it possible for me to finish this project in Groningen. Wil, I am grateful for the fact that you gave me the liberty to carry out this research independently; that you were patient when I was late handing in my chapters; and that you reviewed my drafts critically and with great attention for detail. More importantly, however, I value your guidance and friendship over the last couple of years.

Secondly, I would like to thank my daily supervisor Dr André JJ de Hoogh for reviewing my chapters quickly and carefully, despite a heavy workload and a large number of responsibilities within the Department of International and Constitutional Law. André, I greatly appreciate your aid and comments. Your general knowledge of public international law has helped me out more than once and your dedication to the study of international law is exemplary.

Thirdly, I am honored that Prof Dr M Bothe, Prof Dr HHG Post, and Prof Dr N Schrijver were willing to take a seat on the Manuscript Committee and I am indebted to them for their willingness to read the manuscript during the summer.

And finally, I would like to thank my friends and family, in particular my parents Marnix and Kora Koppe, and my brother and sister, Manuel and Esther, for their love and support. Your faith, enthusiasm, and encouragements have been invaluable during the writing of this thesis!

Contents

Introduction

SINCE 1945, FEW developments have had such a profound impact on international relations, and few issues have drawn as much attention in public international law as nuclear weapons. Innumerable books, articles, resolutions, official statements, and memoranda have dealt with the status, function, and the (il)legality of the use and possession of this category of 'weapons of mass destruction',[1] and almost all of them agree that nuclear weapons are potentially the most destructive weapons ever invented. It is therefore surprising that so few rules of public international law have been adopted to regulate nuclear weapons.

The adoption of this limited number of rules does not stem from lack of interest on the side of the international community of states, however. On the contrary: in its very first Resolution, the United Nations General Assembly established an Atomic Energy Commission (AEC), which was supposed to make proposals, among other things, 'for the elimination from national armaments of atomic weapons and of all other major weapons adaptable to mass destruction'.[2] And in the 1950s, a number of

[1] The United Nations Conventional Armaments Commission defined weapons of mass destruction as including 'atomic explosive weapons, radioactive material weapons, lethal chemical and biological weapons, and any weapons developed in the future which have characteristics comparable in destructive effect to those of the atomic bomb or other weapons mentioned above.' Resolution of the Commission for Conventional Armaments, 12 Aug 1948, on the definition of armaments, para 1, at: <http://www.yale.edu/lawweb/avalon/decade/decad253.htm>.

[2] A/Res/1 (I), adopted unanimously on 24 Jan 1946, on the establishment of a commission to deal with the problems raised by the discovery of atomic energy. The AEC did not manage to table a unanimous proposal despite two far-reaching proposals from the United States (known as the Baruch Plan), and the Soviet Union (known as the Gromyko Plan). Both plans entailed the abolishment of nuclear weapons but differed as to the procedure to be followed. The United States proposed to destroy its existing stockpile after the establishment of an adequate system of control, whereas the Soviet Union would only agree to a system of supervision after the destruction of all existing nuclear weapons. The Soviet proposal stood therefore diametrically opposed to the American plan, and this fact—in combination with a deeply rooted mistrust of each other—doomed both proposals to failure. B Baruch, United States Representative to the AEC of the United Nations, *Control of Atomic Energy; United States Plan*, delivered at the opening session of the Commission, Jun 14, 1946, American Association for the United Nations, Inc, New York, NY, 1946; A Gromyko at the second meeting of the United Nations Atomic Energy Commission on 19 Jun 1946, as quoted in JL Nogee, *Soviet Policy Towards International Control of Atomic Energy*, University of Notre Dame Press, Notre Dame, IN, 1961, p 36.

far-reaching proposals were submitted for comprehensive or 'general and complete disarmament',[3] a phrase which subsequently returned like a mantra in almost every other disarmament or arms control proposal or agreement as the international community's ultimate goal.

Since nuclear disarmament did not appear feasible in the short-term, the focus of attention gradually shifted in the 1960s to a step-by-step approach. By setting more limited and less ambitious goals agreement was less difficult to achieve, and one hoped that these more moderate agreements would then become stepping-stones for more comprehensive ones. This approach became known as 'arms control' and was recognised in the US-Soviet Joint Statement of Agreed Principles[4] of 20 September 1961, also known as the McCloy-Zorin Statement. Paragraph 8 stipulated:

> States participating in the negotiations should seek to achieve and implement the widest possible agreement at the earliest possible date. Efforts should continue without interruption until agreement upon the total program has been achieved, and efforts to ensure early agreement on and implementation of measures of disarmament should be undertaken without prejudicing progress on agreement on the total program and in such a way that these measures would facilitate and form part of that program.

Most agreements that were subsequently concluded with respect to nuclear weapons may be qualified as arms control agreements.[5] They deal with horizontal[6] and vertical[7] non-proliferation, non-

[3] The idea of 'general and complete disarmament' was endorsed by the Soviet Union and the United States as well as by the General Assembly in 1959, by A/Res/1378 (XIV) adopted unanimously on 20 Nov 1959, on general and complete disarmament.

[4] Report of the United States and the Soviet Union to the Sixteenth General Assembly on the Results of the Bilateral Talks: Agreed Statement of Principles, Sep 20, 1961, in: TN Dupuy, GM Hammerman (Eds), *A Documentary History of Arms Control and Disarmament*, TN Dupuy Associates, Dunn Loring, VA, 1973, pp 470–2.

[5] For a recent and comprehensive study on the law of arms control, see G den Dekker, *The Law of Arms Control; International Supervision and Enforcement*, Martinus Nijhoff Publishers, The Hague, 2001.

[6] Horizontal non-proliferation intends to limit the spread of nuclear weapons and is primarily reflected in the Treaty on the Non-Proliferation of Nuclear Weapons, opened for signature on 1 Jul 1968, entered into force 5 Mar 1970, UNTS, Vol. 729, No 10485. Other agreements that reflected the concept of horizontal non-proliferation were the post-World War II peace treaties between the Allies and their former enemies, which prohibited the latter to manufacture or possess nuclear weapons.

[7] Vertical non-proliferation intends to put limits to the production, development and stockpiling of nuclear weapons in existing nuclear-weapon arsenals and is reflected in the Strategic Arms Limitation Talks between the United States and the Soviet Union which produced, among other things, the Interim Agreement between the United States of America and the Union of Soviet Socialist Republics on Certain Measures with respect to the Limitation of Strategic Offensive Arms, together with Protocol and Associated Documents, signed on 26 May 1972, entered into force on 3 Oct, 1972, UNTS, Vol 944, No 13445; and the Treaty between the United States of America and the Union of Soviet Socialist Republics on the Limitation of Strategic Offensive Arms, together with Protocol, Memorandum of Understanding, Joint Statement, and Associated Documents (SALT, also referred to as SALT II), signed on 18 Jun 1979, never entered into force, CD/28 of 27 Jun 1979 and CD/29 of 2 Jul 1979.

nuclearisation,[8] and nuclear testing.[9] Only the United States and the Soviet Union/Russian Federation concluded a number of disarmament agreements in which they agreed to actual reduction and elimination of nuclear warheads and certain nuclear weapon systems.[10]

Where most of these agreements regulate the possession of nuclear weapons and thereby fall under the law of peace, or *ius pacis*, no agreements have been concluded as to the actual use of nuclear weapons during armed conflict under *ius in bello*.[11] Although the United Nations General Assembly declared in 1961 that the use of nuclear weapons was not only illegal under public international law, but would also constitute a crime against mankind and civilisation,[12] and despite the fact that a large

[8] Non-nuclearisation aims to prohibit the presence of nuclear weapons in a particular zone, area, or country. Nuclear-weapon-free zones have been established in Latin America (1967), in the South Pacific (1985), South-East Asia (1995), and Africa (1996). In addition, nuclear weapons may not be deployed on Antarctica (1959), in outer space, on the moon, and on other celestial bodies (1967 and 1979) and on the deep seabed (1971). And the list of countries that have declared themselves nuclear-weapon-free includes Japan, Iceland, Spain, New Zealand, Mongolia, Denmark, Sweden and Norway, and the territory of the former German Democratic Republic.

[9] Regulation of nuclear testing is primarily regulated by the Treaty Banning Nuclear Weapon Tests in the Atmosphere, in Outer Space and Under Water, signed 5 Aug 1963, opened for signature on 8 Aug1963, entered into force on 10 Oct1963, UNTS, Vol 480, No 6964; Comprehensive Nuclear-Test-Ban Treaty, together with Annexes and Protocol, opened for signature on 24 Sept 1996, has not entered into force yet, ILM, Vol 35, 1996, p 1439.

[10] Treaty between the United States of America and the Union of Soviet Socialist Republics on the Elimination of Their Intermediate-Range and Shorter-Range Missiles, together with Protocols, Memorandum of Understanding, and Associated Documents (INF), signed on 8 Dec 1987, entered into force on 1 Jun 1988, UNTS, Vol 1657, No 28521; Treaty between the United States of America and the Union of Soviet Socialist Republics on the Reduction and Limitation of Strategic Offensive Arms, together with Annexes, Protocols, Memorandum of Understanding, and Associated Documents (START I), signed on 31 Jul 1991, entered into force 5 Dec 1994, CD/1192 of 5 Apr 1993; Treaty between the United States of America and the Russian Federation on Further Reduction and Limitation of Strategic Offensive Arms, together with Protocols, Memorandum of Understanding, and Associated Documents (START II), signed on 3 Jan 1993, has not entered into force yet, CD/1194 of 5 Apr 1993; Treaty between the United States of America and the Russian Federation on Strategic Offensive Reductions, signed 24 May 2002, has not entered into force yet (although both the US Senate and the Russian Duma have conditionally approved of ratification), ILM, Vol 41, 2002, p 799.

[11] Some agreements limit the use of nuclear weapons in specific areas, such as in Antarctica and certain nuclear-weapon-free zones. Also the five official nuclear-weapon states have given security assurances to non-nuclear weapon states that are Parties to the Non-Proliferation Treaty.

[12] A/Res/1653 (XVI), adopted on 24 Nov 1961, by 55 to 20, with 26 abstentions; declaration on the illegality of the use of nuclear weapons. In operative para 1, the Assembly declared: '(a) The use of nuclear and thermo-nuclear weapons is contrary to the spirit, letter and aims of the United Nations and, as such, a direct violation of the Charter of the United Nations; (b) The use of nuclear and thermo-nuclear weapons would exceed even the scope of war and cause indiscriminate suffering and destruction to mankind and civilization and, as such, is contrary to the rules of international law and the laws of humanity; (c) The use of nuclear and thermo-nuclear weapons is a war directed not against an enemy or enemies alone but also against mankind in general, since the peoples of the world not involved in such a war will be subjected to all the evils generated by the use of such weapons; (d) Any State using nuclear and thermo-nuclear weapons is to be considered as violating the Charter of the

number of authoritative authors have argued that the use of nuclear weapons is contrary to international law, no such determination has ever been generally accepted in binding form by States.

Therefore, in 1992, a number of non-governmental organisations[13] launched an international campaign under the name 'World Court Project'[14] aimed at influencing member states of the World Health Organization (WHO) and the United Nations to request the International Court of Justice to give an advisory opinion pursuant to article 96 UN Charter on the legality of the use of nuclear weapons.[15] And successfully. On 14 May 1993, the WHO Assembly adopted Resolution 46/40 requesting the Court to consider whether:

> [i]n view of the health and environmental effects, (. . .) the use of nuclear weapons by a State in war or other armed conflict [would] be a breach of its obligations under international law including the WHO Constitution?'[16]

And despite strong opposition, the United Nations General Assembly requested the Court on 15 December 1994 to render an advisory opinion on the following question: 'Is the threat or use of nuclear weapons in any circumstance permitted under international law?'[17]

On 8 July 1996, the International Court of Justice delivered both opinions.[18] It denied the request from the WHO because the legality of the use of nuclear weapons:

United Nations, as acting contrary to the laws of humanity and as committing a crime against mankind and civilization'.

[13] Most prominent among these organizations were the International Physicians for the Prevention of Nuclear War (IPPNW), the International Peace Bureau (IPB), and the International Association of Lawyers Against Nuclear Arms (IALANA).

[14] VP Nanda, D Krieger, *Nuclear Weapons and the World Court*, Transnational Publishers, Ardsley, NY, 1998, pp 69–86.

[15] The General Assembly is entitled *ex* Art 96(1) UN Charter 'to request the International Court of Justice to give an advisory opinion on any legal issue'. The WHO was authorized to request advisory opinions of the Court on legal questions arising within the scope of its activities, in the light of Art 96(2) UN Charter, by Art X(2) of the Agreement between the United Nations and the WHO (A/348), in accordance with Art 76 WHO Constitution. The Agreement was approved by General Assembly Resolution 124 (II) adopted unanimously on 15 Nov 1947, which provided the WHO, with 'Specialized Agency' status in accordance with Art 57 and 63 UN Charter. The foundation of the WHO was laid in New York on 22 Jul 1947 with the signature of the Constitution of the WHO, which entered into force on 7 Apr 1948, UNTS, Vol 14, No 221. This possibility was already suggested by Schwarzenberger in 1958, although he admitted that 'the value of such a pronouncement should not be overestimated.' G Schwarzenberger, *The Legality of Nuclear Weapons*, Stevens & Sons, London, 1958, p 57.

[16] WHA 46/40, adopted on 14 May 1993, request for an advisory opinion from the International Court of Justice on the legality of the use of nuclear weapons.

[17] A/Res/49/75 K, adopted on 15 Dec 1994, by 78 to 43, with 38 abstentions, request for an advisory opinion from the International Court of Justice on the legality of the threat of use of nuclear weapons.

[18] Legality of the Use by a State of Nuclear Weapons in Armed Conflict, Advisory Opinion, 8 Jul1996, ICJReports 1996, p 66 (Nuclear Weapons Opinion (WHO)); Legality of the Threat or Use of Nuclear Weapons, Advisory Opinion, 8 Jul 1996, ICJ Reports 1996, p 226 (Nuclear Weapons Opinion (GA)).

> does not relate to a question which arises "within the scope of activities" of that Organization in accordance with Article 96, paragraph 2, of the Charter.[19]

Although the use of nuclear weapons may have serious effects on human health and the environment, the WHO needs to undertake measures irrespective of the legality of their use. The request from the General Assembly, however, was accepted and discussed in (some) detail, the Court concluding that:

> there is in neither customary nor conventional international law any comprehensive and universal prohibition of the threat or use of nuclear weapons as such;

that any lawful use of nuclear weapons would have to comply both with the law relating to the use of force, or *ius ad bellum*, and with the law applicable during armed conflict, or *ius in bello*; and that:

> [i]t follows from the above-mentioned requirements that the threat or use of nuclear weapons would generally be contrary to the rules of international law applicable in armed conflict, and in particular the principles and rules of humanitarian law; However, in view of the current state of international law, and of the elements of fact at its disposal, the Court cannot conclude definitively whether the threat or use of nuclear weapons would be lawful or unlawful in an extreme circumstance of self-defense, in which the very survival of a State would be at stake.[20]

In addition to *ius ad bellum* and *ius in bello*, which it considered 'the most directly relevant applicable law governing the question of which it was seised', the Court also discussed the legality of the use of nuclear weapons in relation to the right to life and the prohibition of genocide, as well as existing norms relating to the safeguarding and, indeed, protection of the environment. Unfortunately, however, the Court's reasoning was rather brief. According to the Court, the right to life had to be interpreted in light of the rules regulating the conduct of hostilities;[21] and genocide requires intent, which means that it depends on 'the circumstances specific to each case' whether or not a violation of the prohibition can be established.[22] As

[19] Nuclear Weapons Opinion (WHO), para 31, p 84.

[20] Nuclear Weapons Opinion (GA), dicta 2B–E, p 266. The Court's conclusions were severely criticised for various reasons although it is probably fair to say that no matter what the Court would have said, it would have been wrong. The dilemma reminded Judge Shahabuddeen in his Dissenting Opinion of a dilemma with which judges in Persia were once confronted. According to Herodotus, when asked by their king, Cambyses, whether he could marry his sister, the judges took no risks and answered that although they could not find a law that permitted a brother to marry his sister, there would undoubtedly be a law that permitted the king to do whatever he wanted. Dissenting Opinion of Judge Shahabuddeen, Legality of the Threat of Use of Nuclear Weapons, Advisory Opinion, 8 July 1996, ICJ Reports 1996, p 392, n 6. For the whole story, see Herodotus, *Het verslag van mijn onderzoek*, Vert HL van Dolen, SUN, Nijmegen, 2000.

[21] Nuclear Weapons Opinion (GA), paras 24–5, pp 239–40.

[22] Nuclear Weapons Opinion (GA), para 26, p 240.

far as the protection of the environment was concerned, the Court found that:

> while the existing international law relating to the protection and safeguarding of the environment does not specifically prohibit the use of nuclear weapons it indicates important environmental factors that are properly to be taken into account in the context of the implementation of the principles and rules of the law applicable in armed conflict.[23]

The present study means to elaborate on the last conclusion focusing on the question whether or not the use of nuclear weapons during international armed conflict[24] would violate existing norms of public international law relating to the protection and safeguarding of the environment. Although the use of weaponry during armed conflict is usually related to the protection of individuals, the rapidly emerging appreciation of, and the worldwide realisation of the intrinsic value of the natural environment as an indispensable asset for the continuation of life, including human life, on this planet, both for present and future generation, warrants a thorough and extensive study on the question of the (il)legality of the employment of nuclear weapons from the point of view of international environment protection law.

By assessing the legality of the use of nuclear weapons under public international law, and relating it to the protection of the environment during international armed conflict, this research upholds a tradition first established by Prof Dr BVA Röling and later followed by his successor Prof Dr WD Verwey at the Department of International Law at the University of Groningen. Since the 1950s, the Law of International Peace and Security or the Law of War and Peace has played a prominent role in the Department's research program,[25] while the law relating to the protection of the environment was later included as an additional pillar during the 1980s.[26]

Since an international convention prohibiting the use and possession of nuclear weapons seems to be a long shot in the near future,[27] despite the

[23] Nuclear Weapons Opinion (GA), para 33, p 243.

[24] The protection of the environment during non-international armed conflict has been excluded from the scope of the present study.

[25] See WD Verwey, *Bert VA Röling; 1906–1985*, TMC Asser Instituut, The Hague, 1985, pp 8–22 and the latest thesis published within this framework: G Molier, *De (on)rechtmatigheid van humanitaire interventie; Respect voor staatssoevereiniteit versus bescherming van mensenrechten?*, Boom Juridische uitgevers, Den Haag, 2003.

[26] Compare Schrijver's and Nelissen's doctoral theses: N Schrijver, *Sovereignty over Natural Resources: Balancing Rights and Duties in an Interdependent World*, Doctoral Thesis, University of Groningen, 1995; later published as N Schrijver, *Sovereignty over Natural Resources: Balancing Rights and Duties*, Cambridge University Press, Cambridge, 1997; and FA Nelissen, *Scheepswrakken en wrakke schepen; Een volkenrechtelijke beschouwing vanuit milieu-perspectief*, TMC Asser Instituut, Den Haag, 1997.

[27] In 1997, the Lawyers' Committee on Nuclear Policy, a United States based non-governmental organization which is affiliated with the International Association of Lawyers

nuclear-weapon states' obligation to negotiate nuclear disarmament,[28] analyses like the present one are required in order to clarify existing rights and obligations with respect to the potential employment of nuclear weapons under current public international law. Although a nuclear-weapon state may actually not be inclined to allow the ultimate decision to use nuclear weapons to depend on environmental (or even humanitarian considerations),[29] and although ultimately public international law may only play a subordinate role 'where matters of high policy are concerned',[30] a clarification of the law may nevertheless influence public opinion and ultimately national and international decision-making, particularly in times of peace. It is during times of peace that regulation of conduct in times of armed conflict may be more easily achieved. As long as nuclear weapons form part of the weapon arsenals of certain states, and

Against Nuclear Arms, which is based in the Netherlands, released a draft Convention on the Prohibition of the Development, Testing, Production, Stockpiling, Transfer, Use and Threat of Use of Nuclear Weapons and on Their Elimination (through <http://www.lcnp.org/> and <http://www.ialana.org/>), prepared by a large number of lawyers, scientists and other experts and modelled on the 1972 Biological Weapons Convention, and the 1993 Chemical Weapons Convention. The document was enclosed with a letter of 31 October 1997 from the Permanent Representative of Costa Rica to the United Nations Secretary-General and was upon request circulated as an official document of the First Committee of the General Assembly on 17 Nov 1997 (A/C1/52/7). Although the United Nations General Assembly has annually called upon member states to negotiate nuclear disarmament and to conclude a Nuclear Weapons Convention since 1996 (A/Res/51/45 M, adopted on 10 Dec 1996, by 115 to 22, with 32 abstentions; A/Res/52/38 O, adopted on 9 Dec 1997, by 116 to 26, with 24 abstentions; A/Res/53/77 W, adopted on 4 Dec1998, by 123 to 25, with 25 abstentions; A/Res/54/54 Q, adopted on 1 Dec 1999, by 114 to 28, with 22 abstentions; A/Res/55/33 X, adopted on 20 Nov 2000, by 119 to 28, with 22 abstentions; A/Res/56/24 S, adopted on 29 Nov 2001, by 111 to 29, with 21 abstentions: all follow-ups to the Advisory Opinion of the International Court of Justice on the Legality of Nuclear Weapons), and although the draft Convention was deemed to be a helpful instrument and worth of discussion by a variety of persons and national and international institutions, among which were the European Parliament and the United States House of Representatives, a Nuclear Weapons Convention is still far from reality.

[28] According to Art VI of the 1968 Non-Proliferation Treaty, '[e]ach of the Parties to the Treaty undertakes to pursue negotiations in good faith on effective measures relating to cessation of the nuclear arms race at an early date and to nuclear disarmament, and on a Treaty on general and complete disarmament under strict and effective international control.' And in 1996, the International Court of Justice unanimously concluded in *dictum* 2F of the Nuclear Weapons Opinion (GA): 'There exists an obligation to pursue in good faith and bring to a conclusion negotiations leading to nuclear disarmament in all its aspects under strict and effective international control.'

[29] According to Schwarzenberger, 'the first, and most self-denying, duty of the international lawyer is to warn against the dangerous illusion that his findings on the legality or illegality of nuclear weapons are likely to influence one way or the other the decision on the use of these devices of mechanized barbarism.' Schwarzenberger, *The Legality of Nuclear Weapons*, p 58.

[30] I Brownlie, *Some Legal Aspects of the Use of Nuclear Weapons*, International and Comparative Law Quarterly, Vol 14, 1965, p 437. Also Schwarzenberger wrote in 1958 that 'if it should ever come to an all-out contest by force between the super-Powers of our age, it would be sheer day-dreaming to expect that in their fight for survival, and so necessarily world hegemony, they would refrain from the use of any weapon in their arsenal.' Schwarzenberger, *The Legality of Nuclear Weapons*, p 58.

as long as nuclear weapons play a significant role in national and international security strategies, their potential use in practice is not just imaginary but something that has to be dealt with, even after the end of the Cold War.[31]

This book consists of two parts. Part I discusses nuclear weapons from a historical perspective (Chapter I) and deals with nuclear weapons and their effects (Chapter II). Part II generally discusses the protection of the environment during international armed conflict under *ius in bello* (Chapter III), *ius ad bellum* (Chapter IV), and *ius pacis* (Chapter V). Only then will it be possible to assess the use of nuclear weapons under the relevant and applicable rules of public international law that protect and safeguard the environment during international armed conflict (Appraisal and Conclusions).

The findings in Part I are largely based on historical and military literature as well as technical reports dealing with the effects of nuclear weapons. Some of the historical literature is autobiographic and contains first-hand accounts of the developments regarding nuclear energy and nuclear weapons. Most literature, however, contains subsidiary accounts and is based on historical research by the respective authors. The studies used with respect to the long-term effects of nuclear explosions are generally conducted by intergovernmental organisations or *fora*, such as the International Atomic Energy Agency and the Chernobyl Forum.

The findings in Part II are based on research of the primary and subsidiary sources of public international law, as laid down in Article 38 of the Statute of the International Court of Justice, with a particular focus on conventional and customary law, interpreted in conformity with the customary means of interpretation as laid down in Articles 31 and 32 of the Vienna Convention on the Law of Treaties. The methodology with respect to customary international law is discussed in detail in Chapter III, Section 2.3.1. Since the protection of the environment during international armed conflict falls primarily under the laws of war, emphasis in Part II lies on the protection of the environment under *ius in bello* (Chapter III).

[31] See eg, the attempts of the Bush Jr Administration to carry out research on a so-called Robust Nuclear Earth Penetrator (RNEP), also known as the 'Nuclear Bunker Buster', intended to destroy large underground structures and neutralize buried stockpiles of chemical and biological weapons; international concern relating to Iran's uranium enrichment program and alleged nuclear weapons program; international concern relating to North-Korea's nuclear weapons program; and the hostile relationship between two relatively new nuclear-weapon states India and Pakistan.

Part I

I

Nuclear Weapons in Historical Perspective

1—INTRODUCTION

IN ORDER TO gain a better understanding of the subject under discussion, it is first necessary to deal with nuclear weapons from a historical perspective. This includes a brief discussion of nuclear physics and nuclear energy in order to become familiar with the terminology and the technicalities of nuclear weapons (section 2); the development of the atomic bomb by the United States within the framework of the Manhattan Project during World War II (section 3); the development of the hydrogen bomb by the United States after World War II to regain superiority over the Soviet Union (section 4); and finally, certain developments regarding nuclear weapons outside the United States (section 5).

2—NUCLEAR PHYSICS

2.1 Introduction

The development of modern nuclear physics started in Paris in 1896, when Becquerel discovered that uranium[1] minerals had the power to ionise air, which means that they were able to give air-molecules an electrical charge. This ionising capability became known as radioactivity, a term that was first used by Marie Curie, who subsequently attracted the attention of the scientific community through her discovery of several other radioactive elements, some of which were so powerful that they could inflict burns on human skin. It was discovered that there were different kinds of radioactive substances that could be distinguished by reference to their ionising,

[1] Uranium was first discovered in the Joachimsthal mines, on the northern border of the Czech Republic. Here, the German chemist Klaproth found an unusual ore and in 1789 extracted a material which he called uranium to honour an English astronomer who had just a few years earlier discovered a new planet which he named Uranus after the earliest supreme god in Greek mythology. R Rhodes, *The Making of the Atomic Bomb*, Simon and Schuster, New York, 1986, p 118.

and therewith their penetrating power, namely alpha, beta and gamma particles. Alpha particles are Helium nuclei that move relatively slowly (15,000 km per second) due to their large mass; beta particles are high speed electrons (300,000 km per second) whose mass is negligible; and gamma rays are pulses of high-frequency electromagnetic radiation that are similar to X-rays. A quantum of gamma radiation that sometimes acts as a particle is called a photon.[2]

The explanation of radioactivity could only be given after Rutherford and Bohr had unravelled the structure of the atom. The idea of the atom is originally an invention of Greek philosophers such as Leucippus and Democritus and has been discussed over the centuries.[3] Newton, for example, imagined the atom as a miniature billiard ball, solid and massy, but this idea became subject to pressure during the 19th century and was totally reformed in the beginning of the 20th century. In 1911, Rutherford discovered that the mass of atoms was located in a nucleus, and Bohr elaborated on Rutherford's nuclear atom theory with his planetary atomic model in which negative electrons were positioned in orbits around a positive nucleus based on energetic stationary states.[4] The subject of radioactivity had gradually evolved into nuclear physics.[5]

Hodgson describes the atom as follows:

> Using the simple picture, we can imagine a typical atom as composed of a small, hard central core, called the nucleus [where all mass is located], surrounded by a cloud of lighter particles called electrons.[6]

This electron cloud forms the surface of the atom and participates in chemical reactions, leaving the core unaffected. The number of electrons and thus the chemical characteristics of the atom are determined by the

[2] Generally on radioactivity: L Badash, *Scientists and the Development of Nuclear Weapons; From Fission to the Limited Test Ban Treaty 1939–1963*, Humanities Press International, Inc, Atlantic Highlands, New Jersey, 1995, pp 12–14; H Briezeveld, L Mathot, *Scoop; Natuurkunde voor de Bovenbouw 5/6 VWO*, Wolters-Noordhoff, Groningen, 1991, pp 242–3; S Glasstone, PJ Dolan (Eds), *The Effects of Nuclear Weapons*, US Department of Defense and the US Department of Energy, Washington, DC, 1977, pp 18–19; PE Hodgson, *Nuclear Physics in Peace and War*, Hawthorn Books Publishers, New York, 1963, pp 18–20, 23–5; HD Smyth, *Atomic Energy; A General Account of the Development of Methods of Using Atomic Energy for Military Purposes under the Auspices of the United States Government 1940–1945*, US Government Printing Office, Washington, DC; His Majesty's Stationary Office, London, 1945, pp 2–3.

[3] The word 'atom' is derived from the Greek words 'a', which means not, and 'tomnein' which means to cut, to divide or to split. *Collins Cobuild English Dictionary*, HarperCollins Publishers, Glasgow, 1995, p 95.

[4] For his paper 'On the Constitution of Atoms and Molecules', published in 1913, Bohr was awarded the Nobel Prize for Physics in 1922. See: <http://nobelprize.org/>.

[5] Badash, *Scientists and the Development of Nuclear Weapons*, p 14; Glasstone, Dolan (Eds), *The Effects of Nuclear Weapons*, pp 3–4. For a discussion of these early days of nuclear physics and the lives, education and work of Rutherford and Bohr see the chaps 2 and 3 in: Rhodes, *The Making of the Atomic Bomb*, pp 29–77.

[6] Hodgson, *Nuclear Physics*, p 21.

number of positive charges in the nucleus giving the atom its atomic number Z and its place in the Periodic System.[7] These positive charges are called protons. An equal amount of electrons and protons makes sure that the atom as a whole is neutral, ie uncharged.

The mass of the nucleus, however, given by the number A, is always at least twice as great as the atomic number, which means that there must be something else in the nucleus, equal to the difference between A and Z and giving the atom its additional mass. On 3 June 1920, Rutherford suggested in a lecture delivered before the Royal Society of London the potential existence of the 'neutron' and in February 1932, its existence was finally proven by James Chadwick. Neutrons have the same mass as protons but they are uncharged, which makes them highly suitable for penetration as they are not blocked by electric repulsion. Protons and neutrons are both also known as 'nucleons'.[8]

This identification of the third basic constituent of matter, next to protons and electrons, opened up the nucleus for more detailed examination. Most nuclei have an equal amount of protons and neutrons, although the heavier nuclei tend to have an excess of neutrons. As was mentioned above, the number of protons is equal to the atomic number Z and the number of neutrons is equal to the difference between mass number A and atomic number Z. Normally, a certain element in the Periodic System has a fixed amount of neutrons in its nucleus. However, in 1919, Aston discovered that nuclei of the same element, of the same nuclear charge sometimes have different masses. Nuclei of the same nuclear charge and thus with identical chemical properties, but with different mass numbers are called isotopes. Hydrogen, for instance, has three isotopes, namely H (hydrogen; no neutrons), D (deuterium; one neutron) and T (tritium; two neutrons). And also uranium has three isotopes: uranium-238 (U-238), uranium-235 (U-235) and uranium-234 (U-234). The fact that they have identical chemical characteristics makes them extremely difficult to distinguish and to separate, but this issue will be discussed further below.[9]

Within the nucleus there are two sets of forces: on the one hand, there are Coulomb forces or repulsion between the positively charged protons, and on the other hand, there are short-range forces of attraction between

[7] The Periodic System was invented by the Russian chemist Mendeleev, who divided the elements into groups or families and periods, based on their properties. Through: <http://en.wikipedia.org/>.

[8] Badash, *Scientists and the Development of Nuclear Weapons*, pp 15–16; Briezeveld, Mathot, *Scoop*, pp 257–60; Hodgson, *Nuclear Physics*, pp 21–3; Jungk, *Brighter than a Thousand Suns*, Grove Press, Inc, New York, NY, 1958.p 48; Rhodes, *The Making of the Atomic Bomb*, pp 153–67; Smyth, *Atomic Energy*, pp 3–7; EP Wigner, *Roots of the Atomic Age*, in: D Masters, K Way (Eds), *One World or None: A Report to the Public on the Full Meaning of the Atomic Bomb*, McGraw-Hill, New York, 1946, p 13.

[9] Briezeveld, Mathot, *Scoop*, pp 258–9; Glasstone, Dolan, *The Effects of Nuclear Weapons*, p 4; Hodgson, *Nuclear Physics*, pp 20–2; Smyth, *Atomic Energy*, pp 3–7.

all protons and neutrons. The problem is that only a few combinations of neutrons and protons are stable. If they are few in number and their number is about equal, stability is likely to occur. However, larger nuclei with complicated nuclear structures require an increasing amount of neutrons to balance the Coulomb forces. When the number of protons exceeds ninety, such as in the case of uranium, there are no completely stable nuclei.

Already in the early days of nuclear physics, Rutherford and a chemist named Soddy had claimed that atoms were not always stable and that it would keep on transmuting until a stable condition was reached. And indeed, as one later found out, in every mutation one form of radiation is emitted, in the form of either alpha particles (two protons and two neutrons), beta particles (electrons), or gamma rays (photons). This process of transformation or disintegration is called radioactive decay, more popularly known as radioactivity and the rate at which it changes is measured in 'half-lives,' which is the time required for half of the atoms to disintegrate. If these particles knock another atom's electron out of its path, that atom then becomes positively charged. This is the explanation of the process of ionisation that was mentioned at the beginning of this section.[10]

2.2 Nuclear Energy

2.2.1 Introduction

Two principles have generally been regarded as the cornerstones of modern physics, namely the law of the conservation of mass and the law of the conservation of energy. In fact, these principles are two phases of one single principle: energy may sometimes be converted into mass, and, conversely, mass may sometimes be converted into energy. The former phenomenon is believed to be the basis of the creation of the universe and its planets; the latter phenomenon explains what happens in the case of nuclear fission and nuclear fusion, which is the subject of discussion in this section.[11]

Einstein had written as early as 1905 that mass and energy were equivalent and that the amount of energy was expressed by the famous equation $E = \Delta mc^2$, where Δm stands for the difference in mass and c for

[10] Badash, *Scientists and the Development of Nucelar Weapons*, pp 12–16; Briezeveld, Mathot, *Scoop*, pp 264–6; Glasstone, Dolan, *The Effects of Nuclear Weapons*, pp 18–19; Hodgson, *Nuclear Physics*, pp 23–5; Smyth, *Atomic Energy*, pp 3–7.

[11] Badash, *Scientists and the Development of Nuclear Weapons*, pp 17-19; Briezeveld, Mathot, *Scoop*, p 264; Glasstone, Dolan, *The Effects of Nuclear Weapons*, pp 4–5; Smyth, *Atomic Energy*, pp 1–2. Please note that until then, the common sources of power besides sunlight, wind, and water had been confined to regular chemical reactions such as the burning of wood, coal or oil.

the speed of light in vacuum,[12] which is roughly 300,000 km per second. Controlling such a conversion seemed remote at the time but as from the early 1930s experimental evidence began to appear in increasing quantity.[13]

Still the scientific community was sceptical as regards the possibility of releasing the vast stores of energy locked inside the atom and providing the world with unlimited amounts of energy.[14] Rutherford, for example said that anyone looking for a source of consumable energy in the transformation of the atoms was talking 'moonshine'.[15] The founding father of nuclear physics never believed in the release of nuclear energy on a large scale up until his death in 1936. The reason for this scepticism was that in order to release nuclear energy by means of a nuclear reaction protons were accelerated to high speeds by electric fields in an attempt to break up nuclei by collision. These high energies were necessary because the positively charged protons were repelled by the positively charged nuclei they were supposed to break up, and since this process would cost a lot more energy than it would get in return, the process did not seem economical. Optimism returned, however, when Chadwick discovered the neutron in 1932. From that moment on, experimental physicists started to bombard elements with neutrons that were not repelled by electrical charges.[16]

2.2.2 *Nuclear Fission*

On the eve of World War II, the German chemists Hahn and Strassmann made a sensational discovery at the Kaiser Wilhelm Institute for Chemistry in Berlin which caused quite a stir in the scientific community. After bombarding uranium with neutrons in late 1938, they discovered traces of barium, which element has roughly half the weight of uranium. Their assistant Meitner and her nephew Frisch, who had both fled to Sweden, gave a daring explanation, namely that the nuclei of uranium atoms must have been blown to pieces. They argued that the uranium nuclei each must have captured a neutron, and must have therefore become unstable and broken up. They used the term 'fission' by analogy with the division of cells or the multiplication of bacteria on the suggestion

[12] The c stands for the Latin word *celeritas* which means speed.

[13] Smyth, *Atomic Energy*, p 10.

[14] To get an idea of the amount of energy that is released, Briezeveld and Mathot give the example of the atomic bombs dropped on Hiroshima and Nagasaki. In both cases, only 1 gram of fissionable material was converted which is equal to 9.10^{13} Joules of energy. The same amount of energy is released after the combustion of 3 million kilograms of coal. Briezeveld, Mathot, *Scoop*, p 264.

[15] Rhodes, *The Making of the Atomic Bomb*, p 27.

[16] Badash, *Scientists and the Development of Nuclear Weapons*, pp 20–5; L. Badash, *Introduction*, in: L Badash, JO Hirschfelder, HP Broida (Eds), *Reminiscences of Los Alamos 1943–1945*, D Reidel Publishing Company, Dordrecht, 1980, p xi; Hodgson, *Nuclear Physics*, pp 20, 25–31; Jungk, *Brighter than a Thousand Suns*, pp 48–68.

of the American biologist J Arnold.[17] The discovery was announced and published in Nature, early 1939, and from then on the news spread by word of mouth. Within days experiments made all over the world confirmed Hahn's and Stassmann's findings as well as Meitner's and Frisch's conclusions, and the concept of fission was soon generally accepted.[18]

The reason why fission only takes place after bombardment of the heaviest nuclei, is that neutrons function as a kind of cement in order to keep the positively charged protons together, and the larger and the heavier the nucleus, the more difficult it is to keep them together, and the easier it becomes to split them. The reaction is started by a so-called 'slow' neutron whose moving energy is completely absorbed by the nucleus of the target. Similar to putting in golf, a slow shot has a better chance to drop into the hole than a fast one which might overshoot the mark.[19]

The implications of this discovery were that firstly, it appeared to be the long sought key to releasing the energy of the nucleus that is so much larger than any other source known at the time. The masses of the fission products combined were less than the masses of the original uranium nuclei, which meant that, in accordance with Einstein's equation $E=\Delta mc^2$, mass was converted into energy. And secondly, it was discovered that during the fission process of uranium, additional neutrons were emitted, which opened up the possibility of a chain reaction. A chain reaction is an on-going, self-sustaining reaction during which one neutron releases other neutrons during a nuclear reaction, which, on their turn, induce other nuclei to split. If a process could be started during which each fission would release exactly one neutron on average that could be used for further splitting, a continuous, powerful, cheap source of nuclear energy could be made. If, however, on average more than one neutron remained after every fission, an uncontrollable, sudden and violent release of a large amount of energy would occur revealing itself in an explosion.[20]

[17] Badash, *Scientists and the Development of Nuclear Weapons*, pp 23–4; Jungk, *Brighter than a Thousand Suns*, pp 69–70; Rhodes, *The Making of the Atomic Bomb*, pp 263–4.

[18] Badash, *Scientists and the Development of Nuclear Weapons*, pp 23–4; Badash, *Introduction*, in: Badash, Hirschfelder, Broida (Eds), *Reminiscences of Los Alamos 1943–1945*, pp xi–xii; Briezeveld, Mathot, *Scoop*, p 264; Hodgson, *Nuclear Physics*, pp 27–8; Jungk, *Brighter than a Thousand Suns*, pp 66–70; H Krane, *Introductory Nuclear Physics*, John Wiley & Sons, New York, 1988, 478; Smyth, *Atomic Energy*, 14–15. For an elaborate discussion on this discovery and the impact it had on the scientific community, see: Rhodes, *The Making of the Atomic Bomb*, pp 233–5.

[19] Briezeveld, Mathot, *Scoop*, p 267.

[20] Badash, *Scientists and the Development of Nuclear Weapons*, pp 25–7; DP Barash, *Introduction to Peace Studies*, Wadsworth Publishing Company, Belmont, CA, 1991, p 106; Briezeveld, Mathot, *Scoop*, pp 264, 267–8; Glasstone, Dolan, *The Effects of Nuclear Weapons*, pp 1, 6–7, 16–17; Hodgson, *Nuclear Physics*, pp 27–8, 35; Jungk, *Brighter than a Thousand Suns*, pp 70–8; JR Oppenheimer, *The New Weapon: The turn of the Screw*, in: Masters, Way (Eds), *One World or None*, p 23; Smyth, *Atomic Energy*, pp 16, 18, 22, 25–7, 124–6; G Young, *The New Power*, in: Masters, Way (Eds), *One World or None: A Report to the Public on the Full Meaning of the Atomic Bomb*, McGraw-Hill, New York, 1946, pp 16–17; Wigner, *Roots of the Atomic Age*, in: Masters, Way (Eds), *One World or None*, pp 13–14.

2.2.3 *Difficulties*

2.2.3.1 Introduction

There were a number of issues that needed to be clarified, however, before one could even start thinking about the possible uses of nuclear energy, two of which were paramount. The first issue was that of the so-called critical mass (section 2.2.3.2). The second issue was that of isotope separation (section 2.2.3.3).

2.2.3.2 Critical Mass

The critical mass is the exact amount of uranium necessary to sustain a chain reaction. In case of a nuclear reaction, there are basically four simultaneous and competing processes that have to be taken into account, three of which cause neutrons to digress. Firstly, some neutrons will escape from the mass; secondly, some neutrons will be captured by uranium nuclei without causing them to split; thirdly, some neutrons will be absorbed by impurities; and fourthly some neutrons will indeed cause uranium nuclei to split.[21] 'If the loss of the first three processes is less than the surplus produced by the fourth, the chain reaction occurs; otherwise it does not.'[22]

The first problem, namely that of escape, can be minimised by changing the size and shape of the mass, because it depends completely on the area of the surface. Hodgson writes:

> Since the number of neutrons produced is proportional to the volume of the uranium, while the number escaping is proportional to its surface area, the more uranium there is the greater the proportion of the neutrons that do not escape and so are available to carry on the reaction.[23]

Therefore, there must be a minimum amount of material to sustain a chain reaction. Estimates differed widely, however, in the early days of chain reaction research and it did not seem unlikely that the critical size would be too large for practical purposes.[24]

The second and third problem, regarding non-fission capture by uranium and impurities, had to do with the fact that uranium nuclei are only fissioned by slow neutrons and the neutrons that are emitted during the fission process have high speeds; these fast neutrons can be captured by

[21] Smyth, *Atomic Energy*, pp 18–22, 124–5.
[22] Smyth, *Atomic Energy*, p 19.
[23] Hodgson, *Nuclear Physics*, p 29.
[24] Briezeveld, Mathot, *Scoop*, p 268; Glasstone, Dolan, *The Effects of Nuclear Weapons*, pp 13–15; LG Groves, *Now It Can Be Told; The Story of the Manhattan Project*, Andre Deutsch Publishers, London, 1963, p 40; Hodgson, *Nuclear Physics*, p 29; Smyth, *Atomic Energy*, pp 18–19, 23.

one of the isotopes of uranium that is incapable of fissioning. This means that one had to invent ways to slow neutrons down, which can be done by letting them pass through material of low atomic weight so that the collisions would deprive the neutrons of their kinetic energy, or speed, similar to a game of billiards. Furthermore, a good moderator must be practicable, which excludes a gas such as helium and it must have little or no tendency to absorb neutrons. The Italian physicist and Nobel laureate Fermi and the Hungarian physicist Szilard proposed graphite as a moderator because of it was a lot easier and cheaper to produce than other materials despite being an inferior, ie less efficient moderator. The moderator would then be mixed with the uranium in the form of a matrix.[25]

2.2.3.3 Isotope Separation

The second issue that had to be dealt with in order to use nuclear fission as a source of energy was isotope separation. Isotope separation was necessary since it was established, as has been observed above, that uranium had three isotopes, namely uranium-238 (U-238), uranium-235 (U-235) and uranium-234 (U-234), present in nature to the extent of 99.3%, 0.7% and 0.006% respectively,[26] of which U-235 appeared to be most suitable for nuclear fission. U-235 therefore had to be separated from U-238 and U-234 to a sufficient degree of purity. This process is called uranium enrichment. The by-product of this enrichment process is called 'depleted uranium' and largely consists of U-238 with a reduced level of U-235.

Isotope separation or enrichment is extremely difficult since all isotopes have an equal number of protons and electrons, the only difference being the number of neutrons. Therefore, isotopes have identical chemical characteristics, and their physical differences, ie differences in mass, are extremely small. There are four separation techniques that take advantage of these small differences.

The first method was developed by American physicist and Nobel laureate Lawrence and is called electromagnetic separation. For a long time it had been considered impossible due to its complexity, but Lawrence was remarkably successful at it. Basically, electromagnetic separation uses a scaled-up mass spectrometer, and is based on the idea that if nuclei of the same mass pass through an electric field their direction of motion is changed and their curvatures depend on and are determined by their masses. A heavy nucleus is simply more difficult to bend away and will therefore describe a curve of a longer radius than a light nucleus. The disadvantage of this method was that separation occurred atom by atom, so that only very small portions could be obtained.

[25] Glasstone, Dolan, *The Effects of Nuclear Weapons*, pp 13–15; Hodgson, *Nuclear Physics*, pp 28–9; Smyth, *Atomic Energy*, pp 19–20.

[26] Smyth, *Atomic Energy*, p 19.

The second and third approaches looked more promising, however, because one could build on existing petroleum engineering and technology. The centrifuge method and the gaseous diffusion method had both been studied by Urey at Columbia University and the University of Virginia. The latter is based on the idea that if a gas is diffused through a porous barrier, the rate of diffusion is based on its density: light gases have a higher chance to pass through the microscopic holes of a screen than heavy gases. If you create a system of some 5000 barriers, a so-called cascade, you can eventually obtain enriched U-235 of any desired degree of purity. The former is based on the idea that heavy and light components will be separated by centrifugal forces, similar to what happens in washing machines. This method, required thousands of separately driven extremely high-speed centrifuges. Both methods, however, required that uranium had to be transformed into a gaseous substance, which is complicated.

The fourth and last method was based on thermal diffusion in liquids. In September 1940, Abelson, a young Navy Officer and scientist, elaborated a process that had already been pioneered in Germany before the war. Liquid uranium hexa-fluoride was heated in a concentric cylinder inside a long, vertical, and externally cooled tube which would cause the separation of heavy and light nuclei because lighter isotopes tend to diffuse toward hotter regions. By the end of 1941, the initial results seemed superior to the centrifuge and gaseous diffusion processes.[27]

None of the techniques produced a sufficient degree of purity, however. The electromagnetic separation technique, for example, yielded a purity of only 11% while at least 90% is needed for an explosive chain reaction. Only in 1943 did they start to use the various techniques as complementary methods using enriched uranium as feed material for the other techniques.[28]

New opportunities presented themselves, however, in 1941, when a group of scientists under the direction of Seaborg discovered a new fissionable material, which was almost twice as fissionable as uranium and much easier to produce. It had already been established that fast neutrons were captured by U-238 nuclei, but it came as a surprise when they

[27] Generally on methods of isotope separation see: Badash, *Scientists and the Development of Nuclear Weapons*, pp 30–2; Badash, *Introduction*, in: Badash, Hirschfelder, Broida (Eds), *Reminiscences of Los Alamos 1943–1945*, p xiv; Briezeveld, Mathot, *Scoop*, pp 261–2; Glasstone, Dolan, *The Effects of Nuclear Weapons*, p 13; Groves, *Now It Can Be Told*, pp 8–10, 95, 111, 119–20; Hodgson, *Nuclear Physics*, pp 29–31, 38; Rhodes, *The Making of the Atomic Bomb*, pp 487–9, 549–54; Seaborg, *A Chemist in the White House, From the Manhattan Project to the End of the Cold War*, The American Chemical Society, Washington, DC, 1998, 2–7; Smyth, *Atomic Energy*, pp 19, 39–41, 46; Wigner, *Roots of the Atomic Age*, in: Masters, Way (Eds), *One World or None*, pp 12–14. For more detailed information see: Smyth, *Atomic Energy*, ch IX, pp 92–103.

[28] Badash, *Scientists and the Development of Nuclear Weapons*, pp 38–9; Groves, *Now It Can Be Told*, pp 119–20.

discovered that after capture of a neutron, U-238 had changed into a new and heavier element with atomic number 94. In line with tradition to call these new elements after planets, he decided to name it plutonium, after the ninth planet from the sun that was discovered in 1930, after the Greek god of the underworld and of the dead.

Now they had two strings on their bow, and a kind of fissionable material that had different chemical characteristics than its source which meant that it could be separated by the usual chemical methods from the U-238 reaction pile. This was relatively easy and cheap, despite the fact that its high radioactivity and toxicity made remote control necessary.[29]

3—THE MANHATTAN PROJECT

3.1 Introduction

The first time that the possible military application and consequences of nuclear energy were officially discussed by government officials and scientists was during a conference attended by representatives of the United States Navy Department in March 1939. Fermi, the Italian 1938 Nobel laureate who had fled his home country in the late 1930s and who had since been working at Columbia University in New York, suggested the possibility of a controlled chain reaction or a reaction of an explosive character. The first one could be used as a power source for the propulsion of submarines; the second could be used for the production of bombs.

Later in 1939, the military application of nuclear fission was discussed for a second time as a result of the so-called 'Einstein Letter'. Frustrated about the lack of coordination in nuclear research and about the scepticism and lack of appreciation by the British and United States governments, the Hungarian physicist Szilard decided with his fellow Hungarian physicist Wigner to alert the United States government once more. In order to enforce their arguments and to underscore their point of view they asked Einstein to join them. Together they composed a letter which they had had delivered directly and in person to President Roosevelt by Sachs, an acquaintance of the President, on 11 October 1939.

Roosevelt subsequently appointed an Advisory Committee on Uranium, thereby securing the necessary coordination and financing. In June 1940, this Committee was transformed into a subcommittee of the newly established National Defense Research Committee (NDRC) and in the summer

[29] Badash, *Scientists and the Development of Nuclear Weapons*, pp 32–3; Badash, *Introduction*, in: Badash, Hirschfelder, Broida (Eds), *Reminiscences of Los Alamos 1943–1945*, p xiv; Groves, *Now It Can Be Told*, pp 8–9; Hodgson, *Nuclear Physics*, pp 31–4, 39; Rhodes, *The Making of the Atomic Bomb*, pp 352–5, 366; Seaborg, *A Chemist in the White House*, 2–7; Smyth, *Atomic Energy*, pp 22, 78; Wigner, *Roots of the Atomic Age*, in: Masters, Way (Eds), *One World or None*, p 14.

of 1941, the Advisory Committee on Uranium was renamed 'the Uranium Section' or cryptically 'the S-1 Section' of the NDRC. In order to make the organisation more efficient and for a better coordination of scientific work, the NDRC was brought under supervision of the new Office of Scientific Research and Development (OSRD) in 1941, which office is part of the Executive Office of the President. The Uranium Section, however, was placed directly under the OSRD.[30]

After encouraging results with respect to critical mass research, isotope separation, and plutonium research, it was decided in January 1942 to concentrate subsequent work on the chain reaction and plutonium research at the University of Chicago. There, under the University's football-stadium, research was carried out by Fermi, Szilard, Seaborg and many others under the unsuspicious name of the 'Metallurgical Laboratory,' or 'Met Lab'. Finally, on 2 December 1942, they managed to initiate a self-sustaining nuclear chain reaction, to keep it under control, and to stop it after some time.[31]

For practical purposes the nuclear research project was brought under the wings of the Army Corps of Engineers, and received a boost when in September 1942 Brigadier-General Groves took command of the operation. Before that, Groves had been Deputy Chief of Construction for the entire US Army and had just been charged with building the Pentagon. He was supposed to carry the major responsibility to coordinate the whole effort and to keep it focused on the military objectives; to keep the various parts of the project in step, ie securing supply of resources and raw materials, implementation of production schedules, development of the bomb and making arrangements for its use; and finally, to maintain an adequate security environment.[32]

Although initially horrified when he learned more about the operation—'It seemed as if the whole endeavour was founded on possibilities

[30] Badash, *Scientists and the Development of Nuclear Weapons*, pp 27–30; Badash, *Introduction*, in: Badash, Hirschfelder, Broida (Eds), *Reminiscences of Los Alamos 1943–1945*, pp xiii–xiv; Groves, *Now It Can Be Told; The Story of the Manhattan Project*, pp 6–8; Hodgson, *Nuclear Physics*, pp 36–8; Jungk, *Brighter than a Thousand Suns*, pp 78–9, 82–6, 109–13; Rhodes, *The Making of the Atomic Bomb*, pp 304–17; Seaborg, *A Chemist in the White House*, pp 1–2; Smyth, *Atomic Energy*, pp 18, 26–30, 44–7; Seaborg, *A Chemist in the White House*, pp 1–2.

[31] They had found out that a chain reaction would be possible and feasible and that the critical mass of uranium would be between 2.5 and 5 kg, an amount that was significantly less than previously estimated and practically very important in case of explosives. Badash, *Scientists and the Development of Nuclear Weapons*, pp 33–4; Badash, *Introduction*, in: Badash, Hirschfelder, Broida (Eds), *Reminiscences of Los Alamos 1943–1945*, p xiv; F Seitz, H Bethe, *How Close is the Danger*, in: Masters, Way (Eds), *One World or None*, p 42, and in: Bethe, *The Road from Los Alamos*, The American Institute of Physics, New York, NY, 1991, 4–5; Groves, *Now It Can Be Told*, pp 8–9; Rhodes, *The Making of the Atomic Bomb*, pp 399–401, 407–15; Smyth, *Atomic Energy*, pp 46, 52–3.

[32] Badash, *Introduction*, in: Badash, Hirschfelder, Broida (Eds), *Reminiscences of Los Alamos 1943–1945*, p xvii; Jungk, *Brighter than a Thousand Suns*, pp 115–20; Smyth, *Atomic Energy*, p 51.

rather than probabilities'—he did realise its importance for the war effort and immediately took firm steps to secure its progress.[33] Within days, he approved of a directive for the acquisition of a piece of land in Tennessee for the construction of uranium isotope separation plants; secured the uranium ore supply from the Shinkolobwe Mine in the Belgian Congo (Katanga); and assigned first-priority to the activities of his District. 'Time, not money, was becoming the limiting factor in atomic bomb development.'[34] Because the Army's first contact with nuclear research was through its office in Manhattan, the project received the code name of the newly established Manhattan Engineer District (MED), or more popularly, 'the Manhattan Project'. Groves objected to an initial proposal to call the new establishment 'The Laboratory for the Development of Substitute Materials' (DSM) because it would attract too much attention. All atomic research projects that were carried out under the supervision of the Office of Scientific Research were placed under the MED in order to increase efficiency and avoid delays.[35]

3.2 Fissionable Materials

As was mentioned above, the first uranium isotope separation pilot plants were located at one large single site in Tennessee. Although they were located at the same site, they were well separated so that they would not contaminate each other in case of disaster.[36] Eventually, in September 1942, one decided upon a site near a small town called Clinton, Tennessee. The name Oak Ridge that became a common designation for the site was not used until the summer of 1943, when it was chosen for the community's housing area that was being built on a series of ridges overlooking part of the location.[37]

[33] Groves, *Now It Can Be Told*, p 19.

[34] Rhodes, *The Making of the Atomic Bomb*, p 406.

[35] Badash, *Scientists and the Development of Nuclear Weapons*, pp 33–5; Badash, *Introduction*, in: Badash, Hirschfelder, Broida (Eds), *Reminiscences of Los Alamos 1943–1945*, p xvi; Groves, *Now It Can Be Told*, pp ix–xii, 3, 13, 17, 23, 33–4; Jungk, *Brighter than a Thousand Suns*, p 115; Rhodes, *The Making of the Atomic Bomb*, pp 424–8, 486; Seaborg, *A Chemist in the White House*, 11–12; Smyth, *Atomic Energy*, pp 50, 123.

[36] Groves, *Now It Can Be Told*, p 94. This choice had not made things easier for those people who had to select a suitable site, however, due to a list of requirements that had to be satisfied. Groves listed them as follows: they were looking for an area, relatively undeveloped and with reasonable land-prices; an area that had to be located away from both coasts to prevent enemy interference; an area where the heavy requirement for electric power and water would not face any difficulties; an area not too far away from Chicago, New York and Washington; an area with a climate that would permit heavy construction work throughout the year; and finally an area where the necessary construction and operation forces would be available. Groves, *Now It Can Be Told*, pp 13–14.

[37] Badash, *Introduction*, in: Badash, Hirschfelder, Broida (Eds), *Reminiscences of Los Alamos 1943–1945*, p xvii; Hodgson, *Nuclear Physics*, pp 42–3; Groves, *Now It Can Be Told*, pp 25–6, 51; Rhodes, *The Making of the Atomic Bomb*, pp 486–7.

For practical reasons, they opted for the electromagnetic and gaseous diffusion methods at Oak Ridge and not until 1944 did they add a thermal diffusion facility. Construction of the electromagnetic plant, codename Y-12, started in February 1943 and it was the first to start operation. From November 1943 until December 1946 it was the only plant that produced the final product of fully enriched uranium.[38]

The gaseous diffusion plant with codename K-25 initially turned out to be more problematic. It needed a power station of its own because all the motors and pumps required more electricity than an average American city. It was four stories high and shaped in the form of U, each leg of which was half a mile long and 400 feet wide. Based on earlier research in the United Kingdom, this technique was brought to perfection and after the war, gaseous diffusion became common practice in the United States.[39]

Furthermore, it was decided to locate the plutonium production plant at a different location, separate from the enrichment facilities, because it would be on such a large scale and it could generate a large quantity of potentially dangerous radioactivity. For this plant a large site was eventually chosen in January 1943 on the Columbia River near Hanford, Washington, that satisfied the requirements of water and space, as well as a mild climate that would allow unimpeded construction work. Construction started a few months later after the site's acquisition, under the name of the Hanford Engineer Works. They built a reactor in combination with a chemical separation plant that was expected to run early 1945, but went operative late 1944.[40]

3.3 Bomb Design

As soon as it had been established in early 1942 that a chain reaction was theoretically feasible, the need arose to conduct further research on the actual design of an atomic bomb. It was considered essential to start this

[38] Badash, *Scientists and the Development of Nuclear Weapons*, pp 38–9; Badash, *Introduction*, in: Badash, Hirschfelder, Broida (Eds), *Reminiscences of Los Alamos 1943–1945*, p xvii; Hodgson, *Nuclear Physics*, pp 42–3; Groves, *Now It Can Be Told*, pp 11, 95–6, 107–9; Rhodes, *The Making of the Atomic Bomb*, pp 486–7, 490–2.

[39] Badash, *Scientists and the Development of Nuclear Weapons*, pp 37–9; Badash, *Introduction*, in: Badash, Hirschfelder, Broida (Eds), *Reminiscences of Los Alamos 1943–1945*, p xvii; Hodgson, *Nuclear Physics*, pp 42–3; Groves, *Now It Can Be Told*, pp 111, 117; Rhodes, *The Making of the Atomic Bomb*, pp 486–7, 492–6.

[40] Badash, *Scientists and the Development of Nuclear Weapons*, pp 39–41; Badash, *Introduction*, in: Badash, Hirschfelder, Broida (Eds), *Reminiscences of Los Alamos 1943–1945*, p xvii; Hodgson, *Nuclear Physics*, pp 42–3; Groves, *Now It Can Be Told*, pp 69, 74; Rhodes, *The Making of the Atomic Bomb*, pp 486–7, 496–500, 559–60; Seaborg, *A Chemist in the White House*, pp 9–11. More generally on the decision to build the Hanford plant and the problems involved with its operation, see: Smyth, *Atomic Energy*, pp 64–77, 80–92.

work as soon as possible. In June 1942, Robert Oppenheimer,[41] a Professor in theoretical physics at the University of California at Berkeley, and at the California Institute of Technology at Pasadena, was asked to make a study on the design of the bomb, a project that later became known as Project Y. Although he had no administrative experience of any kind, and although he was not a Nobel Prize winner (Lawrence at Berkeley, Urey at Columbia, and Compton at Chicago, were all Nobel laureates), Oppenheimer was appointed as director of the project in October 1942 for his extraordinary qualifications.[42]

Groves endorsed the idea of putting all scientists and engineers who would be working on the design of the bomb together in isolation and to build a laboratory in a remote area that could be easily guarded and that would be conducive to keeping discoveries secret. After months of searching, the area around Albuquerque, New Mexico was eventually selected in November 1942. According to Groves the area had good rail and air service, an excellent climate, it was well isolated and far inland. On the suggestion of Oppenheimer, who knew the area quite well since he had a ranch in the neighbourhood, the final choice fell on an old boarding school at Los Alamos, 35 miles from Santa Fe, up in the Jemez Mountains of New Mexico. It was an isolated site with plenty of room for expansion, and there was testing ground available. Construction started soon after procurement, and as from March 1943, people started to work at the newly constructed laboratory.[43]

The contractor who would carry out the research at and who would operate the Los Alamos laboratory or 'Site Y', was the University of California that provided the core of the Los Alamos personnel. The rest of the team had to be assembled by Oppenheimer, which was not easy, considering the Spartan living conditions, the secrecy,[44] and the insecurities regarding the project. But the excitement of the people asked prevailed and Oppenheimer managed to gather an impressive staff, which included Bethe, Teller, Peierls, Fermi, Bohr, Chadwick, Frisch, Fuchs, Neddermeyer

[41] On Oppenheimer, see: Jungk, *Brighter than a Thousand Suns*, pp 124–55; Rhodes, *The Making of the Atomic Bomb*, pp 119–27, 443–55.

[42] Badash, *Scientists and the Development of Nuclear Weapons*, pp 41–3; Groves, *Now It Can Be Told*, pp 60–3; Hodgson, *Nuclear Physics*, pp 41–2; Rhodes, *The Making of the Atomic Bomb*, pp 127, 415–20, 447–9, 460–1; Smyth, *Atomic Energy*, pp 123–4.

[43] Badash, *Scientists and the Development of Nuclear Weapons*, pp 41–3; Badash, *Introduction*, in: Badash, Hirschfelder, Broida (Eds), *Reminiscences of Los Alamos 1943–1945*, p xvii; Groves, *Now It Can Be Told*, pp 64–7; JO Hirschfelder, *Scientific-Technological Miracle at Los Alamos*, in: Badash, Hirschfelder, Broida (Eds), *Reminiscences of Los Alamos 1943–1945*, p 71; Hodgson, *Nuclear Physics*, pp 41–2; Rhodes, *The Making of the Atomic Bomb*, pp 449–51; Smyth, *Atomic Energy*, p 124.

[44] They used fake names, mail was censored as from Dec 1943 and contact with the outside world was through a postal box in Santa Fe. Jungk, *Brighter than a Thousand Suns*, pp 121–3, 134. See also Groves, *Now It Can Be Told*, pp 138–48; Rhodes, *The Making of the Atomic Bomb*, pp 453–5.

and Kistiakowsky, and most scientists regarded it as an unforgettable experience.[45]

As soon as Oppenheimer had assembled a small scientific community of some thirty persons, mostly youngsters, he started a series of introductory lectures delivered by Serber, a close collaborator of Oppenheimer. The lectures were put together into a report that was called the Los Alamos Primer[46] which more or less became the groundwork for the Los Alamos laboratory. In his lectures Serber discussed, among other things, the efficiency of a nuclear explosion, and the issue of detonation as well as why a nuclear explosion would not ignite the atmosphere which had been something that had preoccupied nuclear physicists for some time.[47]

As far as efficiency is concerned, it has already been mentioned above that one of the major theoretical questions that had to be solved was the time available for a nuclear reaction. The violence of the explosion depended on the number of neutrons released by the chain reaction, but in order to achieve a major detonation the reaction had to be given time to proceed. Otherwise it would not be unthinkable that the bomb would already be blown apart before the bomb would reach its real explosive capacity. One solution to this problem was to surround the core by a casing or tamper in order to hold the material together and delay expansion, and to reflect the escaping neutrons.[48]

The issue of detonation, however, was equally complicated. It was considered necessary to keep the uranium in a subcritical condition in order to prevent an early explosion, or pre-detonation by stray neutrons, for example from cosmic rays, so the core material had to be arranged in such

[45] Badash, *Scientists and the Development of Nuclear Weapons*, pp 43, 46; Badash, *Introduction*, in: Badash, Hirschfelder, Broida (Eds), *Reminiscences of Los Alamos 1943–1945*, pp xix–xx; Badash, Hirschfelder, Broida (Eds), *Reminiscences of Los Alamos 1943–1945*, p ix; Groves, *Now It Can Be Told*, pp 153–60; Jungk, *Brighter than a Thousand Suns*, p 115; Rhodes, *The Making of the Atomic Bomb*, pp 452–5, 460. Not all participants felt happy about building a weapon of mass destruction. Joseph Rotblat, a Polish born nuclear physicist, who had moved to England in 1939, left Los Alamos at the end of 1944, a couple of months after he had joined the team, when it became apparent that Germany had 'abandoned their bomb project'. He found '[w]orking on the Manhattan Project (. . .) a traumatic experience' and spent the rest of his life working in a medical college and hospital on the applicability of nuclear physics to medicine. After the first test of the United States with a military configuration of a thermonuclear weapon in 1954 at Bikini Atoll, he established the Pugwash movement—<http://www.pugwash.org/>—with British philosopher Bertrand Russell. Together with Pugwash, Rotblat received the Nobel Peace Prize in 1995. See: <http://nobelprize.org/>. Rotblat died in 2005. J Rotblat, *Leaving the bomb project*, Bulletin of the Atomic Scientists, August 1985; NRC Handelsblad, 2 Sep 2005.

[46] R Serber, *The Los Alamos Primer; The First Lectures on How to Build an Atomic Bomb*, University of California Press, Berkeley, 1992.

[47] Rhodes, *The Making of the Atomic Bomb*, pp 460–4.

[48] Badash, *Scientists and the Development of Nuclear Weapons*, pp 81–2; Glasstone, Dolan, *The Effects of Nuclear Weapons*, p 15; Groves, *Now It Can Be Told*, pp 157–8; JH Manley, *A New Laboratory Is Born*, in: Badash, Hirschfelder, Broida (Eds), *Reminiscences of Los Alamos 1943–1945*, pp 32; Rhodes, *The Making of the Atomic Bomb*, pp 419, 460–5, 538–49; Smyth, *Atomic Energy*, pp 128–33.

a way that the number of neutrons produced would change from less than one to more than one. In a very short period of time the core had to change from a subcritical mass into a supercritical one.

Eventually, two design proposals remained. The first was called the gun-barrel method, a very straightforward design that seemed to be the simplest option. By this method, one subcritical piece would be fired into another subcritical piece through the barrel of a gun or cannon thereby momentarily producing a supercritical mass of fissionable material that would spontaneously undergo a self-sustaining chain-reaction leading to a nuclear explosion.[49]

One agreed that a gun-barrel assembly might very well work for a bomb using uranium as fission material, but that a bomb using plutonium required a different approach. The reason for this was the unstable nature of the material and its tendency to fission spontaneously. Instead, Neddermeyer came up with a new solution that involved the positioning of a sphere of high explosives around a core of plutonium that would be squeezed together into a tiny, super-dense lump after the ignition of the high explosives by a converging spherical shock-wave travelling through the device with a speed of seven to eight thousand meters per second with a pressure of millions of pounds per square inch, thereby creating a supercritical mass. This would avoid pre-detonation during the assembly of a critical mass. Neddermeyer called this three-dimensional squeezing technique 'implosion'. An advantage of this technique was that it required a lot less fissionable material. One disadvantage, however, was that the technique was extremely difficult to apply and that it had never been carried beyond conversation.[50]

3.4 Test Explosion

Now, the indications for the effectiveness of a gun-type device were strong but the uncertainty on the effectiveness of the implosion technique released a discussion in the fall of 1944 on the question of whether or not

[49] Badash, *Scientists and the Development of Nuclear Weapons*, pp 43–4; Badash, *Introduction*, Badash, Hirschfelder, Broida (Eds), *Reminiscences of Los Alamos 1943–1945*, p xvii; Briezeveld, Mathot, *Scoop*, pp 271–2; Glasstone, Dolan, *The Effects of Nuclear Weapons*, pp 15–16; Groves, *Now It Can Be Told*, p 158; Hirschfelder, *Scientific-Technological Miracle at Los Alamos*, in: Badash, Hirschfelder, Broida (Eds), *Reminiscences of Los Alamos 1943–1945*, pp 71–2; Rhodes, *The Making of the Atomic Bomb*, pp 359, 462–5.

[50] Badash, *Scientists and the Development of Nuclear Weapons*, pp 44, 46; Badash, *Introduction*, Badash, Hirschfelder, Broida (Eds), *Reminiscences of Los Alamos 1943–1945*, p xviii; Briezeveld, Mathot, *Scoop*, pp 271–2; Glasstone, Dolan, *The Effects of Nuclear Weapons*, p 16; Groves, *Now It Can Be Told*, p 158; Hirschfelder, *Scientific-Technological Miracle at Los Alamos*, in: Badash, Hirschfelder, Broida (Eds), *Reminiscences of Los Alamos 1943–1945*, pp 71–2; GB Kistiakowsky, *Reminiscences of Wartime Los Alamos*, in: Badash, Hirschfelder, Broida (Eds), *Reminiscences of Los Alamos 1943–1945*, p 50; Rhodes, *The Making of the Atomic Bomb*, pp 466–7, 548–9, 573–80.

to perform a test. At first, there did not seem to be enough plutonium to carry out a test and the Project could not afford to waste such precious material in a test explosion. Later, however, after solving the problems at Hanford, more plutonium was produced and at a steady rate, thereby paving the way to carry out a test of a plutonium implosion device.[51]

A date for the test, code named Trinity,[52] was deliberately set in July to make sure that Truman had news of the test at the Potsdam Summit from 17 July to 2 August 1945. Originally, the test had been set on 4 July 1945, or Independence Day but it had to be delayed to 16 July 1945 and even then it was doubtful whether the test could take place due to weather conditions. Weather conditions were very important, according to Groves, in view of the effects of the explosion, in particular the radioactive fallout, which is 'the falling to earth of particles of airborne matter [ie dust particles] which have been made radioactive through the effects of a nuclear explosion.'[53] Its danger to life depends on how long these particles retain their radioactivity which varies greatly per element. Rain was undesirable because rain would bring down excessive fallout over a small area instead of permitting it to be widely distributed, and wind was undesirable in view of the distribution of the cloud over populated areas.[54] This aspect, however, will be discussed in more detail in Chapter II.

A site was chosen at a flat, dry, and remote section of the Army Air Corp's Alamogordo Bombing Range, 60 miles northwest from Alamogordo and 100 miles south of Albuquerque, New Mexico. Since the scientists were not so sure that the test would be successful, they first proposed to place the device in a steel container so that if only a small explosion would take place, much of the precious plutonium could be saved.[55] At the time of the test, however, they were confident enough to place the bomb on a steel tower in the open.

The detonation was due at four o'clock in the morning so that the effects of the blast would be most visible and clear in the darkness. At around two, however, a violent thunderstorm blew up that was forecast to lie down at dawn. It was agreed to postpone the test until half past five. As the storm calmed down and the hour approached, the tension mounted.

[51] Groves, *Now It Can Be Told*, p 288; Kistiakowsky, *Reminiscences of Wartime Los Alamos*, in: Badash, Hirschfelder, Broida (Eds), *Reminiscences of Los Alamos 1943–1945*, pp 55–6; Rhodes, *The Making of the Atomic Bomb*, pp 571, 651–2.

[52] The name Trinity was Oppenheimer's idea as he was inspired by a poem of John Donne, 'Hymne to God My God, in my Sicknesse'. This poem as well as another poem by Donne reflect complementarity, which is also present in the power of an atomic bomb, which he had learned to appreciate after conversations with Bohr. According to Bohr and Oppenheimer, 'the bomb (. . .) was a weapon of death that might also end war and redeem mankind'. Rhodes, *The Making of the Atomic Bomb*, pp 571–3.

[53] Groves, *Now It Can Be Told*, p 291, fn 2.

[54] Groves, *Now It Can Be Told*, pp 291–3.

[55] Groves, *Now It Can Be Told*, pp 288–91.

All observers were waiting anxiously to see what was going to happen, and to see the result of their efforts.

What they saw then was almost indescribable; it was something that went completely beyond anybody's imagination.[56] The observers first saw an enormous flash of blinding light[57] and subsequently, a rising multi-colour ball of fire, followed only a few seconds later by the blast that knocked down all those who were standing. As far as the flash is concerned, Teller thought it 'was like opening the heavy curtains of a darkened room to a flood of sunlight'[58] and Bethe said that:

> it looked like a giant magnesium flare which kept on for what seemed a whole minute but was actually one or two seconds.[59]

Somebody else recorded that it was not so much the light that had disturbed him but the heat. 'It was like opening a hot oven with the sun coming out like a sunrise.'[60] The explosion in general was 'a foul and awesome display,' according to Trinity-test director Bainbridge[61] and Serber said afterwards that 'the grandeur and magnitude of the phenomenon were completely breathtaking.'[62]

They found that the bomb's yield had been the equivalent of 18.6 kilotons of conventional high explosives (trinitro-toluene or TNT), which was four times what they had expected. The devastation from a single bomb was indeed comparable to that of a major air raid. The bomb had vaporised the steel tower leaving a huge radioactive crater of green, glassy and fused desert sand. The radioactive fallout was their greatest concern after the test, but the first reports that started to come in half an hour after the test from a network of people equipped with Geiger counters were not alarming. The civilian evacuation plans did not have to be executed.[63]

[56] Badash, *Scientists and the Development of Nuclear Weapons*, p 47; Groves, *Now It Can Be Told*, pp 295–6; Hodgson, *Nuclear Physics*, p 43; Jungk, *Brighter than a Thousand Suns*, pp 196–200; Kistiakowsky, *Reminiscences of Wartime Los Alamos*, in: Badash, Hirschfelder, Broida (Eds), *Reminiscences of Los Alamos 1943–1945*, p 56; Rhodes, *The Making of the Atomic Bomb*, pp 651–78; Seaborg, *A Chemist in the White House*, p 13.

[57] The title of Jungk's book, 'Brighter than a Thousand Suns' refers specifically to this blinding flash of light. It is based on a passage from the Bhagavad-Gita that flashed into Oppenheimer's mind after the successful Trinity test: 'If the radiance of a thousand suns; were to burst into the sky; that would be like; the splendor of the Mighty One'. Jungk, *Brighter than a Thousand Suns*, p 201. Oppenheimer also refers to another passage from the same source for this moment, when Vishnu says: 'Now I am become Death, the destroyer of worlds.' Rhodes, *The Making of the Atomic Bomb*, p 676. Jungk, *Brighter than a Thousand Suns*, p 201.

[58] Teller, in: Rhodes, *The Making of the Atomic Bomb*, p 672.

[59] Bethe, in: Rhodes, *The Making of the Atomic Bomb*, p 673.

[60] Morrison, in: Rhodes, *The Making of the Atomic Bomb*, p 673.

[61] Bainbridge, in: Rhodes, *The Making of the Atomic Bomb*, p 675.

[62] Serber, in: Rhodes, *The Making of the Atomic Bomb*, p 673. For other comments, see: Rhodes, *The Making of the Atomic Bomb*, pp 672–6.

[63] Badash, *Scientists and the Development of Nuclear Weapons*, p 47; Groves, *Now It Can Be Told*, pp 296–301; Rhodes, *The Making of the Atomic Bomb*, pp 676–8.

3.5 Hiroshima and Nagasaki

During the research phase, no one had ever really questioned the ultimate use of the bomb, in any case against Japan.[64] As a matter of fact, most of the memoranda that dealt with the Project used the words 'after or when' it was used and never 'if' it were used. Already in 1944, one had agreed that the target would be Japan in view of the fact that the war in Europe would be over before the bomb would be ready. The only question was how the bomb should be employed. Should there be a demonstration of the bomb's power after which an ultimatum had to be delivered to the Japanese, or should the bomb be used without warning taking the Japanese completely by surprise. A demonstration had been suggested in the Franck Report of 11 June 1945[65] which concluded that military application without warning was inadvisable and proposed, instead, to demonstrate the effects of the bomb to the Japanese leaders in an uninhabited desert or island, either in the US or in Japan.[66] The Report was discussed by the Scientific Advisory Panel consisting of Compton, Fermi, Lawrence and Oppenheimer in mid June 1945 but there were too many practical objections and they rejected the recommendation.[67]

[64] Rhodes gives a comprehensive description of the way the western world looked at Asians and the Japanese in particular. At first, it was found difficult to take them seriously, largely because of their different physical characteristics. Later, when fighting continued and the US had started a slow and bloody push up the Pacific, this changed into a deep aversion to them. They were compared with animals, because of the way they thought, their fear of being captured and the absence of fear of dying, most clearly accentuated in the appearance of kamikazes, which cost so many casualties. The proportion of captured to dead Japanese in the North Burma campaign, for example, was about 1:120, whereas among western nations these ratios are normally 4:1. The Germans at least they could respect, but fighting against the Japanese required a totally new set of skills. This 'bestiality' made it also emotionally easier to kill them, no matter how. Everything was justified in order to save the lives of American soldiers. Flame-throwers were invented and firebombing of Japanese cities became a common event as soon as they came within reach of US bombers. BJ Bernstein, *The Atomic Bombings Reconsidered*, Foreign Affairs, Vol 74, 1995, pp 140–1; Rhodes, *The Making of the Atomic Bomb*, pp 517–21.

[65] Report of the Committee on Political and Social Problems; Manhattan Project; 'Metallurgical Laboratory'; University of Chicago, Jun 11, 1945. The Committee was chaired by Nobel laureate Franck and further consisted of Hughes, Nickson, Rabinowitch, Seaborg, Stearns, and Szilard. Jungk, *Brighter than a Thousand Suns*, App B, pp 348–60, or through: <http://www.atomicarchive.com/>.

[66] A poll at the Met Lab in Chicago showed that 15% of the people preferred to '[u]se the weapon in the manner that is from the military point of view most effective in bringing about prompt Japanese surrender at minimum human cost to our armed forces.' 46% preferred to '[g]ive a military demonstration in Japan, to be followed by renewed opportunity for surrender before full use of the weapon is employed.' 26% preferred to '[g]ive an experimental demonstration in this country, with representatives of Japan present; followed by a new opportunity for surrender before full use of the weapons is employed.' 11% favoured to '[w]ithhold military use of the weapons, but make public experimental demonstration of their effectiveness.' And only 2% wanted to '[m]aintain as secret as possible all development of our new weapons, and refrain from using them in this war.' Through: <http://www.atomicarchive.com/>.

[67] The Scientific Advisory Panel was to advise the Interim Committee which had been established to advise the President on matters of atomic energy. Generally on the discussion

Truman, who had succeeded Roosevelt after his death on 12 April 1945, eventually decided on military use[68] for a number of reasons. First of all, it was believed that the atomic bomb could force Japan to surrender and thereby save tens of thousands of lives.[69] Secondly, these efforts had meanwhile become so costly (around 2 billion dollars, which amounts to some 20 billion dollars at the beginning of the 21st century)[70] involving tens of thousands of people that, according to Groves, 'the government [had become] increasingly committed to the ultimate use of the bomb.'[71] And thirdly, the bomb was needed to put the Soviets on notice and reveal a shift in the balance of powers in post-war international relations.[72]

The next step was the selection of the targets. For this purpose a special Target Committee was established consisting of eight people, three of which came from the Air Force, and the others from the Manhattan Project. Firstly, the targets had to be 'places the bombing of which would most adversely affect the will of the Japanese people to continue the war.'[73] Secondly, it had to be a military target, ie military headquarters, troop concentrations or a military-industrial complex producing equipment and supplies, and in order to be able to identify the effects of the bomb most clearly, the target should not have been damaged by previous air raids. And thirdly, they had to take into account the maximum range of the aircraft, the need for visual bombing in order to aim with certainty and to photograph the effects, which means that they had to contemplate

whether or not to use the bomb: Jungk, *Brighter than a Thousand Suns*, pp 176–86; Rhodes, *The Making of the Atomic Bomb*, pp 634–50.

[68] Groves, *Now It Can Be Told*, p 266; Hirschfelder, *Scientific-Technological Miracle at Los Alamos*, in: Badash, Hirschfelder, Broida (Eds), *Reminiscences of Los Alamos 1943–1945*, p 87; Rhodes, *The Making of the Atomic Bomb*, p 651. On Truman and his first weeks as President of the United States, see: Rhodes, *The Making of the Atomic Bomb*, pp 613–25.

[69] The invasion of Kyushu, the most southern island of Japan was planned for 1 Nov 1945 requiring a force of 36 divisions, or 1,532,000 men. Casualties were expected to be heavy and it was still uncertain whether the civilian population would fight to the death when unconditional surrender meant dethroning the emperor. The invasion and conquest of Iwo Jima on 19 Feb 1945 had produced the highest casualty ratio in the history of the Marine Corps. When fighting ended in late Mar 1945, 6,821 marines were dead and 21,865 were wounded. Groves, *Now It Can Be Told*, pp 263–4; Rhodes, *The Making of the Atomic Bomb*, pp 594–5, 641. Compare also BVA Röling, *Inleiding tot de wetenschap van oorlog en vrede*, Van Gorcum, Assen, 1968, pp 166–7.

[70] At <http://eh.net/hmit/ppowerusd/>.

[71] Groves, *Now It Can Be Told*, p 265. Also: Jungk, *Brighter than a Thousand Suns*, pp 208–9. Compare also Röling who writes that it is a natural inclination to use things for which considerable efforts have been made. Röling, *Inleiding tot de wetenschap van oorlog en vrede*, pp 170–1, 175.

[72] Bernstein, *The Atomic Bombings Reconsidered*, pp 138–9, 145–6, 149; Groves, *Now It Can Be Told*, p 265; Jungk, *Brighter than a Thousand Suns*, pp 176–7; Rhodes, *The Making of the Atomic Bomb*, pp 696–7. Röling believes that this was in fact the most important reason to use the atomic bomb. Röling, *Inleiding tot de wetenschap van oorlog en vrede*, pp 172–3.

[73] Groves, *Now It Can Be Told*, p 267.

the desired weather conditions, and the need to have three targets available per run, ie one primary, and two subsidiary targets.[74]

Finding a city that had not yet been destroyed or heavily damaged by air raids and that could be saved from bombing until the dropping of the atomic bombs was not easy. The first raid on Japan, after the Doolittle raid of 1942 and raids from mainland China, was on 24 November 1944 when B-29s had come within reach of Japan, and Japanese cities had been attacked ever since.[75] In the night of 9 to 10 March 1945, Tokyo was attacked with 334 B-29s dropping more than 2,000 tons of incendiary bombs. The burning of wood-and-paper houses in combination with a strong wind caused a firestorm, destroying an area of around 41 square kilometers and killing more than 100,000 people in less than six hours. In the following days, similar bomber raids devastated the city centres of Nagoya, Osaka and Kobe.[76]

Air strikes on population centres had not been uncommon in the Pacific or in Europe. The Air Force justified the attacks on civilian targets among other things by referring to the fact that both the Japanese and German governments were mobilising the population to fight the Allies, which would make them a legitimate military target.[77] The argument is not convincing, since the principle of distinction, which is one of the fundamental principles of the laws of war, requires that belligerents must always distinguish between military and civilian objects, and it seems far-fetched to regard civilians who have not yet taken up arms against an adversary as combatants. The principles of the laws of war will be discussed, further below, in Chapter III.

In 1945, the principle of distinction was reflected in Article 25 of the Hague Regulations on Land Warfare,[78] which was considered to be customary international law by the Nuremberg Tribunal in 1946,[79] as well as in Article 1 of Hague Convention IX Concerning Bombardment by Naval

[74] Badash, *Scientists and the Development of Nuclear Weapons*, p 51; Bernstein, *The Atomic Bombings Reconsidered*, p 144; Groves, *Now It Can Be Told*, pp 267–8; Rhodes, *The Making of the Atomic Bomb*, pp 626–7.

[75] Jimmy Doolittle's surprise attack on Tokyo in mid Apr 1942 with 16 B-25s from the US carrier Hornet to landing fields in China had been made to boost morale. Rhodes, *The Making of the Atomic Bomb*, pp 407, 588.

[76] Badash, *Scientists and the Development of Nuclear Weapons*, p 55; Bernstein, *The Atomic Bombings Reconsidered*, pp 140–1; Rhodes, *The Making of the Atomic Bomb*, pp 596–600.

[77] Rhodes, *The Making of the Atomic Bomb*, p 596.

[78] Hague Convention (II) with respect to the Laws and Customs of War on Land, with annexed Regs, signed on 29 Jul 1899, entered into force on 4 Sep 1900, AJIL, Vol 1, No 2, supp: Official Documents, 1907, p 129; Hague Convention (IV) Respecting the Laws and Customs of War on Land, with annexed Regs, signed on 18 Oct 1907, entered into force on 26 Jan 1910, AJIL, Vol 2, No 1/2, supp: Official Documents, 1908, p 90.

[79] International Military Tribunal (Nuremberg), *Judgments and Sentences; October 1, 1946*, American Journal of International Law, Vol 41, 1947, pp 248–9.

Forces in Time of War.[80] Furthermore, the principle of distinction was reflected in Articles 22 and 24 of the 1923 Hague Rules of Aerial Warfare.[81] Although these Hague Rules were never adopted as an international agreement, and although there were therefore no specific rules on aerial warfare during World War II, the contents of Articles 22 and 24 reflect the fundamental and customary obligation for belligerents to distinguish between military and civilian objects.[82]

The indiscriminate bombardment of Japanese cities may only be justified by reference to the doctrine of belligerent reprisals,[83] but it is uncertain whether they satisfy the various requirements. Belligerent reprisals must be a response to prior violations of the laws of war, that can be attributed either to the enemy state or, under circumstances, to its allies; they must be proportionate and subsidiary; and they must be undertaken for the purpose of putting an end to these prior wrongful acts.[84] Although Japan had committed atrocities against the civilian population in all of its occupied territories, primarily in China and Korea—after the fall of Nanjing, in December 1937, the Japanese Army massacred between 200,000 and 300,000 civilians[85]—it is unlikely that the

[80] Hague Convention (IX) Concerning Bombardment by Naval Forces in Time of War, signed on 18 Oct 1907, entered into force on 26 Jan 1910, AJIL, Vol 2, No 1/2, Supplement: Official Documents, 1908, p 146.

[81] 1923 Hague Rules of Aerial Warfare, in: A Roberts, R Guelff, *Documents on the Laws of War*, Oxford University Press, Oxford, 2000, pp 141–53. Art 24(1) provided that '[a]erial bombardment is legitimate only when directed at a military objective (. . .)' and Art 22 stated: 'Aerial bombardment for the purpose of terrorizing the civilian population, of destroying or damaging private property not of military character, or of injuring non-combatants is prohibited.'

[82] Similarly the District Court of Tokyo, Japan, on 7 Dec 1963; Ryuchi Shimoda *et al* v The State, in: E Lauterpacht (Ed), International Law Reports, Vol 32, Butterworths, London, 1966, pp 629–31. Post refers to two cases before the Greco-German Mixed Arbitral Tribunal—Coenca Brothers v Germany and Kiriadolou v Germany—from 1927 and 1930 that are exemplary for the application of general rules of the laws of war on aerial warfare. 'The Tribunal found that "there is no reason why the rules adopted for bombardment in war on land should not equally apply to aerial attacks"'. HHG Post, *War Crimes in Air Warfare*, in: N Ronzitti, G Venturini (Eds), *The Law of Air Warfare—Contemporary Issues*, Eleven International Publishing, Utrecht, 2006, pp 160–2. Also G Schwarzenberger, *International Law; As Applied by International Courts and Tribunals; Volume II; The Law of Armed Conflict*, Stevens & Sons, London, 1968, pp 144–50.

[83] F Kalshoven, *Belligerent Reprisals*, AW Sijthoff, Leiden, 1971.

[84] C Greenwood, *The Twilight of the Law of Belligerent Reprisals*, Netherlands Yearbook of International Law, Vol 20, 1989, p 40; Kalshoven, *Belligerent Reprisals*, p 33.

[85] See: <http://en.wikipedia.org/wiki/Nanking_massacre>. The massacre became known as the 'Rape of Nanking'. According to the International Military Tribunal for the Far East, in the case against general Iwane Matsui, 'a long succession of most horrible atrocities committed by the Japanese Army upon the helpless citizens. Wholesale massacres, individual murders, rape, looting and arson were committed by Japanese soldiers. (. . .) This orgy of crime started with the capture of the City on the 13th December 1937 and did not cease until early in February 1938. In this period of six or seven weeks thousands of women were raped, upwards of 100,000 people were killed and untold property was stolen and burned.' Iwane Matsui was sentenced to death by hanging. BVA Röling, CF Rüter, *The Tokyo Judgment; The International Military Tribunal for the Far East (I.M.T.F.E) 29 April 1946–12 November 1948; Volume I*, University Press Amsterdam, Amsterdam 1977, pp 389–91, 453–4, 465.

bombardments in 1944 and 1945 were carried out in order to stop these war crimes.

The cities that were eventually selected were, in order of choice: Hiroshima, because of its large port used by the Japanese Army, its Army headquarters with 25,000 troops in garrison and its large industrial complex; Kokura Arsenal, because of a very large munitions plant; Niigata, because of its heavy industries and its port of increasing importance; and Kyoto, because it was the ancient capital of Japan, it had a population of about 1 million, and displaced industries were moving to this city. Secretary of War Stimson immediately objected to Kyoto and although against the will of the Committee he had it removed from the list because of its great cultural, historical and religious significance, and President Truman concurred with Stimson's decision.[86] Nagasaki was only added in the last week of July, probably because it was one of the last cities that had not yet been bombed and because it was not too far away from Hiroshima and Kokura. Nagasaki was a major military port and was one of the largest shipbuilding and repair cities.[87]

Truman wanted Japan to have sufficient time to consider the ultimatum that the Allied Forces had released at the Potsdam Summit of 17 July till 2 August 1945. In the so-called Potsdam Declaration issued on 26 July 1945, the President of the United States, the Prime Minister of Great Britain and the President of Nationalist China[88] presented an ultimatum to Japan in which they offered Japan the choice between unconditional surrender[89] and total destruction, without mentioning the existence of the atomic bomb:

> We call upon the government of Japan to proclaim now the unconditional surrender of all Japanese armed forces (. . .). The alternative for Japan is prompt and utter destruction.[90]

The ultimatum was rejected the following day.

[86] Badash, *Scientists and the Development of Nuclear Weapons*, pp 51–2; Bernstein, *The Atomic Bombings Reconsidered*, p 147; Groves, *Now It Can Be Told*, pp 272–5, 316; Rhodes, *The Making of the Atomic Bomb*, pp 627–8, 630–2, 639–41.

[87] Groves, *Now It Can Be Told*, pp 342–3; Rhodes, *The Making of the Atomic Bomb*, p 689.

[88] The Soviet Union did not declare war upon Japan until 8 Aug 1945.

[89] It should be noted that Roosevelt had used the phrase 'unconditional surrender' by mistake at the Press Conference after the Casablanca Summit in Jan 1945. Because divergence in statements would have been damaging to the cause, Churchill immediately concurred. From that moment on 'unconditional surrender became official Allied policy.' Rhodes, *The Making of the Atomic Bomb*, p 521. Junk refers to American historian Butow who believes that the war could have been brought to and end by diplomatic means if the Potsdam Declaration had not been issued. Already in the spring of 1945, the United States had significant indications that Japan wanted to surrender if the position of the Emperor would not be affected. The Potsdam Declaration made it difficult for the Japanese Government to capitulate without losing face. Junk, *Brighter than a Thousand Suns*, pp 207–8. Similarly: Röling, *Inleiding tot de wetenschap van oorlog en vrede*, p 170.

[90] Potsdam Declaration; Proclamation Defining Terms for Japanese Surrender Issued, at Potsdam, Jul 26, 1945. Through: <http://www.atomicarchive.com/>. Badash, *Scientists and the Development of Nuclear Weapons*, pp 53–4; Groves, *Now It Can Be Told*, p 311; Rhodes, *The Making of the Atomic Bomb*, pp 692–3.

Bad weather over Japan in early August delayed the first dropping. When the weather improved and the forecasts for the following days indicated good weather over the target cities, it was decided and officially confirmed that the first raid would take place early in the morning of Monday, 6 August 1945. The targets that were presented to the crews, who were only now briefed on the nature of their cargo, were Hiroshima, Kokura, and Nagasaki. The first mission was carried out under the command of Colonel Tibbets, commander of the 509th Composite Group, which had been established in December 1944 for this specific task. He had decided to fly this mission himself and had named the aircraft the *Enola Gay* after his mother, because she had assured him that he would not be killed flying when he told his parents that he was going to be a pilot.[91] Apart from the *Enola Gay*, the entire mission consisted of six other aircraft: one being sent to Iwo Jima, in case the *Enola Gay* would face mechanical problems; three planes to the three targets to appraise the weather condition; and two planes stuffed with measuring and recording equipment were supposed to follow the *Enola Gay* and observe the effects of the explosion. Tibbets took off as scheduled at 2:45 am. There was no flak and there were no fighters; the weather planes reported that Hiroshima was the best target. At an altitude of 31,000 feet and a speed of 328 miles Little Boy was dropped at exactly 8:15:19 am Hiroshima time. Little Boy exploded 43 seconds later at exactly 8:16:02 am at an altitude of 1,900 feet with an equivalent yield of around 12.5 kiloton TNT.[92]

Just as the observers of the Trinity test, the crews of the *Enola Gay* and the observer planes were stunned. As they were diving and turning, the plane was first filled with a bright light from the flash and was then hit by the two shock waves—the first being the direct result of the blast and the second being the reflection from the ground. Tibbets:

> We turned back to look at Hiroshima. The city was hidden by that awful cloud (. . .) boiling up, mushrooming, terrible and incredibly tall.[93]

The observation planes reported that five minutes after the explosion a white column with an enlarged top emerged from the grey cloud that lay over the city. The column looked like a mushroom and rose to a height of 35,000 feet. Another member of the crew, Lewis:

> Where we had seen a clear city two minutes before, we could no longer see the city. We could see smoke and fires creeping up the sides of the mountains.[94]

[91] Groves, *Now It Can Be Told*, p 317; Rhodes, *The Making of the Atomic Bomb*, pp 583, 703.

[92] Badash, *Scientists and the Development of Nuclear Weapons*, p 54; Groves, *Now It Can Be Told*, pp 316–18; Rhodes, *The Making of the Atomic Bomb*, pp 704–11. According to a Report from Los Alamos, the estimated yield was around 15 kilotons. J Malik, *The Yields of the Hiroshima and Nagasaki Nuclear Explosions*, Los Alamos National Laboratory, Sep 1985, p 25. Through: <http://www.atomicarchive.com/>.

[93] Tibbets, in: Rhodes, *The Making of the Atomic Bomb*, p 710.

[94] Lewis, in: Rhodes, *The Making of the Atomic Bomb*, p 710.

Estimates on the number of casualties vary to a certain extent. According to United States Strategic Bombing Survey and the British Mission to Japan in 1946, the casualty estimates were between 70,000 and 90,000 people killed or missing, and about a similar number injured.[95] And Glasstone and Dolan come up with respectively 68,000 and 76,000 casualties, in 1977.[96] At the end of 1945, the death rate had gone up to approximately to 130,000–140,000 people.[97]

As was already observed above, the whole idea behind the use of atomic weapons was to coerce the Japanese to surrender. It was therefore considered important to have the second blow follow quickly after the first, in case Japan refused to surrender, which it did. At first, Fat Man was scheduled for 11 August 1945, but due to bad weather forecasts they had to move up the date to 9 August 1945, one day after the Soviet Union declared war on Japan. Major Sweeney was the pilot of the second strike plane called the *Bock's Car*, after its usual commander Frederick Bock. Sweeney took off at 3:47 am; primary target Kokura Arsenal on the north coast of Kyushu; secondary target Nagasaki, on the north-west coast of Kyushu. At Kokura, Sweeney found out that visual bombing was impossible, in spite of what the weather planes had reported. After three runs over the city, he decided to proceed to Nagasaki which city he found covered with clouds as well. They had only time for one approach, otherwise they would run out of fuel, so contrary to his orders, Sweeney decided to bomb by radar. At the last minute, however, a hole appeared in the clouds revealing part of the target, just enough to allow a twenty-second visual run. Fat Man was aimed one and a half miles north of the original target

[95] United States Strategic Bombing Survey, *The Effects of the Atomic bombs on Hiroshima and Nagasaki*, Chairman's Office, 30 Jun 1946; United States Government Printing Office, Washington, DC, 1946, p 3; British Mission to Japan, *The Effects of the Atomic Bombs at Hiroshima and Nagasaki*, Report of the British Mission to Japan, His Majesty's Stationery Office, London, 1946, p 18.

[96] Glasstone, Dolan, *The Effects of Nuclear Weapons*, p 544. Badash mentions 70,000–80,000 dead and 70,000–80,000 wounded. Badash, *Scientists and the Development of Nuclear Weapons*, p 56.

[97] Rhodes, *The Making of the Atomic Bomb*, pp 733–4. The Committee for the Compilation of Materials on Damage Cause by the Atomic Bombs in Hiroshima and Nagasaki refers to 7 reports from 1945 to 1961, each with different figures. It believes that the report of the Hiroshima Prefecture of 30 Nov 1945 'offers a highly credible death count': 78,150 dead, and 13,983 missing, presumably dead. For the critical stage of 2 to 4 months after 6 Aug 1945, 'the overall estimate for A-bomb deaths in Hiroshima for the initial critical stage is currently set at 90,000–120,000.' Committee for the Compilation of Materials on Damage Cause by the Atomic Bombs in Hiroshima and Nagasaki, *The Impact of the A-Bomb; Hiroshima and Nagasaki, 1945–85*, Iwanami Shoten, Tokyo, 1985, pp 18–21. See also the British Medical Association; Report of the British Medical Association's Board of Science and Education, *The Medical Effects of Nuclear War*, John Wiley & Sons, Chichester, 1983, pp 4, 47; Groves writes that according to the Japanese, the casualties were estimated at 71,000 dead and missing, and 68,000 injured. Groves, *Now It Can Be Told*, p 319. Singh and McWhinney estimate the number of casualties at approximately 70,000 dead and missing (minimum), and 70,000 wounded (minimum). N Singh, E McWhinney, *Nuclear Weapons and Contemporary International Law*, Martinus Nijhoff Publishers, Dordrecht, 1989, p 387.

and dropped from an altitude of 29,000 feet. It exploded 1,650 feet above the city at 11:02 am with an explosive force equivalent to 22 kiloton TNT.[98] Photos showed that 44 per cent of the city had been destroyed;[99] casualties were estimated by the United States Strategic Bombing Survey and the British Mission at between 35,000 and 40,000 dead or missing and a similar number injured in 1946.[100] Glasstone and Dolan mention figures of 38,000 dead or missing and 21,000 injured.[101] Some 60,000–70,000 people had died at the end of 1945;[102] five years later the death rate had increased to 140,000 similar to the death rate in Hiroshima.[103]

Still, Japan refused to accept unconditional surrender. After a few days the United States grew impatient and the Air Force resumed area bombing, pending the completion of another plutonium-implosion device, which would be ready for delivery at around 17 August 1945. Civilian and military leaders were still engaged in a deadlocked debate on surrender, which forced the Emperor to undertake the extraordinary step of interfering. Having gained support from the Imperial Family, he eventually addressed the issue of surrender and instructed his cabinet to stop fighting and to accept the Potsdam Declaration and the surrender of the Japanese Armies on 14 August 1945.[104]

4—THE HYDROGEN BOMB

After the war, attention shifted to the other way of releasing nuclear energy, namely nuclear fusion. Nuclear fusion is a phenomenon in which

[98] According to the Los Alamos Report, the bomb's yield was around 21 kilotons. Malik, *The Yields of the Hiroshima and Nagasaki Nuclear Explosions*, p 25. Badash writes the its yield was 20 kt. Badash, *Scientists and the Development of Nuclear Weapons*, p 55.

[99] Groves, *Now It Can Be Told*, p 346.

[100] United States Strategic Bombing Survey, *The Effects of the Atomic bombs on Hiroshima and Nagasaki*, p 5; The British Mission to Japan gives a figure of around 37,000 killed in 1946. British Mission to Japan, *The Effects of the Atomic Bombs at Hiroshima and Nagasaki*, p 19. Groves refers to the Strategic Bombing Survey mentioning casualty estimates of 35,000 killed and 60,000 injured. Groves, *Now It Can Be Told*, p 346.

[101] Glasstone, Dolan, *The Effects of Nuclear Weapons*, p 544. Badash mentions estimates of 35,000–40,000 dead and 35,000–40,000 wounded; Singh and McWhinney write 35,000 (minimum) respectively 40,000 (minimum). Badash, *Scientists and the Development of Nuclear Weapons*, p 56; Singh, McWhinney, *Nuclear Weapons and Contemporary International Law*, p 387.

[102] The Committee for the Compilation of Materials on Damage Cause by the Atomic Bombs in Hiroshima and Nagasaki refers to 7 reports from 1945 to 1956, each with different figures.

The estimated losses around 1950 were 60,000–70,000 dead. Committee for the Compilation of Materials on Damage Cause by the Atomic Bombs in Hiroshima and Nagasaki, *The Impact of the A-Bomb; Hiroshima and Nagasaki, 1945–85*, pp 18–21. Also British Medical Association; Report of the British Medical Association's Board of Science and Education, *The Medical Effects of Nuclear War*, pp 4, 47; Rhodes, *The Making of the Atomic Bomb*, pp 740–2.

[103] Rhodes, *The Making of the Atomic Bomb*, pp 740–2.

[104] Badash, *Scientists and the Development of Nuclear Weapons*, p 57; Groves, *Now It Can Be Told*, pp 354–5; Rhodes, *The Making of the Atomic Bomb*, pp 742–6; United States Strategic Bombing Survey, *The Effects of the Atomic bombs on Hiroshima and Nagasaki*, pp 22–3.

nuclei are fused together to form a new element under the release of enormous amounts of energy. So, in that sense, it is exactly the opposite of nuclear fission which releases energy by splitting nuclei. Already before the war research had been carried out with respect to the mechanisms that fire stars and one had come to the conclusion that their energy was based on nuclear fusion.[105]

Nuclear fusion is in principle only possible under extremely high temperatures measuring tens of millions degrees Celsius,[106] comparable to those found in the center of the sun. The high temperatures are required to give the nuclei a speed high enough to overcome the electrical barrier that repels elements with the same electrical charge. That is why one usually uses the term thermonuclear fusion. The word thermo comes from the Greek word *thermos*, which means hot. And this is just for the various isotopes of hydrogen, with only one positively charged proton: H (hydrogen; one proton, no neutrons), D (deuterium; one proton, one neutron) and T (tritium; one proton, two neutrons).[107]

The first to recognise the potential of the enormous amount of energy released during an explosion based on nuclear fission was Fermi in September 1941 in the presence of Teller. He suggested that the enormous heat could be used to trigger a nuclear fusion reaction using hydrogen, or H isotopes. A fission bomb would thus function as a detonator for a fusion, hydrogen or H-bomb.[108] An H-bomb would not only be cheaper than a fission bomb due to the fact that hydrogen is abundant in nature, but fusion would also be more efficient than fission in the sense that in principle all reacting material will be used. This implies that bombs of unlimited size could be constructed. In fission, the yield depends on the amount of material that is fissioned before the bomb blows apart setting a maximum explosive yield of an equivalent of about one Megaton TNT.[109]

The idea would never leave Teller. The idea of making a thermonuclear bomb or hydrogen bomb, quickly designated 'Super', was discussed by a

[105] Hans Bethe, the German born physicist, who had headed the Theoretical Division at Los Alamos, had published an article in 1938 on energy production in stars, for which he was awarded the Nobel Prize in 1967. Through: <http://nobelprize.org/>. Bethe died in 2005. NRC Handelsblad, 8 maa 2005.

[106] For years, scientists have tried to realise fusion under extremely low temperature, so-called 'cold fusion', but they have been unsuccessful so far.

[107] Barash, *Introduction to Peace Studies*, pp 106–7; Glasstone, Dolan, *The Effects of Nuclear Weapons*, pp 20–2; Hodgson, *Nuclear Physics*, pp 44–5; Rhodes, *The Making of the Atomic Bomb*, pp 150, 370–1.

[108] Because of these high temperatures, peaceful use of nuclear fusion is practically very difficult. Recently, the People's Republic of China, the European Union and Switzerland (represented by Euratom), India, Japan, the Republic of Korea, the Russian Federation, and the United States have set up an international organization—ITER, or International Fusion Energy Organization—under auspices of the International Atomic Energy Agency, to build an experimental nuclear fusion reactor. ITER is located in France and must be operational in 2016. See: <http://www.iter.org/>.

[109] Badash, *Scientists and the Development of Nuclear Weapons*, p 81.

group of theoretical physicists in Oppenheimer's study group at Berkeley in the summer of 1942 and despite widespread scepticism, many unanswered questions, and too many presumptions, the idea was under serious investigation as from July 1942. As from 1944, Teller worked full-time on the Super, whose theoretical complexity challenged him more than the fission bomb.[110]

Immediately after the war, the United States government did not feel urged to carry on with the development of the Super, and much to the dissatisfaction of Teller,[111] fusion studies were completely stopped on 3 June 1946 after most of the scientific personnel had left. Because the United States had a nuclear monopoly with an increasing number of bombs, there was no need to spend millions of dollars on an even stronger weapon.[112] This feeling changed, however, when the Soviet Union managed to carry out a nuclear test explosion in August 1949. In January 1950, Truman instructed the United States Atomic Energy Commission (AEC), which had been established in 1946,[113] to initiate a crash program to build thermonuclear weapons.[114] The so-called hydrogen bomb should lead the country back to 'superiority'.

It is interesting to note that the AEC's General Advisory Committee (GAC) consisting of scientific advisors and chaired by Oppenheimer unanimously advised not to proceed with the H-bomb.[115] They argued that the bomb's yield would be too large for military targets which left cities as the only possible targets and which would make the Super an indiscriminate weapon. They believed the bomb was 'an evil thing' and

[110] Badash, *Scientists and the Development of Nuclear Weapons*, pp 41, 81; Jungk, *Brighter than a Thousand Suns*, pp 265–70; Rhodes, *The Making of the Atomic Bomb*, pp 374–5, 415–22, 538–47. The first, however, to make this connection was Hagiwara of the University of Kyoto who discussed the matter a few months earlier.

[111] Teller was not only disappointed because of scientific reasons, but also because of his intense mistrust of the Soviet Union. His anti-communist sentiments even led him to testify against Oppenheimer in 1954 before the McCarthy Commission. Later, in his memoirs, Teller would write that the bombing of Nagasaki and Hiroshima had been wrong. Instead, a nightly demonstration over Tokyo would have been the proper choice. Teller died in 2003. NRC Handelsblad, 19 Sep 2003.

[112] The number of bombs that the US produced after the war was anxiously kept secret. They did not want other countries to be able to deduce the United States' atomic bomb production capacity. In the early 1980s they were released and they turned out to be surprisingly small: 1945 (2), 1946 (9), 1947 (13), 1948 (50). Badash, *Scientists and the Development of Nuclear Weapons*, p 75.

[113] The US AEC was established by the Atomic Energy Act which entered into force on 1 Aug 1946. An Act; For the development and control of atomic energy, Public Law 585–79th Congress; 1 Aug 1946. According to s21, 'This Act may be cited as the "Atomic Energy Act of 1946."' The AEC was controlled by civilian authorities and existed until 1974. In 1974, the AEC was replaced by the Energy Research and Development Administration, which was the predecessor of the Department of Energy, established in 1977.
Through: http://www.energy.gov/aboutus/history/.

[114] Statement President Truman on 22 Jan 1950. At: <http://www.atomicarchive.com/Docs/Hydrogen/HBomb.shtml>.

[115] GAC's Reports on Building the H-Bomb; Oct 30, 1949. At: <http://www.atomicarchive.com/Docs/Hydrogen/GACReport.shtml>.

ethically unjustifiable. Convinced of their social responsibility, they even argued for a unilateral commitment never to pursue and develop thermonuclear weapons. Although the AEC adopted the GAC's advice, they were overruled by a subcommittee of the National Security Council.[116]

Research was resumed at the Los Alamos Laboratory. Just after the war, the Los Alamos Laboratory had struggled for survival, but it had been considered important to maintain the laboratory for the further improvement of existing atomic weapon technology.[117] Most of the scientists had left but the development of the Super gave new impetus to scientific life at Los Alamos.[118]

Before they could start with the development of a full-scale thermonuclear weapon, Teller and his group first focused on the 'booster principle'. The 'booster principle' is based on the idea that a large amount of fissionable material may ignite a small portion of thermonuclear fuel; and the larger the portion of thermonuclear fuel, the more the bomb approaches the concept of a hydrogen bomb. In fact, the Super is the final stage in which a relative large portion of hydrogen isotopes is ignited by a small fission device. Successful tests were conducted in May 1951 (boosted fission weapon) and in November 1952 (full-scale thermonuclear weapon). The latter test had taken place at Eniwetok Atoll in the Marshall Islands,[119] in the Pacific Ocean, and it had an equivalent yield of 10 Megaton TNT, ie a thousand times more powerful than Little Boy. The island where Mike had been detonated had vaporised leaving a crater of half a mile deep and two miles wide. A second test was carried out in March 1954 with a military configuration that fitted in an airplane. This H-bomb had an equivalent yield of 15 Megatons TNT and unexpectedly caused substantial radioactive fall-out.[120]

[116] Badash, *Scientists and the Development of Nuclear Weapons*, pp 77, 83–6; Bethe, *The Hydrogen Bomb*, in: Bethe, *The Road from Los Alamos*, pp 16–22; Groves, *Now It Can Be Told*, pp 376, 394; Hodgson, *Nuclear Physics*, p 45; Jungk, *Brighter than a Thousand Suns*, pp 281–96; Rhodes, *The Making of the Atomic Bomb*, pp 768–9; Seaborg, *A Chemist in the White House*, pp 42–4. For a discussion on the first meetings of the GAC, see: Seaborg, *A Chemist in the White House*, pp 21–48. For a discussion on Oppenheimer's role, see: H Bethe, *J. Robert Oppenheimer*, in: Bethe, *The Road from Los Alamos*, pp 221–30. The AEC Personnel Security Board refused to waive Oppenheimer's security clearance in 1954 stigmatising him for the rest of his life until his rehabilitation by Kennedy and Johnson.

[117] The Columbia laboratory had been dismantled, while the Berkeley laboratory would only exist as long as Lawrence lived. Only the Chicago laboratory remained operational although in reduced size. Groves, *Now It Can Be Told*, pp 377–9.

[118] Rhodes, *The Making of the Atomic Bomb*, pp 754–6.

[119] The Marshall Islands were a United Nations Trust Territory placed under United States authority. Trusteeship Agreement for the Former Japanese Mandated Islands; Between the United States and the United Nations Security Council; Approved by the Security Council on 2 Apr 1947, UNTS, Vol 8, No 123; S/RES/21 (1947), adopted unanimously on 2 Apr 1947; on the Trusteeship of Strategic Areas; Trusteeship Agreement for the Trust Territory of the Pacific Islands.

[120] Badash. *Scientists and the Development of Nuclear Weapons*, pp 86–7; Barash, *Introduction to Peace Studies*, pp 106–7; Glasstone, Dolan, *The Effects of Nuclear Weapons*, pp 21–2; Hodgson, *Nuclear Physics*, pp 45–8; Jungk, *Brighter than a Thousand Suns*, pp 294, 297–305; Rhodes, *The Making of the Atomic Bomb*, pp 768–9, 773–8.

5—DEVELOPMENTS OUTSIDE THE UNITED STATES

5.1 Introduction

Outside the United States, nuclear weapons programs have been carried out in a number of other states. These are in the first place, a number of states that already started nuclear weapon research during World War II, namely the United Kingdom (section 5.2), Germany (section 5.3), Japan (section 5.4), and the Soviet Union (section 5.5). And in the second place, a number of states that either developed or pursued a nuclear weapon capacity after World War II (section 5.6).

5.2 The United Kingdom

The United Kingdom had been one of the United States' closest allies during the war. Much nuclear research had already been carried out before the war, but British nuclear scientists had not received much help from their government or industry, due to the fact that there had been greater want for directly applicable war machinery.

Growing US involvement in the war had led to an increasing exchange of information on atomic energy research, particularly in view of British expertise. The first informal discussions between representatives of both sides date back as far as early 1940, but as soon as Manhattan got on its way, the information flow had become one-way traffic and it had been stopped after a while. Exchange of information was resumed, however, after the 1943 Quebec Agreement between the United States, the United Kingdom and Canada[121] which established an official basis for cooperation. Based on the Agreement, a selected number of British scientists such as Chadwick, Frisch and Fuchs had come to the United States to work for the Manhattan Project or the 'Tube Alloys Project' as the British called it, subsequently followed by Niels Bohr and his son Aage who had escaped to England.[122] The German-born physicist Fuchs, who had made signif-

[121] Quebec Agreement between the United States and the United Kingdom, signed and entered into force on 19 Aug 1943. At: <http://www.atomicarchive.com/Docs/ManhattanProject/Quebec.shtml>.

[122] Early 1943 Chadwick had contacted Bohr in Copenhagen through the British intelligence and the Danish underground and had asked him to come to England. When things grew worse in Denmark and Bohr was warned that he would be arrested within a couple of days, the Bohrs fled to Sweden by fishing boat. From there, Bohr was transported to Great Britain in Oct 1943 in the bomb bay of a Mosquito bomber by which the British diplomatic pouch was flown back and forth from Stockholm. It almost went wrong because the helmet did not fit Bohr's head so that he fainted from lack of oxygen. 2 months later he continued his journey to the United States. Rhodes, *The Making of the Atomic Bomb*, pp 481–5. Slightly differently: Jungk, *Brighter than a Thousand Suns*, pp 120–1.

icant contributions to the success of the Project, later turned out to be a spy. He had submitted top-secret information to the Soviet Union since 1942, was arrested in London in 1950, and sentenced to 14 years in prison.[123] After the war he had been head of the Theoretical Physics Division at Harwell, Britain's nuclear establishment.

Within a few years after the war, the United Kingdom had developed its own atomic bomb. It was tested in the Australian desert in October 1952. Five years later it had developed thermonuclear weapons as well.[124]

5.3 Germany

Obviously the other warring parties had not sat still after the discovery of nuclear fission in late 1938 either. This certainly applies to Germany, where the phenomenon of nuclear fission had been discovered in the first place. Despite the exodus of Jewish scientists,[125] Germany was still considered as one of the world's gravity centres of science and there were many highly skilled physicists left with knowledge of nuclear physics.

The driving force behind the German uranium research program was Werner Heisenberg, a physicist and Nobel laureate. He very well understood the possibilities of military application of nuclear fission, both in terms of explosives and energy-sources and he had pushed for government funding. As from April 1939, exports of uranium had been banned, supplies of radium and uranium had been acquired from the Czechoslovakian mines at Joachimsthal and research had been instigated by Diebner under direction of the War Office at the Kaiser Wilhelm Institute of Physics at Berlin. Heisenberg had been asked to head the theoretical division.

After initial experiments and calculations, Heisenberg and his group had also come to the conclusion that isotope separation was necessary to obtain U-235 of sufficient purity in order to build a nuclear reactor, and

[123] Jungk, *Brighter than a Thousand Suns*, pp 186–90.

[124] Badash, *Scientists and the Development of Nuclear Weapons*, pp 28, 91, 105–6; Groves, *Now It Can Be Told*, pp 125–9, 135–6; Rhodes, *The Making of the Atomic Bomb*, pp 522–5, 770; Smyth, *Atomic Energy*, pp 30–1. Groves sums up the British contributions to the Manhattan Project at the end of his report. Groves, *Now It Can Be Told*, pp 406–7. For a timeline, see: <http://www.atomicarchive.com/Timeline/Time1950.shtml>.

[125] Badash compares the exodus of the Jews from Germany with the exodus of Christians from Constantinople in 1453 after the city's seizure by the Turks. The latter exodus provided a boost to intellectual activity in Europe culminating into a Renaissance. The former 'helped to switch the center of gravity of world science from western Europe to the United States.' Nevertheless, there were many highly skilled and talented scientists left and together with the fact that fission had been discovered in Germany, made several people believe in public statements that they were losing the race with respect to the applicability of nuclear energy. Badash, *Scientists and the Development of Nuclear Weapons*, p 11; Badash, *Introduction*, in: Badash, Hirschfelder, Broida (Eds), *Reminiscences of Los Alamos 1943–1945*, p xiii; GT Seaborg, *A Chemist in the White House; From the Manhattan Project to the End of the Cold War*, The American Chemical Society, Washington DC, 1998, pp 1–2.

that a moderator was necessary to slow down the neutrons. Due to miscalculations, however, they thought that graphite would not be as useful as a moderator and instead they had focused on heavy water (deuterium and tritium) to be obtained from an electrochemical plant of Norsk Hydro-Elektrisk Kvaelstofaktieselskab at Vemork west of Oslo. The production of heavy water is very expensive and a very time-consuming process.[126]

The Allies knew from their intelligence agents about this heavy water production and the transports to Germany, and had thus been confirmed in their belief that the Germans were making progress. The factory was attacked by massive air raids and partially destroyed by special forces in 1943. Norwegian saboteurs even succeeded in a bold attack to sink the ferry carrying a large supply of heavy water heading for Germany, thereby damaging the German uranium research project.[127]

When the Allies landed in Italy and in France, the MED immediately sent a Scientific Intelligence Mission, code name ALSOS, into Europe following the advancing armies, investigating all nuclear laboratories and universities and questioning scientists. They concluded that apparently the German efforts had not been as intensive and successful as the American efforts. Indeed, during the war, when the situation at the Eastern Front had become problematic for the Germans, the physicists working on the fission of uranium had been forced to shift to other research. The capacity of the German war economy had reached its limits and the War Office had decided to limit uranium research. The criterion that had been applied to judge requests from scientists was whether there was any chance of success in the near future and that could certainly not be guaranteed with respect to nuclear fission.

Apart from that, and apart from the question whether German scientists had been willing to develop an atomic bomb during the war,[128] it is ques-

[126] Badash, *Scientists and the Development of Nuclear Weapons*, p 28; Rhodes, *The Making of the Atomic Bomb*, pp 296, 311–12, 326–7, 343–6.

[127] Groves, *Now It Can Be Told*, pp 187–9; Jungk, *Brighter than a Thousand Suns*, p 114; Rhodes, *The Making of the Atomic Bomb*, pp 512–17.

[128] After the war, Heisenberg claimed that he never would have wanted Germany to have an atomic bomb and that he had worked on Germany's nuclear program in order to prevent Germany from actually succeeding in developing them. Niels Bohr, however, was not convinced that Heisenberg had moral doubts with respect to his research activities. In a private conversation between Heisenberg and Bohr in Copenhagen in Sept 1941—Heisenberg had studied under Bohr in Copenhagen during the 1920s, Bohr had not sensed any hesitancy with Heisenberg. According to Bohr, Heisenberg was convinced that Germany would win the war and that Bohr and his Copenhagen Institute should not be reticent to all German offers for cooperation. Bohr further had the impression that under Heisenberg's leadership everything was done in Germany to develop atomic weapons. This account appears from personal documents from Niels Bohr pertaining to this particular conversation, including draft letters to Heisenberg that were never sent. These documents were released on 6 Feb 2002 and can be found at the Niels Bohr Institute website at: <http://www.nbi.dk/NBA/release.html>. Heisenberg, on the other hand, had a different account from their conversation. In a letter he wrote to Junk and which is published in 'Brighter than a Thousand Suns', he recalls that he mentioned to Bohr that the construction of an atomic bomb was theoretically feasible but that

tionable whether they would have been able to do so in the first place. When ALSOS moved into Germany and came across the German research laboratories at Stadtilm near Weimar (Diebner) and a rudimentary nuclear reactor at Haigerloch in the Black Forest region (Heisenberg, Hahn), they found that the Germans had not come nearly as far as the Allies, and not nearly as far as one had feared they would be.[129] The German nuclear scientists who had worked on nuclear research and had been detained at Farm Hall in Great Britain were thus surprised and shocked when they heard that the Allies had been able to develop an atomic bomb.[130]

5.4 Japan

As much attention as the Allies had paid to the German research program, as little did they make efforts to obtain information on atomic developments in Japan. Groves sums up a number of reasons why they did not focus on Japan. Firstly, there was no chance that Japan had assembled enough uranium ore; secondly, the industrial effort would exceed Japan's capabilities; and thirdly, the number of qualified scientists was too small.[131]

Still, the Japanese had followed the developments in the field of nuclear fission conscientiously. Upon the request of Yasuda, the director of the Aviation Technology Research Institute of the Imperial Japanese Army, Suzuki had prepared a first report on the possible consequences of nuclear fission in 1940. Based on this report which had focused on the availability

it required a great technical effort, and whether it was right for scientists to work on such a project. From Bohr's reaction, he sensed that Bohr must have assumed that he tried to tell him that Germany had made great progress, which was not true, but Heisenberg did not manage to regain Bohr's trust. Jungk, *Brighter than a Thousand Suns*, pp 102–4. See also: Jungk, *Brighter than a Thousand Suns*, pp 98–102; Rhodes, *The Making of the Atomic Bomb*, pp 383–6. D van Delft, *Alles voor de Duitse bom*, NRC Handelsblad, 9–10 feb 2002, p 37; J Engels, *Een cruciale wandeling*, Trouw, 3 jan 2002, p 11. The conversation between Heisenberg and Bohr even inspired Michael Frayn to write a play on this topic, called 'Copenhagen'. 'Copenhagen' was played by the Royal National Theatre and proclaimed 'Best Play of the Year' in 1998. In 1999–2000, 'Copenhagen' was played by Het Noord Nederlands Toneel, in the Netherlands.

[129] According to German historian Rainer Karlsch, the Germans did in fact test three small atomic bombs. In his book 'Hitlers Bombe', he claims that the 1st test took place on the island Rügen at the end of 1944, followed by 2 other tests in Thüringen at the beginning of 1945. Although Karlsch refers to eyewitness reports, documents from Russian, American, and German archives, and soil samples, his assertions are controversial. NRC Handelsblad, 15 maa 2005; D van Delft, *Broodje bom*, NRC Handelsblad, 19–20 maa 2005.

[130] Groves, *Now It Can Be Told*, pp 194, 249, 333–7; Jungk, *Brighter than a Thousand Suns*, pp 157–70, 216–20; Rhodes, *The Making of the Atomic Bomb*, pp 401–5, 455–7, 600–10, 735. For excerpts from declassified transcripts of secretly recorded conversations at Farm Hall, see: <http://www.atomicarchive.com/Docs/Hiroshima/Farmhall.shtml>. For extensive comments on ALSOS in Italy, France, the Low Countries and finally Germany, see: Groves, *Now It Can Be Told*, pp 185–249.

[131] Groves, *Now It Can Be Told*, pp 186–7.

of uranium ore both in Japan and in Indochina, Yasuda had asked Nishina, the director of Japan's Physical and Chemical Research Institute, who had worked with Bohr in Copenhagen and who was the country's leading physicist, to do some introductory research. Not long after that did the Imperial Army Air Force authorise a full-scale research. Parallel to the steps made by Army Air Force, the Navy had independently started research on the possibilities of nuclear power for propulsion in 1941. In early 1943, they came to the conclusion that fission weapon research would consume a disproportionate share of the economy and that it would take Japan at least 10 years to build a bomb, so they decided to put an end to atomic research and to focus on more immediately valuable research. In Tokyo, Nishina had unsuccessfully pursued isotope separation by means of gaseous diffusion until his laboratory was burnt to the ground in April 1945 after an air raid.[132]

5.5 The Soviet Union

Soviet nuclear research dates from 1939 when Kurchatov, a nuclear physicist, had alerted Moscow on the possibilities of nuclear fission. Soviet physicists suspected that nuclear fission programs were carried out in Germany and in the United States when the names of German physicists and of those physicists who had fled to the United States gradually disappeared from the journals. Research had temporarily been suspended after the German invasion on 22 June 1941, but Kurchatov returned to nuclear physics after the tide had changed at the Battle of Stalingrad in early 1943. Still he was limited to laboratory work. By January 1944, Kurchatov had a staff of only twenty scientists and thirty support personnel.[133]

As has been observed above, Fuch's spying had proved to be very helpful[134] and in a short time Kurchatov and his team had made remarkable achievements and efforts had been doubled when after Hiroshima and Nagasaki, they knew that their goal was feasible. In December 1946, the Soviets succeeded in initiating a controlled chain reaction and in August 1949, they carried out their first plutonium test explosion. The Americans called it Joe-1, after Joseph Stalin, and were shocked when President

[132] Rhodes, *The Making of the Atomic Bomb*, pp 327, 346, 457–9, 580–2, 612.

[133] Badash, *Scientists and the Development of Nuclear Weapons*, pp 77–9; Jungk, *Brighter than a Thousand Suns*, pp 260–4; Rhodes, *The Making of the Atomic Bomb*, pp 327, 500–2.

[134] In 1999, it appeared that apart from Fuchs, also Melita Norwood had played an important role in the Soviet Union's nuclear weapons program. Since 1937, she had spied for the Soviet Union for 40 years, while having access to crucial documentation of the United Kingdom's nuclear weapons program as a secretary with the British Non-Ferrous Metals Association. She died in 2005. NRC Handelsblad, 29 jun 2005.

Truman announced the Russian test on the radio in September 1949.[135] No one had expected it so soon. Spying aircraft had recorded unusual levels of radioactivity which turned out to be fission fragments.

Not long after that, in August 1953, Kurchatov, now assisted by the young Sakharov who would later be awarded the Nobel Peace Prize in 1975[136] produced the Soviet Union's first booster bomb or Joe-4. This was only nine months after the first full thermonuclear test by the United States at Eniwetok Atoll in the Marshall Islands. In November 1955, the Soviet Union detonated its first full-scale thermonuclear weapon followed, by the largest bomb ever in history with an equivalent yield of 58 Megatons TNT, in October 1961.[137] 60 Megatons of TNT is equivalent to almost six thousand Little Boys, and is more than al the explosives used during World War II together.[138]

5.6 Further Proliferation

Implicit threats from the US to use atomic bombs or thermonuclear weapons against China in case of an invasion of Taiwan made Mao Zedong decide to develop his own atomic bomb. With the help of the Soviet Union, China managed to detonate its first fission weapon in 1964, and its first thermonuclear weapon in 1967.[139] France tested its first atomic bomb in 1960 and its first thermonuclear weapon in 1968;[140] India conducted a test in 1974 claiming that it was only meant for peaceful purposes, and five subsequent tests, including one thermonuclear text, in 1998, followed by Pakistan in the same year.[141] Israel is known to have a nuclear capability, but has never officially confirmed that they do; South Africa admitted in the early 1990s that they had developed atomic bombs but that they had dismantled them; and Argentina and Brazil have given up their nuclear weapon programs.[142] After the 1990–1991 Gulf War, Iraq

135 President Truman's Statement Announcing the First Soviet A-Bomb; Sep 23, 1949. At: <http://www.atomicarchive.com/Docs/Hydrogen/SovietAB.shtml>.

136 Through <http://nobelprize.org/>.

137 For a timeline, see: <http://www.atomicarchive.com/Timeline/Time1950.shtml> and <http://www.atomicarchive.com/Timeline/Time1960.shtml>. The 58 Mt Soviet H-bomb is also known as the Tsar Bomb. It weighed 27 tons and was detonated at a height of 4000 meters over the land surface. The fireball touched the ground and was seen 1,000 km away. The cloud rose to an altitude of 60 km. At: <http://en.wikipedia.org/wiki/Tsar_Bomba>.

138 Badash, *Scientists and the Development of Nuclear Weapons*, pp 77, 79, 87–8; Rhodes, *The Making of the Atomic Bomb*, pp 767, 778.

139 See: <http://www.atomicarchive.com/Timeline/Time1960.shtml>.

140 For specifics, see: <http://www.atomicarchive.com/Timeline/Time1960.shtml>.

141 See: <http://www.atomicarchive.com/Timeline/Time1970.shtml> and <http://www.atomicarchive.com/Timeline/Time1990.shtml>.

142 Badash, *Scientists and the Development of Nuclear Weapons*, pp 90–1.

was ordered by the Security Council to dismantle its nuclear weapons program.[143] Currently, only North Korea and Iran are suspected to pursue a nuclear capability.[144]

[143] S/RES/687 (1991), adopted on 3 Apr 1991, by 12 to 1, with 1 abstention, on the situation between Iraq and Kuwait.

[144] The Democratic People's Republic of Korea withdrew from the 1968 Non-Proliferation Treaty—Treaty on the Non-Proliferation of Nuclear Weapons, opened for signature on 1 Jul 1968, entered into force 5 Mar 1970, UNTS, Vol 729, No 10485—on 10 Jan 2003. S/2003/91, 24 Jan 2003, Letter dated 24 Jan 2003 from the Permanent Representative of the Democratic People's Republic of Korea to the United Nations addressed to the President of the Security Council; with Annexes. Iran's nuclear program is under severe scrutiny after two secret nuclear facilities were discovered in 2003 and its subsequent lack of cooperation with the International Atomic Energy Agency. See IAEA Resolution GOV/2006/14, of 4 Feb 2006; Implementation of the NPT Safeguards Agreement in the Islamic Republic of Iran, in which the Board of Governors expresses serious concern on Iran's nuclear program. The Board requests the Director General to report on the implementation of this resolution and to convey this report to the Security Council for its consideration.

II

Nuclear Weapons and Their Effects

1—INTRODUCTION

AFTER THE PRECEDING discussion of nuclear weapons in historical perspective, it seems appropriate to look at nuclear weapon systems and the effects of nuclear explosions in greater detail before continuing to a legal analysis regarding their use. Apart from a discussion of existing nuclear weapon systems (section 2), emphasis will lie on the direct and possible indirect effects of nuclear explosions (section 4), especially those effects that are unique for nuclear weapons and distinguish them from conventional, and other non-conventional weapons.[1] In order to make this comprehensible, however, it is first necessary to explain briefly the physical phenomena during a nuclear explosion and the various types of nuclear explosions (section 3).

[1] In order to delineate its jurisdiction, the Commission for Conventional Armaments advised the Security Council in its Resolution of 12 Aug 1948, that it considered all armaments and armed forces to fall under its jurisdiction, 'except atomic weapons and weapons of mass destruction [*sic*]'. The Commission then states 'that weapons of mass destruction should be defined to include atomic explosive weapons [*sic*], radioactive material weapons, lethal chemical and biological weapons, and any weapons, lethal chemical and biological weapons, and any weapons developed in the future which have characteristics comparable in destructive effect to those of the atomic bomb or other weapons mentioned above.' Both statements are contradictory as far as atomic weapons are concerned which seems to be due to bad drafting. First, atomic weapons are not considered weapons of mass destruction, which is already peculiar and then weapons of mass destruction are defined as a category of weapons that include atomic weapons. Resolution of the Commission for Conventional Armaments, 12 Aug 1948, on the definition of armaments, para 1. Through: <http://www.yale.edu/lawweb/avalon/avalon.htm>. The Conventional Armaments Commission had been established by the Security Council by S/RES/18 (1947), adopted on 13 Feb 1947, by 10 to 0, with 1 abstention; implementation of General Assembly Resolutions on the principles governing the general regulation and reduction of armaments and information on armed forces. For a discussion on the differences between conventional arms and nuclear weapons, see ch 3, N Singh, E McWhinney, *Nuclear Weapons and Contemporary International Law*, Martinus Nijhoff, Dordrecht, 1989, pp 28–32.

2—NUCLEAR WEAPON SYSTEMS

2.1 Introduction

Although they have had a major influence on post-World War II international relations, there are only a few legally significant definitions of 'atomic' or 'nuclear weapons'.[2] The first definition of an atomic weapon in an international legal instrument was laid down in the 1954 Protocol III[3] to the 1948 Brussels Treaty[4] which established the Western European Union (WEU). In Protocol III, the Federal Republic of Germany undertook as a new member of the WEU not to manufacture in its territory atomic, biological or chemical weapons. In Annex II, the Contracting Parties defined 'atomic weapons' as:

> (a) (. . .) any weapon which contains, or is designed to contain or utilise nuclear fuel or radioactive isotopes and which, by explosion or other uncontrolled nuclear transformation of the nuclear fuel, or by radioactivity of the nuclear fuel or radioactive isotopes, is capable of mass destruction, mass injury or mass poisoning. (b) Furthermore, any part, device, assembly or material especially designed for, or primarily useful in, any weapon as set forth under paragraph (a), shall be deemed to be an atomic weapon. (. . .).

Subsequent and similar definitions of 'nuclear weapons' or 'nuclear explosive devices' followed in each of the four nuclear-weapon-free zone (NWFZ) treaties concluded between 1967 and 1996,[5] as well as in a num-

[2] Before the development of thermonuclear weapons in the 1950s, nuclear fission weapons were generally referred to as 'atomic weapons'. Since the 1960s, however, it is more common and more proper to use the term 'nuclear weapons' for all weapons whose explosive energy is derived from a nuclear reaction. S Glasstone, PJ Dolan (Eds), *The Effects of Nuclear Weapons*, US Department of Defence and the US Department of Energy, Washington, DC, 1977, p 6; J Goldblat, *Arms Control; The New Guide to Negotiations and Agreements*, International Peace Research Institute, Oslo; Stockholm International Peace Research Institute; SAGE Publications, London, 2002, pp 41–2. Compare, however, A/Res/1653 (XVI), adopted on 24 Nov 1961, by 55 to 20, with 26 abstentions; declaration on the prohibition of the use of nuclear and thermo-nuclear weapons; which distinguishes between nuclear and thermo-nuclear weapons.

[3] Protocol No III (with annexes) on the Control of Armaments to the Treaty between Belgium, France, Luxembourg, the Netherlands, and the United Kingdom of Great Britain and Northern Ireland for Collaboration in Economic, Social and Cultural Matters and for Collective Self-Defence, signed on 23 Oct 1954, entered into force on 6 May 1955, UNTS, Vol 211, No 304.

[4] Treaty between Belgium, France, Luxembourg, the Netherlands, and the United Kingdom of Great Britain and Northern Ireland for Collaboration in Economic, Social and Cultural Matters and for Collective Self-Defence, signed on 17 Mar 1948, entered into force on 25 Aug 1948, UNTS, Vol 19, No 304.

[5] Treaty for the Prohibition of Nuclear Weapons in Latin America (Tlatelolco Treaty), together with Protocols, signed and opened for signature on 14 Feb 1967, entered into force on 22 Apr 1968, UNTS, Vol 634, No 9068.; South Pacific Nuclear Free Zone Treaty (*sic*) (Rarotonga Treaty), together with Annexes and Protocols, signed and opened for signature on 6 Aug 1985, entered into force on 11 Dec 1986, UNTS, Vol 1445, No 24592; Treaty on the

ber of other agreements.[6] Each of these definitions refers to the capability to release nuclear energy in an uncontrolled manner, but unlike the 1954 definition just quoted above, the NWFZ treaties exclude delivery vehicles from the scope of the definition if such vehicle is not an indivisible part of the weapon.[7]

Finally, also the Model Nuclear Weapons Convention[8] contains a comprehensive definition of nuclear weapons. This Model Convention was drafted in 1997 by a large number of lawyers, scientists and other experts and was modeled on the 1972 Biological Weapons Convention.[9] Although this definition is largely based on the definition on the Tlatelolco Treaty, it also regards radiological weapons as nuclear weapons, which is rather uncommon.[10] Radiological weapons were defined by the United States and the Soviet Union in 1979 as devices:

Southeast Asia Nuclear Weapon-Free Zone (*sic*) (Bangkok Treaty), together with Annex and Protocol, signed and opened for signature on 15 Dec 1995, entered into force on 27 Mar 1997, UNTS, Vol 1981, No 33873; African Nuclear-Weapon-Free Treaty (*sic*) (Pelindaba Treaty), together with Annexes and Protocols, signed and opened for signature on 11 Apr 1996, has not entered into force yet, ILM, Vol 35, 1996, p 698.

[6] Compare, for example, Art XI of the bilateral Agreement between the United States and the United Kingdom for Co-operation on the Uses of Atomic Energy for Mutual Defence Purposes, signed on 3 Jul 1958, entered into force on 4 Aug 1958, UNTS, Vol 326, No 4707.

[7] Art 5 of the 1967 Tlatelolco Treaty, for example, defines 'nuclear weapon' as 'any device which is capable of releasing nuclear energy in an uncontrolled manner and which has a group of characteristics that are appropriate for use for warlike purposes. An instrument that may be used for the transport of propulsion of the device is not included in this definition if it is separable from the device and not an indivisible part thereof.' And according to Art 1(c) of the 1996 Pelindaba Treaty, a 'nuclear explosive device' as 'any nuclear weapon or other explosive device capable of releasing nuclear energy, irrespective of the purpose for which it could be used. The term includes such a weapon or device in unassembled and partly assembled forms, but does not include the means of transport or delivery of such a weapon or device if separable from and not an indivisible part of it'. Art 1(c) of the 1985 Rarotonga Treaty and Art 1(c) of the 1995 Bangkok Treaty are almost similar.

[8] Model Nuclear Weapons Convention; Convention on the Prohibition of the Development, Testing, production, Stockpiling, Transfer, Use and Threat of Use of Nuclear Weapons and on Their Elimination, Apr 1997, Lawyer's Committee on Nuclear Policy. Through: http://www.lcnp.org/ and http://www.ialana.org/. The draft convention was attached to a letter from Costa Rica to the General Assembly and is listed as UN Document A/C.1/52/7, circulated by the United Nations Secretary-General on 17 Nov 1997; Letter dated 31 Oct 1997 from the Chargé d'affaires of the Permanent Mission of Costa Rica to the United Nations addressed to the Secretary-General.

[9] Convention on the Prohibition of the Development, Production and Stockpiling of Bacteriological (Biological) and Toxic Weapons and on Their Destruction, opened for signature on 10 Apr 1972, entered into force on 26 Mar 1975, UNTS, Vol 1015, No 14860.

[10] Art II(6) defines a nuclear weapon as: 'a. Any device which is capable of releasing nuclear energy in an uncontrolled manner and which has a group of characteristics that are appropriate for use for warlike purposes; {Source: Treaty of Tlatelolco, to be updated to refer to weapons with nuclear triggers.}; [OR a. Any explosive device, in assembled or disassembled form, designed for or capable of releasing nuclear energy by fission or fusion;] b. Any radiological weapon; or c. Any weapon which is designed to include a nuclear explosive device as a trigger or other component. An instrument that may be used for the transport or propulsion of the device is not included in this definition if it is separable from the device and not an indivisible part thereof. {Source: Treaty of Tlatelolco}'.

> other than a nuclear explosive device, specifically designed to employ radioactive material by disseminating it to cause destruction, damage or injury by means of the radiation produced by the decay of such material.[11]

Although radiological weapons are regarded as weapons of mass destruction,[12] and although they use radioactivity as weapons of war, they do not derive explosive energy from a nuclear reaction.

Although most definitions exclude delivery vehicles from the definition of nuclear weapons, if they are separable from the device, in daily practice, the term nuclear weapon is often used to refer to both the warhead, containing the nuclear explosive, and the delivery vehicle. Together with the delivery platform, and the supporting system for command and control, one usually speaks of a nuclear weapon system.[13] Both delivery vehicles and warheads will therefore briefly discussed in sections 2.2 and 2.3.

2.2 Delivery Vehicles

2.2.1 Introduction

A common way to distinguish between the various kinds of delivery vehicles is on the ground of their intended use. Although there is no international consensus on the terms strategic, theatre, tactical, and battlefield weapons, international literature often adheres to the terms 'strategic', 'theater', and 'tactical' weapons as used by the Soviet Union and the United States.[14] Because it is difficult to indicate the exact difference

[11] CD/31, 1979, Joint USSR-United States proposal to the Committee on Disarmament on the prohibition of the development, production, stockpiling and use of radiological weapons. Quoted in: J Rotblat, *Nuclear Radiation in Warfare*, Stockholm International Peace Research Institute, Taylor & Francis, London, 1981, p 131. The Conference on Disarmament established an Ad Hoc Committee on radiological weapons, which reported in 1992 (CD/1159). In 2002, the Conference was again seized of the matter by Germany, after reported threats of terrorist attacks with so-called 'dirty weapons'. CD/1681, of 15 Aug 2002; Germany; Discussion Paper; Radiological Weapons. See also: Goldblat, *Arms Control; The New Guide to Negotiations and Agreements*, pp 162–4.

[12] As was observed above, the Conventional Armaments Commission regarded 'atomic explosive weapons [*sic*], radioactive material weapons, lethal chemical and biological weapons, and any weapons, lethal chemical and biological weapons, and any weapons developed in the future which have characteristics comparable in destructive effect to those of the atomic bomb or other weapons mentioned above' as weapons of mass destruction. Resolution of the Commission for Conventional Armaments, 12 Aug 1948, on the definition of armaments, para 1. Through: <http://www.yale.edu/lawweb/avalon/avalon.htm>.

[13] United Nations Organization; UN Department of Disarmament Affairs; Report of the Secretary-General, *Nuclear Weapons: A Comprehensive Study*, United Nations Publication, New York, 1991, p 11.

[14] TB Cochran, WM Arkin, MM Hoenig, *Nuclear Weapons Databook; Volume I, US Nuclear Forces and Capabilities*, Ballinger Publishing Company, Cambridge, Massachusetts, 1984, p 2; United Nations Organization; UN Department of Disarmament Affairs; Report of the Secretary-General, *Nuclear Weapons: A Comprehensive Study*, p 14.

between theatre and tactical weapons, the distinction between 'strategic' and 'non-strategic' weapons, as used by the Stockholm International Peace Research Institute (SIPRI), is more workable.[15]

Collins Dictionary defines 'strategy' as:

> the art or science of the planning and conduct of a war; (. . .). 2. A particular long-term plan for success, (. . .).[16]

Strategic attacks using strategic weapons are therefore aimed at winning the war. Terms that are nowadays used within that context are 'counter-force strikes', which are attacks against launching sites, air bases, and other military installations; and 'countervalue strikes', which are attacks against the enemy's population centers.[17]

Strategic weapons are weapons that have long-range or intercontinental capabilities, usually over 5,500 km; that are employed far beyond the battlefield; and that are aimed at an enemy's military, economic, and sometimes political potential, usually in his homeland.[18] The 5,500 km minimum is a direct and indirect reference to the definitions used for intercontinental ballistic missiles (ICBMs) as one of the strategic nuclear delivery vehicles, or for 'strategic offensive arms' by the United States and the Soviet Union in the 1979 Strategic Arms Limitation Treaty (SALT);[19] in the 1987 Intermediate-Range Nuclear Forces (INF) Treaty;[20] in the 1991

[15] RS Norris, WM Arkin, *Appendix 8A; Tables of Nuclear Forces*, in: Stockholm International Peace Research Institute, *SIPRI Yearbook 2000; Armaments, Disarmament and International Security*, Oxford University Press, Oxford, 2000, pp 478–95; SN Kile, HM Kristensen, *Appendix 12A. World nuclear forces 2005*, in: Stockholm International Peace Research Institute, *SIPRI Yearbook 2005; Armaments, Disarmament and International Security*, Oxford University Press, Oxford, 2005, pp 578–602.

[16] *Collins Dictionary*, HarperCollins Publishers, Glasgow, 1998, p 1516.

[17] D Rauschning, *Nuclear Warfare and Weapons*, in: R Bernhardt (Ed), *Encyclopaedia of Public International Law; Volume Three; Jan Mayen to Pueblo Incident*, Elsevier, Amsterdam, 1997, p 731. In World War II, bombing inaccuracy and air defence forced aircraft to switch to area bombing which was justified as being intended to break the enemy's morale. Since then, strategic bombing became to mean destruction of cities. L Badash, *Scientists and the Development of Nuclear Weapons; From Fission to the Limited Test Ban Treaty 1939–1963*, Humanities Press International, Inc., Atlantic Highlands, New Jersey, 1995, p 98.

[18] Cochran, Arkin, Hoenig, *Nuclear Weapons Databook; Volume I, US Nuclear Forces and Capabilities*, p 2; Stockholm International Peace Research Institute, *SIPRI Yearbook 2000; Armaments, Disarmament and International Security*, p xxxiii; United Nations Organization; UN Department of Disarmament Affairs; Report of the Secretary-General, *Nuclear Weapons: A Comprehensive Study*, p 14.

[19] Treaty between the United States of America and the Union of Soviet Socialist Republics on the Limitation of Strategic Offensive Arms, together with Protocol, Memorandum of Understanding, Joint Statement, and Associated Documents (SALT, also referred to as SALT II), signed on 18 Jun 1979, never entered into force, CD/28 of 27 Jun 1979 and CD/29 of 2 Jul 1979.

[20] Treaty between the United States of America and the Union of Soviet Socialist Republics on the Elimination of Their Intermediate-Range and Shorter-Range Missiles, together with Protocols, Memorandum of Understanding, and Associated Documents (INF), signed on 8 Dec 1987, entered into force on 1 Jun 1988, UNTS, Vol 1657, No 28521.

Strategic Arms Reduction Treaty (START) I;[21] and in the 1993 Strategic Arms Reduction Treaty (START) II.[22] Therefore, in legal practice, a weapon's strategic character is not only determined by its intended use, but also by its physical performance.

According to SIPRI, a non-strategic weapon is a 'weapon with a range up to and including 5500 km' and is '[a]lso referred to as a tactical nuclear weapon.'[23] These weapons are generally employed against selected military targets on or behind the field of battle and whose activities are related to activities on the battlefield, such as airbases, supply depots and reserve forces.[24] The term 'tactics' is defined by Collins Dictionary as:

> 1. (. . .) the art and science of the detailed direction and control of movement or maneuver of forces in battle to achieve an aim or task. 2. the maneuvers used or plans followed to achieve a particular short-term aim.[25]

Hence, non-strategic or tactical weapons are used to win a battle rather than winning the war.

According to Cochran, Arkin, and Hoenig, the term 'theater' weapon received a negative connotation in the late 1970s, early 1980s as a result of its use in the context of the European political and security debate. The term was associated with an alleged American policy to restrict a possible war between the North Atlantic Treaty Organization (NATO) and Warsaw Pact countries to European soil while sparing United States territory.[26]

[21] Treaty between the United States of America and the Union of Soviet Socialist Republics on the Reduction and Limitation of Strategic Offensive Arms, together with Annexes, Protocols, Memorandum of Understanding, and Associated Documents (START I), signed on 31 Jul 1991, entered into force 5 Dec 1994, CD/1192 of 5 Apr 1993.

[22] Treaty between the United States of America and the Russian Federation on Further Reduction and Limitation of Strategic Offensive Arms, together with Protocols, Memorandum of Understanding, and Associated Documents (START II), signed on 3 Jan 1993, has not entered into force yet, CD/1194 of 5 Apr 1993.

[23] Stockholm International Peace Research Institute, *SIPRI Yearbook 2000; Armaments, Disarmament and International Security*, p xxxiii.

[24] Badash, *Scientists and the Development of Nuclear Weapons; From Fission to the Limited Test Ban Treaty 1939–1963*, pp 97–8; Cochran, Arkin, Hoenig, *Nuclear Weapons Databook; Volume I, US Nuclear Forces and Capabilities*, pp 2–3; Rauschning, *Nuclear Warfare and Weapons*, in: Bernhardt (Ed), *Encyclopaedia of Public International Law; Volume Three; Jan Mayen to Pueblo Incident*, p 731; United Nations Organization; UN Department of Disarmament Affairs; Report of the Secretary-General, *Nuclear Weapons: A Comprehensive Study*, p 14.

[25] *Collins Dictionary*, p 1558.

[26] Cochran, Arkin, Hoenig, *Nuclear Weapons Databook; Volume I, US Nuclear Forces and Capabilities*, p 2. Similarly: J Dean, *The INF Treaty Negotiations*, in: Stockholm International Peace Research Institute, *SIPRI Yearbook 1988; World Armaments and Disarmament*, Oxford University Press, 1988, p 380. The talks on intermediate-range nuclear forces in Europe used to be called 'negotiations on Theater Nuclear Forces'. This designation was changed by the Reagan Administration.

2.2.2 *Strategic Delivery Vehicles*

2.2.2.1 Introduction

There are only few intercontinental weapon systems that have the capacity to strike targets with military, economic or political value, far beyond the battlefield. These are long-range bombers and guided missiles. The former will be briefly discussed in section 2.2.2.2; the latter will be discussed in section 2.2.2.3.

2.2.2.2 Bombers

The oldest strategic nuclear weapon is certainly the gravity bomb, two of which were used in combat over Japan. Both bombs were delivered by B-29 aircraft, long-range intercontinental bombers, the first of their kind, and the only aircraft at that time capable of accomplishing the mission. Until the 1960s, long-range strategic bombers remained the backbone of nuclear weapon states' strategic nuclear forces, at first propeller-driven and later jet-engined increasing their speed and operation ceiling.[27] During the 1960s, they lost their leading role to long-range guided missiles which have the advantage that they carry no risk of casualties; that they generally travel large distances, at supersonic speed, which makes defence—detection, identification, course prediction and interception—almost impossible;[28] that there is a large number of missiles ready for immediate launch; and that they have a high probability of survival under nuclear attack.[29] Currently, only the United States and the Russian Federation still employ long-range bombers.[30]

[27] DP Barash, *Introduction to Peace Studies*, Wadsworth Publishing Company, Belmont, CA, 1991, p 115; Cochran, Arkin, Hoenig, *Nuclear Weapons Databook; Volume I, US Nuclear Forces and Capabilities*, pp 3, 39; United Nations Organization; UN Department of Disarmament Affairs; Report of the Secretary-General, *Nuclear Weapons: A Comprehensive Study*, p 13. The first jet-engined aircraft was the German Arado Ar 234 employed with little success during the last months of World War II. During the 1950s, the United States introduced the Boeing B-47 Stratojet, followed by the eight-engined Boeing B-52 Stratofortress, which is still in service; the United Kingdom introduced so-called V-bombers; and the Soviet Union introduced the Tu-16 Badger, the M-4 Bison, and the Tu-95 Bear. Through: <http://en.wikipedia.org/>.

[28] LN Ridenour, *There is no Defence*, in: D Masters, K Way (Eds), *One World or None: A Report to the Public on the Full Meaning of the Atomic Bomb*, McGraw-Hill, New York, 1946, on actual and possible defences against V-1s and V-2s.

[29] Cochran, Arkin, Hoenig, *Nuclear Weapons Databook; Volume I, US Nuclear Forces and Capabilities*, p 100.

[30] The United States has the B-52H Stratofortress (16,000 km) and the B-2 Spirit (11,000 km). The Russian Federation has the Tu-95MS6 Bear-H6 (12,800 km), Tu-95MS16 Bear-H16 (12,800 km), and Tu-160 Blackjack (11,000 km). Norris, Arkin, *Appendix 8A; Tables of Nuclear Forces*, in: Stockholm International Peace Research Institute, *SIPRI Yearbook 2000; Armaments, Disarmament and International Security*, pp 478–95; Kile, Kristensen, *Appendix 12A. World nuclear forces 2005*, in: Stockholm International Peace Research Institute, *SIPRI Yearbook 2005; Armaments, Disarmament and International Security*, pp 580–8.

2.2.2.3 Missiles

2.2.2.3.1 Introduction

Missiles[31] are vehicles designed to deliver explosives with high speed upon a target and are either guided or unguided. Unguided missiles are usually referred to as 'rockets'. Guided missiles are controlled during their flight and must be distinguished on the basis of propulsion, namely ballistic missiles (section 2.2.2.3.2) and cruise missiles (section 2.2.2.3.3).[32]

2.2.2.3.2 Ballistic Missiles

A ballistic missile is a pilotless rocket propelled vehicle 'which follows a ballistic trajectory (part of which may be outside the earth's atmosphere) when thrust is terminated.'[33] The term 'ballistic' refers to the final stage, after separation from the rocket, which is governed by inertia and gravity.[34] According to Collins Dictionary, 'ballistics' is:

> the study of the flight dynamics of projectiles, either through the interaction of the forces of propulsion, the aerodynamics of the projectile, atmospheric resistance, and gravity (exterior ballistics), or through these forces along with the means of propulsion, and the design of the propelling weapon and projectile (interior ballistics).[35]

The first ballistic missile was Germany's *Vergeltungswaffen-2* (V-2), developed largely during World War II by a team led by Werner von Braun and first used against the United Kingdom on 6 September 1944. It was launched from fixed launch platforms and had a range of about 300 km.[36] The first modern ground-launched guided ballistic missile was successfully launched by the Soviet Union in August 1957.[37]

Under continuous pressure of the arms and space race, particularly between the United States and the Soviet Union, ballistic missiles were

[31] The word missile comes from the Latin verb *mittere* which means to send or to throw.

[32] *Collins Dictionary*, p 995; <http://en.wikipedia.org/wiki/Missile>.

[33] Stockholm International Peace Research Institute, *SIPRI Yearbook 2000; Armaments, Disarmament and International Security*, p xxv. Similarly: Art II(1) INF; Art 7 Annex on Terms and Their Definitions START I, II; United Nations Organization; UN Department of Disarmament Affairs; Report of the Secretary-General, *Nuclear Weapons: A Comprehensive Study*, p 12.

[34] United Nations Organization; UN Department of Disarmament Affairs; Report of the Secretary-General, *Nuclear Weapons: A Comprehensive Study*, p 12. Similarly: Cochran, Arkin, Hoenig, *Nuclear Weapons Databook; Volume I, US Nuclear Forces and Capabilities*, p 100. Ballistic missiles have four phases, namely the boost phase, post-boost phase, mid-course phase, and terminal phase. United Nations Organization; UN Department of Disarmament Affairs; Report of the Secretary-General, *Nuclear Weapons: A Comprehensive Study*, p 39, fn 34.

[35] *Collins Dictionary*, p 117.

[36] At: <http://en.wikipedia.org/wiki/V-2_rocket>.

[37] Badash, *Scientists and the Development of Nuclear Weapons; From Fission to the Limited Test Ban Treaty 1939–1963*, pp 93–4.

rapidly improved. Firstly, solid rocket fuel was introduced, which is less explosive and therefore safer than liquid fuel and more appropriate for quick launches.[38] Secondly, the launching capabilities of strategic ballistic missiles were enlarged by the development a technology to launch missiles from submarines and from mobile launch platforms, in the form of railroad cars or trucks. The development of submarine launched ballistic missiles had a significant impact on security strategies, because until then, ballistic missiles could only be launched from fixed, heavily fortified underground silos, which made a preemptive counterforce strike—a so-called 'use-them-or-lose-them scenario'—theoretically possible.[39] With the development of submarine launched ballistic missiles, however, it was possible to develop a second-strike capability by spreading nuclear forces equally among bombers, land-based, and sea-based forces. This became generally known as the so-called triad arrangement,[40] and until recently, all five official nuclear weapon states,[41] with the exception of the United Kingdom, relied on it.[42] The development of mobile launch platforms became necessary when missiles became so accurate that hardening silos

[38] United Nations Organization; UN Department of Disarmament Affairs; Report of the Secretary-General, *Nuclear Weapons: A Comprehensive Study*, pp 32–3.

[39] United Nations Organization; UN Department of Disarmament Affairs; Report of the Secretary-General, *Nuclear Weapons: A Comprehensive Study*, p 30.

[40] In view of a new security environment, the United States changed the meaning of the term 'triad'. In its Nuclear Posture Review drafted by the Department of Defense at the request of Congress and would 'lay out the direction for American nuclear forces over the next five to ten years', the first leg of the New Triad will be the offensive strike leg and will consist of the entire old triad of nuclear ICBMs, SLBMs and long-range bombers integrated with non-nuclear capabilities. The second leg will consist of both active and passive defences, and the third of a new revitalized responsive defence infrastructure. The classified report was submitted to Congress on 31 Dec 2001 and its foreword was published on 9 Jan 2002. Foreword Nuclear Posture Review, by DH Rumsfeld, Secretary of Defense, through: <http://www.defenselink.mil/>, and <http://www.fas.org/>. Similarly, Joint Chiefs of Staff, *Doctrine for Joint Nuclear Operations*, Joint Publication 3-12, Final Coordination (2), 15 Mar 2005, through: <http://www.globalsecurity.org/>.

[41] The phrase 'official nuclear weapon state' refers to the definition of a nuclear weapon state in Art IX(3) of the 1968 Treaty on the Non-Proliferation of Nuclear Weapons (NPT), signed 1 Jul 1968, entered into force 5 Mar 1970, UNTS, Vol 729. It states that '[f]or the purposes of this treaty, a nuclear-weapon State is one which has manufactured and exploded a nuclear weapon or other nuclear explosive device prior to 1 January 1967.' These were the United States, the Soviet Union, the United Kingdom, France and the People's Republic of China. Various states among which Israel, India and Pakistan have as yet refused to sign the treaty and are presumed or known to be in possession of nuclear weapons. They are called unofficial nuclear weapon states.

[42] Norris, Arkin, *Appendix 8A; Tables of Nuclear Forces*, in: Stockholm International Peace Research Institute, *SIPRI Yearbook 2000; Armaments, Disarmament and International Security*, pp 478–95; Kile, Kristensen, *Appendix 12A. World nuclear forces 2005*, in: Stockholm International Peace Research Institute, *SIPRI Yearbook 2005; Armaments, Disarmament and International Security*, pp 578–94; United Nations Organization; UN Department of Disarmament Affairs; Report of the Secretary-General, *Nuclear Weapons: A Comprehensive Study*, p 15. France decided to dismantle its silo-based IRBMs on the Plateau d'Albion in 1996. Norris, Arkin, *Appendix 8A; Tables of Nuclear Forces*, in: Stockholm International Peace Research Institute, *SIPRI Yearbook 2000; Armaments, Disarmament and International Security*, p 488.

was not considered appropriate anymore. Mobility was expected to be a more effective defence against counterforce strikes.[43]

Thirdly, strategic ballistic missiles became increasingly powerful and sophisticated as far as range, guidance, and accuracy are concerned. Some missile categories can now travel distances of over 13,000 km, and improved and sophisticated guidance techniques provided by satellites in geo-stationary orbit have turned them into one of the most dangerous and accurate delivery vehicles of our time.[44] In fact, the Circular Error Probable (CEP), which is:

> defined as the radius of the circle, with the target at its center within which the missile has a 50 per cent probability of landing[,][45]

has improved dramatically over the years. The trend to build increasingly larger warheads to make up for the lack of accuracy was therefore reversed in the 1970s. Before then, strategic ballistic missiles were not considered to be able to hit anything smaller than cities or large industrial or military complexes; nowadays, it is possible to hit targets over thousands of kilometers with a precision of less than 200 meters CEP.[46]

And fourthly, the loading capacity of strategic ballistic missiles has not only increased significantly since the late 1950s, but has also become increasingly sophisticated with the development of missiles carrying multiple warheads. These so-called 'multiple re-entry vehicles' (MRVs) were developed in the 1960s as a result of attempts to develop anti-ballistic missile technology, and were followed by the development of the more advanced 'multiple independently targetable re-entry vehicles' (MIRVs) in the 1970s. The term 're-entry vehicle' (RV) refers to:

> [t]he part of the ballistic missile which carries a nuclear warhead and penetration aids to the target. It re-enters the earth's atmosphere and is destroyed in the final phase of the missile's trajectory.[47]

MRVs are re-entry vehicles that are released from the 'bus', the final physical stage of the missile, follow separate ballistic trajectories and fall within

[43] United Nations Organization; UN Department of Disarmament Affairs; Report of the Secretary-General, *Nuclear Weapons: A Comprehensive Study*, pp 30–3.

[44] United Nations Organization; UN Department of Disarmament Affairs; Report of the Secretary-General, *Nuclear Weapons: A Comprehensive Study*, p 31.

[45] Rotblat, *Nuclear Radiation in Warfare*, p 19. Similarly: United Nations Organization; UN Department of Disarmament Affairs; Report of the Secretary-General, *Nuclear Weapons: A Comprehensive Study*, p 30.

[46] Barash, *Introduction to Peace Studies*, pp 115–17; Cochran, Arkin, Hoenig, *Nuclear Weapons Databook; Volume I, US Nuclear Forces and Capabil*ities, p 100; Rauschning, *Nuclear Warfare and Weapons*, in: Bernhardt (Ed), *Encyclopaedia of Public International Law; Volume Three; Jan Mayen to Pueblo Incident*, p 731; Rotblat, *Nuclear Radiation in Warfare*, p 19; United Nations Organization; UN Department of Disarmament Affairs; Report of the Secretary-General, *Nuclear Weapons: A Comprehensive Study*, pp 28–9.

[47] Stockholm International Peace Research Institute, *SIPRI Yearbook 2000; Armaments, Disarmament and International Security*, p xxxiii.

short distance of the target. MIRVs are re-entry vehicles that are independently aimed at separate targets by equipping the bus with an independent guidance system, a propellant, and a set of thrust devices which allows the bus to maneuver so that each vehicle may follow an independent flight path. Research was planned on the development of third-generation re-entry vehicle technology for maneuverable re-entry vehicles (MARVs), that would behave as separate guided missiles after re-entering the atmosphere.[48]

Ballistic missiles are usually distinguished by reference to delivery platform and range. In the course of history, air-launched ballistic missiles (ALBMs), submarine-launched ballistic missiles (SLMBs) and ground-launched ballistic missiles (GLBMs) have been developed. The latter category has usually been subdivided between intercontinental ballistic missiles (ICBMs) with a range greater than 5,500 km;[49] intermediate-range ballistic missiles (IRBMs) with ranges greater than 1,000 km, but smaller than 5,500 km;[50] and shorter-range ballistic missiles (SRBMs) with ranges between 500 and 1,000 km.[51] Depending on use and circumstances, each type may be regarded as a strategic weapon system. All nuclear powers possess at least one category of ballistic missiles.[52]

2.2.2.3.3 Cruise Missiles

Cruise missiles are pilotless jet-propelled:

> guided weapon-delivery vehicle which sustains flight at subsonic or supersonic speeds through aerodynamic lift, generally flying at very low altitudes to avoid radar detection, sometimes following the contours of the terrain.[53]

[48] Barash, *Introduction to Peace Studies*, pp 115–17; Cochran, Arkin, Hoenig, *Nuclear Weapons Databook; Volume I, US Nuclear Forces and Capabilities*, pp 106–7; <http://en.wikipedia.org/wiki/MIRV> and <http://en.wikipedia.org/wiki/Multiple_Reentry_vehicle>; Rotblat, *Nuclear Radiation in Warfare*, p 21; Singh, McWhinney, *Nuclear Weapons and Contemporary International Law*, p 261; United Nations Organization; UN Department of Disarmament Affairs; Report of the Secretary-General, *Nuclear Weapons: A Comprehensive Study*, pp 12–13, 30–1.

[49] Both the SALT II and the START agreements also distinguish so-called 'heavy ICBMs', defined in terms of launch weight and throw weight: Art II(7) SALT respectively Art 39 Annex on Terms and Their Definitions START I, II.

[50] Compare Art II(5) INF Treaty.

[51] Compare Art II(6) INF Treaty.

[52] Kile, Kristensen, *Appendix 12A. World nuclear forces 2005*, in: Stockholm International Peace Research Institute, *SIPRI Yearbook 2005; Armaments, Disarmament and International Security*, pp 578–602.

[53] Stockholm International Peace Research Institute, *SIPRI Yearbook 2000; Armaments, Disarmament and International Security*, Oxford University Press, Oxford, 2000, p xxvii. Similarly: Art II(8) SALT; Art II(3) Protocol to SALT; Art II(2) INF; Art 13 Annex on Terms and Their Definitions START I, II; Cochran, Arkin, Hoenig, *Nuclear Weapons Databook; Volume I, US Nuclear Forces and Capabilities*, p 172; United Nations Organization; UN Department of Disarmament Affairs; Report of the Secretary-General, *Nuclear Weapons: A Comprehensive Study*, p 13.

It usually flies horizontal, parallel to the ground, more or less like an aircraft. The forerunner of the modern cruise missile was the German *Vergeltungswaffen-1* (V-1) first used in combat on 13 June 1944 and with an average range of about 240 km.[54]

The development of cruise missiles lasted longer as a result of the priority given to ballistic missiles, and their complicated guidance and navigation mechanisms. In principle, guided ballistic missiles only need guidance during the boosting phase; cruise missiles, on the other hand must be guided or navigated throughout the entire flight, using radio, radar, radar map-matching, infra-red and laser devices.[55] The first modern cruise missiles were tested and deployed in the 1960s, primarily as short-range non-strategic weapons intended against surface ships. By the 1980s, cruise missile technology had become so advanced that their range had increased to 2500 km and accuracy to a few tens of meters.[56]

Cruise missiles may be launched from ground-mobile transporters, or so-called transporter-erector-launchers (TELs) (ground-launched cruise missiles or GLCMs),[57] surface vessels and submarines (sea-launched cruise missiles or SLCMs), and aircraft (aircraft-launched cruise missiles or ALCMs).[58] Advanced cruise missiles (ACMs) are the newest generation cruise missiles that have stealth technology and can fly at supersonic speeds. Stealth technology is a combination of design, electronics and coating that enables an object to fly undetected by radar.[59]

Only ALCMs launched from long-range strategic bombers are generally regarded as strategic weapons. The combination of bomber range and missile accuracy is deemed perfect for attacking strategic objects in the hinterland. In addition, it allows bombers to avoid heavy air defences and it has given old bombers such as the United States B-52 and the Russian Bear a second life and increased longevity. Please note that when carrying gravity bombs, bombers are called delivery vehicles, while when carrying missiles they are usually called 'carriers' and serve as delivery plat-

[54] At <http://en.wikipedia.org/wiki/V-1>.

[55] United Nations Organization; UN Department of Disarmament Affairs; Report of the Secretary-General, *Nuclear Weapons: A Comprehensive Study*, pp 31–2, 38, fn 17.

[56] Barash, *Introduction to Peace Studies*, p 117; Cochran, Arkin, Hoenig, *Nuclear Weapons Databook; Volume I, US Nuclear Forces and Capabilities*, pp 172–3; Rauschning, *Nuclear Warfare and Weapons*, in: Bernhardt (Ed), *Encyclopaedia of Public International Law; Volume Three; Jan Mayen to Pueblo Incident*, p 731; United Nations Organization; UN Department of Disarmament Affairs; Report of the Secretary-General, *Nuclear Weapons: A Comprehensive Study*, pp 29–31.

[57] In the 1987 INF Treaty, the United States and the Soviet Union agreed to eliminate all their intermediate and shorter-range ground-launched missiles, including GLCMs.

[58] Barash, *Introduction to Peace Studies*, p 117; United Nations Organization; UN Department of Disarmament Affairs; Report of the Secretary-General, *Nuclear Weapons: A Comprehensive Study*, p 31.

[59] United Nations Organization; UN Department of Disarmament Affairs; Report of the Secretary-General, *Nuclear Weapons: A Comprehensive Study*, p 33.

forms.[60] Depending on the nature of the attack, also ground-launched cruise missiles, sea-launched cruise missiles and submarine-launched cruise missiles could be regarded as strategic weapons.

Of the current nuclear powers, only the United States and the Russian Federation have cruise missiles in their arsenals.[61]

2.2.3 *Non-Strategic Delivery Vehicles*

There is a wide variety of non-strategic delivery vehicles. Non-strategic missiles would generally be armed with single low-yield warheads and may be launched from aircraft, mobile ground stations, surface vessels, and submarines against aircraft, ground forces, surface vessels and submarines. Apart from relatively short-range ballistic missiles and cruise missiles, one may distinguish surface-to-surface missiles (SSMs), surface-to-air missiles (SAMs), short-range-attack missiles (SRAMs), anti-submarine missiles (AS missiles), and torpedoes, which are propeller-driven underwater missiles. Air-to-air missiles (AAMs) are generally not nuclear armed.

Other non-strategic delivery vehicles include various kinds of rockets, gravity bombs, depth charges, artillery fired atomic projectiles (AFAPs) and atomic demolition munition (ADM), which are so-called mini-nukes, that can be carried in a backpack by a single soldier and that are placed by special engineer teams below the surface or near bridges, tunnels or other structural targets.[62]

Of the current nuclear forces, only the People's Republic of China seems to possess a number of non-strategic delivery vehicles, other than SLCMs.[63] On 27 September 1991 President Bush Sr declared that, in view of the expected dissolution of the Soviet Union, the United States would eliminate from its ground forces 'its entire worldwide inventory of

[60] Cochran, Arkin, Hoenig, *Nuclear Weapons Databook; Volume I, US Nuclear Forces and Capabilities*, pp 105–6, 172–3; United Nations Organization; UN Department of Disarmament Affairs; Report of the Secretary-General, *Nuclear Weapons: A Comprehensive Study*, pp 13, 31–4.

It should be noted that although there is a de facto distinction between aircraft as delivery vehicles and aircraft as delivery platforms, this distinction is not made in the Strategic Arms Reduction Treaties. Heavy bombers are regarded as one 'Strategic Nuclear Delivery Vehicle'.

[61] Kile, Kristensen, *Appendix 12A. World nuclear forces 2005*, in: Stockholm International Peace Research Institute, *SIPRI Yearbook 2005; Armaments, Disarmament and International Security*, pp 580–8.

[62] Cochran, Arkin, Hoenig, *Nuclear Weapons Databook; Volume I, US Nuclear Forces and Capabilities*, pp 3, 39, 52–3, 60, 311; through: <http://en.wikipedia.org/>; LW McNaught, *Nuclear Weapons and Their Effects*, Brassey's Defence Publishers, London, 1984, p 26; Rauschning, *Nuclear Warfare and Weapons*, in: Bernhardt (Ed), *Encyclopaedia of Public International Law; Volume Three; Jan Mayen to Pueblo Incident*, p 731; Rotblat, *Nuclear Radiation in Warfare*, p 22; United Nations Organization; UN Department of Disarmament Affairs; Report of the Secretary-General, *Nuclear Weapons: A Comprehensive Study*, pp 12, 15, 19.

[63] The People's Republic of China is believed to have somewhere around 120 warheads in the low kiloton range for artillery, ADMs, and short-range missiles. Kile, Kristensen, *Appendix 12A. World nuclear forces 2005*, in: Stockholm International Peace Research Institute, *SIPRI Yearbook 2005; Armaments, Disarmament and International Security*, p 593.

ground-launched short-range, that is theater nuclear weapons' and that it would withdraw all 'tactical nuclear weapons' from its naval forces, many of which were promised to be destroyed, with a few remaining in storage for possible future crises.[64] The Soviet Union responded by mouth of its President, Gorbachev, on 5 October 1991 announcing similar steps as regards 'tactical nuclear weapons,' namely the elimination of all 'nuclear artillery munitions and nuclear warheads for tactical missiles;' the withdrawal and partial elimination of 'warheads for air defense missiles;' and the removal and storage of all 'tactical nuclear weapons,' from naval forces.[65]

In 2002, however, the Bush Jr Administration announced that it wished to carry out research on a so-called Robust Nuclear Earth Penetrator (RNEP), also known as the 'Nuclear Bunker Buster', intended to destroy large underground structures and neutralise buried stockpiles of chemical and biological weapons. In its request, the Administration asked Congress to repeal a 10 year old moratorium on research on low-yield nuclear weapons, which it did in 2003. After strong protests and thorough examination, however, the program was cancelled in 2004 when the Senate eliminated funds for the RNEP in 2004 and again in 2005.[66]

2.3 Warhead

Apart from delivery platform and delivery vehicle, the third and certainly the most important part of a nuclear weapon system is the nuclear warhead, which is 'the part of a weapon which contains the [nuclear] explosive (. . .).'[67] There are many types of nuclear warheads, made of different fission or fusion materials, with different sizes and yields, and

[64] President of the United States; George Bush, announcement from the White House, 27 Sep 1991, in: *Appendix 2A. The 1991–92 US, Soviet and Russian unilateral nuclear reduction initiative*, Stockholm International Peace Research Institute, *SIPRI Yearbook 1992; World Armaments and Disarmament*, Oxford University Press, Oxford, 1992, p 85.

[65] President of the Soviet Union; Mikhail Gorbachev, televised announcement, 5 Oct 1991, in: *Appendix 2A. The 1991–92 US, Soviet and Russian unilateral nuclear reduction initiative*, Stockholm International Peace Research Institute, *SIPRI Yearbook 1992; World Armaments and Disarmament*, Oxford University Press, Oxford, 1992, p 87.

[66] AJ Grotto, *Nuclear Bunker Busters and Article VI of the Non-Proliferation Treaty*, ASIL Insights, Feb 2005; SN Kile, *Nuclear arms control and non-proliferation*, in: Stockholm International Peace Research Institute, *SIPRI Yearbook 2005; Armaments, Disarmament and International Security*, Oxford University Press, Oxford, 2005, pp 574–6; DG Kimball, *Nuclear Bunker-Buster (As We Know It) is Dead*, though: <http://www.armscontrol.org/>. K Knip, *Mininukes*, NRC Handelsblad, 31 mei–1 jun 2003; E Mourlon-Druol, *Smaller, but smarter? The Robust Nuclear Earth Penetrator (RNEP), the Bush administration and the second nuclear age*, Bofaxe No 257E, 25 Aug 2003. Through: <http://www.ruhr-uni-bochum.de/ifhv/publications/bofaxe/>. The development of the RNEP was considered necessary in the 2001 Nuclear Posture Review as well as in the 2005 Joint Nuclear Doctrine.

[67] Stockholm International Peace Research Institute, *SIPRI Yearbook 2000; Armaments, Disarmament and International Security*, p xxxiv.

made suitable for their respective delivery vehicles. They may also carry highly sophisticated technology, such as micro-processors; chemical high explosives; neutron actuators; arming systems to ready or make safe the warhead; a firing system; a fusing mechanism (radar, pressure sensitive, time) which regulates the detonation of the warhead; and control and safety devices.[68] Despite the technological differences, their explosion characteristics are relatively similar.

3—NUCLEAR EXPLOSIONS

3.1 Introduction

The whole process of nuclear detonation, ie the time period from the first neutron until the end of the chain reaction does not take longer than a microsecond, or a millionth of a second. During that period several tens of generations of neutrons are produced, each generation doubling the energy release. Most of the explosive energy is in the form of kinetic or moving energy of the fission products and the bomb debris resulting in a hot gaseous sphere with a temperature of several tens of millions of degrees Celsius, similar to those in the sun,[69] and a pressure of over a million times the atmospheric pressure. In case of a thermonuclear or boosted fission weapon, this phase is then accompanied or followed by the nuclear fusion of the hydrogen elements and possibly by nuclear fission of the U-238 tamper.

Subsequently a number of phenomena take place that are undetectable by the human eye, but that are worth mentioning, because they explain the effects that will be discussed below. The hot and high pressure sphere immediately starts to radiate so-called 'soft' X-rays that are absorbed by the surrounding air and then re-radiated. Gradually, a transition takes place from X-rays to energy of longer wavelengths which leads to a 'luminous', or 'incandescent' spherical mass, commonly referred to as the fireball whose size depends on the weapon's yield. Because of this radiation emission and the rapid expansion of the fast ascending 'bubble of hot, radioactive gas', the temperature drops to about 300,000 degrees Celsius. At some point a shock wave is formed which breaks away from the hot sphere and moves ahead of the fireball thereby revealing its hot interior. This causes the release of a major flash of radiant energy of visible wavelengths containing almost all of the thermal energy, and whose duration

[68] Cochran, Arkin, Hoenig, *Nuclear Weapons Databook; Volume I, US Nuclear Forces and Capabilities*, p 30.

[69] Compare the maximum temperature of conventional high explosives, which is about 5,000 degrees Celsius. Glasstone, Dolan (Eds), *The Effects of Nuclear Weapons*, pp 6–7.

may last for seconds. This flash is, according to eye witnesses, supposed to be many times more brilliant than a sun at noon.[70]

As the fireball rises rapidly like a 'hot-air balloon', it continues to expand and to cool off. The vaporised materials condense into solid particles and water vapor into cloud and depending on the height of burst, after-winds will suck up dust and debris through the bottom of the sphere, shaped like a donut, and making the whole cloud look like a giant mushroom. After reaching its maximum height after about 10 minutes, movement stops and the cloud will only grow laterally, merging with natural clouds. The speed and height of ascension depend on the height of burst or type of explosion, energy yield and atmospheric and meteorological conditions, variable factors that will come back regularly in the discussion of the direct and indirect effects of nuclear explosions below.[71]

The actual energy distribution of nuclear weapons is dependent on four variables: the type of explosion; the weapon design; the meteorological conditions, such as temperature, humidity, wind, precipitation, and atmospheric pressure; and the nature of the terrain. The type of explosion requires separate discussion because it always reflects a definite choice (section 3.2); the others will be dealt with within the framework of the effects of nuclear weapons, which will be discussed in a subsequent section (section 4).

3.2 Types of Nuclear Explosions

3.2.1 Introduction

One may differentiate the various types of nuclear explosions both on the basis of quality and on the basis of quantity of the surrounding environment. In the first case we should think of nuclear explosions in air, ground,

[70] British Medical Association; Report of the British Medical Association's Board of Science and Education, *The Medical Effects of Nuclear War*, John Wiley & Sons, Chichester, 1983, pp 31–3; Glasstone, Dolan (Eds), *The Effects of Nuclear Weapons*, pp 6–8, 27–8, 64; CS Grace, *Nuclear Weapons; Principles, Effects and Survivability*, Brassey's, London, 1994, pp 25–7; PE Hodgson, *Nuclear Physics in Peace and War*, Hawthorn Books Publishers, New York, 1963, pp 93–4; International Council of Scientific Unions; Scientific Committee on Problems of the Environment 28; AB Pittock, TP Ackerman,PJ. Crutzen, MC MacCracken, CS Shapiro, RP Turco, *Environmental Consequences of Nuclear War; Volume I: Physical and Atmospheric Effects*, John Wiley & Sons, Chichester, 1986, pp 5–6; DS Kothari (et al), *Nuclear Explosions and Their Effects*, The Publications Division, Ministry of Information and Broadcasting, New Delhi, 1958, pp 40–1; McNaught, *Nuclear Weapons and Their Effects*, pp 28–9, 73; R Rhodes, *The Making of the Atomic Bomb*, Simon and Schuster, New York, 1986, pp 670–2; Rotblat, *Nuclear Radiation in Warfare*, pp 12–14.

[71] Glasstone, Dolan, *The Effects of Nuclear Weapons*, pp 28–33; Hodgson, *Nuclear Physics in Peace and War*, pp 93–4; International Council of Scientific Unions; Scientific Committee on Problems of the Environment 28; Pittock, Ackerman, Crutzen, MacCracken, Shapiro, Turco, *Environmental Consequences of Nuclear War; Volume I: Physical and Atmospheric Effects*, p 12.

water, or in relative vacuum (exo-atmospheric burst); and in the second case we should think of differences in density, or easier, height or depth of burst. Also the temperature, pressure and composition of the surrounding medium should be taken into consideration.[72]

According to McNaught, '[t]he type of burst is classified by the position of the fireball at its maximum diameter in relation to the ground.' Based on this definition, one could basically distinguish three main categories, namely air (section 3.2.2), surface (section 3.2.3), and sub-surface bursts (section 3.2.4).[73] The type of explosion that is eventually chosen for depends on the nature of the target and the seriousness and magnitude of the damage that needs to be inflicted.[74]

3.2.2 Air Burst

An air burst is defined by Glasstone and Dolan as:

> one in which the weapon is exploded in the air at an altitude below 100,000 feet, but at such a height that the fireball (at roughly maximum brilliance in its later stages) does not touch the surface of the earth.

Because of this, they explain later on, 'no appreciable quantities of surface materials are taken up into the fireball.'[75] This latter consequence has major implications for the delayed direct effects of nuclear explosions.

This main characteristic of the fireball not touching the ground returns in most of the definitions from other writers. Glasstone's and Dolan's somewhat arbitrary 100,000 feet barrier is based on their distinction between air bursts and high-altitude bursts.[76] Others have subdivided air bursts into low-, high-, and exo-atmospheric bursts,[77] in low-air bursts

[72] Glasstone, Dolan, *The Effects of Nuclear Weapons*, pp 63–4; Rotblat, *Nuclear Radiation in Warfare*, p 11.

[73] Glasstone, Dolan, *The Effects of Nuclear Weapons*, pp 33–63; McNaught, *Nuclear Weapons and Their Effects*, p 26. Compare Art I of the 1963 Partial Test Ban Treaty which distinguishes between nuclear explosions in outer space, in the atmosphere, under water, and in 'any other environment'. Treaty Banning Nuclear Weapon Tests in the Atmosphere, in Outer Space and Under Water (Partial Test Ban Treaty), signed 5 Aug 1963, opened for signature on 8 Aug 1963, entered into force on 10 Oct 1963, UNTS, Vol 480, No 6964.

[74] Glasstone, Dolan, *The Effects of Nuclear Weapons*, p 26; Hodgson, *Nuclear Physics in Peace and War*, pp 106–7; Kothari, *Nuclear Explosions and Their Effects*, pp 53–60.

[75] Glasstone, Dolan, *The Effects of Nuclear Weapons*, pp 9, 409. Similarly Kothari, *Nuclear Explosions and Their Effects*, pp 52–3; A Tucker, J Gleisner, *Crucible Despair: The Effects of Nuclear War*, The Menard Press, London, 1982, pp 19–20.

[76] Glasstone, Dolan, *The Effects of Nuclear Weapons*, p 10. Similarly: Tucker, Gleisner, *Crucible Despair: The Effects of Nuclear War*, pp 19–20.

[77] McNaught, *Nuclear Weapons and Their Effects*, p 26. Please note that McNaught defines exoatmospheric bursts as bursts above an altitude of 35 km, which is according to Westing in the upper stratosphere and therefore part of the lower atmosphere. The earth's atmosphere extends upward to approximately 150 km. AH Westing, *Weapons of Mass Destruction and the Environment*, Stockholm International Peace Research Institute, Taylor & Francis Ltd., London, 1977, p 26, fn 4.

and exo-atmospheric bursts,[78] into air bursts and low-altitude bursts,[79] into tropospheric and stratospheric bursts,[80] and into atmospheric bursts and bursts in outer space.[81] They all have in common that the reason for their distinction are the different circumstances at high-altitudes. However, whether you draw the line at 30 km, at 35 km, or no line at all,[82] or whether you distinguish between two or three types of air bursts is just a matter of preference of the author emphasising different aspects. It is not of great importance and does therefore not need further deliberation.

Where the energy distributions of regular air bursts remain generally the same, and their quantitative aspects merely depend on the yield of the explosion, explosions at higher altitudes tend to show significant differences. Because of the low air density, the interaction of the explosive energy with the surrounding air is different, leaving less room for blast and shock because there are simply less molecules to move. Because of the slow growth of the shock wave, the fireball has time to grow rapidly and to radiate more thermal energy. Because of the fact that the amount of nuclear radiation is independent of the surrounding material and of the type of burst, one may conclude that the proportion of thermal energy increases at higher altitudes. Also, the thermal and nuclear radiations are allowed to travel a lot further, although the effective thermal and nuclear radiation received on the ground decreases at the same time with increasing altitude due to attenuation by the air through which they travel. Fireballs of high-altitude explosions are known to be extremely bright and visible hundreds of miles away. The longer reach of nuclear radiation on its turn leads to a more significant and widespread impact of the electromagnetic pulse (EMP), which is a direct effect of nuclear explosions and which will be discussed in greater detail further below.[83]

Low air bursts are most likely to be used in warfare if one wants to inflict immediate damage over specific areas. Both the explosions over Hiroshima and Nagasaki, for example, were low air bursts, set at altitudes of respectively 1,900 and 1,650 feet. High-altitude bursts may be used to destroy electrical equipment, in particular the enemy's command, control,

[78] Grace, *Nuclear Weapons; Principles, Effects and Survivability*, ch 3.
[79] Kothari, *Nuclear Explosions and Their Effects*, pp 53–60.
[80] Westing, *Weapons of Mass Destruction and the Environment*, pp 2–3.
[81] Art I(1)(a) PTBT.
[82] Art I(1)(a) PTBT states that nuclear explosions are prohibited 'in the atmosphere; beyond its limits, including outer space.' The reason for doing so is that no agreed upon definition existed.
[83] Glasstone, Dolan, *The Effects of Nuclear Weapons*, pp 6–11, 45–8, 64, 73; Grace, *Nuclear Weapons; Principles, Effects and Survivability*, p 32; Westing, *Weapons of Mass Destruction and the Environment*, pp 2–3.

communication and intelligence facilities, making use of an explosion's electromagnetic pulse,[84] or to destroy incoming ballistic missiles.[85]

3.2.3 *Surface Burst*

Glasstone and Dolan define the surface burst as 'one which occurs either at or slightly above the actual surface of land or water.'[86] Typical of surface bursts is that in this case the fireball does touch the surface, in which case the consequences vary with the material of which the underground consists. Using this definition and this characteristic, one prevents a transition or gray area between air bursts and surface bursts. This means that a low-air burst whose fireball touches the surface should be regarded a surface burst instead of an air burst.

The fireball vaporises everything it touches, and in combination with the strong afterwinds that suck up large amounts of material, it could leave a crater whose size will depend on yield, actual height of burst, and surface material. So, in fact, the main difference between air and surface bursts is the large amount of vaporised or sucked up material in the radioactive mushroom cloud, the consequences of which will be discussed further below.[87]

Nuclear detonation on or close to the water surface has an additional effect which was discovered during a nuclear test at Bikini Atoll in the Marshall Islands in July 1946. After the column or plume of water in the form of a hollow cylinder with a mushroom or cauliflower head and consisting of millions of tons of water had reached its highest point and started to collapse, a white ring of mist, or a donut shaped condensation cloud rolled out at the bottom of the stem moving at about 50 miles per hour. This is known as the 'base surge' and is quite dangerous for surface vessels because of its radioactivity. Water-bursts also create a series of

[84] Grace, *Nuclear Weapons; Principles, Effects and Survivability*, p 47; LG Groves, *Now It Can Be Told; The Story of the Manhattan Project*, Andre Deutsch Publishers, London, 1963, p 286; H Krane, *Introductory Nuclear Physics*, John Wiley & Sons, New York, 1988, p 523; McNaught, *Nuclear Weapons and Their Effects*, pp 26, 30; United Nations Organization; UN Department of Disarmament Affairs; Report of the Secretary-General, *Nuclear Weapons: A Comprehensive Study*, p 75.

[85] The United States developed nuclear-armed anti-ballistic missiles during the Cold War, but abandoned the program when it did not turn out to be cost-effective. Russia removed the nuclear warheads from its anti-ballistic missile system around Moscow in 1998, and replace them with conventional warheads. Through: <http://www.fas.org/nuke/guide/index.html>.

[86] Glasstone, Dolan, *The Effects of Nuclear Weapons*, p 11.

[87] British Medical Association; Report of the British Medical Association's Board of Science and Education, *The Medical Effects of Nuclear War*, pp 8–9; Glasstone, Dolan, *The Effects of Nuclear Weapons*, pp 33–6, 232–6; Grace, *Nuclear Weapons; Principles, Effects and Survivability*, p 31; Kothari, *Nuclear Explosions and Their Effects*, pp 53–60; McNaught, *Nuclear Weapons and Their Effects*, p 26; Rotblat, *Nuclear Radiation in Warfare*, p 16; Tucker, Gleisner, *Crucible Despair: The Effects of Nuclear War*, pp 19–20; Westing, *Weapons of Mass Destruction and the Environment*, pp 2–3.

waves moving outward at high speed causing serious flooding if the burst were close enough to the shore.[88]

Surface bursts cause severe damage over a small area around ground-zero, which is:

> the point on the surface of land [or water] vertically below or above the center of a burst of a nuclear (or atomic) weapon.[89]

They are most likely to be used against specific hard targets, such as factories, (nuclear) power plants, air ports, ships, and most importantly, missile silos.[90]

3.2.4 *Sub-surface Burst*

Of sub-surface bursts, the explosion's center is beneath the ground for underground bursts or under the water-surface for underwater bursts. Some writers make a distinction between these two; others discuss them together because most of the phenomenology is relatively comparable.[91] Similar to what has been said above about preventing a transition area between air bursts and surface bursts, the same holds good for surface bursts and shallow underground bursts. Surface bursts and shallow underground bursts have generally the same characteristics, and therefore, Glasstone and Dolan define both types of explosions as:

> those in which either the fireball or the hot, high-pressure gases generated by the explosion intersect or break through the earth's surface.[92]

This section only deals with regular sub-surface bursts.

In case of a sub-surface burst, the fireball solely consists of vaporised bomb materials, fission products, nuclear radiation and vaporised rock or water and remains relatively small. In case of an underground burst, a cavity could be produced that disintegrates when gases vent through cracks in the soil and the earth above, loosened and displaced by a

[88] Glasstone, Dolan, *The Effects of Nuclear Weapons*, pp 48–55; Grace, *Nuclear Weapons; Principles, Effects and Survivability*, p 31; Kothari, *Nuclear Explosions and Their Effects*, pp 53–60.

[89] Glasstone, Dolan, *The Effects of Nuclear Weapons*, p 634. For surface or sub-surface bursts, one generally uses the term 'surface zero' or 'surface ground zero'. Glasstone, Dolan, *The Effects of Nuclear Weapons*, p 39, fn 5. Similarly, Grace, *Nuclear Weapons; Principles, Effects and Survivability*, p 132; McNaught, *Nuclear Weapons and Their Effects*, p 26. The SCOPE-ENUWAR Report makes use of the word 'hypocenter' instead of ground-zero: International Council of Scientific Unions; Scientific Committee on Problems of the Environment 28; Pittock, Ackerman, Crutzen, MacCracken, Shapiro, Turco, *Environmental Consequences of Nuclear War; Volume I: Physical and Atmospheric Effects*, pp 314–15.

[90] British Medical Association; Report of the British Medical Association's Board of Science and Education, *The Medical Effects of Nuclear War*, pp 8–9; Krane, *Introductory Nuclear Physics*, p 523; McNaught, *Nuclear Weapons and Their Effects*, p 26.

[91] Glasstone, Dolan, *The Effects of Nuclear Weapons*, p 11. Similarly: Tucker, Gleisner, *Crucible Despair: The Effects of Nuclear War*, p 20.

[92] Glasstone, Dolan, *The Effects of Nuclear Weapons*, p 231.

reflected shock wave, collapses. In case of an underwater burst, the fireball shortly illuminates the water. The laws of nature make sure that the large bubble of hot, high pressure radioactive gases, vapors and steam eventually reaches the surface, but at that time the temperature has dropped to such level that there is no appreciable emission of thermal radiation. In both cases large quantities of earth or water will be contaminated, a phenomenon that will be discussed below within the context of delayed direct effects of nuclear explosions.

As far as the direct impact of a subsurface burst is concerned, one could say that in general, most of the thermal and initial nuclear radiation is absorbed at close distances from the explosion because of the relatively large density of the surrounding environment. Therefore, most of the damage to underground or underwater structures and objects results from the shock wave. Depending on yield, depth of burst, nature of the soil, and for water-bursts also the depth and surface area of the water, and the composition and contour of the bottom, some of this shock energy might pop up thereby producing a so-called throw-out crater or a 'spray dome', which is a hollow column of broken water. An underwater burst, may also cause a series of surface waves, and a limited air blast just like surface bursts. There may even be a second 'spray dome' when the shock wave is reflected from the bottom, a base surge or condensation cloud and a series of high waves, and, if the burst is close enough to the bottom and the bubble hits the bottom, there may be even underwater cratering. Underwater bursts whose shock wave break through the surface, therefore, do resemble water surface bursts.[93]

Although sub-surface bursts generally have little military use, they could be used as environmental modification techniques to create earthquakes or tsunamis,[94] to destroy sub-surface structures, such as underground missile silos and bunkers, or to destroy submerged submarines or even surface vessels.[95] Recently, sub-surface nuclear explosions have received renewed attention after the Bush Administration announced in 2002 that it wished to carry out research on bunker busters to destroy hardened deeply buried targets. Since 1961 most nuclear tests have been carried out underground at great depth due to increased awareness of

[93] Glasstone, Dolan, *The Effects of Nuclear Weapons*, pp 11, 48–55, 58–63, 232–6, 244–52; Grace, *Nuclear Weapons; Principles, Effects and Survivability*, p 31; Kothari, *Nuclear Explosions and Their Effects*, pp 53–60; McNaught, *Nuclear Weapons and Their Effects*, p 26; Westing, *Weapons of Mass Destruction and the Environment*, pp 2–3.

[94] The use of environmental modification techniques was prohibited by the Convention on the Prohibition of Military or any Other Hostile Use of Environmental Modification Techniques (ENMOD), opened for signature on 18 May 1977, entered into force on, 5 Oct 1978, UNTS, Vol 1108, No 17119. Earthquakes and tsunamis were specifically referred to in an Understanding Relating to Art II, as phenomena that could be caused by the use of environmental modification techniques. ENMOD will be further discussed in Ch III.

[95] Glasstone, Dolan, *The Effects of Nuclear Weapons*, pp 58, 61; Grace, *Nuclear Weapons; Principles, Effects and Survivability*, pp 31, 60–3.

negative environmental and health effects and in 1963, the United States, the Soviet Union and the United Kingdom agreed to prohibit all nuclear tests in the atmosphere, in outer space, under water, and in any other environment:

> if such explosion causes radioactive debris to be present outside the territorial limits of the State under whose jurisdiction or control such explosion is conducted.[96]

4—THE EFFECTS OF NUCLEAR EXPLOSIONS

4.1 Introduction

Having dealt with the energy output of nuclear explosions and the different types of bursts, it will be easier to explain the 'interactions of the output of the exploding weapon with its environment'.[97] The events which follow the very large and extremely rapid energy release in a nuclear explosion are mainly the consequences of the interaction of the moving energy of the fission fragments and the thermal radiation with the surrounding medium of the explosion.[98] Here, these events or consequences will be referred to as direct effects (section 4.2). In addition, nuclear war or multiple nuclear explosions may have long-term consequences for the global economy and the global environment. These consequences will be referred to as indirect effects and will be discussed further below (section 4.3).

4.2 Direct Effects

4.2.1 Introduction

One can distinguish four direct effects, namely blast or shock (section 4.2.2), thermal radiation (section 4.2.3), electromagnetic pulse or EMP (section 4.2.4), and nuclear radiation (section 4.2.5). Blast, heat and EMP may be considered prompt effects; nuclear radiation, however, is more generic by nature and manifests itself both promptly and in the long-term.[99]

[96] Art I of the 1963 Partial Test Ban Treaty.

[97] Glasstone, Dolan, *The Effects of Nuclear Weapons*, p 26.

[98] Glasstone, Dolan, *The Effects of Nuclear Weapons*, pp 1, 6–8, 26.

[99] H von Arx, T Marauhn, *Nuclear Tests*, in: R Bernhardt (Ed), *Encyclopaedia of Public International Law; Volume Three; Jan Mayen to Pueblo Incident*, Elsevier, Amsterdam, 1997, p 723; Congress of the United States; Office of Technology Assessment, *The Effects of Nuclear War*, Allanheld, Osmun & Co. Publishers, Inc, Montclair, NJ, 1980, pp 15–23. Also published as M Riordan (Ed), *The Day after Midnight; The Effects of Nuclear War*, Cheshire Books, Palo Alto, California, 1982; Glasstone, Dolan, *The Effects of Nuclear Weapons*, pp 6–8; Kothari, *Nuclear Explosions and Their Effects*, pp 39–40; Krane, *Introductory Nuclear Physics*, pp 522–3; McNaught, *Nuclear Weapons and Their Effects*, pp 27–8; United Nations Organization;

4.2.2 Blast

Depending on the surrounding medium, the shock wave that escapes from the fireball is either in the form of an air blast, an underground shock, or an underwater shock. In regular air bursts, the blast wave of a fission weapon carries 50 per cent of the explosive energy which percentage progressively declines at increasing altitudes. For hydrogen weapons this percentage is a couple of points higher, around 54 per cent. Although it travels slower than the pulses of thermal and nuclear radiation, it initially travels at a speed that is many times the speed of sound, which is approximately 330 meters per second. Because of the long duration (up to several seconds for nuclear weapons in the megaton range), nuclear blasts are generally more destructive than blasts from conventional explosives.[100]

As has been observed above, the air blast results from an enormous build-up of pressure in the vaporised material and a subsequent rapid expansion of gases, and it gives rise to a high-pressure wave traveling rapidly away from the fireball, generally at supersonic speed. This is the primary or incident shock wave. If close enough to the surface of a more dense medium, this wave may merge with a reflected shock wave to form what is known as the Mach stem or fused shock.[101] Under ideal circumstances the peak-pressure or overpressure, could be twice the value of the pressure at ground-zero. Factors that have to be taken into consideration are the nature of the surface, the angle at which it strikes the surface, strength of the incident wave, yield of detonation, and height of burst. In

UN Department of Disarmament Affairs; Report of the Secretary-General, *Nuclear Weapons: A Comprehensive Study*, pp 71–2.

[100] Barash, *Introduction to Peace Studies*, pp 108–9; British Medical Association; Report of the British Medical Association's Board of Science and Education, *The Medical Effects of Nuclear War*, pp 3–5; Congress of the United States; Office of Technology Assessment, *The Effects of Nuclear War*, pp 15–16; Glasstone, Dolan, *The Effects of Nuclear Weapons*, pp 6–8; Grace, *Nuclear Weapons; Principles, Effects and Survivability*, pp 28–9; Hodgson, *Nuclear Physics in Peace and War*, pp 96–7; International Council of Scientific Unions; Scientific Committee on Problems of the Environment 28; Pittock, Ackerman, Crutzen, MacCracken, Shapiro, Turco, *Environmental Consequences of Nuclear War; Volume I: Physical and Atmospheric Effects*, p 6; Kothari, *Nuclear Explosions and Their Effects*, pp 43–6; McNaught, *Nuclear Weapons and Their Effects*, pp 27–9, 73–7; Rotblat, *Nuclear Radiation in Warfare*, pp 11, 16–18; Tucker, Gleisner, *Crucible Despair: The Effects of Nuclear War*, pp 21–2; United Nations Organization; UN Department of Disarmament Affairs; Report of the Secretary-General, *Nuclear Weapons: A Comprehensive Study*, p 72; United Nations Organization; UN Department of Disarmament Affairs; Report of the Secretary-General, *Study on the Climatic and Other Global Effects of Nuclear War*, United Nations Publication, New York, 1989, p 40; Westing, *Weapons of Mass Destruction and the Environment*, pp 3–7, 24–5, fn 2; World Health Organization; Report of the WHO Management Group on Follow-up of resolution WHA36.28: 'The Role of Physicians and Other Health Workers in the Preservation and Promotion of Peace . . .', *Effects of Nuclear War on Health and Health Services*, World Health Organization, Geneva, 1987, p 13.

[101] The reflected shock wave travels faster through the heated air which enables it to catch up with the primary wave. If the burst is close enough to the surface, some of the blast energy may be absorbed causing a shock wave that may be strong enough to damage even subsurface structures or objects.

case of a surface burst, the incident and reflected shock waves merge instantly.[102]

The blast wave consists two phases, namely a positive phase and a negative phase. The positive phase is formed by the shock front traveling rapidly away from the fireball 'behaving like a moving wall of highly compressed air',[103] and accounts for most of the structural damage. This shock front, which is experienced as a sudden and shattering gigantic hammer blow, is accompanied by very damaging hurricane-force drag winds taking down everything still standing. In terms of pressure, one could say that there is a sharp rise in pressure until it reaches its peak, which is basically static by nature, followed by a steady decrease as the shock wave moves on. This steady decrease in pressure is dynamic by nature. Both Grace and McNaught illustrate the difference between the two by considering a box-like target. The overpressure tries to crush the object, whereas the dynamic pressure tries to move the object.

The negative phase is characterised by reduced pressure, underpressure, or negative overpressure, ie below the normal atmospheric pressure, longer duration, and winds blowing in the opposite direction to fill the vacuum after the mass movement of air molecules. McNaught compares this reaction with an overextended spring that tries to re-establish equilibrium. Despite its duration it has little military value.[104]

The area destroyed by the blast wave is basically circular and depends on, besides weather conditions, the yield of the nuclear weapon and the altitude at which it was detonated. With respect to the latter, the relationship is as follows: the higher the altitude, the larger the area destroyed, but

[102] British Medical Association; Report of the British Medical Association's Board of Science and Education, *The Medical Effects of Nuclear War*, pp 4–5, 8–9; Glasstone, Dolan, *The Effects of Nuclear Weapons*, pp 38–40, 80–1, 86–7, 91; Grace, *Nuclear Weapons; Principles, Effects and Survivability*, pp 47–56; International Council of Scientific Unions; Scientific Committee on Problems of the Environment 28; Pittock, Ackerman, Crutzen, MacCracken, Shapiro, Turco, *Environmental Consequences of Nuclear War; Volume I: Physical and Atmospheric Effects*, pp 10–11; Kothari, *Nuclear Explosions and Their Effects*, pp 43–6; McNaught, *Nuclear Weapons and Their Effects*, pp 77–80; Rotblat, *Nuclear Radiation in Warfare*, pp 16–18; United Nations Organization; UN Department of Disarmament Affairs; Report of the Secretary-General, *Study on the Climatic and Other Global Effects of Nuclear War*, p 40; World Health Organization; Report of the WHO Management Group on Follow-up of resolution WHA36.28: 'The Role of Physicians and Other Health Workers in the Preservation and Promotion of Peace . . .', *Effects of Nuclear War on Health and Health Services*, p 13.

[103] Glasstone, Dolan, *The Effects of Nuclear Weapons*, p 38.

[104] Barash, *Introduction to Peace Studies*, pp 108–9; British Medical Association; Report of the British Medical Association's Board of Science and Education, *The Medical Effects of Nuclear War*, pp 4–5, 32–3; Congress of the United States; Office of Technology Assessment, *The Effects of Nuclear War*, pp 16–19; Glasstone, Dolan, *The Effects of Nuclear Weapons*, pp 80–1, 86–7; Grace, *Nuclear Weapons; Principles, Effects and Survivability*, pp 28–9, 47–56; Hodgson, *Nuclear Physics in Peace and War*, pp 96–7; International Council of Scientific Unions; Scientific Committee on Problems of the Environment 28; Pittock, Ackerman, Crutzen, MacCracken, Shapiro, Turco, *Environmental Consequences of Nuclear War; Volume I: Physical and Atmospheric Effects*, pp 10–11; Kothari, *Nuclear Explosions and Their Effects*, pp 43–4; McNaught, *Nuclear Weapons and Their Effects*, pp 29, 73–7, 80–7.

also the less intense the damage inflicted. In order to cause maximum damage, target analysts must try and find a balance between size and intensity. For every nuclear weapon with a specific yield, there is one altitude, one height of burst, that will produce the greatest overpressure, or the most efficient Mach stem. This altitude is called the 'Optimum Height of Burst'.[105] The optimum height for a 1 kt bomb would be 320 meters; the optimum height for a 1 Mt bomb would 3,200 meters.[106]

With respect to the former, it is generally considered that the area destroyed increases with increasing yield, but not in direct proportion to it. It is found that the area destroyed increases with the two-thirds power of the increase in energy release, or $\Delta E^{2/3}$, where ΔE stands for the increase in yield. This means that a ten-fold increase in yield produces roughly a five-fold increase; a hundred-fold increase in yield, produces a twenty-fold increase; and a thousand-fold increase produces a hundred-fold increase in area devastated by blast. Similarly, the radius of destruction by blast increases with the one-thirds power or cube root of the increase in the bomb's yield, or $\Delta E^{1/3}$.[107]

Shock waves in water generally behave similarly as blast waves in air, but there are some differences. Firstly, the peak overpressure does not fall off as rapidly with distance as in air, and secondly, the duration of the wave in water is shorter than in the air, but its velocity is greater. Also, when the shock wave reaches the surface and meets a much less dense medium, part of the energy is sent back as a reflection wave which

[105] British Medical Association; Report of the British Medical Association's Board of Science and Education, *The Medical Effects of Nuclear War*, pp 8–9; Congress of the United States; Office of Technology Assessment, *The Effects of Nuclear War*, pp 16–19; Glasstone, Dolan, *The Effects of Nuclear Weapons*, p 542; Grace, *Nuclear Weapons; Principles, Effects and Survivability*, pp 28–9; Hodgson, *Nuclear Physics in Peace and War*, pp 106–7; International Council of Scientific Unions; Scientific Committee on Problems of the Environment 28; Pittock, Ackerman, Crutzen, MacCracken, Shapiro, Turco, *Environmental Consequences of Nuclear War; Volume I: Physical and Atmospheric Effects*, pp 10–11; Kothari, *Nuclear Explosions and Their Effects*, pp 43–6; McNaught, *Nuclear Weapons and Their Effects*, pp 77–80; Rhodes, *The Making of the Atomic Bomb*, p 631; Rotblat, *Nuclear Radiation in Warfare*, pp 16–18; United Nations Organization; UN Department of Disarmament Affairs; Report of the Secretary-General, *Nuclear Weapons: A Comprehensive Study*, p 75; World Health Organization; Report of the WHO Management Group on Follow-up of resolution WHA36.28: 'The Role of Physicians and Other Health Workers in the Preservation and Promotion of Peace . . .', *Effects of Nuclear War on Health and Health Services*, p 9.

[106] Rotblat, *Nuclear Radiation in Warfare*, p 18.

[107] H Bethe, *The Hydrogen* Bomb, in: H. Bethe, *The Road from Los Alamos*, The American Institute of Physics, New York, 1991, p 15; Glasstone, Dolan, *The Effects of Nuclear Weapons*, p 213; JO Hirschfelder, *Scientific-Technological Miracle at Los Alamos*, in: L Badash, JO Hirschfelder, HP Broida (Eds), *Reminiscences of Los Alamos 1943–1945*, D Reidel Publishing Company, Dordrecht, 1980, p 87; Hodgson, *Nuclear Physics in Peace and War*, pp 94–7; Krane, *Introductory Nuclear Physics*, p 553; JR Oppenheimer, *The New Weapon: The Turn of the* Screw, in: Masters, Way (Eds), *One World or None: A Report to the Public on the Full Meaning of the Atomic Bomb*, McGraw-Hill, New York, 1946; United Nations Organization; UN Department of Disarmament Affairs; Report of the Secretary-General, *Nuclear Weapons: A Comprehensive Study*, p 75.

decreases the positive shock wave. This phenomenon is called the 'surface cut-off.' The other part breaks through the surface and may cause an air blast and a series of surface waves.[108]

Ground shocks can be produced in two ways. Not only can they be generated 'by direct coupling of explosive energy to the ground in the neighborhood of the crater', which is the most common cause, but also 'by pressure of the air blast wave as it runs over the earth's surface.'[109] Regular underground bursts, where much energy is used to form the cavity, may result in a series of seismic waves, similar to earthquakes, although so far no evidence has been found that earthquakes are stimulated by nuclear explosions. The actual number of shock waves, their speed, their strength, their direction, and the damage they inflict depends on yield, depth of burst and geological circumstances.[110]

The damage resulting from a nuclear blast wave is much larger than from a conventional blast due to the combination of high peak overpressure, drag winds and duration. Most buildings and structures will be demolished or heavily damaged; many people will be killed. Casualties will result from two different types of blast injuries, namely:

> direct (or primary) injuries associated with exposure of the body to the environmental pressure variations accompanying a blast wave, and indirect injuries resulting from impact of penetrating and non-penetrating missiles on the body or as the consequences of displacement of the body as a whole.[111]

Westing distinguishes between primary, secondary, and tertiary blast effects, where primary stands for overpressure, secondary for flying

[108] Glasstone, Dolan, *The Effects of Nuclear Weapons,* pp 244–52; Grace, *Nuclear Weapons; Principles, Effects and Survivability,* pp 60–3; International Council of Scientific Unions; Scientific Committee on Problems of the Environment 28; Pittock, Ackerman, Crutzen, MacCracken, Shapiro, Turco, *Environmental Consequences of Nuclear War; Volume I: Physical and Atmospheric Effects,* p 11.

[109] Glasstone, Dolan, *The Effects of Nuclear Weapons,* pp 236–7. Also: Grace, *Nuclear Weapons; Principles, Effects and Survivability,* pp 60–3.

[110] Glasstone, Dolan, *The Effects of Nuclear Weapons,* pp 236–43; International Council of Scientific Unions; Scientific Committee on Problems of the Environment 28; Pittock, Ackerman, Crutzen, MacCracken, Shapiro, Turco, *Environmental Consequences of Nuclear War; Volume I: Physical and Atmospheric Effects,* p 13.

[111] Glasstone, Dolan, *The Effects of Nuclear Weapons,* p 548. Similarly: International Council of Scientific Unions; Scientific Committee on Problems of the Environment 28; Pittock, Ackerman, Crutzen, MacCracken, Shapiro, Turco, *Environmental Consequences of Nuclear War; Volume I: Physical and Atmospheric Effects,* pp 11–12; International Council of Scientific Unions; Scientific Committee on Problems of the Environment 28; MA Harwell, TC Hutchinson (Eds), *Environmental Consequences of Nuclear War; Volume II: Ecological and Agricultural Effects,* John Wiley & Sons, Chichester, 1985, pp 430–2; Tucker, Gleisner, *Crucible Despair: The Effects of Nuclear War,* pp 39–40; United Nations Organization; UN Department of Disarmament Affairs; Report of the Secretary-General, *Study on the Climatic and Other Global Effects of Nuclear War,* p 40; World Health Organization; Report of the WHO Management Group on Follow-up of resolution WHA36.28: 'The Role of Physicians and Other Health Workers in the Preservation and Promotion of Peace . . .', *Effects of Nuclear War on Health and Health Services,* p 14.

objects, and tertiary for body displacement, ie 'to having the body slammed into some object'.[112]

All human injuries are mechanical of nature, namely fractures, soft tissue wounds, crush injuries and concussions. In built-up areas, most people fall victim to indirect or secondary and tertiary blast injuries because men are surprisingly resistant to overpressure. Man's most sensitive organs are his eardrums and thanks to the flexibility of the rib cage, people can withstand large overpressures before his vital organs, such as heart and lungs, are fatally wounded. The human body can withstand overpressures of more than two atmospheres, which is approximately 200 kPa, or 30 psi (pounds per square inch), but only for a short period of time.[113]

The environmental damage resulting from blast can be substantial. According to Westing the following figures apply to air and surface bursts of various yields. The blast wave of an 18 kt air burst will blown down most trees within an area of 565 ha[114] and most vertebrates will be killed within an area of 43 ha; the blast wave of a 0.91 Mt air burst will blow down most trees within an area of 14,100 ha and kill most vertebrates within an area of 591 ha; and the blast wave of a 9.1 Mt air burst will blow down most trees within an area of 82,000 ha and kill most vertebrates within an area of 2,740 ha. For surface bursts these numbers are somewhat lower: most trees will be blown down within an area of 362 ha (18 kt), 9,040 ha (0.9 Mt) and 52,500 (9.1 Mt); and most vertebrates will be killed within areas of 24 ha (18 kt); 332 ha (0.91 Mt); and 1,540 (9.1 Mt).[115]

4.2.3 Thermal Radiation

The second largest energy output after the blast or shock is in the form of thermal radiation and comprises approximately 35 per cent of the total energy yield for fission weapons. For thermonuclear weapons, this

[112] Westing, *Weapons of Mass Destruction and the Environment*, pp 3–7.

[113] Congress of the United States; Office of Technology Assessment, *The Effects of Nuclear War*, pp 16–19; Glasstone, Dolan, *The Effects of Nuclear Weapons*, pp 154–7, 541; Grace, *Nuclear Weapons; Principles, Effects and Survivability*, pp 56–60; D Holdstock, L Waterston, *Nuclear weapons, a continuing threat to health*, The Lancet, Vol 355, 2000, p 1544; International Council of Scientific Unions; Scientific Committee on Problems of the Environment 28; Harwell, Hutchinson, *Environmental Consequences of Nuclear War; Volume II: Ecological and Agricultural Effects*, pp 430–2; Kothari, *Nuclear Explosions and Their Effects*, pp 43–6; McNaught, *Nuclear Weapons and Their Effects*, pp 80–7; Rotblat, *Nuclear Radiation in Warfare*, pp 16–18; United Nations Organization; UN Department of Disarmament Affairs; Report of the Secretary-General, *Nuclear Weapons: A Comprehensive Study*, pp 72, 81–2. For empirical data and an elaborate analysis of structural damage from and medical consequences of air blast, see: Glasstone, Dolan, *The Effects of Nuclear Weapons*, pp 154–230; 548–59.

[114] 1 ha equals 10,000 square meters.

[115] Westing, *Weapons of Mass Destruction and the Environment*, pp 16–17, Tables 1.12 and 1.13.

percentage is around 38 per cent. This large proportion of thermal energy, which comes in the form of heat—extremely high temperatures—and light—a blinding flash, is one of the characteristic differences with conventional weapons. In case of air bursts, this percentage increases at the expense of blast energy at high altitudes; together, blast energy and thermal radiation always account for 85 per cent (fission) or 92 per cent (fusion) of the total energy output of fission and fusion weapons. Thermal radiation travels at the speed of light—which makes it the first noticeable effect of nuclear explosions—and the duration of the pulse varies with the energy yield: the pulse from a 1 kt air burst may last for 0.4 seconds, whereas the pulse from a 10 Mt air burst could last for about 20 seconds.[116]

The origin of the thermal energy lies in the development of the fireball. As soon as the chain reaction stops, a gaseous sphere remains of extremely high temperature that immediately starts to emit thermal radiation in the form of X-rays. Glasstone and Dolan call this primary thermal radiation. These X-rays are absorbed by the surrounding medium and subsequently re-radiated in the form of ultraviolet, visible and infra-red rays that have longer wavelengths. Glasstone and Dolan call this secondary thermal radiation. The emission of ultraviolet radiation causes a first surface temperature pulse that does not pose a significant hazard, as it contains only 1 per cent of the total thermal radiation. After further cooling, there is a second pulse which lasts longer, carries the remaining 99 per cent of the thermal radiation and which consists of visible and infra-red radiation. This second pulse leads to the formation of the visible fireball, incandescent, bright, luminous, and, as was mentioned above, of an intensity that is supposed to be many times more than that of the sun at noon.[117]

[116] Barash, *Introduction to Peace Studies*, p 108; British Medical Association; Report of the British Medical Association's Board of Science and Education, *The Medical Effects of Nuclear War*, pp 3–5; Congress of the United States; Office of Technology Assessment, *The Effects of Nuclear War*, pp 15–16, 20–2; Glasstone, Dolan, *The Effects of Nuclear Weapons*, pp 6–8, 10–11, 64, 73, 276–7; Grace, *Nuclear Weapons; Principles, Effects and Survivability*, pp 25–7, 36–40; International Council of Scientific Unions; Scientific Committee on Problems of the Environment 28; Pittock, Ackerman, Crutzen, MacCracken, Shapiro, Turco, *Environmental Consequences of Nuclear War; Volume I: Physical and Atmospheric Effects*, p 6; Kothari, *Nuclear Explosions and Their Effects*, p 41; McNaught, *Nuclear Weapons and Their Effects*, p 27; Rotblat, *Nuclear Radiation in Warfare*, p 11; Tucker, Gleisner, *Crucible Despair: The Effects of Nuclear War*, pp 21–2; United Nations Organization; UN Department of Disarmament Affairs; Report of the Secretary-General, *Nuclear Weapons: A Comprehensive Study*, p 72; United Nations Organization; UN Department of Disarmament Affairs; Report of the Secretary-General, *Study on the Climatic and Other Global Effects of Nuclear War*, pp 40–1; Westing, *Weapons of Mass Destruction and the Environment*, pp 7–10, 25 fn 2; World Health Organization; Report of the WHO Management Group on Follow-up of resolution WHA36.28: 'The Role of Physicians and Other Health Workers in the Preservation and Promotion of Peace . . .', *Effects of Nuclear War on Health and Health Services*, p 14.

[117] British Medical Association; Report of the British Medical Association's Board of Science and Education, *The Medical Effects of Nuclear War*, pp 31–3; Glasstone, Dolan, *The Effects of Nuclear Weapons*, pp 40–1, 63–4, 276; Grace, *Nuclear Weapons; Principles, Effects and Survivability*, pp 25–7; Hodgson, *Nuclear Physics in Peace and War*, pp 94–6; Kothari, *Nuclear Explosions and Their Effects*, pp 41–3; International Council of Scientific Unions; Scientific

Thermal radiation appears as heat and light and may travel, in straight lines, considerable distances in air. The actual damage inflicted, however, depends on the amount of radiation received, which will be less at larger distances due to distribution over a larger area and loss of energy. Loss of energy or attenuation is due to absorption and scattering and depends on the density, composition and condition of the atmosphere. Fog, for example, may largely reduce the intensity of the heat flash.

As far as energy distribution over large areas is concerned, the energy dose received at a certain place or radiation intensity depends on the distance from and the yield of the explosion. For a given yield, the energy dose is determined by the inverse square law which is given by the formula: $E/4\pi r^2$, where E stands for a given energy yield, r for radius, which is the distance from the point of explosion, and $4\pi r^2$ for the surface area of a sphere. With increasing yield, the radius increases not in direct proportion to it, but by the square root of the energy difference, which is the same as $\Delta E^{1/2}$, where ΔE stands for the increase in yield. This increase is at a higher rate than that of the blast, which varies with the cube root of the power, or $\Delta E^{1/3}$. This means that the effect of thermal radiation becomes relatively more important with increasing weapon yields, whereas the blast wave is dominant in case of low yield weapons.[118]

The intense and blinding flash has various direct or primary effects on the human body. Firstly, it may cause considerable damage to the eyes, such as incurable retinal burns, and it may even lead to permanent loss of sight, although this is likely to be rare. These effects are commonly called flash blindness. The time of day and the degree of visibility are in that respect important factors as they determine the size of the eye pupils. For example, a 1 Mt nuclear weapon could cause flash blindness at 21 km on a clear day, but at a distance of 85 km on a clear night.[119] Secondly, the flash may 'photograph' objects leaving shadows on the ground or on people's bodies, a phenomenon called 'pigmentation'. Thirdly, the immense pulse of heat caused by absorption of thermal energy may cause various degrees of skin burns or carbonisation of objects. These wounds are called flash

Committee on Problems of the Environment 28; Pittock, Ackerman, Crutzen, MacCracken, Shapiro, Turco, *Environmental Consequences of Nuclear War; Volume I: Physical and Atmospheric Effects*, pp 5–6; McNaught, *Nuclear Weapons and Their Effects*, pp 28–9, 37–41; Rotblat, *Nuclear Radiation in Warfare*, pp 12–16; United Nations Organization; UN Department of Disarmament Affairs; Report of the Secretary-General, *Nuclear Weapons: A Comprehensive Study*, p 72.

[118] Bethe, *The Hydrogen Bomb*, in: Bethe, *The Road from Los Alamos*, p 15; Glasstone, Dolan, *The Effects of Nuclear Weapons*, pp 277–8, 282; Grace, *Nuclear Weapons; Principles, Effects and Survivability*, pp 25–7; Hodgson, *Nuclear Physics in Peace and War*, pp 94–6, 107–8; McNaught, *Nuclear Weapons and Their Effects*, pp 28–9, 37–41; Rotblat, *Nuclear Radiation in Warfare*, pp 14–16; United Nations Organization; UN Department of Disarmament Affairs; Report of the Secretary-General, *Nuclear Weapons: A Comprehensive Study*, pp 72–5.

[119] Congress of the United States; Office of Technology Assessment, *The Effects of Nuclear War*, pp 20–2.

burns as opposed to flame burns that are caused by fire. Flash burns are produced within a fraction of a second; flame burns develop more slowly and may have a more damaging effect on internal organs. If you are too close to ground-zero, evaporation, carbonisation of body parts and boiling away of internal organs may occur. In Hiroshima, about 30 to 50 per cent of all casualties were caused by flash burns.

The pulse may also ignite flammable and combustible materials, which is known as a secondary or indirect effect. Factors that should be taken into consideration are the nature, colour, thickness and moisture content of the material, as well as the rate of delivery and the duration of exposure. Wool, for example is more resistant than cotton. Subsequently, a large number of fires may develop into a firestorm or a conflagration,[120] depending on the circumstances, such as available fuel, vegetation, and weather conditions. These fires generate additional casualties, not only by the flames, but also by the production of asphyxiating and toxic gases. Both flash and flame burns need intensive treatment; if there is no treatment at all, mortality will be high. In Hiroshima and Nagasaki, most of the fires were started by the breaking of gas lines and the knocking over of stoves and furnaces as a result of the blast wave.

The damage to the environment will be significant. According to Westing, the surface area within which most (dry) vegetation is ignited by thermal radiation in case of an air burst is 1170 ha (18 kt yield), 33,300 ha (0.91 Mt yield), and 183,000 (9.1 Mt yield); and in case of a surface burst 749 ha (18 kt yield), 21,300 (0.91 Mt), and 117,000 (9.1 Mt yield). The surface area within which most vertebrates will be killed after an air burst is 1570 ha (18 kt yield), 42,000 (0.91 Mt yield), and 235,000 (9.1 Mt); and for a surface burst 1000 ha (18 kt yield), 26,900 ha (0.91 Mt yield), and 150,000 ha (9.1 Mt).[121]

Despite large scale destruction by fires McNaught observes that:

> [t]hermal effects are so easily attenuated that they are not considered sufficiently reliable as casualty producers to be taken into account in nuclear target analysis.

Protection from nuclear radiation is not too difficult with solid or opaque materials.[122]

[120] 'In a firestorm many fires merge to form a single convective column of hot gases rising from the burning area and strong, fire-induced, radial (inwardly directed) winds are associated with the convective column. (. . .). Conflagrations, as distinct from firestorms, have moving fire fronts which can be driven by the ambient wind.' Glasstone, Dolan, *The Effects of Nuclear Weapons*, pp 299–300. Similarly: Congress of the United States; Office of Technology Assessment, *The Effects of Nuclear War*, pp 20–2; Rhodes, *The Making of the Atomic Bomb*, pp 596–600.

[121] Westing, *Weapons of Mass Destruction and the Environment*, pp 16–17, Tables 1.12 and 1.13.

[122] Barash, *Introduction to Peace Studies*, p 108; Bethe, *The Hydrogen* Bomb, in: Bethe, *The Road from Los Alamos*, p 15; Congress of the United States; Office of Technology Assessment, *The Effects of Nuclear War*, pp 20–2; Glasstone, Dolan, *The Effects of Nuclear Weapons*, pp 155,

4.2.4 *Electromagnetic Pulse*

The third prompt effect of nuclear explosions is the generation of a so-called EMP. Although an EMP was expected to exist because also conventional high explosives were known to cause electromagnetic signals, its seriousness was not realised until the 1960s. It is caused by the interaction of gamma radiation and X-rays with air molecules. The gamma rays and X-rays cause intense ionisation of the air creating a 'large current of negative electrons flowing outward from the point of the explosion'.[123] This results into an extremely powerful electromagnetic field that propagates outwards and takes the form of a short pulse of radiofrequency energy trailing off within about one thousandth of a second. This pulse contains waves with a wide variety of amplitudes and a wide variety of frequencies, from a few hundred Hertz to up to several hundred MHz.[124]

277–8, 281–2, 285–91, 290–6, 541, 560–74; Grace, *Nuclear Weapons; Principles, Effects and Survivability*, pp 40–5; Hodgson, *Nuclear Physics in Peace and War*, pp 94–6, 107–8; International Council of Scientific Unions; Scientific Committee on Problems of the Environment 28; Pittock, Ackerman, Crutzen, MacCracken, Shapiro, Turco, *Environmental Consequences of Nuclear War; Volume I: Physical and Atmospheric Effects*, pp 6–9; International Council of Scientific Unions; Scientific Committee on Problems of the Environment 28; Harwell, Hutchinson, *Environmental Consequences of Nuclear War; Volume II: Ecological and Agricultural Effects*, 1985, pp 432–3; McNaught, *Nuclear Weapons and Their Effects*, pp 28–9, 42–6; Rauschning, *Nuclear Warfare and Weapons*, in: Bernhardt (Ed), *Encyclopaedia of Public International Law; Volume Three; Jan Mayen to Pueblo Incident*, p 731; Rhodes, *The Making of the Atomic Bomb*, pp 714–33; Rotblat, *Nuclear Radiation in Warfare*, pp 14–16; Tucker, Gleisner, *Crucible Despair: The Effects of Nuclear War*, pp 41–3; United Nations Organization; UN Department of Disarmament Affairs; Report of the Secretary-General, *Nuclear Weapons: A Comprehensive Study*, pp 72, 82; United Nations Organization; UN Department of Disarmament Affairs; Report of the Secretary-General, *Study on the Climatic and Other Global Effects of Nuclear War*, pp 40–1; Westing, *Weapons of Mass Destruction and the Environment*, pp 7–10; World Health Organization; Report of the WHO Management Group on Follow-up of resolution WHA36.28: 'The Role of Physicians and Other Health Workers in the Preservation and Promotion of Peace . . .', *Effects of Nuclear War on Health and Health Services*, pp 14–15.

[123] Krane, *Introductory Nuclear Physics*, p 556.

[124] H Briezeveld, L Mathot, *Scoop; Natuurkunde voor de Bovenbouw 5/6 VWO*, Wolters-Noordhoff, Groningen, 1991, p 272; Congress of the United States; Office of Technology Assessment, *The Effects of Nuclear War*, pp 15–16, 22; Glasstone, Dolan, *The Effects of Nuclear Weapons*, pp 10–11, 43, 514–17; Grace, *Nuclear Weapons; Principles, Effects and Survivability*, pp 25, 91–105; International Council of Scientific Unions; Scientific Committee on Problems of the Environment 28; Pittock, Ackerman, Crutzen, MacCracken, Shapiro, Turco, *Environmental Consequences of Nuclear War; Volume I: Physical and Atmospheric Effects*, pp 16–19; McNaught, *Nuclear Weapons and Their Effects*, pp 25, 30, 95–106; Rotblat, *Nuclear Radiation in Warfare*, pp 18–19; J Rotblat, *Physical Effects of Nuclear War*, in: World Health Organization, *Effects of Nuclear War on Health and Health Services*, Annex 1, pp 47–8; United Nations Organization; UN Department of Disarmament Affairs; Report of the Secretary-General, *Nuclear Weapons: A Comprehensive Study*, p 73; World Health Organization; Report of the WHO Management Group on Follow-up of resolution WHA36.28: 'The Role of Physicians and Other Health Workers in the Preservation and Promotion of Peace . . .', *Effects of Nuclear War on Health and Health Services*, p 11.

As explained above, at high-altitudes X-rays and gamma rays are allowed to travel large distances due to a lack of attenuation thereby generating much larger electromagnetic fields and affecting large areas of the earth's surface. For example, a single exo-atmospheric burst of 1 Mt at an altitude of about 400 km would affect an area extending out to 2200 km in all directions, ie the whole of Europe. Grace writes:

> Indeed the EMP is the only significant effect on the ground for a high-altitude burst, even though the EMP energy amounts to little more than 0.01 per cent of the total weapon output.[125]

The EMP can be extremely damaging to electronics and electrical equipment, depending on height of burst, yield, and range to the target. The electromagnetic energy travels at the speed of light and may be collected by metallic or other conductors. 'The energy of the radiation can then be converted into strong electric currents and high voltages.'[126] If the equipment with which the collector is connected is not protected by resistors, it will be destroyed as if it were struck by lightning. Also, the widespread ionisation of the atmosphere may severely disturb radio and radar traffic, the virtual eyes and mouth of defence systems. As was mentioned above, high-altitude bursts are therefore very likely to be used against the enemy's command, control, communication and intelligence facilities, and appealing as a preemptive strike.[127]

In principle, electromagnetic radiation does not have harmful effects on man, except for cases where people are dependent on the well-functioning of electronic equipment, such as pacemakers and other medical equipment used in hospitals.[128]

[125] Glasstone, Dolan, *The Effects of Nuclear Weapons*, pp 45–8; Grace, *Nuclear Weapons; Principles, Effects and Survivability*, pp 91–105; Krane, *Introductory Nuclear Physics*, p 556; McNaught, *Nuclear Weapons and Their Effects*, pp 30, 95–106; Rotblat, *Nuclear Radiation in Warfare*, pp 18–19; J Rotblat, *Physical Effects of Nuclear War*, in: World Health Organization, *Effects of Nuclear War on Health and Health Services*, Annex 1, pp 47–8; United Nations Organization; UN Department of Disarmament Affairs; Report of the Secretary-General, *Nuclear Weapons: A Comprehensive Study*, pp 74–6; World Health Organization; Report of the WHO Management Group on Follow-up of resolution WHA36.28: 'The Role of Physicians and Other Health Workers in the Preservation and Promotion of Peace . . .', *Effects of Nuclear War on Health and Health Services*, p 11.

[126] Glasstone, Dolan, *The Effects of Nuclear Weapons*, pp 516.

[127] Cables, wires and electrical equipment can be protected by coating and shielding them with specific materials. Radios and satellites, however, will remain vulnerable. At: http://en.wikipedia.org/wiki/Electromagnetic_pulse.

[128] British Medical Association; Report of the British Medical Association's Board of Science and Education, *The Medical Effects of Nuclear War*, pp 12–14; Congress of the United States; Office of Technology Assessment, *The Effects of Nuclear War*, pp 15–16, 22; Glasstone, Dolan, *The Effects of Nuclear Weapons*, pp 10–11, 43–8, 461, 515–17; Grace, *Nuclear Weapons; Principles, Effects and Survivability*, pp 91–105; International Council of Scientific Unions; Scientific Committee on Problems of the Environment 28; Pittock, Ackerman, Crutzen, MacCracken, Shapiro, Turco, *Environmental Consequences of Nuclear War; Volume I: Physical and Atmospheric Effects*, pp 16–20; McNaught, *Nuclear Weapons and Their Effects*, pp 25, 30, 95–106; Rotblat, *Nuclear Radiation in Warfare*, pp 18–19; J Rotblat, *Physical Effects of Nuclear*

4.2.5 *Nuclear Radiation*

4.2.5.1 Introduction

Although both the blast and the thermal radiation are significantly larger than any other effect of nuclear and conventional explosions, a nuclear weapon's most distinguishing characteristic is undoubtedly the emission of nuclear radiation.[129] Generally, there is a distinction between initial nuclear radiation and residual nuclear radiation, the former being a prompt effect of a nuclear explosion, and the latter being a delayed effect of a nuclear explosion. Residual nuclear radiation will be dealt with further below (section 4.2.5.3); the following section will focus on initial nuclear radiation (section 4.2.5.2).

4.2.5.2 Initial Nuclear Radiation

According to Rotblat:

> [i]nitial nuclear radiation is generally defined as that emitted from both the fireball and the radioactive cloud within the first minute after the explosion.[130]

Most writers admit that this line of demarcation, this time period is arbitrary, but it is practicable and it is connected with the effective range of gamma rays.[131] Rotblat explains:

War, in: World Health Organization, *Effects of Nuclear War on Health and Health Services*, Annex 1, pp 47–8; United Nations Organization; UN Department of Disarmament Affairs; Report of the Secretary-General, *Nuclear Weapons: A Comprehensive Study*, p 73; World Health Organization; Report of the WHO Management Group on Follow-up of resolution WHA36.28: 'The Role of Physicians and Other Health Workers in the Preservation and Promotion of Peace . . .', *Effects of Nuclear War on Health and Health Services*, p 11. For a more elaborate discussion of the ionization of the atmosphere, effects on radio and radar signals, and theory and characteristics of the electromagnetic pulse, see: Glasstone, Dolan, *The Effects of Nuclear Weapons*, pp 462–89, 517–39.

[129] Please note that '[t]he more general expression 'ionizing radiations' is often employed instead of nuclear radiations, since this permits the inclusion of radiations of nonnuclear origin, e.g. X-rays, having similar biological effects.' Glasstone, Dolan, *The Effects of Nuclear Weapons*, p 575, fn 6.

[130] Glasstone, Dolan, *The Effects of Nuclear Weapons*, pp 42–3. Similarly: Grace, *Nuclear Weapons; Principles, Effects and Survivability*, pp 29–30; Hodgson, *Nuclear Physics in Peace and War*, pp 97–8; International Council of Scientific Unions; Scientific Committee on Problems of the Environment 28; Pittock, Ackerman, Crutzen, MacCracken, Shapiro, Turco, *Environmental Consequences of Nuclear War; Volume I: Physical and Atmospheric Effects*, p 237; International Council of Scientific Unions; Scientific Committee on Problems of the Environment 28; Harwell, Hutchinson, *Environmental Consequences of Nuclear War; Volume II: Ecological and Agricultural Effects*, 1985, p 196; Kothari, *Nuclear Explosions and Their Effects*, pp 46–7; McNaught, *Nuclear Weapons and Their Effects*, pp 28–9, 49–50; Rauschning, *Nuclear Warfare and Weapons*, in: Bernhardt (Ed), *Encyclopaedia of Public International Law; Volume Three; Jan Mayen to Pueblo Incident*, p 731; Rotblat, *Nuclear Radiation in Warfare*, p 59; Westing, *Weapons of Mass Destruction and the Environment*, Table 1.8, n d, p 10.

[131] Glasstone, Dolan, *The Effects of Nuclear Weapons*, p 324.

The reason for this convention is that after one minute the fireball has risen to such a great height that only a negligible fraction of the emitted radiation will reach the ground.[132]

Independent of the type of burst, initial nuclear radiation from fission weapons contains approximately 5 per cent of the total energy yield—in case of thermonuclear weapons this is about 2.5 per cent—and consists mainly of gamma rays, which is electromagnetic radiation of high energy, and neutrons. Both are generated by the fission and/or fusion reactions preceding or following the explosion. Neutrons and gamma rays may travel large distances through air at the speed of light, and they have a large penetrating capacity.[133] The properties of various kinds of radiation are explained in the preceding chapter.[134]

These energy percentages are remarkably different in case of an Enhanced Radiation Weapon, more popularly known as the Neutron Bomb. Neutron bombs are intended to release as much nuclear radiation as possible and their percentage of initial nuclear radiation is therefore increased to between 50–60 per cent, and in theory even as high as 80 per cent of the total energy output. This weapon design:

has a very small yield in terms of thermal and/or blast but has a greatly enhanced output of neutrons giving rise to the more accurate name of Enhanced Radiation/Reduced Blast weapons (ER/RB).[135]

Stimulation of neutron emission is achieved by using a fusion weapon technology with a small fission-fusion ratio and a special kind of coating that instead of reflecting fast neutrons produced during the fusion reaction, allows neutrons to escape. In most cases they simply remove the

[132] Rotblat, *Nuclear Radiation in Warfare*, p 59. Similarly: Glasstone, Dolan, *The Effects of Nuclear Weapons*, pp 387–8; McNaught, *Nuclear Weapons and Their Effects*, p 51.

[133] Barash, *Introduction to Peace Studies*, pp 109–10; British Medical Association; Report of the British Medical Association's Board of Science and Education, *The Medical Effects of Nuclear War*, pp 3–5; Glasstone, Dolan, *The Effects of Nuclear Weapons*, pp 6–8, 10–11, 41–2, 324–9, 340–2; Grace, *Nuclear Weapons; Principles, Effects and Survivability*, pp 29–30; International Council of Scientific Unions; Scientific Committee on Problems of the Environment 28; Pittock, Ackerman, Crutzen, MacCracken, Shapiro, Turco, *Environmental Consequences of Nuclear War; Volume I: Physical and Atmospheric Effects*, pp 6, 13; Kothari, *Nuclear Explosions and Their Effects*, pp 47–52; McNaught, *Nuclear Weapons and Their Effects*, pp 20–2, 28–9; Rotblat, *Nuclear Radiation in Warfare*, pp 63–8; United Nations Organization; UN Department of Disarmament Affairs; Report of the Secretary-General, *Nuclear Weapons: A Comprehensive Study*, pp 72–3; Westing, *Weapons of Mass Destruction and the Environment*, pp 10–15, 25, fn 2; World Health Organization; Report of the WHO Management Group on Follow-up of resolution WHA36.28: 'The Role of Physicians and Other Health Workers in the Preservation and Promotion of Peace . . .', *Effects of Nuclear War on Health and Health Services*, p 15.

[134] See also: Glasstone, Dolan, *The Effects of Nuclear Weapons*, pp 329–30; Grace, *Nuclear Weapons; Principles, Effects and Survivability*, pp 64–77; Groves, *Now It Can Be Told; The Story of the Manhattan Project*, p 87; Hodgson, *Nuclear Physics in Peace and War*, pp 54–5; McNaught, *Nuclear Weapons and Their Effects*, pp 49–50.

[135] McNaught, *Nuclear Weapons and Their Effects*, pp 20–2.

U-238 tamper and other components. By doing so, one could construct a weapon with a blast yield of 1 kt, but with a neutron flux that would result from a 10 kt explosion.[136]

In vacuum gamma rays and neutrons would travel in straight lines, but while traveling through the atmosphere they are scattered and attenuated which decreases their intensity and changes their direction. If the air is disturbed, for example by blast, there is less attenuation. This is a phenomenon known as 'hydrodynamic enhancement'.

Attenuation is caused by absorption by the surrounding medium which is determined by the mass of material through which it travels. This means that a distinction between initial and residual nuclear radiation is less meaningful in case of sub-surface bursts, because all initial nuclear radiation will be immediately absorbed. In case of surface bursts, there is no definite demarcation either, due to the presence of large amounts of surface material in the radioactive cloud. Here, initial and residual radiation categories gradually merge into one another. In case of air bursts, however, there is a clear distinction between initial and residual nuclear radiation.[137]

In air, the intensity of initial nuclear radiation at certain distances depends on weapon design,[138] weapon yield and distance, and would under perfect circumstances, ie in vacuum, be given by the same inverse square law as for thermal radiation, namely $E/4\pi r^2$. The relationship between lethal distance and yield, however, is significantly different for initial nuclear radiation. The radius or 'effective injury range' increases much more slowly with yield than the cube root or square root of blast and thermal radiation. Therefore, in case of high-yield explosions, thermal radiation and blast are the dominating effects, whereas for low-yield explosions, initial nuclear radiation has the greater effective range. In the range of 1 kt and below, such as in the case of Enhanced Radiation Weapons, the lethal radius of initial nuclear radiation far exceeds the

[136] Briezeveld, Mathot, *Scoop; Natuurkunde voor de Bovenbouw 5/6 VWO*, p 272; Cochran, Arkin, Hoenig, *Nuclear Weapons Databook; Volume I*, US Nuclear Forces and Capabilities, pp 28–9; Grace, *Nuclear Weapons; Principles, Effects and Survivability*, pp 22–3, 32–4; Krane, *Introductory Nuclear Physics*, pp 555–6; Rauschning, *Nuclear Warfare and Weapons*, in: Bernhardt (Ed), *Encyclopaedia of Public International Law; Volume Three; Jan Mayen to Pueblo Incident*, p 731; Rotblat, *Nuclear Radiation in Warfare*, pp 11, 70–3; United Nations Organization; UN Department of Disarmament Affairs; Report of the Secretary-General, *Nuclear Weapons: A Comprehensive Study*, pp 28–9; World Health Organization; Report of the WHO Management Group on Follow-up of resolution WHA36.28: 'The Role of Physicians and Other Health Workers in the Preservation and Promotion of Peace . . .', *Effects of Nuclear War on Health and Health Services*, p 15.

[137] Glasstone, Dolan, *The Effects of Nuclear Weapons*, pp 387–8.

[138] Fat Man, for example, hardly had a neutron flux, because of the presence of hydrogen in the high explosives surrounding the core. Hydrogen slows down and absorbs neutrons. Rotblat, *Nuclear Radiation in Warfare*, pp 59–63. For Enhanced Radiation Weapons, see above and further below.

destructive radius of blast. Also, at larger distances, more and more neutrons are absorbed by the atmosphere thereby increasing the proportion of gamma radiation.[139]

Nuclear radiation could be very damaging to living organisms, the environment in general and to electrical equipment due to its ionising capacity. Ionisation is, as was explained in the preceding chapter, the process of knocking electrons out of their path thereby leaving a positively charged atom. The effects of neutron radiation is a little bit more complex. Neutrons may collide with nuclei which may result in bouncing off, slowing down, displacement or absorption.[140] This section focuses on short-term human injuries and effects caused by acute whole-body or less than whole-body exposure to initial nuclear radiation. The long-term consequences of chronic exposure to small doses of (residual) radiation will be discussed in the following section.

As far as human beings are concerned, the actual damage inflicted depends on the sensitivity of the receiving tissue, the reception dose, the rate of delivery, the exposure time, and the type of radiation. The type of radiation is important because alpha and beta particles, neutrons and gamma rays all have a different Relative Biological Effectiveness (RBE). The RBE of alpha particles, for example, is 20 times that of a gamma ray; and the RBE of a neutron is 10 times that of a gamma ray. As was mentioned above, the nuclear radiation that is emitted during the first minute generally consists of gamma rays and neutrons. Human beings are particularly sensitive to neutron radiation because of their large penetrating powers and because of the presence of large quantities of water in the human body which may take over all kinetic energy of the penetrating neutrons. Gamma radiation is highly penetrating as well and it has the capacity to travel over large distances.

[139] Cochran, Arkin, Hoenig, *Nuclear Weapons Databook; Volume I, US Nuclear Forces and Capabilities*, pp 28–9; Congress of the United States; Office of Technology Assessment, *The Effects of Nuclear War*, pp 19–20; Glasstone, Dolan, *The Effects of Nuclear Weapons*, pp 9–11, 324–5, 332–8, 343–8, 541–2; Grace, *Nuclear Weapons; Principles, Effects and Survivability*, pp 33–4, 64–77; International Council of Scientific Unions; Scientific Committee on Problems of the Environment 28; Pittock, Ackerman, Crutzen, MacCracken, Shapiro, Turco, *Environmental Consequences of Nuclear War; Volume I: Physical and Atmospheric Effects*, p 13; McNaught, *Nuclear Weapons and Their Effects*, pp 51–3; Rotblat, *Nuclear Radiation in Warfare*, pp 59–70, table 12; Tucker, Gleisner, *Crucible Despair: The Effects of Nuclear War*, pp 21–2; United Nations Organization; UN Department of Disarmament Affairs; Report of the Secretary-General, *Nuclear Weapons: A Comprehensive Study*, p 75; World Health Organization; Report of the WHO Management Group on Follow-up of resolution WHA36.28: 'The Role of Physicians and Other Health Workers in the Preservation and Promotion of Peace . . .', *Effects of Nuclear War on Health and Health Services*, p 15. Kothari, on the other hand, writes that 'for a nuclear weapon in the kilotons range the radiological effects, compared to blast and heat effects, are relatively of minor importance, in the case of megaton weapons the radiological effects far outweigh anything else.' Kothari, *Nuclear Explosions and Their Effects*, pp 38–9. Presumably, Kothari here refers to both initial and residual nuclear radiation.

[140] McNaught, *Nuclear Weapons and Their Effects*, pp 49–50.

During the first minute, the intensity of the radiation flux will be high and so will be the doses received by those who survived the combined effects of blast and thermal radiation. On its passage through, neutron and gamma radiation may damage hundreds of thousands of molecules whose reparation might eventually become beyond the capacity of the affected cells. The cell will then be unable to divide and multiply and will eventually die. This is called somatic damage, which is experienced by the individual, and which must be distinguished from genetic damage which could be experienced by future generations and which will be discussed further below. Particularly sensitive are those cells that multiply rapidly, such as stem cells in the bone marrow, which produces various types of blood cells; cells in the lymphoid tissue; cells in the organs of reproduction; and cells in the gastro-intestinal organs. The skin, lungs and liver are less sensitive; muscles, nerves, and adult bones are least sensitive.

The ensuing syndrome is called radiation sickness and can lead to death within a time span varying from a few hours to a couple of weeks, mainly due to damage to the blood forming system. Its symptoms are based on information from Hiroshima and Nagasaki victims, experiences with laboratory, reactor, and testing accidents, and depend on the actual dose. It includes irritation of the skin, a general feeling of nausea and malaise, dizziness, headache, anorexia, loss of hair, internal and skin hemorrhages, diarrhea, vomiting, fever, and sometimes seizures. In case of extremely high doses, incapacitation will be immediate. Recovery is hardly feasible especially in combination with other injuries and depends among other things on age and sex. Treatment would mainly consist of attempting to prevent or reverse infections by providing a clean environment, using antibiotics, and blood transfusions, none of which is likely to be available after a nuclear attack.[141] In Hiroshima and Nagasaki, some 5 to 15 per cent

[141] Generally, on the early effects of nuclear radiation on living organisms, see: Von Arx, Marauhn, *Nuclear Tests*, in: Bernhardt (Ed), *Encyclopaedia of Public International Law; Volume Three; Jan Mayen to Pueblo Incident*, p 723; Bethe, *The Hydrogen* Bomb, in: Bethe, *The Road from Los Alamos*, p 15; Briezeveld, Mathot, *Scoop; Natuurkunde voor de Bovenbouw 5/6 VWO*, p 272; British Medical Association; Report of the British Medical Association's Board of Science and Education, *The Medical Effects of Nuclear War*, pp xii-xiii, 33–5, 45; British Mission to Japan, *The Effects of the Atomic Bombs at Hiroshima and Nagasaki*, pp 15–17; Glasstone, Dolan, *The Effects of Nuclear Weapons*, pp 545–8, 575–88, 614–7; Grace, *Nuclear Weapons; Principles, Effects and Survivability*, pp 68–90; Groves, *Now It Can Be Told; The Story of the Manhattan Project*, pp 87, 204–5; Hodgson, *Nuclear Physics in Peace and War*, pp 56–8, 60–2; Holdstock, Waterston, *Nuclear weapons, a continuing threat to health*, p 1544; International Council of Scientific Unions; Scientific Committee on Problems of the Environment 28; Harwell, Hutchinson, *Environmental Consequences of Nuclear War; Volume II: Ecological and Agricultural Effects*, pp 433–5; Kothari, *Nuclear Explosions and Their Effects*, pp 66–8, 87–93, 96; McNaught, *Nuclear Weapons and Their Effects*, pp 51, 57–61; Rhodes, *The Making of the Atomic Bomb*, p 731; Rotblat, *Nuclear Radiation in Warfare*, pp 26–39, 51–7; Tucker, Gleisner, *Crucible Despair: The Effects of Nuclear War*, pp 43–8; United Nations Organization; UN Department of Disarmament Affairs; Report of the Secretary-General, *Nuclear Weapons: A Comprehensive Study*, pp 82–4; United Nations Organization; UN Department of Disarmament Affairs; Report of the Secretary-General, *Study on the Climatic and Other Global Effects of Nuclear War*, pp 41–2;

of all fatalities were believed to have died from radiation sickness;[142] roughly 30 per cent of all fatalities are believed to have received lethal doses.[143]

Damage to the environment in general depends on species, since each organism has a different sensitivity to nuclear radiation. Generally, one could say that 'the higher the species on the evolutionary scale the greater the sensitivity.'[144] Mammals are most sensitive, followed by birds; plants; fish; amphibians; reptiles; crustaceans; insects; moss, lichen, algae; bacteria; protozoa; mollusks; and viruses.[145] Although most categories overlap and consist of species that are either very sensitive or not very sensitive, this order of sensitivity is set by the most sensitive kind of each group.

According to Westing, mortality resulting from initial radiation after an air burst is significant. For an 18 kt air burst most trees will be killed by nuclear radiation within an area of 129 ha; all vegetation will be killed within an area of 18 ha; and most vertebrates will be killed within an area of 318 ha. For a 0.91 Mt burst these numbers are 648 ha (trees), 312 ha (vegetation), and 1080 ha (vertebrates); for a 9.1 Mt burst these numbers are 1250 ha (trees), 759 ha (vegetation), and 1840 ha (vertebrates).[146] The

United States Strategic Bombing Survey, *The Effects of the Atomic bombs on Hiroshima and Nagasaki*, Chairman's Office, 30 June 1946; United States Government Printing Office, Washington, DC, 1946, pp 18–20; World Health Organization; Report of the WHO Management Group on Follow-up of resolution WHA36.28: 'The Role of Physicians and Other Health Workers in the Preservation and Promotion of Peace . . .', *Effects of Nuclear War on Health and Health Services*, pp 18–20.

[142] The United States Strategic Bombing Survey estimated that 15–20% of the deaths were from radiation. United States Strategic Bombing Survey, *The Effects of the Atomic bombs on Hiroshima and Nagasaki*, p 15.

[143] According to the WHO Report, the dose needed to kill 50% of the people within 60 days after exposure, also known as the LD-50 value, or the Lethal Dose-50%, is smaller than previously estimated, which means that in case of nuclear war the number of radiation victims would be considerably higher. T Ohkita, J Rotblat, *Biological Effects of Nuclear War; Acute Effects of Radiation; The LD-50 Value*, in: World Health Organization; Report of the WHO Management Group on Follow-up of resolution WHA36.28: 'The Role of Physicians and Other Health Workers in the Preservation and Promotion of Peace . . .', *Effects of Nuclear War on Health and Health Services*, p 85; World Health Organization; Report of the WHO Management Group on Follow-up of resolution WHA36.28: 'The Role of Physicians and Other Health Workers in the Preservation and Promotion of Peace . . .', *Effects of Nuclear War on Health and Health Services*, p 19. Also: United Nations Organization; UN Department of Disarmament Affairs; Report of the Secretary-General, *Study on the Climatic and Other Global Effects of Nuclear War*, p 42.

[144] Rotblat, *Nuclear Radiation in Warfare*, p 100. For a more detailed analysis of the effects of fallout on animal and plant life, see: Rotblat, *Nuclear Radiation in Warfare*, pp 100–2. See also: Chernobyl Forum, *Environmental Consequences of the Chernobyl Accident and Their Remediation: Twenty Years of Experience*, Report of the UN Chernobyl Forum Expert Group 'Environment' (EGE), Aug 2005, pp 191–4. Through: <http://www.iaea.org/>.

[145] Chernobyl Forum, *Environmental Consequences of the Chernobyl Accident and Their Remediation: Twenty Years of Experience*, p 192. Also Rotblat, *Nuclear Radiation in Warfare*, pp 101–2; Westing, *Weapons of Mass Destruction and the Environment*, pp 11–12.

[146] Westing, *Weapons of Mass Destruction and the Environment*, pp 16–17, Tables 1.12 and 1.13.

consequences of surface bursts will likely stem from residual radioactivity, this will be referred to further below.

As far as damage to equipment is concerned, this applies only to electronics. The effect of neutrons and gamma rays is called transient radiation effect on electronics (TREE). It has to be distinguished from the EMP that was dealt with in the preceding section. The TREE is caused by direct interaction between neutrons and gamma rays with the electronic components of apparatus, whereas the EMP is an indirect effect of the emitted gamma and X-ray flux. The damage is devastating within close vicinity of the burst, although protection is not too difficult and very likely in the case of military installations.[147]

4.2.5.3 Residual Nuclear Radiation

4.2.5.3.1 Introduction

The previous direct effects of nuclear explosions were all prompt effects, the duration of which does not last longer than one minute. Residual nuclear radiation is the only direct effect of which the consequences appear over a longer period of time, ranging from hours to decades. It is therefore called a delayed effect of nuclear explosions. Residual nuclear radiation is by definition radiation emitted later than one minute after the burst, and it contains approximately 10 per cent of the total energy yield for regular fission weapons and approximately 5 per cent for thermonuclear weapons. It appears in two forms, namely fallout and neutron induced activity (NIA), the latter being a consequence of the interaction between neutrons emitted during the first minute and the surrounding environment and is less significant than fallout.[148] The former will be discussed in section 4.2.5.3.2; the latter will be discussed in section 4.2.5.3.3.

[147] Glasstone, Dolan, *The Effects of Nuclear Weapons*, pp 349–53; Grace, *Nuclear Weapons; Principles, Effects and Survivability*, pp 68–90; McNaught, *Nuclear Weapons and Their Effects*, pp 28–9, 55–6.

[148] Barash, *Introduction to Peace Studies*, pp 110–11; British Medical Association; Report of the British Medical Association's Board of Science and Education, *The Medical Effects of Nuclear War*, pp 3–6; Glasstone, Dolan, *The Effects of Nuclear Weapons*, pp 6–8, 36, 387; Grace, *Nuclear Weapons; Principles, Effects and Survivability*, pp 29–30, 64–81; International Council of Scientific Unions; Scientific Committee on Problems of the Environment 28; Pittock, Ackerman, Crutzen, MacCracken, Shapiro, Turco, *Environmental Consequences of Nuclear War; Volume I: Physical and Atmospheric Effects*, pp 6, 237–8; International Council of Scientific Unions; Scientific Committee on Problems of the Environment 28; Harwell, Hutchinson, *Environmental Consequences of Nuclear War; Volume II: Ecological and Agricultural Effects*, p 196; Kothari, *Nuclear Explosions and Their Effects*, pp 46–7; McNaught, *Nuclear Weapons and Their Effects*, pp 27–8, 49–50, 61–2; Rotblat, *Nuclear Radiation in Warfare*, pp 73–80; Westing, *Weapons of Mass Destruction and the Environment*, pp 10–15.

4.2.5.3.2 Fallout

4.2.5.3.2.1 Introduction

Fallout is generally described as residual nuclear radiation emitted later than one minute after the explosion arising:

> mainly from the weapon debris, that is, from the fission products and, to a lesser extent, from the uranium and plutonium which have escaped fission.[149]

Glasstone and Dolan, as well as other authors, only refer to radioactivity from fission products, since unlike nuclear fission, nuclear fusion does not leave radioactive products. This means that apart from the small fission trigger, pure fusion weapons, including Enhanced Radiation Weapons, are relatively clean weapons with relatively little fallout, which explains the reduced nuclear energy percentages for fusion weapons. The remaining 5 per cent residual nuclear radiation is due to the fission trigger and Neutron Induced Activity.[150]

On the other hand, weapons that are in a so-called 'three-decker' configuration could be extremely dirty. Glasstone and Dolan explain that the terms 'clean' and 'dirty' are:

> often used to describe the amount of radioactivity produced by a fusion weapon (or hydrogen bomb) relative to that from what might be describe as a 'normal' weapon. (. . .). If special steps were taken in the design of a fusion device, e.g. by salting (. . .), it would be described as 'dirty'.[151]

'Three-decker' configuration weapons are boosted fission (fission weapons with a small amount of fusion material), or thermonuclear weapons whose U-238 tamper is fissioned by neutrons emitted during the fusion process. Apart from the fact that this latter process accounts for the bulk of the explosive energy, it also produces so many additional fission products with lengthy half-lives that it could generate a significant amount of fallout.

This was observed after the first military hydrogen bomb test at Bikini Atoll in the Marshall Islands in March 1954.[152] A 15 Mt thermonuclear

[149] Glasstone, Dolan, *The Effects of Nuclear Weapons*, p 387.

[150] Glasstone, Dolan, *The Effects of Nuclear Weapons*, p 387; Kothari, *Nuclear Explosions and Their Effects*, pp 141–2; Krane, Introductory Nuclear Physics, p 555; McNaught, *Nuclear Weapons and Their Effects*, p 20.

[151] Glasstone, Dolan, *The Effects of Nuclear Weapons*, pp 408–9.

[152] It should be noted that the Marshall Islands had been placed under United Nations trusteeship in 1947 with the United States as administrator. The tests at Bikini Atoll in 1946 were therefore conducted outside US territory. Trusteeship Agreement for the Former Japanese Mandated Islands; Between the United States and the United Nations Security Council; Approved by the Security Council on 2 Apr 1947, UNTS, Vol 8, No 123; S/RES/21 (1947), adopted unanimously on 2 Apr 1947; on the Trusteeship of Strategic Areas; Trusteeship Agreement for the Trust Territory of the Pacific Islands. See also: E Margolis, *The Hydrogen Bomb Experiments and International Law*, The Yale Law Journal, Vol 64, 1955, p 630.

weapon, the first that was dropped from an airplane, unexpectedly caused substantial fallout that started to come down some three-and-a-half hours after the explosion covering an area of several thousands square miles. A Japanese fishing boat the No 5 Fukurayu Maru (the Fortunate or Lucky Dragon), which sailed in the neighborhood, but still outside the 90-mile warning area, was contaminated, killing at least one of the fishermen.[153] Also 28 American soldiers as well as 239 Marshallese were accidentally exposed. The contamination of Bikini Atoll was so severe that in 1979 and again in 1998, it was still considered to be generally too radioactive for habitation.[154]

In order to enhance or boost this process one could add to the U-238 tamper:

> some material which has a reasonably high avidity for neutrons and which, on neutron capture, is transformed into a radioactive element emitting hard gamma rays[155]

and which has a long half-life. Various salts have this capacity among which Cobalt-60 is most well-known. This process is called 'salting' and it could be used to produce extremely dirty weapons, close to radiological weapons. Limited salting has been used in the past to produce tracers to study fallout patterns.[156]

[153] The damage was settled by Exchange of Notes Constituting an Agreement Relating to the Settlement of Japanese Claims for Personal and Property Damages Resulting from Nuclear Tests in the Marshall Islands in 1954, Tokyo 4 Jan 1955, UNTS, Vol 237, No 3346.

[154] R Ferm, *Appendix 12B; Nuclear Explosions, 1945–98*, in: Stockholm International Peace Research Institute, *SIPRI Yearbook 1999; Armaments, Disarmament and International Security*, Oxford University Press, Oxford, 1999, p 559; Glasstone, Dolan, *The Effects of Nuclear Weapons*, pp 84–90; Hodgson, *Nuclear Physics in Peace and War*, pp 45–8, 98–9; R Jungk, *Brighter than a Thousand Suns*, Grove Press, Inc, New York, 1958, pp 309–12; International Council of Scientific Unions; Scientific Committee on Problems of the Environment 28; Pittock, Ackerman, Crutzen, MacCracken, Shapiro, Turco, *Environmental Consequences of Nuclear War; Volume I: Physical and Atmospheric Effects*, pp 14–16; Kothari, *Nuclear Explosions and Their Effects*, pp 129–36; Margolis, *The Hydrogen Bomb Experiments and International Law*, pp 637–9; McNaught, *Nuclear Weapons and Their Effects*, p 20; Rotblat, *Nuclear Radiation in Warfare*, pp 87–8; p Stegnar, *Review at Bikini Atoll; Assessing Radiological Conditions at Bikini Atoll and the Prospects for Resettlement*, IAEA Bulletin, Vol 40(4), 1998, pp 15–17. Von Arx and Marauhn refer to a similar incident after a Soviet thermonuclear test when radioactive rain fell down, again on Japan. Von Arx, Marauhn, *Nuclear Tests*, in: Bernhardt (Ed), *Encyclopaedia of Public International Law; Volume Three; Jan Mayen to Pueblo Incident*, p 724. Also: United States Arms Control and Disarmament Agency, *Arms control and Disarmament Agreements; Texts and Histories of the Negotiations*, US Government Printing Office, Washington, DC, 1996, p 24.

[155] Kothari, *Nuclear Explosions and Their Effects*, pp 121–3.

[156] Glasstone, Dolan, *The Effects of Nuclear Weapons*, pp 388–90; Hodgson, *Nuclear Physics in Peace and War*, pp 45–8; Kothari, *Nuclear Explosions and Their Effects*, pp 20, 121–3; Rauschning, *Nuclear Warfare and Weapons*, in: Bernhardt (Ed), *Encyclopaedia of Public International Law; Volume Three; Jan Mayen to Pueblo Incident*, p 731; Rotblat, *Nuclear Radiation in Warfare*, p 3.

The term fallout is solely reserved for air and surface bursts.

> As the violent disturbance due to the explosion subsides, the contaminated particles and droplets gradually descend to earth. This phenomenon is referred to as 'fallout' and the same name is applied to the particles themselves when they reach the ground.[157]

For sub-surface bursts, one could use the general term residual nuclear radiation.

There are three types of fallout, each of which is related to the area affected and the time period involved: local fallout, intermediate fallout, and global fallout. Local fallout will be discussed first, in section 4.2.5.3.2.2; intermediate and global fallout will be discussed together in section 4.2.5.3.2.3.[158] The extent, nature and distribution of fallout depend on the height of burst, energy yield, weapon design, nature of the surface, geographic features of the terrain, time of day, season of the year, and most importantly, the meteorological conditions.[159]

4.2.5.3.2.2 Local Fallout

Local fallout only occurs in significant amounts in cases of surface bursts, where the fireball touches the surface, and low air bursts, where the strong afterwinds suck up large amounts of dust or other surface material into the radioactive cloud.[160] Both have in common that the fission products mix with dust particles or water droplets thereby creating large amounts of airborne and volatile radioactive material that is capable of contaminating large areas downwind way beyond the areas affected by blast,

[157] Glasstone, Dolan, *The Effects of Nuclear Weapons*, p 36.

[158] Glasstone and Dolan prefer to speak of early fallout and delayed fallout. Early fallout then corresponds with local fallout; and delayed fallout corresponds with intermediate and global fallout. Glasstone, Dolan, *The Effects of Nuclear Weapons*, pp 387–90, 442–3.

[159] Von Arx, Marauhn, *Nuclear Tests*, in: Bernhardt (Ed), *Encyclopaedia of Public International Law; Volume Three; Jan Mayen to Pueblo Incident*, p 723; Briezeveld, Mathot, *Scoop; Natuurkunde voor de Bovenbouw 5/6 VWO*, 1991, p 272; Glasstone, Dolan, *The Effects of Nuclear Weapons*, pp 36–8, 387–8, 390–1, 410; International Council of Scientific Unions; Scientific Committee on Problems of the Environment 28; Pittock, Ackerman, Crutzen, MacCracken, Shapiro, Turco, *Environmental Consequences of Nuclear War; Volume I: Physical and Atmospheric Effects*, p 237; Rotblat, *Nuclear Radiation in Warfare*, p 3; United Nations Organization; UN Department of Disarmament Affairs; Report of the Secretary-General, *Nuclear Weapons: A Comprehensive Study*, p 75; United Nations Organization; UN Department of Disarmament Affairs; Report of the Secretary-General, *Study on the Climatic and Other Global Effects of Nuclear War*, p 42; Westing, *Weapons of Mass Destruction and the Environment*, pp 10–15; World Health Organization; Report of the WHO Management Group on Follow-up of resolution WHA36.28: 'The Role of Physicians and Other Health Workers in the Preservation and Promotion of Peace . . .', *Effects of Nuclear War on Health and Health Services*, pp 9–11.

[160] The critical height for local fallout to occur is, according to the WHO Report, given by the formula $H=55\ W^{0.4}$, where H is the altitude in meters, and W the yield in kilotons. World Health Organization; Report of the WHO Management Group on Follow-up of resolution WHA36.28: 'The Role of Physicians and Other Health Workers in the Preservation and Promotion of Peace . . .', *Effects of Nuclear War on Health and Health Services*, p 48.

thermal, and initial nuclear radiation. This uncontrollability thus poses an additional and significant threat towards survivors and rescue teams that may last for an extended period of time.

The mixing of fission products and surface material especially occurs in cases of surface bursts. As was explained above, the fireball vaporises everything it touches, which means that significant amounts of surface material are incorporated into the mushroom-shaped radioactive cloud. As soon as the cloud starts to cool down, vaporised fission products mix or fuse with vaporised surface material to form new solid particles or they condense on the surface of solid or molten dust particles or water droplets. In both cases, these particles become heavily radioactive.[161]

Because of the abundant presence of surface particles, the new particles are relatively big and heavy, which causes the heaviest to fall down by the force of gravity soon after the explosion, relatively close to the area of detonation, and in relatively large concentrations. This is why it is called *local* fallout. In case of a water surface burst, the particles will likely be lighter because of difference in specific gravity of water and sea salts, and therefore there will be less local fallout.[162]

[161] Barash, *Introduction to Peace Studies*, pp 110–11; Briezeveld, Mathot, *Scoop; Natuurkunde voor de Bovenbouw 5/6 VWO*, 1991, p 272; British Medical Association; Report of the British Medical Association's Board of Science and Education, *The Medical Effects of Nuclear War*, pp 8–9; Congress of the United States; Office of Technology Assessment, *The Effects of Nuclear War*, pp 19, 22–5; Glasstone, Dolan, *The Effects of Nuclear Weapons*, pp 9–10, 36, 387–90, 409, 415–16; Grace, *Nuclear Weapons; Principles, Effects and Survivability*, pp 64–81; International Council of Scientific Unions; Scientific Committee on Problems of the Environment 28; Pittock, Ackerman, Crutzen, MacCracken, Shapiro, Turco, *Environmental Consequences of Nuclear War; Volume I: Physical and Atmospheric Effects*, pp 14–16, 238; Kothari, *Nuclear Explosions and Their Effects*, pp 99–104; McNaught, *Nuclear Weapons and Their Effects*, pp 62–8; Rauschning, *Nuclear Warfare and Weapons*, in: Bernhardt (Ed), *Encyclopaedia of Public International Law; Volume Three; Jan Mayen to Pueblo Incident*, p 731; Rotblat, *Nuclear Radiation in Warfare*, pp 12–14, 73–4; United Nations Organization; UN Department of Disarmament Affairs; Report of the Secretary-General, *Nuclear Weapons: A Comprehensive Study*, pp 73–5; United Nations Organization; UN Department of Disarmament Affairs; Report of the Secretary-General, *Study on the Climatic and Other Global Effects of Nuclear War*, p 42; World Health Organization; Report of the WHO Management Group on Follow-up of resolution WHA36.28: 'The Role of Physicians and Other Health Workers in the Preservation and Promotion of Peace . . .', *Effects of Nuclear War on Health and Health Services*, pp 9–11, 48.

[162] Congress of the United States; Office of Technology Assessment, *The Effects of Nuclear War*, pp 19, 22–5; Glasstone, Dolan, *The Effects of Nuclear Weapons*, pp 36–8, 409–14; Grace, *Nuclear Weapons; Principles, Effects and Survivability*, pp 64–81; International Council of Scientific Unions; Scientific Committee on Problems of the Environment 28; Pittock, Ackerman, Crutzen, MacCracken, Shapiro, Turco, *Environmental Consequences of Nuclear War; Volume I: Physical and Atmospheric Effects*, pp 14–16, 238, 240; International Council of Scientific Unions; Scientific Committee on Problems of the Environment 28; Harwell, Hutchinson, *Environmental Consequences of Nuclear War; Volume II: Ecological and Agricultural Effects*, p 199; Kothari, *Nuclear Explosions and Their Effects*, pp 99–106; Rotblat, *Nuclear Radiation in Warfare*, pp 12–14, 73–4, 84–90; United Nations Organization; UN Department of Disarmament Affairs; Report of the Secretary-General, *Nuclear Weapons: A Comprehensive Study*, pp 73–5; United Nations Organization; UN Department of Disarmament Affairs; Report of the Secretary-General, *Study on the Climatic and Other Global Effects of Nuclear War*, p 42; World Health Organization; Report of the WHO Management Group on Follow-up of

Glasstone and Dolan characterise those particles that come down within 24 hours after the explosion as early fallout.[163] Although this time barrier is somewhat arbitrary, they distinguish between early fallout and delayed fallout because during the first 24 hours, the radioactive decay of the various fission products is still at a high level and as soon as these products reach the earth, they pose an immediate threat to the surrounding ecosystem. It is assumed that a large proportion of the total radioactivity, ranging from 40–70 per cent, is in the early fallout. The rest comes down as delayed fallout.[164] Fallout particles are relatively harmless as long as they are airborne, due to the limited range of the various forms of nuclear radiation.[165]

The properties of local fallout depend mainly on the diversity and number of fission products. Generally, a mixture is produced of about 400 different types of radioactive fission products, some 400 hundred isotopes of some 36 elements, all with their own decay periods measured in half-lives, ie the time required for half of the atoms to disintegrate, and varying from

resolution WHA36.28: 'The Role of Physicians and Other Health Workers in the Preservation and Promotion of Peace . . .', *Effects of Nuclear War on Health and Health Services*, pp 9–11, 48.

[163] Glasstone, Dolan, *The Effects of Nuclear Weapons*, pp 36–8, 387–8, 409. Similarly: British Medical Association; Report of the British Medical Association's Board of Science and Education, *The Medical Effects of Nuclear War*, pp 8–9 (early fallout within hours or days); International Council of Scientific Unions; Scientific Committee on Problems of the Environment 28; Pittock, Ackerman, Crutzen, MacCracken, Shapiro, Turco, *Environmental Consequences of Nuclear War; Volume I: Physical and Atmospheric Effects*, pp 14–16, 237 (first day or 24 hours); International Council of Scientific Unions; Scientific Committee on Problems of the Environment 28; Harwell, Hutchinson, *Environmental Consequences of Nuclear War; Volume II: Ecological and Agricultural Effects*, p 199 (24 to 48 hours); Westing, *Weapons of Mass Destruction and the Environment*, pp 10–11, Table 1.8, ne d, p 10 (first day or first 24 hours). The UN Report on Nuclear Weapons uses the term immediate fallout in this context. United Nations Organization; UN Department of Disarmament Affairs; Report of the Secretary-General, *Nuclear Weapons: A Comprehensive Study*, p 75. The WHO Report links the 24 hours time barrier with the area where the fallout is deposited: 'Local fallout is the deposition on the ground of radioactivity within 24 hours after the explosion.' World Health Organization; Report of the WHO Management Group on Follow-up of resolution WHA36.28: 'The Role of Physicians and Other Health Workers in the Preservation and Promotion of Peace . . .', *Effects of Nuclear War on Health and Health Services*, pp 16–18, 48.

[164] After 24 hours, however, 'the activity will have decayed to such an extent that only 20 per cent of the total dose remains to be delivered.' Rotblat, *Nuclear Radiation in Warfare*, p 94. Also Glasstone, Dolan, *The Effects of Nuclear Weapons*, pp 404, 410–15; International Council of Scientific Unions; Scientific Committee on Problems of the Environment 28; Pittock, Ackerman, Crutzen, MacCracken, Shapiro, Turco, *Environmental Consequences of Nuclear War; Volume I: Physical and Atmospheric Effects*, pp 14–16; International Council of Scientific Unions; Scientific Committee on Problems of the Environment 28; Harwell, Hutchinson, *Environmental Consequences of Nuclear War; Volume II: Ecological and Agricultural Effects*, p 199; Rotblat, *Nuclear Radiation in Warfare*, pp 84–90; World Health Organization; Report of the WHO Management Group on Follow-up of resolution WHA36.28: 'The Role of Physicians and Other Health Workers in the Preservation and Promotion of Peace . . .', *Effects of Nuclear War on Health and Health Services*, pp 16–18, 48.

[165] United Nations Organization; UN Department of Disarmament Affairs; Report of the Secretary-General, *Nuclear Weapons: A Comprehensive Study*, pp 73–5.

fractions of a second to several years. Another source of radioactivity is uranium or plutonium particles that escaped fission.[166]

Determining the eventual duration of this delayed effect of a nuclear explosion is therefore very difficult, almost impossible. An easy rule of thumb that is usually applied to give an indication of the intensity of radioactivity for the first six months after a nuclear explosion is the so-called 'Seven-Ten Law'. This means that '(. . .) for every sevenfold increase in time after the explosion, the dose rate decreases by a factor of ten.'[167] So, seven hours after the explosion, the radiation rate is one-tenth of the emission rate right after the explosion; after 49 hours, it is one-hundredth; after 343 hours, or two weeks, it is reduced to one-thousandth. Although the radiation rate seems to decrease rapidly after the explosion, the emission of nuclear radiation in case of megaton yield explosion, may be of such an extent that radioactivity may be still be lethal after 24 hours and remain dangerous for decades.

In practice, surveys of nuclear testing and nuclear accident sites show mixed results.[168] Firstly, Bikini Atoll in the Marshall Islands was still found to be generally unsafe for habitation decades after 16 tests had been carried out over a time span of 12 years, all of which were air bursts or surface bursts, including shallow underwater bursts. This was established first in 1978, after 139 Bikinians had started a lawsuit in the United States against the federal government after resettlement in the early 1970s; and again in 1998 by the International Atomic Energy Agency (IAEA)[169] upon request of the Government of the Republic of the Marshall Islands, ie 40 years after testing had been terminated in 1958.[170] The conclusion was based on the assumption that Bikinians would almost entirely consume locally produced food which would lead to an annual dose that was considered to be too high.[171]

[166] Glasstone, Dolan, *The Effects of Nuclear Weapons*, pp 390–1, 407–8; Kothari, *Nuclear Explosions and Their Effects*, pp 29–35; McNaught, *Nuclear Weapons and Their Effects*, pp 62–8; Tucker, Gleisner, Crucible Despair: The Effects of Nuclear War, pp 22–3.

[167] Glasstone, Dolan, *The Effects of Nuclear Weapons*, p 391. Similarly: Grace, *Nuclear Weapons; Principles, Effects and Survivability*, pp 64–81; International Council of Scientific Unions; Scientific Committee on Problems of the Environment 28; Pittock, Ackerman, Crutzen, MacCracken, Shapiro, Turco, *Environmental Consequences of Nuclear War; Volume I: Physical and Atmospheric Effects*, pp 14–16, 239; Kothari, *Nuclear Explosions and Their Effects*, pp 29–35; McNaught, *Nuclear Weapons and Their Effects*, pp 30–1, 62–8; Rotblat, *Nuclear Radiation in Warfare*, pp 80–4; Tucker, Gleisner, *Crucible Despair: The Effects of Nuclear War*, pp 22–3.

[168] For other surveys, see: Westing, *Weapons of Mass Destruction and the Environment*, pp 20–2.

[169] Statute of the International Atomic Energy Agency, signed on 26 Oct 1956, entered into force on 29 Jul 1957, UNTS, Vol 276, No 3988. As of Nov 2005, the IAEA has 139 member states. Its headquarters are located in Vienna, Austria. Through <http://www.iaea.org>.

[170] Glasstone, Dolan, *The Effects of Nuclear Weapons*, pp 390–1, 415–16; Rotblat, *Nuclear Radiation in Warfare*, pp 87–8; Tucker, Gleisner, *Crucible Despair: The Effects of Nuclear War*, p 23.

[171] Ferm, *Appendix 12B; Nuclear Explosions, 1945–98*, in: Stockholm International Peace Research Institute, *SIPRI Yearbook 1999; Armaments, Disarmament and International Security*, p 559; Stegnar, *Review at Bikini Atoll; Assessing Radiological Conditions at Bikini Atoll and the Prospects for Resettlement*, pp 15–17. Currently, part of the Atoll has been rehabilitated. See:

Secondly, the IAEA investigated the radiological conditions of two other nuclear test sites between 1993 and 1998. These were the Semipalatinsk area in north-eastern Kazakhstan upon the request of the Government of Kazakhstan, and the Mururoa and Fangataufa Atolls in French Polynesia upon the request of the French Government. The findings were published in separate reports in 1998 in which it was concluded that most of the Semipalatinsk area, where about 460 tests had been conducted according to the IAEA investigators, both underground and above the ground for more than 40 years, had little or no residual radioactivity except for a few places where surface tests had been carried out or where radioactive material had been vented into the atmosphere after underground tests. The annual dose that resettled people would receive, however, would be too high, primarily through external exposure, and because there is too little money to for remedial action, it is recommended that access is restricted to this area.[172] At Mururoa Atoll and Fangataufa Atoll, where 178 nuclear tests had been conducted according to the IAEA investigators—both underground and in the atmosphere—between 1966 and 1996, hardly any residual radioactivity or radiation effects was found.[173]

Thirdly, the Chernobyl Forum issued a comprehensive report on the health, environmental and socio-economic impact of the Chernobyl accident in 2005,[174] almost 20 years after the nuclear power plant exploded on 26 April 1986. The Chernobyl Forum is an initiative of the IAEA in cooperation with six other intergovernmental organisations and three national states,[175] and was established in 2003. As far as the surroundings of Chernobyl are concerned, a surface area of more than 200,000 square

<http://www.bikiniatoll.com/> and the Marshall Islands Program of the United States Department of Energy, through: <http://www.eh.doe.gov/>.

172 Ferm, *Appendix 12B; Nuclear Explosions, 1945–98*, in: Stockholm International Peace Research Institute, *SIPRI Yearbook 1999; Armaments, Disarmament and International Security*, p 559; p Stegnar, T. Wrixon, *Semipalatinsk Revisited; Radiological Evaluation of the Former Nuclear Test Site*, IAEA Bulletin, Vol 40(4), 1998, pp 12–14.

173 Ferm, *Appendix 12B; Nuclear Explosions, 1945–98*, in: Stockholm International Peace Research Institute, *SIPRI Yearbook 1999; Armaments, Disarmament and International Security*, pp 559–60; E. Gail de Planque, *The Mururoa Study; International Study of the Radiological Situation at the Atolls of Mururoa and Fangataufa*, IAEA Bulletin, Vol 40(4), 1998, pp 21–3.

174 Chernobyl Forum, *Chernobyl's Legacy: Health, Environmental and Socio-Economic Impacts; and Recommendations to the Governments of Belarus, the Russian Federation and Ukraine*, Sep 2005; Chernobyl Forum, *Environmental Consequences of the Chernobyl Accident and Their Remediation: Twenty Years of Experience*, Report of the UN Chernobyl Forum Expert Group 'Environment' (EGE), Aug 2005, through: <http://www.iaea.org/>. Generally on Chernobyl: <http://www.iaea.org/NewsCenter/Focus/Chernobyl/index.shtml>.

175 These are the World Health Organization (WHO), Food and Agriculture Organization (FAO), United Nations Development Program (UNDP), United Nations Environment Program (UNEP), United Nations Office for the Coordination of Humanitarian Affairs (UN-OCHA), United Nations Scientific Committee on the Effects of Atomic Radiation (UNSCEAR), and the World Bank Group. The three states represented in the Chernobyl Forum are Belarus, the Russian Federation, and Ukraine.

kilometers of Europe was contaminated. Most contamination occurred within 100 km of the reactor, however, and increased mortality and adverse effects were found in plants and animals in certain 'hot spots' of up to 20–30 km from the explosion, especially during the first two months. In 2005, the levels of radiation had decreased to such levels that most areas were accessible and inhabitable, although medical and environmental monitoring and research, and awareness of persistence of radioactive contamination in food products—both agricultural and forest products—are still required.

As has been observed above, the distribution of fallout depends primarily on the meteorological conditions, in particular on the speed and direction of the wind. This applies to local fallout and to a lesser extent to intermediate fallout. Global fallout on the other hand is relatively independent of meteorological conditions, as will be explained further below. Under normal circumstances, fallout patterns are in the shape of a cigar, with steadily decreasing concentrations and could be rather large. In practice, however, anomalies occur due to irregularities in the terrain, and due to precipitation. Precipitation is the deposition of condensed water vapor on the earth's surface and can be in the form of rain, snow, hail, or dew. It is called rainout or snowout when the particles are located within the clouds; it is called washout when the particles are located below the clouds. It is also possible that rain is induced as a result of the heat of the explosion. This occurred both in Hiroshima and Nagasaki and was called 'black rain'. For intermediate fallout, precipitation is the main source of fallout; for local fallout precipitation can be the cause of so-called local 'hot spots', or places that are much more contaminated than the immediate surroundings.[176]

The effects of local fallout, as distinct from the effects of intermediate and global fallout, are relatively similar to the effects of initial nuclear

[176] Barash, *Introduction to Peace Studies*, pp 110–11; British Medical Association; Report of the British Medical Association's Board of Science and Education, *The Medical Effects of Nuclear War*, pp 71–4; Congress of the United States; Office of Technology Assessment, *The Effects of Nuclear War*, pp 22–5; Glasstone, Dolan, *The Effects of Nuclear Weapons*, pp 36–8, 414–21; Grace, *Nuclear Weapons; Principles, Effects and Survivability*, pp 64–81; Hodgson, *Nuclear Physics in Peace and War*, pp 98–9; Holdstock, Waterston, *Nuclear weapons, a continuing threat to health*, pp 1544–5; International Council of Scientific Unions; Scientific Committee on Problems of the Environment 28; Pittock, Ackerman, Crutzen, MacCracken, Shapiro, Turco, *Environmental Consequences of Nuclear War; Volume I: Physical and Atmospheric Effects*, pp 16, 106, 240–50; International Council of Scientific Unions; Scientific Committee on Problems of the Environment 28; Harwell, Hutchinson, *Environmental Consequences of Nuclear War; Volume II: Ecological and Agricultural Effects*, pp 199–202; Kothari, *Nuclear Explosions and Their Effects*, pp 52–3, 105–6, 115, 129–36, 143–4; McNaught, *Nuclear Weapons and Their Effects*, pp 62–8; Rotblat, *Nuclear Radiation in Warfare*, pp 73–4, 84–90; Tucker, Gleisner, *Crucible Despair: The Effects of Nuclear War*, pp 29–33; World Health Organization; Report of the WHO Management Group on Follow-up of resolution WHA36.28: 'The Role of Physicians and Other Health Workers in the Preservation and Promotion of Peace . . .', *Effects of Nuclear War on Health and Health Services*, pp 9–11, 17. 49–50. For a discussion of various fallout models, see: Glasstone, Dolan, *The Effects of Nuclear Weapons*, pp 422–39.

radiation. Because of the large size of the local fallout particles, the dangers are mostly external by nature, from sources outside the body, and they appear in the form of beta and gamma radiation. Radioactive decay in the form of neutron emission hardly ever happens, and alpha radiation has little penetrating power. What should be taken into account, however, is the accumulation of doses due to continuous exposure to radioactive radiation. Although a slowly accumulated dose is considered to be less harmful than a large instantaneous dose, and despite the generally rapid decrease of activity according to the 'Seven-Ten Law', local fallout and early fallout are considered to be very dangerous.

As far as damage to living organisms is concerned, Rotblat observes:

> Of the main injurious agents of nuclear weapons—blast, heat and ionizing radiations—one aspect of the last agent, fallout, is the least amenable to quantitative assessment, owing to its dependence on a number of unpredictable factors.[177]

Still one generally agrees that '[l]ocal fallout, (. . .), could be highly consequential to natural and agricultural systems and to humans',[178] although the actual sensitivity to nuclear radiation differs per species.[179]

According to studies by Westing, the surface area within which most mortality will occur after a surface burst is substantial. The surface areas related to initial radiation have been referred to above. Nuclear radiation after an 18 kt surface burst will kill most trees within an area of 148 ha; kill all vegetation within 43 ha; and kill most vertebrates within 674 ha. For a 0.91 Mt surface burst, these numbers are 12,800 ha (trees), 2830 ha (vegetation), 36,400 ha (vertebrates). And for a 9.1 Mt burst, the surface areas are 63,800 ha (trees), 12,100 ha (vegetation), and 177,000 ha (vertebrates).[180]

As regards the effects on the biosphere, in the following years, no significant effects on the environment were found by the United States Strategic Bombing Survey and the British Mission to Japan which investigated the effects of both nuclear explosions. According to the former, the radiation:

> had not lasting effects on the soil or vegetation: Seeds later planted within a few hundred feet of ground zero grew normally. Examination of subsurface soil in the immediate area showed presence of earthworms and other life only a few inches below the surface.[181]

[177] Rotblat, *Nuclear Radiation in Warfare*, p 139.

[178] International Council of Scientific Unions; Scientific Committee on Problems of the Environment 28; Harwell, Hutchinson, *Environmental Consequences of Nuclear War; Volume II: Ecological and Agricultural Effects*, p xxiii.

[179] Rotblat, *Nuclear Radiation in Warfare*, p 100. For a more detailed analysis of the effects of fallout on animal and plant life, see: Rotblat, *Nuclear Radiation in Warfare*, pp 100–2. See also: Chernobyl Forum, *Environmental Consequences of the Chernobyl Accident and Their Remediation: Twenty Years of Experience*, pp 191–4.

[180] Westing, *Weapons of Mass Destruction and the Environment*, pp 16–17, Tables 1.12 and 1.13.

[181] United States Strategic Bombing Survey, *The Effects of the Atomic bombs on Hiroshima and Nagasaki*, Chairman's Office, 30 Jun 1946; United States Government Printing Office, Washington, DC, 1946, p 28.

And the latter stated that 'in spite of stories to the contrary, plant life was flourishing in both cities.'[182]

According to the Chernobyl Forum, fallout caused increased mortality and adverse effects in plants and animals in certain 'hot spots' of up to 20–30 km from the explosion, especially during the first two months. By next growing season, however:

> population viability of plants and animals [had] substantially recovered as a result of the combined effects of reproduction and immigration. A few years were needed for recovery from major radiation-induced adverse effects in plants and animals.[183]

Furthermore, and paradoxically, since the area surrounding Chernobyl, also known as the Exclusion Zone, is still closed for human activity, the environment has actually become 'a unique sanctuary for biodiversity.'[184]

Where people and animals might suffer from radiation sickness after receiving large doses in a short period of time, other syndromes could occur after exposure to smaller doses over a more protracted period of time. For example, beta radiation causes general incapacitation and disintegration of the skin, the recovery of which may take a couple of months up to a year. The somatic effects of protracted exposure to small doses of gamma radiation are more long-term and may be latent for years or decades. Hiroshima, Nagasaki, nuclear testing, and nuclear accidents, have shown that nuclear radiation causes increased incidence of various forms of cancer,[185] of

[182] British Mission to Japan, *The Effects of the Atomic Bombs at Hiroshima and Nagasaki*, Report of the British Mission to Japan, His Majesty's Stationery Office, London, 1946, p 15.

[183] Chernobyl Forum, *Environmental Consequences of the Chernobyl Accident and Their Remediation: Twenty Years of Experience*, p 203. Compare also the conclusion of the United States Strategic Bombing Survey who wrote in 1946 that the atomic bombs over Hiroshima and Nagasaki 'apparently had no lasting effects on the soil or vegetation: Seeds later planted within a few hundred feet of ground zero grew normally.' United States Strategic Bombing Survey, *The Effects of the Atomic bombs on Hiroshima and Nagasaki*, p 28. And the Report of the British Mission stated that 'in spite of stories to the contrary, plant life was flourishing in both cities. Thus residual radio-activity is not a danger from these bombs exploded at such heights.' British Mission to Japan, *The Effects of the Atomic Bombs at Hiroshima and Nagasaki*, p 15.

[184] Chernobyl Forum, *Chernobyl's Legacy: Health, Environmental and Socio-Economic Impacts; and Recommendations to the Governments of Belarus, the Russian Federation and Ukraine*, pp 24, 15–24, 39–46. Chernobyl Forum, *Environmental Consequences of the Chernobyl Accident and Their Remediation: Twenty Years of Experience*, pp 194–209.

[185] Cancer is defined by King as 'a set of diseases characterized by unregulated cell growth leading to invasion of surrounding tissues and spread (metastasis) to other parts of the body', and is caused by changes in the DNA sequence—mutations—that may be generated by a number of factors, one of which is ionizing radiation. In the latter case, changes may result from a deficient repair of DNA bonds that were broken under the influence of highly energetic ionizing radiations. As in the case of initial nuclear radiation, this occurs first in the most sensitive organs leading to leukemia, lung cancer and cancer of the intestines. RJB King, *Cancer Biology*, Pearson Education, Harlow, 2000, pp 1–7, 110–13. A recent study on thyroid disease under a group of Hiroshima and Nagasaki atomic bomb survivors showed that '55 to 58 years after radiation exposure, a significant linear close-response relationship existed in the prevalence of not only malignant thyroid tumors but also benign thyroid nodules and that the relationship was significantly higher in those exposed at younger ages.' M Imaizumi

cataracts, of intra-uterine death or birth defects,[186] of decreased immunological resistance and general life shortening.[187]

Some claim that nuclear radiation even causes genetic defects appearing over some generations, but, according to the Secretary-General's comprehensive study on nuclear weapons, a direct relationship is difficult to assess:[188]

> If the germ cells of a person—as distinct from the somatic cells—receive a dose of ionizing radiation, changes may occur which would manifest themselves in the offspring of the exposed person or in future generations (. . .).[189]

Although Rotblat admits that the only irradiated population large enough to be studied, namely the Japanese, did not show any statistical difference

(et al), *Radiation Dose-Response Relationships for Thyroid Nodules and Autoimmune Thyroid Diseases in Hiroshima and Nagasaki Atomic Bomb Survivors 55–58 Years After Radiation Exposure*, Journal of the American Medical Association, Vol 295, 2006, No 9, 1 Mar 2006, pp 1021, 1011–22. The Chernobyl Forum estimated that of the 600,000 people who worked or lived in the most contaminated areas some 4,000 people will die as a result of ionizing radiation. These include around 50 emergency workers who died of radiation sickness shortly after contamination in 1986, and 9 children who died of thyroid cancer. Since 25% of these 600,000 people will die from spontaneous cancer, it will be difficult to monitor the exact relationship between the contamination and these people's deaths. Chernobyl Forum, *Chernobyl's Legacy: Health, Environmental and Socio-Economic Impacts; and Recommendations to the Governments of Belarus, the Russian Federation and Ukraine*, pp 10–11.

186 *Intra uterine* death, first-year mortality, congenital malformations, and mental retardation and malformation, may occur especially when a foetus is exposed during the first 4 months of pregnancy.

187 On the delayed effects of nuclear radiation on living organisms see: Von Arx, Marauhn, *Nuclear Tests*, in: Bernhardt (Ed), *Encyclopaedia of Public International Law; Volume Three; Jan Mayen to Pueblo Incident*, p 723; Briezeveld, Mathot, *Scoop; Natuurkunde voor de Bovenbouw 5/6 VWO*, p 272; British Medical Association; Report of the British Medical Association's Board of Science and Education, *The Medical Effects of Nuclear War*, pp 33–5, 100–4; Congress of the United States; Office of Technology Assessment, *The Effects of Nuclear War*, pp 19–20, 22–5; Glasstone, Dolan, *The Effects of Nuclear Weapons*, pp 442, 590–614; Grace, *Nuclear Weapons; Principles, Effects and Survivability*, pp 64–81; Hodgson, *Nuclear Physics in Peace and War*, pp 62–6, 102–4; Holdstock, Waterston, *Nuclear weapons, a continuing threat to health*, pp 1544–5; International Council of Scientific Unions; Scientific Committee on Problems of the Environment 28; Pittock, Ackerman, Crutzen, MacCracken, Shapiro, Turco, *Environmental Consequences of Nuclear War; Volume I: Physical and Atmospheric Effects*, pp 13–16, 239; International Council of Scientific Unions; Scientific Committee on Problems of the Environment 28; Harwell, Hutchinson, *Environmental Consequences of Nuclear War; Volume II: Ecological and Agricultural Effects*, pp 203–30; Kothari, *Nuclear Explosions and Their Effects*, pp 84–7, 96, ch VII; McNaught, *Nuclear Weapons and Their Effects*, pp 49–50, 57–62; Rauschning, *Nuclear Warfare and Weapons*, in: Bernhardt (Ed), *Encyclopaedia of Public International Law; Volume Three; Jan Mayen to Pueblo Incident*, p 735; Rotblat, *Nuclear Radiation in Warfare*, pp 26, 39–49, 80–4; Tucker, Gleisner, *Crucible Despair: The Effects of Nuclear War*, pp 43–8; United Nations Organization; UN Department of Disarmament Affairs; Report of the Secretary-General, *Nuclear Weapons: A Comprehensive Study*, pp 82–3; World Health Organization; Report of the WHO Management Group on Follow-up of resolution WHA36.28: 'The Role of Physicians and Other Health Workers in the Preservation and Promotion of Peace . . .', *Effects of Nuclear War on Health and Health Services*, pp 16–20.

188 United Nations Organization; UN Department of Disarmament Affairs; Report of the Secretary-General, *Nuclear Weapons: A Comprehensive Study*, p 84.

189 Rotblat, *Nuclear Radiation in Warfare*, p 49.

with non-exposed people,[190] he says that the conclusion that there are no genetic effects of radiation in man 'cannot be taken seriously'.[191] In 2005, the Chernobyl Forum Expert Group 'Environment' indeed observed genetic defects in plants in animals in the zone surrounding the Chernobyl reactor, both in somatic and germ cells:

> [I]n the exclusion zone, and beyond, different cytogenetic anomalies attributable to radiation continue to be reported from experimental studies performed on plants and animals. Whether the observed cytogenetic anomalies in somatic cells have any detrimental biological significance is not known.[192]

The Chernobyl Forum did not find hereditary effects among the human population of affected areas. Although there has been:

> a modest but steady increase in reported congenital malformations in both contaminated and uncontaminated areas of Belarus since 1986 (. . .), [t]his does not appear to be radiation-related and may be the result of increased registration.[193]

4.2.5.3.2.3 *Intermediate and Global Fallout*

Those particles that do not come down within 24 hours and therefore are not in the relative vicinity of the explosion site, fall into the categories of intermediate and global fallout, or delayed fallout. As has been explained above, the speed of descent strongly depends on the size of the particles. In case of a surface burst, some particles, and in case of an air burst, most particles, are so small that they may remain up in the atmosphere for days, sometimes even years, until they reach the earth, mainly through precipitation. According to Glasstone and Dolan it has been estimated that for an air burst almost all fallout is delayed; for a ground burst this is about 40 per cent; for a water burst, this is about 70 per cent. Most estimates are

[190] See, eg, Committee for the Compilation of Materials on Damage Cause by the Atomic Bombs in Hiroshima and Nagasaki, *The Impact of the A-Bomb; Hiroshima and Nagasaki, 1945–85*, Iwanami Shoten, Tokyo, 1985, pp 141–2.

[191] Rotblat, *Nuclear Radiation in Warfare*, pp 49–50. Similarly: British Medical Association; Report of the British Medical Association's Board of Science and Education, *The Medical Effects of Nuclear War*, p 104.

[192] Chernobyl Forum, *Environmental Consequences of the Chernobyl Accident and Their Remediation: Twenty Years of Experience*, pp 209, 203–5; Chernobyl Forum, *Chernobyl's Legacy: Health, Environmental and Socio-Economic Impacts; and Recommendations to the Governments of Belarus, the Russian Federation and Ukraine*, p 23.

[193] Chernobyl Forum, *Chernobyl's Legacy: Health, Environmental and Socio-Economic Impacts; and Recommendations to the Governments of Belarus, the Russian Federation and Ukraine*, p 14. See also, the United Nations Scientific Committee on the Effects of Atomic Radiation, *UNSCEAR 2001 Report; Annex Hereditary effects of radiation*, p 4. Through: <http://www.unscear.org/>.

based on the results of atmospheric testing in the late 1940s, 1950s and early 1960s.[194]

The difference between intermediate and global fallout is related to the existence of various relatively separate layers in the atmosphere. According to Westing, the earth's atmosphere is generally divided into two parts: the so-called lower atmosphere extending up to 55 km and containing some 99 per cent of the atmospheric mass; and the so-called upper-atmosphere extending from 55 km up to roughly 150 km and containing the remaining 1 per cent of the atmospheric mass. The latter may be subdivided into the mesosphere, extending from 55 km up to 80 km, and the ionosphere, extending from 80 km up to 150 km.[195] Except for the electromagnetic pulse, a nuclear explosion in the upper atmosphere will not have significant military or strategic effects, making upper-atmospheric bursts less likely to occur. The lower-atmosphere, however, is therefore all the more interesting. It consists of two layers, namely the troposphere extending up to 12 km and containing more than 87 per cent of the atmospheric mass, and the stratosphere, extending from 12 km up to 55 km and containing 12 per cent of the atmospheric mass. The latter, finally, may be subdivided into a lower stratosphere (12–30 km) in which part most of the ozone layer is situated,[196] and an upper stratosphere (30–55km). It should be noted that the altitudes given are mere indications and vary with longitude, latitude and season. The troposphere and stratosphere are separated from each other by a turbulent and imaginary boundary layer, called the tropopause.

Each layer has its own characteristics such as temperature and convective motion. In the troposphere, for example, the temperature drops with increasing altitude, whereas the temperature remains stable or rises with increasing altitude in the stratosphere. These stable or rising temperatures in the stratosphere cause very little convective motion which means that in the stratosphere, the air is relatively stable. The troposphere, on the other hand, is very dynamic. The troposphere sees large differences in temperature and high moisture contents causing convective movement

[194] British Medical Association; Report of the British Medical Association's Board of Science and Education, *The Medical Effects of Nuclear War*, pp 8–9; Glasstone, Dolan, *The Effects of Nuclear Weapons*, pp 387–8, 442; Rotblat, *Nuclear Radiation in Warfare*, pp 73–4, 94–9; United Nations Organization; UN Department of Disarmament Affairs; Report of the Secretary-General, *Nuclear Weapons: A Comprehensive Study*, p 75; World Health Organization; Report of the WHO Management Group on Follow-up of resolution WHA36.28: 'The Role of Physicians and Other Health Workers in the Preservation and Promotion of Peace . . .', *Effects of Nuclear War on Health and Health Services*, p 48.

[195] Collins Dictionary refers to the ionosphere as that part of the atmosphere extending from 60 km to some 1000 km altitude, where there is a high concentration of free electrons as a result of ionising radiation coming from outer space. *Collins Dictionary*, p 809.

[196] The ozone layer is 'the region of the stratosphere with the highest concentration of ozone molecules [(O_3)] which by absorbing high-energy solar ultraviolet radiation protects organisms on earth.' *Collins Dictionary*, p 1112.

and creating clouds and rainfall. In fact, '[m]ost of the visible phenomena associated with weather occur in the troposphere.'[197]

It therefore makes a big difference if a particle is blown into the stratosphere or in the troposphere. As was mentioned above, those particles that do not come down the first day and that are so small that gravity can hardly get a hold of them mainly come down by means of precipitation which only occurs in the troposphere. This means that as soon as a particle has entered the stratosphere it might stay up there for years traveling around the globe and only coming down when it eventually re-enters the troposphere. That is why this type of fallout is called global or stratospheric fallout. Stratospheric fallout will only occur in cases of explosions in the stratosphere and in cases of large-yield tropospheric detonations where the radioactive cloud enters the stratosphere. Those particles that did not pass by the tropopause and remain in the troposphere will be precipitated within a few weeks or months. This is called intermediate or tropospheric fallout and is also capable of covering the entire globe. Considering the fact that most particles will come down by precipitation, however, dry areas will receive considerably less fallout than wet regions.[198]

A distinction between intermediate and global fallout was considered necessary due to the differences in deposition rates. Although fallout particles are relatively harmless as long as they are airborne, and although most particles will have lost most of their activity and will be scattered over a large area, there is a significant difference between fallout particles that come down within weeks after the explosion and particles that come down in a time span of years. These differences make it impossible to

[197] Glasstone, Dolan, *The Effects of Nuclear Weapons*, p 443. On the structure of the atmosphere, see: Glasstone, Dolan, *The Effects of Nuclear Weapons*, pp 443–5; Westing, *Weapons of Mass Destruction and the Environment*, p 26, fn 4.

[198] British Medical Association; Report of the British Medical Association's Board of Science and Education, *The Medical Effects of Nuclear War*, pp 8–9; Glasstone, Dolan, *The Effects of Nuclear Weapons*, pp 442–8; Grace, *Nuclear Weapons; Principles, Effects and Survivability*, pp 64–81; International Council of Scientific Unions; Scientific Committee on Problems of the Environment 28; Harwell, Hutchinson, *Environmental Consequences of Nuclear War; Volume II: Ecological and Agricultural Effects*, pp 200–2; Kothari, *Nuclear Explosions and Their Effects*, pp 99–116, 143–4; Rotblat, *Nuclear Radiation in Warfare*, pp 73–4, 94–7; United Nations Organization; UN Department of Disarmament Affairs; Report of the Secretary-General, *Nuclear Weapons: A Comprehensive Study*, p 75; United Nations Organization; UN Department of Disarmament Affairs; Report of the Secretary-General, *Study on the Climatic and Other Global Effects of Nuclear War*, pp 42–3; World Health Organization; Report of the WHO Management Group on Follow-up of resolution WHA36.28: 'The Role of Physicians and Other Health Workers in the Preservation and Promotion of Peace . . .', *Effects of Nuclear War on Health and Health Services*, pp 16–18, 48–51. The SCOPE-28 Report (Vol I) sets more strict time limits: 'Global fallout will be further subdivided into an intermediate time scale, sometimes called tropospheric, of 1 to 30 days; and a long-term (beyond 30 days) stratospheric component.' International Council of Scientific Unions; Scientific Committee on Problems of the Environment 28; Pittock, Ackerman, Crutzen, MacCracken, Shapiro, Turco, *Environmental Consequences of Nuclear War; Volume I: Physical and Atmospheric Effects*, pp 237, 250.

lump all delayed fallout together and 'justify the introduction of the tropospheric fallout as a separate intermediate type.'[199]

Due to the loss of activity, the hazards from intermediate and global fallout are mainly internal and come primarily from sources inside the body of a human, an animal or another living creature. Especially particles that have relatively long half-lives are dangerous, such as strontium-90, cesium-137, iodine-131, and uranium and plutonium, pose a threat. They enter the body through inhalation, injection (wounds and absorption), but primarily ingestion. Once inside, some of it will be deposited in the bones if they are chemically similar to calcium (bone-seekers) or in the thyroid gland,[200] from where they may start their damaging work, in which case alpha-emitters, such as uranium and plutonium can be extremely destructive. Alpha particles have little to no penetrating power, but they are most harmful once they are inside, because they are relatively heavy and have therefore considerable ionising powers.[201] Ingestion occurs once fallout particles enter the food chain; human beings, for instance, could be contaminated by 'eating meat or drinking milk from animals which had ingested radioactive substances, or by eating vegetarian food from plants which had incorporated such substances, or by drinking contaminated water.'[202] According to a report of the IAEA on Depleted Uranium, which is a rest-product after uranium enrichment, and which consists mostly of U-238, bio-accumulation of uranium in plants and animals is small and is therefore not effectively transported in the food chain. A large percentage of uranium particles that are ingested leave the body through the faeces.[203]

[199] World Health Organization; Report of the WHO Management Group on Follow-up of resolution WHA36.28: 'The Role of Physicians and Other Health Workers in the Preservation and Promotion of Peace . . .', *Effects of Nuclear War on Health and Health Services*, p 49.

[200] 'Thus, in a real sense, our very bones carry in them the signatures of the nuclear test explosions.' Kothari, *Nuclear Explosions and Their Effects*, p 157.

[201] Briezeveld, Mathot, *Scoop; Natuurkunde voor de Bovenbouw 5/6 VWO*, p 272; Glasstone, Dolan, *The Effects of Nuclear Weapons*, pp 439–42, 594–609; Hodgson, *Nuclear Physics in Peace and War*, pp 54–5, 98–9; International Council of Scientific Unions; Scientific Committee on Problems of the Environment 28; Pittock, Ackerman, Crutzen, MacCracken, Shapiro, Turco, *Environmental Consequences of Nuclear War; Volume I: Physical and Atmospheric Effects*, pp 14–16, 263–4; Kothari, *Nuclear Explosions and Their Effects*, pp 123–7; International Council of Scientific Unions; Scientific Committee on Problems of the Environment 28; Harwell, Hutchinson, *Environmental Consequences of Nuclear War; Volume II: Ecological and Agricultural Effects*, pp 197–9; McNaught, *Nuclear Weapons and Their Effects*, pp 49–50; Rotblat, *Nuclear Radiation in Warfare*, pp 28–9, 54–5; Tucker, Gleisner, *Crucible Despair: The Effects of Nuclear War*, p 32; United Nations Organization; UN Department of Disarmament Affairs; Report of the Secretary-General, *Nuclear Weapons: A Comprehensive Study*, p 83; Westing, *Weapons of Mass Destruction and the Environment*, p 11; World Health Organization; Report of the WHO Management Group on Follow-up of resolution WHA36.28: 'The Role of Physicians and Other Health Workers in the Preservation and Promotion of Peace . . .', *Effects of Nuclear War on Health and Health Services*, pp 16–18, 29, 48. Extensively: Kothari, *Nuclear Explosions and Their Effects*, pp 144–225.

[202] Rotblat, *Nuclear Radiation in Warfare*, p 80. Similarly: Glasstone, Dolan, *The Effects of Nuclear Weapons*, p 442; Rotblat, *Nuclear Radiation in Warfare*, p 103.

[203] International Atomic Energy Agency, *Features: Depleted Uranium*, paragraphs 2, 9, 12, 14. At: <http://www.iaea.org/NewsCenter/Features/DU/du_qaa.shtml>.

However, despite the fact that it is often only very small doses that are ingested, the consequences can be devastating in the longer term because of accumulation in certain organs—some of which are very sensitive—and therefore amounts to chronic exposure.[204] Hodgson illustrates this by referring to the case of the girls who painted the dials of luminous clocks at the beginning of the 20th century. By licking their brushes to get a sharp point they ingested minute doses of radium and some of them died painful deaths around 20 years after they had stopped painting.[205] The consequences of nuclear radiation from internal sources are no different from the consequences of external sources and do therefore not need separate discussion.

4.2.5.3.3 Neutron Induced Activity

Apart from fallout, residual nuclear radiation also appears in the form of so-called NIA. It is caused by the capture of neutrons released during the first second of the explosion by fission products, weapon residues, and substances in the atmosphere and on the surface. After capturing neutrons, most substances become radioactive and start emitting beta particles and gamma rays, some of them for an extended period of time. Except for a small, circular area around ground-zero, however, they normally contribute little to the overall nuclear radiation. Obviously, in case of Enhanced Radiation Weapons or neutron bombs, and in case of irregular bomb designs or bomb materials, the activity may be significantly different. In view of their reach and the presence of material to induce, only surface burst may generally produce sufficient Neutron Induced Activity to pose a threat to the surrounding ecosystem.[206]

4.3 Indirect Effects

Apart from direct effects, a large exchange of nuclear weapons may also have significant indirect effects on the environment and the world's

204 International Council of Scientific Unions; Scientific Committee on Problems of the Environment 28; Pittock, Ackerman, Crutzen, MacCracken, Shapiro, Turco, *Environmental Consequences of Nuclear War; Volume I: Physical and Atmospheric Effects*, pp 14–16; Rotblat, *Nuclear Radiation in Warfare*, pp 54–5; United Nations Organization; UN Department of Disarmament Affairs; Report of the Secretary-General, *Nuclear Weapons: A Comprehensive Study*, p 83.

205 Hodgson, *Nuclear Physics in Peace and War*, pp 54–5.

206 Glasstone, Dolan, *The Effects of Nuclear Weapons*, pp 329, 405–7; Grace, *Nuclear Weapons; Principles, Effects and Survivability*, 64–81; International Council of Scientific Unions; Scientific Committee on Problems of the Environment 28; Harwell, Hutchinson, *Environmental Consequences of Nuclear War; Volume II: Ecological and Agricultural Effects*, p 197; Kothari, *Nuclear Explosions and Their Effects*, pp 96–9; McNaught, *Nuclear Weapons and Their Effects*, p 28; Rotblat, *Nuclear Radiation in Warfare*, pp 77, 79–80.

economy. Research of the long-term consequences of multiple nuclear explosions for the environment was instigated in the 1960s and received a boost after the 1972 Stockholm Conference on the Human Environment.[207] Since then, various studies have been carried out dealing with the impact of nuclear explosions on the ozone layer, and climate change. Of these, the ambitious study on the environmental consequences of nuclear war, carried out within the framework of the International Council of Scientific Unions, by the Scientific Committee on Problems of the Environment (SCOPE 28 Report) from 1985 and 1986, is generally regarded as very comprehensive.[208]

The long-term effects of all-out nuclear war were considered to be so dramatic that a group of scientists invented the term 'nuclear winter' in 1983.[209] Originally, the focus of research had been on the input of large quantities of dust into the atmosphere, but in the early 1980s attention shifted to an additional element, namely the injection of black smoke into the atmosphere caused by widespread petroleum, city and forest fires ignited by the nuclear explosions. Smoke particles are much smaller than dust particles, remain longer in the atmosphere, and absorb more sunlight. The presence of possibly millions of tons of light-absorbing matter in the atmosphere could reduce solar energy by up to 80 per cent, leading to a significant drop in temperature, considerable darkening, and large-scale reduction of photosynthesis in plants and other organisms for as long as the material remains in the atmosphere. Although on a much smaller scale, some of this did occur after giant volcanic eruptions in the 19th and 20th century.[210]

[207] A/CONF.48/14/Rev.1, Report of the United Nations Conference on the Human Environment, Stockholm, 5–16 Jun 1972, Declaration of the United Nations Conference on the Human Environment, United Nations, New York, 1973.

[208] International Council of Scientific Unions; Scientific Committee on Problems of the Environment 28; AB Pittock, TP Ackerman, PJ Crutzen, MC MacCracken, CS Shapiro, RP Turco, *Environmental Consequences of Nuclear War; Volume I: Physical and Atmospheric Effects*, John Wiley & Sons, Chichester, 1986; International Council of Scientific Unions; Scientific Committee on Problems of the Environment 28; MA Harwell, TC Hutchinson (Eds), *Environmental Consequences of Nuclear War; Volume II: Ecological and Agricultural Effects*, John Wiley & Sons, Chichester, 1985. See also: United Nations Organization; UN Department of Disarmament Affairs; Report of the Secretary-General, *Nuclear Weapons: A Comprehensive Study*, p 85; United Nations Organization; UN Department of Disarmament Affairs; Report of the Secretary-General, *Study on the Climatic and Other Global Effects of Nuclear War*, pp 1–3, 8–10.

[209] RP Turco, OB Toon, TP Ackerman, JP Pollack, C Sagan, *Nuclear Winter: Global Consequences of Multiple Nuclear Explosions*, Science, Volume 222, 1983, pp 1283–92, also known as the TTAPS study, after the first letters of the authors' last names.

[210] Compare the eruptions of the Krakatau in Indonesia, late Aug 1883. The eruption was one of the most violent eruptions in modern history and had an equivalent yield of 200 Mt TNT. The resulted in spectacular sunsets everywhere in the world, and caused a global drop in temperature of 1.2 degrees Celsius on average. The weather returned to normal in 1888. At: <http: //en.wikipedia.org / wiki / Krakatau>.

In addition, large amounts of toxic substances could cause widespread pollution and large amounts of nitrogen oxides (NO_xs) produced by the fireballs of high-yield nuclear explosions could cause a significant depletion of the (stratospheric) ozone layer. The ozone layer protects the earth from harmful carcinogenic ultraviolet radiation. Depending on the total yield of nuclear explosions and the time of year, estimates on the depletion of the ozone layer vary from 10 to 50 per cent.[211]

Although the nuclear winter hypothesis has been criticised from various angles, it is generally agreed that major nuclear war would entail a high risk of global environmental disruption, global change of climate, depletion of the ozone layer, global economic crisis and widespread social chaos. This would be the case for both belligerent and non-belligerent states alike, and this would be greatest in case of a summer attack on large cities and industries in the Northern Hemisphere.[212] The Committee on the Environmental Consequences of Nuclear War concludes in a study undertaken for the government of Canada that:

> although the modelling results must be interpreted with care, a prima facie case has been made that a nuclear winter will indeed follow a wide range of attacks.[213]

[211] Barash, *Introduction to Peace Studies,* pp 112–13; British Medical Association; Report of the British Medical Association's Board of Science and Education, *The Medical Effects of Nuclear War,* pp 97–9; Congress of the United States; Office of Technology Assessment, *The Effects of Nuclear War,* pp 112–14; PJ Crutzen, *Climatic Effects of Nuclear War,* in: World Health Organization, *Effects of Nuclear War on Health and Health Services,* Annex 2, pp 65–71; Krane, *Introductory Nuclear Physics,* p 556; International Council of Scientific Unions; Scientific Committee on Problems of the Environment 28; Pittock, Ackerman, Crutzen, MacCracken, Shapiro, Turco, *Environmental Consequences of Nuclear War; Volume I: Physical and Atmospheric Effects,* pp 13, 39–86, 120–4, 143–7, 215–35; Rotblat, *Nuclear Radiation in Warfare,* p 100; The Royal Society of Canada; Report of the Committee on the Environmental Consequences of Nuclear War, *Nuclear Winter and Associated Effects; A Canadian Appraisal of the Environmental Impact of Nuclear War,* The Royal Society of Canada, Ottawa, Ontario, 1985, pp 22–7; United Nations Organization; UN Department of Disarmament Affairs; Report of the Secretary-General, *Nuclear Weapons: A Comprehensive Study,* pp 85–6; United Nations Organization; UN Department of Disarmament Affairs; Report of the Secretary-General, *Study on the Climatic and Other Global Effects of Nuclear War,* pp 3–5, 10–25; Westing, *Weapons of Mass Destruction and the Environment,* pp 18–20; World Health Organization; Report of the WHO Management Group on Follow-up of resolution WHA36.28: 'The Role of Physicians and Other Health Workers in the Preservation and Promotion of Peace . . .', *Effects of Nuclear War on Health and Health Services,* pp 5, 12–13.

[212] United Nations Organization; UN Department of Disarmament Affairs; Report of the Secretary-General, *Nuclear Weapons: A Comprehensive Study,* p 85; United Nations Organization; UN Department of Disarmament Affairs; Report of the Secretary-General, *Study on the Climatic and Other Global Effects of Nuclear War,* pp vi, 6–7. For a discussion of critique on the hypothesis, see: The Royal Society of Canada; Report of the Committee on the Environmental Consequences of Nuclear War, *Nuclear Winter and Associated Effects; A Canadian Appraisal of the Environmental Impact of Nuclear War,* pp 32–4.

[213] The Royal Society of Canada; Report of the Committee on the Environmental Consequences of Nuclear War, *Nuclear Winter and Associated Effects; A Canadian Appraisal of the Environmental Impact of Nuclear War,* p 29.

The impact of global nuclear war involving multiple nuclear exchange and possibly leading to a nuclear winter is tremendous. Harwell and Hutchinson write: 'Nuclear war represents the most significant threat of our times.'[214] Although most of the consequences will be limited to the Northern Hemisphere, the Southern Hemisphere will receive its share within a relatively short period of time, due to monsoon-like winds and through interhemispheric transport.[215]

Apart from expected short-term atmospheric, climatic and meteorological changes, it is the biosphere that will be most affected.[216] A study on the 'Long-Term Biological Consequences of Nuclear War' concludes that:

> [s]ubfreezing temperatures, low light levels, and high doses of ionizing and ultraviolet radiation extending for many months after a large-scale nuclear war could destroy the biological support systems of civilizations.

Many life-forms may cease to exist and 'extinction of the human species itself cannot be excluded.'[217]

As far as flora is concerned, temperature fluctuations may have devastating effects, depending on the sensitivity of the species and the time of year. In winter, for example, many plants and seeds are cold hardened and may endure very low temperatures, but in summer, even a sudden small drop in temperature could be fatal. Large-scale fires, fallout and plagues of insects that are less sensitive to radiation will add to the disturbance and impair recovery. Those plants that survived will experience a severe decrease in productivity as a result of reduced photosynthesis and will be exposed to damaging radioactive and solar ultraviolet radiation, smog and acid rains. Phytoplankton which is at the bottom of the food chain in marine ecosystems is particularly sensitive to reduced solar energy and to ultraviolet radiation.

As far as surviving animals and humans are concerned, the severe cold and continuous darkness, in combination with widespread death and destruction, would cause severe distress and mortality. Reduced crop yields, such as rice, wheat, maize and soybean, reduced seed availability, loss of experienced farmers, loss of agricultural production material, loss

[214] International Council of Scientific Unions; Scientific Committee on Problems of the Environment 28; Harwell, Hutchinson, *Environmental Consequences of Nuclear War; Volume II: Ecological and Agricultural Effects*, p 3.

[215] Turco, Toon, Ackerman, Pollack, Sagan, *Nuclear Winter: Global Consequences of Multiple Nuclear Explosions*, pp 1289–90.

[216] For an extensive discussion of Meteorological and Climatic Effects, see: International Council of Scientific Unions; Scientific Committee on Problems of the Environment 28; Pittock, Ackerman, Crutzen, MacCracken, Shapiro, Turco, *Environmental Consequences of Nuclear War; Volume I: Physical and Atmospheric Effects*, ch 5, 149–214.

[217] PR Ehrlich, J Harte, MA Harwell, PH Raven, C Sagan, GM Woodwell, J Berry, ES Ayensu, AH Ehrlich, T Eisner, SJ Gould, HD Grover, R Herrera, RM May, E Mayr, CP McKay, HA Mooney, N Myers, D Pimentel, JM Teal, *Long-Term Biological Consequences of Nuclear War*, Science, 1983, Vol 222, p 1293.

of livestock, loss of eatable vegetation, and lack of clean and fresh water will lead to severe competition among survivors for the remaining products and could lead to widespread epidemic disease, malnutrition, famine[218] and eventually mass starvation. Injured casualties will be deprived of health care and will be vulnerable to infections,[219] and nuclear and ultraviolet radiation are likely to account for a steadily increasing number of casualties.

Finally, although the magnitude of the economic consequences of nuclear war are difficult to assess, the impairment of economic productivity, the collapse of socio-economic infrastructure, the collapse of trade, and the collapse of the world economy in general as a result of a large and still increasing interdependence, are expected to affect the entire global society and to bring untold sorrow to mankind.[220]

[218] The United States and Canada are the world's largest cereal exporters.

[219] More extensively on post-nuclear war health care scenarios: British Medical Association; Report of the British Medical Association's Board of Science and Education, *The Medical Effects of Nuclear War*, pp 37–45; United Nations Organization; UN Department of Disarmament Affairs; Report of the Secretary-General, *Study on the Climatic and Other Global Effects of Nuclear War*, pp 44–5.

[220] Barash, *Introduction to Peace Studies*, pp 111–12; British Medical Association; Report of the British Medical Association's Board of Science and Education, *The Medical Effects of Nuclear War*, pp 92–104; Ehrlich, Harte, Harwell, Raven, Sagan, Woodwell, Berry, Ayensu, Ehrlich, Eisner, Gould, Grover, Herrera, May, Mayr, McKay, Mooney, Myers, Pimentel, Teal, *Long-Term Biological Consequences of Nuclear War*, pp 1293–9; Glasstone, Dolan, *The Effects of Nuclear Weapons*, pp 618–27; International Council of Scientific Unions; Scientific Committee on Problems of the Environment 28; Harwell, Hutchinson, *Environmental Consequences of Nuclear War; Volume II: Ecological and Agricultural Effects*, p 3; The Royal Society of Canada; Report of the Committee on the Environmental Consequences of Nuclear War, *Nuclear Winter and Associated Effects; A Canadian Appraisal of the Environmental Impact of Nuclear War*, pp 35–51; United Nations Organization; UN Department of Disarmament Affairs; Report of the Secretary-General, *Nuclear Weapons: A Comprehensive Study*, pp 71, 85–7; United Nations Organization; UN Department of Disarmament Affairs; Report of the Secretary-General, *Study on the Climatic and Other Global Effects of Nuclear War*, pp 6–7, 26–40, 44–7; Westing, *Weapons of Mass Destruction and the Environment*, pp 20–2; World Health Organization; Report of the WHO Management Group on Follow-up of resolution WHA36.28: 'The Role of Physicians and Other Health Workers in the Preservation and Promotion of Peace . . .', *Effects of Nuclear War on Health and Health Services*, p 5.

For a detailed and technical discussion of see: International Council of Scientific Unions; Scientific Committee on Problems of the Environment 28; Harwell, Hutchinson, *Environmental Consequences of Nuclear War; Volume II: Ecological and Agricultural Effects*, John Wiley & Sons, Chichester, 1985.

Part II

III

The Protection of the Environment During International Armed Conflict Under Ius in Bello

1—INTRODUCTION

1.1 Introduction

> Attached to force are certain self-imposed imperceptible limitations hardly worth mentioning, known as international law and custom but they scarcely weaken it. . . . Kind-hearted people might . . . think there was some ingenious way to disarm or defeat an enemy without too much bloodshed, and might imagine that is the true goal of the art of war. Pleasant as it sounds, it is a fallacy that must be exposed: war is such a dangerous business that the mistakes which come from kindness are the very worst.[1]

Thus wrote Von Clausewitz in his 1832 treatise '*On War*'. Almost 1900 years earlier, Cicero had more or less said the same thing, though under very different circumstances and with a very different object. In his defence of Titus Annius Milo, Cicero stated: '*Silent leges inter arma*' which basically means that as soon as the weapons speak, the laws remain silent.[2]

A lot has changed since 52 BC and 1832. For the better, although the truth requires one to say that the opinions of Cicero, Von Clausewitz and others belonged to a respected minority. It was and still is a fact that the amount of force used during armed conflict is not unlimited, and that the various limitations are deeply rooted in many cultures and religions going back thousands of years. Early examples of rules of warfare can be found in Judaism,[3]

[1] C Von Clausewitz, *On War*, in: LC Green, *The Contemporary Law of Armed Conflict*, Manchester University Press, Manchester, 2000, p 1.

[2] Cicero, *De Milone*, §11, in: F Ahlheid, H Bremer, S Kemper,P Rijke, T van de Vliet, *Res Loquitur Ipsa; Cicero's pleidooi voor Titus Annius Milo en de retorische traditie*, Hermaion, Emmeloord, 1994.

[3] Deuteronomy 20:19, on the protection of the environment; Kings 6:22-3 on the treatment of prisoners. See also Flavius Josephus, *De Oude Geschiedenis van de Joden (Antiquitates Judaicae)*, Vertaling FJAM Meijer, MA Wes, Ambo, Amsterdam, 2005, Boek IV, 294–306, Hoofdstuk 8, para 42 [299], pp 398–9, on the prohibition to cut down cultivated trees. Josephus writes: '*Is een kamp eenmaal ingericht, dan moeten jullie oppassen dat jullie je in geen enkel opzicht schuldig maken aan misdadige acties. Wanneer jullie een stad belegeren en gebrek hebben aan*

Hinduism,[4] Christianity,[5] Islam[6] and in Greek,[7] and Chinese[8] literature.[9] And also the fathers of modern public international law gave detailed accounts on what is permissible in war, including Grotius in his most famous treaties *De Iure Belli ac Pacis* published in 1625.[10]

1.2 Historical Development

The development of modern *ius in bello* starts in the second half of the 19th century, both in Europe and in the United States. In Switzerland, Henri Dunant[11] establishes the predecessor of the independent International

hout voor de vervaardiging van oorlogsmachines, mogen jullie geen kaalslag plegen en gecultiveerde bomen omhakken. Die moeten jullie sparen, in de gedachte dat die zijn ontwikkeld tot nut van de mensen en dat zij, als ze zouden kunnen spreken, zich tegenover jullie zouden hebben verdedigd door erop te wijzen dat zij op geen enkele manier verantwoordelijk waren voor de oorlog en nu onterecht werden mishandeld, en dat zij als ze de mogelijkheid daartoe hadden gehad zeker waren verhuisd en vertrokken naar een ander land.' (Once a camp has been set up, then you should be careful that you will not be responsible for any criminal action. When you lay siege to a city and you are short of wood for the creation of war machinery, you may not cause deforestation and cut down trees that have been cultivated Those you must spare, bearing in mind that they have been developed for the benefit of people and that they, if they could speak, would have argued against you by referring to the fact that they are not in any way responsible for the war and that they are now mistreated, and that they, if they had been able to, would certainly have moved and left for another country. EVK).

[4] Ramayana and the Mahabharata, concerning the use of certain kinds of weapons. In both the Ramayana and the Mahabharata warring princes get the opportunity to use super-destructive weapons; both refuse, however, because mass destruction was not in conformity with ethics and forbidden by religion and the old laws of war, despite the fact that their adversaries were fighting unjust wars.

[5] Deuteronomy 20:19, Kings 6:22-3, and the second Lateran Council of 1139 which prohibited the use of the crossbow. The crossbow was considered disgraceful, diabolical, and in contravention of the law of God.

[6] Koran, LXXVII.8 on the treatment of prisoners.

[7] Homer, *The Odyssey*, Bk I, on a wide variety of rules.

[8] Sun Tzu, *The Art of War*, 4th century BC, on attacking civilians.

[9] Examples from Green, *The Contemporary Law of Armed Conflict*, pp 18–27; Dissenting Opinion of Judge Weeramantry, Legality of the Threat or Use of Nuclear Weapons, Advisory Opinion, 8 Jul 1996, ICJ Reports 1996, p 226, at pp 478–81. Compare also the literature references by Greenwood in: C Greenwood, *International Humanitarian Law (Laws of War); Revised Report for the Centennial Commemoration of the First Hague Peace Conference 1899*, London School of Economics and Political Science, London, 1999, p 7, fn 2.

[10] H Grotius, *De Iure Belli ac Pacis*, The Classics of International Law, Clarendon Press, Oxford, 1925. In particular Book III deals with the rights and duties of those who wage a just war.

[11] Henri Dunant was a Swiss business man who had witnessed as a bystander the Battle of Solferino in 1859 between an Austrian and a Franco-Sardinian army. Shocked by the cruelties both during and after the hostilities, he wrote down his experiences in 'A Memory of Solferino', which he published in 1862, and in which he called for the establishment of national relief organisations—the national Red Cross Societies—and the development of international rules on the treatment of the wounded in the field and the protection of aid workers. His book shook public consciousness and marked the first step towards the development of international humanitarian law. Through <http://en.wikipedia.org/>.

Committee of the Red Cross in 1863,[12] and paves the way for the 1864 Convention for the Amelioration of the Condition of the Wounded in Armies in the Field.[13] This document constitutes the first international convention on international humanitarian law. In the United States, President Lincoln promulgates in 1863 the 'Instructions for the Government of Armies of the United States in the Field', better known as the 'Lieber Code', named after Francis Lieber who prepared the instructions. Although the Lieber Code is only a military manual and therefore only an internal document, it represents the first comprehensive codification of the laws of war and it became a source of inspiration for subsequent efforts at the international level.[14]

Before 1864,[15] rules on warfare were generally unwritten and based on custom. After 1864, many rules were laid down in a large number of conventions on a wide variety of topics. For the sake of clarity, it is common to make a general distinction between on the one hand rules that deal with:

> the rights and duties of belligerents in their conduct of operations and [limit] the choice of methods and means of injuring the enemy in an international armed conflict;[16]

and on the other hand, rules that protect:

> the victims of war and [aim] to provide safeguards for disabled armed forces personnel and persons not taking part in the hostilities.[17]

The former set of rules is generally referred to as 'Hague law', named after two fundamental codifications on the conduct of war on land at the 1899 and 1907 Peace Conferences in The Hague.[18] The latter set of rules is

[12] See <http://www.icrc.org/>.

[13] Geneva Convention for the Amelioration of the Condition of the Wounded in Armies in the Field, signed on 22 Aug 1864, entered into force on 22 Jun 1865, AJIL, Vol 1, No 2, Supplement: Official Documents, 1907, p 90.

[14] F Kalshoven, L Zegveld, *Constraints on the Waging of War; An Introduction to International Humanitarian Law*, International Committee of the Red Cross, Geneva, 2001, pp 19–20.

[15] Greenwood refers to the 1856 Declaration of Paris as the first international treaty concerning the laws of war. Greenwood, *International Humanitarian Law (Laws of War); Revised Report for the Centennial Commemoration of the First Hague Peace Conference 1899*, p 7. The Declaration was signed upon the conclusion of the 1856 Treaty of Paris which ended the 1853–1856 Crimean War and contains a restatement of four rules on maritime law. These four rules were 'the outcome of a *modus vivendi* which was adopted between France and Great Britain in 1854 and was originally intended for the Crimean War only.' D Schindler, J Toman (Eds), *The Laws of Armed Conflicts; A Collection of Conventions, Resolutions and Other Documents*, Martinus Nijhoff Publishers, Dordrecht, 1988, p 787.

[16] Legality of the Threat or Use of Nuclear Weapons, Advisory Opinion, 8 Jul 1996, ICJ Reports 1996, p 226, at p 256, para 75.

[17] Legality of the Threat or Use of Nuclear Weapons, Advisory Opinion, 8 Jul 1996, ICJ Reports 1996, p 226, at p 256, para 75.

[18] These were the so-called Hague Regulations on land warfare annexed to 1899 Hague Convention II and 1907 Hague Convention IV Because they are almost similar, they are usually referred to as Hague Regulations. 1899 Hague Convention (II) with respect to the Laws and Customs of War on Land, with annexed Regulations, signed on 29 Jul 1899, entered into force on 4 Sep 1900, AJIL, Vol 1, No 2, Supplement: Official Documents, 1907, p 129; and the

generally referred to as 'Geneva law', named after the place where the majority of these humanitarian rules were codified, most notably the first 1864 Convention and the Four Geneva Conventions of 1949.[19]

It may look paradoxical nowadays that rules were created for the conduct of warfare, but one has to keep in mind that warfare used to play a very different role in international politics before 1945.[20] During the Middle Ages war was considered legal if fought for 'just' reasons; after the Middle Ages and with the birth of the modern Nation State, war was considered a sovereign right, or rather an attribute of sovereignty. Furthermore, according to Malanczuk, before the 20th century wars 'were seldom fought for ideological reasons and tended not to rouse the same intensity of passion' as nowadays.[21] The object and purpose of warfare was therefore not the complete annihilation of the enemy, including its ideology—after all, 'a state's enemy today might be its ally tomorrow'[22]—but merely the submission of its armed forces and to alleviate as much as

1907 Hague Convention (IV) Respecting the Laws and Customs of War on Land, with annexed Regulations, signed on 18 Oct 1907, entered into force on 26 Jan 1910, AJIL, Vol 2, No 1/2, Supplement: Official Documents, 1908, p 90.

[19] On the protection of wounded in the field:1864 Geneva Convention for the Amelioration of the Condition of the Wounded in the Field, signed on 22 Aug 1864, entered into force on 22 Jun 1865, AJIL, Vol 1, No 2, Supplement: Official Documents, 1907, p 90; replaced by the 1906 Geneva Convention, signed on 6 Jul 1906, entered into force on 9 Aug 1907, AJIL, Vol 1, No 2, Supplement: Official Documents, 1907, p 201; replaced by the 1929 Geneva Convention, signed on 27 Jul 1929, entered into force on 19 Jun 1931, AJIL, Vol 27, No 2, Supplement: Official Documents, 1933, p 43. On the protection of wounded at sea: 1899 Hague Convention (III), for the Adaptation to Maritime War of the Principles of the Geneva Convention of 22 Aug 1864, signed on 29 Jul 1899, entered into force on 4 Sep 1900, AJIL, Vol 1, No 2, Supplement: Official Documents, 1907, p 159; replaced by 1907 Hague Convention (X) for the Adaptation to Maritime Warfare of the Principles of the Geneva Convention, signed on 18 Oct 1907, entered into force on 26 Jan 1910, AJIL, Vol 2, No 1/2, Supplement: Official Documents, 1908, p 153. On the treatment of Prisoners of War: 1929 Geneva Convention relative to the Treatment of Prisoners of War, signed on 27 Jul 1929, entered into force on 19 Jun 1931, AJIL, Vol 27, No 2, Supplement: Official Documents, 1933, p 59. And naturally the 1949 Geneva Convention (I) for the Amelioration of the Condition of the Wounded and Sick in Armed Forces in the Field; Convention (II) for the Amelioration of the Condition of Wounded, Sick and Shipwrecked Members of Armed Forces at Sea; Convention (III) relative to the Treatment of Prisoners of War; Convention (IV) relative to the Protection of Civilian Persons in Time of War, signed on 12 Aug 1949, entered into force on 21 Oct 1950, UNTS, Vol 75, No 970–3.

[20] In 1945, the drafters of the United Nations Charter prohibited in Art 2(4) the threat of use of force in international relations against the territorial integrity or political independence of United Nations member states, or in any other way inconsistent with the purposes of the United Nations. Before World War II, the High Contracting Parties to the 1928 Pact of Paris or Kellogg-Brian Pact renounced in Art I recourse to war as an instrument of international policy. United Nations Charter, signed on 26 Jun 1945, entered into force on 24 Oct 1945, AJIL, Vol 39, No 3, Supplement: Official Documents, 1945, p 190; Treaty between the United States and Other Powers Providing for the Renunciation of War as an Instrument of National Policy, signed on 27 Aug 1928, entered into force on 24 Jul 1929, AJIL, Vol 22, No 4, Supplement: Official Documents, 1928, p 171.

[21] P Malanczuk, *Akehurst's Modern Introduction to International Law*, Routledge, London, 1997, pp 342–3.

[22] Malanczuk, *Akehurst's Modern Introduction to International Law*, p 343.

possible the calamities of warfare; not only for practical and economical reasons, but also because of humanitarian concerns.

1.3 Foundations of *Ius in Bello*

Both the object and purpose of warfare and the ratio behind the laws of war were recognised by the drafters of the 1868 St. Petersburg Declaration.[23] The St. Petersburg Declaration constitutes the first modern prohibition of the use of a specific weapon under international law by renouncing the use of a then newly invented type of rifle ammunition that exploded or ignited upon impact and which had been adapted for anti-personnel use. Because of its devastating effects upon troops, its use was considered undesirable in times of war between 'Civilized Nations,[24] and not in conformity with basic requirements under the laws of war.

In the Preamble of the Declaration, the drafters explained the rationale of the prohibition by referring to the underlying and fundamental principles of the laws of warfare in general and those regarding means and methods of warfare in particular:

> Considering that the progress of civilization should have the effect of alleviating as much as possible the calamities of war,

the Contracting Parties stated that:

> the only legitimate object which States should endeavour to accomplish during war is to weaken the military forces of the enemy

and that for that purpose it was 'sufficient to disable the greatest possible number of men'. According to the drafters, the use of explosive bullets would exceed that purpose and their employment would only 'uselessly aggravate the sufferings of disabled men, or render their death inevitable'. Therefore, their employment would be 'contrary to the laws of humanity'

[23] St Petersburg Declaration Renouncing the Use, in Time of War, of Explosive Projectiles Under 400 Grammes Weight, signed on 11 Dec 1868, entered into force on 11 Dec 1868, AJIL, Vol 1, No 2, Supplement: Official Documents, 1907, p 95.

[24] This meant that the prohibition would not apply in wars between civilised nations and non-civilised nations or peoples. Non-civilised nations included nations that were not recognised as civilised by the so-called Circle of Civilized Nations as well as people under colonial domination. The Circle of Civilized Nations consisted of European nations and the United States (the former Circle of Christian Nations) and the Ottoman Empire. Compare for example Art 38(1)(c) of the Statute of the International Court of Justice for similar terminology. Art 38(1)(c) states that one of the three primary sources of international law are 'the general principles of law recognized by civilized nations'. For the distinction between the Circles of Christian, Civilized and later Peace-loving Nations, see, BVA Röling, *International Law in an Expanded World*, Djambatan, Amsterdam, 1960, pp xv, 17–55; BVA Röling, *Volkenrecht en Vrede*, Kluwer, Deventer, 1985, pp 27–8.

which, under these circumstances, had to prevail over 'the necessities of war'.[25]

In other words, the progress of civilisation entails a specific set of rules and limitations which are intended to lessen the scourge of war. In order to achieve that, the laws of war strike a balance between the 'necessities of war' on the one hand, and the 'laws of humanity' on the other.[26] The former reflects the fundamental justification for a state and its armed forces to do things in times of war that would normally be illegal during peacetime.[27] The latter reflects the general exception or limitation to this

[25] St Petersburg Declaration, preambular paras 1–6.

[26] Compare also Y Dinstein, *Military Necessity*, in: R Bernhardt (Ed), *Encyclopaedia of Public International Law; Vol Three; Jan Mayen to Pueblo Incident*, Elsevier, Amsterdam, 1997, p 395; D Momtaz, *La Recours à l'Arme Nucléaire et la Protection de l'Environnement: l'Apport de la Cour Internationale de Justice*, in: L Boisson de Chazournes,P Sands (Eds), *International Law, the International Court of Justice and Nuclear Weapons*, Cambridge University Press, Cambridge, 1999, p 362; S Oeter, *Methods and Means of Combat*, in: D Fleck (Ed), *The Handbook of Humanitarian Law in Armed Conflicts*, Oxford University Press, Oxford, 1995, p 112; A Roberts, R Guelff, *Documents on the Laws of War*, Oxford University Press, Oxford, 2000, p 10; Y Sandoz, C Swinaraski, B Zimmerman (Eds), *Commentary on the Additional Protocols; of 8 Jun 1977 to the Geneva Conventions of 12 Aug 1949*, International Committee of the Red Cross, Martinus Nijhoff Publishers, Geneva, 1987, pp 392–3 (the Commentary is also available through <http://www.icrc.org/>); RG Tarasofsky, *Legal Protection of the Environment during International Armed Conflict*, Netherlands Yearbook of International Law, Vol 24, 1993, p 24; and the Dissenting Opinion of Judge Higgins, Legality of the Threat or Use of Nuclear Weapons, Advisory Opinion, 8 Jul 1996, ICJ Reports 1996, p 226, at p 586. According to Schwarzenberger it is important to realise that 'by and large, the rules of warfare are the result of a tug-of-war between two major formative agencies: the necessities of war and the requirements of the standard of civilisation.' G Schwarzenberger, *International Law; As Applied by International Courts and Tribunals; Vol II; The Law of Armed Conflict*, Stevens & Sons, London, 1968, p 4.

[27] According to Schwarzenberger, '[t]he necessities of war are but a negative in positive guise. (. . .). In the relations between belligerent States, sovereignty is no longer limited by the ensemble of the rules governing the other six fundamental principles of international law [sovereignty, recognition, consent, good faith, freedom of the seas, international responsibility, and self-defense. EVK], but solely by the rules of warfare. Thus, wartime sovereignty comes nearest to pristine and prelegal sovereignty, and the rules of warfare constitute the only remaining barrier against sovereignty in its most violent and anarchic form.' And later, he adds 'The necessities of war share with necessity as a defence against he allegation of the commission of an international tort [cf Art 25 of the 2001 ILC Draft Articles on State Responsibility] but one common feature: the absence of legal responsibility. (. . .) In the cases of necessities of war and sovereignty at large, however, prohibitory rules of international law are altogether lacking.' Schwarzenberger, *International Law; As Applied by International Courts and Tribunals; Vo II; The Law of Armed Conflict*, pp 13–14, 128. According to Greenwood, many 'supposed "belligerent rights" are not rights in the true legal sense at all', since they often do not have correlative duties. 'What the law actually confers in such a case is a liberty; the person (or state) concerned may exercise that liberty without violating the law but others are under no duty to cooperate with him or even to abstain from obstructing him. (. . .) The notion that the *ius in bello* leaves states and individuals free to act in a particular way without giving them a 'right' to do so is one aspect of a fundamental principle of that law. That principle is that war (or armed conflict) is not an institution established by international law but a fact which the law has always recognized and attempted to contain. (. . .) Thus, each side in a conflict might lawfully kill the other's soldiers in open combat, not because international law gave it a right to kill but because international law left it alone to kill or not according to its ability and inclination.' C Greenwood, *The Relationship between ius ad bellum and ius in bello*,

freedom of action and requires that the actions taken shall be in conformity with the 'laws of humanity',[28] such as the prohibition of unnecessary suffering.[29] The balance between military necessity and humanitarian values forms the foundation of *ius in bello*.[30]

In addition to this general restriction imposed by the laws of humanity, the necessities of war are also inherently limited by the recognised object and purpose of warfare, namely the weakening of the armed force of the adversary.[31] This seems to be confirmed by Article 1 of the authoritative 1880 *Oxford Manual on the Law of War on Land*[32] adopted by the *Institut de Droit International*,[33] which states that '[t]he state of war does not

Review of International Studies, Vol 9, 1983, pp 228–9. Nowadays, the principle of military necessity serves also as a 'defense against excessive military force'. According to Baker, this doctrine 'has evolved from authorizing any barbaric act of armed conflict to being the measure of whether a military action may be sanctioned as an unacceptable act of war.' B Baker, *Legal Protections for the Environment in Times of Armed Conflict*, Virginia Journal of International Law, Vol 33, 1993, p 360. Compare, however, Schmitt and Rogers who either deny or ignore the primary meaning of the principle of necessity. Schmitt writes that military necessity operates in the paradigm that prohibits acts that are not militarily necessary. '[I]t is a principle of limitation, not authorization. In its legal sense, military necessity justifies nothing.' And Rogers refers to the threefold significance of military necessity in the laws of war. Firstly, military necessity prohibits any action which is not militarily necessary; secondly, military necessity sometimes allows for exceptions to its rules; thirdly, military necessity is an element of the principle of proportionality (rather than vice versa. EVK). MN Schmitt, *Green War: An Assessment of the Environmental Law of International Armed Conflict*, Yale Journal of International Law, Vol 22, 1997, p 54; APV Rogers, *Law on the Battlefield*, Manchester University Press, Manchester, 2004, p 6.

[28] The laws of humanity have also been recognised in the so-called 'Martens clause' that was first incorporated in the Preamble of Hague Convention (II) with respect to the Laws and Customs of War on Land, with annexed Regulations of 1899, and repeated in the Preamble of Hague Convention (IV) of 1907; Arts 63, respectively 62, 142, and 158 of the four Geneva Convention of 1949; Art 1(2) of Additional Protocol I of 1977; and in the Preamble of Additional Protocol II of 1977. Art 1(2) of Additional Protocol I provides: 'In cases not covered by this Protocol or by other international agreements, civilians and combatants remain under the protection and authority of the principles of international law derived from established custom, from the principles of humanity and from the dictates of public conscience.' On the relativity of 'humanity', see: F Kalshoven, *Arms, Armaments and International Law*, Recueil des Cours; Collected Courses of the Hague Academy of International Law, Vol 191, 1985-II, Martinus Nijhoff Publishers, Dordrecht, 1986, pp 208–13.

[29] The general prohibition of unnecessary suffering has been recognised and codified in Art 23(e) of the Hague Regulations and in Art 35(2) of Additional Protocol I.

[30] Similarly: J Gardam, *Necessity and Proportionality in Jus ad Bellum and Jus in Bello*, in: L Boisson de Chazournes, P Sands (Eds), *International Law, the International Court of Justice and Nuclear Weapons*, Cambridge University Press, Cambridge, 1999, pp 276, 282.

[31] The principle of necessity was recognised among others by Grotius in the 17th century and is reflected in Art 22 of the Hague Regulations and Art 35(1) of Additional Protocol I. The former states: 'The right of belligerents to adopt means of injuring the enemy is not unlimited' The latter states: 'In any armed conflict, the right of the Parties to the conflict to choose methods or means of warfare is not unlimited'

[32] Schindler, Toman (Eds), *The Laws of Armed Conflicts; A Collection of Conventions, Resolutions and Other Documents*, pp 35–48.

[33] The Institute was founded in Ghent in 1873 by Baron Rolin-Jacquemyns and Gustave Moynier together with 9 other international lawyers for the purpose of promoting the development of international law. It is a scientific society whose members are chosen from the international legal community and which was awarded the Nobel Peace Prize in 1904. The

admit of acts of violence, save between the armed forces of belligerent States' and by the United States Military Tribunal in Nuremberg. In the Trial of Wilhelm List and Others, or the 'Hostages Trial', the Tribunal stated:

> Military necessity has been invoked by the defendants as justifying the killing of innocent members of the population and the destruction of villages and towns in the occupied territory. *Military necessity permits a belligerent, subject to the laws of war, to apply any amount and kind of force to compel the complete submission of the enemy with the least possible expenditure of time, life and money*. In general, it sanctions measures by an occupant necessary to protect the safety of this forces and to facilitate the success of his operations. It permits the destruction of life of armed enemies and other persons whose destruction is incidentally unavoidable by the armed [conflict]; it allows the capturing of armed enemies and others of peculiar danger, but it does not permit the killing of innocent inhabitants for purposes of revenge of the satisfaction of a lust to kill. The destruction of property to be lawful must be imperatively demanded by the necessities of war. Destruction as an end in itself is a violation of International Law. There must be some reasonable connection between the destruction of property and the overcoming of the enemy forces[34] (emphasis added).

1.4 Principles of *Ius in Bello*

In terms of principles of *ius in bello*, it seems therefore that the 'necessities of war' are embodied in the 'principle of necessity', and that the 'principle of humanity' finds its origin in the 'laws of humanity'. Because the principle of necessity requires that military action shall only be employed in order to submit or weaken the military forces of the enemy,[35] distinction shall be made between military and civilian objects and collateral damage to civilian objects must be kept to a minimum. The former limitation is known as the principle of distinction or discrimination; the latter limita-

Oxford Manual was 'drafted by Gustave Moynier and unanimously adopted by the Institute.' Schindler, Toman (Eds), *The Laws of Armed Conflicts; A Collection of Conventions, Resolutions and Other Documents*, p 35. See also the Institute's website at <http://www.idi-iil.org/>.

[34] United States Military Tribunal (Nuremberg), *Case No 47; The Hostages Trial; Trial of Wilhelm List and Others; 8th Jul, 1947–19th Feb, 1948; The Judgment of the Tribunal; No (ix) The Plea of Military Necessity*, in: The United Nations War Crimes Commission, *Law Reports of Trials of War Criminals; Volume VIII*, His Majesty's Stationary Office, London, 1949, p 66.

[35] Compare Simonds' definition of the principle of necessity, based on United States military manuals and the above-quoted Nuremberg Hostages Case . '[T]he principle of necessity justifies measures not forbidden by international law which are indispensable for securing the prompt submission of the enemy with the least possible loss of economic and human resources.' SN Simonds, *Conventional Warfare and Environmental Protection: A Proposal for International Legal Reform*, Stanford Journal of International Law, Vol 29, 1992, p 169.

tion is better known as the principle of proportionality.[36] Although these principles are usually identified as original principles of *ius in bello*, it is therefore arguable that the principles of discrimination and proportionality ultimately find their origin in the principle of necessity.[37]

In addition to the principles of necessity and humanity, it may be possible to distinguish a third fundamental principle of *ius in bello*, namely the principle of environmental protection.[38] It is arguable that this principle

36 The obligations under the principle of proportionality should not be confused with the prohibition of unnecessary suffering which is a reflection of the principle of humanity and aims at the protection of combatants. Similarly, Y Dinstein, *The Conduct of Hostilities under the Law of International Armed Conflict*, Cambridge University Press, Cambridge, 2004, p 59. Schmitt, however, writes that the principle of humanity is 'theoretically implicit in both military necessity and proportionality' and discusses humanity in the context of possible negative consequences of means and methods of warfare on people in general. Schmitt, *Green War: An Assessment of the Environmental Law of International Armed Conflict*, pp 61–2. Also Gardam believes that 'proportionality is the basis of the prohibition of means and methods of warfare that are of a nature to cause unnecessary suffering or superfluous injury to combatants' in addition to 'the delimitation of civilian casualties in armed conflict'. Gardam, *Necessity and Proportionality in Jus ad Bellum and Jus in Bello*, in: Boisson de Chazournes, Sands (Eds), *International Law, the International Court of Justice and Nuclear Weapons*, pp 276, 284. And Verwey refers in his tribute to Röling that one of the 'new basic principles of modern *ius in bello* [that] ought to be recognized' was the principle of proportionality 'implying, in its *new* form, a prohibition on weapons and military acts which cause disproportionate, and not just unnecessary, suffering (emphasis added). WD Verwey, *Bert VA Röling; 1906–1985*, TMC Asser Instituut, The Hague, 1985. Compare also the discussion of the principles of necessity, proportionality, discrimination, humanity and unnecessary suffering by Higgins, Dissenting Opinion of Judge Higgins, Legality of the Threat or Use of Nuclear Weapons, Advisory Opinion, 8 Jul 1996, ICJ Reports 1996, p 226, at pp 584–9.

37 Compare, eg, Oeter who writes: 'Flowing from the general principle of "limited warfare" (limited to what is militarily absolutely necessary in order to achieve the military objectives) several sub-principles have developed historically, giving the rule of military necessity its specific contours.' These sub-principles are, according to Oeter, the principle of discrimination and the prohibition of unnecessary suffering; the principle of proportionality is regarded as a supplement to the principle of necessity. Oeter, *Methods and Means of Combat*, in: Fleck (Ed), *The Handbook of Humanitarian Law in Armed Conflicts*, pp 112, 112–14. Also Schmitt, *Green War: An Assessment of the Environmental Law of International Armed Conflict*, p 55. The ICRC Report that was submitted by the Secretary-General to the General Assembly seems to indicate a similar relationship between necessity and proportionality when it referred to the 'Balance between protection of the environment and military necessity (including the principle of proportionality)'. A/48/269, Report of the Secretary-General to the General Assembly on the Protection of the Environment in the Environment in Times of Armed Conflict, of 29 Jul 1993, p 14. Rogers and Schmitt, however, believe that the principle of proportionality is a balancing test between military and humanitarian interests. Rogers, *Law on the Battlefield*, p 17 and MN Schmitt, *War and the Environment: Fault Lines in the Prescriptive Landscape*, in: JE Austin, CE Bruch (Eds), *The Environmental Consequences of War*, Cambridge University Press, Cambridge, 2000, p 103. Dinstein, on the other hand, rejects any link between the principle of unnecessary suffering, and thus the principle of humanity, and the principle of proportionality. Dinstein, *The Conduct of Hostilities under the Law of International Armed Conflict*, p 59.

38 Also Röling recognised this principle as one of the 'new basic principles of modern *ius in bello* (. . .) (c) *the principle of the protection of the environment* (implying a prohibition on weapons and techniques with a destructive effect on the natural balance, or which introduce destructive and irrevocable ecological processes)'. Verwey, *Bert VA. Röling; 1906–1985*, p 15. See also WA Solf, in: M Bothe, KJ Partsch, WA Solf, *New Rules for Victims of Armed Conflicts; Commentary on the Two 1977 Protocols Additional to the Geneva Conventions of 1949*, Martinus Nijhoff Publishers, The Hague, 1982, p 193.

emerged during the 1970s stemming from a general and worldwide concern for the environment as reflected in the 1972 Stockholm Declaration:[39]

> Considering that the progress of civilization should have the effect of alleviating as much as possible the calamities of war,[40]

this principle of environmental protection or responsibility has influenced the development of the laws of war, similar to the principles of necessity and humanity. This principle is reflected in the conclusion in 1977 of a convention on so-called environmental modification techniques and in two environmental protection provisions in Additional Protocol I. These treaty rules were established in view of international concern for the use of certain means and methods of warfare during the war in Vietnam and since they cannot be reduced to either the principle of necessity, or the principle of humanity, the existence of a new and third fundamental principle of *ius in bello,* focused on environmental protection, must be assumed.

Rather than using the principles of necessity, humanity, environmental protection, and necessity's sub-principles of discrimination and proportionality as separate customary rules of international law,[41] it is preferable to consider them as the foundation of the modern laws of war.[42] They are the cornerstones that have shaped *ius in bello*[43] and should be regarded as framework concepts or umbrella norms from which specific customary and conventional rules of international law are derived.[44] This is not

[39] A/CONF.48/14/Rev1, Report of the United Nations Conference on the Human Environment, Stockholm, 5–16 Jun 1972, Declaration of the United Nations Conference on the Human Environment, United Nations, New York, 1973, pp 3–5. The Report was taken note of with satisfaction by the General Assembly by A/Res/2994 (XXVII), adopted on 15 Dec 1972, by 112 to 0, with 10 abstentions; United Nations Conference on the Human Environment.

[40] St Petersburg Declaration, preambular para 1.

[41] Compare, however, Roberts, who writes that each of the four principles underlying the laws of war—proportionality, discrimination, necessity and humanity—, 'strongly points to the conclusion that actions resulting in massive environmental destruction (. . .) would be questionable on many grounds, even in the absence of specific rules of war addressing environmental matters in detail. When the four principles are taken together, such a conclusion would seem inescapable.' A Roberts, *Environmental Issues in International Armed Conflict: The Experience of the 1991 Gulf War,* in: RJ Grunawalt, JE King, RS McClain (Eds), *Protection of the Environment during Armed Conflict,* International Law Studies 1996, Vol 69, Naval War College, Newport, RI, 1996, p 228.

[42] Compare L Low, D Hodgkinson, *Compensation for Wartime Environmental Damage: Challenges to International Law After the Gulf War,* Virginia Journal of International Law, Vol 35, 1995, pp 424–5.

[43] Compare the reference from Weeramantry to Dias' *Jurisprudence* from 1976 in his Dissenting Opinion in the Nuclear Weapons Opinion of the International Court of Justice upon request of the General Assembly. 'The rules of every legal order have an enveloping blanket of principles and doctrines as the earth is surrounded by air, and these not only influence the operation of rules but sometimes condition their very existence.' Dissenting Opinion of Judge Weeramantry, Legality of the Threat or Use of Nuclear Weapons, Advisory Opinion, 8 Jul 1996, ICJ Reports 1996, p 226, at p 493.

[44] Schwarzenberger chooses to identify four types of rules flowing from the 'tug-of-war' between the necessities of war and the laws of humanity. The first category consists of absolute prohibitions that do not conflict with the necessities of war. The second category

only more proper in view of the differences in meaning between 'principle' and 'rule',[45] but it also provides clarity and keeps the customary rules of the law of armed conflict flexible, as will be explained further below.

This seems to be confirmed by the International Court of Justice in the 1986 Nicaragua Case[46] and partly recognised in its 1996 Advisory Opinion on the threat or use of nuclear weapons, submitted upon request of the General Assembly (Nuclear Weapons Opinion (GA)).[47] In the Nicaragua Case the Court established that the Geneva Conventions were 'in some respects a development, and in other respects no more than the expression' of 'the fundamental general principles of humanitarian law'.[48] And although the Court referred in the Nuclear Weapons Opinion (GA) only to the principles of distinction and the principle of unnecessary suffering,[49] and characterised them as 'intransgressible principles of international

'sets limitations to warfare in cases in which considerations of civilization demand priority over military interests.' The third category consist of rules that form 'a true compromise between the requirements of civilization and the necessities of war' such as the prohibition of explosive ammunition below 400 grams under the St Petersburg Declaration. The fourth category is 'a formal compromise between the standard of civilization and the necessities of war. Here, in fact, the rule of force is supreme.' These rules 'expressly proclaim the necessities of war as overriding or are emasculated by 'as far as possible' clauses'. Schwarzenberger, *International Law; As Applied by International Courts and Tribunals; Volume II; The Law of Armed Conflict*, pp 10–13.

[45] *Collins Dictionary* defines 'principle', among other things, as 'a fundamental or general truth or law', 'the essence of something', 'a source or fundamental cause; origin', and as 'an underlying or guiding theory or belief'. And *Black's Law Dictionary* defines 'principle' as follows: 'A fundamental truth or doctrine, as of law; a comprehensive rule or doctrine which furnishes a basis or origin for others; (. . .). That which constitutes the essence of a body or its constituent parts. (. . .).' A 'rule' is primarily defined by *Black's Law Dictionary* as '[a]n established standard, guide, or regulation' and by *Collins Dictionary* as 'an authoritative regulation or direction concerning method or procedure (. . .)'. *Collins Dictionary*, HarperCollins Publishers, Glasgow, 1998, pp 1229, 1345; HC. Black (et al), *Black's Law Dictionary*, West Publishing, St Paul, MN, 1991, pp 828, 925.

[46] Military and Paramilitary Activities in and against Nicaragua (Nicaragua v United States of America), Merits, Judgment, 27 Jun 1986, ICJ Reports 1986, p 14.

[47] Legality of the Threat or Use of Nuclear Weapons, Advisory Opinion, 8 Jul 1996, ICJ Reports 1996, p 226.

[48] Military and Paramilitary Activities in and against Nicaragua (*Nicaragua v United States of America*), Merits, Judgment, 27 Jun 1986, ICJ Reports 1986, p 14, para 218, p 113.

[49] The first principle 'is aimed at the protection of the civilian population and civilian objects and establishes the distinction between combatants and non-combatants; States must never make civilians the object of attack and must consequently never use weapons that are incapable of distinguishing between civilian and military targets. According to the second principle, it is prohibited to cause unnecessary suffering to combatants: it is accordingly prohibited to use weapons causing them such harm or uselessly aggravating their suffering. In application of that second principle, States do not have unlimited freedom of choice of means in the weapons they use.' Legality of the Threat or Use of Nuclear Weapons, Advisory Opinion, 8 Jul 1996, ICJ Reports 1996, p 226, para 78, at p 257. The Court also refers in relation to both principles to the Martens Clause, referred to above, as laid down most recently in Art 1(2) Additional Protocol I. There is no reference to the principles of necessity, proportionality or humanity.

customary law',[50] it stated that the principles of distinction and unnecessary suffering were 'cardinal principles contained in the texts' and constitute 'the fabric of humanitarian law'. Subsequently:

> [i]n conformity with the aforementioned principles, humanitarian law, at a very early stage, prohibited certain types of weapons either because of their indiscriminate effect on combatants and civilians or because of the unnecessary suffering caused to combatants, that is to say, a harm greater than that unavoidable to achieve legitimate military objectives.[51]

1.5 Terminology

The terminology used in this area of international law is diverse and has developed over time. Before 1949, this area of international law was usually designated as 'the laws and customs of war' or by the Latin phrase *ius in bello*.[52] After 1949, it is more accurate to refer to the law of armed conflict, since the common Article 2 of the four 1949 Geneva Conventions[53] requires the existence of an 'armed conflict' for the applicability of the Conventions. Unlike the existence of a state of war, the existence of an international armed conflict is only determined by factual circumstances

[50] Legality of the Threat or Use of Nuclear Weapons, Advisory Opinion, 8 Jul 1996, ICJ Reports 1996, p 226, para 79, at p 257. In the 2004 Wall Opinion, the Court observes that 'these rules incorporate obligations which are essentially of an *erga omnes* character'. Legal Consequences of the Construction of a Wall in the Occupied Palestinian Territory, Advisory Opinion, 9 Jul 2004, ICJ Reports 2004, para 157, p 61.

[51] Legality of the Threat or Use of Nuclear Weapons, Advisory Opinion, 8 Jul 1996, ICJ Reports 1996, p 226, para 78, at p 257.

[52] The term *ius in bello* must be clearly distinguished from the term *ius ad bellum*, which refers to the law on the use of force and regulates under which circumstances a state may resort to the use of force. Although both terms appear to be of Roman origin, 'they were only coined at the time of the League of Nations and were rarely used in doctrine or practice until after the Second World War, in the late 1940s to be precise.' Both terms may well be coined by Kunz in 1934 and were adopted by Verdross in 1937, and by Guggenheim after World War II. From earliest times until after the Middle Ages, emphasis had always been on the reasons for going to war under the just war doctrine; there was no general *ius in bello*. The rights and duties of warring parties depended on their just cause. Kolb: 'A belligerent without a just cause had no rights; he was simply a criminal who might be executed.' Only after warfare became a sovereign right, or an attribute of warfare, emphasis shifted to the regulation of warfare. R. Kolb, *Origin of the twin terms jus ad bellum/jus in bello*, International Review of the Red Cross, 1997. Also through <http://www.icrc.org/>. Compare also Kolb's reference to the variety of terms used for the regulation of warfare before the term *ius in bello* became customary in the 20th century.

[53] Geneva Convention (I) for the Amelioration of the Condition of the Wounded and Sick in Armed Forces in the Field, signed on 12 Aug 1949, entered into force on 21 Oct 1950, UNTS, Vol 75, No 970; Geneva Convention (II) for the Amelioration of the Condition of Wounded, Sick and Shipwrecked Members of Armed Forces at Sea, signed on 12 Aug 1949, entered into force on 21 Oct 1950, UNTS, Vol 75, No 971; Geneva Convention (III) relative to the Treatment of Prisoners of War, signed on 12 Aug 1949, entered into force on 21 Oct 1950, UNTS, Vol 75, No 972; Geneva Convention (IV) relative to the Protection of Civilian Persons in Time of War, signed on 12 Aug 1949, entered into force on 21 Oct 1950, UNTS, Vol 75, No 973.

and does not depend on an official declaration of war. Although a declaration of war used to be self-evident, the Hague Peace Conference of 1907 adopted a Convention Relative to the Opening of Hostilities,[54] after Japan had attacked Russia by surprise in 1904. In Article 1 of this Convention, the Contracting Powers recognize:

> that hostilities between themselves must not commence without previous and explicit warning, in the form either of a declaration of war, or of an ultimatum with conditional declaration of war.

In addition to this more accurate designation of this area of international law since 1949, the increasing importance of the protection of the victims of war since 1949, in particular relating to disabled armed forces and civilians, has led to an increasing popularity of the name 'international humanitarian law'. This development was reinforced by the adoption of the two Additional Protocols to the 1949 Geneva Conventions in 1977 by the Diplomatic Conference on the Reaffirmation and Development of International Humanitarian Law Applicable in Armed Conflicts that had convened in Geneva between 1974 and 1977. Although in fact only dealing with a specific area of *ius in bello*[55]—the protection of victims of armed conflict—the designation 'international humanitarian law' has nowadays become equivalent to the more general designations.[56]

In literature, all terms are used interchangeably. Kalshoven, Zegveld and the ICRC, for example, refer to 'international humanitarian law';[57] Dinstein, Green, and Schindler and Toman refer to the 'law of armed conflict' or 'international law of armed conflict';[58] Detter, Roberts and Guelff,

[54] Hague Convention (III) Relative to the Opening of Hostilities, signed on 18 Oct 1907, entered into force on 26 Jan 1910, AJIL, Vol 2, No 1/2, Supplement: Official Documents, 1908, p 85.

[55] Roberts and Guelff, for example, refer to the law of neutrality that does not have a humanitarian character. Roberts, Guelff, *Documents on the Laws of War*, p 2. Also C Greenwood, *Historical Development and Legal Basis*, in: D Fleck (Ed), *The Handbook of Humanitarian Law in Armed Conflicts*, Oxford University Press, Oxford, 1995, pp 8–10.

[56] Compare the International Court of Justice in the Nuclear Weapons Advisory Opinion upon request of the General Assembly. According to the Court, both 'branches of the law applicable in armed conflict [namely Hague and Geneva Law] have become so closely interrelated that they are considered to have gradually formed one single complex system, known today as international humanitarian law.' Legality of the Threat or Use of Nuclear Weapons, Advisory Opinion, 8 Jul 1996, ICJ Reports 1996, p 226, at p 256.

[57] F Kalshoven, L Zegveld, *Constraints on the Waging of War; An Introduction to International Humanitarian Law*, International Committee of the Red Cross, Geneva, 2001; J -M Henckaerts, L Doswald-Beck (Eds), *Customary International Humanitarian Law; Vol I: Rules*, International Committee of the Red Cross, Cambridge University Press, Cambridge, 2005; J -M Henckaerts, L Doswald-Beck (Eds), *Customary International Humanitarian Law; Vol II: Practice; Part 1*, International Committee of the Red Cross, Cambridge University Press, Cambridge, 2005.

[58] Y Dinstein, *The Conduct of Hostilities under the Law of International Armed Conflict*, Cambridge University Press, Cambridge, 2004; L C Green, *The Contemporary Law of Armed Conflict*, Manchester University Press, Manchester, 2000; D Schindler, J Toman (Eds), *The Laws of Armed Conflicts; A Collection of Conventions, Resolutions and Other Documents*, Martinus Nijhoff Publishers, Dordrecht, 1988.

and Solf prefer the designation 'law of war';[59] and others make a combination, such as Delissen and Tanja as well as Fleck who refer to 'international humanitarian law of armed conflict'.[60] In this section, the terms *ius in bello*, law or laws of war, law of armed conflict and international humanitarian law are used most of time.

1.6 Format

This chapter deals with the protection of the environment during international armed conflict under *ius in bello*. For the benefit of clarity, this section distinguishes between direct protection of the environment and indirect protection of the environment, the difference being the intention of the drafters or the *ratio* behind the specific rule. Rules that directly protect the environment were intended to do so by the drafters; rules that indirectly protect the environment were not intended to do so, but may nevertheless be conducive to environmental protection. Although indirect protection of the environment may provide significant protection, emphasis in this section lies on rules that are intended to protect the environment.

The first part focuses on direct protection under *ius in bello*, both under conventional and customary law (section 2). The second part seeks to identify rules indirectly protecting the environment under *ius in bello* by reference to the protection of civilian objects under the laws of war as well as to protection of neutral territory under the law of neutrality (section 3).

2—DIRECT PROTECTION

2.1 Introduction

There are only few rules under *ius in bello* which deal specifically with the protection of the environment during international armed conflict. Because the general principles of law as referred to in Article 38(1)(c) of the Statute of the International Court of Justice tend to play only a marginal

[59] I Detter, *The Law of War*, Cambridge University Press, Cambridge, 2000; A Roberts, R Guelff, *Documents on the Laws of War*, Oxford University Press, Oxford, 2000. According to Almond, Solf 'insisted that the law regulating states in war was the law of war and avoided the ambiguous expression "international humanitarian law" because he saw that he law of war itself was aimed at reducing the "unnecessary suffering" that arises out of the hostilities.' H H Almond, Jr, *Waldemar Solf (1913–1987)*, American Journal of International Law, Vol 82, 1988, p 563.

[60] A J M Delissen, G J Tanja (Eds), *Humanitarian Law of Armed Conflict; Challenges Ahead; Essays in Honour of Frits Kalshoven*, Martinus Nijhoff Publishers, Dordrecht, 1991; D Fleck (Ed), *The Handbook of Humanitarian Law in Armed Conflicts*, Oxford University Press, Oxford, 1995.

role in the establishment of legal rights and duties under public international law, the focus of attention will be on international conventions and international custom as primary sources, with additional reference to judicial decisions and literature as subsidiary sources of international law. Because conventional and treaty law are independent sources of public international law, they will be discussed separately in sections 2.2 and 2.3.

2.2 Treaty Law

2.2.1 Introduction

Direct protection of the environment in written form is provided only by four relatively recent conventions. These are, in chronological order, the 1977 Convention on the Prohibition of Military or Any Other Hostile Use of Environmental Modification Techniques (ENMOD),[61] the 1977 Additional Protocol I to the 1949 Geneva Conventions (Additional Protocol I),[62] the 1981 Certain Conventional Weapons Convention, in particular the Convention's Third Protocol on Incendiary Weapons (the Incendiary Weapons Protocol),[63] and the 1998 Statute of the International Criminal Court (the ICC Statute).[64] Although all four conventions make use of similar terminology, they were concluded for different purposes and must therefore be dealt with and interpreted separately and independently.

[61] Convention on the Prohibition of Military or any Other Hostile Use of Environmental Modification Techniques, opened for signature on 18 May 1977, entered into force on, 5 Oct 1978, UNTS, Vol 1108, No 17119.

[62] Protocol Additional to the Geneva Conventions of 12 Aug 1949, and Relating to the Protection of Victims of International Armed Conflicts, opened for signature on 12 Dec 1977, entered into force on 7 Dec 1978, UNTS, Vol 1125, No 17512.

[63] Protocol on Prohibitions or Restrictions on the Use of Incendiary Weapons (Protocol III) to the Convention on Prohibitions or Restrictions on the Use of Certain Conventional Weapons Which May be Deemed To Be Excessively Injurious or To Have Indiscriminate Effects, opened for signature on 10 Apr 1981, entered into force on 2 Dec 1983, UNTS, Vol 1342, No 22495. Some authors refer to the Certain Conventional Weapons Convention as the Weaponry Convention, the UN Weapons Convention, the Weapons Convention, the Inhumane Weapons Convention or the Dubious Conventional Weapons Convention. Also writings differ as to the year that is attached to the Convention. Some authors refer to 1980 as the year in which the text of the Convention was adopted; others refer to 1981 as the year in which the treaty was opened for signature. The Convention itself only provides that the Convention is opened for signature on 10 Apr 1981. Vierdag refers in his article on the conclusion of multilateral treaties to two examples in the practice of the United Nations in which the date on which the Convention is opened for signature is different from the date of adoption. E.W. Vierdag, *The Time of the 'Conclusion' of a Multilateral Treaty: Article 30 of the Vienna Convention on the Law of Treaties and Related Provisions*, British Year Book of International Law, Vol 59, 1988, pp 78–9.

[64] Rome Statute of the International Criminal Court, opened for signature on 17 Jul 1998, entered into force 1 Jul 2002, UNTS, Vol 2187, No 38544.

2.2.2 The Environmental Modification Convention

2.2.2.1 Introduction

ENMOD was the final result of primarily bilateral negotiations between the United States and the Soviet Union against the background of the Vietnam War, and against the background of a growing national and international concern for the environment.[65] In the early 1970s, both states were studying and actually developing sophisticated techniques to manipulate environmental processes, such as earthquakes and precipitation, in order to be able to use these processes as possible weapons of war, and the United States is supposed to have actually applied one of these techniques in Vietnam.[66] By manipulating climate conditions through 'cloud-seeding'[67], it had attempted to induce rainfall in order to flood and muddy the supply routes from North Vietnam that curved through the woods, and which were vital for the provisioning of the North-Vietnamese forces. This rain-making and other large-scale destruction of vegetation in Vietnam by chemical and physical means provoked national and international concern for the consequences for the world's ecological system, and raised voices calling for the prohibition of such means of warfare.[68]

[65] Although international conventions regarding protection of the environment had been adopted as from the beginning of the 20th century, the attitude of national governments and states changed dramatically at the end of the 1960s with the United Nations Conference on the Human Environment in Stockholm in 1972 as a turning or rather starting point for international environmental law. A Kiss, D Shelton, *International Environmental Law*, Transnational Publishers, Ardsley, NY, 2004, pp 39–66. For the Stockholm Declaration, see: A/CONF.48/14/Rev1, Report of the United Nations Conference on the Human Environment, Stockholm, 5–16 Jun 1972, Declaration of the United Nations Conference on the Human Environment, United Nations, New York, 1973, pp 3–5.

[66] According to Chinese sources, cloud-seeding or rainmaking was already applied by the United States and elsewhere in the 1950s. E Cody, *Chinese Rainmakers Competing for Clouds; Widespread Drought Leads to Regional Rivalries*, The Washington Post, 2 Aug 2004.

[67] Cloud-seeding can be carried out by adding silver-iodide or liquid nitrogen to clouds that will induce freezing and subsequently rainfall because of the weight of the particles. There is no ensuing chemical pollution. The technique is used by a number of states for peaceful purposes. The People's Republic of China recently resorted to cloud-seeding by silver-iodide to induce rainfall in order to bring relief to the city of Shanghai during the heat wave that lasted for weeks during the summer of 2004 (NRC Handelsblad of 18 Aug 2004) and again over Beijing in May 2006. As a matter of fact, the People's Republic of China has an extensive government program for weather modification and has meanwhile become 'the world's leading rainmaker, using aircraft, rockets, and even antiaircraft guns to seed the clouds for precious moisture.' Cody, *Chinese Rainmakers Competing for Clouds; Widespread Drought Leads to Regional Rivalries*, The Washington Post, 2 Aug 2004. Thailand has used similar techniques since 1956. NRC Handelsblad of 19 Mar 2005.

[68] H Blix, *Arms Control Treaties Aimed at Reducing the Military Impact on the Environment*, in: J Makarczyk (Ed), *Essays in International Law in Honour of Judge Manfred Lachs*, Martinus Nijhoff Publishers, The Hague, 1984, p 708; D Bodansky, *Legal Regulation of the Effects of Military Activity on the Environment*, Environmental Research of the Federal Ministry of the Environment, Nature Conservation and Nuclear Safety; Research Report 201 18 103; UBA—FB 000499—On Behalf of the Federal Environmental Agency, Erich Schmidt Verlag, Berlin, 2003, p 29; J Goldblat, *Arms Control; The New Guide to Negotiations and Agreements*,

2.2.2.2 Drafting History

The United States Government unilaterally renounced the use of climate modification techniques for hostile purposes in 1972, and in 1973 US Congress called for an international agreement prohibiting environmental modification techniques as methods of war.[69] It was the Soviet Union, however, that took the diplomatic initiative. In 1974, it transmitted a draft treaty to the General Assembly,[70] which then referred the issue to the Conference of the Committee on Disarmament in Geneva.[71]

The Conference of the Committee on Disarmament was one in a chain of successors to the Ten-Nation Disarmament Committee,[72] established in 1959 to provide for a negotiation forum for arms control and disarmament measures outside the framework of the United Nations. It may seem peculiar that the General Assembly chose to refer the item to this forum rather

International Peace Research Institute, Oslo; Stockholm International Peace Research Institute; SAGE Publications, London, 2002, p 158; L Juda, *Negotiating a treaty on environmental modification warfare: the convention on environmental warfare and its impact upon arms control negotiations*, International Organization, Vol 32, 1978, pp 976–7; L Lijnzaad, G J Tanja, *Protection of the Environment in Times of Armed Conflict: The Iraq-Kuwait War*, Netherlands International Law Review, Vol 40, 1993, p 186; Roberts, Guelff, *Documents on the Laws of War*, p 407; B K Schafer, *The Relationship between the International Laws of Armed Conflict and Environmental Protection: The Need to Reevaluate what Types of Conduct are Permissible during Hostilities*, California Western International Law Journal, Vol19, 1989, p 312; Schmitt, *Green War: An Assessment of the Environmental Law of International Armed Conflict*, p 82; M N Schmitt, *Humanitarian Law and the Environment*, Denver Journal of International Law and Policy, Vol 28, 2000, p 268; Tarasofsky, *Legal Protection of the Environment during International Armed Conflict*, p 43.

[69] Roberts, Guelff, *Documents on the Laws of War*, p 407; United States Arms Control and Disarmament Agency, *Arms control and Disarmament Agreements; Texts and Histories of the Negotiations*, US Government Printing Office, Washington, D.C., 1996, p 153.

[70] The move was surprising, because in 1974, the United States and the Soviet Union had agreed to discuss the issue bilaterally. See the Joint Statement by the United States and the Soviet Union of 3 Jul 1974, through: <http://www.sunshine-project.org/enmod/primer.html>. Juda gives two possible explanations for the Soviet Union's initiative. Firstly, they may have thought that the United States was not serious to reach agreement and secondly, they may have thought it was time for another 'dramatic Soviet initiative in the General Assembly' and that this initiative would embarrass the United States. Juda, *Negotiating a treaty on environmental modification warfare: the convention on environmental warfare and its impact upon arms control negotiations*, pp 977–8.

[71] A/Res/3264 (XXIX), adopted on 9 Dec 1974, by 126 to 0, with 5 abstentions, on the prohibition of action to influence the environment and climate for military and other purposes incompatible with the maintenance of international security, human well-being and health; Annex Draft Convention on the Prohibition of Action to Influence the Environment and Climate for Military and Other Purposes Incompatible with the Maintenance of International Security, Human Well-Being and Health

[72] The Ten-Nation Disarmament Committee (1959–1960) was succeeded by the Eighteen-Nation Committee on Disarmament (1961–1969), the Conference of the Committee on Disarmament (1969–1978), the Committee on Disarmament (1979–1983), and the Conference on Disarmament (1983), which is still active and consists of 66 member states. J Goldblat, *Arms Control; A Guide to Negotiations and Agreements*, International Peace Research Institute, Oslo, SAGE Publications, London, 1994, p 8; Goldblat, *Arms Control; The New Guide to Negotiations and Agreements*, p 14; through <http://www.unog.ch/> and <http://disarmament.un.org/>.

than the Diplomatic Conference on the Reaffirmation and Development of International Humanitarian Law Applicable in Armed Conflicts, which was also convened in Geneva upon the initiative of the International Committee of the Red Cross (ICRC) to prepare protocols additional to the 1949 Geneva Conventions.[73] Despite references to disarmament in ENMOD's Preamble,[74] the use of environmental modification techniques as methods of warfare is typically a topic that belongs to the laws of war, and should therefore have been discussed by the Diplomatic Conference, whereas arms control and disarmament measures fall under the laws of peace,[75] and deal with the possession of weapons.[76]

The reason for referral to the Conference of the Committee on Disarmament, however, may lie in the fact that the original Soviet proposal did not only intend to prohibit the use of environmental manipulation methods, but also 'not *to develop* meteorological, geophysical or any other scientific or technological means of influencing the environment' (emphasis added).[77] And prohibiting the development of a specific weapon of warfare is preeminently a disarmament measure, comparable to the 1972 Biological Weapons Convention[78] and the 1993 Chemical Weapons Convention.[79] Both Conventions were negotiated and drafted within the

[73] It should be noted that environmental modification techniques were briefly discussed at one of the Conferences of Government Experts in the early 1970s prior to the Diplomatic Conference. Solf, in: Bothe, Partsch, Solf, *New Rules for Victims of Armed Conflicts; Commentary on the Two 1977 Protocols Additional to the Geneva Conventions of 1949*, p 344.

[74] Preambular paras 1 and 2.

[75] Goldblat believes that prevention of the use of environmental modification techniques could be valuable both for arms control measures and for the law of armed conflict. Goldblat, *Arms Control; The New Guide to Negotiations and Agreements*, p 161.

[76] According to Mrs Thorsson, of the Swedish delegation in the First Committee of the United Nations General Assembly, '[t]he convention in fact does not prescribe any form of disarmament. It does prohibit certain use. But it does not envisage the elimination from the arsenals of States of the technique, or rather devices, necessary to carry out the technique. Neither does it prevent experiments with such techniques.' CCD/479, 24 Feb 1976, Sweden, Comments on draft convention on the 'Prohibition of Military or any other hostile use of environmental modification techniques' (CCD/471, CCD/472) made in a statement by Mrs Inga Thorsson in the First Committee of the United Nations General Assembly, 14 Nov 1975, in: A/31/27, Report of the Conference of the Committee on Disarmament; Vol II, United Nations, New York, p 7.

[77] Art I of the Draft Convention on the Prohibition of Action to Influence the Environment and Climate for Military and Other Purposes Incompatible with the Maintenance of International Security, Human Well-Being and Health, Annex to A/Res/3264 (XXIX). Goldblat and Juda incompletely write that the original Soviet proposal only prohibits the use of all environmental modification techniques. Goldblat, *Arms Control; The New Guide to Negotiations and Agreements*, p 160; Juda, *Negotiating a treaty on environmental modification warfare: the convention on environmental warfare and its impact upon arms control negotiations*, p 978.

[78] Convention on the Prohibition of the Development, Production and Stockpiling of Bacteriological (Biological) and Toxic Weapons and on Their Destruction, opened for signature on 10 Apr 1972, entered into force on 26 Mar 1975, UNTS, Vol 1015, No 14860.

[79] Convention on the Prohibition of the Development, Production, Stockpiling and Use of Chemical Weapons and on Their Destruction, together with Annexes, opened for signature on 13 Jan 1993, entered into force on 29 Apr 1997, UNTS, Vol 1975, No 33757.

framework of this negotiation forum and must primarily be regarded as disarmament agreements, because they prohibit the development, production and stockpiling of these weapons while the Chemical Weapons Convention also regulates the destruction of existing stockpiles.[80]

The final version of ENMOD, however, only prohibits the use of environmental modification techniques and should therefore be characterised as a law-of-war agreement. Unfortunately, commentators and States Parties generally keep referring to ENMOD as an arms limitation and disarmament agreement,[81] as evidenced, for example, by the Final Declarations of both ENMOD's Review Conferences.[82]

The United States and the Soviet Union came to an agreement relatively easily and relatively fast. They submitted identical proposals to the Conference of the Committee on Disarmament in 1975,[83] had their proposals accepted after modification,[84] adopted by the Conference in 1976 and approved and referred to all States for signature and ratification by the General Assembly on 10 December 1976.[85] Currently the treaty has 88

[80] The use of biological and chemical weapons had already been prohibited by the 1925 Geneva Protocol. Geneva Protocol for the Prohibition of the use in War of Asphyxiating, Poisonous or Other Gases, and of Bacteriological Methods of Warfare, signed 17 Jun 1925, entered into force on 8 Feb 1928, AJIL, Vol 25, No 2, Supplement: Official Documents, 1931, p 94. The treaty was a protocol to the 1925 Convention for the Supervision of the International trade in Arms and Ammunition and in Implements of War that never entered into force.

[81] The Report of the United States Department of Defense to Congress after the 1990–1991 Gulf War, however, refers to ENMOD as a law of war treaty. United States Department of Defence, *Conduct of the Persian Gulf War; Final Report to Congress; Pursuant to Title V of the Persian Gulf Conflict Supplemental Authorization and Personnel Benefits Act of 1991 (Public Law 102–25)*, US Government Printing Office, Washington, DC, 1992, p 606. Also published as: United States Department of Defence, *Report to Congress on the Conduct of the Persian Gulf War—Appendix on the Role of the law of War*, in: International Legal Materials, Vol 31, 1992, p 616.

[82] ENMOD/CONF.I/13/II; First Review Conference of the Parties to the Convention on the Prohibition of Military or Any Other Hostile Use of Environmental Modification Techniques; Final Document; Part II; Final Declaration; ENMOD/CONF.II/12/II; Second Review Conference of the Parties to the Convention on the Prohibition of Military or Any Other Hostile Use of Environmental Modification Techniques; Final Document; Part II; Final Declaration. Compare also Sandoz, Swinaraski, Zimmerman (Eds), *Commentary on the Additional Protocols; of 8 Jun 1977 to the Geneva Conventions of 12 Aug 1949*, p 420. The Commentary is also available through <http://www.icrc.org/>.

[83] According to the Report of the Conference of the Committee on Disarmament; Vol I, on the Conference's deliberations and submitted to the General Assembly and the Disarmament Commission, the proposals are registered under CCD/471 and CCD/472. A/31/27, Report of the Conference of the Committee on Disarmament; Vol I, United Nations, New York, p 61.The submission of identical proposals to the Conference was noted with satisfaction by the General Assembly by Resolution 3475 (XXX), adopted without a vote on 11 Dec 1975.

[84] See for the comments on the US-SU draft convention, both general and per Article, and both within the framework of a plenary session and in the Working Group established on 1 Jul 1976 for informal deliberations on the draft convention. A/31/27, Report of the Conference of the Committee on Disarmament; Vol I, United Nations, New York, pp 1–5, 61–96.

[85] A/Res/31/72, adopted on 10 Dec 1976, by 96 to 8, with 30 abstentions, on the Convention on the Prohibition of Military or any Other Hostile Use of Environmental Modification Techniques; Annex: Convention on the Prohibition of Military or Any Other Hostile Use of Environmental Modification Techniques.

States Parties, including six states that possess nuclear weapons: the People's Republic of China, the Russian Federation, the United Kingdom, the United States, India, and Pakistan.[86]

The relatively low number of states parties is probably due to the fact that the prohibited means and methods of warfare did not and still do not belong to the regular military arsenals of most states. On the contrary, only a few highly industrialised states are believed to be capable of development; only the United States and the Soviet Union are believed to have investigated their military relevance; and, apparently, only the United States has actually used one of those methods during international armed conflict. And besides, the potential military value of these weapon techniques was and still is debatable. That is probably also the reason why the United States and the Soviet Union reached agreement so easily at a time when it was difficult for both of them to reach agreement on matters of strategic arms control: they did not have to sacrifice much, it would not affect their security interests, and it made a good impression on the general public.

ENMOD consists of 10 Articles and one Annex to the Convention on the establishment of a consultative committee of experts. The first two Articles contain the substantive obligations of ENMOD. The other eight Articles deal with the peaceful use of environmental modification techniques,[87] implementation, consultation, enforcement, duration, amendment, review and some treaty-technical matters. Not part of the Convention, but important and relevant as to its interpretation are four 'Understandings Regarding the Convention' relating to Articles I, II, III, and VIII. These Understandings were included in the Report that was prepared by the Conference of the Committee on Disarmament and sent to the General

[86] On the negotiating history of ENMOD, see among others: Blix, *Arms Control Treaties Aimed at Reducing the Military Impact on the Environment*, in: Makarczyk, *Essays in International Law in Honour of Judge Manfred Lachs*, pp 708–9; Lijnzaad, Tanja, *Protection of the Environment in Times of Armed Conflict: The Iraq-Kuwait War*, p 186.

[87] The States Parties realised 'that the use of environmental modification techniques for peaceful purposes could improve the interrelationship of man and nature and contribute to the preservation and improvement of the environment for the benefit of present and future generation[.]' ENMOD, preambular para 5. The Understanding Relating to Article III, however, seems to indicate the possibility that certain uses of environmental modification techniques may not be in accordance with generally recognised principles and applicable rules of international law. The Understanding states that it does not deal with the question whether or not a given environmental modification technique is in accordance with existing rules of international law. Goldblat gives a few examples of environmental modification techniques that may have peaceful applications such as cloud dispersion at airports, the manipulation of storms to limit damages from hurricanes and rainmaking to relieve drought or to extinguish forest fires. Goldblat, *Arms Control; The New Guide to Negotiations and Agreements*, p 161. As was observed above, the People's Republic of China is said to have an extensive government program for rainmaking. Cody, *Chinese Rainmakers Competing for Clouds; Widespread Drought Leads to Regional Rivalries*, The Washington Post, 2 Aug 2004. The provision reminds of Art IV of the Treaty on the Non-Proliferation of Nuclear Weapons, opened for signature on 1 Jul 1968, entered into force 5 Mar 1970, UNTS, Vol 729, No 10485.

Assembly and the Disarmament Commission in 1976.[88] Because of their importance in the interpretation of specific terms, their status will be discussed separately further below.

2.2.2.3 Article I ENMOD

> Recognizing (. . .) that military or any other hostile use of such techniques could have effects extremely harmful to human welfare:

and wishing 'to eliminate the dangers to mankind from such use,'[89] the States Parties undertake in Article I(1) 'not to engage in military or any other hostile use of environmental modification techniques'. In paragraph 2, they agree not to assist, encourage or induce other states or international organisations to engage in these activities, in order to prevent circumvention. Environmental modification techniques are defined in Article II as:

> any technique for changing—through the deliberate manipulation of natural processes—the dynamics, composition or structure of the Earth, including its biota, lithosphere, hydrosphere and atmosphere, or of outer space.

Biota means plant and animal life, and the lithosphere, hydrosphere and atmosphere refer respectively to the earth's ground, its waters and its air.[90]

In order to clarify the definition of Article II, the drafters or 'the Committee'[91] included an illustrative list of 'phenomena that could be caused by the use of environmental modification techniques' in the 'Understanding Relating to Article II'. These include:

> earthquakes, tsunamis; an upset in the ecological balance of a region; changes in weather patterns (clouds, precipitation, cyclones of various types and tornadic storms); changes in climate patterns; changes in ocean currents; changes in the state of the ozone layer; and changes in the state of the ionosphere.

Tsunamis are large and destructive sea waves caused by submarine earthquakes or volcanic eruptions; the ozone layer is:

[88] A/31/27, Report of the Conference of the Committee on Disarmament; Vol I and II, United Nations, New York. United States Arms Control and Disarmament Agency, *Arms control and Disarmament Agreements; Texts and Histories of the Negotiations*, p 158; <http://disarmament2.un.org/TreatyStatus.nsf>.

[89] ENMOD, preambular paras 6–7. These paragraphs refer to the effect of the use of these environmental modification techniques on human welfare and mankind which seems to indicate that ENMOD is essentially anthropocentric of character.

[90] *Collins Dictionary*, HarperCollins Publishers, Glasgow, 1998, pp 95, 758, 905.

[91] The 'Committee' refers to the Conference of the Committee on Disarmament. See A/31/27, Report of the Conference of the Committee on Disarmament; Vol I, United Nations, New York, p 1. See also, Blix, *Arms Control Treaties Aimed at Reducing the Military Impact on the Environment*, in: Makarczyk, *Essays in International Law in Honour of Judge Manfred Lachs*, p 709; I. Detter, *The Law of War*, Cambridge University Press, Cambridge, 2000, p 270; Juda, *Negotiating a treaty on environmental modification warfare: the convention on environmental warfare and its impact upon arms control negotiations*, p 983, who take this interpretation for granted.

> the region of the stratosphere with the highest concentration of ozone molecules [(O_3)] which by absorbing high-energy solar ultraviolet radiation protects organisms on earth

and, the ionosphere is that part of the atmosphere extending from 80 km up to 150 km.[92]

It is not easy to see how these phenomena could be used as actual weapons of warfare. The majority have a high futuristic and science-fiction caliber,[93] and according to Dinstein, the techniques do not even reflect existing capabilities.[94] The potential military relevance of changing weather patterns became clear during the Vietnam War, and it is also not difficult to imagine the potential military value of the ability to create earthquakes or tsunamis. More difficult to grasp, however, is the usefulness of changing the composition of the Earth's biota in order to upset the ecological balance of a region. The delegations of the United States and the Soviet Union indeed admitted that the list contained examples that were only theoretically conceivable, but that 'it was important to preclude their use before they were perfected'; and that, even though 'some of the techniques listed were inconceivable today, they could be rapidly developed.' They also stated that the list was the result of careful consideration by many scientific specialists of all the possible natural phenomena that humans could cause or influence.[95]

After the 1990–1991 Gulf War, a number of states appeared to be unhappy with the scope of Articles I and II in view of the burning of oil wells and the spilling of oil in the Persian Gulf. Jordan attempted to initiate a revision of the law on environmental protection during international armed conflict through the United Nations General Assembly, among other things because ENMOD 'was revealed as being painfully inadequate during the Gulf conflict.'[96] For that purpose, it requested the inclusion of

[92] *Collins Dictionary*, pp 1641, 1112. *Collins Dictionary* refers to the ionosphere as that part of the atmosphere extending from 60 km to some 1000 km altitude, where there is a high concentration of free electrons as a result of ionising radiation coming from outer space. *Collins Dictionary*, p 809.

[93] See also: CCD/479, 24 Feb 1976, Sweden, Comments on draft convention on the 'Prohibition of Military or any other hostile use of environmental modification techniques' (CCD/471, CCD/472) made in a statement by Mrs Inga Thorsson in the First Committee of the United Nations General Assembly, 14 Nov 1975, in: A/31/27, Report of the Conference of the Committee on Disarmament; Vol II, United Nations, New York, pp 5, 8.

[94] Dinstein, *The Conduct of Hostilities under the Law of International Armed Conflict*, p 181.

[95] A/31/27, Report of the Conference of the Committee on Disarmament; Vol I, United Nations, New York, pp 73–4.

[96] A/46/141, 8 Jul 1991, Request for the inclusion of an additional item in the provisional agenda of the forth-sixth session; Exploitation of the Environment as a Weapon in Times of Armed Conflict and the Taking of Practical Measures to Prevent Such Exploitation; Annex: Explanatory Memorandum, p 2, para 2. Compare also the statements from the representative from Austria, A/C.6/46/SR.19, Summary Record of the 19th meeting of the Sixth Committee of the General Assembly on 23 Oct 1991, p 3, para 5.

an additional item into the provisional agenda of the General Assembly's forty-sixth session entitled:

> Exploitation of the environment as a weapon in times of armed conflict and the taking of practical measures to prevent such exploitation.[97]

Since the object and purpose of the discussion was environmental protection in general, this was later changed into the more general title 'Protection of the environment in times of armed conflict'.[98]

Subsequently, in 1992, at ENMOD's Second Review Conference in 1992,[99] a number of states expressed their unhappiness about the fact that it was not clear to what extent ENMOD was applicable to the setting on fire of oil wells and the spilling of oil into the Persian Gulf.[100] Discussions were carried out based on a working paper submitted by Finland and the Netherlands,[101] and concentrated on the question whether, in addition to high-tech means such as weather manipulation, also low-tech measures such as the use of herbicides and the setting on fire of oil wells might fall under the definition of Article II. If these so-called low-tech measures were recognised as environmental modification techniques, ENMOD's scope would be significantly extended.

Proponents of an extended scope referred to the illustrative list of phenomena in the Understanding regarding Article II which includes upsetting of the ecological balance in a region. Adversaries of an extended scope focused on the definition of environmental modification techniques

[97] A/46/141, 8 Jul 1991, Request for the inclusion of an additional item in the provisional agenda of the forth-sixth session; Exploitation of the Environment as a Weapon in Times of Armed Conflict and the Taking of Practical Measures to Prevent Such Exploitation; Annex: Explanatory Memorandum. Jordan's proposal would eventually lead to A/Res/47/37, adopted without a vote on 25 Nov 1992, on the protection of the environment in times of armed conflict, that will be discussed further below.

[98] A/C.6/46/SR.18, Summary Record of the 18th meeting of the Sixth Committee of the General Assembly on 22 Oct 1991, p 3, para 10; A/C.6/46/L.13, Draft Decision proposed by the Chairman of the 6th Committee of the General Assembly of 21 Nov 1991.

[99] The First Review Conference was held in 1984 in accordance with Art VIII with limited attendance. Despite various proposals as to the scope and as to the complaint and review process of the Convention, the Final Declaration reflected satisfaction and only called upon signatory states and non-signatory states to become party to the Convention. ENMOD/CONF.I/13/II; First Review Conference of the Parties to the Convention on the Prohibition of Military or Any Other Hostile Use of Environmental Modification Techniques; Final Document; Part II; Final Declaration; through <http://www.sunshine-project.org/>.

[100] Iraq had only signed ENMOD. Through <http://disarmament2.un.org/TreatyStatus.nsf>.

[101] ENMOD/CONF.II/8 of 8 Sep 1992; Second Review Conference of the Parties to the Convention on the Prohibition of Military or Any Other Hostile Use of Environmental Modification Techniques; Working Paper Submitted by Finland and the Netherlands; through <http://documents.un.org/> and <http://www.sunshine-project.org/>.

in Article II, according to which such techniques must be 'through the deliberate manipulation of natural processes'.[102]

In view of the text of the Convention and its Understandings and the purpose of its drafters, the latter opinion seems more appealing.[103] The examples listed in the Understanding to Article II are merely:

> illustrative of phenomena that could be caused by the use of environmental modification techniques as defined in Article II of the Convention.[104]

It is therefore wrong to conclude that certain activities comprise environmental modification techniques because the results of these measures fall under the illustrative list of phenomena. The argument put forward to compromise both views by claiming that certain low-tech measures deliberately manipulated natural processes such as the blocking of photosynthesis by chemical means or by soot in the atmosphere resulting from burning oil wells appears artificial.

Nevertheless, the States Parties seem to have extended the scope of the Convention to a limited extent by confirming in their Final Declaration that the military use of herbicides:

> as an environmental modification technique in the meaning of Article II is a method of warfare prohibited by Article I if such use of herbicides upsets the ecological balance of a region.[105]

The burning of oil wells remained unmentioned.

[102] Although the United States referred to the use of herbicides in the 1970s as possibly falling under the Convention, it is nowadays a strong adversary of including low-tech methods under the prohibition of ENMOD. See JB Berger III, D Grimes, ET Jensen and others (Eds), *Operational Law Handbook (2004)*, International and Operational Law Department, The Judge Advocate General's Legal Center and School, Charlottesville, VA, 2004, p 194. The Operational Law Handbook warns on the same page against different and wider interpretations of possible coalition states, such as Australia. The Australian Defence Force Publication on the Laws of Armed Conflict from 1994 states that the ENMOD Convention prohibits 'any means or method of attack which is likely to cause widespread, long-term or severe damage to the natural environment' which is a 'gross overstatement', according to the Operational Law Handbook, and which 'serves as an example of the type of misinformation that requires U.S. Judge Advocates to the conversant in treaties like the ENMOD Convention.' Berger III, Grimes, Jensen and others, *Operational Law Handbook (2004)*, p 194, fn 292. Also Rogers, *Law on the Battlefield*, pp 165–6.

[103] Schmitt seems to share this view when he writes that there is general consensus on the fact that because of this definition, the activities of Iraq during the Gulf War of 1990–1991 would not be covered by ENMOD, even if Iraq would be party to the Convention. Schmitt, *Green War: An Assessment of the Environmental Law of International Armed Conflict*, p 84; Schmitt, *Humanitarian Law and the Environment*, p 280. Similarly Tarasofsky: Tarasofsky, *Legal Protection of the Environment during International Armed Conflict*, pp 44–5. Also but more ambiguous: LC Green, *The Environment and the Law of Conventional Warfare*, The Canadian Yearbook of International Law, Vol 29, 1991, pp 231–2.

[104] Understanding Relating to Article II.

[105] ENMOD/CONF.II/12/II; Second Review Conference of the Parties to the Convention on the Prohibition of Military or Any Other Hostile Use of Environmental Modification Techniques; Final Document; Part II; Final Declaration, pp 11–12; through <http://documents.un.org/>. and <http://www.sunshine-project.org/>.

Despite strong arguments against, the reference to herbicides in the Final Declaration was not completely new. Back in 1976, during the ENMOD negotiations, the United States had already referred to this possibility,[106] and it had subsequently been brought forward at regular intervals.[107] The choice for the word 'confirm' also seems to point into the direction of an already existing *communis opinio*. Nevertheless, the Final Declaration leaves sufficient ambiguity by referring to the military use of herbicides 'as an environmental modification technique *in the meaning of Article II*'.

The scope of ENMOD was brought up again in the context of the two Advisory Opinions on the legality of the use of nuclear weapons.[108] On the one hand, Egypt[109] and Iran[110] believed that the use of nuclear weapons would violate the Convention, a view apparently shared by Mexico[111] and left open by the Solomon Islands.[112] On the other hand, the United Kingdom and the United States adamantly opposed this view. Although nuclear weapons can be used for the modification of the environment, their use does not necessarily entail the deliberate manipulation of the environment as required by Article II of the Convention. Environmental

[106] A/31/27, Report of the Conference of the Committee on Disarmament; Vol I, United Nations, New York, p 73; Goldblat, *Arms Control; The New Guide to Negotiations and Agreements*, p 160; Juda, *Negotiating a treaty on environmental modification warfare: the convention on environmental warfare and its impact upon arms control negotiations*, p 982; Tarasofsky, *Legal Protection of the Environment during International Armed Conflict*, p 45, fn 130.

[107] Green also seems to interpret the manipulation of natural processes and the dynamics, composition or structure of the earth, including its biota, as including the prohibition of long-term defoliation. LC Green, *The Contemporary Law of Armed Conflict*, Manchester University Press, Manchester, 2000, p 157, fn 244.

[108] Legality of the Use by a State of Nuclear Weapons in Armed Conflict, Advisory Opinion, 8 Jul 1996, ICJ Reports 1996, p 66 upon the request of the World Health Organization (WHA 46/40, adopted on 14 May 1993, request for an advisory opinion from the International Court of Justice on the legality of the use of nuclear weapons); Legality of the Threat or Use of Nuclear Weapons, Advisory Opinion, 8 Jul 1996, ICJ Reports 1996, p 226, upon the request of the United Nations General Assembly (A/Res/49/75 K, adopted on 15 Dec 1994, by 78 to 43, with 38 abstentions, request for an advisory opinion from the International Court of Justice on the legality of the threat of use of nuclear weapons).

[109] Written Comments of the Government of Egypt on other Written Statements of Sep 1995; on request for an advisory opinion submitted to the International Court of Justice by the General Assembly on the Legality of the Threat or Use of Nuclear Weapons (GA), p 31, para 72. Through: <http://www.icj-cij.org/>.

[110] CR 95/26, Oral Plea of the Government of the Islamic Republic of Iran, of 6 Nov 1995, on the Legality of the Use by a State of Nuclear Weapons in Armed Conflict and on the Legality of the Threat or Use of Nuclear Weapons (WHO and GA), p 33, para 57. Through: <http://www.icj-cij.org/>.

[111] Written Statement of the Government of Mexico of 9 Jun 1994; on the request for an advisory opinion submitted to the International Court of Justice by the World Health Assembly on the Legality of the Use by a State of Nuclear Weapons in Armed Conflict (WHO), p 11, para 40. Through: <http://www.icj-cij.org/>.

[112] Written Statement of the Government of the Solomon Islands of 10 Jun 1994 (WHO), p 63, para 3.70. Through: <http://www.icj-cij.org/>.

damage resulting from the use of nuclear weapons does not necessarily entail a violation of ENMOD.[113]

Unfortunately, the International Court of Justice did not provide clarity on this point. In the WHO Opinion, it did not go into the substance of the matter because it believed that the question of the legality of the use by a state of nuclear weapons in armed conflict did not fall within the scope of the WHO's activities, as required by Article 96(2) of the United Nations Charter.[114] In the General Assembly Opinion, the Court referred to both points of view, but refrained from choosing sides. The Court's silence on this point may be interpreted, however, as an implicit denial of the principal applicability of ENMOD to the use of nuclear weapons.

2.2.2.4 Damage Threshold

ENMOD does not prohibit the use of all military environmental modification techniques, however. Firstly, it only prohibits those techniques that are used for military or hostile purposes, which does not exclude application in times of peace, ie in the absence of an armed conflict.[115] Secondly, there must be damage or injury inflicted upon 'any other State Party.' And thirdly, the techniques employed must have 'widespread, long-lasting or severe effects'.

The first condition is rather self-explanatory. The second condition indicates that the prohibition only applies to the States Parties inter se,[116] which reminds of early 20th century conventions on the prohibition of certain

[113] Written Statement of the Government of the United Kingdom (WHO), p 91; Written Comments of the Government of the United Kingdom on other Written Statements of 16 Jun 1995 (WHO), p 56, para 3.75; Written Statement of the Government of the United Kingdom of 16 Jun 1995 (GA), p 56, para 3.75; Written Statement of the Government of the United States of America of 10 Jun 1994 (WHO), p 30, para 8; Written Statement of the Government of the United States of America of 20 Jun 1995 (GA), p 29; CR 95/34, Oral Plea of the Government of the United States of America, of 15 Nov 1995 (WHO and GA), p 72. All statements through: <http://www.icj-cij.org/>.

[114] Legality of the Use by a State of Nuclear Weapons in Armed Conflict, Advisory Opinion, 8 Jul 1996, ICJ Reports 1996, p 66, at p 84, para 31.

[115] Application of ENMOD, even without the existence of an armed conflict, was specifically envisaged by both the United States and the Soviet Union. A/31/27, Report of the Conference of the Committee on Disarmament; Vol I, United Nations, New York, pp 66, 69, 72. It should be noted that the necessity of the phrase 'military use' was questioned by various delegations. A/31/27, Report of the Conference of the Committee on Disarmament; Vol I, United Nations, New York, p 69.

[116] The delegations from the Soviet Union, Canada, Mongolia, and Bulgaria believed that otherwise there would not be an incentive for states not party to the convention to accede. The delegations of the Netherlands, Iran, Japan, Egypt, Yugoslavia, and Mexico preferred application to all states. A/31/27, Report of the Conference of the Committee on Disarmament; Vol I, United Nations, New York, p 71; Goldblat, *Arms Control; The New Guide to Negotiations and Agreements*, p 161. The Netherlands declared upon ratification that 'The Kingdom of the Netherlands accepts the obligations laid down in Article 1 of the said Convention as extending to states which are not a party to the Convention and which act in conformity with Article 1 of the Convention.' Through: <http://disarmament2.un.org/TreatyStatus.nsf> and <http://untreaty.un.org/>.

means and methods of warfare, such as the 1925 Geneva Protocol on the prohibition of the use of chemical and bacteriological weapons.[117] The scope of application of the Convention is therefore limited. It should be observed, however, that the state to which damage is inflicted does not necessarily have to be a belligerent, but can also be a third or neutral party.[118]

The third condition, establishing a damage threshold, is most interesting, however. Although it was criticised by various delegations, both during and outside the sessions of the Conference of the Committee on Disarmament,[119] it remained part of the text. This threshold must be clearly distinguished from a seemingly similar triple standard used in Additional Protocol I, as will be explained further below. In ENMOD, all criteria are listed alternatively as a result of the word 'or', whereas in Additional Protocol I, the criteria are listed cumulatively, due to the word 'and'. The difference between both standards means that a violation of ENMOD can be established if the resulting damage meets either of the three criteria, whereas under Additional Protocol I, the resulting damage must meet all three requirements. The damage threshold of ENMOD is therefore lower than the threshold of Additional Protocol I, which means that a violation of ENMOD can more easily be established.[120]

As to the interpretation of these unspecified terms, the 'Understanding Relating to Article I' offers helpful support. It states that the term 'widespread' must be understood as 'encompassing an area on the scale of several hundred square kilometres'; that the term 'long-lasting' must be understood as 'lasting for a period of months, or approximately a season'; and that the term 'severe' must be understood as 'involving serious or significant disruption or harm to human life, natural and economic resources or other assets.'[121] The Understanding adds that this interpretation is

[117] Geneva Protocol for the Prohibition of the use in War of Asphyxiating, Poisonous or Other Gases, and of Bacteriological Methods of Warfare, signed 17 Jun 1925, entered into force on 8 Feb 1928, AJIL, Vol 25, No 2, Supplement: Official Documents, 1931, p 94.

[118] Dinstein, *The Conduct of Hostilities under the Law of International Armed Conflict*, p 180.

[119] See eg the statements from The Netherlands, Argentina, Iran and Mexico: A/31/27, Report of the Conference of the Committee on Disarmament; Vol I, United Nations, New York, pp 66–7, 93; CCD/516, 1 Sep 1976, Mexico, Working paper on the scope of a prohibition of military or any other hostile use of environmental modification techniques, in: A/31/27, Report of the Conference of the Committee on Disarmament; Vol II, United Nations, New York, p 294.

[120] Bothe writes that the AP I provisions are a less stringent restraint than ENMOD, which means that as far as the threshold is concerned, states have more latitude under AP I than under ENMOD. M Bothe, *War and Environment*, in: R Bernhardt (Ed), *Encyclopaedia of Public International Law; Vol Four; Quirin, Ex Parte to Zones of Peace*, Elsevier, Amsterdam, 2000, p 1344.

[121] These meanings were already given to the terms by the United States and the Soviet Union as co-sponsors of their draft Convention as appears from the statement of the delegation of Mexico during the deliberations in the Conference of the Committee on Disarmament. The definitions were included in the Understanding when various western states proposed to have them laid down in an annex, or interpretative declaration or agreed minutes. A/31/27, Report of the Conference of the Committee on Disarmament; Vol I, United Nations, New York, pp 64, 66–7, 73.

exclusively intended for ENMOD and does not prejudice the interpretation of similar terms in any other international agreement. Obviously this refers to Additional Protocol I which makes use of the same terminology, but which is interpreted differently as will be discussed further below.

Furthermore, the 'Understanding Relating to Article II' assumes that the 'widespread, long-term or severe' standard is met under specific circumstances. The Understanding Relating to Article II stipulates that the illustrative list of phenomena that could be caused by the use of environmental modification techniques 'would result or could reasonably be expected to result, in widespread, long-lasting or severe destruction, damage or injury.' Therefore, the hostile use of environmental modification techniques as defined in Article II:

> so as to cause those phenomena as a means of destruction, damage or injury to another State Party, would be prohibited.[122]

2.2.2.5 Understandings

In view of its extensive use as a source for interpretation, it is worth saying a few words on the legal value of the Understandings in light of current rules of the law of treaties. As was stated above, the Understandings of the Committee were not incorporated into the Convention, but merely included in the Report of the Conference of the Committee on Disarmament that was sent to the General Assembly in 1976. Their legal status in terms of interpretation is not exactly clear, however.

Some authors believe that they should be understood as part of the negotiating history of ENMOD,[123] but it is questionable whether this is true or even desirable in view of the rules on interpretation of treaties. Article 32 of the Vienna Convention on the Law of Treaties[124] provides that the preparatory works of a treaty must be regarded as mere supplementary means of interpretation, when the textual, contextual and teleological means of interpretation of Article 31 leave the meaning of the treaty ambiguous or obscure, or when they lead to results that are manifestly absurd or unreasonable. Recourse to the preparatory works of a convention is therefore not easily to be assumed. Although the Vienna Convention on the Law of Treaties, does not apply to ENMOD because it only entered into force for states parties on 27 January 1980,[125] Articles 31

[122] Understanding Relating to Article II.

[123] Bodansky, *Legal Regulation of the Effects of Military Activity on the Environment*, p 29; Detter, *The Law of War*, p 270; Goldblat, *Arms Control; The New Guide to Negotiations and Agreements*, p 158; Simonds, *Conventional Warfare and Environmental Protection: A Proposal for International Legal Reform*, p 186, fn 97; United States Arms Control and Disarmament Agency, *Arms control and Disarmament Agreements; Texts and Histories of the Negotiations*, p 158.

[124] Vienna Convention on the Law of Treaties, signed on 23 May 1969, entered into force on 27 Jan 1980, UNTS, Vol 1155, No 18232.

[125] Art 4 Vienna Convention on the Law of Treaties.

and 32 regarding interpretation of treaties are generally considered to reflect customary international law.[126] This has been confirmed by the International Court of Justice on various occasions, most recently in 2002 in the Case between Indonesia and Malaysia on the sovereignty over Pulau Ligitan and Pulau Sipadan.[127]

In view of the wording of the Understandings,[128] the fact that part of the contents was originally included in the main text,[129] and the meaning given to them, both during the negotiations in the Conference of the Committee on Disarmament in 1976 and during both Review Conferences,[130] it would seem preferable or more appropriate to consider them as:

> [agreements] relating to the treaty which was made between all the parties in connection with the conclusion of the treaty.

According to Article 31(2)(a), such agreements form an essential part of the context, necessary for the interpretation of the terms of a treaty in the

[126] M Fitzmaurice, *The Practical Working of the Law of Treaties*, in: MD Evans, *International Law*, Oxford University Press, Oxford, 2003, p 186; DJ Harris, *Cases and Materials on International Law*, Sweet & Maxwell, London, 2004, p 836; MN Shaw, *International Law*, Cambridge University Press, Cambridge, 2003, p 839. See also Aust's comments on the frequent references to the Vienna Convention's Articles by non-state parties in practice and the fact that even courts and tribunals take the Vienna Convention as their starting point. A Aust, *Modern Treaty Law and Practice*, Cambridge University Press, Cambridge, 2000, pp 10–11.

[127] Case Concerning Sovereignty over Pulau Ligitan and Pulau Sipadan (Indonesia/Malaysia), Merits, Judgment, 17 Dec 2002, ICJICJ Reports 2002, para 37, p 23. See also the Court's Advisory Opinion on the use of nuclear weapons upon request of the World Health Organization, Legality of the Use by a State of Nuclear Weapons in Armed Conflict, Advisory Opinion, 8 Jul 1996, ICJ Reports 1996, p 66, at p 75.

[128] The Understandings state that the interpretations reflect the opinion of 'the Committee', which is, the Conference of the Committee on Disarmament.

[129] Juda, *Negotiating a treaty on environmental modification warfare: the convention on environmental warfare and its impact upon arms control negotiations*, p 979.

[130] Most states that participated in the Conference of the Committee's negotiations stressed the importance of the Understandings. A/31/27, Report of the Conference of the Committee on Disarmament; Vol I, United Nations, New York, pp 65–8, 73–5, 82–5, 93; ENMOD/CONF.I/13/II; First Review Conference of the Parties to the Convention on the Prohibition of Military or Any Other Hostile Use of Environmental Modification Techniques; Final Document; Part II; Final Declaration; ENMOD/CONF.II/12/II; Second Review Conference of the Parties to the Convention on the Prohibition of Military or Any Other Hostile Use of Environmental Modification Techniques; Final Document; Part II; Final Declaration; through <http://www.sunshine-project.org/>. Also Tarasofsky refers to the authority given to the understandings by the States Parties. Tarasofsky, *Legal Protection of the Environment during International Armed Conflict*, p 46, fn 134. Please note, however, that not every state supported the interpretation given by the Committee. Ex post facto, that is. When Turkey (not a member of the Conference of the Committee on Disarmament at the time) signed the Convention on 18 May 1977, it added a reservation as to the interpretation of the terms widespread, long lasting and severe, stating that the terms needed to be more clearly defined and that until that would happen it would rely on its own interpretation of the terms. Turkey, however, never deposited its instruments of ratification and therefore never became a party to ENMOD. Schmitt, *Green War: An Assessment of the Environmental Law of International Armed Conflict*, p 82, fn 396; reservation through <http://disarmament2.un.org/TreatyStatus.nsf> and <http://untreaty.un.org/>. However, the fact that Turkey added a reservation to its signature does not change the legal status of the Understandings.

sense of Article 31(1), and must therefore be considered as primary means of interpretation. Interpretative documents like these are usually not considered as part of the preparatory works.

This view is held, for example, by Aust who seems to take it for granted,[131] and is not contradicted by the words of the Department for Disarmament Affairs of the United Nations Secretariat. In its overview of the Status of Multilateral Arms Regulation and Disarmament Agreements, the Understandings are introduced as 'Documents pertaining to the Convention'.[132]

Finally, Goldblat and Tarasofsky are of the opinion that the interpretation given to the various Articles may be changed at any future Review Conference.[133] This view is probably correct as the Declarations adopted by the various Review Conferences may be regarded as 'subsequent agreements between the parties regarding the interpretation of the treaty or the application of its provisions' which must be taken into account together with the context of the treaty, in accordance with Article 31(3)(a) of the Vienna Convention.

2.2.2.6 Lacunae

Although ENMOD is a valuable contribution to the laws of war, and to the protection of the environment during international armed conflict in particular, and although the Convention is observed well, there are nevertheless a few shortcomings regarding its scope. By applying the maxim *expressio unius est exclusio alterius*,[134] it is justified to draw the following list of activities that are not prohibited under the Convention. These include: research, development, manufacture, possession and testing of environmental modification techniques; the threat to use environmental modification techniques; non-military use of environmental modification

[131] Aust, *Modern Treaty Law and Practice*, p 190.

[132] Through <http://disarmament2.un.org/TreatyStatus.nsf>. The Report is recorded as A/31/27, Report of the Conference of the Committee on Disarmament; Vol I, United Nations, New York.

[133] Comments Goldblat in Round Table Session I on General Principles and methods for Executing a New Convention, in: G Plant (Ed), *Environmental Protection and the Law of War; A 'Fifth Geneva' Convention on the Protection of the Environment in Time of Armed Conflict*, Belhaven Press, London, 1992, p 111; Tarasofsky, *Legal Protection of the Environment during International Armed Conflict*, p 46.

[134] '[E]xpress mention excludes other items[.]' I Brownlie, *Principles of Public International Law*, Oxford University Press, Oxford, 2003, p 604. See generally McNair on the use of 'General Words and Special Words: the *ejusdem generis* Doctrine: *expressio unius est exclusio alterius*' for the interpretation and application of treaties: AD McNair, *The Law of Treaties*, Clarendon Press, Oxford, 1961, ch 22, pp 393–410. McNair also refers to other forms of the maxim, for instance: '*inclusio unius est exclusio alterius; expressum facit cessare tacitum*. It seems that the application of the argument *a contrario* achieves substantially the same result as the maxim cited above, and perhaps on the Continent of Europe the term *a contrario* is more frequently used.' McNair, *The Law of Treaties*, p 400.

techniques, even if that results in damage to another State Party; military use that results in damage to another State Party, but that does not meet either of the three conditions, widespread, long-term or severe; and finally, military use that does not result in damage to another State Party, but to the actor state itself, to areas outside the limits of national jurisdiction,[135] or, more importantly, to states that have not become party to the Convention.[136] As far as the last *lacuna* is concerned, however, it is theoretically possible that such activities are covered by the provisions of Additional Protocol I, as will be discussed further below. With respect to the others, obligations under other conventions or customary international law may preclude such activities.

2.2.3 *Additional Protocol I*

2.2.3.1 Introduction

A second treaty providing for direct protection of the environment is Additional Protocol I of 1977. Additional Protocol I is the latest comprehensive codification of the laws of war, merging the classic means and methods law of The Hague with the humanitarian law of Geneva, while elaborating the protection of civilians during armed conflict.[137] As has been observed above, the term Hague law primarily relates to the 1899 and 1907 Hague Regulations on Land Warfare; the term Geneva law primarily relates to the 1949 Geneva Conventions and a number of other conventions dating from the 19th century, and focuses on the protection of the victims of armed conflict. Although the distinction between Hague and Geneva Law has often been subject to criticism, since both branches con-

[135] Heintschel von Heinegg and Donner believe that ENMOD only relates to use of modification techniques 'directed at land and sea areas that are covered by the opponent's sovereignty.' W Heintschel von Heinegg, M Donner, *New Developments in the Protection of the Natural Environment in Naval Armed Conflicts*, German Yearbook of International Law, Vol 37, 1994, p 294.

[136] See also for comments and criticism on ENMOD: Bodansky, *Legal Regulation of the Effects of Military Activity on the Environment*, pp 27–8; Y Dinstein, *Protection of the Environment in International Armed Conflict*, in: JA Frowein, R Wolfrum (Eds), *Max Planck Yearbook of United Nations Law*, Vol 5, 2001, Kluwer Law International, The Hague, 2001, pp 526–30; Dinstein, *The Conduct of Hostilities under the Law of International Armed Conflict*, pp 178–81; Goldblat, *Arms Control; The New Guide to Negotiations and Agreements*, pp 159–60, 162; Juda, *Negotiating a treaty on environmental modification warfare: the convention on environmental warfare and its impact upon arms control negotiations*, pp 989–97; Roberts, Guelff, *Documents on the Laws of War*, p 408; Schmitt, *Green War: An Assessment of the Environmental Law of International Armed Conflict*, p 85; SN Simonds, *Conventional Warfare and Environmental Protection: A Proposal for International Legal Reform*, Stanford Journal of International Law, Vol 29, 1992, pp 186–7; Tarasofsky, *Legal Protection of the Environment during International Armed Conflict*, p 47.

[137] Kalshoven, Zegveld, *Constraints on the Waging of War; An Introduction to International Humanitarian Law*, pp 19–36; Schmitt, *Humanitarian Law and the Environment*, pp 275–6, fn 46.

tain comparable rules,[138] and although the distinction has now become outdated with Additional Protocol I, it is still common to distinguish between both branches for the sake of clarity.

The 1949 Geneva Conventions had left a number of issues unresolved, in particular the protection of the civilian population during armed conflict and the modernisation of regulations of the conduct of warfare. The XIXth Red Cross Conference,[139] held in New Delhi in 1957, attempted to remedy these *lacunae*, but the ICRC's detailed proposals,[140] although adopted by the Conference, did not trigger enough enthusiasm to convene a diplomatic conference. The main reason for their lack of interest lay in the fact that the so-called 'Delhi Rules' addressed, among other things, the use of nuclear weapons,[141] which was not considered appropriate at that time.[142] At the next Red Cross Conference, held in Vienna in 1965, four general principles were adopted[143] and the ICRC was asked to continue its efforts to further develop International Humanitarian Law,[144] but no direct steps were undertaken for their implementation.

[138] Detter, *The Law of War*, pp 158–9; Dinstein, *The Conduct of Hostilities under the Law of International Armed Conflict*, pp 9–11. Also Fleck, in: D Fleck (Ed), *The Handbook of Humanitarian Law in Armed Conflicts*, Oxford University Press, Oxford, 1995, p xiii; Sandoz, Swinaraski, Zimmerman, *Commentary on the Additional Protocols; of 8 Jun 1977 to the Geneva Conventions of 12 Aug 1949*, p xxvii.

[139] The International Conference of the Red Cross is 'the supreme deliberative body' of the International Red Cross and Red Crescent Movement (hereinafter the Movement), according to Art 8 of the Statutes (*sic*) of the International Red Cross and Red Crescent Movement, which consists of the National Red Cross and Red Crescent Societies, their International Federation of Red Cross and Red Crescent Societies, and the International Committee of the Red Cross (Art 1). The International Conference of the Red Cross is composed of this Movement, together with the States Parties to the Geneva Conventions (Art 9) and meets in principle every four years (Art 11). Statutes of the International Red Cross and Red Crescent Movement, through <http://www.icrc.org/>.

[140] Draft Rules for the Limitation of the Dangers Incurred by the Civilian Population in Time of War, International Committee of the Red Cross, 1956, in: Schindler, Toman (Eds), *The Laws of Armed Conflicts; A Collection of Conventions, Resolutions and Other Documents*, pp 251–7.

[141] Art 14 of the ICRC Draft Rules provided that '[w]ithout prejudice to the present or future prohibition of certain specific weapons, the use is prohibited of weapons whose harmful effects—resulting in particular from the dissemination of incendiary, chemical, bacteriological, radioactive or other agents—could spread to an unforeseen degree or escape, either in space or in time, from the control of those who employ them, thus endangering the civilian population. (. . .).'

[142] Sandoz, Swinaraski, Zimmerman, *Commentary on the Additional Protocols; of 8 Jun 1977 to the Geneva Conventions of 12 Aug 1949*, p xxix.

[143] The XXth International Conference of the Red Cross solemnly declared that 'all Governments and other authorities responsible for action in armed conflicts should conform at least to the following principles: that the right of the parties to a conflict to adopt means and methods of injuring the enemy is not unlimited; that it is prohibited to launch attacks against the civilian populations as such; that distinction must be made at all times between persons taking part in the hostilities and members of the civilian population to the effect that the latter be spared as much as possible; that the general principles of the Law of War apply to nuclear and similar weapons'. in: Schindler, Toman, *The Laws of Armed Conflicts; A Collection of Conventions, Resolutions and Other Documents*, pp 259–60.

[144] Resolution XXVIII adopted by 64, 0, with 2 abstentions, by the XXth International Conference of the Red Cross, Vienna, 1965, on the protection of civilian populations against

Although the ICRC had traditionally been the instigator of most of the progressive development and codification of the laws of war, the momentum that was needed to set in motion a process that would lead to the adoption of both Additional Protocols came from the UN General Assembly.[145] The process was triggered by two developments: firstly, there was increased attention for human rights and secondly, the nature of armed conflict had changed as a result of the decolonisation struggle.[146]

The process of decolonisation, the recognition of the right of self-determination of peoples, and their right to struggle,[147] made a revision of the laws of war necessary because it had taken armed conflict from the classic inter-state level to the intra-state level. Since the early 1950s, the General Assembly had consistently underscored the right of self-determination of peoples, and when the use of force in an anti-colonial setting became increasingly frequent, the General Assembly stated that national liberation struggle was justified and had to be regarded as international armed conflicts, therewith endowing liberation fighters with certain protective rights under the laws of war.[148] The increased attention for human rights led the General Assembly to request the Secretary-General in 1968 to undertake studies, in cooperation with the ICRC, investigating how to promote the application of international humanitarian law in all forms of armed conflict, and assessing the need for new international humanitarian conventions to improve the protection of civilians.[149]

the dangers of indiscriminate warfare, in: Schindler, Toman, *The Laws of Armed Conflicts; A Collection of Conventions, Resolutions and Other Documents*, pp 259–60.

[145] M Bothe, KJ Partsch, in: Bothe, Partsch, Solf, *New Rules for Victims of Armed Conflicts; Commentary on the Two 1977 Protocols Additional to the Geneva Conventions of 1949*, p 2.

[146] Kalshoven, Zegveld, *Constraints on the Waging of War; An Introduction to International Humanitarian Law*, p 30–2.

[147] A/Res/1514 (XV), adopted on 14 Dec 1960, by 89 to 0, with 9 abstentions; declaration on the granting of independence to colonial countries and peoples; A/Res/1541 (XV), adopted on 15 Dec 1960, by 69 to 2, with 21 abstentions; principles which should guide Members in determining whether or not an obligation exists to transmit the information called for under Art 73(e) of the Charter; A/Res/2625 (XXV), adopted without a vote on 24 Oct 1970; Declaration on Principles of International Law concerning Friendly Relations and Co-operation among States in accordance with the Charter of the United Nations.

[148] Bothe, Partsch, in: Bothe, Partsch, Solf, *New Rules for Victims of Armed Conflicts; Commentary on the Two 1977 Protocols Additional to the Geneva Conventions of 1949*, pp 2–3; Kalshoven, Zegveld, *Constraints on the Waging of War; An Introduction to International Humanitarian Law*, pp 30–2. On the relationship between self-determination and *ius ad bellum*, see: WD Verwey, *Humanitarian Intervention under International Law*, Netherlands International Law Review, Vol 32, 1985, pp 381–3.

[149] A/Res/2444 (XXIII), adopted unanimously on 19 Dec 1968, on the respect for human rights in armed conflicts. The Assembly responded by this Resolution to the request of the 1968 International Conference on Human Rights that was held in Teheran in that same year. Bothe, Partsch, in: Bothe, Partsch, Solf, *New Rules for Victims of Armed Conflicts; Commentary on the Two 1977 Protocols Additional to the Geneva Conventions of 1949*, p 3; Kalshoven, Zegveld, *Constraints on the Waging of War; An Introduction to International Humanitarian Law*, pp 30–1; Sandoz, Swinaraski, Zimmerman, *Commentary on the Additional Protocols; of 8 Jun 1977 to the Geneva Conventions of 12 Aug 1949*, p xxx.

It is interesting to note that from then onwards, these activities of the Assembly were carried out under the banner of the promotion of respect for human rights during armed conflict.[150] According to Kalshoven and Zegveld, this may not only indicate the historical origin of these activities, but also their justification, since under the Charter, 'the promotion and protection of human rights are among its main functions.'[151] Still, this designation is unfortunate, because it confuses the direct protection of civilians during armed conflict under the laws of war with the potential protection of individuals under peacetime human rights law in times of armed conflict. As regards the potential protection of individuals under human rights law, it is first necessary to determine the relationship between *ius pacis* and *ius in bello* in general and then, more specifically, the relationship between human rights law and international humanitarian law.[152] This will be addressed further below in Chapter V.

2.2.3.2 Drafting History

After several reports from the Secretary-General, several resolutions from the General Assembly, two Conferences of Red Cross Experts and two Conferences of Government Experts, the ICRC drafted two Protocols additional to the Geneva Conventions in 1973.[153] One year later, in February 1974, the Swiss Government convened a Diplomatic Conference on the Reaffirmation and Development of International Humanitarian Law Applicable in Armed Conflicts, which met four times between 1974 and 1977. Discussions were held on the basis of the two draft Protocols,[154] by a large number of states and international organisations. Between 107 and 124 states participated, as well as 11 national liberation movements and 51 intergovernmental and non-governmental organisations.[155] Only states had the right to vote on the Conference's proposals.

[150] Compare also the name of the 1968 Teheran Resolution of the International Conference on Human Rights.

[151] Kalshoven, Zegveld, *Constraints on the Waging of War; An Introduction to International Humanitarian Law*, p 31.

[152] Detter, *The Law of War*, pp 160–3; Dinstein, *The Conduct of Hostilities under the Law of International Armed Conflict*, pp 20–5.

[153] ICRC, *Draft Additional Protocols to the Geneva Conventions of Aug 12, 1949; Commentary*, ICRC, Geneva, 1973.

[154] The sessions were held from 20 Feb to 29 Mar 1974; from 3 Feb to 18 Apr 1975; from 21 Apr to 11 Jun 1976; and from 17 Mar to 10 Jun 1977. ICRC, *Protocols Additional to the Geneva Conventions of 12 Aug 1949*, ICRC, Geneva 1996, p 123.

[155] Bothe, Partsch, in: Bothe, Partsch, Solf, *New Rules for Victims of Armed Conflicts; Commentary on the Two 1977 Protocols Additional to the Geneva Conventions of 1949*, pp 3–4; Sandoz, Swinaraski, Zimmerman, *Commentary on the Additional Protocols; of 8 Jun 1977 to the Geneva Conventions of 12 Aug 1949*, pp xxx–xxxiii.

The Diplomatic Conference set up its own rules of procedure, divided the workload over a number of separate Committees,[156] and managed to adopt the texts of two new treaties by consensus on 8 June 1977, after long negotiations:[157] the Protocol Additional to the Geneva Conventions of 12 August 1949, and Relating to the Protection of Victims of International Armed Conflicts (Additional Protocol I) and a second Protocol on the non-international armed conflict (Additional Protocol II).[158] Both protocols were opened for signature for a period of twelve months on 12 December 1977, and entered into force on 7 December 1978.[159]

In the summer of 2006, Additional Protocol I had been ratified by 166 states—including France, the People's Republic of China, the Russian Federation, and the United Kingdom—and signed by five others.[160] Notably absent among the State Parties are India, Israel, Pakistan, and the United States that signed the Additional Protocol on 12 December 1977, but decided in 1987 not to ratify. Although the United States had been an active participant during the negotiations and had welcomed the adoption

156 3 main plenary committees dealt with various parts of the Protocols (Committee I—general and final provisions, execution of Protocol I and fundamental guarantees of Protocol II; Committee II—provisions relating to the wounded and sick, civil defence and relief; Committee III—means and methods of warfare and protection of the civilian population), one ad hoc committee on conventional weapons, and three specific committees on drafting, credentials and general issues. For practical purposes, the committees were subsequently subdivided in Working Groups in which most of the work was carried out. Bothe, Partsch, in: Bothe, Partsch, Solf, *New Rules for Victims of Armed Conflicts; Commentary on the Two 1977 Protocols Additional to the Geneva Conventions of 1949*, pp 4–5; Sandoz, Swinaraski, Zimmerman, *Commentary on the Additional Protocols; of 8 Jun 1977 to the Geneva Conventions of 12 Aug 1949*, pp xxxiii.

157 The Final Act was not signed until two days later, on 10 Jun 1977, by 102 states. Bothe, Partsch, in: Bothe, Partsch, Solf, *New Rules for Victims of Armed Conflicts; Commentary on the Two 1977 Protocols Additional to the Geneva Conventions of 1949*, p 6.

158 Protocol Additional to the Geneva Conventions of 12 Aug 1949, and Relating to the Protection of Victims of Non-International Armed Conflicts, opened for signature on 12 Dec 1977, entered into force on 7 Dec 1978, UNTS, Vol 1125, No 17513. In 2005, a third Additional Protocol was adopted and opened for signature on an additional distinctive emblem: Protocol Additional to the Geneva Conventions of 12 Aug 1949, and Relating to the Adoption of an Additional Distinctive Emblem (Additional Protocol III), opened for signature on 8 Dec 2005, entered into force on 14 Jan 2007, at <http://www.icrc.org/ihl.nsf/>.

159 Art 92 and Art 95(1) of Additional Protocol I; and Art 20 of Additional Protocol II. Bothe, Partsch express surprise as to the two-step approach chosen by the drafters of the Protocols: first the Final Act of the Conference is signed on 10 Jun 1977, and then the Protocols are opened for signature 6 months later. Bothe, Partsch, in: Bothe, Partsch, Solf, New Rules for Victims of Armed Conflicts; Commentary on the Two 1977 Protocols Additional to the Geneva Conventions of 1949, p 6. The authors refer to the fact that Art 10(b) of the Vienna Convention on the Law of Treaties recognises both methods as equivalent methods of authenticating the text of a treaty and that it seemed that the Diplomatic Conference was of the opinion that the signature of the text is more important. They fail to recognise, however, that according to Art 10(a) of the Vienna Convention, the authentication of a text by signature of a Final Act of a particular conference only becomes relevant in the absence of a 'procedure provided for in the text' of the treaty. Art 92 of AP I and Art 20 of AP II do provide for such a procedure and Art 10(b) Vienna Convention therefore does not seem to be applicable in this case.

160 Through <http://www.icrc.org/> and <http://www.eda.admin.ch/>.

of the Protocol, the Reagan Administration decided that it did not wish to become a Party. While submission to the Senate for approval only seemed a matter of time in the early 1980s, President Reagan notified the Senate in 1987 that it would not ask for its consent.[161] The rationale given in Reagan's Letter of Transmittal was that, although the Protocol contained 'certain meritorious elements', the Protocol was 'fundamentally and irreconcilably flawed', among other things, because of the extension of international armed conflicts to so-called 'wars of national liberation.' According to the Reagan Administration, the question whether or not a certain conflict is an international armed conflict should be based on objective criteria and not on 'one's view of the moral qualities of each conflict'. Furthermore the Protocol extended the criteria for the status of combatant to so-called irregular forces which was considered unacceptable, as it would benefit terrorists and endanger civilians.[162]

The size of Protocol I is substantial. It consists of 102 Articles divided in six parts on respectively General Provisions (I), Wounded, Sick and Shipwrecked (II), Methods and Means of Warfare,[163] and Combatant and Prisoner-of-War Status (III), Civilian Population (IV), Execution of the Conventions and of This Protocol (V), and Final Provisions (VI). In addition, the Protocol contains two Annexes: one on Regulations Concerning Identification (I) and one with a model Identity Card for Journalists on Dangerous Professional Missions (II).

2.2.3.3 Articles 35(3) and 55 Additional Protocol I

2.2.3.3.1 Drafting History

Among the Protocol's 102 Articles, two provisions are directly related to the protection of the environment: Articles 35 and 55. The former is included in Section I, Part III of the Protocol and deals with 'Basic Rules'

[161] R Reagan, *Letter of Transmittal; The White House, Jan 29, 1987*, published in the American Journal of International Law, Vol 81, 1987, pp 910–2.

[162] R Reagan, *Letter of Transmittal; The White House, Jan 29, 1987*, p 911. See for more arguments from the State Department's Legal Adviser Sofaer, AD Sofaer, *The Rationale for the United States Decision*, The American Journal of International Law, Vol 82, 1988, pp 784–7, and for a rebuttal from the Head of the US Delegation at the Diplomatic Conference in Geneva, Ambassador Aldrich, GH Aldrich, *Prospects for United States Ratification of Additional Protocol I to the 1949 Geneva Conventions*, American Journal of International Law, Vol 85, 1991, pp 1–20, and GH Aldrich, *Why the United States of America Should Ratify Additional Protocol I*, in: AJM Delissen, GJ Tanja (Eds), *Humanitarian Law of Armed Conflict; Challenges Ahead; Essays in Honour of Frits Kalshoven*, Martinus Nijhoff Publishers, Dordrecht, 1991, pp 127–44.

[163] The first amendment as regards environmental protection of Art 35 from the German Democratic Republic was named 'Means and Methods of Combat'. CDDH/III/108, 11 Sep 1974 (III, 155), proposed amendment by the German Democratic Republic, in: HS Levie, *Protection of War Victims: Protocol 1 to the 1949 Geneva Conventions; Vol 2*, Oceana Publications, Dobbs Ferry, NY, 1980, p 254. Although the common designation is 'methods and means of warfare', the phrase 'means and methods of warfare' does sound better.

of Methods and Means of Warfare; the latter deals with the 'Protection of the Environment' in the context of Chapter II ('Civilian Objects') of Section I ('General Protection Against the Effects of Hostilities') of Part IV dealing with the 'Civilian Population'. Both provisions were proposed during the Diplomatic Conference and were not part of the original draft Protocols submitted by the ICRC. Both Articles intend to protect the environment from the consequences of war and seem to be derived from the fundamental principle of environmental protection.[164] As has been explained above, it is arguable that this principle has shaped the laws of war since the 1970s, in addition to the principles of necessity and humanity.

Although the issue had been brought up by a few Eastern European states during the Conference of Government Experts in 1972, the ICRC had decided not to include an environmental protection provision in its draft protocols. According to Kalshoven, this was caused by a lack of interest from western states;[165] according to Solf, this was because of bilateral efforts made by the United States and the Soviet Union to regulate environmental modification techniques.[166]

The reason for the drafting of two separate provisions on more or less the same subject lies in the Protocol's drafting history. Not long before the second session of the Diplomatic Conference in 1975, a number of states proposed the introduction of an Article that would prohibit ecological damage to the environment as a result of warfare, each in different wordings and focusing on different aspects.[167] On 19 March 1974, two amendments were proposed to add a provision in the section dealing with civilian objects: one by Australia for the insertion of a new Article,[168] and one by a group of Central and Eastern European States for an additional paragraph to one of the Articles under discussion.[169] Subsequently, on 11

164 Compare Arts 35(1) and (2) which seem to reflect the principles of necessity and humanity respectively.

165 F Kalshoven, *Reaffirmation and Development of International Humanitarian Law Applicable in Armed Conflicts: the Diplomatic Conference, Geneva, 1974–1977; Part II,* Netherlands Yearbook of International Law, Vol 9, 1978, p 129.

166 Solf, in: Bothe, Partsch, Solf, *New Rules for Victims of Armed Conflicts; Commentary on the Two 1977 Protocols Additional to the Geneva Conventions of 1949,* p 344.

167 Sandoz, Swinaraski, Zimmerman, *Commentary on the Additional Protocols; of 8 Jun 1977 to the Geneva Conventions of 12 Aug 1949,* pp 411–2.

168 CDDH/III/60, 19 Mar 1974 (III, 220), proposed new Art [55] by Australia, in: HS Levie, *Protection of War Victims: Protocol 1 to the 1949 Geneva Conventions; Vol 3,* Oceana Publications, Dobbs Ferry, NY, 1980, p 259. The proposed Art read: '(1) Without prejudice to the rights of a High Contracting Party in its own territory, it is forbidden to despoil the natural environment as a technique of warfare; (2) Attacks against the natural environment by way of reprisal are prohibited; (3) A breach of this Article shall constitute a grave breach of the present Protocol.'

169 CDDH/III/64, 19 Mar 1974 (III, 221), proposed additional para, by Czechoslovakia, German Democratic Republic, Hungary, in: Levie, *Protection of War Victims: Protocol 1 to the 1949 Geneva Conventions; Vol 3,* p 259. The proposed para read: 'It is forbidden to impair or destroy the natural environment as such by any means or methods whatsoever since the maintenance of a balanced environment is essential for the survival of the civilian population. The natural environment shall not be made the subject of reprisals.'

September 1974, the German Democratic Republic proposed to amend the basic rules on means and methods of combat by adding a paragraph that would forbid the use of means and methods of warfare that destroy natural human environmental conditions.[170]

During the negotiations, it appeared that there were two dominant points of view. One group regarded protection of the environment necessary as an objective in itself; the second group regarded environmental protection only in relation to the survival of the civilian population.[171] The former view was new and in a sense revolutionary, because it aims to protect the intrinsic value of the environment. It is therefore also referred to as eco-centric. The latter view took a more traditional international *humanitarian* law approach and connected environmental protection with the protection of the civilian population. This view is therefore referred to as anthropocentric.[172]

A specific but informal working group named the 'Biotope Group' dealt with the issue,[173] unsuccessfully tried to merge both views,[174] then could not choose one view at the expense of the other, and finally advised to work out separate provisions.[175] This recommendation was adopted by

[170] CDDH/III/108, 11 Sep 1974 (III, 155), proposed amendment by the German Democratic Republic, in: Levie, *Protection of War Victims: Protocol 1 to the 1949 Geneva Conventions; Vol 2*, p 254. The amendment read: '(4) It is forbidden to use means and methods which destroy natural human environmental conditions.'

[171] Report to the Third Committee on the Work of the Working Group, Committee III, 3 Apr 1975 (CDDH/III/275), on Art 48 *bis* [present Art 55. EVK] and Art 33 [present Art 35. EVK], para 3, of Protocol I, in: Levie, *Protection of War Victims: Protocol 1 to the 1949 Geneva Conventions; Vol 2*, p 269, and in Levie, *Protection of War Victims: Protocol 1 to the 1949 Geneva Conventions; Vol 3*, p 269; Kalshoven, *Reaffirmation and Development of International Humanitarian Law Applicable in Armed Conflicts: the Diplomatic Conference, Geneva, 1974–1977; Part II*, pp 129–30; Solf, in: Bothe, Partsch, Solf, *New Rules for Victims of Armed Conflicts; Commentary on the Two 1977 Protocols Additional to the Geneva Conventions of 1949*, p 344. Compare also the comments from Mr Fischer of the delegation of the German Democratic Republic (GDR) in the Meeting of Committee III on 27 Feb 1075 (CDDH/III/SR.26), in: Levie, *Protection of War Victims: Protocol 1 to the 1949 Geneva Conventions; Vol 2*, p 257.

[172] Schmitt, *Green War: An Assessment of the Environmental Law of International Armed Conflict*, pp 70–1; Schmitt, *Humanitarian Law and the Environment*, pp 276–7.

[173] The Group was set up in response to the request of the Rapporteur of Committee III, US Ambassador Aldrich. Participating were: Australia, Czechoslovakia, Finland, German Democratic Republic, Hungary, Ireland, Spain, Sweden, The Netherlands, Yugoslavia, and representatives from the ICRC and the UN Environment Program. Levie, *Protection of War Victims: Protocol 1 to the 1949 Geneva Conventions; Vol 2*, p 267; Levie, *Protection of War Victims: Protocol 1 to the 1949 Geneva Conventions; Vol 3*, p 266.

[174] The Rapporteur of Committee III, Ambassador Aldrich, preferred to have the protection of the environment grouped in a single Article. Levie, *Protection of War Victims: Protocol 1 to the 1949 Geneva Conventions; Vol 2*, p 260.

[175] Report of the Chairman of the Group 'Biotope', Committee III, 11 Mar 1975 (CDDH/III/GT/35), in: Levie, *Protection of War Victims: Protocol 1 to the 1949 Geneva Conventions; Vol 2*, p 268, and Levie, *Protection of War Victims: Protocol 1 to the 1949 Geneva Conventions; Vol 3*, p 268. See also: Solf, in: Bothe, Partsch, Solf, *New Rules for Victims of Armed Conflicts; Commentary on the Two 1977 Protocols Additional to the Geneva Conventions of 1949*, p 345; Sandoz, Swinaraski, Zimmerman, *Commentary on the Additional Protocols; of 8 Jun 1977 to the Geneva Conventions of 12 Aug 1949*, pp 414, 663.

the responsible Working Group and led eventually to the adoption of two separate Articles by the Diplomatic Conference at the end.[176] Article 35(3) was included in that part of the Protocol dealing with means and methods of warfare; and Article 55 was included in that part of the protocol dealing with the protection of the civilian population.[177] The former proposal was in the tradition of The Hague; the latter proposal followed the tradition of Geneva.[178]

Both Articles use similar terminology, but differ as to the relationship between environmental damage and the civilian population in Article 55. Article 35(3) states that:

> [i]t is prohibited to employ methods or means of warfare which are intended or may be expected, to cause widespread, long-term and severe damage to the natural environment.

Article 55(1) provides that:

> [c]are shall be taken in warfare to protect the natural environment against widespread, long-term and severe damage. This protection includes a prohibition of the use of methods or means of warfare which are intended or may be expected to cause such damage to the natural environment and thereby to prejudice the health or survival of the population.

In addition, Article 55(2) provides: 'Attacks against the natural environment by way of reprisals are prohibited.'[179]

[176] Report of Committee III, Second Session (CDDH/215), in: Levie, *Protection of War Victims: Protocol 1 to the 1949 Geneva Conventions; Vol 2*, pp 275–7, and in: Levie, *Protection of War Victims: Protocol 1 to the 1949 Geneva Conventions; Vol 3*, p 273; Sandoz, Swinaraski, Zimmerman, *Commentary on the Additional Protocols; of 8 Jun 1977 to the Geneva Conventions of 12 Aug 1949*, pp 412–14.

[177] On 10 Apr 1975, Committee III adopted para 3 of Art 35 with 57 to 4, with 3 abstentions, both paras of Art 55 by consensus, and Arts 35 and 55 as a whole by consensus. Two years later, at the Plenary Meeting of 25 May 1977, the Diplomatic Conference finally adopted both Articles by consensus. In Committee III, both the United Kingdom and the Federal Republic of Germany voted against adoption of Art 35(3) because they believed the topic should only be dealt with in the context of protection of the civilian population and repetition in Art 35 was unnecessary. The Representative from Canada agreed with the UK. Levie, *Protection of War Victims: Protocol 1 to the 1949 Geneva Conventions; Vol 2*, pp 273–5, 278; Levie, *Protection of War Victims: Protocol 1 to the 1949 Geneva Conventions; Vol 3*, pp 271, 275.

[178] Schmitt, *Green War: An Assessment of the Environmental Law of International Armed Conflict*, p 70; Schmitt, *Humanitarian Law and the Environment*, p 275.

[179] The text for both Articles was first suggested by the Rapporteur for Committee III, United States Ambassador Aldrich, on 4 Apr 1975, on the basis of the Report to the Third Committee on the Work of the Working Group of Committee III, of a day earlier, 3 Apr 1975. His proposals were subsequently adopted by the Working Group of Committee III, and after review and slight change by the Drafting Committee, eventually by the Conference in 1977. Proposal by the Rapporteur, 4 Apr 1975 (CDDH/III/276): Art [55] and Proposal by the Rapporteur, Committee III, 4 Apr 1975 (CDDH/III/277): Art [35(3)], respectively in: Levie, *Protection of War Victims: Protocol 1 to the 1949 Geneva Conventions; Vol 3*, pp 270–1, and in: Levie, *Protection of War Victims: Protocol 1 to the 1949 Geneva Conventions; Vol 2*, p 271; Report to the Third Committee on the Work of the Working Group, Committee III, 3 Apr 1975 (CDDH/III/275), in: Levie, *Protection of War Victims: Protocol 1 to the 1949 Geneva Conventions; Vol 2*, pp 269–70.

2.2.3.3.2 Differences between Art. 35(3) and Art. 55

Both provisions intend to protect the environment against the destructive effects of warfare, but do so in different ways. Article 35(3) lays down a general prohibition to use certain means or methods of warfare that damage or could damage the environment, whereas Article 55(1) first introduces a general duty of care in the first sentence,[180] and then specifies this duty by a specific prohibition in the second sentence of that paragraph. That prohibition repeats the general prohibition of Article 35(3) but makes application conditional on harmful effects on the population. The choice for the word 'includes' in the second sentence implies that the prohibition of means and methods of warfare that prejudice the health or survival of the population is illustrative and exemplary for the duty of care of Article 55(1), first sentence and apparently also of the prohibition of Article 35(3).[181] Therefore, both provisions are not believed to duplicate each other, although they certainly partially overlap.[182]

Because both provisions intend to protect the environment during international armed conflict in different ways, there may be differences in scope. Article 35(3) is formulated as a strict prohibition, whereas the first sentence of Article 55(1) is formulated as a duty of care.[183] On the one hand, it may be argued that Article 35(3) is more stringent and has a more general scope than Article 55(1). According to the ICRC's Commentary on the Additional Protocols, it seems that the formula 'care shall be taken in warfare to protect the natural environment' reduces 'the effect of the provision by allowing some latitude of judgment.' The formula is not used in Article 35(3), where the drafters only chose for a prohibition in the style of the first two paragraphs, 'which is therefore more stringent.'[184] Schmitt also writes that 'at first glance' the phrase 'care shall be taken' appears to set a low standard.[185]

[180] Compare also K Hulme, *War Torn Environment: Interpreting the Legal Threshold*, Martinus Nijhoff Publishers, Leiden, 2004, pp 80–1.

[181] See also: Report to the Third Committee on the Work of the Working Group, Committee III, 3 Apr 1975 (CDDH/III/275), on Art 48 *bis* [present Art 55. EVK] and Art 33 [present Art 35. EVK], para 3, of Protocol I, in: Levie, *Protection of War Victims: Protocol 1 to the 1949 Geneva Conventions; Vol 2*, p 270, and in: Levie, *Protection of War Victims: Protocol 1 to the 1949 Geneva Conventions; Vol 3*, p 270. Similarly: Dinstein, *The Conduct of Hostilities under the Law of International Armed Conflict*, p 182.

[182] Sandoz, Swinaraski, Zimmerman, *Commentary on the Additional Protocols; of 8 Jun 1977 to the Geneva Conventions of 12 Aug 1949*, pp 663.

[183] Both provisions are not each other's mirror image. If they had been opposites, the drafters would have made use of antonyms: the antonym of prohibition is obligation, and the antonym of duty of care is negligence.

[184] Sandoz, Swinaraski, Zimmerman, *Commentary on the Additional Protocols; of 8 Jun 1977 to the Geneva Conventions of 12 Aug 1949*, pp 414, 663. Also Lijnzaad, Tanja, *Protection of the Environment in Times of Armed Conflict: The Iraq-Kuwait War*, p 181.

[185] Schmitt, *Green War: An Assessment of the Environmental Law of International Armed Conflict*, pp 73–4.

On the other hand, it is similarly arguable that the first sentence of Article 55(1) has a wider scope of application and entails a larger responsibility. A prohibition only implies abstention and is negative by nature, whereas a duty of care could also involve action or due diligence and is positive by nature.[186] *Black's Law Dictionary* recognises three degrees of care that inversely correspond with the three degrees of negligence, which are each other's complements, and which are dependent on the circumstances of each case. These are slight care, ordinary, reasonable or due care, and great care.[187] Assuming that in this case due or reasonable care is required, this means that:

> [t]hat degree of care [is required] that a reasonable person can be expected to exercise to avoid harm reasonably foreseeable if such care is not taken.[188]

It is not unthinkable that this degree of care requires more than just refraining from the use of means and methods of warfare that are intended or expected to cause damage to the environment, and it may even include preventive action.[189] This interpretation would be supported by the fact that Article 55 continues by illustrating this duty of care by laying down the exemplary prohibition of using means and methods that cause damage to the environment and which prejudice the health and survival of the population.[190]

In this context, Hulme even argues that the process of calculating the potential risks to the environment before an attack is launched 'resembles the concept of environmental impact assessments (EIA) as utilised in environmental law.' Such assessments are, according to her, not alien to the military world since:

> [i]n a similar way, a procedure akin to an impact assessment is required in the balancing of values for the military principle of proportionality.

If that would be case, this would mean that the obligation of care would be ongoing and applicable both in offense and defence; would include taking into account form, type, extent, long-term effects of the damage on flora and fauna and the nature of environment; would have to be detailed to a certain extent and would need to be updated regularly; and might

186 Similarly: Hulme, *War Torn Environment: Interpreting the Legal Threshold*, p 81.

187 HC Black (et. al), *Black's Law Dictionary*, West Publishing, St Paul, MN, 1991, pp 145–6.

188 Black, *Black's Law Dictionary*, p 345.

189 Simonds, however, is very determined that 'Articles 35 and 55 do not include preventive or precautionary measures. They prohibit only demonstrated damage to some element of the environment, not activities that pose environmental hazards. They thus do not reflect preventive theories of environmental law.' Simonds, *Conventional Warfare and Environmental Protection: A Proposal for International Legal Reform*, p 175.

190 Schmitt, *Green War: An Assessment of the Environmental Law of International Armed Conflict*, pp 73–4; Schmitt, *Humanitarian Law and the Environment*, p 277.

even entail further obligations in order to limit the foreseeable damage as much as possible.[191]

Furthermore, liability for not taking action against others for whom one is not directly responsible is not unknown in both national private law and international law. Under the law of state responsibility, for example, states have a general duty of care towards other states not to allow their territories to be used by private individuals, for whom they have no direct responsibility, to the detriment of other states. If a state cannot show due diligence in attempting to prevent these harmful activities, it has been negligent, and is consequently responsible for the resulting damage.[192]

Be that as it may, both Articles 35(3) and 55(1) are believed to cover similar ground,[193] and it has never been claimed by the ICRC or States Parties that Article 55 prohibits more than Article 35.[194] A wide responsibility under Article 55(1) is still an interesting thought though, and the duty of care in the paragraph's first sentence may reflect a customary rule of international law, as will be explained further below.

Finally, Verwey also implies a difference in scope between both provisions. Where Article 35(3) falls under the basic rules on means and methods of warfare, Article 55 is placed in the context of the protection of civilian objects. According to Verwey, this means that the protection of

[191] Hulme, *War Torn Environment: Interpreting the Legal Threshold*, pp 80–8.

[192] According to Max Huber in the Island of Palmas Case, '[t]erritorial sovereignty, as has already been said, involves the exclusive right to display the activities of a state. This right has as corollary a duty: the obligation to protect within the territory the rights of other states, in particular their right to integrity and inviolability in peace and in war (. . .).'The Island of Palmas (or Miangas), Apr 4, 1928, Arbitral Award; rendered by Max Huber, Arbitrator, American Journal of International Law, Vol 22, 1928, p 867, at p 876. See also: Trail Smelter Arbitration (US v Canada); 16 Apr 1938, 11 Mar 1941, in: H Lauterpacht (Ed), *Annual Digest and Reports of Public International Law Cases; Being a Selection from the Decisions of International and National Courts and Tribunals given during the Years 1938–1940*, (also published as International Law Reports, Vol 9), Butterworth & Co. (Publishers), London, 1942, Case No 104 (pp. 315–33), p 317; Case Concerning the Barcelona Traction, Light and Power Company, Limited (Belgium v Spain), Judgment of 5 Feb 1970, ICJICJ Reports, 1970, paras 33–6, pp 32–3.

[193] Solf writes that '[a]rticle 35 reinforces the implication of Art. 35 that care must be taken to avoid collateral catastrophic effects on the natural environment resulting from such methods or means of warfare employed for purposes other than causing such effect on the environment.' Solf, in: Bothe, Partsch, Solf, *New Rules for Victims of Armed Conflicts; Commentary on the Two 1977 Protocols Additional to the Geneva Conventions of 1949*, pp 345–6.

[194] WD Verwey, *Observations on the Legal Protection of the Environment in Times of International Armed Conflict*, Hague Yearbook of International Law, Vol 7, 1994, p 38; WD Verwey, *Protection of the Environment in Times of Armed Conflict: In Search of a New Legal Perspective*, Leiden Journal of International Law, Vol 8, 1995, p 13; WD Verwey, *Comment: Protection of the Environment in Times of Armed Conflict—Do We Need Additional Rules?*, in: RJ Grunawalt, JE King, RS McClain (Eds), *Protection of the Environment during Armed Conflict*, International Law Studies 1996, Vol 69, Naval War College, Newport, RI, 1996, p 561. Also: Dinstein, *Protection of the Environment in International Armed Conflict*, in: Frowein, Wolfrum (Eds), *Max Planck Yearbook of United Nations Law*, p 531; Dinstein, *The Conduct of Hostilities under the Law of International Armed Conflict*, p 182. Schmitt believes that the provision in Art 55 'might be simply hortatory, and merit no formal prescriptive valance beyond that.' Schmitt, *Green War: An Assessment of the Environmental Law of International Armed Conflict*, p 73.

Article 55 does not extend to elements of the environment that may be considered military objects in the sense of Article 52(2) Additional Protocol I. Because:

> this provision ranks under Part IV, chapter III, which is entitled 'Civilian Objects', Article 55, paragraph 1, does not apply to means and methods of warfare affecting non-civilian parts, objects or assets of the environment, even if they would cause triple standard damage to them (. . .). Identifying affected parts, objects or assets of the environment as a military object or as an object of military significance would suffice to exclude the applicability of Article 55.[195]

If this interpretation of Article 55 must be understood as implying that Article 55 does not protect the environment if it is used as a military object, it does not fully convince, however. Chapter III provides general protection to civilian objects under Article 52 and specific protection to a number of particular objects under Articles 53–56. These are cultural objects and places of worship (Article 53), objects that are indispensable to the survival of the civilian population (Article 54), the natural environment (Article 55), and works and installations containing dangerous forces (Article 56). Although each of these particular objects would seem to be a civilian object at first sight, the drafters of Additional Protocol I thought it necessary to lay down specific provisions for these objects and specify the exact conditions for immunity and the exact circumstances under which this immunity shall cease to apply. According to Articles 54(3) and 56(2), these particular civilian objects lose their immunity if they are used for military purposes and therewith become military objects. No such exception was included in Article 55 with respect to the protection of the environment, however, which seems to imply—by reference to the maxim *expressio unius est exclusio alterius*—that the protection of Article 55 is in this respect unconditional, and does not cease to apply in cases where the environment is a military object.[196] Furthermore, it is arguable that Articles 53–56

[195] Verwey, *Protection of the Environment in Times of Armed Conflict: In Search of a New Legal Perspective*, p 13. Similarly, Verwey, *Observations on the Legal Protection of the Environment in Times of International Armed Conflict*, p 38; Verwey, *Comment: Protection of the Environment in Times of Armed Conflict—Do We Need Additional Rules?* in: Grunawalt, King, McClain, *Protection of the Environment during Armed Conflict*, p 562. Also Dinstein emphasises the position of Art 55 in a chapter entitled 'Civilian Objects' and writes: 'In comparison to civilian objects in general, the natural environment is granted special protection (. . .). But the point is that, once classified as a civilian object, the natural environment must not be the object of attack.' If aspects of the environment can be considered military objects, then 'it would be exposed to attack.' He does not refer to Art 55 in case the environment is identified as a military object. Dinstein, *Protection of the Environment in International Armed Conflict*, in: Frowein, Wolfrum (Eds), *Max Planck Yearbook of United Nations Law*, pp 533–4.

[196] Similarly M Bothe, *The Protection of the Environment in Times of Armed Conflict; Legal Rules, Uncertainty, Deficiencies, and Possible Developments*, German Yearbook of International Law, Vol 34, 1991, p 56. 'Thus, Articles 35 and 55 prohibit causing damage to the environment even where the environment constitutes a military objective or where the damage to the environment may be considered as not being excessive in relation to the military advantage anticipated.'

prevail as *leges speciales* over the general protection of Article 52 in accordance with the maxim *lex specialis derogat legi generali*,[197] but this will be discussed in section 3 on indirect protection of the environment during international armed conflict.

2.2.3.3.3 Similarities between Art. 35(3) and Art. 55

Both Article 35 and 55 prohibit the use of means and methods of warfare that are either intended or expected to damage the environment. This means that not only are deliberate or direct attacks on the environment prohibited, but also attacks of which it is reasonably foreseeable that they will lead to environmental damage.[198] This is irrespective of the weapons used and must be well distinguished from ENMOD which is more specific and which intends to protect the environment by prohibiting the use of the environment, or more specifically, the use of natural processes, as a weapon of warfare.[199]

Requiring that the environmental damage is reasonably foreseeable means that those who deploy these means or methods of warfare must know beforehand to a certain extent that they may have detrimental effects on the environment. This implies that if they can not reasonably know that they may have adverse environmental impact and such damage is accidental, no violation of either Article can be established.[200] This interpretation is supported by declarations made by the United Kingdom and France upon ratification of Additional Protocol I, respectively on 28 January 1998 and 11 April 2001.[201] Both states stated that the risk of environmental damage as a result of the use of means and methods of warfare must be assessed 'objectively on the basis of information available at the time'.[202]

[197] Although the maxim *lex specialis derogat legi generali* is one of the general rules of conflict and stems from classic Roman law, it cannot be found in this specific form. The Roman lawyer Papinianus however, described the rule as follows: '*In toto iure generi per speciem derogatur*' (D 50,17,80) and it is found in similar words in canon law in Liber Sextus 5,13,34. Please note that the verb '*derogare*' comes with the dative and not with the ablative or nominative. It is therefore *lex specialis derogat legi generali* and not *lex specialis derogate lege generale*.

[198] Prohibiting the use of means or methods of warfare that are not only intended but also expected to cause damage to the environment was, according to Schmitt, 'obviously designed to preclude any argument that since collateral damage is not "intended", it is not encompassed in the prohibition.' This is nothing new in the law of war. Schmitt, *Green War: An Assessment of the Environmental Law of International Armed Conflict*, p 72.

[199] Sandoz, Swinaraski, Zimmerman, *Commentary on the Additional Protocols; of 8 Jun 1977 to the Geneva Conventions of 12 Aug 1949*, pp 414–15, 420.

[200] M Bothe, *War and Environment*, in: R Bernhardt (Ed), *Encyclopaedia of Public International Law; Vol Four; Quirin, Ex Parte to Zones of Peace*, Elsevier, Amsterdam, 2000, p 1344; Dinstein, *The Conduct of Hostilities under the Law of International Armed Conflict*, p 183.

[201] Through <http://www.icrc.org/>.

[202] Through <http://www.icrc.org/ihl.nsf/>. Also J-M. Henckaerts, L Doswald-Beck (Eds), *Customary International Humanitarian Law; Vol II: Practice; Part 1*, International Committee of the Red Cross, Cambridge University Press, Cambridge, 2005, p 877; UK Ministry of Defence, *The Manual of the Law of Armed Conflict*, Oxford University Press, Oxford,

Verwey points in this context to the two following difficulties. Firstly, certain means and methods may cause harm that is not directly demonstrable, and secondly, it is still extremely difficult to analyse natural processes and to understand how certain activities will impact the environment in the long term:

> [M]any interactive natural processes have not yet been (fully) understood, resulting in the fact that harmful effects which are not (yet) recognized or expected may occur now or in the future. Only quite recently, science has become able to demonstrate that even apparently restricted, relatively short-term and seemingly insignificant forms of environmental impact may subsequently turn out to have triggered serious or significant ecological disruption.[203]

Therefore, although the Protocol does incorporate a precautionary element through the phrase 'or may be expected', this does not seem to go as far as the precautionary approach which is sometimes taken within the framework of peacetime international environmental law.[204] Articles 35(3) and 55 require that certain environmental consequences are reasonably foreseeable, whereas the precautionary principle does not require full scientific certainty or a causal connection between act and environmental degradation.[205]

2004, p 76. France made the same declaration upon ratification with respect to Art 8(2)(b)(iv) of the Statute of the International Criminal Court, that will be discussed further below. Through <http://untreaty.un.org/>.

[203] Verwey, *Protection of the Environment in Times of Armed Conflict: In Search of a New Legal Perspective*, p 12. Also: Verwey, *Observations on the Legal Protection of the Environment in Times of International Armed Conflict*, p 37; Verwey, *Comment: Protection of the Environment in Times of Armed Conflict—Do We Need Additional Rules?*, in: Grunawalt, King, McClain, *Protection of the Environment during Armed Conflict*, p 561.

[204] Rogers, *Law on the Battlefield*, p 169.

[205] The precautionary principle was first laid down in Principle 15 of the 1992 Rio Declaration: 'In order to protect the environment, the precautionary approach shall be widely applied by States according to their capabilities. Where there are threats of serious or irreversible damage, lack of full scientific certainty shall not be used as a reason for postponing cost-effective measures to prevent environmental degradation'. A/CONF.151/26/Rev 1 (Vol I), Report of the United Nations Conference on Environment and Development, Rio de Janeiro, 3–14 Jun 1992, Vol I, Resolutions Adopted by the Conference; Resolution 1, Adoption of Texts on Environment and Development; Annex I, Rio Declaration on Environment and Development, United Nations, New York, 1993. Before 1992, the principle had been applied most notably in the case of the Montreal Protocol on Substances that Deplete the Ozone Layer (Montreal Protocol on Substances that Deplete the Ozone Layer, opened for signature on 16 Sep 1987, entered into force on 1 Jan 1989, as amended in London (27–29 Jun 1990), Nairobi (19–21 Jun 1991) and Copenhagen (23–24 Nov 1992), UNTS, Vol 1522, No 26369. Protocol to the 1985 Vienna Convention for the Protection of the Ozone Layer, opened for signature on 22 Mar 1985, entered into force on 22 Sep 1988, UNTS, Vol 1513, No 26164). The Protocol 'required action on the part of states before the causal link between ozone depletion and CFCs had been conclusively demonstrated.' P Birnie, A Boyle, *International Law & The Environment*, Oxford University Press, Oxford, 2002, p 117.

2.2.3.3.4 The Natural Environment

Despite differences in formulation, and the possibility of different levels of responsibility, both provisions intend to protect the natural environment from the destructive effects of warfare. From the preparatory works, it appears that the phrase 'natural environment' was first used by Australia when it proposed on 19 March 1974 to add a provision on the protection of the natural environment within the framework of depicting certain civilian objects that would be protected in times of international armed conflict.[206] The suggestion by the Australian delegation intended to prohibit 'to despoil the natural environment as a technique of warfare.'

Although the formulation changed over time, the use of the phrase 'natural environment' was later followed by the Biotope Group in its proposal for Article 55,[207] as well as by the Rapporteur for Committee III, United States Representative, Ambassador Aldrich in his proposals first for Article 55 and later for Article 35(3).[208] Earlier proposals for Article 35(3) referred to 'natural human environmental conditions',[209] 'the ecological balance of the human environment',[210] 'the natural conditions of the human environment',[211] and 'the stability of the ecosystem'.[212] Earlier proposals for Article 55 referred to 'a balanced environment'[213], and to 'the stability of the ecosystem',[214] in addition to references to the natural environment.

[206] CDDH/III/60, 19 Mar 1974 (III, 20), proposed new Art [55] by Australia, in: Levie, *Protection of War Victims: Protocol 1 to the 1949 Geneva Conventions; Vol 3*, p 259.

[207] Report of the Chairman of the Group 'Biotope', Committee III, 11 Mar 1975 (CDDH/III/GT/35), in: Levie, *Protection of War Victims: Protocol 1 to the 1949 Geneva Conventions; Vol 3*, p 268.

[208] Proposal by the Rapporteur, 4 Apr 1975 (CDDH/III/276): Art [55] and Proposal by the Rapporteur, Committee III, 4 Apr 1975 (CDDH/III/277): Art [35(3)], respectively in: Levie, *Protection of War Victims: Protocol 1 to the 1949 Geneva Conventions; Vol 3*, pp 270–1, and in: Levie, *Protection of War Victims: Protocol 1 to the 1949 Geneva Conventions; Vol 2*, p 271.

[209] CDDH/III/108, 11 Sep 1974 (III, 155), proposed amendment by the German Democratic Republic, in: Levie, *Protection of War Victims: Protocol 1 to the 1949 Geneva Conventions; Vol 2*, p 254.

[210] CDDH/III/222, 24 Feb 1975 (III, 156), proposed amendment by the Arab Republic of Egypt, Australia, Czechoslovakia, Finland, German Democratic Republic, Hungary, Ireland, Norway, Yugoslavia, and Sudan, in: Levie, *Protection of War Victims: Protocol 1 to the 1949 Geneva Conventions; Vol 2*, p 254.

[211] CDDH/III/238, 25 Feb 1975 (III, 157), proposed amendment by the Democratic Republic of Viet-Nam (*sic*), and Uganda, in: Levie, *Protection of War Victims: Protocol 1 to the 1949 Geneva Conventions; Vol 2*, pp 255–6.

[212] Report of the Chairman of the Group 'Biotope', Committee III, 11 Mar 1975 (CDDH/III/GT/35), in: Levie, *Protection of War Victims: Protocol 1 to the 1949 Geneva Conventions; Vol 2*, p 268.

[213] CDDH/III/64, 19 Mar 1974 (III, 221), proposed amendment by Czechoslovakia, the German Democratic Republic, and Hungary, in: Levie, *Protection of War Victims: Protocol 1 to the 1949 Geneva Conventions; Vol 3*, p 259.

[214] Report of the Chairman of the Group 'Biotope', Committee III, 11 Mar 1975 (CDDH/III/GT/35), in: Levie, *Protection of War Victims: Protocol 1 to the 1949 Geneva Conventions; Vol 3*, p 270; Proposal by the Rapporteur: Art [55], in: Levie, *Protection of War Victims: Protocol 1 to the 1949 Geneva Conventions; Vol 3*, p 268.

Additional Protocol I remains silent on the actual meaning of the phrase, however. Where the environment was described in ENMOD as 'the Earth, including its biota, lithosphere, hydrosphere and atmosphere',[215] and 'outer space', the phrase 'natural environment' is left undefined in the Protocol. Although definitions are usually convenient, they carry not only an inherent danger, 'for there is hardly one which cannot be undermined',[216] but they are also not even always necessary.[217]

Still, it may be useful to clarify the concept to some extent and to see what the drafters meant with the 'natural environment'. *Collins Dictionary* primarily describes the 'environment' as:

> external conditions or surroundings, esp. those in which people live or work; *Ecology*, the external surroundings in which a plant or animal lives, which tend to influence its development and behaviour.[218]

And *Collins Cobuild* distinguishes between a person's personal environment; the human environment that:

> consists of the particular natural surroundings in which you live or exist, considered in relation to their physical characteristics or weather conditions;

and 'the environment' that is defined as 'the natural world or land, sea, air, plants, and animals'.[219]

The same distinction between the human environment and the natural environment which is connected with ecology and natural life is made by the so-called Biotope Group, in the context of Article 35(3) and Article 55. According to this informal working group:

> Article [55] is directed to the protection of the *natural* environment as distinct from the *human* environment. The natural environment relates to external conditions and influences which affect the life, development and the survival of the civilian population and to living organisms. The human environment may be understood to relate only to the immediate surroundings in which the civilian population lives. The natural environment is wider in scope than the human environment

[215] Biota means plant and animal life and the lithosphere, hydrosphere and atmosphere refer respectively to the earth's ground, its waters and its air.

[216] Javolenus, *omnis definitio in iure civili periculosa est, parum est enim ut non subverti possit*, 'every definition in the civil law is dangerous, for there is hardly one which cannot be undermined', Digest (of Justinian), 50.17.202, quoted from Final Report of the International Committee on the Formation of Customary (General) International Law; Principles Applicable to the Formation of General Customary International Law, in: The International Law Association, *Report of the Sixty-Ninth Conference, London, 2000*, p 719, fn 20.

[217] When Justice Stewart of the United States Supreme Court was confronted in 1964 with a case that involved the showing of an obscene motion picture and the freedom of speech in the Constitution's First Amendment and had to interpret the term pornography, he said: 'I shall not today attempt further to define the kinds of material I understand to be embraced within that shorthand description; and perhaps I could never succeed in intelligibly doing so. But I know it when I see it, and the motion picture involved in this case is not that.' Mr Justice Stewart, concurring, in: US Supreme Court; *Jacobellis v Ohio*, 378 US 184 (1964).

[218] *Collins Dictionary*, p 517.

[219] *Collins Cobuild English Dictionary*, HarperCollins Publishers, Glasgow, 1995, p 555.

> and is essential to the existence of the civilian population. It is for this reason that Article [55] seeks to protect the natural environment and to prohibit disturbance of it to the prejudice of the health and survival of the civilian population.[220]

Similarly, according to the ICRC's Commentary:

> [t]he concept of the natural environment should be understood in the widest sense to cover the biological environment in which a population is living. It does not consist merely of the objects indispensable to survival (. . .) but also includes forests and other vegetation (. . .), as well as fauna, flora and other biological or climatic elements.[221]

It seems therefore that the focus of attention of the drafters of Additional Protocol I was on the land environment, ie those parts of nature that were most visible and that had the most direct impact on human civilisation. This is not surprising since the laws of war have always been anthropocentric in character and most of the hostilities between states are carried out on land in the first place. But this focus of the drafters does not necessarily exclude other parts of the natural environment, namely the marine environment and the atmosphere. After all, according to *Collins Cobuild*, the 'environment' includes 'the natural world or land, sea, air, plants, and animals' and the environment on land is only a fraction of the global environment. As a matter of fact, over 70 per cent of the Earth's surface is covered by oceans and the atmosphere is even omnipresent.

It would certainly be desirable to include the marine environment and the atmosphere under the phrase 'natural environment' of Articles 35(3) and 55. Nowadays, states have significant navies and air forces that are capable of causing significant damage to the marine environment and the atmosphere, but it is not self-evident whether navies and air forces fall under the scope of Additional Protocol I in the first place. The laws of war have traditionally distinguished between land, naval and aerial warfare[222] and it seems that as far as the carrying out of hostilities is concerned,

[220] Report of the Chairman of the Group 'Biotope', Committee III, 11 Mar 1975 (CDDH/III/GT/35), in: Levie, *Protection of War Victims: Protocol 1 to the 1949 Geneva Conventions; Vol 2*, p 267, and Levie, *Protection of War Victims: Protocol 1 to the 1949 Geneva Conventions; Vol 3*, p 267.

[221] Sandoz, Swinaraski, Zimmerman, *Commentary on the Additional Protocols; of 8 Jun 1977 to the Geneva Conventions of 12 Aug 1949*, p 662.

[222] Each type of warfare had different purposes and required different techniques. Naval warfare was not intended to subjugate the enemy but rather to gain control over the oceans. Detter, *The Law of War*, p 308; W Heintschel von Heinegg, *The Law of Armed Conflict at Sea*, in: Fleck, *The Handbook of Humanitarian Law in Armed Conflicts*, p 405. Greenwood observes that naval warfare also has larger scope for affecting the rights of neutrals. C Greenwood, *Historical Development and Legal Basis*, in: Fleck, *The Handbook of Humanitarian Law in Armed Conflicts*, p 11. Also Rauch on the specific and peculiar difficulties of the law of naval warfare: E Rauch, *The Protocol Additional to the Geneva Conventions for the Protection of Victims of International Armed Conflicts and the United Nations Convention on the Law of the Sea: Repercussions on the Law of Naval Warfare; Report to the Committee for the Protection of Human Life in Armed Conflict of the International Society for Military Law and Law of War*, Duncker & Humblot, Berlin, 1984, p 59.

Additional Protocol I is primarily aimed at the reaffirmation of the rules with respect to warfare on land. As was mentioned above, Protocol I does not only update and supplement existing rules of international humanitarian law as ultimately laid down in the four Geneva Conventions of 1949,[223] to which the Protocol is additional, but it also reaffirms and develops rules of *ius in bello* with respect to the conduct of warfare. Until 1977, these rules were either of customary nature or laid down in a number of conventions or declarations, the majority of which were concluded at the 1899 and 1907 Peace Conferences in The Hague. Of these documents, only the 1899 and 1907 Hague Regulations on Land Warfare[224] provided a comprehensive framework on the carrying out of hostilities. The other 1899 and 1907 conventions and declarations, and a number of other conventions of later date only focused on specific aspects of warfare, mostly with respect to warfare on sea,[225] or were of humanitarian character. The only other document with general rules on warfare were the 1923 Hague Rules on Aerial Warfare but they never made it to a legally binding document.[226]

[223] Geneva Convention (I) for the Amelioration of the Condition of the Wounded and Sick in Armed Forces in the Field; Geneva Convention (II) for the Amelioration of the Condition of Wounded, Sick and Shipwrecked Members of Armed Forces at Sea; Geneva Convention (III) relative to the Treatment of Prisoners of War; Geneva Convention (IV) relative to the Protection of Civilian Persons in Time of War, all signed on 12 Aug 1949, entered into force on 21 Oct 1950, UNTS, Vol 75, No 970–3.

[224] Hague Convention (II) with respect to the Laws and Customs of War on Land, with annexed Regulations, signed on 29 Jul 1899, entered into force on 4 Sep 1900, AJIL, Vol 1, No 2, Supplement: Official Documents, 1907, p 129, supplemented by Hague Convention (IV) Respecting the Laws and Customs of War on Land, with annexed Regulations, signed on 18 Oct 1907, entered into force on 26 Jan 1910, AJIL, Vol 2, No 1/2, Supplement: Official Documents, 1908, p 90.

[225] For naval warfare a whole variety of conventions and declarations was concluded ranging from the regulation of submarine warfare (1909 London Declaration; 1922 Washington Treaty that never entered into force; 1930 London Treaty; 1936 London Protocol) and the use of automatic submarine contact mines (1907 Hague Convention VIII) to naval bombardment (1907 Hague Convention IX) and the status, conversion and capture of merchant ships or ships in general (1907 Hague Convention VI, VII, and XI).

[226] 1923 Hague Rules of Aerial Warfare, in: Roberts, Guelff, *Documents on the Laws of War*, pp 141–53. An International Commission of Jurists established in 1922 adopted a General Report on the Revision of the Rules of Warfare in 1923, Part II of which dealt with Aerial Warfare. These Hague Rules on Aerial Warfare never made it to an international agreement, however. The only other treaties dealing with aerial warfare were the 1899 Hague Declaration (IV, 1) to Prohibit for the Term of Five Years the Launching of Projectiles and Explosives from Balloons, and Other Methods of a Similar Nature, signed on 29 Jul 1899, entered into force on 4 Sep 1900, D Schindler, J Toman (Eds), *The Laws of Armed Conflicts; A Collection of Conventions, Resolutions and Other Documents*, Martinus Nijhoff Publishers, Dordrecht, 1988, p 201, followed by the 1907 Hague Declaration (XIV) Prohibiting the Discharge of Projectiles and Explosives from Balloons, signed on 18 Oct 1907, entered into force on 27 Nov 1909, AJIL, Vol 2, No 1/2, Supplement: Official Documents, 1908, p 216. In principle only air-to-air warfare is regulated by specific rules on aerial warfare. When aircraft are flying over land and are involved in air-to-land operations, they fall under the rules on land warfare; when they fly over sea and are involved in air-to-sea operations, they fall under the rules on naval warfare. FAF von der Heydte, *Air Warfare*, in: R Bernhardt (Ed), *Encyclopaedia of Public International Law; Vol One; Aalands Islands to Dumbarton Oaks Conference (1944)*, North-Holland Publishing Company, Amsterdam, 1992, p 83.

Although the Protocol seems to focus primarily on land warfare,[227] it does not explicitly say so. As a matter of fact, there is no reference to land, naval or aerial warfare at all in the Protocol's definition of its scope of application. Article 1 of Additional Protocol I only states that:

> [t]his Protocol, which supplements the Geneva Conventions of 12 August 1949 for the protection of war victims, shall apply in the situations referred to in Article 2 common to those Conventions,

ie in 'all cases of declared war' or armed conflict between two or more Contracting Parties, as well as in 'all cases of partial or total occupation of the territory of a High Contracting Party.'

This silence can be interpreted in two ways. On the one hand, it is arguable that it is significant since it shows that the drafters did not intend to discuss the rules on naval and aerial warfare and regarded the primary application of the rules on the conduct of hostilities on land for granted. After all, 'there was no systematic attempt to include three important areas of the laws of war in this updating process',[228] and according to Kalshoven and Zegveld, '[t]he Diplomatic Conference of 1974–1977 had no mandate to include the law of warfare at sea in its work'.[229] On the other hand, it is arguable that the silence in the Protocol's scope of application does not mean anything, because the Protocol is primarily a reaffirmation and development of the law of Geneva as laid down in the Geneva Conventions and the law of Geneva does not deal with the carrying out of hostilities. Furthermore, Geneva Convention II deals with the treatment of wounded, sick and shipwrecked members of armed forces at sea which implies that warfare at sea is included in the phrase 'armed conflict' of Article 1 of Additional Protocol I.

Although it is true that the drafters of Additional Protocol I had no intention to discuss the rules on naval and aerial warfare in detail, the

[227] Compare, eg, Art 49(2) on the scope of application of S I of Part IV of the Protocol on General protection Against Effects of Hostilities: 'The provisions of this Protocol with respect to attacks apply to all attacks in whatever territory conducted, including the national territory belonging to a Party to the conflict but under the control of an adverse party.' The provision was included to stress the fact that the entire civilian population of all warring states had to be granted protection against attack, but also indicated that the provisions of the Protocol dealing with actual hostilities apply in principle to the territories of States Parties, ie on land.

[228] M Bothe, *Commentary—1977 Geneva Protocol I Additional to the Geneva Conventions of 12 Aug 1949, and Relating to the protection of Victims of International Armed Conflicts*, in: N Ronzitti (Ed), *The Law of Naval Warfare; A Collection of Agreements and Documents with Commentaries*, Martinus Nijhoff Publishers, Dordrecht, 1988, p 760. Bothe refers here to the law of neutrality, the law of air warfare and the law of naval warfare.

[229] Kalshoven, Zegveld, *Constraints on the Waging of War; An Introduction to International Humanitarian Law*, p 181. Similarly, D Fleck, *Topical Approaches towards Developing the Laws of Armed Conflict at Sea*, in: AJM Delissen, GJ Tanja (Eds), *Humanitarian Law of Armed Conflict; Challenges Ahead; Essays in Honour of Frits Kalshoven*, Martinus Nijhoff Publishers, Dordrecht, 1991, p 408. See also, Art 49(3), second sentence AP I.

latter interpretation seems more appealing because there are not only certain provisions that deal specifically with naval and aerial warfare, but there are also whole sections in Additional Protocol I that focus on certain aspects of warfare at sea,[230] and in the air. In addition to provisions on the treatment of shipwrecked and aircraft crew in distress,[231] medical transportation over sea and through the air,[232] and a reference to the generally recognised rules on the use of flags,[233] Article 49(3) provides specifically that the rules of Part IV, Section I dealing with the general protection of the civilian population against the effects of hostilities also apply to naval and aerial warfare to the extent that they affect civilians on land. Article 49(3) states:

> The provisions of this Section apply to any land, air or sea warfare which may affect the civilian population, individual civilians or civilian objects on land. They further apply to all attacks from the sea or from the air against objectives on land but do not otherwise affect the rules of international law applicable in armed conflict at sea or in the air.

Article 49(4) furthermore provides that the rules of Part IV, Section I are additional to:

> other rules of international law relating to the protection of civilians and civilian objects on land, at sea or in the air against the effects of hostilities.

Because Article 55 falls under Part IV, Section I, this means that within the framework of those naval and aerial operations that are covered by this section, care must be taken 'to protect the natural environment against widespread, long-term and severe damage' including the marine environment and the atmosphere. Which aspects of naval and aerial warfare fall under the scope of Article 49(3) are not exactly clear, however. The provision seems to be primarily aimed at operations by naval and air forces against targets on land, but it is not necessarily limited to the actual carrying out of hostilities. As far as naval operations are concerned, Rauch claims that a literal interpretation of Article 49(3) can only lead to the conclusion that in addition to these operations just mentioned, also measures against maritime commerce fall under Article 49(3) and even attacks with collateral effects on civilian objects at sea and in the air:

230 Bothe, *Commentary—1977 Geneva Protocol I Additional to the Geneva Conventions of 12 Aug 1949, and Relating to the protection of Victims of International Armed Conflicts*, in: Ronzitti (Ed), *The Law of Naval Warfare; A Collection of Agreements and Documents with Commentaries*, p 760; Rauch, *The Protocol Additional to the Geneva Conventions for the Protection of Victims of International Armed Conflicts and the United Nations Convention on the Law of the Sea: Repercussions on the Law of Naval Warfare; Report to the Committee for the Protection of Human Life in Armed Conflict of the International Society for Military Law and Law of War*, p 57.

231 Additional Protocol I, Part II, Section I (Arts 8–20) and Art 42.

232 Additional Protocol I, Part II, Section II (Arts 21–31).

233 Art 39(3) AP I.

> The provisions of Section I of part IV (. . .) apply to all (. . .) measures against the maritime commerce of the enemy whether under its own flag or under neutral flags; (. . .) apply to all other acts of naval warfare as far as the effects of hostilities on civilian and civilian objects on land, at sea, or in the air are concerned, as regulated by conventional or customary international humanitarian law, including collateral damage of operations against enemy warships and effects of belligerent acts against merchant ships.[234]

The first interpretation of Article 49(3) seems arguable in view of the use of the general term 'sea warfare' in the Article 49(3)'s first sentence, rather than 'attacks', and in view of the use of the word 'further' in the second sentence.[235] The second sentence of Article 49(3) provides:

> [The provisions of this Section] further apply to any land, air or sea warfare which may affect the civilian population, individual civilians or civilian objects on land.

It is therefore not impossible that forceful action against maritime commerce, other than the carrying out of hostilities, falls under the scope of Part IV, Section I as long as it affects the civilian population on land. It should be noted, however, that the drafters of the Protocol did not intend to change the law of naval blockade.[236]

The second interpretation is not convincing since the effects of land, air or sea warfare must be felt by 'the civilian population, individual civilians or civilian objects on land.' It seems far-fetched to include civilians or civil-

[234] Rauch, *The Protocol Additional to the Geneva Conventions for the Protection of Victims of International Armed Conflicts and the United Nations Convention on the Law of the Sea: Repercussions on the Law of Naval Warfare; Report to the Committee for the Protection of Human Life in Armed Conflict of the International Society for Military Law and Law of War*, p 60, 59.

[235] Rauch, *The Protocol Additional to the Geneva Conventions for the Protection of Victims of International Armed Conflicts and the United Nations Convention on the Law of the Sea: Repercussions on the Law of Naval Warfare; Report to the Committee for the Protection of Human Life in Armed Conflict of the International Society for Military Law and Law of War*, p 58. Compare also Bothe on the interpretation of Art 49(3) and his discussion of the phenomenon of naval blockade under Protocol I. Bothe, *Commentary—1977 Geneva Protocol I Additional to the Geneva Conventions of 12 Aug 1949, and Relating to the protection of Victims of International Armed Conflicts*, in: Ronzitti (Ed), *The Law of Naval Warfare; A Collection of Agreements and Documents with Commentaries*, pp 761–4; and Heintschel von Heinegg, *The Law of Armed Conflict at Sea*, in: Fleck, *The Handbook of Humanitarian Law in Armed Conflicts*, pp 470–4. Dinstein strongly disagrees pointing at the original intention of the Diplomatic Conference. Dinstein, *The Conduct of Hostilities under the Law of International Armed Conflict*, p 138.

[236] According to the Report of Committee III of 1975, it is made clear by current Art 49(3) 'that [Article 54(1)] does not change the law of naval blockade'. Report of Committee III, Second Session (CDDH/215/Rev 1; XV, 261), para 73, in: Levie, *Protection of War Victims: Protocol 1 to the 1949 Geneva Conventions; Vol 3*, p 245. Art 54 prohibits starvation and furthermore deals with the protection of objects that are indispensable to the survival of the civilian population. Also Kalshoven, *Reaffirmation and Development of International Humanitarian Law Applicable in Armed Conflicts: the Diplomatic Conference, Geneva, 1974–1977; Part II*, p 126. This view is held 'untenable', however, by Heintschel von Heinegg, because of the language of Arts 49(3) and 54 Additional Protocol I. Heintschel von Heinegg, *The Law of Armed Conflict at Sea*, in: Fleck, *The Handbook of Humanitarian Law in Armed Conflicts*, p 471.

ian objects at sea or in the air in the equation and according to Bothe, Rauch's interpretation is even 'clearly incompatible with the plain meaning of the text.'[237] Furthermore, the original draft proposal of the ICRC did not envisage that civilians in the air and at sea would fall under the protection of Additional Protocol I:

> As regards civilians at sea and in the air (in aircraft, balloons and other objects in flight), they are not deprived of all protection, since other norms of international law, principally customary law, are applicable to them.[238]

There is general agreement, however, that the rules of Part IV, Section I are not applicable to 'attacks from land against ships at sea or aircraft in the superjacent airspace'[239], nor to aerial and naval warfare proper, ie hostilities between military ships, between aircraft, and between ships and aircraft, without impact on the civilian population and civilian objects on land.[240] Although the preparatory works show considerable disagreement between, on the one hand, a number of states that favoured exclusion of the phrase 'on land' in the original draft proposal of the ICRC,[241] and, on

[237] Bothe, *Commentary—1977 Geneva Protocol I Additional to the Geneva Conventions of 12 Aug 1949, and Relating to the protection of Victims of International Armed Conflicts*, in: Ronzitti (Ed), *The Law of Naval Warfare; A Collection of Agreements and Documents with Commentaries*, p 767, endnote 7.

[238] ICRC, *Draft Additional Protocols to the Geneva Conventions of Aug 12, 1949; Commentary*, p 54.

[239] Rauch, *The Protocol Additional to the Geneva Conventions for the Protection of Victims of International Armed Conflicts and the United Nations Convention on the Law of the Sea: Repercussions on the Law of Naval Warfare; Report to the Committee for the Protection of Human Life in Armed Conflict of the International Society for Military Law and Law of War*, p 60. Also Fleck, *Topical Approaches towards Developing the Laws of Armed Conflict at Sea*, in: Delissen, Tanja (Eds), *Humanitarian Law of Armed Conflict; Challenges Ahead; Essays in Honour of Frits Kalshoven*, p 408; Solf, in: Bothe, Partsch, Solf, *New Rules for Victims of Armed Conflicts; Commentary on the Two 1977 Protocols Additional to the Geneva Conventions of 1949*, p 290.

[240] Bothe, *Commentary—1977 Geneva Protocol I Additional to the Geneva Conventions of 12 Aug 1949, and Relating to the protection of Victims of International Armed Conflicts*, in: Ronzitti (Ed), *The Law of Naval Warfare; A Collection of Agreements and Documents with Commentaries*, p 762; Fleck, *Topical Approaches towards Developing the Laws of Armed Conflict at Sea*, in: Delissen, Tanja (Eds), *Humanitarian Law of Armed Conflict; Challenges Ahead; Essays in Honour of Frits Kalshoven*, p 408; Heintschel von Heinegg, *The Law of Armed Conflict at Sea*, in: Fleck, *The Handbook of Humanitarian Law in Armed Conflicts*, p 419; Rauch, *The Protocol Additional to the Geneva Conventions for the Protection of Victims of International Armed Conflicts and the United Nations Convention on the Law of the Sea: Repercussions on the Law of Naval Warfare; Report to the Committee for the Protection of Human Life in Armed Conflict of the International Society for Military Law and Law of War*, p 60; Solf, in: Bothe, Partsch, Solf, *New Rules for Victims of Armed Conflicts; Commentary on the Two 1977 Protocols Additional to the Geneva Conventions of 1949*, p 290.

[241] Romania suggested to delete the limitation 'on land', which amendment was supported in its efforts by states like India, Mongolia, Hungary, Syria, Sudan, Albania, Morocco, and Iraq. The arguments of the former group are scarce. Sudan stated on 12 Mar 1974 that deletion of the words 'on land' 'would not undermine the existing law of sea warfare'. And Romania as the state who proposed to delete the phrase 'on land' stated 1 year later, on 25 Feb 1975, that the phrase unnecessarily limited the scope of the provision and since the UN General Assembly wanted that human rights always had to be respected during armed conflict, the para as suggested by the ICRC 'would introduce unfair discrimination in the protection of the civilian population, for the deciding factor would be its location at a given

the other hand, a number of large navy states that opposed this idea, the phrase was eventually retained.[242] On 24 February 1975, the Working Group that had to deal with this difference of opinion stated that after extensive discussions, there was almost:

> complete agreement that it would be both difficult and undesirable in the time available to try to review and revise the laws applicable to armed conflict at sea and in the air. Moreover, it was clear that [one] should be careful not to revise that body of law inadvertently through this Article.

Therefore, and despite continued dissatisfaction by some delegates, the Working Group proposed to maintain the ICRC draft text and add a second sentence, namely that the provisions in that section:

> do not otherwise affect the existing generally recognized rules of international law applicable to armed conflict at sea or in the air.[243]

In addition, and in order:

> to satisfy those delegations which felt uneasy about the limitation of the scope of this Section of Protocol I to the effects of attacks on objectives on land,[244]

the Conference adopted Article 57(4), which states that:

> [i]n the conduct of military operations at sea or in the air, each Party to the conflict shall (. . .) take all reasonable precautions to avoid losses of civilian lives and damage to civilian objects.

Finally, with respect to the scope of Article 55, Rogers, the editor of the British Military Manual, and also Bothe, submit that the protection of

moment.' CDDH/III/10, 12 Mar 1974 (III, 196), proposed amendment by Romania, in: Levie, *Protection of War Victims: Protocol 1 to the 1949 Geneva Conventions; Vol 3*, p 75; Mr El Sheikh (Sudan), in Meeting of Committee III, 12 Mar 1974 (CDDH/III/SR.3), in: Levie, *Protection of War Victims: Protocol 1 to the 1949 Geneva Conventions; Vol 3*, p 81; Mr Cristescu (Romania), in: Meeting of Committee III, 25 Feb 1975 (CDDH/III/SR.24), in: Levie, *Protection of War Victims: Protocol 1 to the 1949 Geneva Conventions; Vol 3*, p 94.

242 This group included the United States, the United Kingdom, Finland, Belgium, Greece, Sweden, Australia, New Zealand and to a certain extent the Soviet Union. Most delegates refer to the fact that application to naval and aerial warfare was not appropriate since the military experts who had helped to prepare the Conference had not taken these rules into account. Furthermore, the rules regarding naval warfare were too complex and too different from the rules proposed on targeting to be discussed at the Conference without extensive preparation, and the rules on aerial warfare were still uncertain in many respects. Meetings of Committee III, on 12–13 Mar 1974 (CDDH/III/SR.2–4), in: Levie, *Protection of War Victims: Protocol 1 to the 1949 Geneva Conventions; Vol 3*, pp 76–84. See, especially the comments from Sir Hughes-Morgan from the United Kingdom, in: Meeting of Committee III, on 12 Mar 1974 (CDDH/III/SR.3), in Levie, *Protection of War Victims: Protocol 1 to the 1949 Geneva Conventions; Vol 3*, pp 79–80.

243 Report to the Third Commission on the Work of the Working Group, Committee III, 24 Feb 1975 (CDDH/III/224), in: Levie, *Protection of War Victims: Protocol 1 to the 1949 Geneva Conventions; Vol 3*, p 93.

244 Solf, in: Bothe, Partsch, Solf, *New Rules for Victims of Armed Conflicts; Commentary on the Two 1977 Protocols Additional to the Geneva Conventions of 1949*, p 369.

Article 55 also extends to the coastal waters of an enemy state.[245] This is correct if the damage to the environment is the result of land warfare or naval or aerial operations that affect the civilian population or civilian objects on land. However, if this is related to an extended interpretation of the phrase 'on land' this appears to be incorrect.[246] Not only does the term itself seem to exclude territorial waters, also the preparatory works do not leave much room for doubt. According to the ICRC at a meeting of Committee III in 1974:

> the expression "land" meant all national territory, including lakes, rivers, canals and other bodies of water, with the sole exception of territorial seas.[247]

Also the Working Group of Committee III was of the view that 'the words "on land" included rivers, canals, and lakes' and apparently excluded territorial waters,[248] which interpretation was apparently adopted by the Committee.[249] And finally, the United Kingdom stated that the phrase 'on land' included internal waters,[250] and the United States, concurred one day later with the ICRC and explicitly excluded the territorial sea.[251]

Apart from the provisions mentioned above, there are no other provisions dealing specifically with naval or aerial warfare or defining the scope of application of a specific treaty-section. The applicability of Part III, Section I on Methods and Means of Warfare, including Article 35(3), to naval and air warfare is therefore not self-evident. Most of its provisions find their origin in the 1899 and 1907 Hague Regulations on Land Warfare and corresponding rules of customary law so their applicability to land warfare is beyond dispute. However, in view of the general character of this section, it seems likely that the provisions are applicable to all types of

245 Bothe, *The Protection of the Environment in Times of Armed Conflict; Legal Rules, Uncertainty, Deficiencies, and Possible Developments*, p 58. Similarly, Rogers, *Law on the Battlefield*, p 168.

246 See also: H Blix, *Means and Methods of Combat*, in: United Nations Educational, Scientific and Cultural Organization, *International Dimensions of Humanitarian Law*, Martinus Nijhoff Publishers, Dordrecht, 1988, p 142.

247 Mr Mirimanoff-Chilikine (International Committee of the Red Cross), in: Meeting of Committee III, 13 Mar 1974 (CDDH/III/SR.4), in: Levie, *Protection of War Victims: Protocol 1 to the 1949 Geneva Conventions; Vol 3*, p 81.

248 Report of Committee III, First Session (CDDH/50/Rev 1); Art [49(3)] of draft Protocol I, in: Levie, *Protection of War Victims: Protocol 1 to the 1949 Geneva Conventions; Vol 3*, p 91.

249 Mr Herczegh (Hungary), in: Meeting of Committee III, 25 Feb 1975 (CDDH/III/SR.24), in: Levie, *Protection of War Victims: Protocol 1 to the 1949 Geneva Conventions; Vol 3*, p 95.

250 Sir Hughes-Morgan (United Kingdom), in: Meeting of Committee III, 12 Mar 1974 (CDDH/III/SR.3), in: Levie, *Protection of War Victims: Protocol 1 to the 1949 Geneva Conventions; Vol 3*, p 80.

251 Mr Reed (United States of America), in: Meeting of Committee III, 13 Mar 1974 (CDDH/III/SR.4), in: Levie, *Protection of War Victims: Protocol 1 to the 1949 Geneva Conventions; Vol 3*, p 83.

warfare.[252] The title of Part III, Section I speaks of 'warfare' in general, without specification, and the provisions largely reflect general rules of customary international law. Articles 35(1) and (2), for example, stem from the general principles of necessity and humanity by providing that the right to choose means and methods of warfare is not unlimited and that it is prohibited to use means and methods of warfare that cause superfluous injury or unnecessary suffering.[253] These rules, as well as those on perfidy, emblems, quarter and on the protection of combatants that are *hors de combat*, are regarded as generally applicable to all forms of warfare.[254] Only the treatment of aircraft crews in distress and the rules on espionage or the use of flags in naval warfare required specific regulation or mention.

Furthermore, the ICRC explicitly stated in its Commentary to its Draft Additional Protocol of 1973 that would form the basis of the negotiations at the Diplomatic Conference in Geneva that the general provisions on means and methods of warfare in Part III, Section I were applicable to land, naval and aerial warfare. With respect to draft Article 44(1) that would later become Article 49(3), the ICRC stated:

> It should be recalled that Section I of Part III, entitled *Methods and Means of Combat*, which refers mainly to the behaviour of combatants towards each other, extends its scope to military operations as a whole carried out within the general framework of land, air or sea warfare.[255]

The Commentary continued that this could not be said of Section I of Part IV on the general protection of the civilian population against the effects of hostilities that only applied to naval and air warfare to the extent that they affected the civilian population or civilian objects on land.

This view on the applicability of Part III, Section I, including Article 35(3) to naval and air warfare is generally supported in literature although

[252] Rauch states that it is even applicable to warfare in outer space. Rauch, *The Protocol Additional to the Geneva Conventions for the Protection of Victims of International Armed Conflicts and the United Nations Convention on the Law of the Sea: Repercussions on the Law of Naval Warfare; Report to the Committee for the Protection of Human Life in Armed Conflict of the International Society for Military Law and Law of War*, p 141.

[253] Bothe writes that 'although they probably already constitute part of customary international law of naval warfare, their codification in a treaty is new as far as naval warfare is concerned.' Bothe, *Commentary—1977 Geneva Protocol I Additional to the Geneva Conventions of 12 Aug 1949, and Relating to the protection of Victims of International Armed Conflicts*, in: Ronzitti (Ed), *The Law of Naval Warfare; A Collection of Agreements and Documents with Commentaries*, p 762.

[254] It should be noted that 'the [1907] Hague Conference had urged that until regulations for the law of naval warfare were drawn up, Powers should apply as far as possible to war at sea the principles of the Convention Relative to the Laws and Customs of War on Land.' Sandoz, Swinaraski, Zimmerman, *Commentary on the Additional Protocols; of 8 Jun 1977 to the Geneva Conventions of 12 Aug 1949*, p 387.

[255] ICRC, *Draft Additional Protocols to the Geneva Conventions of Aug 12, 1949; Commentary*, p 54.

usually by reference to Article 49(3).[256] Bodansky, Bothe, Dinstein and Heintschel von Heinegg all write in more ore less similar terms that because there is no general provision in Additional Protocol I limiting the scope of the Protocol to land warfare and because Article 49(3) limits the applicability of that particular section to naval and air warfare and because of the fact that other sections and provisions are not similarly circumscribed, it is clear that other provisions apply to all types of warfare.[257] Rogers, Schmitt and the British Military Manual state without further discussion that Article 55 is in principle restricted to land warfare and Article 35 applies to all forms of warfare wherever they are utilised.[258]

Heintschel von Heinegg and Donner, however, write in 1994 that they do not believe that the scope of Article 35(3) extends beyond the limits of the territorial sea. Although they agree that Article 35(3) applies to naval warfare because:

> [a]ccording to a generally held view this provision is to protect the natural environment as such, that means regardless of its importance for the survival of human beings,[259]

they think:

> it is doubtful whether it also protects the natural (marine) environment (. . .) of the continental shelf or of the EEZ.

Because Additional Protocol I primarily reaffirms and progressively develops the laws of land warfare, 'its provisions in principle apply to areas subject to the sovereignty of the parties to the conflict.'[260] In view of the arguments referred to above, this argument fails to convince.

[256] Only Simonds and Kiss and Shelton seem to exclude application of Art 35(3) to naval and aerial warfare. Simonds writes that 'Protocol I's environmental rules inadequately protect enemy or occupied seas because they are limited to two areas: land warfare and air or sea warfare which affects civilian objects on land or which is aimed at military targets on land.' And Kiss and Shelton write that '[u]nfortunately, the Protocols apply only to land warfare and to sea or air warfare that affects the land.' Kiss, Shelton, *International Environmental Law*, p 738; Simonds, *Conventional Warfare and Environmental Protection: A Proposal for International Legal Reform*, p 183.

[257] Bodansky, *Legal Regulation of the Effects of Military Activity on the Environment*, p 46; Bothe, *Commentary—1977 Geneva Protocol I Additional to the Geneva Conventions of 12 Aug 1949, and Relating to the protection of Victims of International Armed Conflicts*, in: Ronzitti (Ed), *The Law of Naval Warfare; A Collection of Agreements and Documents with Commentaries*, pp 761, 762; Dinstein, *The Conduct of Hostilities under the Law of International Armed Conflict*, p 184; Heintschel von Heinegg, *The Law of Armed Conflict at Sea*, in: Fleck, *The Handbook of Humanitarian Law in Armed Conflicts*, p 419.

[258] UK Ministry of Defence, *The Manual of the Law of Armed Conflict*, p 76; Rogers, *Law on the Battlefield*, p 168; Schmitt, *Green War: An Assessment of the Environmental Law of International Armed Conflict*, p 81.

[259] Heintschel von Heinegg, Donner, *New Developments in the Protection of the Natural Environment in Naval Armed Conflicts*, p 287.

[260] Heintschel von Heinegg, Donner, *New Developments in the Protection of the Natural Environment in Naval Armed Conflicts*, p 295. Also Vöneky believes that the provisions of *ius in bello* only protect the territory of belligerent states. The law of armed conflict does not

Therefore, since Article 35(3) applies to all types of warfare, and Article 55 applies to certain aspects of naval and air warfare, the conclusion seems justified that both articles do not only protect the 'natural environment' on land, but also the marine environment and the atmosphere.[261] Although most warfare is still carried out on land, the protection provided by Additional Protocol I to the marine environment and the atmosphere may be significant, not only in view of the size and destructive power of present-day's navies and air forces, as was observed above, but also in view of the scale of the damage that can be inflicted by naval and air forces, especially to the marine environment. Nuclear-powered ships and submarines and supertankers have the potential to cause considerable damage to the marine environment, possibly even widespread, long-term and severe. This appears from the consequences of and the discussions surrounding peaceful accidents with oil-tankers, oil-platforms and nuclear submarines lost at sea.[262]

In addition to Additional Protocol I, air and naval warfare remain regulated by pre-existing conventional and customary international law. In order to remedy the lack of development and clarity with respect to the law on naval warfare, a number of legal and naval experts were convened by the International Institute of Humanitarian Law in San Remo, Italy,[263] to prepare 'a contemporary restatement' of this field of law. After a number of Round Table Conferences from 1988 to 1994, their discussions resulted in the adoption of the so-called San Remo Manual on International Law Applicable to Armed Conflicts at Sea in June 1994.[264] The Manual consists of 183 paragraphs divided in six Parts, ranging from

protect areas beyond national jurisdiction, nor does it protect areas that are not related to a single state, including the ozone layer, the atmosphere, and the world's climate. S Vöneky, *A New Shield for the Environment: Peacetime Treaties as Legal Restraints of Wartime Damage*, Review of European Community and international environmental law, Vol 9, 2000, p 20; S Vöneky, *Peacetime Environmental Law As a Basis of State Responsibility for Environmental Damage Caused by War*, in: JE Austin, CE Bruch (Eds), *The Environmental Consequences of War*, Cambridge University Press, Cambridge, 2000, p 191.

261 According to Bothe, there still remains uncertainty since the discussion on the damage threshold in Geneva only referred to situations on land. Bothe, *Commentary—1977 Geneva Protocol I Additional to the Geneva Conventions of 12 Aug 1949, and Relating to the protection of Victims of International Armed Conflicts*, in: Ronzitti (Ed), *The Law of Naval Warfare; A Collection of Agreements and Documents with Commentaries*, pp 762.

262 Rauch, *The Protocol Additional to the Geneva Conventions for the Protection of Victims of International Armed Conflicts and the United Nations Convention on the Law of the Sea: Repercussions on the Law of Naval Warfare; Report to the Committee for the Protection of Human Life in Armed Conflict of the International Society for Military Law and Law of War*, pp 143–53. Also Heintschel von Heinegg, Donner, *New Developments in the Protection of the Natural Environment in Naval Armed Conflicts*, pp 282, 286.

263 The International Institute of Humanitarian Law was founded in 1970 and is officially recognised by the United Nations as a Non-governmental Organisation with consultative status with the United Nations Economic and Social Council. <http://web.iihl.org/>.

264 San Remo Manual on International Law Applicable to Armed Conflicts at Sea, in: International Review of the Red Cross, Nov-Dec, No 309, 1995, and in: Roberts, Guelff, *Documents on the Laws of War*, pp 574–606.

basic rules and target discrimination to the protection of specific persons, medical transports and medical transports. In addition, the Manual also contains rules with respect to aircraft, making it therefore also an important clarification of Additional Protocol I and the 1923 non-binding Hague Rules on Aerial Warfare.[265]

2.2.3.3.5 Damage Threshold

2.2.3.3.5.1 Similarity with ENMOD

Irrespective of the scope of application of either Article, and similar to ENMOD, Additional Protocol I does not just prohibit any damage to the environment. Both Article 35(3) and 55 require that the damage to the environment is 'widespread, long-term and severe', which reminds of, and is indeed almost similar to the terminology used in ENMOD. Both treaties use a triple standard to qualify the environmental damage: both refer to 'widespread' and 'severe', but differ as to the time element. ENMOD uses the word 'long-lasting', whereas Additional Protocol I uses the term 'long-term'.

The reason for this similarity is that negotiations for ENMOD were carried out at the same time and in the same city as the negotiations for the Additional Protocols, so cross-fertilisation between the Conference of the Committee on Disarmament that dealt with a specific environmental protection convention and the Diplomatic Conference was inevitable. Because the United States and the Soviet Union pulled the cart as far as ENMOD was concerned and tabled identical draft proposals in the Conference of the Committee on Disarmament in 1975, the opinions of both states in the Working Group of Committee III in that same year were most certainly responsible for the wording of the damage threshold.[266] As far as both provisions of Additional Protocol I are concerned, the Report of the Working Group to Committee III seems to indicate that the triple standard was first suggested and adopted within the framework of Article 55, and later also adopted for Article 35 in order to secure consistency between both provisions. Based on the Working Group's Report of 3 April 1975,[267] the Rapporteur for Committee III, United States Ambassador Aldrich,

[265] Air-to-sea and sea-to-air operations fall under the scope of naval warfare. Von der Heydte, *Air Warfare*, in: Bernhardt (Ed), *Encyclopaedia of Public International Law; Vol One; Aalands Islands to Dumbarton Oaks Conference (1944)*, p 83. Generally on the rules with respect to aircraft: Roberts, Guelff, *Documents on the Laws of War*, p 573.

[266] Sandoz, Swinaraski, Zimmerman, *Commentary on the Additional Protocols; of 8 Jun 1977 to the Geneva Conventions of 12 Aug 1949*, p 413, 413, fn 99.

[267] Report to the Third Committee on the Work of the Working Group, Committee III, 3 Apr 1975 (CDDH/III/275), on Art 48 *bis* [present Art 55. EVK] and Art 33 [present Art 35. EVK], para 3, of Protocol I, in: Levie, *Protection of War Victims: Protocol 1 to the 1949 Geneva Conventions; Vol 2*, p 270, and in: Levie, *Protection of War Victims: Protocol 1 to the 1949 Geneva Conventions; Vol 3*, p 269.

drafted two texts for Article 35 and 55 one day later, on 4 April 1975, both using the triple standard.[268] Both proposals were virtually the same and eventually adopted by the Diplomatic Conference.

2.2.3.3.5.2 *Differences with ENMOD*

Although the terms are generally the same in ENMOD and in Additional Protocol I, there are two major differences that have to be taken into account. Firstly, the qualifications for the environmental damage are alternative in the context of ENMOD, and cumulative in the context of Additional Protocol I.[269] As was mentioned above, ENMOD requires that the effects must be widespread, long-lasting, *or* severe, which means that proof of either one of them would be sufficient to fulfill the requirement. Additional Protocol I, on the other hand, establishes a higher threshold by requiring that the damage to the natural environment is widespread, long-term *and* severe. This means that the damage must meet all three criteria in order establish a violation of the prohibition.[270]

The other major difference between the standards of both conventions is that the terms are believed to have different meanings. The Report of the Conference of the Committee on Disarmament that was sent to the General Assembly and the Disarmament Commission in 1976 with the Draft Convention on the Prohibition of Military or Any Other Hostile Use of Environmental Modification Techniques contained a number of Understandings regarding the interpretation of the terms 'widespread', 'long-lasting' and 'severe'. Although the Understandings are not an integral part of the Convention, they are nevertheless authoritative and should be seen as agreements 'relating to the treaty which was made between all the parties in connection with the conclusion of the treaty' in accordance with Article 31(2)(a) of the Vienna Convention on the Law of Treaties. The term widespread is understood as covering an area of several hundred square kilometers; long-lasting as a period of months or a season; and severe as involving serious or significant disruption or harm to human life, natural and economic resources or other assets. The Understanding added that the interpretation given can only be used for ENMOD and does not prejudice the interpretation of similar terms used in connection with other agreements.

[268] Proposal by the Rapporteur, Committee III, 4 Apr 1975, (CDDH/III/276), Art [55], and (CDDH/III/277), Art [35(3)], respectively in: Levie, *Protection of War Victims: Protocol 1 to the 1949 Geneva Conventions; Vol 3*, pp 270–1 and Levie, *Protection of War Victims: Protocol 1 to the 1949 Geneva Conventions; Vol 2*, p 271.

[269] Solf uses the terms conjunctive for Additional Protocol I and disjunctive for ENMOD. Solf, in: Bothe, Partsch, Solf, *New Rules for Victims of Armed Conflicts; Commentary on the Two 1977 Protocols Additional to the Geneva Conventions of 1949*, p 346.

[270] Sandoz, Swinaraski, Zimmerman, *Commentary on the Additional Protocols; of 8 Jun 1977 to the Geneva Conventions of 12 Aug 1949*, p 418.

Unfortunately, Additional Protocol I does not have a similar instrument with straightforward definitions. For an analysis of the terms of Articles 35 and 55, one therefore needs to establish, independently, the ordinary meaning of the terms in accordance with the general rules of international law on treaty interpretation. According to *Collins Dictionary*, widespread primarily means 'extending over a wide area'; long-term, which somehow appears to be longer than ENMOD's 'long-lasting', means 'lasting, staying, or extending over a long time'; and 'severe' means, among other things, 'critical or dangerous' and 'causing misery or discomfort by its harshness'.[271] Still, these definitions do not add much and do not provide for much practical concretisation. And there is no case-law or other material available to provide clarity.

More help can be derived from the preparatory works to Additional Protocol I. In the international field, resort to the preparatory works has always been widespread, although not preferably as a main basis of interpretation.[272] In the Vienna Convention on the Law of Treaties, therefore, reference to the preparatory works is included in Article 32 and may only be used as a subsidiary method of interpretation to confirm the literal and teleological interpretation of the provision in question as laid down in Article 31, or in case the literal, contextual, and teleological interpretation leaves ambiguity or leads to absurd or unreasonable results. Although the 1969 Vienna Convention would in principle not be applicable in view of Article 4 of the Convention, the International Court of Justice has on various occasions stated that the rules of interpretation as laid down in Articles 31 and 32 reflect customary law which also allows them to be referred to with respect to the Additional Protocol. Because neither of the definitions from *Collins Dictionary*, nor the object and purpose of both provisions, provide sufficient clarity, reference to the preparatory works seems justified.

The records of the Conference as collected by Howard Levie contain some references to the kind of damage that was intended to be covered by the provisions and regarding the interpretation of the triple standard. References by state representatives are mostly limited to declarations that the provisions of Additional Protocol I do not prejudice their states' positions on ENMOD or on other agreements with a different focus and different scope of application. These declarations were made by Argentina, Egypt, the Federal Republic of Germany, Italy, Mexico, Peru and Venezuela.[273] Only Vietnam gave an extensive account of the damage done to the natural environment by the United States during the Vietnam

[271] *Collins Dictionary*, respectively at pp 1742, 914, and 1408.

[272] McNair, *The Law of Treaties*, pp 411–23.

[273] Levie, *Protection of War Victims: Protocol 1 to the 1949 Geneva Conventions; Vol 2*, pp 277–80; Levie, *Protection of War Victims: Protocol 1 to the 1949 Geneva Conventions; Vol 3*, pp 274–5.

War, which it believed to be illustrative for the environmental paragraphs it proposed to add in February 1975.[274] The United Kingdom commented very briefly on the damage threshold in relation to Article 55 stating that the Article struck the necessary balance between environmental protection against severe damage:

> while not making for instance, a tank commander whose tank flattened a clump of tree liable as a war criminal.[275]

It should be noted that neither Article 35(3) nor Article 55 provide for military necessity exceptions.[276]

References in concluding reports are more elaborate and more subject-focused. The Report of the Chairman of the above-mentioned Biotope Group to the Third Committee, for example, states that acts of warfare that cause short-term damage to the environment, such as artillery bombardment, were not intended to be covered by the prohibition of Article 55. The Group concluded that the idea behind the Article was that the disturbance of the environment had to be significant, 'perhaps for ten years or more.'[277] This view was subsequently adopted by the Working Group involved in its Report to the Third Committee. Damage such as cutting down or destruction of trees as a result of artillery fire was not considered to fall under both provisions, because neither was cratering.[278]

The most extensive account on the interpretation of the damage threshold in Articles 35 and 55, however, is laid down in the general Report of the Second Session of Committee III. The account starts by referring to the

[274] Levie, *Protection of War Victims: Protocol 1 to the 1949 Geneva Conventions; Vol 2*, pp 258–9.

[275] Levie, *Protection of War Victims: Protocol 1 to the 1949 Geneva Conventions; Vol 3*, p 272. According to Kalshoven, '[i]t seems clear, therefore, that the man in the field will not easily come into conflict with this provision; rather it is addressed to higher levels of authority where the major decisions about the use of particular means and methods of warfare are taken.' Kalshoven, *Reaffirmation and Development of International Humanitarian Law Applicable in Armed Conflicts: the Diplomatic Conference, Geneva, 1974–1977; Part II*, p 130. Solf writes that both Articles seem 'primarily directed to high level policy decision makers'. Solf, in: Bothe, Partsch, Solf, *New Rules for Victims of Armed Conflicts; Commentary on the Two 1977 Protocols Additional to the Geneva Conventions of 1949*, p 348. Also: Tarasofsky, *Legal Protection of the Environment during International Armed Conflict*, p 52.

[276] This could be of concern to the operational commander writes Schmitt. Environmental concerns may override military advantages and even human values. Schmitt, *Green War: An Assessment of the Environmental Law of International Armed Conflict*, pp 72–3.

[277] Report of the Chairman of the Group 'Biotope', Committee III, 11 Mar 1975 (CDDH/III/GT/35), in: Levie, *Protection of War Victims: Protocol 1 to the 1949 Geneva Conventions; Vol 2*, pp 267–8, and Levie, *Protection of War Victims: Protocol 1 to the 1949 Geneva Conventions; Vol 3*, p 267.

[278] Report to the Third Committee on the Work of the Working Group, Committee III, 3 Apr 1975 (CDDH/III/275), on Art 48 *bis* [present Art 55. EVK] and Art 33 [present Art 35. EVK], para 3, of Protocol I, in: Levie, *Protection of War Victims: Protocol 1 to the 1949 Geneva Conventions; Vol 2*, p 270, and in Levie, *Protection of War Victims: Protocol 1 to the 1949 Geneva Conventions; Vol 3*, pp 269–70.

three elements of the formula of duration, scope and severity, all three of which were extensively discussed. Then, the Report continues:

> The time or duration required (. . .) was considered by some to be measured in decades. References to twenty or thirty years were made by some representatives as being a minimum. Others referred to battlefield destruction in France in the First World War as being outside the scope of the prohibition.

The Report also referred to the Biotope Report which stated that damage from artillery bombardment was not intended to be prohibited and that the period that is referred to and intended might perhaps 10 years or more. The Committee then comments, however, that:

> it is impossible to say with certainty what period of time might be involved. It appeared to be a widely shared assumption that battlefield damage incidental to conventional warfare would not normally be proscribed by this provision.[279]

It seems, therefore, that the drafters intended to raise a high threshold for application of both environmental protection provisions. They envisaged application only in cases with damage that would last for decades, and which could not be the result of ordinary conventional battlefield damage.[280] Even the widespread destruction of northern France and Belgium during the First World War was not considered to fall under both prohibitions.

According to Kalshoven, the provisions allow belligerents to continue to wage conventional warfare, and belligerents should only worry:

> when they have recourse to rather less conventional modes of warfare, such as the use of herbicides or other methods or means specifically designed to damage the environment.[281]

Solf also writes that the Articles seem to be written to prevent damage that would be intentional and a result of certain non-conventional means of warfare, such as 'massive use of herbicides or chemical agents'.[282] And Tarasofsky believes that both environmental protection provisions 'appear limited to proscribing systematic environmental warfare through the use of unconventional means, such as herbicides and chemicals.'[283]

[279] Report of Committee III, Second Session (CDDH/215/Rev 1), in: Levie, *Protection of War Victims: Protocol 1 to the 1949 Geneva Conventions; Vol 2*, pp 276–7.

[280] Problematic, of course, is that is very difficult in practice to estimate the severity and duration of environmental damage, especially long-term damage. A/48/269, Report of the Secretary-General to the General Assembly on the Protection of the Environment in the Environment in Times of Armed Conflict, of 29 Jul 1993, p 7; Tarasofsky, *Legal Protection of the Environment during International Armed Conflict*, p 51.

[281] Kalshoven, *Reaffirmation and Development of International Humanitarian Law Applicable in Armed Conflicts: the Diplomatic Conference, Geneva, 1974–1977; Part II*, p 130.

[282] Solf, in: Bothe, Partsch, Solf, *New Rules for Victims of Armed Conflicts; Commentary on the Two 1977 Protocols Additional to the Geneva Conventions of 1949*, p 348.

[283] Tarasofsky, *Legal Protection of the Environment during International Armed Conflict*, p 51.

Such an interpretation is not undisputed though. Green seems to reject this view,[284] the British Military Manual states that Additional Protocol I exclusively applies to conventional weapons,[285] and Simonds even writes that this 'evaluation is bizarre'.[286] When the ICRC presented its draft Protocols, it stated that it did not intend to 'broach' the problems relating to atomic, bacteriological, and chemical weapons that were subject to other international agreements or negotiations.[287] This note, in combination with a number of understandings and declarations, has sometimes been interpreted as precluding the applicability of both Protocols to these kinds of weapons. Especially the reference to nuclear weapons is relevant for the purpose of this research and will be discussed in the Appraisal and Conclusions at the end of this research. Furthermore, Verwey believes that the provisions were not intended:

> to condemn retroactively the kind of environmental damage—no matter how serious, from a retrospective point of view, this may have been—inflicted by US armed forces in Vietnam.[288]

The absence of any link with the damage inflicted by the United States in Vietnam was necessary to keep the US in favor of Protocol I.

As far as herbicides are concerned, the critique on the evaluation of Kalshoven and Solf may not be completely valid, however. Just like so-called 'riot control agents', herbicides have always been a problematic category in the discussion on chemical weapons. A herbicide is 'a chemical that destroys plants, [especially] one used to control weeds',[289] but it is not prima facie clear whether a herbicide is tantamount to a chemical weapon under international law.

The United States, for example, adheres to a narrow interpretation of the 1925 Geneva Protocol and contends that the Protocol did not cover the use of 'irritants' and anti-plant chemicals.[290] As far as herbicides are con-

[284] Green, *The Environment and the Law of Conventional Warfare*, p 228.

[285] UK Ministry of Defence, *The Manual of the Law of Armed Conflict*, p 76.

[286] Simonds, *Conventional Warfare and Environmental Protection: A Proposal for International Legal Reform*, p 175. It should be noted, however, that she refers to herbicides herself as well, on p 176, as an example of means of warfare that may destroy the environment.

[287] According to *Collins Dictionary*, 'to broach' means primarily 'to initiate (a topic) for discussion'. *Collins Dictionary*, p 201.

[288] Verwey, *Protection of the Environment in Times of Armed Conflict: In Search of a New Legal Perspective*, p 14. Also: Verwey, *Observations on the Legal Protection of the Environment in Times of International Armed Conflict*, p 38; Verwey, *Comment: Protection of the Environment in Times of Armed Conflict—Do We Need Additional Rules?*, in: Grunawalt, King, McClain, *Protection of the Environment during Armed Conflict*, p 562.

[289] *Collins Dictionary*, p 722.

[290] Goldblat, *Arms Control; The New Guide to Negotiations and Agreements*, pp 135–6. According to Verwey, however, the United States originally adopted an extensive interpretation of the Protocol, since '*at least as far as the US is concerned the Protocol at the time of its creation was considered to ban all chemical weapons in war.*' This appears from 'the records of Congressional discussions in 1926 on the question of ratification of the Protocol.' Verwey refers, for example, to a statement by Senator Reed, who opposed ratification because '*it*

cerned, this is rejected by Verwey. After weighing the pros and cons of applicability, he writes that the strongest arguments point towards the conclusion that 'the prohibition of anti-plant agents was included within the original meaning of the Geneva Protocol.'[291] Verwey also concludes that the large majority of States Parties to the Protocol already held in the 1970s that herbicides were prohibited by it.[292]

Unfortunately, the resulting 1993 Chemical Weapons Convention is not unambiguous either, even though the United States unilaterally renounced, in principle, the first use of herbicides in warfare in 1975, and even though the use of herbicides during the Vietnam War was one of the reasons for the start of negotiations for a comprehensive Chemical Weapons Convention. In the Preamble to the Convention, the States Parties recognize:

> the prohibition, embodied in the pertinent agreements and relevant principles of international law, of the use of herbicides as a method of warfare,

but this recognition does not seem to be reflected in their definitions of the terms 'chemical weapons' and 'toxic chemical' in Article II(2). A 'Toxic Chemical' means:

> Any chemical which through its chemical action on life processes can cause death, temporary incapacitation or permanent harm to humans or animals.

Apparently, and by applying the maxim *expressio unius est exclusio alterius*, toxic chemicals that can cause death or temporary or permanent harm to plants, or flora in general, are not considered chemical weapons in the meaning of the Convention.[293]

According to Dinstein, the preambular paragraph:

> was part of a 'compromise package', whereby herbicides were simultaneously omitted from the definition of banned chemical weapons in the operative clauses of the CWC.[294]

Apparently, the drafters wanted to distinguish between the use and the possession of herbicides and chose to recognise only a prohibition of the use of herbicides. The phrase 'pertinent agreements' seems to refer to ENMOD and Additional Protocol I,[295] and possibly to the Geneva

includes tear gases.' WD Verwey, *Chemical Warfare in Vietnam: Legal or Illegal?*, Netherlands International Law Review, Vol 18, 1971, p 224.

291 WD Verwey, *Riot Control Agents and Herbicides in War; Their Humanitarian, Toxicological, Ecological, Military, Polemological, and Legal Aspects*, AW Sijthoff, Leyden, 1977, pp 239–41.

292 Verwey, *Riot Control Agents and Herbicides in War; Their Humanitarian, Toxicological, Ecological, Military, Polemological, and Legal Aspects*, pp 253–5.

293 Goldblat, *Arms Control; The New Guide to Negotiations and Agreements*, p 151.

294 Dinstein, *Protection of the Environment in International Armed Conflict*, in: Frowein, Wolfrum (Eds), *Max Planck Yearbook of United Nations Law*, p 539.

295 Dinstein, *Protection of the Environment in International Armed Conflict*, in: Frowein, Wolfrum (Eds), *Max Planck Yearbook of United Nations Law*, p 539.

Protocol, and the choice for the word 'recognizing' has the 'inescapable connotation (. . .) that the prohibition is now predicated on customary law.'[296]

A further complicating factor could be the fact, that since the Second Review Conference in 1992, States Parties to ENMOD regard the use of herbicides under certain circumstances as environmental modification techniques. This could also be interpreted as putting herbicides in a special category of weaponry, outside the framework of the Chemical Weapons Convention, but nevertheless prohibited under international law. Perhaps this is what the States Parties referred to one year later, in the Preamble of the Chemical Weapons Convention.

Be that as it may, according to Solf, the interpretations of the damage threshold in the Report of the Committee and the interpretations made in declarations are 'well established and uncontradicted'.[297] Virtually all authors refer to the preparatory works and many attach importance to them and confirm the reading given above. Furthermore, there is no indication that a change of interpretation has occurred or is even considered in practice.[298] The extensive damage to the land and marine environment caused by Iraq during the 1990–1991 Gulf War[299] has generally been regarded as not reaching the damage threshold of Additional Protocol I, even if the Protocol would have been applicable,[300] and despite the fact

[296] Dinstein, *Protection of the Environment in International Armed Conflict*, in: Frowein, Wolfrum (Eds), *Max Planck Yearbook of United Nations Law*, p 539.

[297] Solf, in: Bothe, Partsch, Solf, *New Rules for Victims of Armed Conflicts; Commentary on the Two 1977 Protocols Additional to the Geneva Conventions of 1949*, p 348.

[298] Compare the reference by Iran to the 'Understanding of the Conference of Disarmament' of 'the terms "widespread, longstanding, and severe"' (*sic*) when it states that '[i]t is quite clear that the use of nuclear weapons will cause widespread, long-term and severe damage to the natural environment' which seems to be a mistake. CR 95/26, Oral Plea of the Government of the Islamic Republic of Iran, of 6 Nov 1995, on the Legality of the Use by a State of Nuclear Weapons in Armed Conflict and on the Legality of the Threat or Use of Nuclear Weapons, p 33, fn 39. Through: <http://www.icj-cij.org/>.

[299] According to the Final Report of the United States Department of Defense, '[b]etween seven and nine million barrels of oil were set free in the Gulf by Iraqi action. Five hundred ninety oil well heads were damaged or destroyed. 508 were set on fire, and 82 were damaged so that oil was flowing freely from them.' United States Department of Defense, *Conduct of the Persian Gulf War; Final Report to Congress; Pursuant to Title V of the Persian Gulf Conflict Supplemental Authorization and Personnel Benefits Act of 1991 (Public Law 102–25)*, p 624; United States Department of Defense, *Report to Congress on the Conduct of the Persian Gulf War—Appendix on the Role of the law of War*, p 636.

[300] The Report of the US Department of Defense to Congress of 1992 refers to the conclusions of the Conference of Experts invited by the Canadian Ministry of Foreign Affairs from 9 to 12 Jul 1992 in Ottawa. United States Department of Defense, *Conduct of the Persian Gulf War; Final Report to Congress; Pursuant to Title V of the Persian Gulf Conflict Supplemental Authorization and Personnel Benefits Act of 1991 (Public Law 102–25)*, pp 624–5; United States Department of Defense, *Report to Congress on the Conduct of the Persian Gulf War—Appendix on the Role of the law of War*, pp 636–7. Also Bodansky, *Legal Regulation of the Effects of Military Activity on the Environment*, p 28; Schmitt, *Green War: An Assessment of the Environmental Law of International Armed Conflict*, p 75; Simonds, *Conventional Warfare and Environmental Protection: A Proposal for International Legal Reform*, p 207; Rogers, *Law on the Battlefield*, pp 181–2.

that the consequences were so serious that the acts were designated as 'environmental terrorism'.[301]

More recently, a Special Committee established by the Prosecutor of the International Criminal Tribunal for the Former Yugoslavia ex Article 18 of the Tribunal's Statute[302] to review the NATO bombing campaign against Yugoslavia in 1999, agreed that the campaign had caused damage to the environment but concluded that:

> on the basis of information currently in its possession, (. . .) the environmental damage caused during the NATO bombing campaign [did] not reach the Additional Protocol I threshold.[303]

According to the Committee:

> it [was] thought that the notion of 'long-term' damage in Additional protocol I would need to be measured in years rather than months, and that as such, ordinary battlefield damage of the kind caused to France in World War I would not be covered.[304]

Their ultimate assessment of whether the damage from the bombing campaign had reached the damage threshold was based on the conclusions of the Balkan Task Force established by the United Nations Environment Program (UNEP).[305] They concluded that the campaign had not caused an environmental catastrophe, and stated that the serious pollution at

[301] Schmitt, *Humanitarian Law and the Environment*, p 309; United States Department of Defence, *Conduct of the Persian Gulf War; Final Report to Congress; Pursuant to Title V of the Persian Gulf Conflict Supplemental Authorization and Personnel Benefits Act of 1991 (Public Law 102–25)*, p 624; United States Department of Defense, *Report to Congress on the Conduct of the Persian Gulf War—Appendix on the Role of the law of War*, p 636. In the Sixth Committee of the General Assembly, the Austrian representative implicitly referred to environmental terrorism in 1991. A/C.6/46/SR.19, Summary Record of the 19th meeting of the Sixth Committee of the General Assembly on 23 Oct 1991, p 3, para 5. The representative of Nepal went even further by designating the acts as using the environment as a 'weapon of mass destruction'. A/C.6/46/SR.20, Summary Record of the 20th meeting of the Sixth Committee of the General Assembly on 24 Oct 1991, p 8, para 27.

[302] S/25704, 3 May 1993, Report of the Secretary-General Pursuant to Para 2 of Security Council Resolution 808 (1993), on the Statute of an International Criminal Tribunal For the Former Yugoslavia, approved of by the Security Council under ch VII of the Charter by S/RES/827 (1993), adopted unanimously on 25 May 1993, on the establishment of an international tribunal for the Former Yugoslavia.

[303] International Criminal Tribunal for the Former Yugoslavia (ICTY), *Final Report to the Prosecutor by the Committee Established to Review the NATO Bombing Campaign against the Federal Republic of Yugoslavia*, International Legal Materials, Vol 39, 2000, p 1262.

[304] ICTY, *Final Report to the Prosecutor by the Committee Established to Review the NATO Bombing Campaign against the Federal Republic of Yugoslavia*, International Legal Materials, Vol 39, 2000, p 1262.

[305] Balkan Task Force; United Nations Environment Program/United Nations Center for Human Settlements, *The Kosovo Conflict: Consequences for the Environment & Human Settlements*, UNEP/UNCHS, Nairobi, 1999. Also available through: <http://www.grid.unep.ch/btf/> and <http://postconflict.unep.ch/>.

certain hot spots could not be unambiguously attributed to the bombing campaign.[306]

That does not mean, however, that the focus on the preparatory works for the interpretation of the damage threshold is without criticism. With respect to the Committee Report of the Ad Hoc International Criminal Tribunal for the Former Yugoslavia (ICTY), Marauhn states that the Committee:

> could have taken into account recent tendencies to interpret the term used in the ENMOD Convention and the term used in Articles 35, paragraph 3, and 55 of Protocol I as both meaning a period of several months.[307]

Unfortunately, Marauhn only refers to one author to support this view and does not further explicate these 'recent tendencies'.

More generally, Verwey and Bothe criticise the focus on the preparatory works in the first place. Verwey is skeptical, because the terms have not been defined in the Protocol, and because the preparatory works only clarify the term 'long-term':

> no authoritative answer can be given to the question when and where an specific damage inflicted upon the natural environment should be deemed to violate the terms of this provision.[308]

Bothe warns in 1991 that '[f]or the purpose of interpretation it would be highly dangerous to rely too heavily on the negotiating history' because the drafters had only very limited experience and only a few examples in mind;[309] and in 1995, he writes that 'the meaning of those terms is very controversial' and that the damage threshold is 'unacceptably high'.[310]

306 Balkan Task Force; United Nations Environment Program/United Nations Center for Human Settlements, *The Kosovo Conflict: Consequences for the Environment & Human Settlements*, p 10; ICTY, *Final Report to the Prosecutor by the Committee Established to Review the NATO Bombing Campaign against the Federal Republic of Yugoslavia*, International Legal Materials, Vol 39, 2000, pp 1261–4.

307 T Marauhn, *Environmental Damage in Times of Armed Conflict—not 'really' a Matter of Criminal Responsibility?*, International Review of the Red Cross, 2000, para 3. In para 6, he concludes that the difference is unfortunate and that the meaning of the standard in Additional Protocol I should be brought in line with the Understandings of ENMOD. This 'could contribute to a clearer understanding of the proportionality requirement under general humanitarian law'.

308 Verwey, *Observations on the Legal Protection of the Environment in Times of International Armed Conflict*, p 36; Verwey, *Protection of the Environment in Times of Armed Conflict: In Search of a New Legal Perspective*, p 10; Verwey, *Comment: Protection of the Environment in Times of Armed Conflict—Do We Need Additional Rules?*, in: Grunawalt, King, McClain, *Protection of the Environment during Armed Conflict*, p 560.

309 Bothe, *The Protection of the Environment in Times of Armed Conflict; Legal Rules, Uncertainty, Deficiencies, and Possible Developments*, p 56.

310 M Bothe, *Protection of the Environment in Times of Armed Conflict*, in: N Al-Nauimi, R Meese (Eds), *International Legal Issues Arising Under the United Nations Decade of International Law; Proceedings of the Qatar International Law Conference '94*, Martinus Nijhoff Publishers, The Hague, 1995, p 100.

It is indeed possible and even desirable that the interpretation of the various terms and this focus on the preparatory works will change over time. After all, reference to the preparatory works is a subsidiary method of treaty interpretation and moreover, *tempora mutantur, nos et mutamur in illis*.[311] Our knowledge of the environment and of environmental problems has increased tremendously since the 1970s as well as our concern for and appreciation of the environment. Peacetime international environmental law has been one of the fastest growing fields in international law and has dramatically changed in character,[312] and environmental considerations tend to play an increasingly important role in other areas of international law, such as European law, international trade and investment law, the law of state responsibility, treaty law, and even the law of individual criminal responsibility. It is therefore not unthinkable that all these developments will lead to a less restrictive interpretation of these terms.[313]

According to Australia in the Sixth Committee of the General Assembly in 1991, there had been agreement at the Conference of Experts on the Use of the Environment as a Tool of Conventional Warfare that was hosted by the Canadian Government in Ottawa in July 1991 that:

> the application and development of the law of armed conflict must take account of the evolution of environmental concerns generally.[314]

[311] Times change and we change with them. According to Van Dale Dictionary, the origin of the proverb is not clear, but some attribute it to Emperor Lotharius (795–855). G Geerts, T den Boon (et al) (Eds), *Van Dale; Groot Woordenboek der Nederlandse Taal*, Van Dale Lexicografie, Utrecht, 1999, p 4227. Lotharius was the eldest son of Louis the Pious, who was the son and heir to the throne of Charles the Great (742 of 747–814), King of the Franks, self-proclaimed Frank successor of the Roman Emperors, and founder of the Holy Roman Empire.

[312] Bothe, *The Protection of the Environment in Times of Armed Conflict; Legal Rules, Uncertainty, Deficiencies, and Possible Developments*, p 57.

[313] Bothe, *The Protection of the Environment in Times of Armed Conflict; Legal Rules, Uncertainty, Deficiencies, and Possible Developments*, p 56–8; R Desgagné, *The Prevention of Environmental Damage in Time of Armed Conflict: Proportionality and Precautionary Measures*, in: H Fischer, A McDonald (Eds), *Yearbook of International Humanitarian Law; Vol 3; 2000*, TMC Asser Press, The Hague, 2002, pp 112–13; Hulme, *War Torn Environment: Interpreting the Legal Threshold*, pp 99–100; Momtaz, *La Recours à l'Arme Nucléaire et la Protection de l'Environnement: l'Apport de la Cour Internationale de Justice*, in: Boisson de Chazournes, Sands (Eds), *International Law, the International Court of Justice and Nuclear Weapons*, p 374; Simonds, *Conventional Warfare and Environmental Protection: A Proposal for International Legal Reform*, p 174. Desgagné refers to a contribution of the ICRC at the 1992 Rio Conference on Environment and Development (UNCED) on environmental protection during armed conflict and evolving expectations: 'The question as to what constitutes (prohibited) "widespread, long-term and severe" damage and what is acceptable damage to the environment is open to interpretation. Such interpretation has to take the whole context into account, and will vary with changes in expectations with regard to the general need to protect the environment. Of course, the "travaux préparatoires" have also to be taken into consideration where relevant.' Desgagné, *The Prevention of Environmental Damage in Time of Armed Conflict: Proportionality and Precautionary Measures*, in: Fischer, McDonald, *Yearbook of International Humanitarian Law; Vol 3; 2000*, p 112.

[314] A/C.6/46/SR.20, Summary Record of the 20th meeting of the Sixth Committee of the General Assembly on 24 Oct 1991, p 3, para 8.

And in 1997, the International Court of Justice stated in relation to the dispute between Hungary and Slovakia that:

> [t]he awareness of the vulnerability of the environment and the recognition that environmental risks have to be assessed on a continuous basis have become much stronger in the years since the Treaty's conclusion [in 1977 between Hungary and Czechoslovakia].[315]

And a little later:

> In order to evaluate the environmental risks, current standards must be taken into consideration. (. . .) The Court is mindful that, in the field of environmental protection, vigilance and prevention are required on account of the often irreversible character of damage to the environment and of the limitations inherent in the very mechanism of reparation of this type of damage. Throughout the ages, mankind has, for economic and other reasons, constantly interfered with nature. In the past, this was often done without consideration of the effects upon the environment. Owing to new scientific insights and to a growing awareness of the risks for mankind—for present and future generations—of pursuit of such interventions at an unconsidered and unabated pace, new norms and standards have been developed, set forth in a great number of instruments during the last two decades. Such new norms have to be taken into consideration, and such new standards given proper weight, not only when States contemplate new activities but also when continuing with activities begun in the past.[316]

2.2.3.4 General Differences between Additional Protocol I and ENMOD

Apart from the differences in interpretation of similar terminology used in ENMOD and in Additional Protocol I,[317] and the fact that Additional Protocol intends to prevent damage to the environment that is a result of targeting irrespective of the weapons used, whereas ENMOD intends to protect the environment by prohibiting the use of the natural processes as weapons of warfare, there are also a number of other notable differences.

Firstly, Articles 35(3) and 55 only apply in times of international armed conflict, whereas it is possible that environmental modification techniques

[315] Gabèíkovo-Nagymaros Project (Hungary/Slovakia), Judgment, 25 Sep 1997, ICJ Reports 1997, para 112, pp 67–8.

[316] Gabèíkovo-Nagymaros Project (Hungary/Slovakia), Judgment, 25 Sep 1997, ICJ Reports 1997, para 140, pp 77–8.

[317] The difference is considered unfortunate by Marauhn, who states that the meaning of the standard in Additional Protocol I should be brought in line with the Understandings of ENMOD. This 'could contribute to a clearer understanding of the proportionality requirement under general humanitarian law'. As was mentioned above, Marauhn refers to 'recent tendencies' that this is actually the case. Marauhn, *Environmental Damage in Times of Armed Conflict—not 'really' a Matter of Criminal Responsibility?*, para 6 and 3. Also the ICRC believes that the terms in ENMOD and Additional Protocol I call for interpretation and clarification: A/48/269, Report of the Secretary-General to the General Assembly on the Protection of the Environment in the Environment in Times of Armed Conflict, of 29 Jul 1993, p 20.

are used in conflict situations that have not yet reached the status of an armed conflict.[318] The question whether an international armed conflict exists is primarily determined by factual circumstances, namely when 'there is a resort to armed force between States'.[319] It is not likely that this will happen, but it is nevertheless possible.[320]

Secondly, ENMOD requires that the damage to the environment as a result of the use of environmental modification techniques is done to another State Party. This means that the damage must be both trans-boundary and done to a state that is also Party to ENMOD. These requirements are not applicable with respect to Additional Protocol I. Both Article 35(3) and 55 protect the environment per se, including the environment of the state that may be accused of using prohibited means and methods of warfare, as well as the environment of non-State Parties to Additional Protocol I.

Thirdly, the damage referred to in both Articles in Additional Protocol I relates to the natural environment exclusively, whereas the damage in ENMOD also includes 'injury to economic resources and other assets'.[321] And fourthly, ENMOD does not seem to protect areas beyond national jurisdiction, whereas Additional Protocol I does seem to extend its protection to the marine environment and the atmosphere.

Still, both treaties seem to overlap to a certain extent and are complementary where they do not.[322] Environmental modification techniques used during international armed conflict may very well also fall under the prohibitions of Article 35(3) and 55, since they are means and methods that are intended or may be expected to cause widespread, long-term and severe damage to the environment.[323] This could be a possible solution as

[318] Sandoz, Swinaraski, Zimmerman, *Commentary on the Additional Protocols; of 8 Jun 1977 to the Geneva Conventions of 12 Aug 1949*, pp 415, 420.

[319] ICTY; Prosecutor v Dusko Tadic a/k/a 'Dule' (IT-94-1); Decision on the Defence Motion for Interlocutory Appeal on Jurisdiction, 2 Oct 1995, para 70, p 37, International Legal Materials, Vol 35, 1996, p 54, or at <http://www.un.org/icty/tadic/appeal/decision-e/51002.htm>.

[320] The possibility was explicitly mentioned by the delegations of the Soviet Union and the United States during the deliberations on their identical draft Conventions. A/31/27, Report of the Conference of the Committee on Disarmament; Vol I, United Nations, New York, pp 66, 69, 72.

[321] Schmitt, *Humanitarian Law and the Environment*, p 280.

[322] Bouvier writes that both treaties are complementary and 'far from overlapping'. A Bouvier, *Protection of the Natural Environment in Time of Armed Conflict*, International Review of the Red Cross, 1991, pp 567–8, para II(C)(3).

[323] Solf writes that the prohibition of ENMOD 'is directed at deliberate environmental modification, whereas those of Protocol I *also* include objectively forseeable collateral effects' (emphasis added), Solf, in: Bothe, Partsch, Solf, *New Rules for Victims of Armed Conflicts; Commentary on the Two 1977 Protocols Additional to the Geneva Conventions of 1949*, p 347. This view is also supported by A/48/269, Report of the Secretary-General to the General Assembly on the Protection of the Environment in the Environment in Times of Armed Conflict, of 29 Jul 1993, p 6.

to cases where states would somehow escape responsibility under Article I ENMOD, because not all conditions under this Article are fulfilled. These could include cases in which either the perpetrator is not a State Party to ENMOD, or the victim is not a State Party, or neither state is bound by ENMOD. It could also include cases in which the damage is not transboundary or even done to areas outside national jurisdiction.

In view of the damage threshold, it is not very likely, however, that the use of environmental modification techniques would violate the environmental protection provisions of Additional Protocol I. Only under exceptional circumstances, is it possible that the alternative damage threshold of ENMOD—widespread, long-lasting *or* severe—with the term 'long-lasting' interpreted in terms of months, would meet the cumulative threshold of Additional Protocol I—widespread, long-term and severe—while interpreting 'long-term' in terms of decades.

2.2.4 The Certain Conventional Weapons Convention

2.2.4.1 Introduction

A third treaty that contains specific references to the protection of the environment during armed conflict is the 1981 Convention on Certain Conventional Weapons, in particular its third Protocol on Prohibitions or Restrictions on the Use of Incendiary Weapons (Incendiary Weapons Protocol).[324] Conventional weapons were defined by the Conventional Armaments Commission in the late 1940s,[325] as all armaments 'except

[324] Protocol on Prohibitions or Restrictions on the Use of Incendiary Weapons (Protocol III) to the Convention on Prohibitions or Restrictions on the Use of Certain Conventional Weapons Which May be Deemed To Be Excessively Injurious or To Have Indiscriminate Effects, opened for signature on 10 Apr 1981, entered into force on 2 Dec 1983, UNTS, Vol 1342, No 22495. Some authors refer to the Certain Conventional Weapons Convention as the Weaponry Convention, the UN Weapons Convention, the Weapons Convention, the Inhumane Weapons Convention or the Dubious Conventional Weapons Convention. Also writings differ as to the year that is attached to the Convention. Some authors refer to 1980 as the year of adoption; others refer to 1981 as the year in which the treaty was opened for signature.

[325] The Conventional Armaments Commission was set up by the Security Council by S/RES/18 (1947), adopted on 13 Feb 1947, by 10 to 0, with 1 abstention; implementation of General Assembly Resolutions on the principles governing the general regulation and reduction of armaments and information on armed forces. In 1952 the Conventional Armaments Commission was merged with the Atomic Energy Commission, which was established in 1946 by the General Assembly's very first Resolution of 24 Jan 1946. A/Res/1 (I), adopted unanimously on 24 Jan 1946, on the establishment of a commission to deal with the problems raised by the discovery of atomic energy. Together they formed the United Nations Disarmament Commission, established by the General Assembly by A/Res/502 (VI), adopted on 11 Jan 1952, by 42 to 5, with 7 abstentions, on regulation, limitation, and balanced reduction of all armed forces and all armaments; international control of atomic energy.

atomic weapons and weapons of mass destruction [*sic*]',[326] which definition still seems to be valid today.[327]

The first convention prohibiting the use of a weapon of warfare was the 1868 St Petersburg Declaration.[328] In this Declaration, the States Parties renounce the use of explosive ammunition under 400 grams, not only because the use of this type of weapon would exceed the legitimate purpose of weakening the military forces of the enemy, but also because it would 'uselessly aggravate the sufferings of disabled men, or render their death inevitable'.[329] Hence, the use of explosive bullets would not only exceed the necessities of war, but also violate the laws of humanity and the prohibition therefore finds its origin not only in the principle of necessity, but also in the principle of humanity. As has been explained above, both principles have shaped the laws of war and should be regarded as framework concepts or umbrella norms from which specific rules of international law are derived.

Based upon the same rationale and 'inspired by the sentiments which found expression in the Declaration of St. Petersburg', further prohibitions of specific weapons followed in 1899 on the use of asphyxiating gases,[330] expanding or dum-dum bullets,[331] and poison or poisoned weapons;[332] in 1907 on the use of specific types of naval mines,[333] and in 1925 on the

[326] The Commission defined weapons of mass destruction as including 'atomic explosive weapons [*sic*], radioactive material weapons, lethal chemical and biological weapons, and any weapons developed in the future which have characteristics comparable in destructive effect to those of the atomic bomb or other weapons mentioned above.' The definition of 'conventional weapons' and the definition of 'weapons of mass destruction' are contradictory as far as atomic weapons are concerned, which seems to be due to bad drafting. First, atomic weapons are not considered weapons of mass destruction, which is already peculiar and then weapons of mass destruction are defined as a category of weapons that include atomic weapons. Resolution of the Commission for Conventional Armaments, 12 Aug 1948, on the definition of armaments, para 1.

[327] According to *Collins Dictionary*, 'conventional' in relation to weapons or warfare means 'not nuclear', which does not seem to be correct or at least complete. *Collins Dictionary*, p 348.

[328] St Petersburg Declaration Renouncing the Use, in Time of War, of Explosive Projectiles Under 400 Grammes Weight, signed on 11 Dec 1868, entered into force on 11 Dec 1868, AJIL, Vol 1, No 2, Supplement: Official Documents, 1907, p 95.

[329] St Petersburg Declaration, Preamble.

[330] Hague Declaration (IV, 2) on the Use of Projectiles the Object of Which is the Diffusion of Asphyxiating or Deleterious Gases, signed on 29 Jul 1899, entered into force on 4 Sep 1900, D Schindler, J Toman (Eds), *The Laws of Armed Conflicts; A Collection of Conventions, Resolutions and Other Documents*, Martinus Nijhoff Publishers, Dordrecht, 1988, p 105.

[331] Hague Declaration (IV, 3) on the Use of Bullets Which Expand or Flatten Easily in the Human Body, signed on 29 Jul 1899, entered into force 4 Sep 1900, D Schindler, J Toman (Eds), *The Laws of Armed Conflicts; A Collection of Conventions, Resolutions and Other Documents*, Martinus Nijhoff Publishers, Dordrecht, 1988, p 109.

[332] Art 23(a) Hague Convention (II) with respect to the Laws and Customs of War on Land, with annexed Regulations, signed on 29 Jul 1899, entered into force on 4 Sep 1900, AJIL, Vol 1, No 2, Supplement: Official Documents, 1907, p 129.

[333] Hague Convention (VIII) Relative to the Laying of Automatic Submarine Contact Mines, signed on 18 Oct 1907, entered into force on 26 Jan 1910, AJIL, Vol 2, No 1/2, Supplement: Official Documents, 1908, p 138.

use of chemical and bacteriological weapons.[334] Asphyxiating gases and other chemical and bacteriological weapons nowadays qualify as non-conventional weapons or weapons of mass destruction, which means that until the late 1970s the activities of the international community of states with respect to the position of conventional weapons within the framework of the laws of war had been limited to the use of explosive, inflammable and expandable bullets. Not much in view of the large number of conventional weapon categories, but not surprising in view of the fact that traditionally armies have relied on conventional weaponry, and technological innovations usually meant decisive advantages during warfare.

2.2.4.2 Drafting History

Because the ICRC knew that discussion on the use of specific weapons would be such a delicate issue, it had decided not to include any specific proposals in the draft protocols to the Geneva Conventions which it presented in 1973. As was mentioned above, the ICRC had stated in an introductory note that by presenting these draft texts it did not want to broach the problems relating to non-conventional weapons or weapons of mass destruction that were subject to other international agreements or negotiations,[335] and in view of recent experiences regarding conventional weapons it apparently did not want to broach these weapons either. Reference to the customary rule that the right of states to choose means and methods of warfare is not unlimited was considered to be sufficient for the time being.[336]

The ICRC had attempted to include regulation of specific conventional weapons in the discussions that preceded the Diplomatic Conference on the Reaffirmation and Development of International Humanitarian Law, however. Since the 1950s, the ICRC had drawn attention to the use of conventional weapons and their consequences for the civilian population during armed conflict, and despite implicit warnings, the Committee had added the use of conventional weapons to the agenda of the first Conference of Government Experts of 1971. Discouraged by the discussions, however, it had refrained from doing so for the second Conference in 1972 and it had chosen not to include specific proposals in its draft Protocols.[337]

[334] Geneva Protocol for the Prohibition of the use in War of Asphyxiating, Poisonous or Other Gases, and of Bacteriological Methods of Warfare, signed 17 Jun 1925, entered into force on 8 Feb 1928, AJIL, Vol 25, No 2, Supplement: Official Documents, 1931, p 94.

[335] According to *Collins Dictionary*, 'to broach' means primarily 'to initiate (a topic) for discussion'. *Collins Dictionary*, p 201.

[336] Sandoz, Swinaraski, Zimmerman, *Commentary on the Additional Protocols; of 8 Jun 1977 to the Geneva Conventions of 12 Aug 1949*, p xxxii.

[337] The ICRC explained its choice by referring to the fact that (a) arms and their prohibitions were dealt with by other organisations; (b) the prohibition of weapons were traditionally

Nevertheless, and mainly due to the efforts of the Swedish Delegation, the item returned on the agenda and received a final and decisive push at the 22nd International Conference of the Red Cross in Teheran in 1973.[338] One year before the start of the Diplomatic Conference on the Additional Protocols to the Geneva Conventions, the Conference urged:

> the Diplomatic Conference (. . .) to begin consideration at its 1974 session of the question of the prohibition or restriction of use of conventional weapons which may cause unnecessary suffering or have indiscriminate effects.

And additionally, the Conference invited:

> the ICRC to call in 1974 a conference of government experts to study in depth the question of prohibition or restriction of conventional weapons (. . .) and to transmit a report on the work of the conference to all governments participating in the Diplomatic Conference with a view to assisting them in their further deliberations.[339]

The issue therefore remained topical and became an item at the Diplomatic Conference in Geneva even so, despite the fact that the ICRC had decided not to include any proposal in its draft protocols. As a matter of fact, at its first session in 1974, the Conference set up an Ad Hoc Committee on Conventional Weapons,[340] in addition to the three Main Committees,[341] and provided the mandate for a parallel Conference of Government Experts on the same topic, the establishment of which was requested by the International Conference of the Red Cross in Teheran the year before.[342]

covered by agreements separate from the Geneva Conventions; (c) it would be preferable to include specific weapon restrictions in a separate instrument outside the additional Protocols. Solf, in: Bothe, Partsch, Solf, *New Rules for Victims of Armed Conflicts; Commentary on the Two 1977 Protocols Additional to the Geneva Conventions of 1949*, p 197.

[338] As was explained above, the International Conferences of the Red Cross meets in principle every four years and consist of the ICRC, the International Federation of the Red Cross and Red Crescent Societies, the national societies of the Red Cross and Red Crescent and the State Parties to the Geneva Conventions.

[339] Resolution XIV, adopted by the XXIInd International Conference of the Red Cross, Teheran, 1973, on the prohibition or restriction of use of certain weapons, through the Netherlands Red Cross; Division of International Humanitarian Law. F Kalshoven, *The Conference of Government Experts on the Use of Certain Conventional Weapons, Lucerne, 24 Sep–18 Oct 1974*, Netherlands Yearbook of International Law, Vol 6, 1975, pp 78–82; Kalshoven, *Arms, Armaments and International Law*, pp 225–32.

[340] Kalshoven, *Arms, Armaments and International Law*, pp 247–9.

[341] Committee I dealt with general and final provisions, execution of Protocol I and fundamental guarantees of Protocol II. Committee II dealt with the wounded and the sick, civil defence and relief. Committee III dealt with means and methods of warfare and protection of the civilian population. Bothe, Partsch, in: Bothe, Partsch, Solf, *New Rules for Victims of Armed Conflicts; Commentary on the Two 1977 Protocols Additional to the Geneva Conventions of 1949*, pp 4–5.

[342] 'The purpose of the Conference, under the auspices of the Red Cross, shall be the study in depth, from the humanitarian standpoint, of the question of the prohibition or limitation of the use of conventional weapons that may cause unnecessary suffering or have indiscriminate effects.' And the Conference was not to have any law-making powers: 'The Conference shall not adopt any resolution or recommendation and shall not vote. When differing views

This Conference of Experts met twice, in Lucerne from 26 September till 18 October 1974 and again in Lugano from 28 January till 26 February 1976 and included lawyers, diplomats, officers of the armed forces, and technological and medical experts.[343] Neither Conference managed to reach agreement, however, and nor did the Ad Hoc Committee at the Diplomatic Conference.[344] The limited results were eventually presented to the final session of the Diplomatic Conference, after which the Conference recommended to convene another Conference of Governments within two years, under the auspices of the United Nations. The Conference was convinced that the suffering of the civilian population and combatants could be significantly reduced by a prohibition of the use of certain conventional weapons and stated that work towards this purpose should continue with urgency and should proceed from the areas of agreement. Additionally, the Diplomatic Conference concluded that there was agreement on a prohibition of the use of non-detectable fragment weapons, and a wide area of agreement on landmines and booby-traps, but not yet on incendiary weapons, small caliber weapons, and certain blast and fragmentation weapons.[345]

The United Nations noted this recommendation,[346] and decided to convene a specific United Nations Diplomatic Conference in 1979 and 1980 for the purpose of negotiating a convention on conventional weapons,[347] which resulted in the adoption of the Convention on Prohibition or

are expressed on a point and the discussion does not result in conclusions acceptable to all, note shall be taken of the different opinions expressed.' Kalshoven, *Arms, Armaments and International Law*, pp 232–3.

[343] The first session in Lucerne had a general character and dealt with the legal criteria governing the use of conventional weapons as well as certain specific conventional weapon categories. These categories were: incendiary weapons, small-caliber projectiles, blast and fragmentation weapons, delayed action and treacherous weapons, and future weapons. The second session in Lugano was more specific and was intended to 'study the possibility, contents and form of such proposed bans or restrictions.' Kalshoven, *The Conference of Government Experts on the Use of Certain Conventional Weapons, Lucerne, 24 Sep–18 Oct 1974*, pp 89–93 respectively pp 94–9; Kalshoven, *Arms, Armaments and International Law*, pp 232–40; F Kalshoven, *The Conference of Government Experts on the Use of Certain Conventional Weapons, Second Session, Lugano, 28 Jan–26 Feb 1976*, Netherlands Yearbook of International Law, Vol 7, 1976, p 197; Kalshoven, *Arms, Armaments and International Law*, pp 240–2.

[344] Kalshoven, *Reaffirmation and Development of International Humanitarian Law Applicable in Armed Conflicts: the Diplomatic Conference, Geneva, 1974–1977; Part II*, p 153; Kalshoven, *Arms, Armaments and International Law*, pp 247–9.

[345] Diplomatic Conference on the Reaffirmation and Development of International Humanitarian Law Applicable in Armed Conflicts; Resolution 22; adopted on 9 Jun 1977; follow-up regarding prohibition or restriction of use of certain conventional weapons. International Committee of the Red Cross, *Protocols Additional to the Geneva Conventions of 12 Aug 1949*, ICRC, Geneva, 1996; Sandoz, Swinaraski, Zimmerman, *Commentary on the Additional Protocols; of 8 Jun 1977 to the Geneva Conventions of 12 Aug 1949*, pp 1527–8.

[346] A/Res/32/44, adopted by consensus on 8 Dec 1977, on respect for human rights in armed conflict.

[347] A/Res/32/152, adopted on 19 Dec 1977, by 115 to 0, with 21 abstentions, on incendiary and other specific conventional weapons which may be the subject of prohibitions or restrictions of use for humanitarian reasons.

Restrictions on the Use of Certain Conventional Weapons Which May Be Deemed to Be Excessively Injurious or to have Indiscriminate Effects, supplemented by three additional protocols on 10 October 1980.[348] The Convention and its Protocols were thereupon welcomed by the UN General Assembly and commended to all states for ratification.[349]

The negotiators had reached agreement on weapons containing non-detectable fragments (Protocol I), landmines and booby-traps (Protocol II) and incendiary weapons (Protocol III), although only the use of weapons containing non-detectable fragments was unconditionally prohibited. In order to gain the widest possible support for the Convention, the drafters had decided to construct a framework Convention; ie formal and general provisions regarding the treaty were laid down in a main convention or umbrella treaty, whereas the material obligations were laid down in three annexed and optional protocols.[350] According to Article 4(3) of the Convention, Contracting Parties are allowed to choose by which Protocols they would like to be bound, with a minimum of two.

Currently, the Convention has 97 States Parties, 89 of which are bound by Protocol I, 83 by Protocol II, and 88 by Protocol III.[351] The Convention was amended in 1996,[352] and in 2001,[353] and extended in 1995 by a fourth

[348] Bothe, Partsch, in: Bothe, Partsch, Solf, *New Rules for Victims of Armed Conflicts; Commentary on the Two 1977 Protocols Additional to the Geneva Conventions of 1949*, pp 5–6; Sandoz, Swinaraski, Zimmerman, *Commentary on the Additional Protocols; of 8 Jun 1977 to the Geneva Conventions of 12 Aug 1949*, p xxxii.

[349] A/Res/35/153, adopted without a vote on 12 Dec 1980, on the United Nations Conference on Prohibitions or Restrictions of Use of Certain conventional Weapons Which May Be Deemed to Be Excessively Injurious or to Have Indiscriminate Effects.

[350] Framework treaties are treaties that provide 'a framework for later, and more detailed, treaties (usually called protocols), or national legislation, which elaborate the principles declared in the framework treaty. The term is used particularly in connection with environmental treaties.' Aust, *Modern Treaty Law and Practice*, p 97.

[351] Through <http://www.icrc.org/>.

[352] Amended Protocol on Prohibitions or Restrictions on the Use of Mines, Booby-Traps and Other Devices (Amended Protocol II) to the Convention on Prohibitions or Restrictions on the Use of Certain Conventional Weapons Which May be Deemed To Be Excessively Injurious or To Have Indiscriminate Effects, opened for signature on 3 May 1996, entered into force on 3 Dec 1998, UNTS, Vol 2048, No 22495. It should be noted that independently from the Certain Conventional Weapons Convention, a diplomatic conference concluded another and separate treaty on landmines in 1997: the Convention on the Prohibition of the Use, Stockpiling, Production and Transfer of Anti-Personnel Mines and on Their Destruction, signed on 18 Sep 1997, entered into force on 1 Mar 1999, UNTS, Vol 2056, No 35597. The so-called Ottawa Convention does not only strengthen international regulations on the use of landmines but it also prohibits the manufacture and possession of landmines which makes it primarily a disarmament treaty, similar to the 1993 Chemical Weapons Convention. The Ottawa Convention currently has 144 States Parties.

[353] Amendment to the Convention on Prohibitions or Restrictions on the Use of Certain Conventional Weapons Which May Be Deemed To Be Excessively Injurious or To Have Indiscriminate Effects, signed on 21 Dec 2001, entered into force on 18 May 2004, UNTS, Vol 2260, No 22495.

Protocol on blinding laser weapons,[354] and in 2003 by a fifth Protocol on explosive remnants of war.[355]

2.2.4.3 The CCWC and the Protection of the Environment

2.2.4.3.1 Introduction

The Certain Conventional Weapons Convention and the Incendiary Weapons Protocol contain two explicit references to the protection of the environment during armed conflict. Firstly, in preambular paragraph 4 of the framework Convention, the High Contracting Parties recall:

> that it is prohibited to employ methods or means of warfare which are intended, or may be expected, to cause widespread, long-term and severe damage to the natural environment.

Secondly, the Convention's Incendiary Weapons Protocol provides in Article 2(4) that in principle:

> [i]t is prohibited to make forests or other kinds of plant cover the object of attack by incendiary weapons except when such natural elements are used to cover, conceal or camouflage combatants or other military objectives, or are themselves military objectives.

2.2.4.3.2 Preambular Paragraph 4

The first reference repeats the prohibition of Article 35(3) and partly the prohibition of Article 55 of Additional Protocol I of 1977.[356] Although pre-

[354] Protocol on Blinding Laser Weapons (Protocol IV) to the Convention on Prohibitions or Restrictions on the Use of Certain Conventional Weapons Which May be Deemed To Be Excessively Injurious or To Have Indiscriminate Effects, opened for signature on 13 Oct 1995, entered into force on 30 Jul 1998, UNTS, Vol 2024, No 22495.

[355] Protocol on Explosive Remnants of War (Protocol V) to the Convention on Prohibitions or Restrictions on the Use of Certain Conventional Weapons Which May be Deemed To Be Excessively Injurious or To Have Indiscriminate Effects, opened for signature on 28 Nov 2003, entered into force on 12 Nov 2006, CCW/MSP/2003/2.

[356] This reference caused France to attach a reservation upon signature, and the United States to make a declaration upon ratification stating that the provisions of Additional Protocol I of 1977 only apply to States Parties. Schmitt, *Green War: An Assessment of the Environmental Law of International Armed Conflict*, pp 88–9; Schmitt, *Humanitarian Law and the Environment*, pp 287–8. 'France, which is not bound by Additional Protocol I of 10 Jun 1977 to the Geneva Conventions of 12 Aug 1949: Considers that the fourth para of the preamble to the Convention on Prohibitions or Restrictions on the Use of Certain Conventional Weapons Which May Be Deemed to Be Excessively Injurious or to Have Indiscriminate Effects, which reproduces the provisions of Art 35, para 3, of Additional Protocol I, applies only to States parties to that Protocol[.]' And the United States considered 'that the fourth para of the preamble to the Convention, which refers to the substance of provisions of Art 35 (3) and Art 55 (1) of additional Protocol I to the Geneva Conventions for the Protection of War Victims of Aug 12, 1949, applies only to States which have accepted those provisions.' Through <http://untreaty.un.org/> or <http://www.icrc.org/>.

ambular paragraphs are not intended to create legal rights and duties, they are not without legal significance. Preambles usually reflect the motives of the contracting parties and the rationale of the convention, and therefore they provide a thankful source for interpreting the operative paragraphs in accordance with Article 31 of the Vienna Convention on the Law of Treaties.

The drafters' choice to use the same terminology in the Preamble as in Additional Protocol I is not surprising in view of the legislative history of the Convention and seems to echo the principle of environmental protection. As has been explained above, it is arguable that this third principle has shaped the laws of war since the 1970s, in addition to the principles of necessity and humanity. Although the Convention is primarily based on the principles of humanity, reflected in the prohibition of unnecessary suffering, and on the principles of necessity and discrimination,[357] the principle of environmental protection is reflected in Article 2(4) of the Incendiary Weapons Protocol.

2.2.4.3.3 Article 2(4) Protocol III

The second reference to the protection of the environment is the prohibition in Article 2(4) of the Incendiary Weapons Protocol to attack forests and plant cover with incendiary weapons. The Incendiary Weapons Protocol consists of two Articles and does not have a Preamble: Article 1 embodies definitions and Article 2 stipulates the Protocol's material obligations and is entitled 'Protection of civilians and civilian objects'. Article 2 prohibits the use of incendiary weapons against the civilian population, which is a truism, and prohibits attacks with incendiary weapons against military objectives within or close to civilian objects, except under certain circumstances. Inclusion of paragraph 4 in Article 2, prohibiting attacks with incendiary weapons against forests or other kinds of plant cover can be justified by reference to the definition of 'civilian objects' in Article 1(4): '[A]ll objects which are not military objectives as defined in paragraph 3', similar to the definition in Article 52(1) of Additional Protocol I. Military objects are defined by both Protocols as objects that make 'an effective contribution to military action'[358] and since,

[357] This does not only appear from the title of the Convention but also from its Preamble, at least as far as the prohibition of unnecessary suffering is concerned. In preambular para 3, the High Contracting Parties state that they base themselves on the principle that the right of belligerents to choose means and methods of warfare is not unlimited and on the prohibition of unnecessary suffering. The principle of discrimination is reflected in the Contracting Parties' general statement in para 2 that the civilian population must be protected against the effects of hostilities.

[358] Art 1(3) of Protocol III defines a military object as 'any object which by its nature, location, purpose or use makes an effective contribution to military action and whose total or partial destruction, capture or neutralization, in the circumstances ruling at the time, offers a definite military advantage.' Similarly: Art 52(2) of Additional Protocol I.

in principle, the environment does not contribute to military action, it should be considered as a civilian object.

Although probably inspired by the debates at the Diplomatic Conference in Geneva on environmental protection, which is reflected in the main Convention's Preamble, Article 2(4) is very different from Article 35(3) and Article 55 Additional Protocol I. Firstly, the former provision is more concrete than the latter provisions, because it prohibits attacks by incendiary weapons against forests or other kinds of plant cover,[359] whereas Article 35(3) and 55 protect the environment *in abstracto* from attack in general. Secondly, Article 2(4) only prohibits direct attack upon the environment and does not seem to prohibit collateral damage. Thirdly, damage to forests and plant cover is presumed in case of attack with incendiary weapons and is not qualified by a damage threshold, as in Additional Protocol I. And fourthly, Article 2(4) has an exception clause based on military necessity, as opposed to Articles 35(3) and 55, under which the environment may not be the object of attack under any circumstance. Attack of forests or other kind of plant cover with incendiary weapons is allowed when they are used to camouflage combatants or military objectives or when they are military objectives themselves,[360] although subject to the principle of proportionality.[361]

This means that, on the one hand, Article 2(4) has a wider scope than the provisions of Additional Protocol I and provides more protection because there is no damage threshold. On the other hand, Article 2(4) has a narrower scope than the provisions of Additional Protocol I, because firstly, it only deals with incendiary weapons; secondly, it protects only forests and other plant cover; and thirdly, it provides for an escape clause. In particular, this exception to derogate from the main prohibition could become problematic and undermine the practical significance of the provision. After all, why would a military commander employ incendiary weapons against a forest if there is no military advantage to be achieved.[362] Scorched earth tactics are normally only aimed at objects that may be of use to the enemy.

[359] An incendiary weapon is defined by Art 1(1) of the Protocol as 'any weapon or munition which is primarily designed to set fire to objects or to cause burn injury to persons through the action of flame, heat, or a combination thereof, produced by a chemical reaction of a substance delivered on the target.' Art 1(1) subsequently gives a few illustrative examples under (a) and excludes a number of munitions under (b).

[360] Art 1(3) of the Protocol defines a military objective as 'any object which by its nature, location, purpose or use makes an effective contribution to military action and whose total or partial destruction, capture or neutralization, in the circumstances ruling at the time, offers a definite military advantage.'

[361] Schmitt, *Green War: An Assessment of the Environmental Law of International Armed Conflict*, p 89.

[362] Compare also Dinstein, *The Conduct of Hostilities under the Law of International Armed Conflict*, p 187; Kalshoven, Zegveld, *Constraints on the Waging of War; An Introduction to International Humanitarian Law*, p 164. Detter refers in this context to the disadvantages for states with dense tropical vegetation. Detter, *The Law of War*, p 226.

In any case, the relationship between Article 2(4) and Articles 35(3) and 55 reminds of the relationship between *lex specialis* and *lex generalis*, at least theoretically. The use of incendiary weapons against forests or other kinds of plant cover may be covered both by the Incendiary Weapons Protocol and Additional Protocol I to the Geneva Conventions, since their use may cause considerable damage to the environment. And because the former is more specific, and because the Preamble of the main Convention recalls the environmental protection provisions in the latter, the conclusion of a lex specialis—lex generalis relationship seems justified.

Furthermore, since the drafters did not seem to intend to supplant the environmental protection already in force under Additional Protocol I, it would seem possible to fall back on the general protection of the environment under Articles 35(3) and 55,[363] in case the use of incendiary weapons against forests or other plant cover would not be covered by Article 2(4) of the Protocol. Of course, it will be doubtful under normal circumstances, whether the damage inflicted would be widespread, long-lasting and severe, in the sense adhered to by the States Parties.

2.2.5 The Statute of the International Criminal Court

2.2.5.1 Introduction

The fourth and final treaty that contains an explicit reference to the protection of the environment during armed conflict is the 1998 Statute of the International Criminal Court.[364] Although this reference is not a prohibitive norm similar to the ones in the Environmental Modification Convention, Additional Protocol I and the Certain Conventional Weapons Convention, the provision in question does protect the environment during armed conflict, because it establishes individual criminal responsibility

[363] Application of the *lex specialis* rule may have two opposite results: either the special rule supplants the general rule, or the special rule supplements the general rule. In the latter case, it is possible to fall back on the general rule in case the conditions of the special rule are not met. Compare the Commentary of the International Law Commission (ILC) to Art 55 of the Draft Articles on State Responsibility. Art 55 provides that the Draft Articles are only residual and that they do not apply in cases 'governed by special rules of international law.' According to the ILC, '[i]t will depend on the special rule to establish the extent to which the more general rules on State responsibility set out in the present articles are displaced by that rule. In some cases it will be clear form the language of a treaty or other text that only the consequences specified are to flow. (. . .) In other cases, one aspect of the general law may be modified, leaving other aspects still applicable.' A/56/10, Draft Articles on Responsibility of States for Internationally Wrongful Acts, including Commentaries, adopted by the ILC at its fifty-third session, Nov 2001; Yearbook of the International Law Commission, 2001; Vol II, Part Two, forthcoming, p 357. Through <http://www.un.org/law/ilc/>. Also J Crawford, *The International Law Commission's Articles on State Responsibility; Introduction, Text and Commentaries*, Cambridge University Press, Cambridge, 2002, p 307.

[364] Statute of the International Criminal Court, opened for signature on 17 Jul 1998, entered into force on 1 Jul 2002, UNTS, Vol 2187, No 38544.

for excessive damage to the environment, independently of these conventions.[365] In this sense, the reference to individual responsibility is only secondary to the primary or substantive rules that actually regulate the behavior of states in case of an international armed conflict.[366]

2.2.5.2 Drafting History

The Statute of the International Criminal Court was signed in Rome in 1998 after a cumbersome negotiation process that goes back all the way to the late 1940s when first the ILC,[367] and then an Ad Hoc Committee on International Criminal Jurisdiction,[368] were asked by the General Assembly to look into the possibility of a permanent international criminal court. Just earlier, the temporary International Military Tribunals at Nuremberg[369] and Tokyo[370] had tried high German and Japanese state-officials for war crimes, crimes against the peace and crimes against

[365] Compare also Schmitt, *Humanitarian Law and the Environment*, Denver Journal of International Law and Policy, Vol 28, 2000, pp 272, 283.

[366] M Bothe, *War Crimes*, in: A Cassese,P Gaeta, JRWD Jones (Eds), *The Rome Statue of the International Criminal Court: A Commentary; Vol I*, Oxford University Press, Oxford, 2002, pp 381, 387. Generally on the relationship between individual and collective or state responsibility, see: A Nollkaemper, *De dialectiek tussen individuele en collectieve aansprakelijkheid in het volkenrecht*, Inaugural lecture, Vossiuspers AUP, Amsterdam, 2000.

[367] The ILC was established by the General Assembly under Art 13(1)(a) of the Charter of the United Nations by A/Res/174 (II), adopted on 21 Nov 1947, by 44 to 0, with 6 abstentions; establishment of an international law commission. In 1948, the Commission was asked to 'study the desirability and possibility of establishing an international judicial organ' upon the adoption and approval of the Genocide Convention by A/Res/260A (III), adopted on 9 Dec 1948, by 56 to 0; prevention and punishment of the crime of genocide; Annex: Convention on the Prevention and Punishment of the Crime of Genocide.

[368] The International Committee on International Criminal Jurisdiction was established by the General Assembly under A/Res/489 (V), adopted on 12 Dec 1950, by 42 to 7, with 5 abstentions; international criminal jurisdiction. The Committee was established after the ILC had concluded that an international criminal court was feasible, 'for the purpose of preparing one or more preliminary draft conventions and proposals relating to the establishment and the statute' of such a court.

[369] The International Military Tribunal at Nuremberg was established by Agreement between the Government of the United States of America, the Provisional Government of the French Republic, the Government of the United Kingdom of Great Britain and Northern Ireland and the Government of the Union of Soviet Socialist Republics for the Prosecution and Punishment of the Major War Criminals of the European Axis, signed in London, on 8 Aug 1945, entered into force on 8 Aug 1945, AJIL, Vol 39, No 4, Supplement: Official Documents, 1945, p 257. The Charter of the International Military Tribunal was annexed to this Agreement, which is also known as the London Agreement. It should be noted that in addition to the International Military Tribunal, separate military tribunals were established in each of the four occupation zones for the prosecution of lesser war criminals.

[370] Charter of the International Military Tribunal for the Far East, established by special proclamation of General MacArthur as the Supreme Commander in the Far East for the Allied Powers on 19 Jan 1946, at: <http://www.yale.edu/lawweb/avalon/imtfech.htm>. Its scope of jurisdiction was based on the same principles as the International Military Tribunal in Nuremberg.

humanity,[371] and the time seemed right for a permanent institution.[372] The General Assembly had endorsed the Nuremberg and Tokyo Charters by Resolution 95 (I),[373] and the 1948 Genocide Convention, which had been negotiated within the framework of the United Nations,[374] envisaged the existence of such a court in the near future in Article VI of this Convention.[375]

Both the ILC and the Ad Hoc Committee prepared reports on the establishment of an international criminal court.[376] Subsequent discussion within the United Nations became impossible, however, not only because

[371] Cassese, *From Nuremberg to Rome: International Military Tribunals to the International Criminal Court*, in: Cassese, Gaeta, Jones (Eds), *The Rome Statue of the International Criminal Court: A Commentary; Vol I*, pp 5–8.

[372] Unsuccessful proposals for the establishment of individual responsibility under public international law had been made both before, and after the World War I. Roberts and Guelff refer to a proposal for an international criminal court after the 1870–1871 war between France and Prussia. And Cassese refers to the 'Advisory Committee of Jurists', which proposed in 1920 that the new Permanent Court of International Justice should also have jurisdiction over 'crimes constituting a breach of international public order or against the universal law of nations, referred to it by the Assembly or by the Council of the League of Nations.' Similarly, when the ILC was asked by the General Assembly to look into the possibility of an international criminal court by A/Res/260 (III) on 9 Dec 1948, the Assembly requested that the Commission 'in carrying out this task', should 'pay attention to the possibility of establishing a Criminal Chamber of the International Court of Justice.' Roberts, Guelff, *Documents on the Laws of War*, p 667; A Cassese, *From Nuremberg to Rome: International Military Tribunals to the International Criminal Court*, in: A Cassese, P Gaeta, JRWD Jones (Eds), *The Rome Statue of the International Criminal Court: A Commentary; Vol I*, Oxford University Press, Oxford, 2002, pp 4–5, 9.

[373] A/Res/95 (I), adopted unanimously on 11 Dec 1946; affirmation of the principles of international law recognised by the Charter of the Nürnberg Tribunal.

[374] The drafting of the Genocide Convention must almost exclusively be attributed to Raphael Lemkin, a Polish Jew who had managed to escape from occupied Poland in 1939, via Sweden to the United States. Lemkin, who was a lawyer, had dedicated his life to the criminalisation of mass murder after he had learned of the mass slaughter of Armenians by the Turkish during the World War I. He was appalled by the fact that sovereignty could 'shield men who tried to wipe out an entire minority.' During and after World War II he relentlessly and often alone pursued the drafting of an international convention that would hold people individually criminal responsible for committing mass murder, something he called 'genocide'. Genocide is defined in Art 2 of the Convention as 'any of the following acts committed with intent to destroy, in whole or in part, a national, ethnical, racial or religious group, as such: (a) Killing members of the group; (b) Causing serious bodily or mental harm to members of the group; (c) Deliberately inflicting on the group conditions of life calculated to bring about its physical destruction in whole or in part; (d) Imposing measures intended to prevent births within the group; (e) Forcibly transferring children of the group to another group.' S Power, *A Problem from Hell; America and the Age of Genocide*, Perennial, New York, NY, 2003, pp 1–60. For the first use, origin, and explanation of the term 'genocide', see: R Lemkin, *Axis Rule in Occupied Europe; Laws of Occupation—Analysis of Government—Proposals for Redress*, Carnegie Endowment for International Peace, Washington, DC, 1944, pp 79–95.

[375] Convention on the Prevention and Punishment of the Crime of Genocide, opened for signature on 11 Dec 1948, entered into force on 12 Jan 1951, UNTS, Vol 78, No 1021.

[376] A/CN.4/15, Question of International Criminal Jurisdiction; Report by Ricardo J Alfaro, Special Rapporteur, 3 Mar 1950; Yearbook of the International Law Commission, 1950; Vol II, United Nations, New York, 1957; A/2645, Report of the 1953 Committee on International Criminal Jurisdiction; 27 Jul–20 Aug 1953; General Assembly Official Records: Ninth Session, Supplement No 12, United Nations, New York, 1954.

of the Cold War, but also because the Special Committee which had been charged with the definition of aggression[377] was unable to conclude its work.

Years later, the ILC was once again involved in 1989, requested by the General Assembly to produce a draft statute in 1992,[378] and managed to produce a renewed draft text in 1994.[379] Based on this text, the General Assembly established an Ad Hoc Committee on the Establishment of an International Criminal Court in 1994,[380] a Preparatory Committee in 1995,[381] and decided to convoke:

> a diplomatic conference of plenipotentiaries (. . .) with a view to finalizing and adopting a convention on the establishment of an international criminal court

in Rome, upon the invitation of the Italian Government in 1998.[382]

The Conference convened between 15 June and 17 July 1998 with 160 states participating, as well as the involvement of between 31 and 33 intergovernmental organisations and between 135 and 236 non-governmental organisations, and adopted the Statute on 17 July 1998 with 120 votes against 7, with 21 abstentions.[383] As of November 2005, 100 countries are States Parties to the Statute.[384] Although the United States signed the Statute on 31 December 2000, which was the last possible date for signature, it decided not to become a party on 6 May 2002 by notifying the Secretary-General of its intention not to ratify.[385] The seat of the Court is established in The Hague in the Netherlands, in accordance with Article 3 of the Statute.[386]

[377] A/Res/898 (IX), adopted on 14 Dec 1954, by 34 to 0, with 7 abstentions; international criminal jurisdiction.

[378] A/Res/47/33, adopted without a vote on 25 Nov 1992; Report of the International Law Commission on the work of its 44th session.

[379] A/49/10, Report of the International Law Commission to the General Assembly on the work of its forty-sixth session, 2 May to 22 Jul 1994; Yearbook of the International Law Commission, 1994; Vol II, Part Two, United Nations, Geneva, 1996. Also through <http://www.un.org/law/ilc/>.

[380] A/Res/49/53, adopted without a vote on 9 Dec 1994; establishment of an international criminal court.

[381] A/Res/50/46, adopted by consensus on 11 Dec 1995; establishment of an international criminal court.

[382] A/Res/51/207, adopted without a vote on 17 Dec 1996; establishment of an international court.

[383] Cassese, *From Nuremberg to Rome: International Military Tribunals to the International Criminal Court*, in: Cassese, Gaeta, Jones (Eds), *The Rome Statue of the International Criminal Court: A Commentary; Vol I*, pp 9–10, 16–17; Roberts, Guelff, *Documents on the Laws of War*, p 667; through <http://www.icc-cpi.int/>.

[384] Through <http://untreaty.un.org/> and <http://www.icc-cpi.int/>.

[385] The Secretary-General was informed as follows: 'This is to inform you, in connection with the Rome Statute of the International Criminal Court adopted on Jul 17, 1998, that the United States does not intend to become a party to the treaty. Accordingly, the United States has no legal obligations arising from its signature on Dec 31, 2000. The United States requests that its intention not to become a party, as expressed in this letter, be reflected in the depositary's status lists relating to this treaty.' Through <http://untreaty.un.org/>.

[386] For information on the International Criminal Court, see: <http://www.icc-cpi.int/>.

The process of establishing a permanent International Criminal Court in the 1990s coincided largely with a renewed interest in the implementation of international humanitarian law after bloody conflicts in the former Yugoslavia and Rwanda. The ordinary implementation mechanisms under international humanitarian law through national courts did not suffice, and both world public opinion and states publicly demanded action by the international community of states and the United Nations. The Security Council responded in 1993 by establishing the ICTY,[387] in The Hague in the Netherlands, and in 1994 by establishing an Ad Hoc International Criminal Tribunal for Rwanda (ICTR),[388] in Arusha in Tanzania. Both Tribunals are limited, however, both in scope and in time. Geographically they are confined to the conflicts in the former Yugoslavia and Rwanda; temporarily, they are limited to the extent that they are called upon to take all possible measures to finish their work by 2010.[389]

Their success, however, has not only contributed to the development of international law,[390] but it has also led to the establishment of the International Criminal Court as well as various other internationalised or mixed tribunals for the prosecution of war crimes in other states. Internationalised tribunals are national courts with international features, established for a specific purpose by a national state, usually in cooperation with the United Nations. Such bodies have been established for the prosecution of individuals under international criminal law in Sierra Leone,[391] in Cambodia,[392] in East-Timor,[393] and in Iraq.[394] The Special Court for Sierra Leone and the Extraordinary Chambers in Cambodia were set up under a special agreement with the United Nations;[395] the

[387] S/RES/827 (1993), adopted unanimously on 25 May 1993, on the establishment of an international tribunal for the Former Yugoslavia. For more information on the ICTY, see: <http://www.icty.org/>.

[388] S/RES/955 (1994), adopted on 8 Nov 1994, by 13 to 0, with 1 abstention, on the establishment of an international tribunal for Rwanda and the adoption of the statute of the tribunal. For more information on the ICTR, see: <http://www.ictr.org/>.

[389] S/RES/1503 (2003), adopted unanimously on 28 Aug 2003, on the International Criminal Tribunal for the former Yugoslavia and International Criminal Tribunal for Rwanda.

[390] See LJ van den Herik, *The Contribution of the Rwanda Tribunal to the Development of International Law*, Martinus Nijhoff Publishers, Leiden, 2005.

[391] Special Court for Sierra Leone, <http://www.sc-sl.org/>.

[392] Extraordinary Chambers in the Courts of Cambodia for the Prosecution of Crimes Committed during the Period of Democratic Kampuchea, <http://www.cambodia.gov.kh/krt/english/index.htm>.

[393] Special Panel for Serious Crimes in East Timor, <http://www.jsmp.minihub.org/courtmonitoring/spsc.htm>.

[394] The Iraqi Special Tribunal, <http://www.iraq-istorg/>.

[395] Agreement between the United Nations and the Government of Sierra Leone on the Establishment of the Special Court for Sierra Leone, with annexed Statute, signed on 16 Jan 2002, entered into force on 12 Apr 2002, UNTS, Vol 2178, No 38342; Agreement between The United Nations and The Royal Government of Cambodia Concerning The Prosecution Under Cambodian Law Of Crimes Committed During The Period Of Democratic Kampuchea, signed on 6 Jun 2003, entered into force on 20 Oct 2004, A/Res/57/228B, adopted without a vote on 22 May 2003, on the Khmer Rouge Trials.

Special Panel for Serious Crimes in East Timor was set up by a Regulation adopted by the United Nations Transitional Administration in East Timor (UNTAET),[396] a peacekeeping operation established by the Security Council under Chapter VII of the United Nations Charter;[397] and the Iraqi Special Tribunal was set up by a regulation from the Coalition Provisional Authority or Iraqi Governing Council after the invasion of Iraq in the Spring of 2003.[398]

2.2.5.3 Jurisdiction

2.2.5.3.1 Introduction

The Statute confers complementary jurisdiction to the International Criminal Court for the prosecution of the crime of genocide, crimes against humanity, war crimes, and the crime of aggression. Definitions of genocide, crimes against humanity and war crimes are laid down respectively in Articles 6, 7 and 8; the crime of aggression is yet to be defined.[399] The jurisdiction is complementary because in paragraph 10 of the Preamble the States Parties to the Statute emphasise that 'the International Criminal Court established under this Statute shall be complementary to national criminal jurisdictions'; and Article 17 states that cases are not admissible when they are or have been under genuine investigation or prosecution of a state that has or had jurisdiction over them.

2.2.5.3.2 War Crimes

Where the definition of genocide in Article 6 of the Statute is literally based on Article II of the Genocide Convention,[400] and where the foundation of the definition of crimes against humanity was laid down in Article 6(c) of the Nuremberg Statute,[401] the definition of war crimes in the Statute is 'the

[396] UNTAET/Reg/2000/15, of 6 Jun 2000, On the Establishment of Panels with Exclusive Jurisdiction over Serious Criminal Offences.

[397] UNTAET was established by S/RES/1272 (1999), adopted unanimously on 25 Oct 1999, on the establishment of the United Nations Transitional Authority in East Timor, and succeeded UNAMET that was established by S/RES/1246, adopted unanimously on 11 Jun 1999, on the establishment of a United Nations Mission in East Timor.

[398] Statute of the Iraqi Special Tribunal, proclaimed by the Coalition Provision Authority, effective on 10 Dec 2003, ILM, Vol 43, 2004, p 231.

[399] According to Art 5(2) of the Statute, the Court shall have jurisdiction over the crime of aggression once a definition is adopted including the conditions for jurisdiction in conformity with Art 121 and 123 of the Statute. Art 121 deals with amendment and Art 123 deals with the review of the Statute.

[400] Convention on the Prevention and Punishment of the Crime of Genocide, opened for signature on 11 Dec 1948, entered into force on 12 Jan 1951, UNTS, Vol 78, No 1021.

[401] Cassese is of the opinion that the definition of crimes against humanity in Art 6(c) of the Statute did not reflect customary international law but constituted new law. According to Cassese, the fact that therefore the maxim *nullum crimen sine lege*—no crime without law—was violated was justified by 'superior exigencies' of justice. A Cassese, *Crimes against*

first attempt to clearly and comprehensively define what war crimes are.'[402] Before 1998, the concept of 'war crimes' had been recognised in a large number of agreements. In chronological order, the concept was generally referred to in the 1919 Peace Treaty of Versailles,[403] defined in the 1945 Nuremberg Charter[404] and mentioned in the 1946 Tokyo Charter.[405] Furthermore, the concept was characterised as 'grave breaches' in the 1949 Geneva Conventions, including Additional Protocol I,[406] as 'grave breaches' and 'violations of the laws or customs of war' in the ICTY Statute,[407] and as violations of common Article 3 to the Geneva Conventions and Additional Protocol II of 1977 in the ICTR Statute.[408]

The reason for this patchwork of definitions and descriptions of this concept is the fact that it involves individual criminal responsibility and punishment for violation of a specific rule of *ius in bello*, and states have been reluctant in accepting this phenomenon. As a matter of fact, a large part of the corpus of the laws of war, namely the Hague Conventions of 1899 and 1907, did not even recognise the idea of individual criminal responsibility for violations of the laws of war. This meant that after 1945 one had to rely on the customary equivalents of those rules in order to establish individual responsibility for violation of those rules. Individual criminal responsibility for violation of certain rules of *ius in bello* must be clearly distinguished, however, from state responsibility for violations of international law. Violations of certain rules of *ius in bello* that do not constitute war crimes, might still entail the responsibility of the state to which the violations can be attributed under the general customary rules of state responsibility.[409]

Based on these earlier references, definitions and descriptions in earlier statutes and conventions, and based on the interpretations given to these provisions by both international and national courts, the drafters of the Statute have identified in Article 8(2) a long, detailed and comprehensive

Humanity, in: A Cassese,P Gaeta, JRWD Jones (Eds), *The Rome Statue of the International Criminal Court: A Commentary; Vol I*, Oxford University Press, Oxford, 2002, pp 354–5.

402 Bothe, *War Crimes*, in: Cassese, Gaeta, Jones (Eds), *The Rome Statue of the International Criminal Court: A Commentary; Vol I*, p 381.

403 Art 228 of the Covenant of the League of Nations or Peace Treaty of Versailles, signed on 28 Jun 1919, entered into force on 10 Jan 1920, AJIL, Vol 13, No 2, Supplement: Official Documents, 1919, p 128.

404 Art 6 of the Nuremberg Charter.

405 Art 5 of the Tokyo Charter.

406 Respectively Arts 50, 51, 130, and 147 of the four 1949 Geneva Conventions, and Art 85 of 1977 Additional Protocol I.

407 Arts 2 and 3 of the ICTY Statute.

408 Art 4 of the ICTR Statute. Bothe, *War Crimes*, in: Cassese, Gaeta, Jones (Eds), *The Rome Statue of the International Criminal Court: A Commentary; Vol I*, pp 382–6.

409 On the relationship between state responsibility and individual responsibility and the position of reprisals and the consequences of circumstances precluding wrongfulness under rules of state responsibility, see briefly Bothe, *War Crimes*, in: Cassese, Gaeta, Jones (Eds), *The Rome Statue of the International Criminal Court: A Commentary; Vol I*, p 387.

list of war crimes, classified in four categories. Firstly, grave breaches of the 1949 Geneva Conventions (8 crimes); secondly:

> other serious violations of the laws and customs applicable in international armed conflict, within the established framework of international law

(26 crimes); thirdly, serious violations of common Article 3 of the 1949 Geneva Conventions applicable in non-international armed conflict (4 crimes); and fourthly, serious violations of other laws and customs applicable in non-international armed conflicts (12 crimes).

The original Draft Statute from the ILC did not contain such a detailed list.[410] In Article 20 of the Draft Statute dealing with 'Crimes within the jurisdiction of the Court', the ILC simply referred in paragraph (c) to '[s]erious violations of the laws and customs applicable in armed conflict' and in paragraph (e) to:

> [c]rimes, established under or pursuant to the treaty provisions listed in the Annex, which having regard to the conduct alleged, constitute exceptionally serious crimes of international concern.

The first reference is based on customary international law, reflected in a number of international documents. According to the ILC's commentary on Article 20(c), this category is similar to the category of 'war crimes' overlapping with, but not identical to, the 'grave breaches' of the 1949 and 1977 Geneva Conventions. In view of 'uncertainties about the status of "war" since 1945', however, the Commission preferred reference to 'serious violations of the laws and customs applicable in armed conflict'.[411] The second reference is a variety of remaining crimes under general international law, including 'grave breaches' under the Geneva Conventions and Additional Protocol I. In addition, the ILC listed nine other peacetime conventions of universal scope dealing with crimes with an international character.[412]

Definition of the latter crimes in paragraph (e) and in the Annex to the Statute was not necessary, since they were sufficiently defined in treaties

[410] A/49/10, Report of the International Law Commission to the General Assembly on the work of its forty-sixth session, 2 May to 22 Jul 1994; Yearbook of the International Law Commission, 1994; Vol II, Part Two, United Nations, Geneva, 1996. Also through <http://www.un.org/law/ilc/>.

[411] A/49/10, Report of the International Law Commission to the General Assembly on the work of its forty-sixth session, 2 May to 22 Jul 1994; Yearbook of the International Law Commission, 1994; Vol II, Part Two, p 39.

[412] The nine peacetime conventions the Annex referred to were: the 1970 Convention for the Suppression of Unlawful Seizure of Aircraft; the 1971 Convention for the Suppression of Unlawful Acts against the Safety of Civil Aviation; the 1973 Apartheid Convention; the 1973 Convention on the Prevention and Punishment of Crimes against Internationally Protected Persons; the 1979 Hostage Convention; the 1984 Torture Convention; the 1988 Conventions dealing with the Suppression of Unlawful Acts against the Safety of Maritime Navigation and the Safety of Fixed Platforms on the Continental Shelf; and the 1988 Drugs Convention.

dealing with them.[413] Definition of the former category, 'serious violations of the laws and customs applicable in armed conflict', in paragraph (c) was probably not considered necessary, in view of earlier definitions in international documents, such as the Statute of the ICTY, and because the ILC had been working on that particular aspect within the framework of another project: a draft Code of Offences or Crimes against the Peace and Security of Mankind.

The ILC had been asked to prepare such a draft code immediately upon its establishment in 1947,[414] which project was carried out parallel to the international criminal court project which was initiated one year later.[415] As a matter of fact, the project on the international criminal court seemed to be a spin-off of the former, which is reflected, among other things, by the presentation of the Draft Statute within the framework of the Code on Crimes against the Peace and Security of Mankind (Draft Code) in 1994.[416] The project was suspended in 1954 by the General Assembly in view of the difficulties surrounding the definition of the concept of 'aggression',[417] but was invited to resume its work in 1981,[418] and managed to produce a final draft in 1996,[419] after laborious discussion.

This Draft Code recognised the crime of aggression (Article 16), the crime of genocide (Article 17), crimes against humanity (Article 18), crimes against United Nations and associated personnel (Article 19), and war crimes 'when committed in a systematic manner or on a large scale' (Article 20) as crimes against the peace and security of mankind. All of

[413] As a matter of fact, the ILC's commentary to Art 20(e) states that one of the two criteria for inclusion in the Draft Statute's Annex was that 'the crimes [were] themselves defined by the treaty so that an international criminal court could apply that treaty as law in relation to the crime (. . .).' A/49/10, Report of the International Law Commission to the General Assembly on the work of its forty-sixth session, 2 May to 22 Jul 1994; Yearbook of the International Law Commission, 1994; Vol II, Part Two, p 41.

[414] A/Res/177 (II), adopted on 21 Nov 1947, by 42 to 1, with 8 abstentions; formulation of the principles recognised in the Charter of the Nürnberg Tribunal and in the judgment of the Tribunal.

[415] A/Res/260A (III), adopted on 9 Dec 1948, by 56 to 0; prevention and punishment of the crime of genocide; Annex: Convention on the Prevention and Punishment of the Crime of Genocide.

[416] A/49/10, Report of the International Law Commission to the General Assembly on the work of its forty-sixth session, 2 May to 22 Jul 1994; Yearbook of the International Law Commission, 1994; Vol II, Part Two, p 1.

[417] The ILC submitted a Draft Code of Offences against the Peace and Security of Mankind in 1954, but postponed its consideration temporarily by A/Res/897 (IX), adopted on 4 Dec 1954, by 54 to 0, with 3 abstentions; Draft Code of Offences against the Peace and Security of Mankind. The project on an international criminal court was suspended by A/Res/898 (IX), adopted on 14 Dec 1954, by 34 to 0, with 7 abstentions; international criminal jurisdiction.

[418] A/Res/36/106, adopted on 10 Dec 1981, by 129 to 0, with 17 abstentions; Draft Code of Offences against the Peace and Security of Mankind.

[419] Draft Code of Crimes Against the Peace and Security of Mankind, in: A/51/10, Report of the International Law Commission to the General Assembly on the work of its forty-eighth session (6 May–26 Jul 1996); Yearbook of the International Law Commission, 1996; Vol II, Part II, United Nations, Geneva, 1998. Also through <http://www.un.org/law/ilc/>.

these crimes except aggression would fall in principle, and without prejudice to the jurisdiction of a future international court, under the national jurisdiction of the states parties.

In comparison with its Draft Statute for an International Criminal Court of 1994, the 1996 Draft Code of Crimes against the Peace and Security of Mankind is different in two respects. Firstly, the ILC chose to retain the expression 'war crimes', because it was shorter, despite the fact that the other expressions were legally more correct.[420] And secondly, the ILC gave specific definitions of the crimes that it considered as crimes against the peace and security of mankind. These definitions included a detailed and comprehensive list of war crimes, most of which are 'recognized by international humanitarian law and are listed in different instruments.'[421] In view of the wording of these definitions in the Draft Code and the wording of the definitions in Article 8 of the 1998 Rome Statute of the International Criminal Court, it is unmistakable that the drafters of the Statute and the negotiators in the Ad Hoc and Preparatory Committee preceding the Rome Conference in 1998 were strongly influenced by the ILC's Draft Code of Crimes against the Peace and Security of Mankind.

Although the definition of war crimes in Article 8 of the Rome Statute is only valid for the purpose of the Statute, the listed crimes cannot be seen separately from the primary rules from which they are derived. This is particularly true for the 'grave breaches' of paragraph (a) with its specific reference to the 1949 Geneva Conventions; but it also applies to the crimes enumerated in paragraph (b), the so-called:

> [o]ther serious violations of the laws and customs applicable in international armed conflict, within the established framework of international law.

These latter crimes are derived from a wide variety of international conventions as well as from customary rules on armed conflict,[422] although sometimes their definitions do not exactly correspond with their primary counterparts and their scope is often narrower.[423]

[420] A/51/10, Report of the International Law Commission to the General Assembly on the work of its forty-eighth session (6 May–26 Jul 1996); Yearbook of the International Law Commission, 1996; Vol II, Pt II, p 54.

[421] A/51/10, Report of the International Law Commission to the General Assembly on the work of its forty-eighth session (6 May–26 Jul 1996); Yearbook of the International Law Commission, 1996; Vol II, Pt II, p 54.

[422] Bothe, *War Crimes*, in: Cassese, Gaeta, Jones (Eds), *The Rome Statue of the International Criminal Court: A Commentary; Vol I*, p 396; WJ Fenrick, in: O Triffterer (Ed), *Commentary on the Rome Statute of the International Criminal Court; Observers' Notes, Article by Article*, Nomos Verlagsgesellschaft, Baden-Baden, 1999, p 185.

[423] Bothe, *War Crimes*, in: Cassese, Gaeta, Jones (Eds), *The Rome Statue of the International Criminal Court: A Commentary; Vol I*, p 396.

2.2.5.4 The Statute and the Protection of the Environment—Article 8(2)(b)(iv)

2.2.5.4.1 Introduction

Among this mishmash of 'serious violations of the laws and customs applicable in international armed conflict' in Article 8(2)(b), the drafters included under sub-paragraph (iv) an explicit reference to the environment. The reference is imbedded in the general customary obligation not to launch attacks that cause disproportionate collateral damage to civilians or civilian objects, which stems from one of the cornerstones of the laws of war, the principle of necessity, more specifically, the principle of proportionality. Article 8(2)(b)(iv) reads:

> Intentionally launching an attack in the knowledge that such attack will cause incidental loss of life or injury to civilians or damage to civilian objects or widespread, long-term and severe damage to the natural environment which would be clearly excessive in relation to the concrete and direct overall military advantage anticipated.[424]

2.2.5.4.2 Sources of Inspiration

2.2.5.4.2.1 The Draft Code on Crimes against the Peace and Security of Mankind

The 1994 ILC's Draft Statute for an International Criminal Court did not contain a reference to the environment, but the ILC's 1996 Draft Code on Crimes against the Peace and Security of Mankind did. Article 20(g) of the Code provides:

> Any of the following war crimes constitutes a crime against the peace and security of mankind when committed in a systematic manner or on a large scale: (. . .) In the case of armed conflict, using methods or means of warfare not justified by military necessity with the intent to cause widespread, long-term and severe damage to the natural environment and thereby gravely prejudice the health or survival of the population and such damage occurs.

Article 20(g) almost certainly influenced the adoption and formulation of Article 8(2)(b)(iv). Firstly, they both involve individual criminal

[424] The formulation—'damage to civilian objects or (. . .) damage to the natural environment'—implies that the environment should not be regarded as a civilian object or that the environment has military value. Art 52(1) AP I defines civilian objects as 'objects which are not military objectives as defined in para 2.' Para 2 defines 'military objectives' as 'objects, which by their nature, location, purpose or use make an effective contribution to military action and whose total or partial destruction, capture or neutralization, in the circumstances ruling at the time, offers a definite military advantage.' See also: Bothe, *War Crimes*, in: Cassese, Gaeta, Jones (Eds), *The Rome Statue of the International Criminal Court: A Commentary; Vol I*, p 401.

responsibility for causing damage to the environment in times of armed conflict. Secondly, they use a similar damage threshold: widespread, long-term and severe. Thirdly, they both require a form of intent (Article 20(g) Draft Code), or knowledge (Article 8(2)(b)(iv)), which is comparable to a certain extent.[425] And fourthly, they both contain a military necessity exception.[426] The Statute requires the damage to be 'clearly excessive to the military advantage anticipated', whereas the Draft Code requires that the means or methods used are not justified by military necessity.

Both provisions have also two major differences. Firstly, Article 8(2)(b)(iv) only refers to attacks in the context of 'an international armed conflict',[427] whereas Article 20(g) refers to using means and methods of warfare in 'the case of armed conflict', which may also include non-international armed conflict.[428] Secondly, the Statute refers to collateral damage to the environment, whereas the Draft Code refers to attacks launched directly against the environment. And thirdly, the Draft Code requires that the damage should gravely prejudice the survival of the civilian population, whereas the Statute does not.

2.2.5.4.2.2 Additional Protocol I

Just like Article 20(g) of the 1996 Draft Code,[429] the environmental clause in Article 8(2)(b)(iv) is clearly inspired by the environmental protection provisions in Additional Protocol I of 1977. Firstly, Article 8(2)(b)(iv) uses the same damage threshold as Article 35(3) and 55. Secondly, the Statute

[425] According to Black's Law Dictionary, for example, one of the meanings of the term 'knowingly' is 'intentionally'. Black (et al), *Black's Law Dictionary*, p 603. Compare the discussion on the formulation and adoption of Art 20(g) of the Draft Code during the 2448th meeting on 26 Jun 1996: A/CN.4/SER.A/1996, Yearbook of the International Law Commission, 1996; Vol I; Summary records of the meetings of the forty-eighth session 6 May–26 Jul 1996, United Nations, Geneva, 1998, pp 108–16.

[426] Although they eventually consented to their retention, some members of the Drafting Committee would have preferred their deletion. Compare also the comments made during the subsequent ILC deliberations by Crawford, Tomuschat, Fomba, Güney, Rosenstock, Idris, Al-Baharna and Thiam. Summary Records of the 2448th meeting; Wednesday, 26 Jun 1996; Draft Code of Crimes against the Peace and Security of Mankind, in: A/CN.4/SER.A/1996, Yearbook of the International Law Commission, 1996; Vol I; Summary records of the meetings of the forty-eighth session 6 May–26 Jul 1996, United Nations, Geneva, 1998, pp 109–15.

[427] The *chapeau* of Art 8(2)(b)(iv) provides: 'Other serious violations of the laws and customs applicable in international armed conflict, within the established framework of international law, namely any of the following acts'.

[428] Compare also the Commentary of the ILC to Art 20(g): A/51/10, Report of the International Law Commission to the General Assembly on the work of its forty-eighth session (6 May–26 Jul 1996); Yearbook of the International Law Commission, 1996; Vol II, Part II, p 56.

[429] Summary Records of the 2448th meeting; Wednesday, 26 Jun 1996; Draft Code of Crimes against the Peace and Security of Mankind, in: A/CN.4/SER.A/1996, Yearbook of the International Law Commission, 1996; Vol I; Summary records of the meetings of the forty-eighth session 6 May–26 Jul 1996, United Nations, Geneva, 1998, p 109.

requires that the individuals responsible for launching an attack knew that the attack would cause damage to the environment, which resembles the requirement in Additional Protocol I that the damage is either intended or may be expected. And thirdly, the positioning of the environmental clause in Article 8(2)(b)(iv) in the context of the protection of the civilian population also seems to be a combination of the object and purpose of both Article 35(3) and 55.[430] Not only does it set limits to means and methods of warfare, but it also relates environmental protection to the protection of the civilian population.

There are also two significant differences between the Statute and Additional Protocol I, however, that seem to go further than the minor differences in formulation of the other war crimes of Article 8(2)(b). In the first place, the Statute provides for an escape clause based on military necessity, as was mentioned just earlier, whereas the prohibitions of Article 35(3) and Article 55 are absolute. In the second place, unlike the rest of Article 8(2)(b)(iv), using means and methods of warfare that cause damage to the environment is not recognised as a 'grave breach' in Article 85 of Additional Protocol I entailing individual criminal responsibility.[431] Apparently causing damage to the environment was not considered serious enough to be recognised as such in 1977,[432] only giving rise to state responsibility at the international level to remedy violations of Articles 35(3) and 55.[433]

2.2.5.4.3 Primary Rule

In view of these differences, it is difficult to establish with certainty which primary rule, ie which general prohibition, underlies the individual

[430] See also: K Dörmann, *Elements of War Crimes under the Rome Statute of the International Criminal Court; Sources and Commentary*, International Committee of the Red Cross, Cambridge University Press, Cambridge, 2004, p 166.

[431] Australia's original proposal for Art 55 of 19 Mar 1974 did include a para that provided that breach of the Article would constitute a grave breach of the Protocol. CDDH/III/60, 19 Mar 1974 (III, 220), proposed new Art [55] by Australia, in: Levie, *Protection of War Victims: Protocol 1 to the 1949 Geneva Conventions; Vol 3*, p 259.

[432] Baker fails to convince when she argues that it is possible that Art 55 has implicitly been included in Art 85 when she writes that the civilian objects of Art 57(2)(a)(iii) include the natural environment of Art 55. Baker, *Legal Protections for the Environment in Times of Armed Conflict*, p 379. Also according to Rogers, 'an indiscriminate attack launched in the knowledge that it would cause excessive damage to the environment would be a grave breach.' Rogers, *Law on the Battlefield*, p 168.

[433] Since the environment embodies a common interest, it may very well be that complaint in case of violation is open to all States Parties. Please note, however, that this does not exclude the possibility of individual criminal responsibility under customary international law, which will be discussed in a subsequent section. J-M Henckaerts, *Towards Better Protection for the Environment in Armed Conflict: Recent Developments in International Humanitarian Law*, Review of European Community and international environmental law, Vol 9, 2000, p 16.

criminal responsibility for environmental damage under the Rome Statute.[434] There seem to be two options. Either the primary rule entailing state responsibility is wider and more general than the secondary norm entailing individual criminal responsibility, or the secondary norm is a direct reflection of the primary norm, and there is no difference in scope.

The former is not uncommon under the law of armed conflict and would most probably lead to the conclusion that the prohibitions of Articles 35(3) and 55 of Additional Protocol I underlie Article 8(2)(b)(iv). The latter cannot be excluded and would entail that the primary norm that forms the foundation for the crime of Article 8(2)(b)(iv) is a relatively new and yet unknown rule of customary international law. After all, the *chapeau* of Article 8(2)(b) states that the war crimes listed are 'within the established framework of international law',[435] and according to the United Kingdom, the phrase 'established framework of international law' includes 'customary international law as established by State practice and opinio iuris.'[436] And in view of the differences between Additional Protocol I and Article 8(2)(b)(iv) it is arguable that the customary equivalent of the provision follows from a prohibition under current customary international law for states in general to launch an attack or to use means and methods of warfare in times of international armed conflict that cause long-term, widespread and severe damage to the environment that is excessive in comparison to the military advantages anticipated. In other words, a customary rule of international law protecting the environment during international armed conflict, based on one of the cornerstones of the *ius in bello*, namely the principle of necessity, or more precisely the principle of proportionality, as well as on the principle of environmental protection. As has been explained above, it is arguable that this principle has also shaped the laws of war since the 1970s, in addition to the principles of necessity and humanity. The possible existence of this rule of customary law will be discussed in further detail in the following section (section 2.3) which deals with the direct protection of the environment during international armed conflict under customary international law.

[434] For the relationship between individual and collective or state responsibility, see: A Nollkaemper, *De dialectiek tussen individuele en collectieve aansprakelijkheid in het volkenrecht*, Inaugural lecture, Vossiuspers AUP, Amsterdam, 2000.

[435] According to Fenrick, it is presumed that the expression 'within the established framework of international law' is 'merely intended to confirm that the listed acts are serious violations bearing in mind the existing framework of international law.' Fenrick, in: Triffterer (Ed), *Commentary on the Rome Statute of the International Criminal Court; Observers' Notes, Article by Article*, p 186. See also: Dörmann, *Elements of War Crimes under the Rome Statute of the International Criminal Court; Sources and Commentary*, p 167. The rule of *nullum crimen sine lege* of Art 22 does not refer to the existence of primary rules for the possibility to hold someone criminally liable under the Statute. Art 22(1) says: 'A person shall not be criminally responsible under this Statute unless the conduct in question constitutes, at the time it takes place, a crime within the jurisdiction of the Court.'

[436] Declaration upon ratification by the United Kingdom of Great Britain and Northern Ireland of the Statute of the International Criminal Court, through <http://untreaty.un.org/>.

2.2.5.4.4 Interpretation

This leaves us the interpretation of the provision, in particular the formulation of the damage threshold that is literally taken from Article 35(3) and 55 of Additional Protocol I: 'widespread, long-term and severe'. Because of this link with Additional Protocol I, it is on the one hand possible that the terms will be interpreted in conformity with the similar terms in Additional Protocol I, as discussed earlier. This means that, if one falls back on the preparatory works, the threshold will be very high. With respect to 'long-term', the drafters of Additional Protocol I were rather thinking in terms of decades; with respect to 'severity', one thought that mere battlefield damage would not suffice.[437]

On the other hand, the Court is free to adopt a different interpretation, more in conformity with present standards and values. After all, the Statute is an independent international treaty and may be interpreted likewise, in view of its own object and purpose. This possibility is supported by a comment from Tomuschat within the framework of a discussion in the ILC on Article 20(g) of the Draft Code against the Peace and Security of Mankind in 1996.[438] As was mentioned above, Article 20(g) recognised the use of means and methods of warfare employed with the intent to cause long-term, widespread and severe damage to the environment, with grave consequences for the environment, and not justified by military necessity, as a war crime and as a crime against the peace and security of mankind when committed in a systematic manner or on a large scale. Tomuschat points out that the Commission had not defined the meaning of the term 'long-term', and that it had not referred to the interpretation given by some delegates to the same term in Additional Protocol I during the 1974–1977 Diplomatic Conference.[439] Therefore:

> [s]ince the Commission had not discussed the matter, it could not be said to have endorsed the interpretation given by certain representatives at the Conference.[440]

[437] Compare also Fenrick, in: Triffterer (Ed), *Commentary on the Rome Statute of the International Criminal Court; Observers' Notes, Article by Article*, p 197.

[438] It should be recalled that the ILC's Draft Statute of the International Criminal Court did not contain an environmental clause.

[439] The ILC also kept silent when it commented on environmental provisions in an earlier draft of the Code of Crimes against the Peace and Security of Mankind of 1991. A/46/10, Report of the International Law Commission to the General Assembly on the work of its forty-third session, 29 Apr to 19 Jul 1991; Yearbook of the International Law Commission, 1994; Vol II, Pt Two, United Nations, Geneva, 1994, pp 106–7. Also Dörmann, *Elements of War Crimes under the Rome Statute of the International Criminal Court; Sources and Commentary*, p 175.

[440] Tomuschat at the 2448th meeting of the ILC on 26 Jun 1996, in: A/CN.4/SER.A/1996, Yearbook of the International Law Commission, 1996; Vol I; Summary records of the meetings of the forty-eighth session 6 May–26 Jul 1996, p 115. At the same meeting, Rao remarked that 'it was unfortunate that the proposed provisions were not more precisely targeted.' A/CN.4/SER.A/1996, Yearbook of the International Law Commission, 1996; Vol I; Summary records of the meetings of the forty-eighth session 6 May–26 Jul 1996, p 112.

If the terms are interpreted similarly as in the case of Articles 35(3) and 55 of Additional Protocol I, then the Statute will provide for less deterrence than Additional Protocol I. Even if the damage criteria were met, then still it would be possible that the responsible individuals would not be held accountable, because the military actions were militarily justified and the damage was not 'clearly excessive in relation to the concrete and direct overall military advantage anticipated.' It is difficult to imagine such an attack, but it is definitely, at least theoretically, possible.

2.3 Customary International Law

2.3.1 Introduction

In addition to the protection of the environment during international armed conflict provided by the explicit references in the conventions discussed above, the environment may also be protected by unwritten rules of customary international law. Customary international law is one of the primary sources of international law, as recognised by Article 38 of the Statute of the International Court of Justice, and is not only characterised by the fact that it is unwritten, but also, according to Cassese, that 'it is not a deliberate lawmaking process'; and, that in principle, it is binding upon all members of the international community of states.[441] The first two characteristics make it difficult to grasp, but the third characteristic makes it an important and, for the purposes of this research, a very interesting source of law. Because of its importance and inherent vagueness, it is useful to spend a few words on its history, definition, meaning and relationship to treaty law, before discussing the environmental protection it may provide.

Together with treaties, customary international law has been a principal source of international legal rules since the development of an international community of sovereign nation states.[442] As a matter of fact, for a long time customary law was the most common source of international law, comparable to the importance of customary law in European states prior to the national codifications of the 19th century. In politically more 'primitive' societies without strong centralistic legislative powers, many rules develop from commonly accepted practice and remain unwritten.[443] Nowadays, at the international level, customary law has been overshadowed by written law or international treaties; largely as a result of

[441] A Cassese, *International Law*, Oxford University Press, Oxford, 2001, pp 156–7.

[442] Cassese, *International Law*, p 153.

[443] According to Thirlway, '[i]t is probably a universal characteristic of human societies that many practices which have grown up to regulate day-to-day relationships imperceptibly acquire a status of inexorability: the way things have always been done becomes the way things *must* be done.' H Thirlway, *The Sources of International Law*, in: MD Evans, *International Law*, Oxford University Press, Oxford, 2003.

expanding international relations and interdependency, and a corresponding need for legal clarity. But, it has never lost its importance.

According to Article 38(1)(b) of the Statute, international custom or customary international law is established by 'a general practice accepted as law'. This means that a rule of customary international law needs to fulfill two conditions: an objective or material condition and a subjective or psychological condition. Firstly, the rule must be sustained by a general practice, also known as *usus* or *consuetudo*; and secondly, this practice must be accepted as law, or rather as legal obligatory, which is usually referred to as *opinio iuris*.

The former requirement is implied by the term 'custom' in customary law, and has always been self-evident. The latter requirement, however, was not introduced until the late 19th century, under the influence of the study of private international law in Germany,[444] and was intended to distinguish practice susceptible of legal sanction from ordinary every day usage.[445] It is not exactly clear when it was used for the first time in the context of public international law, however. According to Shaw, the phrase was first formulated by a French author François Gény in 1899,[446] but according to Guggenheim, it was Alphonse Rivier who first used a definition for customary international law that corresponded with the civil origin of the rule in 1896.[447] He wrote:

> La coutume ou l'usage des nations est la manifestation de la conscience juridique internationale qui s'opère par des faits répétés continuellement avec la conscience de leur nécessité.[448]

The phrase *opinio iuris* is a shortened version of *opinio iuris sive necessitatis*, which means recognition as law or as necessity.[449] In the 19th

[444] The German historical school led by Von Savigny regarded the *Volksgeist* as the actual source of law and believed that each rule of law was only a reflection of that *Volksgeist* L Strikwerda, *Inleiding tot het Nederlandse internationaal privaatrecht*, Wolters-Noordhoff, Groningen, 1997, p 38.

[445] P Guggenheim, *L'origine de la notion de l'«opinio juris sive necessitatis» comme deuxième élément de la coutume dans l'histoire du droit des gens*, in: H Accioly (et al), *Hommage d'une Génération de Juristes au Président Basdevant*, Éditions A Pedone, Paris, 1960, pp 258–61. For the difference in meaning between 'custom' and 'usage', see I Brownlie, *Principles of Public International Law*, p 6.

[446] Shaw, *International Law*, p 71.

[447] Guggenheim, *L'origine de la notion de l'«opinio juris sive necessitatis» comme deuxième élément de la coutume dans l'histoire du droit des gens*, in: Accioly (et al), *Hommage d'une Génération de Juristes au Président Basdevant*, p 261.

[448] A Rivier, *Principes du droit des gens*, Arthur Rousseau, Paris, 1896, p 35, quoted in : Guggenheim, *L'origine de la notion de l'«opinio juris sive necessitatis» comme deuxième élément de la coutume dans l'histoire du droit des gens*, in: Accioly (et al), *Hommage d'une Génération de Juristes au Président Basdevant*, p 261.

[449] Brownlie refers to *opinio iuris et necessitatis*. Brownlie, *Principles of Public International Law*, p 8. Sometimes one comes across the phrase *opinio iuris sine necessitatis* which means recognition as law *without* necessity, which is confusing because it means almost the opposite. It is likely that these are spelling mistakes. See, eg, TMC Asser Instituut, *Elementair Internationaal Recht 2005*, TMC Asser Press, Den Haag, p 299.

century, when the subjective element was introduced in the framework of customary law, both *opinio iuris* and *opinio necessitatis* were apparently regarded as interchangeable and provided proof that a practice was obligatory and therefore subject to legal consequences. This is confirmed by Rivier's reference to a '*conscience de (. . .) nécessité*' or *opinio necessitatis* in his definition as a constitutive element of customary international law. Nowadays, the Statute of the International Court of Justice only requires that a certain practice is 'accepted as law',[450] or *opinio iuris*.

The definition of the Statute therefore implies that the reference to necessity in the extended version has lost most of its relevance in the context of customary international law, although Cassese has tried to give the concept a new meaning. In his handbook on international law, he states that a practice with a corresponding *opinio necessitatis* is a practice that is 'imposed by social or economic or political needs'. Only when this practice:

> does not encounter strong and consistent opposition from other States, but is increasingly accepted, or acquiesced in, a customary rule gradually crystallizes. At this later stage it may be held that the practice is dictated by international law (*opinio iuris*).[451]

In other words, according to Cassese, *opinio necessitatis* is only a first step in the process of development of a rule of customary international law and may in time evolve into *opinio iuris*. Practice based on *opinio necessitatis*, therefore, only reflects so-called nascent rules of customary international law that do not have the same legal consequences as full-fledged rules of customary international law. Although Cassese's interpretation is creative, and attractive for providing a legal foundation for nascent customary rules, it does not seem to reflect a common understanding of the concept, nor does it seem to be consistent with the original and historical meaning of the phrase *opinio necessitatis*. As was mentioned above, the phrase *opinio necessitatis*, was used interchangeably with the phrase *opinio iuris*, and did not distinguish between the two.

In any case, it is generally agreed that both elements are important and required for the development of a rule of customary international law, but there is disagreement as to the relative importance of either element in the process of its creation. Worth mentioning in this context is the final report

[450] It was included in 1920 in the definition of customary international law by the Consultative Committee of Jurists for the Statute of the Permanent Court of International Justice which was literally copied into the present Statute of the International Court of Justice and it was applied for the first time by the PCIJ in the Lotus Case in 1927. Guggenheim, *L'origine de la notion de l'«opinio juris sive necessitatis» comme deuxième élément de la coutume dans l'histoire du droit des gens*, in: Accioly (et al), *Hommage d'une Génération de Juristes au Président Basdevant*, pp 261–2. The Case of the SS 'Lotus', 7 Sep 1927, Publications of the Permanent Court of International Justice, Collection of Judgments, Series A—No 10, AW Sijthoff's Publishing Company, 1927.

[451] Cassese, *International Law*, p 157.

of a Sub-Committee of the International Law Association (ILA)[452] on customary international law, which was adopted by Resolution 16/2000[453] at the 69th ILA's world conference of 2000.[454] Although both practice and *opinio iuris* are explicitly required by Article 38(1)(b) Statute and generally recognised in international jurisprudence and literature, the Committee on the Principles Applicable to the Formation of General Customary International Law chose not to expressly refer to *opinio iuris* in its definition of customary international law. In its commentary, the Committee recognised that *opinio iuris* was traditionally included in definitions of customary law, but after thorough research, it believed that it was 'not usually necessary' to prove its existence 'before a customary rule can be said to have come into being.'[455] The Committee admits that this statement:

> is contrary to a substantial body of doctrine and more importantly, *appears* to be contrary to a number of *dicta* of the International Court,[456]

but, according to the Committee, these cases are taken out of context. In some circumstances, the psychological element was used to disqualify a certain practice as relevant, such as acts of comity; in other circumstances, a lack of *opinio iuris* was used to deny that a certain practice had binding force.[457] Not often has *opinio iuris* been used to prove the existence of a rule of customary international law. Instead, according to the Committee, a general practice implies consent, belief or recognition, and therefore proof of its existence is no longer necessary:[458]

[452] The ILA is a non-governmental organisation, established in 1873 by international lawyers for the study, clarification and development of both public and private international law. Currently, the ILA has around 50 branches all over the world. See: <http://www.ila-hq.org/>.

[453] ILA Resolution No 16/2000, in: The International Law Association, *Report of the Sixty-Ninth Conference, London, 2000*, ILA, London, 2000, p 39.

[454] Final Report of the International Committee on the Formation of Customary (General) International Law; Principles Applicable to the Formation of General Customary International Law, in: The International Law Association, *Report of the Sixty-Ninth Conference, London, 2000*, pp 712–90. The Report is also available through <http://www.ila-hq.org/>.

[455] Final Report of the International Committee on the Formation of Customary (General) International Law; Principles Applicable to the Formation of General Customary International Law, in: The International Law Association, *Report of the Sixty-Ninth Conference, London, 2000*, pp 720–1.

[456] Final Report of the International Committee on the Formation of Customary (General) International Law; Principles Applicable to the Formation of General Customary International Law, in: The International Law Association, *Report of the Sixty-Ninth Conference, London, 2000*, p 744.

[457] Final Report of the International Committee on the Formation of Customary (General) International Law; Principles Applicable to the Formation of General Customary International Law, in: The International Law Association, *Report of the Sixty-Ninth Conference, London, 2000*, p 745–9.

[458] According to the Committee, it seems clear that 'if there is a good deal of State practice, the need (if such there be) also to demonstrate the presence of the subjective element is likely to be dispensed with.' Final Report of the International Committee on the Formation of Customary (General) International Law; Principles Applicable to the Formation of General Customary International Law, in: The International Law Association, *Report of the Sixty-Ninth Conference, London, 2000*, p 751. Compare in this context also Shaw's references to the

It may often be present, or it may be possible to infer it; but it is not a requirement that its existence be demonstrated.[459]

In other words, the Committee does not deny the relevance of *opinio iuris* for customary international law and admits that there are circumstances in which more proof of an existing *opinio iuris* is required than of practice,[460] but it merely puts its practical value as far as evidence is concerned in perspective.[461] Although the Committee's research has been extensive, it seems that that its conclusion, drafted by Prof Mendelson, is also partly the result of fundamental differences of opinion with respect to legal theory, in particular with respect to the creation of law. It states that the continental theories of the 19th century from which the requirement of *opinio iuris* stemmed were of 'dubious validity even in the context of domestic, let alone international, law'; that they 'have long since been rejected'; but that their 'language lingers on to muddy the waters of customary international law.'[462]

The Committee's Working Definition in Principle 1, therefore, focuses primarily on practice:

(i) (. . .) a rule of customary international law is one which is created and sustained by the constant and uniform practice of States and other subjects of international law in or impinging upon their international legal relations, in circumstances which give rise to a legitimate expectation of similar conduct in the future; (ii) If a sufficiently extensive and representative number of States participate in such a practice in a consistent manner, the resulting rule is one of

Dissenting Opinion of Judge Tanaka in the North Sea Continental Shelf Cases and comments from Lauterpacht. Shaw, *International Law*, p 83. Also Brownlie, *Principles of Public International Law*, pp 8–10. Malanczuk even writes that 'the modern tendency is not to look for direct evidence of a state's psychological convictions, but to infer *opinio iuris* indirectly from the actual behaviour of states.' Malanczuk, *Akehurst's Modern Introduction to International Law*, p 44.

[459] Final Report of the International Committee on the Formation of Customary (General) International Law; Principles Applicable to the Formation of General Customary International Law, in: The International Law Association, *Report of the Sixty-Ninth Conference, London, 2000*, p 742, and generally pp 740–9.

[460] Final Report of the International Committee on the Formation of Customary (General) International Law; Principles Applicable to the Formation of General Customary International Law, in: The International Law Association, *Report of the Sixty-Ninth Conference, London, 2000*, principle 19, pp 751–3.

[461] Also according to Brownlie, it seems to depend on the nature of the issues and the discretion of the Court how much proof is required with respect to *opinio iuris*. Brownlie, *Principles of Public International Law*, pp 8–10. Similarly Dixon, who writes that international law might require different levels of proof of *opinio iuris* for different substantive rules of customary law, in the same way as national criminal law does not require the same intention for every criminal offense. M Dixon, *Textbook on International Law*, Blackstone Press, London, 2000, p 33.

[462] Final Report of the International Committee on the Formation of Customary (General) International Law; Principles Applicable to the Formation of General Customary International Law, in: The International Law Association, *Report of the Sixty-Ninth Conference, London, 2000*, p 743.

> 'general customary international law'. (. . .) such a rule is binding on all States; (iii) Where a rule of general customary international law exists, for any particular State to be bound by that rule it is not necessary to prove either that State's consent to it or its belief in the rule's obligatory or (as the case may be) permissive character.[463]

With respect to the interpretation of both elements, there is relative agreement in literature and jurisprudence that practice generally requires a material fact, ie an act or an abstention, that it is general, relatively uniform, consistent, lengthy and that includes the most relevant states.[464] *Opinio iuris* generally requires that a state acts in a certain way in the conviction that it is in accordance with or even required by international law, ie the state believes that with respect to its behavior, it has a right to act or a duty to abstain.

The essential problem, however, with both elements is one of proof. It is not only difficult to establish how much proof of either element is required, as was noted by the ILA Committee on customary international law, but it is perhaps even more difficult to establish where to exactly find evidence for practice and *opinio iuris*. As far as practice is concerned, one may find primary evidence both in the actual behavior or 'physical acts' of states and by so-called 'verbal acts'.[465] Physical acts include, for example, exploitation of the continental shelf, use of military force, or, with respect to the laws of war, 'battlefield behaviour, the use of certain weapons and the treatment provided to different categories of persons.'[466] Verbal acts include:

> military manuals,[467] national legislation, national case-law, instructions to armed and security forces, military communiqués during war, diplomatic

[463] Final Report of the International Committee on the Formation of Customary (General) International Law; Principles Applicable to the Formation of General Customary International Law, in: The International Law Association, *Report of the Sixty-Ninth Conference, London, 2000*, p 719.

[464] Compare the ILA's principles 3–15, Final Report of the International Committee on the Formation of Customary (General) International Law; Principles Applicable to the Formation of General Customary International Law, in: The International Law Association, *Report of the Sixty-Ninth Conference, London, 2000*, pp 724–40.

[465] The use of both physical and verbal acts as evidence of state practice is based on state practice and is followed by international judicial bodies and organisations, including the International Court of Justice, ICTY, the International Law Commission and the ILA. J-M Henckaerts, L Doswald-Beck (Eds), *Customary International Humanitarian Law; Vol I: Rules*, International Committee of the Red Cross, Cambridge University Press, Cambridge, 2005, pp xxxii–xxxiii.

[466] Henckaerts, Doswald-Beck (Eds), *Customary International Humanitarian Law; Vol I: Rules*, p xxxii. Similarly J-M Henckaerts, *Study on customary international law: A contribution to the understanding and respect for the rule of law in armed conflict*, International Review of the Red Cross, Vol 87, 2005, p 179.

[467] On the importance of military manuals for the development of the customary law of armed conflict, see: HG Post, *Some Curiosities in the Sources of the Law of Armed Conflict Conceived in a General International Legal Perspective*, Netherlands Yearbook of International Law, Vol 25, 1994, pp 97–101; HHG Post, *The Role of State Practice in the Formation of Customary*

> protests, opinions of official legal advisers, comments by governments on draft treaties, executive decisions and regulations, pleadings before international tribunals, statements in international organizations and at international conferences and government positions taken with respect to resolutions of international organizations.[468]

In addition, the practice of international organisations may 'contribute to the formation of customary international law', since they have an international legal personality and 'participate in international relations in their own capacity, independently of their member States.'[469] This includes the practice of the ICRC in the form of appeals and memoranda[470] as well as the 'negotiation and adoption of resolutions by international organizations or conferences, together with the explanations

International Humanitarian Law, in: IF Dekker, HHG. Post (Eds), *On the Foundations and Sources of International Law,* TMC Asser Press, The Hague, 2003, pp 142–5. Post compares the value of military manuals for the development of customary international humanitarian law with the 'more 'ordinary' national regulations or instructions as they exist for several other areas of activity, like the use of the seas and oceans, of Antarctica, or of air and space. Post, *The Role of State Practice in the Formation of Customary International Humanitarian Law,* in: Dekker, Post (Eds), *On the Foundations and Sources of International Law,* p 141. Also on the value of military manuals in the development of customary international law of armed conflict, Schwarzenberger, *International Law; As Applied by International Courts and Tribunals; Vol II; The Law of Armed Conflict,* pp 15–16.

[468] Henckaerts, Doswald-Beck (Eds), *Customary International Humanitarian Law; Vol I: Rules,* p xxxii; Henckaerts, *Study on customary international law: A contribution to the understanding and respect for the rule of law in armed conflict,* p 179. For similar and other examples, see: Brownlie, *Principles of Public International Law,* p 6; Dixon, *Textbook on International Law,* p 29; Malanczuk, *Akehurst's Modern Introduction to International Law,* pp 39–41; Shaw, *International Law,* pp 77–80 and, in detail, the Final Report of the International Committee on the Formation of Customary (General) International Law; Principles Applicable to the Formation of General Customary International Law, in: The International Law Association, *Report of the Sixty-Ninth Conference, London, 2000,* principles 3–11, pp 724–30. Special Rapporteur Hudson refers in his report to the ILC in 1950 to the texts of international instruments, decisions of international and national courts, national legislation, diplomatic correspondence, opinions of national legal advisers, and practice of international organisations. A/CN.4/16, Art 24 of the Statute of the International Law Commission; Ways and means for making the evidence of customary international law more readily available; Working Paper by Manley O. Hudson, Special Rapporteur, 3 Mar 1950; Yearbook of the International Law Commission, 1950; Vol. II, United Nations, New York, 1957. The Report of was largely adopted by the ILC by A/CN.4/34; Report of the International Law Commission on its Second Session, 5 Jun to 29 Jul 1950. Both documents also through: <http://www.un.org/law/ilc/>.

[469] Henckaerts, Doswald-Beck (Eds), *Customary International Humanitarian Law; Vol I: Rules,* p xxxv. Similarly Brownlie, *Principles of Public International Law,* p 6 ('the practice of international organs'; Shaw, *International Law,* p 78 ('International organizations in fact may be instrumental in the creation of customary law.'); A/CN.4/16, Art 24 of the Statute of the International Law Commission; Ways and means for making the evidence of customary international law more readily available; Working Paper by Manley O Hudson, Special Rapporteur, 3 Mar 1950.

[470] ICRC practice has been used by the ICTY as an important factor. Henckaerts, Doswald-Beck (Eds), *Customary International Humanitarian Law; Vol I: Rules,* p xxxv.

of vote'.[471] Since decisions of international and national judicial institutions[472] are an independent albeit supplementary source of public international law (Article 38(1)(d) Statute ICJ), it might not be proper to use them as evidence of state practice or customary international law in general, although their findings may nevertheless be influential.[473]

As far as *opinio iuris* is concerned, this is even more difficult to determine since it concerns proof of a specific state of mind which can only be inferred from certain behavior,[474] and from the circumstances of each case, or presumed by reference to the motivation of a state's behavior.[475] At any rate, practice must be inspired by a sense of obligation or legality and it is not sufficient if they are merely carried out for political reasons or moral reasons.[476]

Since it is difficult to distinguish between state practice and *opinio iuris*, and '[m]ore often than not, one and the same act reflects [both] practice

[471] Henckaerts, Doswald-Beck (Eds), *Customary International Humanitarian Law; Vol I: Rules*, p xxxv; Henckaerts, *Study on customary international law: A contribution to the understanding and respect for the rule of law in armed conflict*, p 179. Similarly Brownlie, *Principles of Public International Law*, p 6. For other aspects dealing with the assessment of state practice, see Henckaerts, Doswald-Beck (Eds), *Customary International Humanitarian Law; Vol I: Rules*, pp xxxii–xxxix. See also the use of Resolutions of the General Assembly and the Organization of American States as evidence of customary international law: Military and Paramilitary Activities in and against Nicaragua (Nicaragua v United States of America), Merits, Judgment, 27 Jun 1986, ICJ Reports 1986, p 14, paras 188–205, pp 99–108. According to the Arbitrator in the 1977 Texaco Case, the legal value of General Assembly Resolutions depends on the circumstances of their adoption, in particular the voting conditions, and the contents of the provisions involved. Texaco Overseas Petroleum Company and California Asiatic Oil Company v The Government of the Libyan Arab Republic; Dupuy, Sole Arbitrator; Arbitral Award on the Merits, 19 Jan 1977, in: H Lauterpacht (Ed), *International Law* Reports, Vol 53, Grotius Publications Limited, Groningen, Cambridge, 1979, pp 483–95.

[472] The ICRC Study regards decisions of national courts as evidence of state practice, since they are state organs. Henckaerts, Doswald-Beck (Eds), *Customary International Humanitarian Law; Vol I: Rules*, pp xxxii–xxxiv; Henckaerts, *Study on customary international law: A contribution to the understanding and respect for the rule of law in armed conflict*, p 179.

[473] Henckaerts, Doswald-Beck (Eds), *Customary International Humanitarian Law; Vol I: Rules*, pp xxxiv–xxxv; Henckaerts, *Study on customary international law: A contribution to the understanding and respect for the rule of law in armed conflict*, p 179. Compare, however, Brownlie, *Principles of Public International Law*, p 6; Shaw, *International Law*, p 78; A/CN.4/16, Art 24 of the Statute of the International Law Commission; Ways and means for making the evidence of customary international law more readily available; Working Paper by Manley O Hudson, Special Rapporteur, 3 Mar 1950.

[474] See eg Military and Paramilitary Activities in and against Nicaragua (Nicaragua v United States of America), Merits, Judgment, 27 Jun 1986, ICJ Reports 1986, p 14, para 188, pp 99–100. According to the International Court of Justice, an *opinio iuris* may 'with all due caution, be deduced from, *inter alia*, the attitude of the Parties and the attitude of States towards certain General Assembly resolutions.'

[475] Compare: Malanczuk, *Akehurst's Modern Introduction to International Law*, p 44.

[476] Shaw, *International Law*, pp 80–4. More specifically on *opinio iuris*: Final Report of the International Committee on the Formation of Customary (General) International Law; Principles Applicable to the Formation of General Customary International Law, in: The International Law Association, *Report of the Sixty-Ninth Conference, London, 2000*, principles 16–19, pp 743–53.

and legal conviction', it is not always necessary to strictly separate both elements.[477] Instead, one could generally refer to evidence of 'custom' in order to establish the existence of a rule of customary international law.[478]

Because the sources of international law are not mutually exclusive, it is possible that certain substantive rules of international law stem from more than one source. This overlap is most likely in the case of customary and treaty law and may happen in two ways.[479] Either a rule of customary international law is codified into a treaty provision,[480] or a rule laid down

[477] Henckaerts, Doswald-Beck (Eds), *Customary International Humanitarian Law; Vol I: Rules*, p xl; Henckaerts, *Study on customary international law: A contribution to the understanding and respect for the rule of law in armed conflict*, p 182. 'When there is sufficiently dense practice, an *opinio juris* is generally contained within that practice and, as a result, it is not usually necessary to demonstrate separately the existence of an *opinio juris. Opinio juris* plays an important role, however, in certain situations where the practice is ambiguous, in order to decide whether or not that practice counts towards the formation of custom.' Henckaerts, Doswald-Beck (Eds), *Customary International Humanitarian Law; Vol I: Rules*, p xl; Henckaerts, *Study on customary international law: A contribution to the understanding and respect for the rule of law in armed conflict*, p 182.

[478] Compare, eg, Art 24 of the Statute of the International Law Commission (A/Res/174 (II), adopted on 21 Nov 1947, by 44 to 0, with 6 abstentions; establishment of an international law commission), which provides: 'The Commission shall consider ways and means for making the evidence of customary international law more readily available, such as the collection and publication of documents concerning State practice and of the decisions of national and international courts on questions of international law, and shall make a report to the General Assembly on this matter.' Subsequently, Special Rapporteur Manley O Hudson similarly refers only to evidence of customary international law in his Working Paper on Art 24 of the Statute of 3 Mar 1950. A/CN.4/16, Art 24 of the Statute of the International Law Commission; Ways and means for making the evidence of customary international law more readily available; Working Paper by Manley O Hudson, Special Rapporteur, 3 Mar 1950; A/CN.4/34; Report of the International Law Commission on its Second Session, 5 Jun to 29 Jul 1950. Also through: <http://www.un.org/law/ilc/>. During the discussion of Hudson's Working Paper, both Mr Sandström and Mr Kerno were of the opinion that the Commission did not have to define custom and to go into detail with respect to distinction between practice and *opinio iuris*. All it had to do is 'establish a general conception of what constituted a rule of customary law.' A/CN.4/SR.40, Summary record of the 40th meeting; Ways and means for making the evidence of customary international law more readily available, Yearbook of the International Law Commission, 1950; Vol I, paras 34 and 35, p 6. Also through: <http://www.un.org/law/ilc/>. Brownlie and Malanczuk also refer to a number of material sources as evidence of international custom in general, thereby circumventing the problem of distinguishing between elements of proof for either practice or *opinio iuris*. Brownlie, *Principles of Public International Law*, p 6; Malanczuk, *Akehurst's Modern Introduction to International Law*, pp 39–41.

[479] Thirlway and the ILA Committee also mention a third way by referring to the International Court of Justice in the North Sea Continental Shelf Cases (North Sea Continental Shelf, Judgment, ICJ Reports 1969, p 3). In these landmark Cases with respect to customary international law, the Court states that treaties sometimes reflect an emerging or nascent norm of customary law and therefore may have a crystallising effect. Principle 26 in the Final Report of the International Committee on the Formation of Customary (General) International Law; Principles Applicable to the Formation of General Customary International Law, in: The International Law Association, *Report of the Sixty-Ninth Conference, London, 2000*, pp 760–1; Thirlway, *The Sources of International Law*, in: Evans, *International Law*, p 135.

[480] Compare principles 20–3 in the Final Report of the International Committee on the Formation of Customary (General) International Law; Principles Applicable to the Formation of General Customary International Law, in: The International Law Association, *Report of the Sixty-Ninth Conference, London, 2000*, pp 754–6.

in a specific treaty develops into a rule of customary international law.[481] Codification is the older of the two[482] and has been recognised, for example, with respect to provisions of the Vienna Convention on the Law of Treaties and the Vienna Convention on Diplomatic Relations. The development of treaty provisions into customary law, 'constitutes (. . .) one of the recognized methods by which new rules of customary international law may be formed',[483] but is usually only recognised in cases of so-called 'law-making' treaties. Treaty provisions that are recognised as customary international law need to be of 'fundamentally norm-creating character'; must enjoy general and widespread practice of non-party states, including those which are specially affected;[484] and must be accompanied by a strong sense of *opinio iuris*.[485] This has happened with respect to certain provisions from the 1899 and 1907 Hague Regulations,[486] and a number of other conventions on the laws of war,[487] as well as with respect to provisions from the Charter of the United Nations, sometimes without or at least with limited examination of subsequent state practice.[488] Once the customary status of a treaty provision has been established by an authoritative international tribunal, 'its customary law status tends to be assumed in subsequent discussion.'[489]

Because sources are not mutually exclusive, as was mentioned above, and because there is no hierarchy among them, each norm continues to

[481] Compare principles 24–25 in the Final Report of the International Committee on the Formation of Customary (General) International Law; Principles Applicable to the Formation of General Customary International Law, in: The International Law Association, *Report of the Sixty-Ninth Conference, London, 2000*, pp 757–9.

[482] Compare also the national codifications of customary law in Europe in the late 18th and early 19th century.PAJ van den Berg, *The Politics of European Codification; A History of the Unification of Law in France, Prussia, the Austrian Monarchy and the Netherlands*, Europa Law Publishing, Groningen, 2006.

[483] North Sea Continental Shelf, Judgment, ICJ Reports 1969, p 3, at p 41, para 71.

[484] North Sea Continental Shelf, Judgment, ICJ Reports 1969, p 3, at pp 41–4, para 72, 73 and 77. Shaw, *International Law*, pp 90–1.

[485] Compare the ILA Committee's comments on the possibility that a strong sense of *opinio iuris* requires less proof of a general practice. Final Report of the International Committee on the Formation of Customary (General) International Law; Principles Applicable to the Formation of General Customary International Law, in: The International Law Association, *Report of the Sixty-Ninth Conference, London, 2000*, pp 752–3.

[486] C Greenwood, *Customary Law Status of the 1977 Geneva Protocols*, in: AJM Delissen, GJ Tanja (Eds), *Humanitarian Law of Armed Conflict; Challenges Ahead; Essays in Honour of Frits Kalshoven*, Martinus Nijhoff Publishers, Dordrecht, 1991, p 98.

[487] Greenwood, *Customary Law Status of the 1977 Geneva Protocols*, in: Delissen, Tanja (Eds), *Humanitarian Law of Armed Conflict; Challenges Ahead; Essays in Honour of Frits Kalshoven*, p 98.

[488] See also De Hoogh on a particular decision of the Trial Chamber of the ICTY on command responsibility. AJJ de Hoogh, *Commentary*, in: A Klip, G Sluiter (Eds), *Annotated Leading Cases of International Criminal Tribunals; Vol VII: The International Criminal Tribunal for the Former Yugoslavia 2001*, Intersentia, Antwerp, 2005, pp 24–5.

[489] Greenwood, *Customary Law Status of the 1977 Geneva Protocols*, in: Delissen, Tanja (Eds), *Humanitarian Law of Armed Conflict; Challenges Ahead; Essays in Honour of Frits Kalshoven*, p 99.

exist independently and is applicable by itself.[490] In case of codification, the treaty provision is only binding for states parties, while the underlying customary norm remains applicable to all states. In case of customary development of treaty provisions, the treaty provision is only binding for the states parties, but the new customary norm also becomes applicable to non-state parties. Because of their independent status, it is possible that there are differences in content and that both norms move into different directions,[491] but it is likely that in practice both norms will be regarded as complementary by means of interpretation.[492]

It may be clear from the above that customary international law is surrounded by mystery and uncertainty and is one of the most difficult and intangible topics of international law. Nevertheless, this section will focus on two possibilities. Firstly, the question whether or not the explicit treaty provisions discussed above reflect customary international law (section 2.3.2). Secondly, the question whether there are any customary rules directly protecting the environment during international armed conflict, which may have come into existence, independently from these explicit treaty provisions (section 2.3.3).

2.3.2 *Customary Status Treaty Provisions*

2.3.2.1 Introduction

The sources of international law are not mutually exclusive and it is therefore possible that the environmental protection provisions of ENMOD, Additional Protocol I, the Incendiary Weapons Protocol and the Rome Statute may have customary equivalents. Overlap between treaty law and customary law may result either from the fact that these provisions were declaratory of pre-existing norms of customary international law, or from the fact that they have developed into customary international law.

2.3.2.2 ENMOD

2.3.2.2.1 Pre-Existing Customary International Law

It is unlikely that ENMOD was a codification of a pre-existing rule of customary international law that prohibited the use of environmental

[490] Shaw, *International Law*, p 91. For a detailed discussion, see: Military and Paramilitary Activities in and against Nicaragua (Nicaragua v United States of America), Merits, Judgment, 27 Jun 1986, ICJ Reports 1986, p 14, paras 175–81, pp 93–7.

[491] According to the International Court of Justice in the 1986 Nicaragua Case, however, practice that deviates from a treaty norm should in principle be regarded as a breaches of that rules, and 'not as indications of the recognition of a new rule.' Military and Paramilitary Activities in and against Nicaragua (Nicaragua v United States of America), Merits, Judgment, 27 Jun 1986, ICJ Reports 1986, p 14, para 186, p 98.

[492] Dixon, *Textbook on International Law*, p 37.

modification techniques. First of all, the environment did not receive major international attention until the early 1970s, which rules out the possibility of a customary prohibition. Secondly, practice shows that only a small number of states have studied and developed techniques to manipulate environmental processes.[493] Only the United States is said to have actually employed such techniques in practice during the Vietnam War, and no subsequent accusations were made by other states that the United States had violated public international law. Thirdly, neither the original proposal submitted by the Soviet Union,[494] which was primarily a disarmament proposal, nor ENMOD itself suggest in any form that the treaty codified pre-existing customary law.

The absence of a pre-existing customary prohibition was also asserted by the United Kingdom in 1995 before the International Court of Justice and is confirmed in literature. In one of its Written Statements, the United Kingdom stated among other things that the preparatory works of ENMOD indicated that ENMOD dealt with new means of warfare.[495] And Spieker refers to statements made by the United States and the Soviet Union regarding their proposal to ban *new* means of warfare and to a number of statements from a variety of other delegations and concludes that:

> [in] der Gesamtschau kann mithin ein Konsens der Vertragsstaaten dahingehend festgestellt werden, dass es sich bei dem Regelungsgegenstand der ENMOD-Konvention um einen neuen handelte. Das Übereinkommen stellt daher keine Kodifikation eines bereits bestehenden Gewohnheitsrechtssatzes dar.'[496]

2.3.2.2.2 Customary Development

It is furthermore uncertain whether the prohibition to use environmental modification techniques has meanwhile developed into a rule of customary

[493] These are the United States, the Soviet Union, Thailand, and the People's Republic of China. For China, see: Cody, *Chinese Rainmakers Competing for Clouds; Widespread Drought Leads to Regional Rivalries,* The Washington Post, 2 Aug 2004, and NRC Handelsblad of 18 Aug 2004. For Thailand, see: NRC Handelsblad of 19 Mar 2005.

[494] A/Res/3264 (XXIX), adopted on 9 Dec 1974, by 126 to 0, with 5 abstentions, on the prohibition of action to influence the environment and climate for military and other purposes incompatible with the maintenance of international security, human well-being and health; Annex Draft Convention on the Prohibition of Action to Influence the Environment and Climate for Military and Other Purposes Incompatible with the Maintenance of International Security, Human Well-Being and Health. The 1974 Joint Statement by the United States and the Soviet Union expressed the desired 'to limit the potential danger to mankind from possible *new* means of warfare' (emphasis added). Through: <http://www.sunshine-project.org/enmod/primer.html>.

[495] Written Statement of the Government of the United Kingdom of 16 Jun 1995 (GA), p 56, para 3.76. Through: <http://www.icj-cij.org/>.

[496] H Spieker, *Völkergewohnheitsrechtlicher Schutz der Natürlichen Umwelt im internationalen bewaffneten Konflikt; Waffenwirkung und Umwelt I,* Universitätsverlag Brockmeyer, Bochum, 1992, p 371. Also Dinstein, in: Dinstein, *Protection of the Environment in International Armed Conflict,* in: Frowein, Wolfrum (Eds), *Max Planck Yearbook of United Nations Law,* p 530; Dinstein, *The Conduct of Hostilities under the Law of International Armed Conflict,* p 181.

international law. Although it is arguable that the prohibition of the use of environmental modification techniques is of 'fundamentally norm-creating character', despite the Convention's inter se clause,[497] and although practice is arguably widespread and general,[498] despite the average number of state parties,[499] it is doubtful whether this general practice of abstention results from or is accompanied by a sense of obligation. It is more likely that it has more pragmatic reasons. The large majority of states either does not have the technological capabilities to develop these weapons, or is not interested in developing them, because they do not seem to be very practical during armed conflict.

Yet, the International Committee of the Red Cross is ambiguous as far as the customary status of ENMOD is concerned. On the one hand, it concludes in its 2005 Study on Customary International Humanitarian Law[500] that it is unclear whether the provisions of ENMOD have developed into

[497] Art I provides that the prohibition only extends to hostile use of environmental modification techniques having widespread, long-lasting or severe effects 'to any other State Party.' The *inter partes* and *si omnes* clauses of 1899 Hague Convention II and Hague Convention IV of 1907 were no impediment for the International Military Tribunal at Nuremberg to conclude that certain provisions had developed into customary international law. Final Report of the International Committee on the Formation of Customary (General) International Law; Principles Applicable to the Formation of General Customary International Law, in: The International Law Association, *Report of the Sixty-Ninth Conference, London, 2000*, p 757. Art 2 of 1907 Hague Convention IV provided: 'The provisions contained in the Regulations (. . .), as well as in the present Convention, do not apply except between Contracting powers, and then only if all the belligerents are parties to the Convention.' Art 2 of 1899 Hague Convention II provided: "The provisions contained in the Regulations (. . .) are only binding on the Contracting Powers, in case of war between two or more of them. These provisions shall cease to be binding from the time when, in a war between Contracting Powers, a non-Contracting Power joins one of the belligerents.'

[498] It should be noted, however, that the People's Republic of China used cloud seeding techniques in order to generate rainfall in the summer of 2004 for peaceful purposes. NRC Handelsblad of 18 Aug 2004.

[499] ENMOD has 70 States Parties in the Summer of 2005, <http://disarmament2.un.org/TreatyStatus.nsf>.

[500] This long-awaited study was carried out by the ICRC upon the request of the 26th International Conference of the Red Cross and Red Crescent in Geneva in 1995. The ICRC was asked to 'prepare, with the assistance of experts in international humanitarian law representing various geographical regions and different legal systems, and in consultation with experts from governments and international organizations, a report on customary rules of international humanitarian law applicable in international and non-international armed conflicts, and to circulate the report to States and competent international bodies.' Recommendation II of the Intergovernmental Group of Experts for the Protection of War Victims that met in Geneva from 23 till 27 Jan 1995 and that was endorsed by the Conference by Resolution 1. Through: <http://www.icrc.org/>. Also in: Henckaerts, Doswald-Beck (Eds), *Customary International Humanitarian Law; Vol I: Rules*, p x. The ICRC's research was written and edited by Henckaerts and Doswald-Beck and involved over 100 eminent experts from a large number of states. According to the ICRC, 'the study does indeed present an accurate assessment of the current state of customary international humanitarian law.' Henckaerts, Doswald-Beck (Eds), *Customary International Humanitarian Law; Vol I: Rules*, p xi.

customary rules of international law;[501] on the other hand, it states in Customary Rule 45 that '[d]estruction of the natural environment may not be used as a weapon.'[502] Although Rule 45 does not mention the use of environmental modification techniques, its reference to the use of the environment as a weapon of warfare nevertheless, seems to imply more.[503]

Before 2005, the ICRC had included environmental modification prohibitions in two non-binding yet influential documents. These were, the 1993 'Guidelines for Military Manuals and Instructions on the Protection of the Environment in Times of Armed Conflict'[504] and the 1999 'Model Manual on the Law of Armed Conflict for Armed Forces' named 'Fight it Right'.[505] The Guidelines were finalised within the framework of a general report of the ICRC to the Secretary-General on its activities regarding the protection of the environment in times of armed conflict. The ICRC report and the guidelines were subsequently included in its entirety in the report of the Secretary-General to the General Assembly on the Protection of the Environment in Times of Armed Conflict of 29 July 1993,[506] prepared upon its request by Resolution 47/37 of 25 November

[501] Henckaerts, Doswald-Beck (Eds), *Customary International Humanitarian Law; Vol I: Rules*, p 155.

[502] Henckaerts, Doswald-Beck (Eds), *Customary International Humanitarian Law; Vol I: Rules*, p 151.

[503] On the one hand, the military manuals of Australia, Canada, New Zealand, Russia and Spain, all of which are parties to the Convention—<http://disarmament2.un.org/TreatyStatus.nsf>—as well as the manuals of Israel and South Korea seem to indicate that ENMOD only binds Contracting Parties. Indonesia, on the other hand, which is not a party to the Convention has voluntarily included the prohibition in its military manual of 1982, which may suggest that the obligation is also accepted outside the treaty context. Henckaerts, Doswald-Beck (Eds), *Customary International Humanitarian Law; Vol I: Rules*, p 155; J-M Henckaerts, L Doswald-Beck (Eds), *Customary International Humanitarian Law; Vol II: Practice; Part 1*, International Committee of the Red Cross, Cambridge University Press, Cambridge, 2005, pp 904–7. Also the British Military Manual suggests that the prohibition to use ENMOD techniques only apply to '[s]tates party to the Convention'. The United Kingdom became a party to the Convention in 1978. UK Ministry of Defence, *The Manual of the Law of Armed Conflict*, Oxford University Press, Oxford, 2004, pp 74–5. The Dutch Manual also refers to ENMOD in ch 4.13, paras 0476–0474. The Netherlands became a state party in 1983. VS 27-412, *Humanitair Oorlogsrecht*, internal publication, Koninklijke Landmacht, Ministerie van Defensie, Den Haag, Jan 2005, p 53.

[504] A/48/269, Report of the Secretary-General to the General Assembly on the Protection of the Environment in the Environment in Times of Armed Conflict, of 29 Jul 1993, with Annexed the ICRC Guidelines for Military Manuals and Instructions on the Protection of the Environment in Times of Armed Conflict.

[505] APV Rogers,P Malherbe, *Fight it Right; Model Manual on the Law of Armed Conflict for Armed Forces*, International Committee of the Red Cross, ICRC, Geneva, 1999.

[506] A/48/269, Report of the Secretary-General to the General Assembly on the Protection of the Environment in the Environment in Times of Armed Conflict, of 29 Jul 1993.

1992[507] and implicitly endorsed by the United Nations General Assembly in 1994.[508]

The Guidelines[509] consist of twenty principles subdivided into four sections dealing with preliminary remarks, general principles of international law, specific rules on the protection of the environment and implementation and dissemination and they:

> are drawn from existing international legal obligations and from State practice concerning the protection of the environment against the effects of armed conflict,

according to principle 1. The sources of these existing obligations have been listed at the end of the Guidelines and include ENMOD.

Principle 12 provides that:

> [t]he military or any other hostile use of environmental modification techniques having widespread, long-lasting or severe effects as the means of destruction, damage or injury to any other State party is prohibited. The term 'environmental modification techniques' refers to any technique for changing—through the deliberate manipulation of natural processes—the dynamics, composition or structure of the Earth, including its biota, lithosphere, hydrosphere and atmosphere, or of outer space.[510]

Principle 12 is a combination of Article II of ENMOD and a summary of Article I and shows that the IRCR regards the prohibition of ENMOD as one of the rules that protect the environment during armed conflict and that states should incorporate it in their military manuals. However, in

[507] A/Res/47/37, adopted without a vote on 25 Nov 1992, on the protection of the environment in times of armed conflict. In operative para 4, the General Assembly requested 'the Secretary-General to invite the International Committee of the Red Cross to report on activities undertaken by the Committee and other relevant bodies with regard to the protection of the environment in times of armed conflict, and to submit to the General Assembly at its forty-eighth session, under the item entitled 'United Nations Decade of International Law', a report on activities reported by the Committee.'

[508] A/Res/49/50, adopted without a vote on 9 Dec 1994, on the United Nations Decade of International Law, operative para 11, which reads: 'The General Assembly (. . .) Invites all States to disseminate widely the revised guidelines for military manuals and instructions on the protection of the environment in times of armed conflict received from the International Committee of the Red Cross and to give due consideration to the possibility of incorporating them into their military manuals and other instructions addressed to their military personnel'. A/49/323, Report of the Secretary-General on the United Nations Decade of International Law, of 19 Aug 1994.

[509] A/48/269, Report of the Secretary-General to the General Assembly on the Protection of the Environment in the Environment in Times of Armed Conflict, of 29 Jul 1993, with Annexed the ICRC Guidelines for Military Manuals and Instructions on the Protection of the Environment in Times of Armed Conflict, pp 24–7. Also but slightly different in: A/49/323, Report of the Secretary-General on the United Nations Decade of International Law, of 19 Aug 1994, pp 49–53; Roberts, Guelff, *Documents on the Laws of War*, pp 609–14.

[510] This quotation is taken from the version included by the Secretary-General in his report on the United Nations Decade of International Law. A/49/323, Report of the Secretary-General on the United Nations Decade of International Law, of 19 Aug 1994, pp 49–53; Roberts, Guelff, *Documents on the Laws of War*, pp 609–14.

view of the circumstances referred to above, it is more likely that principle 12 does not reflect state practice but is rather intended to induce it.

The ICRC's 1999 Model Military Manual was written by Rogers and Malherbe and published in 1999 fifty years after the signing of the Geneva Conventions in order to assist States Parties in their obligation under the Geneva Conventions to disseminate the text of the Geneva Conventions and their Additional Protocols as widely as possible in their respective countries, in particular to the armed fighting forces.[511] The Manual consists of three Parts, the first part of which contains the actual model rules and deals with the law of armed conflict for the commanding officer. Section II of this part deals with 'Integration of the Law of Armed Conflict into the Assessment of the Military Situation' and contains one chapter on the 'Military Environment'. Paragraph 702 'summarises' the law on 'protection of the natural environment' including one provision on environmental modification techniques. Paragraph 702(a) states:

> Natural processes must not be deliberately manipulated for hostile purposes if that would have widespread, long lasting or severe effects.

It may be typical that most commentators remain silent on the possibility of a customary prohibition of the use of environmental modification techniques. Rogers merely refers to comments from Szasz at a Conference in Ottawa in 1991 that it might be worth examining whether the essential terms of the Convention have already developed into customary law;[512] and only Green, Spieker, Oeter and Dinstein actually conclude at various times that ENMOD has not yet developed into customary international law. Green states in 1991 that 'it cannot be argued that [ENMOD] has established anything in the nature of general or universal international law';[513] Spieker writes in 1992 in relation to ENMOD's First Review Conference of 1984 that:

> [die] Teilnehmerstaaten der Revisionskonferenz gingen (. . .) nicht davon aus, dass Nicht-Vertragsparteien bereits durch die in der ENMOD-Konvention niedergelegten Grundsätze gebunden würden. Auch im Jahr 1984 nahmen sie mithin keine gewohnheitsrechtliche Geltung des Umweltkriegsübereinkommens an;[514]

Oeter believes in 1995 that 'the specific prohibitions against environmental warfare in ENMOD (. . .) probably still have no customary

[511] Arts 47 GC I, 48 GC II, 127 GC III, 144 GC IV, 83 AP I and 19 AP II.

[512] APV Rogers, *Law on the Battlefield*, Manchester University Press, Manchester, 2004, p 166; PC Szasz, *Study of and Proposals for Improvements to Existing Legal Instruments Relating to the Environment and Armed Conflicts*, draft Art 21 Jun 1991; Conference on the use of the environment as a tool of conventional warfare, Ottawa, 1991, not published, p 10.

[513] Green, *The Environment and the Law of Conventional Warfare*, p 232.

[514] Spieker, *Völkergewohnheitsrechtlicher Schutz der Natürlichen Umwelt im internationalen bewaffneten Konflikt; Waffenwirkung und Umwelt I*, p 372. Also, after an analysis of the environmental damage during the Gulf War, p 458.

equivalents';[515] and Dinstein writes in 2004 that it was 'manifest' that the drafters of ENMOD 'deemed the text innovative' and nothing 'has happened since the adoption of the ENMOD Convention to suggest that the legal position has changed in this regard.'[516]

Therefore, in view of significant uncertainty regarding the customary status of ENMOD, it seems unlikely that the Convention's prohibition to use environmental modification techniques has a customary equivalent under public international law.

2.3.2.3 Additional Protocol I

2.3.2.3.1 Pre-Existing Customary International Law

As far as the environmental protection provisions of Additional Protocol I are concerned, there is general agreement that, unlike many other provisions of the Protocol, neither Article 35(3) nor Article 55 reflect pre-existing rules of customary international law.[517] Apart from the fact that international concern for the environment in general only stems from the early 1970s, and apart from the fact before 1977 conventions on the laws of war were silent with respect to the environment, this appears from the Protocol's and the provisions' legislative history, is supported by state practice, and is confirmed in literature.

The legislative history provides evidence in three ways. In the first place, although a proposal for environmental protection during international armed conflict had been brought up by a few Eastern European states during the Conference of Government Experts in 1972, none of the draft proposals from the ICRC in the years preceding the Diplomatic Conference contained an environmental protection clause, including the Draft Additional Protocols to the Geneva Conventions that served as the basis for discussion in Geneva.[518] The fact that the ICRC chose not to mention the environment in its draft proposals,[519] all of which were intended

[515] Oeter, *Methods and Means of Combat*, in: D Fleck (Ed), *The Handbook of Humanitarian Law in Armed Conflicts*, p 118.

[516] Dinstein, *The Conduct of Hostilities under the Law of International Armed Conflict*, p 181 and later p 193. Similarly: Dinstein, *Protection of the Environment in International Armed Conflict*, in: Frowein, Wolfrum (Eds), *Max Planck Yearbook of United Nations Law*, p 530.

[517] It should be noted that '[a]lthough the formulation is new, and the protections granted by Protocol I are greater, this prohibition is so basic that it must be construed as being inherent to a general principle of law and thus, general international law.' WA Solf, *Protection of Civilians Against the Effects of Hostilities under Customary International Law and Under Protocol I*, American University Journal of International Law & Policy, Vol 1, 1986, p 134.

[518] International Committee of the Red Cross, *Draft Additional Protocols to the Geneva Conventions of Aug 12, 1949; Commentary*, ICRC, Geneva, 1973.

[519] According to Solf, one of the reasons for not including any reference to the environment was the fact that environmental modification techniques were already under consideration at the Conference of the Committee on Disarmament. Solf, in: Bothe, Partsch, Solf, *New Rules for Victims of Armed Conflicts; Commentary on the Two 1977 Protocols Additional to the Geneva Conventions of 1949*, p 344.

not only to reaffirm but also to develop international humanitarian law is a strong indication that the ICRC did not consider the protection of the environment during international armed conflict as a separate rule of customary international law.

In the second place, proposals for environmental protection were not introduced before the start of the second session of the Diplomatic Conference in 1975,[520] and none of the proposals suggested that they were attempts to codify pre-existing customary international law.[521] On the contrary, when Australia introduced its amendment, it stated that 'adoption of the Article might well fill a gap in humanitarian law applicable in armed conflicts.'[522] And when Hungary introduced a similar amendment on behalf of the sponsoring states, it stated that 'ecological warfare and the destruction of the environment through military operations' was 'unfortunately now no longer theoretical but had become a reality in modern warfare'.[523]

Thirdly, none of the other comments on the environmental clauses referred to pre-existing customary law. Most statements made in connection with Articles 35(3) and 55 simply acknowledged the importance of environmental protection and dealt with the wording of the provisions and the position of an environmental protection clause in Additional Protocol I.[524] Therefore, because one usually did refer to the customary origins of other treaty provisions such as with respect to Article 35(1) and 35(2), the conclusion seems justified that both environmental protection provisions were regarded as progressive development of international humanitarian law. This is confirmed by statements from Ireland and the Federal Republic of Germany. The former stated that the adoption of Article 35(3) and Article 55 was 'an event in the history of international humanitarian law'.[525] The latter stated with respect to Article 35 that it regarded paragraph 1 and 2 as a reaffirmation of customary international law:

> while paragraph 3 of this Article is an important new contribution to the protection of the natural environment in times of international armed conflict.[526]

[520] The German Democratic Republic proposed an amendment that would later become Art 35(3); Australia and a group consisting of Czechoslovakia, Hungary and the Germany Democratic Republic both proposed a new Article that would later become Art 55. Levie, *Protection of War Victims: Protocol 1 to the 1949 Geneva Conventions; Vol 2*, p 254, respectively Levie, *Protection of War Victims: Protocol 1 to the 1949 Geneva Conventions; Vol 3*, p 259.

[521] Levie, *Protection of War Victims: Protocol 1 to the 1949 Geneva Conventions; Vol 2*, p 257; Levie, *Protection of War Victims: Protocol 1 to the 1949 Geneva Conventions; Vol 3*, p 263.

[522] Levie, *Protection of War Victims: Protocol 1 to the 1949 Geneva Conventions; Vol 3*, p 263.

[523] Levie, *Protection of War Victims: Protocol 1 to the 1949 Geneva Conventions; Vol 3*, p 259.

[524] Levie, *Protection of War Victims: Protocol 1 to the 1949 Geneva Conventions; Vol 2*, pp 256–80; Levie, *Protection of War Victims: Protocol 1 to the 1949 Geneva Conventions; Vol 3*, pp 259–77.

[525] Levie, *Protection of War Victims: Protocol 1 to the 1949 Geneva Conventions; Vol 2*, p 274; Levie, *Protection of War Victims: Protocol 1 to the 1949 Geneva Conventions; Vol 3*, p 272.

[526] Levie, *Protection of War Victims: Protocol 1 to the 1949 Geneva Conventions; Vol 2*, p 279.

In addition to the legislative history of Articles 35(3) and 55, further evidence for the improbability of any pre-existing customary rule in this respect can be found in state practice. Firstly, this appears from the absence of environmental protection provisions in military manuals before 1977. For example, when the United States amended its 1956 Field Manual on the Law of Land Warfare in 1976,[527] and wrote its Pamphlet for the Air Force,[528] the United States chose 'to incorporate language taken directly from Protocol I', in particular with respect to the protection of the civilian population and thereby 'clearly acknowledged the customary law status' of these basic principles.[529] The provisions on the protection of the environment, however, were not included.

Secondly, evidence of state practice can be found in statements and comments made before the International Court of Justice in the mid 1990s within the framework of both Nuclear Weapons Advisory Opinions.[530] Not one single state claimed that both provisions codified pre-existing customary law. On the contrary, six states made both explicit and implicit references to the opposite. The United Kingdom[531] and the United States[532] each explicitly referred to the innovative character of the environmental provisions of Additional Protocol I in their statements before the Court, and so did France in one of its written statements.[533] Egypt claimed in its Oral Plea that Article 35(3) was obviously innovative;[534] Malaysia referred to Article 55 as an example of 'development' of international

[527] FM 27–10, *The Law of Land Warfare*, Department of the Army, Washington, DC, 1956, as changed in 1976. Also through: <http://www.afsc.army.mil/>.

[528] Air Force Pamphlet 110-31, *International Law—The Conduct of Armed Conflict and Air Operations*, Department of the Air Force, Washington, D.C., 1976. Please note, however, the caveat at the beginning of the pamphlet saying that as 'an Air Force pamphlet, it does not promulgate official US Government policy although it does refer to US, DOD and Air Force policies.'

[529] Greenwood, *Customary Law Status of the 1977 Geneva Protocols*, in: Delissen, Tanja (Eds), *Humanitarian Law of Armed Conflict; Challenges Ahead; Essays in Honour of Frits Kalshoven*, p 102.

[530] Legality of the Use by a State of Nuclear Weapons in Armed Conflict, Advisory Opinion, 8 Jul 1996, ICJ Reports 1996, p 66; Legality of the Threat or Use of Nuclear Weapons, Advisory Opinion, 8 Jul 1996, ICJ Reports 1996, p 226.

[531] Written Statement of the Government of the United Kingdom (WHO), p 91, para 43; Written Comments of the Government of United Kingdom on other Written Statements of 16 Jun 1995 (WHO), p 57, para 3.77; Written Statement of the Government of the United Kingdom of 16 Jun 1995 (GA), p 57, para 3.77; CR 95/34, Oral Plea of the Government of the United Kingdom, of 15 Nov 1995 (WHO and GA), pp 36–7. Through: <http://www.icj-cij.org/>.

[532] Written Statement of the Government of the United States of America of 10 Jun 1994 (WHO), p 30, para 8; Written Comments of the Government of the United States of America of 20 Jun 1995 (WHO), pp 23–4; Written Statement of the Government of the United States of America of 20 Jun 1995 (GA), p 25; CR 95/34, Oral Plea of the Government of the United States of America, of 15 Nov 1995 (WHO and GA), p 73. Through: <http://www.icj-cij.org/>.

[533] Written Statement of the Government of Republic of France of 20 Jun 1995 (GA), p 41.

[534] CR 95/23, Oral Plea of the Government of the Arab Republic of Egypt, of 1 Nov 1995 (WHO and GA), p 32.

humanitarian law in Additional Protocol I;[535] and Nauru wrote that 'now' Protocol I must 'be regarded as customary international law which is binding on all States'; which implies that at least part of the Protocol did not yet have this character in 1977.[536]

Finally, the innovative character of Articles 35(3) and 55 seems to be implied by the International Court of Justice, has been acknowledged by the ICRC and is further endorsed in literature. Firstly, the International Court of Justice stated in 1996 in its Nuclear Weapons Advisory Opinion (GA) that Articles 35(3) and 55 of Additional Protocol I were 'powerful constraints for all the States having subscribed to these provisions.'[537] This seems to imply that the Court does not believe that both provisions reflected pre-existing rules of customary international law. Secondly, the International Committee of the Red Cross stated twice that both provisions were new. In its 2005 Study on Customary International Humanitarian Law, it stated that '[t]hese provisions were clearly new when they were adopted.'[538] And in its 1987 Commentary of the Additional Protocols, the Committee wrote that Article 35(3) was an 'absolutely new' provision with no equivalent in earlier conventions and with respect to Article 55 that 'this is a new feature'.[539] And thirdly, the innovative character of both provisions is generally shared in literature.[540] Spieker, for example, concludes in

[535] Written Comments of the Government of Malaysia on other Written Statements of 19 Jun 1995 (WHO), p 19.

[536] Written Statement of the Government of Nauru of 19 Sep 1994, Memorial III (WHO), p 22.

[537] Legality of the Threat or Use of Nuclear Weapons, Advisory Opinion, 8 Jul 1996, ICJ Reports 1996, p 226, at p 242, para 31.

[538] Henckaerts, Doswald-Beck (Eds), *Customary International Humanitarian Law; Vol I: Rules*, p 152.

[539] Sandoz, Swinaraski, Zimmerman, *Commentary on the Additional Protocols; of 8 Jun 1977 to the Geneva Conventions of 12 Aug 1949*, pp 387 and 662.

[540] Compare A/48/269, Report of the Secretary-General to the General Assembly on the Protection of the Environment in the Environment in Times of Armed Conflict, of 29 Jul 1993, para 38, p 7, by implication; Bodansky, *Legal Regulation of the Effects of Military Activity on the Environment*, p 27, on the innovative ecocentric character of Art 35(3); Bothe, *The Protection of the Environment in Times of Armed Conflict; Legal Rules, Uncertainty, Deficiencies, and Possible Developments*, p 56; Dinstein, *Protection of the Environment in International Armed Conflict*, in: Frowein, Wolfrum (Eds), *Max Planck Yearbook of United Nations Law*, p 534; Dinstein, *The Conduct of Hostilities under the Law of International Armed Conflict*, p 185; Green, *The Environment and the Law of Conventional Warfare*, p 232, implying that the provisions did not codify customary law; LC Green, *The Contemporary Law of Armed Conflict*, Manchester University Press, Manchester, 2000, p 127; Greenwood, *Customary Law Status of the 1977 Geneva Protocols*, in: Delissen, Tanja (Eds), *Humanitarian Law of Armed Conflict; Challenges Ahead; Essays in Honour of Frits Kalshoven*, pp 101, 104–5, on the innovative character of Arts 35(3) and 55, and the lack of proof of a pre-existing customary rule; K Hulme, *War Torn Environment: Interpreting the Legal Threshold*, Martinus Nijhoff Publishers, Leiden, 2004, p 103; Kalshoven, *Reaffirmation and Development of International Humanitarian Law Applicable in Armed Conflicts: the Diplomatic Conference, Geneva, 1974–1977; Part II*, p 129, on the progressive development of international humanitarian law with respect to Art 35(3) and 55; Lijnzaad, Tanja, *Protection of the Environment in Times of Armed Conflict: The Iraq-Kuwait War*, pp 181–2, stating that the Protocol provisions provide a different standard than prior customary rules

the early 1990s that based on the legislative history, both provisions are new.[541] And Solf writes in the leading Commentary on the Additional Protocols—other than the ICRC Commentary—that Article 35:

> reaffirms two basic principles which underly [sic] customary international humanitarian law (paras. 1 and 2), and declares a new principle (. . .) (para. 3).[542]

With respect to Article 55, he states that where most of the provisions dealing with the protection of the civilian population against the effects of hostilities are 'reaffirmations and clarifications of existing conventional and customary law, it also includes significant development which change existing law' including Articles 35(3) (*sic*) and 55.[543]

2.3.2.3.2 Customary Development

Apart from the fact that it is highly unlikely that Articles 35(3) and 55 codified pre-existing rules of customary international law, it is doubtful whether subsequent practice arising from or accompanied by *opinio iuris* has led to the development of a customary rule of international law as reflected in both Articles. According to the International Court of Justice, this can only be presumed when treaty provisions have a fundamentally norm-creating character resulting in a widespread practice of non-party states, accompanied by a strong sense of *opinio iuris*.[544] Although there are ample indications that both provisions are widely considered important

of necessity and proportionality; JH McNeill, *Protection of the Environment in Times of Armed Conflict: Environmental Protection in Military Practice*, Hague Yearbook of International Law, Vol 6 1993, p 81; A Roberts, *The Law of War and Environmental Damage*, in: JE Austin, CE Bruch (Eds), *The Environmental Consequences of War*, Cambridge University Press, Cambridge, 2000, p 62; Schmitt, *Green War: An Assessment of the Environmental Law of International Armed Conflict*, p 73, on the fact that the environment-specific prescriptions were not intended 'to forgo protection already in place', and p 76, by implication; Schmitt, *Humanitarian Law and the Environment*, p 268, fn 16; Schmitt, *War and the Environment: Fault Lines in the Prescriptive Landscape*, in: Austin, Bruch (Eds), *The Environmental Consequences of War*, p 93; Simonds, *Conventional Warfare and Environmental Protection: A Proposal for International Legal Reform*, p 177, referring to the opinion of most commentators; also in principle Solf, *Protection of Civilians Against the Effects of Hostilities under Customary International Law and Under Protocol I*, p 134, on the new formulation of both provisions; Tarasofsky, *Legal Protection of the Environment during International Armed Conflict*, p 41; Verwey, *Observations on the Legal Protection of the Environment in Times of International Armed Conflict*, p 39 Verwey, *Protection of the Environment in Times of Armed Conflict: In Search of a New Legal Perspective*, p 15; Verwey, *Comment: Protection of the Environment in Times of Armed Conflict—Do We Need Additional Rules?*, in: Grunawalt, King, McClain, *Protection of the Environment during Armed Conflict*, p 563, implying that both provisions did not codify customary law.

541 Spieker, *Völkergewohnheitsrechtlicher Schutz der Natürlichen Umwelt im internationalen bewaffneten Konflikt; Waffenwirkung und Umwelt I*, pp 373–404.

542 Solf, in: Bothe, Partsch, Solf, *New Rules for Victims of Armed Conflicts; Commentary on the Two 1977 Protocols Additional to the Geneva Conventions of 1949*, p 193.

543 Solf, in: Bothe, Partsch, Solf, *New Rules for Victims of Armed Conflicts; Commentary on the Two 1977 Protocols Additional to the Geneva Conventions of 1949*, pp 278–9.

544 North Sea Continental Shelf, Judgment, ICJ Reports 1969, p 3, para 72, 72 and 77, pp 41–4. Shaw, *International Law*, pp 90–1.

and that they might eventually develop into rules of customary international law, this does not yet seem to be the case.[545] And since there seems to be reasonable doubt, it seems proper to fall back on the principle that restrictions upon the independence of states cannot be presumed.[546]

2.3.2.3.2.1 State Practice and Opinio Iuris

There is as little evidence of relevant state practice by non States Parties as there is from States Parties to the Protocol; and there is even less evidence that practice, as far as it can be ascertained, is based on a strong sense of *opinio iuris*. Relevant evidence of state practice in this regard can be found in actual behavior or physical acts, or in so-called 'verbal acts', such as military manuals and public statements made by high government officials.

As far as actual behavior is concerned, there are only a few occasions on which reference was made to Articles 35(3) and 55. Firstly, both Articles were invoked by Iran in the war between Iraq and Iran in the 1980s, although neither state was a party to Additional Protocol I. Yet, both states 'attacked environmentally sensitive targets when [they] had the capacity to do so.'[547] Secondly, both Articles were referred to after the Gulf War of 1990–1991, when Iraq set fire to hundreds of oil wells in Kuwait and released millions of barrels of oil into the Persian Gulf, but both actions were not considered a breach of Articles 35(3) and 55.[548] Thirdly, reference was made to Articles 35(3) and 55 by belligerents at the beginning of the

[545] Only the first part of the first sentence of Art 55(1) may be found to reflect customary international law as will be explained in s 2.3.3.2. The first sentence of Art 55(1) stipulates that '[c]are shall be taken in warfare to protect the natural environment (. . .).'

[546] The Case of the SS 'Lotus', 7 Sep 1927, Publications of the Permanent Court of International Justice, Collection of Judgments, Series A—No 10, AW Sijthoff's Publishing Company, 1927, p 18.

[547] Greenwood, *Customary Law Status of the 1977 Geneva Protocols,* in: Delissen, Tanja (Eds), *Humanitarian Law of Armed Conflict; Challenges Ahead; Essays in Honour of Frits Kalshoven,* p 101. The Security Council called upon both parties in Resolution 540 'to refrain from any action that may endanger peace and security as well as marine life in the region of the Gulf.' S/RES/540 (1983), adopted on 31 Oct 1983, by 12 to 0, with 3 abstentions, on the situation between Iraq and the Islamic Republic of Iran.

[548] The Report of the US Department of Defense to Congress of 1992 refers to the conclusions of the Conference of Experts invited by the Canadian Ministry of Foreign Affairs from 9 to 12 Jul 1992 in Ottawa. United States Department of Defense, *Conduct of the Persian Gulf War; Final Report to Congress; Pursuant to Title V of the Persian Gulf Conflict Supplemental Authorization and Personnel Benefits Act of 1991 (Public Law 102–25),* pp 624–5; United States Department of Defense, *Report to Congress on the Conduct of the Persian Gulf War—Appendix on the Role of the law of War,* pp 636–7. Also Bodansky, *Legal Regulation of the Effects of Military Activity on the Environment,* p 28; Schmitt, *Green War: An Assessment of the Environmental Law of International Armed Conflict,* p 75; Simonds, *Conventional Warfare and Environmental Protection: A Proposal for International Legal Reform,* p 207; Rogers, *Law on the Battlefield,* pp 181–2. It should be noted that a number of Arab states proposed an amendment to current Art 56 AP I to extend the protection of specific civilian objects containing dangerous forces to 'oil rigs, petroleum storage facilities, and oil refineries'. The amendment was generally rejected. Kalshoven, *Reaffirmation and Development of International Humanitarian Law Applicable in Armed Conflicts: the Diplomatic Conference, Geneva, 1974–1977; Part II,* p 136.

war in the Former Yugoslavia in 1991 and 1992 in a memorandum of understanding and an agreement on the application of international humanitarian law.[549] Croatia and Bosnia-Herzegovina were at that time not yet parties to Additional Protocol I. And fourthly, both provisions were brought up in connection with the bombardments during the Kosovo campaign in 1999 and the use of Depleted Uranium by Allied Forces, including non-state parties to the Protocol, during the Gulf War in 1991, in Kosovo 1999, and again against Iraq in 2003. With respect to the bombing campaign over Kosovo in 1999, a Special Committee established by the Prosecutor of the International Criminal Tribunal for the Former Yugoslavia concluded in 2000 that violation of Articles 35(3) and 55 could not be established.[550]

The number of occasions on which references were made is thus small, and it is difficult to determine whether any of these references were accompanied by a sense of legal obligation or *opinio iuris*.[551] Furthermore, because there have not been that many more international armed conflicts during the period described than the ones just mentioned, it would be difficult to relate the abstention or restraint of non-state parties to a sense of legal obligation.

Also, as far as references to either or both provisions in the military manuals of non-state parties as well as State Parties are concerned, no convincing evidence can be found that the rules of Articles 35(3) and 55 may have developed into rules of customary international law. The ICRC Study on Customary International Humanitarian Law refers to the military manuals or handbooks of nineteen States Parties to Additional Protocol I that contain references to Articles 35(3) and 55.[552] These are: Argentina, Australia, Belgium, Benin, Canada, Colombia, France, Germany,[553] Italy, Kenya, the

[549] Henckaerts, Doswald-Beck (Eds), *Customary International Humanitarian Law; Vol II: Practice; Part 1*, p 879.

[550] ICTY, *Final Report to the Prosecutor by the Committee Established to Review the NATO Bombing Campaign against the Federal Republic of Yugoslavia*, International Legal Materials, Vol 39, 2000, p 1262.

[551] Spieker concluded in 1992 that in literature the international response to the environmental damage during the Gulf War of 1990–1991 had led to the conclusion that a customary rule of international law on the protection of the environment as reflected in Additional Protocol I and ENMOD did not (yet) exist. Spieker, *Völkergewohnheitsrechtlicher Schutz der Natürlichen Umwelt im internationalen bewaffneten Konflikt; Waffenwirkung und Umwelt I*, p 456.

[552] Henckaerts, Doswald-Beck (Eds), *Customary International Humanitarian Law; Vol I; Rules*, p 152, fn 52; Henckaerts, Doswald-Beck (Eds), *Customary International Humanitarian Law; Vol II: Practice; Part 1*, pp 879–83.

[553] ZDv 15/2, *Humanitäres Völkerrecht in bewaffneten Konflikten*, Bundesministerium der Verteidigung, Bonn, 1991. Or DSK AV207320065, *Humanitäres Völkerrecht in bewaffneten Konflikten—Handbuch*, Bundesministerium der Verteidigung—Verwaltung und Recht II 3, Bonn, 1992. Para 401 of the German Military Manual, for example, states that '*Es ist insbesondere verboten, Mittel oder Methoden anzuwenden, die dazu bestimmt oder geeignet sind, (. . .) ausgedehnte, langanhaltende und schwere Schäden der Natürlichen Umwelt zu verursachen*'. DSK AV207320065, *Humanitäres Völkerrecht in bewaffneten Konflikten—Handbuch*, p 39. In translation: 'It is particularly prohibited to employ means or methods which are intended or of a

Netherlands,[554] New Zealand, Russia, Serbia and Montenegro, Spain, Sweden, Switzerland, Togo, and the United Kingdom.[555]

These statements are largely irrelevant, however, in terms of customary law development, since fifteen states were already bound to observe both obligations when they included it in their manuals, because they had become party to the Protocol;[556] and two states were bound to be bound, because they had signed the Protocol.[557] Only Kenya and Serbia/Montenegro seem to have included similar provisions in their manuals before acceding to the Protocol.[558] Furthermore their number is too limited to imply proof of a general and widespread practice accepted as law. After all, 164 countries have become States Parties to Additional Protocol I.[559]

This view is confirmed to a certain extent by Spieker who analysed a number of military manuals of Canada, the Federal Republic of Germany and the United States in the early 1990s. She found explicit and implicit references to Articles 35(3) and 55 and also to ENMOD in manuals of the former two states, whereas the 1989 manual on naval warfare of the latter state was silent on the subject. Although the references show concern for the environment during international armed conflict, none provides for an

nature: (. . .) to cause widespread, long-term, and severe damage to the natural environment (arts. 35, para. 3, and 55, para. 1 Additional Protocol I (. . .))'. D. Fleck (Ed), *The Handbook of Humanitarian Law in Armed Conflicts*, Oxford University Press, Oxford, 1995, p 111; Henckaerts, Doswald-Beck (Eds), *Customary International Humanitarian Law; Vol II: Practice; Part 1*, p 881.

554 VS 27-412, *Humanitair Oorlogsrecht*, internal publication, Koninklijke Landmacht, Ministerie van Defensie, Den Haag, Jan 2005. Section 0404 of the Dutch Military Manual states: '*Daarnaast is het verboden methoden of middelen te gebruiken die omvangrijke, langdurige en ernstige schade aan het natuurlijk milieu toebrengen, of die dergelijke schade, naar verwachting, zullen toebrengen ((. . .) AP I artikel 35)*'. VS 27-412, *Humanitair Oorlogsrecht*, internal publication, p 39. In addition, it is prohibited to use methods or means of warfare that cause widespread, long-term and severe to the natural environment, or that are expected to cause such damage. ((. . .) Additional Protocol I Art 35). Similarly, but referring to an older manual: Henckaerts, Doswald-Beck (eds), *Customary International Humanitarian Law; Vol II: Practice; Part 1*, p 881.

555 UK Ministry of Defence, *The Manual of the Law of Armed Conflict*, Oxford University Press, Oxford, 2004. The British Military Manual discusses in para 5.29 and 5.29.1 in detail the prohibition to use methods of warfare that may cause widespread, long-term and severe damage to the environment as laid down in Arts 35(3) and 55, and states in para 6.3 that '[i]t is prohibited to employ weapons that are intended, or may be expected, to cause widespread, long-term, and severe damage to the natural environment.' UK Ministry of Defence, *The Manual of the Law of Armed Conflict*, pp 75–7, 104. Similarly, but referring to an older manual: Henckaerts, Doswald-Beck (Eds), *Customary International Humanitarian Law; Vol II: Practice; Part 1*, p 882.

556 Henckaerts, Doswald-Beck (Eds), *Customary International Humanitarian Law; Vol I: Rules*, p 152; Henckaerts, Doswald-Beck (Eds), *Customary International Humanitarian Law; Vol II: Practice; Part 1*, pp 879–83. Ratifications through <http://www.icrc.org/ihl>.

557 These were Belgium and the United Kingdom. Both states signed the Protocol on 12 Dec 1977. Through <http://www.icrc.org/ihl>.

558 Henckaerts, Doswald-Beck (Eds), *Customary International Humanitarian Law; Vol I: Rules*, p 152; Henckaerts, Doswald-Beck (Eds), *Customary International Humanitarian Law; Vol II: Practice; Part 1*, pp 879–83. Ratifications through <http://www.icrc.org/ihl>.

559 Through <http://www.icrc.org/ihl> and <http://www.eda.admin.ch/>.

explicit or even implicit *opinio iuris*,[560] ie the feeling that the prescriptions are required under general international law.

Because the United States did not start the procedure for ratification of Additional Protocol I in the 1980s and because it is nowadays probably the strongest and most significant military power in the world, it is relevant to take a closer look at the military manuals and handbooks of the United States. Although the United States' approach in its military publications towards environmental protection is not unambiguous, the general tendency seems to be that the United States does not consider the contents of Articles 35(3) and 55 as rules of customary international law. This does not mean that the United States believes that the environment does not warrant protection during armed conflict, however. It only means that it does not recognise the standard of Additional Protocol I as a rule of customary international law.[561]

The United States has not issued one single military manual for all its armed forces, although a cooperative effort is underway to draft such a joint manual, in which the protection of the environment is expected to be addressed.[562] Nowadays, only US regulations on naval warfare explicitly prescribe environmental protection during armed conflict, at least to a certain extent. The United States' Commander's Handbook on the Law of Naval Operations of 1995[563] contains an explicit environmental protection paragraph, but it does not use similar language as in Additional Protocol I. Protection of the environment is embedded in rules that reflect the principles of necessity and proportionality. According to paragraph 8.1.3, it is 'not unlawful to cause collateral damage to the natural environment during an attack upon a legitimate military objective', but:

> the commander has an affirmative obligation to avoid unnecessary damage to the environment to the extent that it is practicable to do so consistent with mission accomplishment. To that end, and as far as military requirements permit, methods or means of warfare should be employed with due regard to the protection and preservation of the natural environment.

Furthermore, '[d]estruction of the natural environment not necessitated by mission accomplishment and carried out wantonly is prohibited.'[564] Paragraph 8.6.2.3, finally, refers to paragraph 8.1.3 for environmental

560 Spieker, *Völkergewohnheitsrechtlicher Schutz der Natürlichen Umwelt im internationalen bewaffneten Konflikt; Waffenwirkung und Umwelt I*, pp 413–23.

561 Compare also: Spieker, *Völkergewohnheitsrechtlicher Schutz der Natürlichen Umwelt im internationalen bewaffneten Konflikt; Waffenwirkung und Umwelt I*, p 418.

562 Schmitt, *Humanitarian Law and the Environment*, p 271, fn 31; Schmitt, *Green War: An Assessment of the Environmental Law of International Armed Conflict*, p 34.

563 NWP 1-14M, *The Commander's Handbook on the Law of Naval Operations*, Department of the Navy, Norfolk, VA, 1995. Through: <http://www.nwc.navy.mil/>. Also in: AR Thomas, JC Duncan (Eds), *Annotated Supplement to The Commander's Handbook on the Law of Naval Operations*, International Law Studies 1999, Vol 73, Naval War College, Newport, RI, 1999.

564 NWP 1-14M, *The Commander's Handbook on the Law of Naval Operations*, p 8–2.

considerations within the framework of land warfare, since the Navy Commander's Handbook also pays attention 'to relevant principles and concepts common to the whole of the law of armed conflict.'[565]

With respect to land and aerial warfare, United States regulations and documentation are less clear. Paragraph 8.6.2.3 of the Navy Commander's Handbook seems to suggest that current US regulations on land warfare do include environmental considerations; the Army Field Manual on Land Warfare has not been updated since 1976 and remains conspicuously silent on the protection of the environment;[566] and the Air Force Publications are ambiguous. On the one hand, the Air Force Commander's Handbook of 1980[567] and the 2002 Judge Advocate General's 'Air Force Operations & the Law' do refer to environmental considerations.[568] On the other hand, the above-mentioned Air Force Pamphlet of 1976[569] and the Air Force's 'Military Commander and the Law'[570] do not refer to environmental protection in the context of the Law of Armed Conflict.

Additionally, the US Operational Law Handbook of 2004,[571] which is intended for use by Judge Advocates of all branches practicing operational law refers to and discusses Articles 35(3) and 55, but states that these provisions go far beyond the Geneva Conventions or the Hague Rules and are therefore not enforceable.[572] And the 'Law of War Handbook',[573]

[565] Thomas, Duncan (Eds), *Annotated Supplement to The Commander's Handbook on the Law of Naval Operations*, p xxxv.

[566] FM 27-10, *The Law of Land Warfare*, Department of the Army, Washington, DC, 1956, as changed in 1976. Also through: <http://www.afsc.army.mil/>.

[567] Air Force Pamphlet 110–34, *Commander's Handbook on the Law of Armed Conflict*, Department of the Air Force, Washington, DC, 1980, para 6-2(c), in: Henckaerts, Doswald-Beck (Eds), *Customary International Humanitarian Law; Vol II: Practice; Part 1*, pp 882–3. The Pamphlet refers to the new environmental protection principle in Additional Protocol I but states that it is not believed that 'any presently employed conventional weapon would violate this rule.'

[568] TS Tudor, JK Walker, NS Richards and others (Eds), *Air Force Operations and the Law; A Guide for Air and Space Forces*, United States Air Force; Judge Advocate General's Department; International and Operations Law Division, Air Force Pentagon, Washington, DC, 2002, p 43. Although the Guide states that 'localized environmental side effects resulting from aerial bombardment will seldom rise to the level of widespread, long-lasting, and severe', it does require that 'foreseeable environmental collateral damage, like any type of collateral effect that may have an adverse effect on the civilian population, must be considered when determining the proportionality of a contemplated attack.' In any case, the Guide continues, the United States specifically objects to Arts 35(3) and 55 of Additional Protocol I.

[569] Air Force Pamphlet 110–31, *International Law—The Conduct of Armed Conflict and Air Operations*, Department of the Air Force, Washington, DC, 1976.

[570] TL Strand, MW Goldman and others (Eds), *The Military Commander and the Law*, Air Force Judge Advocate General School, Maxwell, AL, 2004. Through: <http://milcom.jag.af.mil/>.

[571] JB Berger III, D Grimes, ET Jensen and others (Eds), *Operational Law Handbook (2004)*, International and Operational Law Department, The Judge Advocate General's Legal Center and School, Charlottesville, VA, 2004. Through: <https://www.jagcnet.army.mil/>.

[572] Berger III, Grimes, Jensen and others (Eds), *Operational Law Handbook (2004)*, p 194–6.

[573] *Law of War Handbook*, Center for Law and Military Operations (CLAMO), Charlottesville, VA, 2005. Through: <https://www.jagcnet.army.mil/>.

provided by the Center for Law and Military Operations (CLAMO),[574] states explicitly that the United States does not regard Articles 35(3) and 55 as customary international law, and that it 'specifically objects' to these Articles.[575]

Besides actual behavior of states and incorporation of rules of law into military manuals, a third potentially relevant source of evidence of state practice are public statements by government officials, made within or outside the framework of international organisations. An example of the latter is the statement of Matheson, deputy legal adviser of the United States Department of State, in 1987. Presumably expressing the opinion of the United States Government, he stated that the United States supported the first two paragraphs of Article 35, but:

> [w]e (. . .) consider that another principle in Article 35, which also appears later in the Protocol, namely that the prohibition of methods or means of warfare intended or expected to cause widespread, long-term and severe damage to the environment, is too broad and ambiguous and is not a part of customary law.[576]

Examples of the former are the written and oral statements by states before the International Court of Justice within the framework of both Nuclear Weapons Advisory Opinions,[577] submitted by the International Court of Justice upon the request of the World Health Organization and the General Assembly.[578] According to the website of the International Court of Justice, 43 states[579] and one intergovernmental organisation[580] responded and sent in either written statements, commented on other

[574] CLAMO was established in 1988 by the US Army and is located at the Judge Advocate General's Legal Center and School of the US Army in Virginia.

[575] *Law of War Handbook*, Center for Law and Military Operations (CLAMO), pp 23–4, 173.

[576] Remarks of MJ Matheson at *Session One: The United States Position on the Relation of Customary International Law to the 1977 Protocols Additional to the 1949 Geneva Conventions*, in: MD Dupuis, JQ Heywood, MYF Sarko, *The Sixth Annual American Red Cross—Washington College of Law Conference on International Humanitarian Law: A Workshop on Customary International Law and the 1977 Protocols Additional to the 1949 Geneva Conventions*, American University Journal of International Law & Policy (currently American University International Law Review), Vol 2, 1987, p 424 and again at p 436.

[577] Legality of the Use by a State of Nuclear Weapons in Armed Conflict, Advisory Opinion, 8 Jul 1996, ICJ Reports 1996, p 66; Legality of the Threat or Use of Nuclear Weapons, Advisory Opinion, 8 Jul 1996, ICJ Reports 1996, p 226.

[578] WHA 46/40, adopted on 14 May 1993, request for an advisory opinion from the International Court of Justice on the legality of the use of nuclear weapons; A/Res/49/75 K, adopted on 15 Dec 1994, by 78 to 43, with 38 abstentions, request for an advisory opinion from the International Court of Justice on the legality of the threat of use of nuclear weapons.

[579] These states were: Australia, Bosnia and Herzegovina, Burundi, Colombia, Costa Rica, the Democratic People's Republic of Korea, Ecuador, Egypt, Finland, France, Germany, India, Indonesia, Iran, Ireland, Italy, Japan, Kazakhstan, Lesotho, Lithuania, Malaysia, Marshall Islands, Mexico, Moldova, Nauru, The Netherlands, New Zealand, Norway, Papua New Guinea, Philippines, Qatar, Russia, Samoa, San Marino, Saudi Arabia, Solomon Islands, Sri Lanka, Sweden, Uganda, Ukraine, The United Kingdom, The United States and Zimbabwe.

[580] The World Health Organization was allowed to explain the Organization's request and set forth its views before the Court.

statements, or pleaded before the Court.[581] 31 states submitted written statements regarding the WHO's request, while nine states submitted written comments on these statements. 28 states submitted written statements regarding the General Assembly's request, while two states submitted written comments on these statements. And 22 states pleaded before the Court in both Cases.[582]

As already observed above, the United Kingdom, the United States and France were very definite in their view that the Protocol's environmental protection provisions reflected progressive development of international law; while Egypt, Malaysia and Nauru seemed to share that view. Of these states, only the United Kingdom, the United States and France still believed that both provisions did not yet reflect customary international law by the mid 1990s. This appears from their explicit and repeated statements on the innovative character of Articles 35(3) and 55 and the absence of references to subsequent practice.[583] As regards the other states, only Qatar seemed to have explicitly excluded the possibility of customary law development, albeit only with respect to Article 35(3), which is 'treaty-based'.[584]

On the other hand, four other states argued or at least implied that both provisions had developed into customary international law and one state argued that both provisions might reflect customary law. According to New Zealand:

> [i]t would be a matter of consideration by the Court whether the avoidance of widespread, long-term and severe damage to the environment during war could yet be regarded as itself a rule of customary law.[585]

[581] The Court ruled by Orders of 20 Jun 1994 and 1 Feb 1995 that states that were entitled to appear before the Court were allowed to furnish information on the question, and subsequently decided later to hold public hearings. International Court of Justice, *Legality of the Use by a State of Nuclear Weapons in Armed Conflict (Request for Advisory Opinion)*, Order of 13 Sep 1993, 1993 General List No 93; International Court of Justice, *Legality of the Use by a State of Nuclear Weapons in Armed Conflict (Request for Advisory Opinion)*, Order of 20 Jun 1994, 1994 General List No 93 (extension time limit); International Court of Justice, *Legality of the Threat or Use of Nuclear Weapons (Request for Advisory Opinion)*, Order of 1 Feb 1995, 1995 General List No 95.

[582] Through: <http://www.icj-cij.org/>.

[583] United Kingdom: Written Statement of the Government of the United Kingdom (WHO), p 91, para 43; Written Comments of the Government of the United Kingdom on other Written Statements of 16 Jun 1995 (WHO), p 57, para 3.77; Written Statement of the Government of the United Kingdom of 16 Jun 1995 (GA), p 57, para 3.77; CR 95/34, Oral Plea of the Government of the United Kingdom, of 15 Nov 1995 (WHO and GA), pp 36–7. United States: Written Statement of the Government of the United States of America of 10 Jun 1994 (WHO), p 30, para 8; Written Comments of the Government of the United States of America of 20 Jun 1995 (WHO), pp 23–4; Written Statement of the Government of the United States of America of 20 Jun 1995 (GA), p 25; CR 95/34, Oral Plea of the Government of the United States of America, of 15 Nov 1995 (WHO and GA), p 73. France: Written Statement of the Government of Republic of France of 20 Jun 1995 (GA), p 41. Through: <http://www.icj-cij.org/>.

[584] CR 95/29, Oral Plea of the Government of Qatar, of 13 Nov 1995 (WHO and GA), p 32, para 27. Through: <http://www.icj-cij.org/>.

[585] Written Statement of the Government of New Zealand of 20 Jun 1995 (GA), p 18. Through: <http://www.icj-cij.org/>.

The four states that seemed to be of the opinion that Articles 35(3) and 55 did reflect customary international law were the Solomon Islands, Malaysia, Nauru and Qatar (the latter only with respect to Article 55). The Solomon Islands wrote that any use of nuclear weapons would violate Articles 35(3) and 55 'and the customary obligation reflected therein.'[586] Malaysia wrote that numerous treaties and instruments of customary international law existed:

> which prohibit the use of methods or means of warfare which are intended, or [may] be expected, to cause widespread, long-term and severe damage to the environment, as laid down in Protocol I (1977).[587]

Nauru wrote with respect to the environmental protection provisions that since Protocol I had been ratified by over 70 states by the mid 1990s 'we can say that it must now be regarded as customary international law which is binding on all States.'[588] And Qatar, finally, stated before the Court with respect to Article 55 that it had been 'accepted by all States; it thus reflects a rule of customary law.'[589]

In addition, a number of states stated before the Court that international law included a general prohibition on causing widespread, long-term and severe damage to the environment,[590] which could indicate that these states also believed that both provisions had developed into one general rule of customary international law. In addition to the Solomon Islands,[591]

[586] Written Statement by the Government of the Solomon Islands of 10 Jun 1994 (WHO), p 62, para 3.69. Similarly: Written Comments of the Government of the Solomon Islands on other Written Statements of 20 Jun 1995 (WHO), p 67, para 4.93; Written Statement of the Government of the Solomon Islands of 20 Jun 1995 (GA), p 63, para 3.78. Through: <http://www.icj-cij.org/>.

[587] Malaysia: Written Statement by the Government of the Malaysia (WHO), p 11. Through: <http://www.icj-cij.org/>.

[588] Nauru: Written Statement of the Government of Nauru of 19 Sep 1994, Memorial III (WHO), p 22. Through: <http://www.icj-cij.org/>.

[589] Qatar (only 55; Art 35(3) is 'treaty-based'): CR 95/29, Oral Plea of the Government of Qatar, of 13 Nov 1995 (WHO and GA), p 36, para 33. Through: <http://www.icj-cij.org/>.

[590] India, Malaysia, and Nauru refer in this context to the principle of environmental security or safety, which seems to confirm the existence of a third fundamental principle of *ius in bello*, as has been argued in s 1.

[591] The Solomon Islands repeatedly stated that customary international humanitarian law included a prohibition against causing widespread, long-term and severe damage to the environment, which rule was well-established and found its source in many of the classical instruments of *ius in bello*. In its oral plea before the Court, the Solomon Islands referred to a 'customary norm prohibiting significant environmental damage in war.' Written Statement of the Government of the Solomon Islands of 10 Jun 1994 (WHO), p 25, para 3.2; p 63, para 3.70; p 69, para 3.81; p 75, paras 3.94 and 3.95; Written Statement of the Government of the Solomon Islands of 19 Jun 1995 (GA), p 27, para 3.13; p 76, para 3.103; CR 95/32, Oral Plea of the Government of the Solomon Islands, of 14 Nov 1995 (WHO and GA), p 58. Through: <http://www.icj-cij.org/>.

Malaysia,[592] and Nauru[593], which already regarded Articles 35(3) and 55 as reflecting customary law, these states were India,[594] Samoa,[595] Zimbabwe,[596] and New Zealand.[597]

Unfortunately, some of the references provided by the ICRC in its 2005 Study on Customary International Humanitarian Law in this context are unsatisfactory.[598] Its references to statements made by the Solomon Islands, Nauru and New Zealand are incomplete and its references to statements made by Australia, Ecuador, Lesotho, the Marshall Islands,

[592] Malaysia regarded as one of the 6 fundamental principles of the laws of war that '[i]t is prohibited to use weapons or tactics that cause widespread, long-term and severe damage to the natural environment' and believed that this prohibition fell under the so-called principle of environmental safety. Written Statement of the Government of Malaysia of 1994 (WHO), pp 4, 10. Through: <http://www.icj-cij.org/>.

[593] And Nauru similarly referred to a principle of environmental security, which entailed that '[i]t is forbidden to use weapons that cause widespread, long-term and severe damage to the environment' and that 'there clearly exists a rule of customary international law that prohibits the use of methods or means of warfare that are intended or may be expected, to cause widespread, long-term, and severe damage to the environment.' Subsequently, it stated that the use of nuclear weapons would violate a principle of customary international law that prohibited the use of weapons 'that cause severe damage to the environment'. Written Statement of the Government of Nauru of Sep 1994 (WHO), p 36; Written Comments of the Government of Nauru on other Written Statements of 15 Jun 1995 (WHO), Memorial I, p 11. Similarly: Written Comments of the Government of Nauru on other Written Statements of 15 Jun 1995 (WHO), Memorial II, p 2. Through: <http://www.icj-cij.org/>.

[594] India claimed that international humanitarian law contains among other things a 'prohibition against causing widespread, long term severe [*sic*] damage to the environment' which is one of the rules that are 'well established' and that find their 'sources in many of the classical instruments governing ius-in-bello'. It also stated that the principle of environmental security required that '[i]t is forbidden to use weapons that cause widespread, long-term and severe damage to the environment' and that '[t]he customary as well as conventional law of war prohibits the use of methods and means of war fare [*sic*] that may cause widespread, long-term and severe damage to the environment.' Written Comments of the Government of India on other Written Statements of 20 Jun 1995 (WHO), pp 6, 12. Through: <http://www.icj-cij.org/>.

[595] Samoa referred to the prohibition under customary and conventional law to use weapons that cause widespread, long-term and severe damage to the environment. 'Samoa considers that the use of nuclear weapons by a state in war or other armed conflict would be a violation of international customary law and conventions, including the Hague Conventions and the Geneva Conventions. Such law and conventions prohibit the use of weapons (. . .) which cause widespread, long-term and severe damage to the environment'. Written Statement of the Government of Samoa of 16 Sep 1994 (WHO), p 3. Through: <http://www.icj-cij.org/>.

[596] Zimbabwe stated before the Court that it shared the analysis of other states that the use of nuclear weapon would violate general principles of international humanitarian law that prohibited among other things the use of means or methods of warfare that 'cause long term and severe damage to the environment.' CR 95/35, Oral Plea of the Government of Zimbabwe, of 15 Nov 1995 (WHO and GA), p 27. Through: <http://www.icj-cij.org/>.

[597] And New Zealand, finally, stated first that according to customary law '[m]ethods and means of war *should* not cause widespread, long-term and severe damage to the environment.' Subsequently, however, New Zealand stated that one of the principles of international humanitarian law provided that 'parties to a conflict *must* not use methods or means of warfare which are intended or may be expected to cause widespread, long term and severe damage to the natural environment.' Written Statement of the Government of New Zealand of 20 Jun 1995 (GA), p 17, para 73 (emphasis added); CR 95/28, Oral Plea of the Government of New Zealand, of 9 Nov 1995 (WHO and GA), p 27. Through: <http://www.icj-cij.org/>.

[598] Henckaerts, Doswald-Beck (Eds), *Customary International Humanitarian Law; Vol I: Rules*, p 152, fns 55 and 56.

Rwanda, Sweden and Ukraine are inappropriate and legally not relevant. Australia merely referred to the incompatibility of weapons with potentially disastrous effects on the environment and the civilian population 'with the dictates of public conscience.'[599] Ecuador only stated that, because of their effects on the environment, the use of nuclear weapons would be contrary to humanitarian conditions that prohibit the destruction of the environment.[600] Sweden sent in a translation of some parts of the Annual Report on Disarmament by the Standing Committee on Foreign Affairs of the Swedish Parliament, which the Committee referred to the existence of an established basic principle that was expressed among other places in the 1972 Stockholm Declaration that 'there [were] impediments to the use of weapons which cause extensive, long-term and serious damage to the environment.'[601] Lesotho, the Marshall Islands, and Rwanda only made general references to international humanitarian law and the laws of war.[602] And finally, Ukraine only observed that in view of health and environmental effects, it was convinced that the use of nuclear weapons would violate obligations under international law in general.[603]

In conclusion, this means that, on the one hand, of the 43 states that commented upon both requests, only three states explicitly stated that Articles 35(3) and 55 had customary equivalents (Solomon Islands, Malaysia and Nauru); one state believed that only Article 55 had developed into customary law (Qatar); and four states insinuated that both provisions had a common customary equivalent (India, Samoa, Zimbabwe and New Zealand), of which one explicitly left it for the Court to decide whether this was indeed the case (New Zealand). On the other hand, three states adamantly denied the existence of customary counterparts of either pro-

[599] Henckaerts, Doswald-Beck (Eds), *Customary International Humanitarian Law; Vol II: Practice; Part 1*, p 887, para 223. CR 95/22, Oral Plea of the Government of Australia, of 30 Oct 1995 (WHO and GA), p 48, para 33. Through: <http://www.icj-cij.org/>. The ICRC erroneously referred to para 31 and combined two separate quotes by adding the phrase 'reflected in general principles of humanity'.

[600] Henckaerts, Doswald-Beck (Eds), *Customary International Humanitarian Law; Vol II: Practice; Part 1*, p 888, para 226. Written Statement of the Government of Ecuador of 20 Jun 1995 (GA), p 2, para D. Through: <http://www.icj-cij.org/>.

[601] Henckaerts, Doswald-Beck (Eds), *Customary International Humanitarian Law; Vol II: Practice; Part 1*, p 894, para 259. Written Statement of the Government of Sweden of Jun 1994 (WHO), p 5; Written Statement of the Government of Sweden of 20 Jun 1995 (GA), p 5. Through: <http://www.icj-cij.org/>.

[602] Henckaerts, Doswald-Beck (Eds), *Customary International Humanitarian Law; Vol II: Practice; Part 1*, respectively at p 891, para 247; p 892, para 248; p 892, para 253. Written Statement of the Government of Lesotho of 20 Jun 1995 (GA), p 2; Written Statement of the Government of the Marshall Islands of 22 Jun 1995 (GA), pp 3–4. Through: <http://www.icj-cij.org/>. The Written Statement of the Government of Rwanda is not available at <http://www.icj-cij.org/>.

[603] Henckaerts, Doswald-Beck (Eds), *Customary International Humanitarian Law; Vol II: Practice; Part 1*, p 894, para 261. Written Statement of the Government of the Ukraine of 16 May 1994 (WHO), p 1. Through: <http://www.icj-cij.org/>.

vision (the United Kingdom, the United States and France). The others remained silent on this issue.

The opposing sides are remarkably different from each other in terms of direct interests. The opponents of customary equivalents of Articles 35(3) and 55 represent three of the most powerful military nations of the world, each of which has continuously resisted and denied legal developments in this field. The proponents of customary development, on the other hand, include small island states in the Pacific Ocean that were represented before the Court by a number of western scholars and experts, known for their 'progressive' views on international law, with links to the non-governmental movement for the abolition of nuclear weapons. Be that as it may, the very limited number of states pronouncedly supporting the existence of a customary rule of law; the explicit opposition by some military powerful states and the silence of the vast majority of states together do not justify the conclusion that either or both provisions have resulted in any widespread practice accepted as law.

2.3.2.3.2.2 Emerging Custom

Although the previous examples of state practice do certainly not justify the conclusion that both Article 35(3) and 55 have developed into customary law, there are certainly indications that both provisions may be developing into rules of customary international law. These are, in the first place, the Preamble of the Certain Conventional Weapons Convention of 10 April 1981;[604] in the second place, the Secretary-General's Bulletin of 6 August 1999, on the 'Observance by United Nations forces of international humanitarian law';[605] in the third place, the Draft Code of Crimes against the Peace and Security of Mankind of 1996,[606] and the 1998 ICC Statute;[607] in the fourth place, the ICRC Guidelines of 1993 for 'Military Manuals and Instructions on the Protection of the Environment in Times of Armed Conflict'[608] that were

[604] Convention on Prohibitions or Restrictions on the Use of Certain Conventional Weapons Which May be Deemed To Be Excessively Injurious or To Have Indiscriminate Effects and Protocols, opened for signature on 10 Apr 1981, entered into force on 2 Dec 1983, UNTS, Vol 1342, No 22495.

[605] ST/SGB/1999/13, 6 Aug 1999, Secretary-General's Bulletin, on the observance by United Nations forces of international humanitarian law.

[606] Draft Code of Crimes Against the Peace and Security of Mankind, in: A/51/10, Report of the International Law Commission to the General Assembly on the work of its forty-eighth session (6 May–26 Jul 1996); Yearbook of the International Law Commission, 1996; Vol II, Pt II, United Nations, Geneva, 1998. Also through <http://www.un.org/law/ilc/>.

[607] Rome Statute of the International Criminal Court, opened for signature on 17 Jul 1998, entered into force 1 Jul 2002, UNTS, Vol 2187, No 38544.

[608] A/48/269, Report of the Secretary-General to the General Assembly on the Protection of the Environment in the Environment in Times of Armed Conflict, of 29 Jul 1993, with Annexed the ICRC Guidelines for Military Manuals and Instructions on the Protection of the Environment in Times of Armed Conflict; A/49/323, Report of the Secretary-General on the United Nations Decade of International Law, of 19 Aug 1994; Roberts, Guelff, *Documents on the Laws of War*, pp 609–14.

implicitly recognised by the United Nations General Assembly in 1994;[609] and in the fifth place, the ICRC Model Manual on the Law of Armed Conflict for Armed Forces of 1999.[610]

Firstly, the Preamble of the framework Convention on Certain Conventional Weapons contains an explicit reference to the protection of the environment in similar terminology as Additional Protocol I. In preambular paragraph 4, the High Contracting Parties recall:

> that it is prohibited to employ methods or means of warfare which are intended, or may be expected, to cause widespread, long-term and severe damage to the natural environment.

This is an obvious reference to Articles 35(3) and 55 of Additional Protocol I concluded just four years earlier and could indicate that the High Contracting Parties considered environmental protection in this context possibly as a nascent rule of customary international law. After all, preambles often reflect the object and purpose of a treaty and are generally considered as a useful source for interpretation of the operative text. It is not likely, however, that this reference implies anything more than concern for the environment and an expression of the desirability of a corresponding norm of customary law. Spieker concluded in this context in 1992 that the preambular paragraph and the limited environmental protection provided by Article 2(4) of the Incendiary Weapons Protocol contributes to the development of a customary environmental protection rule as far as practice is concerned, but that the preparatory works of the Convention do not show that the participating states were incited by a corresponding *opinio iuris*.[611]

Being concerned that this paragraph might indeed be (ab)used by proponents as evidence of a general practice accepted as law by the High Contracting Parties, France and the United States issued official statements with respect to this paragraph, neither of them being party to Additional Protocol I at the time. France stated in a reservation upon signature that it considered:

> the fourth paragraph of the preamble to the Convention (. . .) which reproduces the provisions of Article 35, paragraph 3, of Additional Protocol I, [applied] only to States parties to that Protocol.[612]

[609] A/Res/49/50, adopted without a vote on 9 Dec 1994, on the United Nations Decade of International Law, operative para 11. A/49/323, Report of the Secretary-General on the United Nations Decade of International Law, of 19 Aug 1994.

[610] APV Rogers,P Malherbe, *Fight it Right; Model Manual on the Law of Armed Conflict for Armed Forces*, International Committee of the Red Cross, ICRC, Geneva, 1999.

[611] Spieker, *Völkergewohnheitsrechtlicher Schutz der Natürlichen Umwelt im internationalen bewaffneten Konflikt; Waffenwirkung und Umwelt I*, pp 405–12, at 412.

[612] Through <http://untreaty.un.org/>. Also: Henckaerts, Doswald-Beck (Eds), *Customary International Humanitarian Law; Vol II: Practice; Part 1*, p 878.

The United States attached a declaration to its act of ratification stating that:

> the United States [considered] that the fourth paragraph of the Preamble to the Convention, which refers to the substance of provisions of Article 35(3) and Article 55(1) of additional Protocol I (. . .) [applied] only to States which have accepted those provisions.[613]

Meanwhile France has become party to Additional Protocol I[614] which leaves only the declaration of the United States as significant.

Secondly, the Bulletin of the Secretary-General of 6 August 1999, on the 'Observance by United Nations forces of international humanitarian law' contains a clear but implicit reference to the prohibition of Articles 35(3) and 55 of Additional Protocol I. Section 6.3. of the Bulletin which deals with 'Means and methods of combat' states:

> The United Nations force is prohibited from employing methods of warfare (. . .) which are intended, or may be expected to cause, widespread, long-term and severe damage to the natural environment.

The Bulletin's introduction suggests that it is based on customary international law by stating that it contains 'fundamental principles and rules of international humanitarian law', but this is not necessarily so. According to Zwanenburg, it appears, on the one hand, that not all customary rules of international humanitarian law were intended to be included in the Bulletin, while on the other hand, it must be presumed that several rules in the Bulletin are not rules of customary law at all. 'From the perspective of the content of the substantive rules', he writes, it looks as if it contains a 'summary of what were considered the most important rules in the context of peace support operations.'[615] Therefore, it is not certain whether the Bulletin's reference in Section 6.3 reflects customary international humanitarian law in the eyes of the Secretary-General and the experts involved in the drafting of the Bulletin. In any case, there is enough doubt surrounding the legal status of Section 6.3 for it to be considered as supporting evidence of the customary nature of the environmental protection provisions of Additional Protocol I.

[613] Through <http://untreaty.un.org/>. Also: Henckaerts, Doswald-Beck (Eds), *Customary International Humanitarian Law; Vol II: Practice; Part 1*, p 878.

[614] France ratified Additional Protocol I on 11 Apr 2001 and became a party on 11 Oct that same year. The declaration upon ratification dealing with the environment—declaration 6—only states that the risk of damage to the environment should be analysed objectively on the basis of information available at the time of appreciation. Through: <http://www.icrc.org/ihl.nsf/>.

[615] MC Zwanenburg, *Accountability under International Humanitarian Law for United Nations and North Atlantic Treaty Organization Peace Support Operations*, Doctoral Thesis, University of Leiden, EM Meijers Instituut, 2004, p 183. Later published as MC Zwanenburg, *Accountability of Peace Support Operations*, Martinus Nijhoff Publishers, Leiden, 2005.

Furthermore, the Bulletin has only internal application and does not necessarily reflect state practice accepted as law. According to Section 1.1(a) of the Secretary-General's Bulletin on 'Procedures for the Promulgation of Administrative Issuances' of 28 May 1997,[616] Bulletins of the Secretary-General are administrative documents, subject to amendment, and intended for United Nations staff members only. Section 2.2 states:

> Staff members at all levels shall be responsible for observing the provisions of administrative issuances promulgated in accordance with the present bulletin.

Since the Bulletin on the observance by United Nations forces of international humanitarian law does not seem to fall under the matters that require the issuance of a Secretary-General's Bulletin as enumerated in Section 3.1,[617] it is likely that this bulletin is 'promulgated in connection with [an] important decision of policy, as decided by the Secretary-General' as stated in Section 3.2. Administrative issuances from the Secretary-General are subsidiary instruments elaborating Staff Rules issued by the Secretary-General, which in turn elaborate Staff Regulations 'which embody the fundamental conditions of service and the basic rights, duties and obligations of the Secretariat.'[618]

Zwanenburg also refers in this context to the fact that the Bulletin is mainly intended as a teaching instrument 'to acquaint members of UN peace support operations with the principles and rules of international humanitarian law.'[619] He supports his argument by referring to a statement by the Secretary-General of September 1999 in which he refers to the bulletin as:

> instructing [United Nations forces] on the basic principles and rules governing means and methods of warfare and the protection of civilians and other protected persons.[620]

[616] ST/SGB/1997/1, 28 May 1997, Secretary-General's Bulletin, on procedures for the promulgation of administrative issuances.

[617] Section 3.1 states: 'The following matters shall require the issuance of a Secretary-General's bulletin: (a) Promulgation of rules for the implementation of regulations, resolutions and decisions adopted by the General Assembly, including: (i) Promulgation of financial regulations and rules and publication of consolidated texts thereof; (ii) Promulgation of staff regulations and rules and publication of consolidated texts thereof; (iii) Promulgation of regulations and rules governing programme planning, the programme aspects of the budget, the monitoring of implementation and the methods of evaluation, and publication of consolidated texts thereof; (b) Promulgation of regulations and rules, as required, for the implementation of resolutions and decisions adopted by the Security Council; (c) Organization of the Secretariat; (d) Establishment of specially funded programmes.'

[618] Zwanenburg, *Accountability under International Humanitarian Law for United Nations and North Atlantic Treaty Organization Peace Support Operations*, p 184.

[619] Zwanenburg, *Accountability under International Humanitarian Law for United Nations and North Atlantic Treaty Organization Peace Support Operations*, p 184.

[620] Zwanenburg, *Accountability under International Humanitarian Law for United Nations and North Atlantic Treaty Organization Peace Support Operations*, p 184, fn 195.

Thirdly, the 1996 ILC Draft Code of Crimes against the Peace and Security of Mankind and the 1998 Statute of the International Criminal Court both intend to prevent widespread, long-term and severe damage to the environment which is not justified by military necessity, by holding individuals criminally responsible for such results. The Draft Code provides in Article 20(g) that any individual is individually responsible for committing a crime against the peace and security of mankind when he uses in a systematic manner or on a large scale means or methods of warfare not justified by military necessity with the intent to cause widespread, long-term and severe damage to the natural environment and thereby gravely prejudice the health or survival of the population and such damage occurs. And in Article 8(2)(b)(iv), the Rome Statute holds anyone criminally responsible for committing a war crime in launching an attack in the knowledge that such attack will cause widespread, long-term and severe damage to the natural environment which would be clearly excessive in relation to the concrete and direct overall military advantage anticipated.

An earlier draft of the Code of Crimes against the Peace and Security of Mankind submitted by the ILC in 1991[621] contained a specific provision for individual criminal responsibility for violating an obligation not to commit acts described in Articles 35(3) and 55 Additional Protocol I.[622] Article 22(d) regarded the act of:

> employing methods or means of warfare which are intended or may be expected to cause widespread, long-term and severe damage to the natural environment

as an 'exceptionally serious war crime'. Article 22(d) was eventually dropped and reformulated into Article 20(g) of the final Draft of 1996.

The references to the same damage threshold as in Additional Protocol I in the Statute of the ICC and the Draft Code of 1996, as well as the exact reflection of the language of both provisions in Article 22(d) of the Draft Code of 1991 indicate that both provisions are gaining acceptance and are used as a source of inspiration with respect to the protection of the environment during international armed conflict. It could also indicate that they may be developing into rules of customary law, while keeping in mind that

621 A/46/10, Report of the International Law Commission to the General Assembly on the work of its forty-third session, 29 Apr to 19 Jul 1991; Yearbook of the International Law Commission, 1994; Vol II, Pt Two, United Nations, Geneva, 1994.

622 Commentary ILC to Art 22(d) Draft Code, in: A/46/10, Report of the International Law Commission to the General Assembly on the work of its forty-third session, 29 Apr to 19 Jul 1991; Yearbook of the International Law Commission, 1994; Vol II, Pt Two, United Nations, Geneva, 1994, para 9, p 106.

the references to military necessity[623] in both the Draft Code and in the Statute constitute a significant deviation of both Protocol I provisions.

Furthermore, in the course of drafting Article 20(g) of the 1996 Draft Code, there had been general agreement in the ILC's Drafting Committee that:

> in proposing such a provision, [the ILC] was engaged in progressively developing the law. For that reason, the opening clause of the subparagraph, contrary to the subparagraphs preceding it, did not speak of violations of international humanitarian law. The wording used, 'in the case of armed conflict', indicated that the provision was *lex ferenda*.[624]

One has to be very careful therefore to interpret these Articles as providing evidence of the customary nature of Articles 35(3) and 55.

Fourthly, the ICRC Guidelines for Military Manuals and Instructions on the Protection of the Environment in Times of Armed Conflict of 1993 also provide an indication that Articles 35(3) and 55 may in time develop into rules of customary international law. Principle 11 of the Guidelines states:

> Care shall be taken in warfare to protect and preserve the natural environment. It is prohibited to employ methods or means of warfare which are intended, or may be expected, to cause widespread, long-term and severe damage to the natural environment and thereby prejudice the health or survival of the population.[625]

Although, at first sight, the text seems to be literally taken from Article 55, it is actually a combination of Articles 55 and 35(3). The first sentence is derived from Article 55, although the verb 'to preserve' is new; the first part of the second sentence is a literal quotation of Article 35(3); and finally, the second part of the second sentence reflects the final part of Article 55(1).

The position of principle 11, among the other principles, is conspicuous and could be interpreted as an indication that the ICRC did not regard both provisions as rules of customary international law. In the first place,

[623] The military necessity clause was criticised during the deliberations in the International Law Commission. Summary Records of the 2448th meeting; Wednesday, 26 Jun 1996; Draft Code of Crimes against the Peace and Security of Mankind, in: A/CN.4/SER.A/1996, Yearbook of the International Law Commission, 1996; Vol I; Summary records of the meetings of the forty-eighth session 6 May–26 Jul 1996, United Nations, Geneva, 1998, pp 109–15.

[624] Calero Rodrigues (Chairman of the Drafting Committee) at the 2448th meeting of the International Law Commission on 26 Jun 1996. Summary Records of the 2448th meeting; Wednesday, 26 Jun 1996; Draft Code of Crimes against the Peace and Security of Mankind, in: A/CN.4/SER.A/1996, Yearbook of the International Law Commission, 1996; Vol I; Summary records of the meetings of the forty-eighth session 6 May–26 Jul 1996, United Nations, Geneva, 1998, para 14, p 109.

[625] This quotation is taken from the version that was included by the Secretary-General in his report on the United Nations Decade of International Law. A/49/323, Report of the Secretary-General on the United Nations Decade of International Law, of 19 Aug 1994, pp 49–53; Roberts, Guelff, *Documents on the Laws of War*, pp 609–14.

the principle is not included in the general principles of international law in section II of the Guidelines; and in the second place, principle 11 is only fourth in line in section III of the Guidelines on Specific Rules on the Protection of the Environment. The Guidelines first refer to the prohibition to destroy the environment not justified by military necessity; the prohibition to destroy civilian objects, unless justified by military necessity; and the prohibition of the indiscriminate laying of landmines.

Fifthly, and finally, the ICRC's Model Military Manual of 1999 contains a specific reference to the environment. Paragraph 702(g) on the Protection of the Natural Environment says:

> It is prohibited to employ methods or means of warfare which are intended, or may be expected, to cause widespread, long-term and severe damage to the environment and so prejudice the health or survival of the population.[626]

Although paragraph 702(g) clearly refers to Articles 35(3) and 55 Additional Protocol I, it is actually last in line; and there is no indication that the authors of the Manual might have considered this norm as a rule of customary international law.

2.3.2.3.2.3 Fundamentally Norm-Creating Character

It seems therefore that, by and large, there is no evidence of either widespread practice or *opinio iuris* with respect to a customary prohibition to use means and methods of warfare that are intended or expected to cause widespread, long-term and severe damage to the environment, and it is thus unlikely that Articles 35(3) and 55 of Additional Protocol I have already developed into rules of customary international law. Furthermore, although both provisions were new and unquestionably norm-creating, they should probably not be regarded as having a *fundamentally* norm-creating character. According to the International Court of Justice in the North Sea Continental Shelf Cases, it is necessary for a conventional rule to pass 'into the general *corpus* of international law' that it has 'at all events potentially, (. . .) a fundamentally norm-creating character.'[627] Although it is difficult to establish which rules do and which do not have such character, the opinion of international judicial bodies and law-promoting organs of international organisations may be indicative in this connection. Even though the Special ICTY Committee, established in 1999 to investigate NATO's bombing campaign over Kosovo, stated that Article 55 'may (. . .) reflect current customary law',[628] a number of authoritative

626 Rogers, Malherbe, *Fight it Right; Model Manual on the Law of Armed Conflict for Armed Forces*, pp 37–8.

627 North Sea Continental Shelf, Judgment, ICJ Reports 1969, p 3, para 71–2, pp 41–2.

628 ICTY, *Final Report to the Prosecutor by the Committee Established to Review the NATO Bombing Campaign against the Federal Republic of Yugoslavia*, International Legal Materials, Vol 39, 2000, p 1262.

statements by the General Assembly, the ICRC, and, most importantly, the International Court of Justice in the 1990s seem to point in a different direction.

Firstly, the General Assembly stated in the Preamble of its Resolution 47/37 of 25 November 1992 on the Protection of the Environment in Times of Armed Conflict that, contrary to the provisions applicable to the protection of the environment in times of international armed conflict in the Hague Regulations and Geneva Conventions, the applicable provisions in Additional Protocol I did not have universal applicability, and were therefore apparently not of customary nature.[629]

Secondly, the 1993 ICRC study, carried out upon the request of the Secretary-General, and subsequently submitted to the General Assembly by the Secretary-General, concluded that Articles 35(3) and 55 had not yet developed into rules of customary law.[630] It states in paragraph 34 that, because Protocol I did not cover all cases of damage to the environment and because not all states were party to it, the earlier conventions and customary rules remained very important. And in paragraph 38, it states that, although the provisions on environmental protection of Protocol I were binding for a majority of states, this did not apply to all of them.[631]

Thirdly, the International Court of Justice drew a similar conclusion in 1996 when discussing both provisions *in abstracto* in the Nuclear Weapons Opinion (GA).[632] After considering the legal relevance of the environment within the framework of the principles of necessity and proportionality, the Court noted with respect to Articles 35(3) and 55 that they provided additional protection for the environment and that they provided 'powerful constraints for all the States having subscribed to these provisions.'[633]

2.3.2.3.2.4 Literature and Experts

In literature, only a few authors have argued that both provisions reflected customary international law. Their argumentation is usually questionable, however, and otherwise unconvincing. Van Hegelsom, for example, writes in 1992 that Kalshoven had stated in a prior contribution that Article 35(3) had become a rule of customary law,[634] but this seems to be

[629] A/Res/47/37, adopted without a vote on 25 Nov 1992, on the protection of the environment in times of armed conflict, preambular para 2.

[630] A/48/269, Report of the Secretary-General to the General Assembly on the Protection of the Environment in the Environment in Times of Armed Conflict, of 29 Jul 1993.

[631] A/48/269, Report of the Secretary-General to the General Assembly on the Protection of the Environment in the Environment in Times of Armed Conflict, of 29 Jul 1993, p 7.

[632] Legality of the Threat or Use of Nuclear Weapons, Advisory Opinion, 8 Jul 1996, ICJ Reports 1996, p 226.

[633] Legality of the Threat or Use of Nuclear Weapons, Advisory Opinion, 8 Jul 1996, ICJ Reports 1996, p 226, para 31, p 242.

[634] GJF van Hegelsom, *Comments*, in: IF Dekker, HHG. Post (Eds), *The Gulf War of 1980–1988*, Martinus Nijhoff Publishers, Dordrecht, 1992, p 125.

an incorrect interpretation of Kalshoven's words. Kalshoven had only referred to the normative character of Article 35(3), but had acknowledged that it probably only had force as treaty law.[635] Gupta writes in 1993 with respect to Articles 35(3) and 55 that:

> '[a]lthough other sections of the Protocol are not universally recognized as part of customary law, the (. . .) provisions have generally been accepted as incorporated into customary international law';

but she does not submit any evidence except for referring to two other authors.[636] Sands believes in 1995 that the environmental protection provisions in Additional Protocol I:

> given the large number of parties and views expressed by states, may now reflect a rule of customary international law,[637]

without further evidence.

And Hulme, finally, concludes in 2004, after analysing state practice both before and after the Gulf war, that 'it is still a difficult task to judge the current status of Articles 35(3) and 55(1) of Protocol I' and that:

> it is <u>not</u> clear if the prohibition on environmental damage contained in Article 35(3) and/or 55(1) has attained customary status.[638]

She explains that before the Gulf War of 1990–1991, it is difficult to find sufficient state practice that justify a customary status;[639] while after the Gulf War, a number of references to environmental protection during international armed conflict can be found in a number of internationally relevant documents.[640] Hulme's examples, however, suffer from the fact that, although the references referred to do reflect concern for the environment, their terminology in part differs from the language of Articles 35(3) and 55 to justify regarding them as evidence of state practice accepted as law.

In addition, Judge Weeramantry concluded in his Dissenting Opinion in the Nuclear Weapons Opinion (GA) that Articles 35(3) and 55 were

[635] F Kalshoven, *Prohibitions or restrictions on the use of methods and means of warfare*, in: I.F. Dekker, HHG. Post (Eds), *The Gulf War of 1980–1988*, Martinus Nijhoff Publishers, Dordrecht, 1992, p 100, fn 18.

[636] S Gupta, *Iraq's Environmental Warfare in the Persian Gulf*, Georgetown International Environmental Law Review, Vol 6, 1993, p 260.

[637] P Sands, *Principles of international environmental law; Vol I; Frameworks, standards and implementation*, Cambridge University Press, Cambridge, 2003, p 314.

[638] Hulme, *War Torn Environment: Interpreting the Legal Threshold*, p 108.

[639] Hulme, *War Torn Environment: Interpreting the Legal Threshold*, p 104.

[640] Hulme refers to Security Council Resolution 687 of 1991, the Statute of the International Criminal Court of 1998, the ILC's Draft Arts on State Responsibility of 1996, the ILC's Draft Code of Crimes Against the Peace and Security of Mankind of 1996, the Secretary-General's Bulletin of 1999 on the observance of international humanitarian law by UN forces and the Report to the Prosecutor of the ICTY of 2000. Hulme, *War Torn Environment: Interpreting the Legal Threshold*, pp 105–7.

'undisputed principles of customary international law.'[641] And the ICRC concludes in its 2005 Study on Customary International Humanitarian Law that both provisions have achieved customary status. Rule 45 in Chapter 14 of the study on 'The Natural Environment' partly reads:

> The use of methods or means or warfare that are intended, or may be expected, to cause widespread, long-term and severe damage to the natural environment is prohibited.[642]

Rule 45 is based on Articles 35(3) and 55(1) of Additional Protocol I and although both provisions were new in 1977, according to the ICRC, 'since then, significant practice has emerged to the effect that this prohibition has become customary.'[643] The report claims furthermore that:

> [p]ractice, as far as methods of warfare (. . .) [is] concerned, shows a widespread, representative and virtually uniform acceptance of the customary law nature of the rule found in Articles 35(3) and 55(1) of Additional Protocol.[644]

Despite significant evidence to the contrary,[645] the ICRC concludes that both provisions have developed into rules of customary international law and regards France, the United Kingdom, and the United States as persistent objectors with respect to both rules and only 'as far as any use of nuclear weapons is concerned.'[646]

However, the view that Articles 35(3) and 55 have not yet developed into rules of customary international law is widely supported in literature. Greenwood, for example, writes in 1991 that:

> there is little or no subsequent practice which might have had the effect of incorporating the principle stated therein into customary law,

while observing that nevertheless the core of the principle of Article 35(3) 'may well reflect an emerging norm of international law.'[647] According to

[641] Dissenting Opinion of Judge Weeramantry, Legality of the Threat or Use of Nuclear Weapons, Advisory Opinion, 8 Jul 1996, ICJ Reports 1996, p 226, at p 505.

[642] Henckaerts, Doswald-Beck (Eds), *Customary International Humanitarian Law; Vol I: Rules*, p 151.

[643] Henckaerts, Doswald-Beck (Eds), *Customary International Humanitarian Law; Vol I: Rules*, p 152.

[644] Henckaerts, Doswald-Beck (Eds), *Customary International Humanitarian Law; Vol I: Rules*, p 154.

[645] The ICRC refers here to the statements made by the United States and the United Kingdom before the International Court of Justice during the Nuclear Weapons Cases; the statements of the ICJ in the Advisory Opinion on the Legality of the Threat or Use of Nuclear Weapons; the interpretative statements of France and the United States upon ratification of the Certain Conventional Weapons Convention; and the Final Report of the Committee Established to Review the NATO Bombing Campaign against the Federal Republic of Yugoslavia. Henckaerts, Doswald-Beck (Eds), *Customary International Humanitarian Law; Vol I: Rules*, pp 153–4.

[646] Henckaerts, Doswald-Beck (Eds), *Customary International Humanitarian Law; Vol I: Rules*, pp 154–5.

[647] Greenwood, *Customary Law Status of the 1977 Geneva Protocols*, in: Delissen, Tanja (Eds), *Humanitarian Law of Armed Conflict; Challenges Ahead; Essays in Honour of Frits Kalshoven*, p 105.

Bothe in the same year, it is 'somewhat doubtful' whether Articles 35(3) and 55 form part of customary international law.[648] Spieker implicitly concluded in 1992 that both provisions had not yet become full-fledged rules of customary international law, but a development into this direction was promoted by the Gulf War.[649] A Swedish Report from the Ministry of Foreign Affairs from 1992 concludes that 'the relevant Articles of Additional Protocol I did not reflect customary rules at the time of the Gulf War.'[650] Verwey maintains in various contributions on the subject published in the early 1990s that there is general agreement that both provisions have not yet developed into customary international law, *e.g.* in view of large number of states that at that time had not become party to Additional Protocol I.[651] In the late 1990s, also Schmitt believes that the better view with respect to Articles 35(3) and 55 is that, although there may be an operational code with respect to environmental protection 'it is premature to assert that customary law in the classic sense has solidified.'[652] And Dinstein dismisses all claims of customary nature in 2001[653] and again in 2004 stating that 'the relevant Protocol's clauses have not yet crystallized as customary international law'.[654]

2.3.2.4 The CCWC and the Statute of the International Criminal Court

Finally, as far as the Certain Conventional Weapons Convention is concerned, it is unlikely that the references to the protection of the

[648] Bothe, *The Protection of the Environment in Times of Armed Conflict; Legal Rules, Uncertainty, Deficiencies, and Possible Developments,* p 56.

[649] Spieker, *Völkergewohnheitsrechtlicher Schutz der Natürlichen Umwelt im internationalen bewaffneten Konflikt; Waffenwirkung und Umwelt I,* pp 458–9.

[650] Quoted by Lijnzaad, Tanja, *Protection of the Environment in Times of Armed Conflict: The Iraq-Kuwait War,* p 182.

[651] Verwey, *Observations on the Legal Protection of the Environment in Times of International Armed Conflict,* p 39; Verwey, *Protection of the Environment in Times of Armed Conflict: In Search of a New Legal Perspective,* p 15; Verwey, *Comment: Protection of the Environment in Times of Armed Conflict—Do We Need Additional Rules?,* in: Grunawalt, King, McClain, *Protection of the Environment during Armed Conflict,* p 563.

[652] Schmitt, *Green War: An Assessment of the Environmental Law of International Armed Conflict,* p 76.

[653] Dinstein, *Protection of the Environment in International Armed Conflict,* in: Frowein, Wolfrum (Eds), *Max Planck Yearbook of United Nations Law,* pp 534–5.

[654] Dinstein, *The Conduct of Hostilities under the Law of International Armed Conflict,* pp 185, 193. Compare, in addition to the authors referred to: Green, *The Environment and the Law of Conventional Warfare,* p 232; Kalshoven, *Prohibitions or restrictions on the use of methods and means of warfare,* in: Dekker, Post (Eds), *The Gulf War of 1980–1988,* p 100, fn 18; McNeill, *Protection of the Environment in Times of Armed Conflict: Environmental Protection in Military Practice,* p 81; Oeter, *Methods and Means of Combat,* in: Fleck (Ed), *The Handbook of Humanitarian Law in Armed Conflicts,* p 118; Schmitt, *Humanitarian Law and the Environment,* p 268, fn 16; Schmitt, *War and the Environment: Fault Lines in the Prescriptive Landscape,* in: Austin, Bruch (Eds), *The Environmental Consequences of War,* p 93; Simonds, *Conventional Warfare and Environmental Protection: A Proposal for International Legal Reform,* p 177; Tarasofsky, *Legal Protection of the Environment during International Armed Conflict,* p 41.

environment during armed conflict in its Preamble and in Article 2(4) of the Incendiary Weapons Protocol may be taken as reflecting customary international law.[655] In view of the legislative history of the Convention and its Protocol, it is hardly conceivable that it was either considered declaratory of pre-existing customary international law, or that it has meanwhile developed into rules of customary international law.

It is not unlikely, on the other hand, that Article 8(2)(b)(iv) of the Statute of the International Criminal Court reflects customary international law, as will be discussed in the following paragraph.

2.3.3 Other Customary Rules Directly Protecting the Environment

2.3.3.1 Introduction

In addition, it is possible that perhaps other rules of customary law related to direct environmental protection have come into existence. In view of the lack of interest of the international community of states in the environment in the past, it is highly unlikely that rules of customary international law directly protecting the environment during armed conflict existed before the 1970s. Certainly, there were some rules before the 1970s that did protect the environment to a certain extent, but they did so more by accident than by intention and would therefore have to be considered as indirect protection. Indirect protection of the environment will be discussed in a subsequent paragraph.

As has been explained above, it is arguable that in the 1970s a new fundamental principle of *ius in bello* has emerged in addition to the principles of necessity and humanity, namely the principle of environmental protection or responsibility. Stemming from a general and worldwide concern for the protection of the environment, which is reflected in the 1972 Stockholm Declaration,[656] this principle has given rise to a number of environmental protection provisions in the laws of war, and it may have generated the development of customary international law, independent of the specific treaty provisions.

In the first place, it is arguable that a general customary duty of care for the environment during armed conflict has emerged. This appears from the development of international regulations protecting the environment in general and from repeated expressions of concern that will be discussed below, in particular. In the second place, it is not unlikely that, in view of

[655] Compare Dinstein, *Protection of the Environment in International Armed Conflict*, in: Frowein, Wolfrum (Eds), *Max Planck Yearbook of United Nations Law*, p 537; Dinstein, *The Conduct of Hostilities under the Law of International Armed Conflict*, p 187.

[656] A/CONF.48/14/Rev1, Report of the United Nations Conference on the Human Environment, Stockholm, 5–16 Jun 1972, Declaration of the United Nations Conference on the Human Environment, United Nations, New York, 1973, pp 3–5.

the frequent references to the principles of necessity, distinction, and proportionality within the context of environmental protection during international armed conflict, these principles have found new manifestations in the form of two new rules of customary international law: a prohibition to cause wanton or willful damage to the environment not justified by military necessity, and a prohibition to cause excessive collateral damage to the environment. The former is a reflection of the principle of necessity, in particular the principle of distinction or discrimination and is similar to the customary prohibition:

> to destroy or seize the enemy's property, unless such destruction or seizure be imperatively demanded by the necessities of war,

as laid down in Article 23(g) of the Hague Regulations of 1899 and 1907.[657] The latter is also a reflection of the principle of necessity, more particularly the principle of proportionality, and is related to the meanwhile customary prohibition embodied in Article 51(5)(b) Additional Protocol I, to launch:

> an attack which may be expected to cause incidental loss of civilian life, injury to civilians, damage to civilian objects, or a combination thereof, which would be excessive in relation to the concrete and direct military advantage anticipated.[658]

As has already been explained in section 1, it is arguable that the principles of distinction and proportionality ultimately find their origin in

[657] The prohibition has also been recognised in Art 53 of Geneva Convention (IV) relative to the Protection of Civilian Persons in Time of War of 1949 and in Art 48 of Additional Protocol I of 1977. Art 48 AP I states: 'In order to ensure respect for and protection of the civilian population and civilian objects, the Parties to the conflict shall at all times distinguish between the civilian population and combatants and between civilian objects and military objectives and accordingly shall direct their operations only against military objectives.' Violation of both provisions partly entails individual criminal responsibility. Art 147 of the Convention states that 'extensive destruction and appropriation of property, not justified by military necessity and carried out unlawfully and wantonly' is considered a grave breach. And in addition, Art 85(3)(a) regards 'making the civilian population or individual civilians the object of attack' a grave breach 'when committed wilfully, in violation of the relevant provisions of this Protocol, and causing death or serious injury to body or health'. More recently, the individual criminal responsibility was confirmed in the Statutes of the International Criminal Tribunal for the Former Yugoslavia and the International Criminal Court (Art 8(2)(a)(iv) and in Arts 20(a)(iv) and 20(e)(ii) of the Final Draft Code of Crimes against the Peace and Security of Mankind of 1996.

[658] According to Dinstein, in the past 'once an attack was directed at an indisputable military objective, any unavoidable injury or damage cause to civilians or civilian objects was accepted as 'collateral damage'.' Dinstein, *The Conduct of Hostilities under the Law of International Armed Conflict*, p 119. Failure to refrain from launching an indiscriminate attack which may be expected to cause excessive collateral damage is considered a grave breach of the Protocol according to Art 85(3)(b) AP I and has been branded a war crime in the Statute of the International Criminal Court.

the principle of necessity.[659] The Contracting Parties to the Declaration of St Petersburg of 1868[660] believed that:

> the only legitimate object which States should endeavour to accomplish during war is to weaken the military forces of the enemy

and that for that purpose it was 'sufficient to disable the greatest possible number of men'. This seems to reflect the purpose and the 'necessities of war',[661] which inherently entails distinction between military and civilian objects and limitation of collateral damage.

This development shows exactly the practical dynamics of principles of *ius in bello*. As has been explained above, it is preferable to regard the principles of necessity, humanity, environmental protection, and necessity's sub-principles of distinction, and proportionality as cornerstones and framework norms from which specific rules of the law of armed conflict are derived. Principles have the ability to incorporate new perspectives, new practice, and new concerns into the laws of war.

2.3.3.2 Duty of Care

Probably sufficient evidence exists to support the conclusion that a customary duty of care for the environment during international armed

[659] Compare also Oeter who writes: 'Flowing from the general principle of "limited warfare" (limited to what is militarily absolutely necessary in order to achieve the military objectives) several sub-principles have developed historically, giving the rule of military necessity its specific contours.' These sub-principles are, according to Oeter, the principle of discrimination and the prohibition of unnecessary suffering; the principle of proportionality is regarded as a supplement to the principle of necessity. Oeter, *Methods and Means of Combat*, in: Fleck (Ed), *The Handbook of Humanitarian Law in Armed Conflicts*, pp 112, 112–14. Also Schmitt, *Green War: An Assessment of the Environmental Law of International Armed Conflict*, p 55. The ICRC Report that was submitted by the Secretary-General to the General Assembly seems to indicate a similar relationship between necessity and proportionality where it refers to the 'Balance between protection of the environment and military necessity (including the principle of proportionality'. A/48/269, Report of the Secretary-General to the General Assembly on the Protection of the Environment in the Environment in Times of Armed Conflict, of 29 Jul 1993, p 14. Compare, however, with respect to the relationship between proportionality and the other principles Rogers and Schmitt, who believe that the principle of proportionality is a balancing test between military and humanitarian interests. Rogers, *Law on the Battlefield*, p 17 and Schmitt, *War and the Environment: Fault Lines in the Prescriptive Landscape*, in: Austin, Bruch (Eds), *The Environmental Consequences of War*, p 103. Dinstein, on the other hand, rightly rejects any link between the principle of unnecessary suffering and thus the principle of humanity and the principle of proportionality. Dinstein, *The Conduct of Hostilities under the Law of International Armed Conflict*, p 59.

[660] St Petersburg Declaration Renouncing the Use, in Time of War, of Explosive Projectiles Under 400 Grammes Weight, signed on 11 Dec 1868, entered into force on 11 Dec 1868, AJIL, Vol 1, No 2, Supplement: Official Documents, 1907, p 95.

[661] Compare Simonds' definition of the principle of necessity, based on United States military manuals and Nuremberg case law. '[T]he principle of necessity justifies measures not forbidden by international law which are indispensable for securing the prompt submission of the enemy with the least possible loss of economic and human resources.' Simonds, *Conventional Warfare and Environmental Protection: A Proposal for International Legal Reform*, p 169.

conflict has developed since the early 1970s.[662] International concern for the environment appears from several conventions on the law of armed conflict concluded since 1977, general principles proclaimed by various United Nations conferences on the environment, and a number of General Assembly Resolutions. National concern for the environment appears from references in military manuals, model manuals drafted by the ICRC and the Institute of International Humanitarian Law, and from statements made by official state representatives, both within and outside the framework of the United Nations.

It is arguable that a duty of care appears from each of the treaty provisions that have been concluded since 1977 with respect to the protection of the environment during international armed conflict. This is most explicitly reflected in the first sentence of Article 55(1) of Additional Protocol I: '*Care* shall be taken in warfare to protect the natural environment against widespread, long-term and severe damage' (emphasis added).

Evidence of a customary duty of care for the environment during armed conflict also appears from the final declarations adopted by four United Nations conferences on the environment, held at regular intervals since 1972. Although such declarations are non-binding, they are nevertheless influential, considering the fact that a large majority of states supported them.

Firstly, principle 26 of the Stockholm Declaration that concluded the United Nations Conference on the Human Environment in 1972,[663] states: 'Man and his environment must be spared the effects of nuclear weapons and all other means of mass destruction. (. . .).'[664]

Secondly, the United Nations General Assembly proclaimed in paragraph 5 of its World Charter for Nature of 1982[665] that '[n]ature shall be secured against degradation caused by warfare or other hostile activities.' This statement is one of the five 'general principles' recognised by the General Assembly and must be implemented, according to paragraph 20, by an obligation to avoid all military activities that are damaging to

662 This duty of care would stem directly from the fundamentally principle of environmental protection or responsibility which arguably emerged during the 1970s and which has shaped the laws of war.

663 A/CONF.48/14/Rev 1, Report of the United Nations Conference on the Human Environment, Stockholm, 5–16 Jun 1972, Declaration of the United Nations Conference on the Human Environment, United Nations, New York, 1973, pp 3–5. The Report was taken note of with satisfaction by the General Assembly by A/Res/2994 (XXVII), adopted on 15 Dec 1972, by 112 to 0, with 10 abstentions; United Nations Conference on the Human Environment.

664 Compare also para 6 of the first of the Declaration, in which the Conference proclaims that 'A point has been reached in history when we must shape our actions throughout the world with a more prudent care for their environmental consequences. Through ignorance or indifference we can do massive and irreversible harm to the earthly environment on which our life and well-being depend.'

665 A/Res/37/7, adopted on 28 Oct 1982, by 111 to 1, with 18 abstentions; World Charter for Nature; Annex: World Charter for Nature.

nature. The World Charter for Nature was drafted by an Ad Hoc Group of Experts established by the Secretary-General in the early 1980s and submitted to the General Assembly in 1982.[666]

Thirdly, also the Rio Declaration on Environment and Development of 1992[667] seems to imply a general duty of care for the environment during armed conflict. Principle 24 states:

> Warfare is inherently destructive of sustainable development. States shall therefore respect international law providing protection for the environment in times of armed conflict and cooperate in its further development, as necessary.

Although not expressly referring to a duty of care, the Declaration expresses an obligation to observe existing obligations and calls upon states to face their responsibilities and duties with respect to the environment. In addition, the Conference's program of action provides in paragraph 39.6:

> Measures in accordance with international law should be considered to address, in times of armed conflict, large-scale destruction of the environment that cannot be justified under international law.[668]

The appropriate forum for this would be the United Nations General Assembly, in particular its Sixth Committee, while taking into account the specific supporting role of the ICRC.

This Declaration was the final proclamation of the United Nations Conference on Environment and Development (UNCED), adopted 10 years after the World Charter for Nature and 20 years after the Stockholm Conference. The General Assembly had decided to convene UNCED in 1989[669] following the Report of the World Commission on Environment and

[666] See for the use of Resolutions of the intergovernmental organisations as evidence of customary international law: Military and Paramilitary Activities in and against Nicaragua (Nicaragua v United States of America), Merits, Judgment, 27 Jun 1986, ICJ Reports 1986, p 14, paras 188–205, pp 99–108. According to the Arbitrator in the 1977 Texaco Case, the legal value of General Assembly Resolutions depends on the circumstances of their adoption, in particular the voting conditions, and the contents of the provisions involvEd Texaco Overseas Petroleum Company and California Asiatic Oil Company v The Government of the Libyan Arab Republic; Dupuy, Sole Arbitrator; Arbitral Award on the Merits, 19 Jan 1977, in: H Lauterpacht (Ed), *International Law* Reports, Vol 53, Grotius Publications Limited, Groningen, Cambridge, 1979, pp 483–95.

[667] A/CONF.151/26/Rev 1 (Vol I), Report of the United Nations Conference on Environment and Development, Rio de Janeiro, 3–14 Jun 1992, Vol I, Resolutions Adopted by the Conference; Resolution 1, Adoption of Texts on Environment and Development; Annex I, Rio Declaration on Environment and Development, United Nations, New York, 1993, pp 3–8.

[668] A/CONF.151/26/Rev 1 (Vol I), Report of the United Nations Conference on Environment and Development, Rio de Janeiro, 3–14 Jun 1992, Vol I, Resolutions Adopted by the Conference; Resolution 1, Adoption of Texts on Environment and Development; Annex II, Agenda 21, United Nations, New York, 1993, p 471.

[669] A/Res/44/228, adopted without a vote on 22 Dec 1989; United Nations Conference on Environment and Development.

Development entitled 'Our Common Future',[670] also known as the Brundtland Report. Both the Report and the Declaration were endorsed by the General Assembly.[671]

And fourthly, the Final Declaration of the third and most recent general conference on the environment, the World Summit on Sustainable Development, held in Johannesburg from 2 to 4 September 2002,[672] merely hints at the existence of a duty of care. Paragraph 19 in the Declaration's section on commitments to sustainable development says:

> We reaffirm our pledge to place particular focus on, and give priority attention to, the fight against the worldwide conditions that pose severe threats to the sustainable development of our people, which include[s]: (. . .) armed conflict.[673]

In addition, international concern for the environment was expressed by the United Nations General Assembly, most specifically in Resolution 56/4 of 5 November 2001,[674] in which it declared 6 November the 'International Day for Preventing the Exploitation of the Environment in War and Armed Conflict'.[675] The Assembly referred to the Millennium Declaration of 8 September 2000,[676] that had emphasised the necessity of safeguarding nature for future generations and considered that:

> damage to the environment in times of armed conflict impairs ecosystems and natural resources long beyond the period of conflict, and often extends beyond the limits of national territories and the present generation.

National concern for the protection of the environment appears from references in military manuals, and from statements made by official state representatives. Examples of the latter will be discussed further below; examples of the former are the United States Commander's Handbook on the Law of Naval Operations and the British Military Manual in the context of air operations. While the Dutch and the German military manuals

[670] A/42/427, Report of the World Commission on Environment and Development, of 4 Aug 1987. The Brundtland Report was welcomed with appreciation by the General Assembly by A/Res/42/187, adopted without a vote on 11 Dec 1987; Report of the World Commission on Environment and Development.

[671] A/Res/47/190, adopted without a vote on 22 Dec 1992; Report of the United Nations Conference on Environment and Development.

[672] A/CONF.199/20, Report of the World Summit on Sustainable Development, Johannesburg, South Africa, 26 Aug–4 Sep 2002, Resolution 1; Annex: Johannesburg Declaration on Sustainable Development United Nations, New York, 2002, pp 1–5.

[673] The Report of the World Summit was taken note of with satisfaction and the Johannesburg Declaration was endorsed by the by the General Assembly by A/Res/57/253, adopted without a vote on 21 Feb 2003; World Summit on Sustainable Development.

[674] A/Res/56/4, adopted without a vote on 5 Nov 2001; Observance of the International Day for Preventing the Exploitation of the Environment in War and Armed Conflict.

[675] 6 Nov 2001 marked the 10th anniversary of the extinguishing of the last oil well fire in Kuwait. WJ Hybl, Representative of the United States, in Press Release GA/9946 of 5 Nov 2001, through <http://www.unis.unvienna.org/>.

[676] A/Res/55/2, adopted without a vote on 8 Sep 2000; Millennium Declaration.

limit themselves to repeating their contractual obligations under ENMOD and Additional Protocol I, which in itself may be taken to reflect consciousness of a duty of care for the environment, the US and British military manuals are the only manuals that explicitly refer to a duty of care. The US Naval Handbook of 1995 prescribes that:

> as far as military requirements permit, methods or means of warfare should be employed with due regard to the protection and preservation of the natural environment.[677]

The British Military Manual similarly recognises as a basic rule for air operations that:

> [m]ethods and means of warfare should be employed with due regard for the natural environment, taking into account the relevant rules of international law.[678]

Although 'due regard'[679] may not be identical to a duty of care, both terms are no doubt related.[680]

Similarly, the 1994 San Remo Manual on International Law Applicable to Armed Conflicts at Sea,[681] prepared by international lawyers and naval experts, as well as the 1999 ICRC Model Military Manual refer to a duty of care for the environment during armed conflict. Both manuals are generally considered as influential.[682] The latter provides in paragraph 702(c): 'In the conduct of military operations, care must be taken to spare the environment.'[683] The former contains three references to a duty of care. Firstly, paragraph 44 states that:

> [m]ethods and means of warfare should be employed with due regard for the natural environment taking into account the relevant rules of international law.

Secondly, paragraph 11 provides:

> The parties to the conflict are encouraged to agree that no hostile actions will be conducted in marine areas containing: (a) rare or fragile ecosystems; *or* (b) the habitat of depleted, threatened or endangered species or other forms of marine life.

677 NWP 1-14M, *The Commander's Handbook on the Law of Naval Operations*, p 8–2.

678 UK Ministry of Defence, *The Manual of the Law of Armed Conflict*, para 12.24, p 315.

679 According to Schmitt, '"due regard" is a familiar concept in maritime law and practicc.' Schmitt, *Green War: An Assessment of the Environmental Law of International Armed Conflict*, p 34.

680 According to *Black's Law Dictionary*, 'due regard' means '[c]onsideration in a degree appropriate to demands of the particular case.' Black (et al), *Black's Law Dictionary*, p 347.

681 San Remo Manual on International Law Applicable to Armed Conflicts at Sea, in: International Review of the Red Cross, Nov-Dec, No 309, 1995, and in: Roberts, Guelff, *Documents on the Laws of War*, pp 574–606.

682 It should be noted that the San Remo Manual is believed to reflect 'the law which is currently applicable'. Introductory Note, San Remo Manual on International Law Applicable to Armed Conflicts at Sea, in: International Review of the Red Cross, Nov-Dec, No 309, 1995, and in: Roberts, Guelff, *Documents on the Laws of War*, p 574.

683 Rogers, Malherbe, *Fight it Right; Model Manual on the Law of Armed Conflict for Armed Forces*, p 37.

Paragraph 11 is included in Section IV of the Manual on Areas of Naval Warfare and expresses concern for the environment by encouraging belligerents to pay due regard to the environment by agreeing that no military action is taken in certain areas.[684] And thirdly, principle 46(c) provides that:

> they shall furthermore take all feasible precautions in the choice of methods and means in order to avoid or minimize collateral casualties or damage.

According to principle 13(c), 'collateral damage' includes 'damage to or the destruction of the natural environment'.

Further evidence of state practice at the national level is provided by public statements made by official representatives, both within and outside the framework of international organisations. An example of the latter is provided by a memorandum of 12 July 1991 from the Legal Bureau of the Department of External Affairs of Canada, stating:

> The customary laws of war, in reflecting the dictates of public conscience, now include a requirement to avoid unnecessary damage to the environment. This includes consideration of environmental effects in the planning of military operations.[685]

Although Mawhinney warns that the:

> statements of law and practice should not necessarily be regarded as a definitive statement by the Department of External Affairs of that law or practice,

the memorandum is nonetheless indicative of recognition of the existence of a duty of care for the environment during armed conflict.

Examples of public statements made by official representatives within the framework of international organisations are provided by a number of comments made before the International Court of Justice in the context of both Advisory Opinions on the use of nuclear weapons (WHO and GA) in 1994 and 1995. Sri Lanka referred to the protection of the environment as an established principle of international law,[686] while Iran, Sweden, and New Zealand explicitly expressed a concern for the environment during armed conflict.[687] The statements by Costa Rica, Egypt, Malaysia, Mexico,

[684] Such agreements resemble the agreements referred to in Art 60 of Additional Protocol I to establish so-called 'demilitarized zones'.

[685] Canadian Department of External Affairs, Legal Bureau, *Memorandum; 12 Jul 1991; Armed Conflict and the Environment*, in: B Mawhinney (Ed), *Canadian Practice in International Law; At the Department of External Affairs in 1991–92*, The Canadian Yearbook of International Law, Vol XXX, 1992, p 347.

[686] Written Statement of the Government of Sri Lanka of the Summer of 1994 (WHO), p 3. Through: <http://www.icj-cij.org/>.

[687] Written Statement of the Government of the Islamic Republic of Iran of 19 Jun 1995 (GA), p 4; Written Statement of the Government of Sweden of Jun 1994 (WHO), p 5; Written Statement of the Government of Sweden of 20 Jun 1995 (GA), p 5; Written Statement of the Government of New Zealand of 20 Jun 1995 (GA), pp 17–18. Through: <http://www.icj-cij.org/>.

Qatar and the Solomon Islands that the ICRC refers to in this context in its 2005 Study[688] predominantly refer to the protection of the environment in general.

Moreover, a number of states claimed the existence of a general customary principle of 'environmental security' or 'safety' which would supposedly combine elements of both international environmental law and the law of armed conflict.[689] Although their claim did not receive much support from other states commenting on either request[690] and was not recognised by the International Court of Justice, it seems to confirm the existence of a third fundamental principle of *ius in bello*—the principle of environmental protection—which has arguably shaped the laws of war since the 1970s, in addition to the principles of necessity and humanity.

Finally, the existence of a duty of care with respect to the environment seems to be confirmed by the International Court of Justice in its 1996 Advisory Opinion on the Legality of the Threat or Use of Nuclear Weapons submitted upon request of the General Assembly.[691] Commenting on the relevance of international environmental law with respect to the use of nuclear weapons, the Court stated that:

> States must take environmental considerations into account when assessing what is necessary and proportionate in the pursuit of legitimate military objectives. Respect for the environment is one of the elements that go to assessing whether an action is in conformity with the principle proportionality.[692]

In paragraph 32, the Court refers to:

> the general view according to which environmental considerations constitute one of the elements to be taken into account in the implementation of the principles of the law applicable in armed conflict[693]

[688] Henckaerts, Doswald-Beck (Eds), *Customary International Humanitarian Law; Vol I: Rules*, p 148, fn 32; Henckaerts, Doswald-Beck (Eds), *Customary International Humanitarian Law; Vol II: Practice; Part 1*, respectively at p 862, para 87; p 862, para 88; p 865, para 97; p 865, para 98; p 865, para 102; and p 864, para 103.

[689] These were Nauru, Malaysia, India, and Iran. Written Statement of the Government of Nauru of Sep 1994 (WHO), Memorial I, pp 36–45; Memorial III, pp 22–3; Written Comments of the Government of Nauru on other Written Statements of 15 Jun 1995 (WHO), Memorial II, pp 27–8; Written Statement of the Government of Malaysia of Sep 1994 (WHO), pp 10–11; Written Comments of the Government of Malaysia on other Written Statements of 19 Jun 1995 (WHO), pp 27–9; Written Comments of the Government of India on other Written Statements of 20 Jun 1995 (WHO), pp 12–13; Written Statement of the Government of India of 20 Jun 1995 (GA), p 5; CR 95/26, Oral Pleas of the Governments of the Islamic Republic of Iran, of 6 Nov 1995 (WHO and GA), pp 35–6. Through: <http://www.icj-cij.org/>.

[690] The claim was even explicitly rejected by some states. CR 95/34, Oral Plea of the Government of the United States of America, of 15 Nov 1995 (WHO and GA), pp 65–6. Through: <http://www.icj-cij.org/>.

[691] Legality of the Threat or Use of Nuclear Weapons, Advisory Opinion, 8 Jul 1996, ICJ Reports 1996, p 226.

[692] Legality of the Threat or Use of Nuclear Weapons, Advisory Opinion, 8 Jul 1996, ICJ Reports 1996, para 30, p 242.

[693] Legality of the Threat or Use of Nuclear Weapons, Advisory Opinion, 8 Jul 1996, ICJ Reports 1996, para 32, p 242.

and observes in paragraph 33:

> The Court thus finds that while the existing international law relating to the protection and safeguarding of the environment does not specifically prohibit the use of nuclear weapons, it indicates important environmental factors that are properly to be taken into account in the context of the implementation of the principles and rules of the law applicable in armed conflict.[694]

The 'environmental considerations' and the 'important environmental factors' that need to be taken into account in assessing whether or not a certain course of action is allowed under international law suggest the existence of a general duty of care for the environment.

The International Committee of the Red Cross seems to have come to a similar conclusion in its 2005 Study on customary international humanitarian law. Rule 44 says:

> Methods and means of warfare must be employed with due regard to the protection and preservation of the natural environment. In the conduct of military operations, all feasible precautions must be taken to avoid, and in any event to minimise, incidental damage to the environment. (. . .).[695]

The ICRC observes that over the last few decades the international community of states has expressed concern about the degradation of the environment, and has developed rules to protect it.[696]

References in literature are generally scarce. Although authors usually recognise international concern for the environment during armed conflict in general, only Greenwood, Heintschel von Heinegg and Donner, and Hulme refer to a duty of care. Greenwood wrote in 1996 that:

> customary international law is widely considered to include (. . .) a requirement that a belligerent show due regard for the protection of the environment,

but he only refers to the US Navy's Commander's Handbook on Naval Operations to support this claim.[697] Heintschel von Heinegg and Donner refer to the condition that:

[694] Legality of the Threat or Use of Nuclear Weapons, Advisory Opinion, 8 Jul 1996, ICJ Reports 1996, para 33, p 243.

[695] Henckaerts, Doswald-Beck (Eds), *Customary International Humanitarian Law; Vol I: Rules*, p 147.

[696] In addition to most of the items discussed above, the ICRC found evidence in a number of military manuals, such as Australia's Defence Force Manual and South Korea's Operational Law Manual and general condemnations and public statements going back all the way to the early 1970s. Henckaerts, Doswald-Beck (Eds), *Customary International Humanitarian Law; Vol I: Rules*, pp 147–8; Henckaerts, Doswald-Beck (Eds), *Customary International Humanitarian Law; Vol II: Practice; Part 1*, pp 861–7.

[697] C Greenwood, *State Responsibility and Civil Liability for Environmental Damage Caused by Military Operations*, in: RJ Grunawalt, JE King, RS McClain (Eds), *Protection of the Environment during Armed Conflict*, International Law Studies 1996, Vol 69, Naval War College, Newport, RI, 1996, p 399.

> so far as military requirements permit, methods and means of naval warfare should be employed with due regard to the environment.[698]

And Hulme recently recognised the existence of a general duty of care for the environment during armed conflict. Where she does not rule out the possibility of Articles 35(3) and 55(1) having developed into rules of customary international law, she is confident that 'the environment as an entity has become recognised as something worthy of protection in time of armed conflict.' Therefore:

> all states when making military decisions must now recognise the basic customary obligation to have regard to protection of the environment. For state parties, this customary obligation may correspond with that contained in the first sentence of Article 55(1) of Protocol I.[699]

2.3.3.3 Prohibition of Wanton Destruction of and Excessive Collateral Damage to the Environment during Armed Conflict

2.3.3.3.1 Introduction

In addition to the possible existence of an admittedly rather abstract, or perhaps even illusive duty of care for the environment during armed conflict, it is not unlikely that from the principle of necessity and its sub-principles of distinction and proportionality two new customary rules of international law have developed.[700] The International Court of Justice hinted at this possibility when it stated in general terms that:

> States must take environmental considerations into account when assessing what is necessary and proportionate in the pursuit of legitimate military objectives. Respect for the environment is one of the elements that go to assessing whether an action is in conformity with the principles of necessity and proportionality.[701]

In the first place, this would be the prohibition of wanton or willful destruction of the environment not justified by military necessity, ie the prohibition to attack the environment as such without military justification; in the second place, this would be the prohibition to cause disproportionate or excessive collateral damage to the environment. Although these customary rules are strongly related to the well-known customary prohibitions to willfully and wantonly destroy property and to cause

[698] Heintschel von Heinegg, Donner, *New Developments in the Protection of the Natural Environment in Naval Armed Conflicts*, p 294.

[699] Hulme, *War Torn Environment: Interpreting the Legal Threshold*, p 108.

[700] It is likely that this development has been influence by the principle of environmental protection which arguably emerged in the 1970s in addition to the fundamental principles of necessity and humanity.

[701] Legality of the Threat or Use of Nuclear Weapons, Advisory Opinion, 8 Jul 1996, ICJ Reports 1996, p 226, at p 242, para 30.

excessive collateral damage to civilian objects and property, both rules are new and must be distinguished in view of their specific focus on the environment.[702]

Evidence of the existence of both new customary prohibitions that directly protect the environment is of relatively recent origin and can be found in international legal instruments, national legal instruments, and influential documents. Both rules are strongly related and are often mentioned together. Therefore, the evidence for their existence found in public statements and in literature will be discussed together (sections 2.3.3.3.4 and 2.3.3.3.6); the evidence found in international instruments and military manuals warrant separate discussion (sections 2.3.3.3.2 and 2.3.3.3.3).

2.3.3.3.2 The Prohibition of Wanton Destruction of the Environment

As far as the prohibition of willful or wanton destruction of the environment is concerned, strong evidence is provided by General Assembly Resolution 47/37 of 25 November 1992,[703] the Assembly's first resolution that specifically dealt with the protection of the environment in times of armed conflict. Adopted without a vote, it stresses in preambular paragraph 5:

> that destruction of the environment, not justified by military necessity and carried out wantonly, is clearly contrary to existing international law.

Although the resolution implies that this was already a generally accepted notion in international law, this statement found recognition and implicit confirmation by members of the International Law Commission[704] and by the International Court of Justice in its 1996 Nuclear Weapons Advisory Opinion (GA). In paragraph 32 the Court refers to Resolution 47/37 quoting preambular paragraph 5 and stating that the Resolution:

[702] It should be noted that it is not uncommon to relate new crimes to the prohibition of wanton destruction. In 1945, the drafters of the Charter of the International Military Tribunal at Nuremberg included in Art 6(b) the crime of 'devastation' that would involve individual criminal responsibility. The crime of devastation was obviously related to the prohibition to destroy property under Art 23(g) of the Hague Regulations and customary international law, but the crime itself was not limited to any specific object. Art 6(b) read: '*War crimes*: namely, violations of the laws or customary of war. Such violations shall include, but not be limited to (. . .) plunder of public or private property, wanton destruction of cities, towns or violates, or devastation not justified by military necessity.'

[703] A/Res/47/37, adopted without a vote on 25 Nov 1992, on the protection of the environment in times of armed conflict. The discussions in the Sixth Committee that preceded adoption of this resolution will be discussed further below.

[704] Rosenstock at the 2448th meeting of the International Law Commission on 26 Jun 1996. Summary Records of the 2448th meeting; Wednesday, 26 Jun 1996; Draft Code of Crimes against the Peace and Security of Mankind, in: A/CN.4/SER.A/1996, Yearbook of the International Law Commission, 1996; Vol I; Summary records of the meetings of the forty-eighth session 6 May–26 Jul 1996, United Nations, Geneva, 1998, para 26, pp 110–11.

> affirms the general view according to which environmental considerations constitute one of the elements to be taken into account in the implementation of the principles of the law applicable in armed conflict.[705]

Further evidence of this new customary prohibition can be found in the object and purpose of Article 2(4) of the Incendiary Weapons Protocol.[706] Article 2(4) states that in principle:

> [i]t is prohibited to make forests or other kinds of plant cover the object of attack by incendiary weapons except when such natural elements are used to cover, conceal or camouflage combatants or other military objectives, or are themselves military objectives.

Attack of forests and plant cover without military justification is similar to wanton or willful destruction and can therefore be regarded as an early indication of a new customary prohibition based on the principle of necessity.

Additional support can be found in the discussions related to the preparation of the Draft Code of Crimes against the Peace and Security of Mankind in the International Law Commission. Firstly, an early draft from 1991[707] stipulated that:

> [a]n individual who wilfully causes or orders the causing of widespread, long-term and severe damage to the natural environment shall, on conviction thereof, be sentenced [to . . .].[708]

Secondly, a special Working Group of the ILC, established in 1996 under the chairmanship of Tomuschat and dealing with the issue of willful and severe damage to the environment, also produced three draft proposals[709] two of

[705] Legality of the Threat or Use of Nuclear Weapons, Advisory Opinion, 8 Jul 1996, ICJ Reports 1996, p 242.

[706] Protocol on Prohibitions or Restrictions on the Use of Incendiary Weapons (Protocol III) to the Convention on Prohibitions or Restrictions on the Use of Certain Conventional Weapons Which May be Deemed To Be Excessively Injurious or To Have Indiscriminate Effects, opened for signature on 10 Apr 1981, entered into force on 2 Dec 1983, UNTS, Vol 1342, No 22495.

[707] A/46/10, Report of the International Law Commission to the General Assembly on the work of its forty-third session, 29 Apr to 19 Jul 1991; Yearbook of the International Law Commission, 1994; Vol II, Pt Two, United Nations, Geneva, 1994.

[708] 1991 Draft Code; Art 26. Please note that Art 26 is not limited to armed conflict and therefore also covers willful damage to the environment in peacetime. According to Mikulka at the 2430th meeting of the International Law Commission on 17 May 1996, the '[c]onsideration of the question outside the framework of armed conflicts would be a purely academic and speculative exercise, for the existence of such a crime in peace time [is] quite hypothetical.' Summary Records of the 2430th meeting; Friday, 17 May 1996; Draft Code of Crimes against the Peace and Security of Mankind, in: A/CN.4/SER.A/1996, Yearbook of the International Law Commission, 1996; Vol I; Summary records of the meetings of the forty-eighth session 6 May–26 Jul 1996, United Nations, Geneva, 1998, pp 11–12.

[709] ILC(XLVIII)/DC/CRD.3. The text of this document was supposed to be reproduced in Yearbook of the International Law Commission, 1996; Vol II, Part I. Unfortunately, Part I has been forthcoming since 1998 and may never be published despite having an ISBN and a UN Sales Number: ISBN: 92-1-133598-1; Sales No: E.98.V.9.

which referred to willful damage.[710] And thirdly, the Final Draft Code of 1996[711] considers in Article 20(g) the systematic or large-scale use of:

> methods or means of warfare not justified by military necessity with the intent to cause widespread, long-term and severe damage to the natural environment and thereby gravely prejudice the health or survival of the population and such damage occurs

as crimes against the peace and security of mankind entailing individual criminal responsibility.

Although none of the draft Articles specifically prohibits wanton destruction of the environment, not justified by military necessity, all Articles contain elements thereof. The choice for the word 'willful' in the early proposals as well as the inclusion of a military necessity exception in the final draft, certainly suggests that the drafters were inspired by the principle of military necessity and the customary prohibition to willfully or wantonly destroy property.

Further evidence of the existence of the customary prohibition under discussion can also be found at the national level, particularly in military manuals. The United States' Commander's Handbook on the Law of Naval Operations states in section 8.1.3 that '[d]estruction of the natural environment not necessitated by mission accomplishment and carried out wantonly is prohibited.'[712] And the British Military Manual similarly accepts as a basic rule for air operations that '[d]amage to or destruction of the natural environment not justified by military necessity and carried out wantonly is prohibited.'[713]

In addition, there are a few influential yet non-binding sources that provide supportive evidence. Firstly, the 1994 San Remo Manual on International Law Applicable to Armed Conflicts at Sea states in paragraph 44 not only that '[m]ethods and means of warfare should be employed with

[710] These were firstly, a proposal for a crime against the environment within the framework of an article on war crimes (draft Art 22(2)(a)(iii)(*bis*)). Secondly, a proposal for a crime against the environment within the framework of crimes against humanity (draft Art 21(2)(h)(*bis*)). And thirdly, a proposal for an autonomous crime against the environment (draft Art 26). Summary Records of the 2430th meeting; Friday, 17 May 1996; Draft Code of Crimes against the Peace and Security of Mankind, in: A/CN.4/SER.A/1996, Yearbook of the International Law Commission, 1996; Vol I; Summary records of the meetings of the forty-eighth session 6 May–26 Jul 1996, United Nations, Geneva, 1998, pp 11–12. According to Tomuschat, the Working Group believed that the time was not yet ripe for 'declaring attacks on nature as such crimes against the peace and security of mankind' and adopted therefore a more anthropocentric approach. C Tomuschat, *Crimes Against the Environment*, Environmental Policy & Law, Vol 26, 1996, p 243.

[711] A/51/10, Report of the International Law Commission to the General Assembly on the work of its forty-eighth session (6 May–26 Jul 1996); Yearbook of the International Law Commission, 1996; Vol II, Part II, United Nations, Geneva, 1998. Also through <http://www.un.org/law/ilc/>.

[712] NWP 1-14M, *The Commander's Handbook on the Law of Naval Operations*, p 8–2.

[713] UK Ministry of Defence, *The Manual of the Law of Armed Conflict*, para 12.24, p 315.

due regard for the natural environment', but also that '[d]amage to or destruction of the natural environment not justified by military necessity and carried out wantonly is prohibited.'[714] Secondly, principle 8 of the 1993/1994 ICRC Guidelines for Military Manuals and Instructions on the Protection of the Environment in Times of Armed Conflict provides: 'Destruction of the environment not justified by military necessity violates international humanitarian law.'[715] Principle 8 is listed as the first and apparently most basic principle in Section III of the Guidelines on 'Specific Rules on the Protection of the Environment'. Thirdly, the ICRC's Model Military Manual of 1999 provides in paragraph 702(b) that '[t]he environment as such may not be attacked' and in paragraph 702(d) that '[d]amage which is not militarily necessary may not be inflicted.'[716]

And finally, the existence of a customary rule that directly protects the environment by prohibiting the willful and wanton destruction of the environment, not justified by military necessity, is also confirmed by the ICRC in its 2005 Study on Customary International Humanitarian Law. The ICRC concludes in Customary Rule 43:

> The general principles on the conduct of hostilities apply to the natural environment: A. No part of the natural environment may be attacked, unless it is a military objective. B. Destruction of any part of the natural environment is prohibited, unless required by imperative military necessity.[717]

According to the ICRC, rule 43 is an established norm of customary international law, evidence for which it finds in treaties and other international instruments, national practice, practice of intergovernmental organisations and conferences, practice of international judicial and quasi-judicial bodies and practice of the International Red Cross and Red Crescent Movement, and other practice.[718]

714 San Remo Manual on International Law Applicable to Armed Conflicts at Sea, in: International Review of the Red Cross, Nov-Dec, No 309, 1995, and in: Roberts, Guelff, *Documents on the Laws of War*, pp 574–606.

715 This quotation is taken from A/49/323, Report of the Secretary-General on the United Nations Decade of International Law, of 19 Aug 1994, p 50; Roberts, Guelff, *Documents on the Laws of War*, p 610. The original 1993 ICRC Guidelines provided in principle 8: 'The natural environment is not a legitimate object of attack. Destruction of the environment not justified by military necessity may be punishable as a violation of international law'. A/48/269, Report of the Secretary-General to the General Assembly on the Protection of the Environment in the Environment in Times of Armed Conflict, of 29 Jul 1993, with Annexed the ICRC Guidelines for Military Manuals and Instructions on the Protection of the Environment in Times of Armed Conflict, p 25.

716 Rogers, Malherbe, *Fight it Right; Model Manual on the Law of Armed Conflict for Armed Forces*, p 37.

717 Henckaerts, Doswald-Beck (Eds), *Customary International Humanitarian Law; Vol I: Rules*, p 143. Compare also customary Rule 45 which provides: 'Destruction of the natural environment may not be used as a weapon.'

718 Henckaerts, Doswald-Beck (Eds), *Customary International Humanitarian Law; Vol II: Practice; Part 1*, pp 844–59.

2.3.3.3.3 Prohibition of Excessive Collateral Damage to the Environment

As far as evidence for the existence of a customary prohibition of excessive collateral damage to the environment is concerned, strong evidence is provided by the formulation of Article 8(2)(b)(iv) of the 1998 Statute of the International Criminal Court.[719] This provision recognises as a war crime the launching of an attack:

> in the knowledge that such attack will cause incidental loss of life or injury to civilians or damage to civilian objects or widespread, long-term and severe damage to the natural environment which would be clearly excessive in relation to the concrete and direct overall military advantage anticipated.

Until 1998, international law had not specifically regarded damage to the environment as a war crime entailing individual criminal responsibility, but in view of growing concern for the environment in general and for the environment during international armed conflict in particular, especially after the 1990–1991 Gulf War, the drafters of the Statute thought it necessary to include an environmental clause in the Statute. Although they were clearly inspired by Articles 35(3) and 55 of Additional Protocol I, they decided not to incorporate a paragraph that literally reflected these provisions. Instead, they were embedded in the general obligation to prevent excessive damage while launching an attack, which stems from the principles of necessity and distinction, in particular the principle of proportionality and is generally recognised as one of the fundamental customary rules of the law of armed conflict. The obligation has been codified in Article 51(5)(b) of Additional Protocol I and violation of this obligation involves individual criminal responsibility under Article 85(3) of Additional Protocol I.

Although the addition of the environment to the proportionality obligation is new, and although no direct individual criminal responsibility for damage to the environment was recognised before 1998, the *chapeau* of Article 8(2)(b) seems to suggest that this paragraph finds its basis in pre-existing rules of international law. The *chapeau* of Article 8(2) paragraph (b) reads:

> For the purpose of this statute, "war crimes" means: (. . .) Other serious violations of the laws and customs applicable in international armed conflict, within the established framework of international law.

The 'established framework of international law' includes both conventional and customary international law and the word 'established' seems to

[719] As of Nov 2005, the Statute has 100 States Parties. Through <http://untreaty.un.org/> and <http://www.icc-cpi.int/>. For the relationship between individual and collective or state responsibility, see: A Nollkaemper, *De dialectiek tussen individuele en collectieve aansprakelijkheid in het volkenrecht*, Inaugural lecture, Vossiuspers AUP, Amsterdam, 2000.

exclude the possibility of progressive development. This is confirmed by the United Kingdom that declared upon ratification of the Statute that it:

> understands the term "the established framework of international law", used in Article 8(2)(b) and (e), to include customary international law as established by State practice and opinio iuris.[720]

This would then mean that the individual criminal responsibility for launching attacks that cause widespread, long-term and severe damage to the environment that is clearly excessive in relation to the military advantage anticipated within the framework of the principle of proportionality reflects customary international law. Article 8(2)(b)(iv) was generally accepted by the Diplomatic Conference and none of the current 100 States Parties has adopted an interpretative declaration questioning the legal validity of an environmental war crime clause in Article 8(2)(b)(iv) of the Statute.

Furthermore, evidence can also be found at the national level, such as in the United States Commander's Handbook on the Law of Naval Operations. The United States is not party to Additional Protocol I and decided on 6 May 2002 not to ratify the Statute of the International Criminal Court. Nevertheless, Section 8.1.3 of its 1995 Navy Handbook acknowledges that:

> [i]t is not unlawful to cause collateral damage to the natural environment during an attack upon a legitimate military objective. However, the commander has an affirmative obligation to avoid unnecessary damage to the environment to the extent that it is practicable to do so consistent with mission accomplishment.[721]

Also, the 1994 San Remo Manual on International Law Applicable to Armed Conflicts at Sea,[722] the 1993 ICRC Guidelines,[723] and the 1999 ICRC Model Manual on the Law of Armed Conflict[724] presume the existence of a customary prohibition to cause excessive collateral damage to the environment. Since they reflect the views of internationally recognised experts, they are widely considered influential. Firstly, the San Remo Manual stipulates in paragraph 46(d) that:

[720] Declaration upon ratification by the United Kingdom of Great Britain and Northern Ireland of the Statute of the International Criminal Court, through <http://untreaty.un.org/>.

[721] NWP 1-14M, *The Commander's Handbook on the Law of Naval Operations*, p 8–2.

[722] San Remo Manual on International Law Applicable to Armed Conflicts at Sea, in: International Review of the Red Cross, Nov-Dec, No 309, 1995, and in: Roberts, Guelff, *Documents on the Laws of War*, pp 574–606.

[723] A/48/269, Report of the Secretary-General to the General Assembly on the Protection of the Environment in the Environment in Times of Armed Conflict, of 29 Jul 1993, with Annexed the ICRC Guidelines for Military Manuals and Instructions on the Protection of the Environment in Times of Armed Conflict.

[724] APV Rogers,P Malherbe, *Fight it Right; Model Manual on the Law of Armed Conflict for Armed Forces*, International Committee of the Red Cross, ICRC, Geneva, 1999.

> an attack shall not be launched if it may be expected to cause collateral casualties or damage which would be excessive in relation to the concrete and direct military advantage anticipated from the attack as a whole; an attack shall be cancelled or suspended as soon as it becomes apparent that the collateral casualties or damage would be excessive.[725]

According to paragraph 13(c), collateral damage also includes 'damage to or the destruction of the natural environment'.

Secondly, the ICRC Guidelines contain indications that the principle of proportionality has inspired the development of a new customary rule protecting the environment. Principle 4 states:

> In addition to the specific rules set out below, the general principles of international law applicable in armed conflict—such as the principle of distinction and the principle of proportionality—provide protection to the environment. In particular, only military objectives may be attacked and no methods or means of warfare which cause excessive damage shall be employed. Precautions shall be taken in military operations as required by international law.[726]

And thirdly, the 1999 ICRC Model Manual contains two paragraphs that imply a prohibition of excessive damage to the environment. Paragraph 702(e) provides:

> When attacking a military objective, methods or means should be chosen which, commensurate with military success, cause the least environmental damage.

Paragraph 702(f) provides: 'Any environmental damage caused must be proportionate to the military objective to be attained.'[727]

Finally, the prohibition of excessive collateral damage to the environment is confirmed by the Committee that was established by the Prosecutor of the ICTY to review the NATO bombing campaign against the Federal Republic of Yugoslavia in 1999, and by the ICRC in its 2005 Study on Customary International Humanitarian Law. After concluding that the effects of the bombing campaign can best be 'considered from the underlying principles of the law of armed conflict such as necessity and proportionality', the former states:

> Even when targeting admittedly legitimate military objectives, there is a need to avoid excessive long-term damage to the economic infrastructure and natural environment with a consequential adverse effect on the civilian population. Indeed, military objectives should not be targeted if the attack is likely to cause

[725] The Manual further contains collateral damage prohibitions in principles 51(d), 52(d) and 57(d).

[726] This quotation is taken from the version that was included by the Secretary-General in his report on the United Nations Decade of International Law. A/49/323, Report of the Secretary-General on the United Nations Decade of International Law, of 19 Aug 1994, pp 49–53; Roberts, Guelff, *Documents on the Laws of War*, pp 609–14.

[727] Rogers, Malherbe, *Fight it Right; Model Manual on the Law of Armed Conflict for Armed Forces*, p 37.

> collateral environmental damage which would be excessive in relation to the direct military advantage which the attack is expected to produce.[728]

The latter concludes in Customary Rule 43:

> The general principles on the conduct of hostilities apply to the natural environment: (. . .) C. Launching an attack against a military objective which may be expected to cause incidental damage to the environment which would be excessive in relation to the concrete and direct military advantage anticipated is prohibited.[729]

According to the ICRC, rule 43 is an established norm of customary international law, the evidence for which can be found in a large number of authoritative instruments.[730]

2.3.3.3.4 Public Statements

Evidence for the existence of both customary status of both propositions can also be found in a number of public statements made by governmental representatives, both within and outside the framework of intergovernmental organisations. Examples of unilateral statements are a memorandum from the Canadian Department of External Affairs in 1991 and a memorandum from a United States official in 1987. The former held:

> The customary laws of war, in reflecting the dictates of public conscience, now include a requirement to avoid unnecessary damage to the environment.[731]

The latter concerned a statement by the Legal Deputy of the United States Department of State in 1987 that although Article 55 was 'too broad and too ambiguous for effective use in military operations' it would still be possible that:

[728] ICTY *Final Report to the Prosecutor by the Committee Established to Review the NATO Bombing Campaign against the Federal Republic of Yugoslavia*, International Legal Materials, Vol 39, 2000, paras 15 and 18, pp 1262–3.

[729] Henckaerts, Doswald-Beck (Eds), *Customary International Humanitarian Law; Vol I: Rules*, p 143.

[730] Henckaerts, Doswald-Beck (Eds), *Customary International Humanitarian Law; Vol II: Practice; Pt 1*, pp 844–59.

[731] Canadian Department of External Affairs, Legal Bureau, *Memorandum; 12 Jul 1991; Armed Conflict and the Environment*, in: B Mawhinney (Ed), *Canadian Practice in International Law; At the Department of External Affairs in 1991–92*, The Canadian Yearbook of International Law, Vol XXX, 1992, p 347. Although the memo statements may not be necessarily regarded as statements from Canada, they are nevertheless indicative. Canadian Department of External Affairs, Legal Bureau, *Memorandum; 12 Jul 1991; Armed Conflict and the Environment*, in: B Mawhinney (Ed), *Canadian Practice in International Law; At the Department of External Affairs in 1991–92*, The Canadian Yearbook of International Law, Vol XXX, 1992, p 347.

> the means and methods of warfare that have such a severe effect on the natural environment so as to endanger the civilian population may be inconsistent with the other general principles, such as the rule of proportionality.[732]

Examples of comparable public statements made within the framework of intergovernmental organisations, were made in the course of the debates held in the Sixth Committee of the General Assembly in 1991 and 1992 and in written and oral statements made before the International Court of Justice in connection with the two Nuclear Weapons Opinions (WHO and GA) in 1994 and 1995. The discussions in the Sixth Committee in 1991 and 1992 were instigated by a proposal from Jordan for inclusion of an agenda item on the 'Exploitation of the Environment as a Weapon in Times of Armed Conflict and the taking of Practical Measures to Prevent Such Exploitation'.[733] The proposal was triggered by the 1990–1991 Gulf War that had had 'an impact of tragic proportions' on the environment and that had revealed that the existing regulations for the protection of the environment were inadequate. In view of the narrow scope of the original title, the item was later changed upon instigation from Jordan into 'Protection of the Environment in Times of Armed Conflict'.[734] The discussion eventually led to the adoption of General Assembly Resolution 47/37[735] discussed above.

During the discussions that took place in New York in 1991 and in 1992, a number of states discussed the damage inflicted upon the environment by Iraq by reference to the principles of necessity and proportionality. Canada,[736] the United States,[737] Iran,[738] and the ICRC (as

[732] Remarks of Matheson at *Session One: The United States Position on the Relation of Customary International Law to the 1977 Protocols Additional to the 1949 Geneva Conventions*, in: Dupuis, Heywood, Sarko, *The Sixth Annual American Red Cross—Washington College of Law Conference on International Humanitarian Law: A Workshop on Customary International Law and the 1977 Protocols Additional to the 1949 Geneva Conventions*, p 436.

[733] A/46/141, 8 Jul 1991, Request for the inclusion of an additional item in the provisional agenda of the forth-sixth session; Exploitation of the Environment as a Weapon in Times of Armed Conflict and the Taking of Practical Measures to Prevent Such Exploitation; Annex: Explanatory Memorandum.

[734] A/C.6/46/SR.18, Summary Record of the 18th meeting of the Sixth Committee of the General Assembly on 22 Oct 1991, p 3, para 10; A/C.6/46/L.13, Draft Decision proposed by the Chairman of the 6th Committee of the General Assembly of 21 Nov 1991.

[735] A/Res/47/37, adopted without a vote on 25 Nov 1992, on the protection of the environment in times of armed conflict.

[736] A/C.6/46/SR.18, Summary Record of the 18th meeting of the Sixth Committee of the General Assembly on 22 Oct 1991, p 4, para 12 and in particular para 14; A/C.6/47/SR.8, Summary Record of the 8th meeting of the Sixth Committee of the General Assembly on 1 Oct 1992, p 6, para 20.

[737] A/C.6/46/SR.18, Summary Record of the 18th meeting of the Sixth Committee of the General Assembly on 22 Oct 1991, pp 8–9, paras 36–7; A/C.6/47/SR.9, Summary Record of the 9th meeting of the Sixth Committee of the General Assembly on 6 Oct 1992, p 11, paras 50–1.

[738] A/C.6/46/SR.18, Summary Record of the 18th meeting of the Sixth Committee of the General Assembly on 22 Oct 1991, p 6, para 27 and pp 6–7, para 28. The Iranian representative also stated that for a number of reasons, 'his delegation was convinced that there were well-established rules of both customary and treaty law which held a party to a conflict responsible for unnecessary damage to the environment' A/C.6/46/SR.18, Summary Record of the 18th meeting of the Sixth Committee of the General Assembly on 22 Oct 1991, pp 7–8, para 32.

observer),[739] were most outspoken in their statements. Australia,[740] Austria,[741] Jordan,[742] Nepal,[743] the Netherlands on the behalf of the European Community,[744] New Zealand,[745] and Russia,[746] also provided comments. Other states referred to customary international law containing norms protecting the environment, without referring to the principles of necessity and proportionality.[747]

Canada stated, for example:

> In effect, the practice of States, generally accepted environmental principles and public consciousness about the environment had combined with the traditional armed conflict rules on the protection of civilians and their property to produce a customary rule of armed conflict prohibiting the infliction of unnecessary damage on the environment in wartime.[748]

And one year later, it said:

> An important evolution was thus taking place which reflected the importance of the ecological point of view and which should be brought to bear on other questions, such as that of proportionality (the need to strike a balance between the protection of the environment and the needs of war) or that of the distinction between military and non-military objectives. Under the same principle, the environment as such should not be the object of direct attack, and his delegation

[739] A/C.6/46/SR.18, Summary Record of the 18th meeting of the Sixth Committee of the General Assembly on 22 Oct 1991, p 11, para 49; A/C.6/47/SR.8, Summary Record of the 8th meeting of the Sixth Committee of the General Assembly on 1 Oct 1992, p 3, para 7.

[740] A/C.6/46/SR.20, Summary Record of the 20th meeting of the Sixth Committee of the General Assembly on 24 Oct 1991, p 3, para 7.

[741] A/C.6/46/SR.19, Summary Record of the 19th meeting of the Sixth Committee of the General Assembly on 23 Oct 1991, p 3, para 5; A/C.6/47/SR.8, Summary Record of the 8th meeting of the Sixth Committee of the General Assembly on 1 Oct 1992, p 9, para 37.

[742] A/C.6/46/SR.18, Summary Record of the 18th meeting of the Sixth Committee of the General Assembly on 22 Oct 1991, pp 2–3, para 5, without referring explicitly to necessity.

[743] A/C.6/46/SR.20, Summary Record of the 20th meeting of the Sixth Committee of the General Assembly on 24 Oct 1991, p 8, para 28. Only reference to the violation of customary law by Iraq.

[744] A/C.6/46/SR.20, Summary Record of the 20th meeting of the Sixth Committee of the General Assembly on 24 Oct 1991, p 2, para 1, implicitly.

[745] A/C.6/46/SR.20, Summary Record of the 20th meeting of the Sixth Committee of the General Assembly on 24 Oct 1991, p 6, para 18.

[746] A/C.6/47/SR.9, Summary Record of the 9th meeting of the Sixth Committee of the General Assembly on 6 Oct 1992, p 4, para 16.

[747] These were Uruguay, the United Arab Emirates and Brazil. A/C.6/46/SR.20, Summary Record of the 20th meeting of the Sixth Committee of the General Assembly on 24 Oct 1991, pp 7–8, para 26 and p 12, para 47; A/C.6/47/SR.9, Summary Record of the 9th meeting of the Sixth Committee of the General Assembly on 6 Oct 1992, p 3, para 12.

[748] A/C.6/46/SR.18, Summary Record of the 18th meeting of the Sixth Committee of the General Assembly on 22 Oct 1991, p 4, para 14. Also in: Canadian Department of External Affairs, Legal Bureau, *Memorandum; 12 Jul 1991; Armed Conflict and the Environment*, in: B Mawhinney (Ed), *Canadian Practice in International Law; At the Department of External Affairs in 1991–92*, The Canadian Yearbook of International Law, Vol XXX, 1992, p 347.

> would like to see that point reflected in the resolution to be adopted after discussion of the item.[749]

Japan, on the other hand, stated that it was important that the Sixth Committee discussed this item:

> while bearing in mind that legal rules aimed at protecting the environment had not yet been established under customary international law.[750]

And Sweden stated that the acts of destruction perpetrated by Iraq had been clear violations of customary and treaty law, but:

> the existing rules of international law were not without shortcomings in that they did not make specific reference to environmental damage.[751]

Also before the International Court of Justice a number of states recognised the protection of the environment under customary law by reference to the principles of necessity and proportionality. These were Egypt,[752] India,[753] Ireland,[754] the Marshall Islands,[755] Nauru,[756] New Zealand,[757] the Solomon Islands,[758] the United States[759] and Iran. Iran, for example, stated that:

> [a]s far as the law of armed conflict is concerned, both the customary rules and the provisions of treaty law prohibit belligerent parties, directly or indirectly, from inflicting unnecessary damage on the environment. Parties to the armed conflict are obliged, in accordance with well-established rules of customary law pertaining to armed conflict, to protect the environment in time of armed

[749] A/C.6/47/SR.8, Summary Record of the 8th meeting of the Sixth Committee of the General Assembly on 1 Oct 1992, p 6, para 20.

[750] A/C.6/46/SR.20, Summary Record of the 20th meeting of the Sixth Committee of the General Assembly on 24 Oct 1991, p 5, para 16.

[751] A/C.6/46/SR.20, Summary Record of the 20th meeting of the Sixth Committee of the General Assembly on 24 Oct 1991, pp 6–7, para 22.

[752] Written Comments of Egypt on other Written Statements of Sep 1995 (GA), pp 22–4, in particular paras 53 and 55. Through: <http://www.icj-cij.org/>.

[753] Written Statement of the Government of India of Jun 1994 (WHO), p 2. Through: <http://www.icj-cij.org/>.

[754] Written Statement of the Government of Ireland of Jun 1994 (WHO), p 1, para 2. Through: <http://www.icj-cij.org/>.

[755] CR 95/32, Oral Plea of the Government of the Marshall Islands, of 14 Nov 1995 (WHO and GA), pp 23–4. Through: <http://www.icj-cij.org/>.

[756] Written Statement of the Government of Nauru of Sep 1994 (WHO), p 36. According to Nauru, the environment enjoyed protection as a 'civilian object' by the customary rule of proportionality. Also: Written Comments of the Government of Nauru on other Written Statements of 15 Jun 1995 (WHO), pp 17–18. Through: <http://www.icj-cij.org/>.

[757] Written Statement of the Government of New Zealand of 20 Jun 1995 (GA), p 17, fn 70. Through: <http://www.icj-cij.org/>.

[758] Written Statement of the Government of the Solomon Islands of 10 Jun 1994 (WHO), p 52, para 3.50. Written Statement of the Government of the Solomon Islands of 20 Jun 1995 (GA), p 55, para 3.63. Through: <http://www.icj-cij.org/>.

[759] CR 95/34, Oral Plea of the Government of the United States of America, of 15 Nov 1995 (WHO and GA), pp 70–1. Through: <http://www.icj-cij.org/>.

conflict. These rules include proportionality and the prohibition on military operations not directed against legitimate military targets, as well as the prohibition of destruction of enemy property not imperatively demanded by the necessities of war.[760]

2.3.3.3.5 Damage Standard

As regards the scope of environmental damage, it is not impossible that customary international law requires a certain level of environmental damage. Often reference is made to the triple standard of Articles 35(3) and 55 of Additional Protocol I, and it is plausible that the same or a similar standard applies to the customary prohibition of wanton or excessive collateral damage to the environment.

Both international instruments and national statements regularly refer to 'widespread, long-term and severe' damage, to one or two of these criteria or to similar thresholds such as 'extensive', 'serious', or 'significant'. In addition to the Rome Statute, and the negotiating history and final result of the 1996 Draft Code of Crimes against the Peace and Security of Mankind, these references can particularly be found in the public statements made by states before the International Court of Justice. These were: India,[761] Iran,[762] Lesotho,[763] Malaysia,[764] The Marshall Islands,[765] Nauru,[766] New Zealand,[767] Samoa,[768] San Marino,[769] The Solomon

[760] CR 95/26, Oral Plea of the Government of the Islamic Republic of Iran, of 6 Nov 1995 (WHO and GA), p 34. Through: <http://www.icj-cij.org/>.

[761] Written Comments of the Government of India on other Written Statements of 20 Jun 1995 (WHO), p 12; Written Statement of the Government of India of 20 Jun 1995 (GA), p 4. Through: <http://www.icj-cij.org/>.

[762] CR 95/26, Oral Plea of the Government of the Islamic Republic of Iran, of 6 Nov 1995 (WHO and GA), p 33. Through: <http://www.icj-cij.org/>.

[763] Written Statement of the Government of Lesotho of 20 Jun 1995 (GA), p 2. Through: <http://www.icj-cij.org/>.

[764] Written Statement of the Government of Malaysia of Sep 1994 (WHO), pp 4, 10; Written Comments of the Government of Malaysia on other Written Statements of 19 Jun 1995 (WHO), p 1; CR 95/27, Oral Plea of the Government of Malaysia, of 7 Nov 1995 (WHO and GA), p 59. Through: <http://www.icj-cij.org/>.

[765] Written Statement of the Government of the Marshall Islands of 22 Jun 1995 (GA), p 4; CR 95/32, Oral Plea of the Government of the Marshall Islands, of 14 Nov 1995 (WHO and GA), p 23. Through: <http://www.icj-cij.org/>.

[766] Written Statement of the Government of the Nauru of Sep 1994 (WHO), p 36; Written Comments of the Government of Nauru on other Written Statements of 15 Jun 1995 (WHO), Memorial I, p 11 and Memorial II, p 2. Through: <http://www.icj-cij.org/>.

[767] Written Statement of the Government of New Zealand of 20 Jun 1995 (GA), pp 17–18; CR 95/28, Oral Plea of the Government of New Zealand, of 9 Nov 1995 (WHO and GA), p 27. Through: <http://www.icj-cij.org/>.

[768] Written Statement of the Government of Samoa of 16 Sep 1994 (WHO), p 3. Through: <http://www.icj-cij.org/>.

[769] CR 95/31, Oral Plea of the Government of San Marino, of 13 Nov 1995 (WHO and GA), p 20. Through: <http://www.icj-cij.org/>.

Islands,[770] and Sweden.[771] It should be noted, however, that the interpretation of a damage threshold in this context is not necessarily limited to the interpretation of the triple standard under Additional Protocol I.

2.3.3.3.6 Expert opinions

The existence of two customary rules directly protecting the environment by prohibiting the willful and wanton destruction of the environment as well as excessive damage to the environment was not only confirmed by the ICRC, but also by the 1991 Conference of Experts, convened in Ottawa, and a number of experts in 1993 within the framework of an investigation by the ICRC upon request of the UN Secretary-General. The Ottawa Conference concluded that:

> [t]here was a shared view that wanton destruction of the environment with no legitimate military objective is clearly contrary to existing international law.

Furthermore, they considered that the principles of proportionality and necessity 'can have direct implications for the protection of the environment' and concluded that

> [t]here was a shared view that the law of armed conflict has to be seen in the context of the evolution of environmental concerns generally. The customary laws of war, in reflecting the dictates of public conscience, now include a requirement to avoid unnecessary damage to the environment.[772]

The ICRC experts recalled that '[t]he obligation to respect proportionality between the expected military advantage and the incidental damage to the environment.' And subsequently they stated:

> Customary rules are of great importance. Indeed, some experts even felt that these rules were the key to protecting the environment in times of armed conflict, in particular as they prohibited attack on the environment as such.[773]

[770] Written Statement of the Government of the Solomon Islands of 10 Jun 1994 (WHO), pp 25, 62, 63, 69; Written Statement of the Government of the Solomon Islands of 19 Jun 1995 (GA), pp 27, 63; CR 95/32, Oral Plea of the Government of the Solomon Islands, of 14 Nov 1995 (WHO and GA), pp 30, 54–5, 58. Through: <http://www.icj-cij.org/>.

[771] Written Statement of the Government of Sweden of Jun 1994 (WHO), p 5; Written Statement of the Government of Sweden of 20 Jun 1995 (GA), p 5. Through: <http://www.icj-cij.org/>.

[772] Declaration of the chairman of the 'Conference of Experts on the Use of the Environment as a Tool of Conventional Warfare' (Ottawa, 9–12 Jul 1991), summarising the views expressed at the Conference, quoted in Heintschel von Heinegg, Donner, *New Developments in the Protection of the Natural Environment in Naval Armed Conflicts*, p 292, fn 38, paras 5, 6 and 9. Compare also: Momtaz, *La Recours à l'Arme Nucléaire et la Protection de l'Environnement: l'Apport de la Cour Internationale de Justice*, in: Boisson de Chazournes, Sands (Eds), *International Law, the International Court of Justice and Nuclear Weapons*, p 364, fn 32.

[773] A/48/269, Report of the Secretary-General to the General Assembly on the Protection of the Environment in the Environment in Times of Armed Conflict, of 29 Jul 1993, with Annexed the ICRC Guidelines for Military Manuals and Instructions on the Protection of the Environment in Times of Armed Conflict, p 14.

Finally, the suggestion of direct protection of the environment under customary law is referred to in literature as well. Some authors directly recognise direct protection of the environment under customary law, including Desgagné, Dinstein, Dörmann, Greenwood, Heintschel von Heinegg and Donner, Henckaerts, Lijnzaad and Tanja, McNeill, Momtaz, and Simonds; of which Simonds, Lijnzaad and Tanja, Henckaerts, Heintschel von Heinegg and Donner, Momtaz, and Desgagné are most complete in their analysis.

Simonds refers in 1992 to the principles of proportionality, humanity, discrimination and necessity and concludes that:

> [t]ogether, these guidelines outlaw wanton environmental damage by prohibiting widespread destruction disproportionate to an anticipated military goal.[774]

Lijnzaad and Tanja write in 1993 that:

> [t]here are indeed good reasons for interpreting the general principles of the laws of war to include at present a prohibition on causing an unnecessary and disproportionate adverse environmental impact.[775]

Support for this statement they find in the above-mentioned conclusions of the 1991 Ottawa Conference of Experts on the Use of the Environment as a Tool of Conventional Warfare in Ottawa, in 1991 that:

> the customary laws of war, in reflecting the dictates of public conscience, now include a requirement to avoid unnecessary damage to the environment.

Henckaerts refers in 2000 to the preliminary conclusions of the ICRC Study on customary international humanitarian law that:

> confirm that damage to the environment in violation of the principle of proportionality and damage to the environment not justified by military necessity are prohibited in both international and non-international conflict. As explained above, the prohibition of these acts is, in fact, much more relevant than the reference to widespread, long-term and severe damage in Additional Protocol I.[776]

Heintschel von Heinegg and Donner write, with respect to naval warfare, that wanton destruction of the natural environment not justified by military necessity is prohibited:

> In other words, because of its principal inclusion in the protective scope of the customary laws of armed conflict the natural environment is protected against

[774] Simonds, *Conventional Warfare and Environmental Protection: A Proposal for International Legal Reform*, pp 169–70.

[775] Lijnzaad, Tanja, *Protection of the Environment in Times of Armed Conflict: The Iraq-Kuwait War*, p 184.

[776] J-M Henckaerts, *Towards Better Protection for the Environment in Armed Conflict: Recent Developments in International Humanitarian Law*, Review of European Community and international environmental law, Vol 9, 2000, p 18.

damages caused by the use of methods and means of naval warfare insofar as these damages are excessive in relation to the military advantages anticipated.[777]

Evidence for the 'principal inclusion of the natural environment in the protective scope of the customary laws of armed conflict' they find in the revised version of the United States Commander's Handbook on the Law of Naval Operations and the San Remo Manual.[778]

Momtaz refers to the widely accepted applicability of the principles of necessity and proportionality to the environment as a civilian object by authors in the aftermath of the 1990–1991 Gulf War;[779] and Desgagné writes in 2000 that:

> [i]t is not excluded (. . .) that the general principle of prohibition of wanton destruction has been expanded to include the natural environment.[780]

And a little further:

> There is, however, a trend to consider the environmental as falling outside the military-civilian dichotomy and to apply the proportionality principle directly to environment collateral damage as such.[781]

McNeill, Greenwood, Dinstein and Dörmann only refer to the existence of a customary prohibition of wanton destruction of the environment not justified by military necessity. According to McNeill in 1993:

> the international community can draw upon a considerable body of existing law to prohibit wanton destruction of the environment during wartime.[782]

Greenwood claims in 1996 that 'customary international law is widely considered to include a prohibition on unnecessary and wanton destruction of the environment'.[783] Dinstein considers in 2001 and 2004:

[777] Heintschel von Heinegg, Donner, *New Developments in the Protection of the Natural Environment in Naval Armed Conflicts*, p 294.

[778] Heintschel von Heinegg, Donner, *New Developments in the Protection of the Natural Environment in Naval Armed Conflicts*, p 293.

[779] Momtaz, *La Recours à l'Arme Nucléaire et la Protection de l'Environnement: l'Apport de la Cour Internationale de Justice*, in: Boisson de Chazournes, Sands (Eds), *International Law, the International Court of Justice and Nuclear Weapons*, pp 363–5.

[780] Desgagné, *The Prevention of Environmental Damage in Time of Armed Conflict: Proportionality and Precautionary Measures*, in: Fischer, McDonald (Eds), *Yearbook of International Humanitarian Law; Vol 3; 2000*, p 115.

[781] Desgagné, *The Prevention of Environmental Damage in Time of Armed Conflict: Proportionality and Precautionary Measures*, in: Fischer, McDonald (Eds), *Yearbook of International Humanitarian Law; Vol 3; 2000*, p 116.

[782] McNeill, *Protection of the Environment in Times of Armed Conflict: Environmental Protection in Military Practice*, p 81.

[783] Greenwood, *State Responsibility and Civil Liability for Environmental Damage Caused by Military Operations*, in: Grunawalt, King, McClain (Eds), *Protection of the Environment during Armed Conflict*, p 399.

> the prohibition of damage or destruction to the natural environment 'not justified by military necessity and carried out wantonly' is an accurate reflection of customary international law today.[784]

And Dörmann writes that:

> it should be noted that there is a third rule based on customary international law which provides that '[d]amage to or destruction of the natural environment not justified by military necessity and carried out wantonly is prohibited.'[785]

Other authors only hint at the possibility or refer to the protection of the environment as a civilian object. Spieker, for example, hints in 1992 at the possibility that, in view of state practice after the 1990–1991 Gulf War, the international community of states will become bound by a customary rule of international law that may deviate from Additional Protocol I and that may even distinguish between damage to the marine and land environment.[786] And Bothe states in 1982 that the protection provided by the rule of proportionality lay in the fact that damage to the environment affects the civilian population rather than regarding the environment as a non-military object in itself;[787] refers in 1991 to the practical meaning of the classic prohibition of wanton destruction of property for the environment and the protection of the environment as a civilian object provided by the rule of proportionality;[788] and argues in 1995 that there are a few fundamental rules restraining means and methods of warfare, 'the effect of which is a certain protection of environmental values.' These include the prohibition of wanton destruction of property as laid down in Article 23(g) of the Hague Regulations, which 'also protects the environment against wanton destruction', and which therefore renders it a grave breach of the Geneva Conventions; the prohibition to attack civilian objects; and the prohibition to cause damage to civilian objects that is excessive in relation to the military advantage anticipated.[789] Schmitt, finally, applies the principles of necessity and proportionality to environmental damage but

[784] Dinstein, *The Conduct of Hostilities under the Law of International Armed Conflict*, p 193. Similarly: Dinstein, *Protection of the Environment in International Armed Conflict*, in: Frowein, Wolfrum (Eds), *Max Planck Yearbook of United Nations Law*, p 545.

[785] K Dörmann, *Elements of War Crimes under the Rome Statute of the International Criminal Court; Sources and Commentary*, International Committee of the Red Cross, Cambridge University Press, Cambridge, 2004, p 167.

[786] Spieker, *Völkergewohnheitsrechtlicher Schutz der Natürlichen Umwelt im internationalen bewaffneten Konflikt; Waffenwirkung und Umwelt I*, pp 458–9.

[787] M Bothe, *War and Environment*, in: R. Bernhardt (Ed), *Encyclopaedia of Public International Law; Vol Four; Quirin, Ex Parte to Zones of Peace*, Elsevier, Amsterdam, 2000, p 1343.

[788] Bothe, *The Protection of the Environment in Times of Armed Conflict; Legal Rules, Uncertainty, Deficiencies, and Possible Developments*, pp 55–6.

[789] M Bothe, *Protection of the Environment in Times of Armed Conflict*, in: N Al-Nauimi, R Meese (Eds), *International Legal Issues Arising Under the United Nations Decade of International Law; Proceedings of the Qatar International Law Conference '94*, Martinus Nijhoff Publishers, The Hague, 1995, p 98.

remains in abstracto. He does not refer to specific customary rules of environmental protection.[790]

2.3.3.4 Legal appraisal

The probable existence of three additional customary rules providing direct protection to the environment during international armed conflict is important for three reasons. First of all, they are, in principle, binding on all states. Secondly, they reinforce environmental protection during international armed conflict, in a manner that is in conformity with the traditional laws of war. And thirdly, they provide protection, independently from the various conventions, since they emerged from a general international concern for the environment during armed conflict on the one hand, and from two cornerstone principles of *ius in bello*, on the other hand.

This means therefore that these customary norms do not supplant or override these treaty provisions which they might have done if there had been a symbiotic relationship between both treaty and customary law. Instead, they are additional, supplementary or complementary to ENMOD, Additional Protocol I, the Incendiary Weapons Protocol, and, to a certain extent, the Statute of the International Criminal Court.

Furthermore, this means that there is no lex specialis—lex generalis relationship between the treaty and customary norms involved. The customary and the conventional provisions protect the environment separately and from different angles and there is no indication that either level is more specific or more general vis-à-vis the other.

Since both customary norms emerged after 1977, however, and came to be recognised in the 1990s, both customary rules need to be addressed first, in accordance with the basic principle of law that new law prevails over old law, or *lex posterior derogat legi priori*. Then, if no violation can be established under customary law, treaty law may provide subsidiary protection against states that have become party to these conventions.[791] This seems to be confirmed by the International Court of Justice in its Nuclear Weapons Opinion (GA). The Court notes that 'Articles 35, paragraph 3,

[790] Schmitt, *Green War: An Assessment of the Environmental Law of International Armed Conflict*, pp 52–61; Schmitt, *War and the Environment: Fault Lines in the Prescriptive Landscape*, in: Austin, Bruch (Eds), *The Environmental Consequences of War*, pp 101–4.

[791] Momtaz is skeptical of the supplementary protection provided by Additional Protocol I and believes that customary principles of international environmental and humanitarian law will provide sufficient protection. 'Ces principes tirés du droit international de l'environnement et du droit international humanitaire, s'ils étaient appliqués conjointement et de bonne foi, pourraient offrir une protection suffisante à l'environnement.' Momtaz, *La Recours à l'Arme Nucléaire et la Protection de l'Environnement: l'Apport de la Cour Internationale de Justice*, in: Boisson de Chazournes, Sands (Eds), *International Law, the International Court of Justice and Nuclear Weapons*, p 374.

and 55 of Additional Protocol I provide *additional* protection for the environment'(emphasis added).[792]

Bothe,[793] Rogers,[794] Schmitt[795] and the 1985 Expert Report submitted by Bothe, Cassese, Kalshoven, Kiss, Salmon and Simmonds for the European Commission[796] come to similar conclusions with respect to the supplementary or complementary value of the principles of necessity and proportionality, although their reasoning is not always quite clear. Bothe refers to the protection of the environment during armed conflict as a civilian object under customary law before referring to Articles 35(3) and 55 of Additional Protocol I. According to him, both provisions were not intended to lower the standard of protection under customary law, but to enhance it since customary law only prohibits attacking the environment without military justification and causing excessive collateral damage to the environment, whereas:

> Articles 35 and 55 prohibit causing damage to the environment even where the environment constitutes a military objective or where the damage to the environment may be considered as not being excessive in relation to the military advantage anticipated.[797]

The 1985 Expert Report adopts a similar approach,[798] and so does Rogers when he emphasises Bothe's point that:

> Arts. 35 and 55 only come into play once the military planner has surmounted two hurdles: first that the object to be attacked is a military objective and, second, that the rule of proportionality will not be violated.[799]

However, if customary international law already protected the environment as a civilian object before 1977, as these authors suggest, this would

[792] Legality of the Threat or Use of Nuclear Weapons, Advisory Opinion, 8 Jul 1996, ICJ Reports 1996, p 226, at p 242, para 31.

[793] Bothe, *The Protection of the Environment in Times of Armed Conflict; Legal Rules, Uncertainty, Deficiencies, and Possible Developments*, pp 55–6.

[794] Rogers, *Law on the Battlefield*, p 167.

[795] Schmitt, *Green War: An Assessment of the Environmental Law of International Armed Conflict*, p 73.

[796] M Bothe, A Cassese, F Kalshoven, A Kiss, J Salmon, KR Simmonds, *Protection of the Environment in Times of Armed Conflict*, Report prepared upon request of the European Commission, SJ/110/85, Brussels, 1985, p 70.

[797] Bothe, *The Protection of the Environment in Times of Armed Conflict; Legal Rules, Uncertainty, Deficiencies, and Possible Developments*, p 56.

[798] Bothe, Cassese, Kalshoven, Kiss, Salmon, Simmonds, *Protection of the Environment in Times of Armed Conflict*, pp 67–70.

[799] Rogers, *Law on the Battlefield*, p 167. Heintschel von Heinegg and Donner do not believe that the natural environment can be regarded as a civilian object and therefore do not share this what they call 'dynamic interpretation'. Arts 35(3) and 55 limit protection of the environment to those means and methods that cause widespread, long-term and severe damage to the environment. 'The States parties to AP I can, therefore, not be said to have agreed upon a general protection of the natural environment against negative effects of warfare.' Heintschel von Heinegg, Donner, *New Developments in the Protection of the Natural Environment in Naval Armed Conflicts*, p 289.

mean that the provisions of Additional Protocol I would have to be regarded as more specific and detailed in character than the more general and mere indirect customary protection under customary law. This would then not only mean that both 1977 provisions would prevail over, and not supplement, preceding customary law in accordance with the maxim *lex posterior derogat legi priori* because they are of later date, but also that they would prevail over the customary norms, in accordance with the maxim *lex specialis derogat legi generali*. This conflict rule would not only apply because they are more specific and provide direct protection to the environment, but also because Articles 35(3) and 55 Additional Protocol I seemed to be intended to be the only protection in force in 1977.[800]

And if that were the case, Verwey rightly states that:

> the provision may, in practice, very well result in lowering traditional standards of protection, for, the cumulative triple standard may now render permissible what before would have been forbidden by reference to general legality requirements like that of proportionality and the prohibition of unnecessary suffering.[801]

Lijnzaad and Tanja similarly claim that:

> it seems difficult to deny that the older customary rule has lost some of its relevance and is, with respect to the environment, being taken over by the improved rule based on 'widespread, long-term and severe'. (. . .) Damage falling short of the cumulative requirements may nevertheless cause a rather substantive adverse environmental impact, though not prohibited under Additional Protocol I.[802]

After all, Articles 35(3) and 55 do seem to allow the use of means and methods of warfare that do not cause widespread, long-term and severe damage to the environment, even if they are used to cause wanton destruction of the environment or excessive collateral damage.[803]

Schmitt disagrees with Verwey's argument and his interpretation of the lex specialis rule. He believes that the better view is that the Protocol complements the proportionality and necessity principles since they are both 'designed to further humanitarian concerns' and the *lex specialis* rule only 'applies in situations in which norms appear to conflict' because it is 'a

[800] It should be noted that international concern for the environment only emerged in the early 1970s. Compare also Heintschel von Heinegg, Donner, *New Developments in the Protection of the Natural Environment in Naval Armed Conflicts*, p 289.

[801] Verwey, *Observations on the Legal Protection of the Environment in Times of International Armed Conflict*, pp 36–7; Verwey, *Protection of the Environment in Times of Armed Conflict: In Search of a New Legal Perspective*, p 11; Verwey, *Comment: Protection of the Environment in Times of Armed Conflict—Do We Need Additional Rules?*, in: Grunawalt, King, McClain, *Protection of the Environment during Armed Conflict*, p 560.

[802] Lijnzaad, Tanja, *Protection of the Environment in Times of Armed Conflict: The Iraq-Kuwait War*, p 182.

[803] Arts 35(3) and 55 do not contain a military necessity exception like the classic rules of customary law that protect the civilian population and civilian objects. This might under circumstances enhance protection of the environment in comparison with pre-existing protection.

principle of resolution'. Furthermore, Schmitt believes, similar to Bothe, that the drafters did not intend 'to forego protection already in place.'[804]

Both arguments are difficult to uphold, however, and otherwise fail to convince. First of all, the argument that the drafters did not intend 'to lower the standard of protection' or 'to forego protection already in place' seem to be based on the fact that it is difficult to trace references in the preparatory works of the Diplomatic Conference on protection of the environment during armed conflict under the principles of necessity and proportionality. It is more likely, however, that this silence should be interpreted as implying that the drafters had not even thought of the possibility that any customary protection of the environment under general principles of the law of war already existed. If the drafters had believed that such protection already existed, it surely would have come up at the Conference during the discussions on Articles 35(3) and 55.

In the second place, assuming that general principles of *ius in bello* did indeed protect the environment before 1977, this would mean that after 1977, with the drafting of Articles 35(3) and 55, the environment would be protected by two separate sets of rules. When these sets of rules are applicable at the same time, there is a so-called conflict of laws, which can only be solved by so-called rules of conflict, such as the *lex specialis* or the *lex posterior* rule. This is similar to a legal situation in which two or more national legal systems claim jurisdiction and which conflict has to be solved by the rules of conflict under international private law.

For the applicability of rules of conflict, including the *lex specialis* rule, therefore, it is not necessary that both sets of rules lead to conflicting or opposite results. According to Koskenniemi in his outline paper for the Study Group of the ILC on Fragmentation of International Law, application of the principle 'need not be limited to conflict',[805] and the Study Group itself concluded that only '[a] narrower view considered *lex specialis* to apply only where the special rule was in conflict with the general law.'[806]

The solution to a conflict of laws by means of the *lex specialis* rule ultimately determines which rule should be applied and seems to depend on the object and purpose of each rule, on the intention of the drafters when

[804] Schmitt, *Green War: An Assessment of the Environmental Law of International Armed Conflict*, p 73.

[805] Koskenniemi, *Fragmentation of International Law*, Outline for Study Group, International Law Commission, 55th session, 2003, p 4. At: <http://www.un.org/law/ilc/sessions/55/55sess.htm>.

[806] A/CN.4/L.644, Report of the Study Group on Fragmentation of International Law: Difficulties arising from the Diversification and Expansion of International Law, of 18 Jul 2003; International Law Commission, fifty-fifth session, Geneva, 5 May–6 Jun 2003 and 7 Jul–8 Aug 2003, p 8, para 21. At: <http://www.un.org/law/ilc/sessions/55/55sess.htm>.

written rules are involved and on the circumstances of the case.[807] As has been observed above, it is likely that the drafters intended Articles 35(3) and 55 of Additional Protocol I to be the only set of rules that would protect the environment during international armed conflict. This appears from the explicit text of both provisions, the preparatory works, and the spirit of the time.

Application of the *lex specialis* rule leads in this case, therefore, to a result in which one rule or one set of rules sets aside another rule of set of rules. Setting aside of the general rule by the special rule is not necessarily the case, however. Koskenniemi refers to the European Court of Human Rights as an example in which two rules that are simultaneously applicable do not set each other aside. According to the Court, '[t]he former did not set aside the latter but was to be "taken into account" when applying the latter.'[808] A similar approach was adopted by the International Court of Justice in 1996 in its Nuclear Weapons Opinion (GA) with respect to the relationship between international human rights law and international humanitarian law,[809] and to a lesser extent in 2004 in its Wall Opinion,[810] and in 2005 in its Judgment in the case between the Democratic Republic of Congo and Uganda.[811] This relationship between both sets of law will be briefly discussed further below in Chapter V. In practice, however, it may well be that 'taking into account' and 'setting aside' are not that different from each other.

It seems that the customary rules directly protecting the environment that have arguably emerged after 1977 and matured in the 1990s were never intended to override treaty obligations already in force. On the contrary, both rules emerged in the knowledge that Additional Protocol I contained two specific rules on the protection of the environment and

807 According to the Commentary of the ILC on Art 55 of the Draft Articles on State Responsibility dealing with *leges speciales* with respect to state responsibility, '[i]t will depend on the special rule to establish the extent to which the more general rules on State responsibility set out in the present articles are displaced by that rule. In some cases it will be clear form the language of a treaty or other text that only the consequences specified are to flow. (...) In other cases, one aspect of the general law may be modified, leaving other aspects still applicable.' A/56/10, Draft Articles on Responsibility of States for Internationally Wrongful Acts, including Commentaries, adopted by the International Law Commission at its fifty-third session, Nov 2001; Yearbook of the International Law Commission, 2001; Vol II, Pt Two, forthcoming, p 357. Through <http://www.un.org/law/ilc/>. Also J Crawford, *The International Law Commission's Articles on State Responsibility; Introduction, Text and Commentaries*, Cambridge University Press, Cambridge, 2002, p 307.

808 Koskenniemi, *Fragmentation of International Law*, Outline for Study Group, International Law Commission, 55th session, 2003, p 4.

809 Legality of the Threat or Use of Nuclear Weapons, Advisory Opinion, 8 Jul 1996, ICJ Reports 1996, para 25, p 240.

810 Legal Consequences of the Construction of a Wall in the Occupied Palestinian Territory, Advisory Opinion, 9 Jul 2004, ICJ Reports 2004, pp 41–2.

811 Case Concerning Armed Activities on the Territory of the Congo (Democratic Republic of the Congo v Uganda), Merits, Judgment, 19 Dec 2005, ICJICJ Reports 2005, para 216, pp 69–70.

seem to be intended as merely complementary to these treaty provisions. Therefore there is no lex specialis—*lex generalis* relationship, but rather a primary and secondary protection level relationship. This means that if a state would not violate its obligations to protect the environment during international armed conflict under customary international law, it might still very well violate its obligations under treaty law.[812] Similarly, if a state violated its obligation under customary international law, its actions are not necessarily in contravention of obligations under treaty law.

3—INDIRECT PROTECTION

3.1 Introduction

In addition to treaty and customary law that provides direct protection to the environment during international armed conflict, there may also be a number of provisions that provide indirect protection to the environment. These provisions are not intended to protect the environment but their implementation may nevertheless have a beneficial impact on the environment. Although it is arguable that by that rationale, most rules of *ius in bello* can be regarded as indirectly protecting the environment,[813] there are a number of rules that have specific value in this context. These are the rules on the protection of civilian objects and the law on neutrality.[814] By

[812] This seems to be in accordance with the Court's view referred to above that the protection of Arts 35(3) and 55 AP I provide additional protection.

[813] A cynic could argue that the use and subsequent non-removal of landmines in particular environmental areas may actually benefit the environment, ie flora and small animals, because it prevents any human activity in that area.

[814] The 1993 ICRC Report to the Secretary-General also refers to the 1925 Geneva Protocol; the 1972 Biological Weapons Convention; the 1993 Chemical Weapons Convention; the 1954 Hague Convention for the Protection of Cultural Property in the Event of an Armed Conflict; the 1972 Convention Concerning the Protection of the World Cultural and Natural Heritage; and the 1981 Certain Conventional Weapons Convention, including protocols. 'Furthermore, all other international rules limiting the development, protection, testing or use of weapons of mass destruction make a significant contribution to the protection of the environment in times of armed conflict.' A/48/269, Report of the Secretary-General to the General Assembly on the Protection of the Environment in the Environment in Times of Armed Conflict, of 29 Jul 1993, pp 7–8. Similarly, Roberts, *Environmental Issues in International Armed Conflict: The Experience of the 1991 Gulf War*, in: Grunawalt, King, McClain (Eds), *Protection of the Environment during Armed Conflict*, pp 230–1; Schmitt, *Green War: An Assessment of the Environmental Law of International Armed Conflict*, pp 85–90; and Verwey, reservedly, Verwey, *Observations on the Legal Protection of the Environment in Times of International Armed Conflict*, p 39–40; Verwey, *Protection of the Environment in Times of Armed Conflict: In Search of a New Legal Perspective*, pp 15–16; Verwey, *Comment: Protection of the Environment in Times of Armed Conflict—Do We Need Additional Rules?*, in: Grunawalt, King, McClain, *Protection of the Environment during Armed Conflict*, p 563. Deduction of indirect protection of the environment during armed conflict from these international documents seems rather far-fetched, however. Some experts also refer to the Martens clause, most recently codified in Art 1(2) Additional Protocol I. Schwarzenberger however, warns against abuse of this provision. 'As becomes apparent from the history of this Clause, its purpose was to forestall an unintended

reference to the general rules of interpretation as reflected in Articles 31 and 32 of the Vienna Convention on the Law of Treaties, they may either be interpreted as encompassing elements of the natural environment or arguably entail protection for the environment during international armed conflict. There is no need to deal with the rules of customary international law separately from the conventional rules.

3.2 The Protection of Civilian Objects

3.2.1 Introduction

The obligation to protect civilian objects, and thus to distinguish between military and civilian objects, is a manifestation of the principle of distinction or discrimination, which in itself seems to be derived from the principle of necessity. Considering the 'necessities of war', the drafters of the 1868 St Petersburg Declaration, stated that 'the progress of civilization should have the effect of alleviating as much as possible the calamities of war'; that 'the only legitimate object which States should endeavour to accomplish during war is to weaken the military forces of the enemy' and that for this purpose it is 'sufficient to disable the greatest possible number of men'. The only legitimate object of warfare is thus to weaken the military forces of the enemy. This implies, firstly, that in principle civilian objects and the civilian population may not be primary objects of attack, and, secondly, that they must be spared the consequences of warfare as much as possible. The former reflects the principle of discrimination; the latter reflects the principle of proportionality.

The protection of civilian objects is one of the older obligations of the laws of war[815] and now constitutes one of the cornerstones of modern

and cynical argument *a contrario*. Because the Regulations on Land Warfare were not exhaustive, the Parties wished to avoid the interpretation that anything that was not expressly prohibited by these Regulations was allowed. (. . .) What (. . .) this Clause was not meant to settle with binding force for the Parties was how rules of warfare came into existence. Its only function was to preserve intact any pre-existing rules of warfare, on whatever law-creating process they happened to rest.' G Schwarzenberger, *The Legality of Nuclear Weapons*, Stevens & Sons, London, 1958, pp 10–11. Similarly, Schwarzenberger, *International Law; As Applied by International Courts and Tribunals; Vol II; The Law of Armed Conflict*, pp 21–3. This interpretation is confirmed by the context of the first edition of the Martens Claus in the Preamble of the 1899 Hague Regulations. Preambular paras 7 and 8 which precede the Martens clause provide: 'It has not, however, been possible to agree forthwith on provisions embracing all the circumstances which occur in practice. On the other hand, it could not be intended by the High Contracting Parties that the cases not provided for should, for want of a written provision, be left to the arbitrary judgment of the military commanders.'

[815] Compare the references, among others, to Deuteronomy, Sun Tzu, Islamic authors, the medieval law of chivalry in Shakespeare, King Richard II's code, Coligny, Gentili, and England's 17th century Articles of War in LC Green, *The Contemporary Law of Armed Conflict*, Manchester University Press, Manchester, 2000, pp 20–9.

international humanitarian law. In the past, it may have been self-evident that warfare was primarily waged against the armed forces of the enemy,[816] but the concept of total war,[817] which implicated the entire population in the war machinery, the technological progress that enabled states to conduct total warfare and attack strategic objects in the enemy's hinterland, and the development of guerilla warfare increasingly left the civilian population and civilian objects vulnerable and in need of more effective protection. Since 1977, Additional Protocol I contains a large number of specific and detailed provisions dealing with the protection of the civilian population and of civilian objects. Before 1977, civilian objects were merely granted marginal protection under the 1899 and 1907 Hague Regulations (HR),[818] and the 1949 Fourth Geneva Convention (GC IV),[819] most importantly by prohibiting the seizure or destruction of property during hostilities and during occupation.

3.2.2 Protection of Civilian Objects before 1977

Although the protection of property was not stipulated in binding form before the 1899 and 1907 Hague Regulations, draft provisions had been laid down in the 1874 Brussels Declaration,[820] which was never ratified,

[816] Similarly, Rogers, *Law on the Battlefield*, pp 58–9.

[817] Schwarzenberger defines 'total war' as 'war conducted in such a manner that the necessities of war form the overriding test of belligerent action.' Schwarzenberger, *International Law; As Applied by International Courts and Tribunals; Vol II; The Law of Armed Conflict*, p 150. For a general discussion of the concept, see: <http://en.wikipedia.org/wiki/Total_war>.

[818] Hague Convention (II) with respect to the Laws and Customs of War on Land, with annexed Regulations, signed on 29 Jul 1899, entered into force on 4 Sep 1900, AJIL, Vol 1, No 2, Supplement: Official Documents, 1907, p 129; Hague Convention (IV) Respecting the Laws and Customs of War on Land, with annexed Regulations, signed on 18 Oct 1907, entered into force on 26 Jan 1910, AJIL, Vol 2, No 1/2, Supplement: Official Documents, 1908, p 90.

[819] Geneva Convention (IV) relative to the Protection of Civilian Persons in Time of War, signed on 12 Aug 1949, entered into force on 21 Oct 1950, UNTS, Vol 75, No 973.

[820] Final Protocol of the Brussels Conference, with the Project of an International Declaration concerning the Laws and Customs of War, signed on 27 Aug 1874, never entered into force, AJIL, Vol 1, No 2, Supplement: Official Documents, Apr 1907, p 96. The Brussels Declaration was adopted by the Brussels Conference in 1874, 6 years after the 1868 St Petersburg Declaration. The Conference had been assembled by the Russian Czar, Alexander II, was attended by 15 states, generally adopted his 'Project of International Rules on the Laws and Usages of War'. The text was never ratified, however, because some of the 15 states participating did not wish to see it as a binding convention. Schindler, Toman (Eds), *The Laws of Armed Conflicts; A Collection of Conventions, Resolutions and Other Documents*, p 25. The Declaration consists of 56 Articles covering all major aspects of warfare, including occupation, combatants, means and methods of warfare, the treatment of prisoners of war and the treatment of wounded and the sick. With respect to the protection of property during hostilities, Art 13(g) forbids '[a]ny destruction or seizure of the enemy's property that is not imperatively demanded by the necessity of war.' With respect to the protection of property during occupation, Art 7 provides that '[t]he occupying State shall be regarded only as administrator and usufructuary of public buildings, real estate, forests, and agricultural estates belonging to the hostile State, and situated in the occupied country. It must safeguard the capital of these properties, and administer them in accordance with the rules of usufruct.'

and subsequently in the 1880 Oxford Manual[821] of the International Institute of International Law. The Hague Regulations are arguably the most significant results of both Hague Peace Conferences in 1899 and 1907, which were convened upon instigation of the Russian Czar, then Nicholas II, and United States President Theodore Roosevelt.[822] Although the main focus of the 1899 Peace Conference was on other topics, such as the prevention of war, the maintenance of peace, disarmament, and dispute resolution, the Conference also discussed the general rules of warfare. One of the documents adopted was the 'Regulations Respecting the Laws and Customs of War on Land'. These so-called Hague Regulations were annexed to Hague Convention (II) with Respect to the Laws and Customs of War on Land, were largely based on the Brussels Declaration of 1874 and the Oxford Manual of 1880 and were slightly revised at the Peace Conference of 1907.

Article 23(g) prohibits the unnecessary destruction or seizure of property during hostilities by providing that:

> [i]n addition to the prohibitions provided by special Conventions, it is especially forbidden (. . .) [t]o destroy or seize the enemy's property, unless such destruction or seizure be imperatively demanded by the necessities of war.

For the treatment of property during occupation, Article 47 prohibits 'pillage' and Article 55 provides:

> The occupying State shall be regarded only as administrator and usufructuary of public buildings, real estate, forests, and agricultural estates belonging to the hostile State, and situated in the occupied country. It must safeguard the capital of these properties, and administer them in accordance with the rules of usufruct.

After World War II, the drafters of the Geneva Conventions chose not to revise the general laws of warfare but limited themselves to the treatment of the wounded and sick on land (Geneva Convention I), the wounded,

[821] Manual on the Laws of War on Land, published by the Institute of International Law (Oxford Manual), adopted by the Institute of International Law at Oxford, 9 Sep 1880. D Schindler, J Toman (Eds), *The Laws of Armed Conflicts; A Collection of Conventions, Resolutions and Other Documents*, Martinus Nijhoff Publishers, Dordrecht, 1988, pp 35–48. The Manual was drafted by Gustave Moynier and subsequently adopted by the Institute. As far as the protection of property during hostilities is concerned, Art 32(b) states that is forbidden '[t]o destroy public or private property, if this destruction is not demanded by an imperative necessity of war'. During occupation Art 52 provides with respect to public property that '[t]he occupant can only act in the capacity of provisional administrator in respect to real property, such as buildings, forests, agricultural establishments, belonging to the enemy State. It must safeguard the capital of these properties and see to their maintenance.' With respect to private property, Art 54 states that '[p]rivate property, whether belonging to individuals or corporations, must be respected, and can be confiscated only under the limitations contained in the following Articles.' Schindler, Toman (Eds), *The Laws of Armed Conflicts; A Collection of Conventions, Resolutions and Other Documents*, pp 37–48.

[822] Schmitt, *Green War: An Assessment of the Environmental Law of International Armed Conflict*, pp 62–3.

sick and shipwrecked at sea (Geneva Convention II), prisoners of war (Geneva Convention III), and civilians in time of war, in particular under occupation (Geneva Convention IV). Only the latter Convention contains two provisions protecting property in times of occupation: Article 33 prohibits pillaging and Article 53:

> Any destruction by the Occupying Power of real or personal property belonging individually or collectively to private persons, or to the State, or to other public authorities, or to social or cooperative organizations, is prohibited, except where such destruction is rendered absolutely necessary by military operations.

According to Article 147 GC IV 'extensive destruction and appropriation of property' is regarded as a 'grave breach' of the Convention, involving individual criminal responsibility.

All of these provisions have in common that they reflect the principle of necessity, and that they are intended to alleviate 'as much as possible the calamities of war' required by 'the progress of civilization'.[823] Although they are arguably inspired by economics rather than by environmental concerns,[824] they can nevertheless be interpreted as protecting the natural environment. Even if this is 'far-fetched', according to Lijnzaad and Tanja,[825] and 'a tricky interpretative exercise', according to Verwey,[826] there are a number of arguments why protection of property in the Hague Regulations and Geneva Convention IV do indeed indirectly protect the environment.

[823] Compare preambular para 1 of the 1868 St Petersburg Declaration which largely reflects the rationale behind the laws of war in general.

[824] Compare Art 55 HR, second sentence, which refers to the 'capital of these properties'.

[825] Lijnzaad and Tanja find interpreting Art 23(g) as encompassing an obligation to protect the environment 'far-fetched', although they still acknowledge that Arts 23(g) and 55 of the Hague Regulations 'might be helpful since willful destruction of real or personal property is prohibited.' Lijnzaad, Tanja, *Protection of the Environment in Times of Armed Conflict: The Iraq-Kuwait War*, p 176.

[826] According to Verwey, 'the question arises whether it is justified at all to inject such provisions with an environment protection-oriented meaning. For, establishing a link between them and the modern objective of environment protection is, both factually and legally, disputable at best: all the "Hague" and "Geneva" Conventions and Protocols were drafted and entered into force at "pre-ecological" times, i.e. at times when environmental concern and ecological awareness were (virtually) non-existent, in particular with respect to armed conflict. (. . .) Consequently, any effort aimed at a retroactive *hineininterpretieren* of an environmental connotation into such old-fashioned, general treaty provisions, is bound to be a tricky interpretative exercise, which cannot be performed without running the risk of provoking substantial criticism—an observation which, at the time, exposes its questionable evidential value.' Verwey, *Protection of the Environment in Times of Armed Conflict: In Search of a New Legal Perspective*, p 21. Also: Verwey, *Observations on the Legal Protection of the Environment in Times of International Armed Conflict*, pp 43–4; Verwey, *Comment: Protection of the Environment in Times of Armed Conflict—Do We Need Additional Rules?*, in: Grunawalt, King, McClain, *Protection of the Environment during Armed Conflict*, p 566.

Firstly, the concept of 'property' in Article 23(g) HR is so broad that it could encompass almost anything[827] including elements of the environment.[828] *Collins Dictionary* defines 'property' as 'something of value (. . .); a piece of land or real estate'.[829] And *Black's Law Dictionary* describes property as 'that which belongs exclusively to one' and subsequently provides an extensive overview of the different meanings of 'property' under common law.[830] Secondly, Articles 55 HR and 53 GC IV on the treatment of property during occupation even explicitly refer to public property and to assets that nowadays have a clear environmental connotation to illustrate the concept of property. Article 55 HR refers to 'real estate, forests, and agricultural estates' and Article 53 GC IV refers to 'real or personal property belonging individually or collectively to private persons, or to the State' all of which need to be administered in accordance with the rules of *usufruct*.[831] Real property is all immovable property and includes land for example.

In practice, the protection of property during belligerent occupation has indeed been applied in an environmental context. After World War II, the

[827] The 1954 Hague Convention for the Protection of Cultural Property in the Event of Armed Conflict only relates to cultural property, which unlikely encompasses the natural environment. Cultural property is defined in Art 1 as '(a) movable or immovable property of great importance to the cultural heritage of every people, such as monuments of architecture, art or history, whether religious or secular; archaeological sites; groups of buildings which, as a whole, are of historical or artistic interest; works of art; manuscripts, books and other objects of artistic, historical or archaeological interest; as well as scientific collections and important collections of books or archives or of reproductions of the property defined above; (b) buildings whose main and effective purpose is to preserve or exhibit the movable cultural property defined in sub-para (a) such as museums, large libraries and depositories of archives, and refuges intended to shelter, in the event of armed conflict, the movable cultural property defined in subpara (a); (c) centres containing a large amount of cultural property as defined in subparas (a) and (b), to be known as "centres containing monuments".' Convention for the Protection of Cultural Property in the Event of Armed Conflict, signed on 14 May 1954, entered into force on 7 Aug 1956, UNTS, Vol 249, No 3511.

[828] Similarly Bothe, *The Protection of the Environment in Times of Armed Conflict; Legal Rules, Uncertainty, Deficiencies, and Possible Developments*, p 55; M Bothe, *Criminal Responsibility for Environmental Damage in Times of Armed Conflict*, in: RJ Grunawalt, JE King, RS McClain (Eds), *Protection of the Environment during Armed Conflict*, International Law Studies 1996, Vol 69, Naval War College, Newport, RI, 1996, p 475; Bothe, *Protection of the Environment in Times of Armed Conflict*, in: Al-Nauimi, Meese (Eds), *International Legal Issues Arising Under the United Nations Decade of International Law; Proceedings of the Qatar International Law Conference '94*, p 98. Compare also Bothe, Cassese, Kalshoven, Kiss, Salmon, Simmonds, *Protection of the Environment in Times of Armed Conflict*, p 67.

[829] *Collins Dictionary*, p 1238.

[830] Black, *Black's Law Dictionary*, pp 845–7. It should be noted that the concept of property under common law is not equivalent to the Roman concept of *dominium* under civil law. Art 5:1 of the Dutch Civil Code defines '*eigendom*' as '*het meest omvattende recht dat een persoon op een zaak kan hebben.*' A '*zaak*' is defined by Art 3:2: '*Zaken zijn de voor menselijke beheersing vatbare stoffelijke objecten.*' The Dutch Civil Code entered into force on 1 Jan 1992, through <http://wetten.overheid.nl/>.

[831] *Usufruct* means 'the right to use and derive profit from a piece of property belonging to another, provided the property itself remains undiminished and uninjured in any way'. *Collins Dictionary*, p 1678.

violation of the prohibition to destroy forests, presumably was considered to be a war crime for which people could be held individually responsible.[832] The Committee on Facts and Evidence (Committee I) of the United Nations War Crimes Commission[833] found prima facie evidence that nine Germans:

> all of whom had been heads of various Departments in the Forestry Administration in Poland during the German occupation (1939–1944), could be listed as war criminals on a charge of pillaging Polish public property.

Although Germany had been among the first nations who had advanced scientific forestry, the accused had 'wilfully felled the Polish forests without the least regard to the basic principles of forestry.' Cutting of forests had been far in excess of what was necessary and this had caused the Polish nation losses of about 6,525,000,000 zloty,[834] which shows that the protection of property regulations primarily have an economic rationale. And in 2005, the International Court of Justice held Uganda responsible for 'looting, plundering and exploitation of natural resources', including diamonds, gold and coffee, in the territory of the Democratic Republic of Congo, which it regarded as pillaging, prohibited under Articles 47 of the Hague Regulations and 33 of the Fourth Geneva Convention.[835]

To which extent the natural environment is protected from damage under this concept is uncertain, however. 'Property' certainly seems to encompass all immovable or real property which is in principle all land

[832] The individual criminal responsibility was based on the prohibition of pillaging of public property and is most likely related to Art 55 of the Hague Regulations. Schmitt writes that the Commission cited Art 23(g) HR in this context, but it is more likely that the Commission referred to Art 55 HR, since the cutting of forests presumably took place during the occupation. Schmitt, *Green War: An Assessment of the Environmental Law of International Armed Conflict*, p 64. See also Art 6(b) of the Nuremberg Charter which includes under war crimes 'plunder of public or private property' and the discussion of this crime by the Tribunal in its Final Judgment: International Military Tribunal (Nuremberg), *Judgments and Sentences; Oct 1, 1946*, American Journal of International Law, Vol 41, 1947, pp 235–8.

[833] The United Nations War Crimes Commission had been established in Oct 1943 for the investigation of war crimes. The United Nations War Crimes Commission, *History of the United Nations War Crimes Commission and the Development of the Laws of War*, His Majesty's Stationary Office, London, 1948, pp 109–35.

[834] Commission No 7150, in: The United Nations War Crimes Commission, *History of the United Nations War Crimes Commission and the Development of the Laws of War*, His Majesty's Stationary Office, London, 1948, p 496.

[835] Case Concerning Armed Activities on the Territory of the Congo (Democratic Republic of the Congo v Uganda), Merits, Judgment, 19 Dec 2005, ICJ Reports 2005, para 245, p 77. For a more detailed discussion of the protection of natural resources under belligerent occupation, within the context of Art 55 HR (rather than Art 47 HR), see: N Schrijver, *Sovereignty over Natural Resources: Balancing Rights and Duties*, Cambridge University Press, Cambridge, 1997, pp 266–9.

and that which is affixed to land.[836] This means that a large part of the natural environment, including vegetation, is covered by the Hague Regulations and the Fourth Geneva Convention,[837] since it is likely that all land is either privately or publicly owned.[838] Problematic, however, may be the protection of the natural environment as far as wildlife, the atmosphere, and open waters are concerned.[839] Wildlife may be considered *res nullii* under certain legal systems,[840] the atmosphere may not always be

[836] *Black's Law Dictionary* describes real or immovable property as '[l]and, and generally whatever is erected or growing upon or affixed to land. Also rights issuing out of, annexed to, and exercisable within or about land. A general term for lands, tenements, and hereditaments; property which, on the death of the owner intestate, passes to his heir.' Black, *Black's Law Dictionary*, p 847. Compare Art 3:3 of the Dutch Civil Code: 'Onroerend zijn de grond, de nog niet gewonnen delfstoffen, de met de grond verenigde beplantingen, alsmede de gebouwen en werken die duurzaam met de grond zijn verenigd, hetzij rechtstreeks, hetzij door vereniging met andere gebouwen of werken.'

[837] Compare Boelaert-Suominen, SAJ Boelaert-Suominen, *International Environmental Law and Naval War; The Effect of Marine Safety and Pollution Conventions During International Armed Conflict*, Newport Paper Number Fifteen, Naval War College Press, Newport, RI, 2000, pp 54–6. Also through: <http://www.nwc.navy.mil/press/>. Desgagné writes that inclusion of 'ecological concepts such as ecosystems or biological diversity, may indeed unreasonably overstretch the notion of "property"' but that it is not excluded that the natural environment is included in Art 23(g) HR. Desgagné, *The Prevention of Environmental Damage in Time of Armed Conflict: Proportionality and Precautionary Measures*, in: Fischer, McDonald (Eds), *Yearbook of International Humanitarian Law; Vol 3; 2000*, p 115. According to Schmitt, in 2000, '[c]omponents of the environment such as land, water, flora, and fauna should readily be considered protected property.' Schmitt, *War and the Environment: Fault Lines in the Prescriptive Landscape*, in: Austin, Bruch (Eds), *The Environmental Consequences of War*, p 111.

[838] Compare, for example, Art 5:24 of the Dutch Civil Code, which provides: 'Aan de Staat behoren onroerende zaken die geen andere eigenaar hebben.' Simonds is confusing when she first writes that the Hague Regulations only protect civilian property and subsequently writes that Art 23(g) prohibits destruction of public property. Simonds, *Conventional Warfare and Environmental Protection: A Proposal for International Legal Reform*, p 171. Compare also Schwarzenberger on the distinction between the protection of public and private property during occupation. Schwarzenberger, *International Law; As Applied by International Courts and Tribunals; Vol II; The Law of Armed Conflict*, ch 20, pp 259–65.

[839] Similarly Low, Hodgkinson, *Compensation for Wartime Environmental Damage: Challenges to International Law After the Gulf War*, pp 438–41; Roberts, *The Law of War and Environmental Damage*, in: Austin, Bruch (Eds), *The Environmental Consequences of War*, p 57. Bothe writes: 'One can then argue that the elements of the environment which are damaged as a consequence of the destruction are also property within the meaning of that provision. This may be so if land owned by somebody is damaged. But where the marine environment or certain species living on land are the victim, it is at least not a matter of course to conclude that this damage to the environment also constitutes a destruction of property.' Bothe, *Criminal Responsibility for Environmental Damage in Times of Armed Conflict*, in: Grunawalt, King, McClain (Eds), *Protection of the Environment during Armed Conflict*, p 476.

[840] Compare Schmitt, who refers to straddling stock of fish or migratory bird species. Schmitt, *Green War: An Assessment of the Environmental Law of International Armed Conflict*, p 64; Schmitt, *War and the Environment: Fault Lines in the Prescriptive Landscape*, in: Austin, Bruch (Eds), *The Environmental Consequences of War*, p 111. As far as straddling stock of fish are concerned, see further below on the protection of interests in the Exclusive Economic Zone and the Continental Shelf.

susceptible of ownership,[841] and it is not self-evident that surface water falls under the concept of 'property'.

Under Dutch law, for example, animals that do not have an owner are considered *res nullii* that will become the property of the person that catches them, even if that person did not have a right to hunt or fish.[842] This follows from Article 5:4 of the Dutch Civil Code.[843] The atmosphere is in principle not susceptible to ownership, under Dutch law, since Article 5:1 of the Dutch Civil Code defines '*eigendom*' as '*het meest omvattende recht dat een persoon op een zaak kan hebben.*' According to Article 3:2 Civil Code, '*zaken*' are '*voor menselijke beheersing vatbare stoffelijke objecten*' and need to be capable of 'individualization' according to jurisprudence. Without technical processing, this is impossible with respect to air and to the atmosphere in general.[844]

The same problem exists for surface waters. In principle surface water is incapable of 'individualization', it can therefore not be regarded as a '*zaak*' and is thus not susceptible to ownership. The Dutch Civil Code makes two exceptions on this. Article 5:20(c) states that the ownership of land includes groundwater that has come to the surface through a spring, well, or pump; and Article 5:20(d) states that the ownership of land includes surface water that is not connected with surface water on someone else's property.

Open surface waters can therefore not be owned under Dutch law. That does not mean that their use is open to everyone, however. Article 5:21(1) states that a landowner has in principle the exclusive right to use the space underneath and above the surface, including surface water. And since the

[841] Where Schmitt only refers in this context to the difficulties with respect to the atmosphere, climate and the ozone layer, Simonds and Desgagné are more determined. On the one hand, Simonds writes that 'property' encompasses land and airspace, but not outer space. Desgagné, on the other hand, believes that including the atmosphere under Art 23(g) 'may (. . .) unreasonably overstretch the notion of "property" as it is used in the Regulations.' Desgagné, *The Prevention of Environmental Damage in Time of Armed Conflict: Proportionality and Precautionary Measures*, in: Fischer, McDonald (Eds), *Yearbook of International Humanitarian Law; Vol 3; 2000*, p 115; Schmitt, *Green War: An Assessment of the Environmental Law of International Armed Conflict*, p 64; Schmitt, *War and the Environment: Fault Lines in the Prescriptive Landscape*, in: Austin, Bruch (Eds), *The Environmental Consequences of War*, p 111; Simonds, *Conventional Warfare and Environmental Protection: A Proposal for International Legal Reform*, p 171. Roberts, finally, writes that 'some environmental 'goods', such as the air we breathe, are not property.' Roberts, *Environmental Issues in International Armed Conflict: The Experience of the 1991 Gulf War*, in: Grunawalt, King, McClain (Eds), *Protection of the Environment during Armed Conflict*, p 237.

[842] CC van Dam, FHJ Mijnssen, AA van Velten (Eds), *Mr C Asser's Handleiding tot de Beoefening van het Nederlands Burgerlijk Recht; Vol 3—Goederenrecht; Band II—Zakelijke Rechten*, veertiende druk, Kluwer, Deventer, 2002, No 60.

[843] *Nederlands Burgerlijk Wetboek*, or Dutch Civil Code, entered into force on 1 Jan 1992, through <http://wetten.overheid.nl/>.

[844] FHJ Mijnssen,P de Haan (Eds), *Mr C Asser's Handleiding tot de Beoefening van het Nederlands Burgerlijk Recht; Vol 3—Goederenrecht; Band I—Algemeen Goederenrecht*, veertiende druk, WEJ Tjeenk Willink, Deventer, 2001, No 54.

bottom of the territorial sea belongs to the State,[845] all land underneath internal public waterways is presumed to belong to the State,[846] and all land that is not privately owned is the property of the State,[847] all surface waters fall under the exclusive user's right of the State.[848] Although this exclusive right to use water does not fall under the Dutch, and likely also the civil, legal concept of ownership, it might very well fall under the broader common law concept of 'property'.[849]

Furthermore, it is uncertain whether the living resources in the Exclusive Economic Zones (EEZ) of coastal states and the mineral resources in its Continental Shelf fall under the concept of 'property'. Although, coastal states do not have sovereignty over these sea areas, they do have exclusive rights of exploitation of both natural and mineral resources in both zones, according to Articles 56 and 77 of the United Nations Convention on the Law of the Seas.[850] Because of these exclusive user's rights, the living and mineral resources in the EEZ and Continental Shelf might still fall under the concept of property.[851] This would only be relevant, however, for Article 55 HR and Article 53 GC IV, since Article 23(g) HR only focuses on the conduct of hostilities on land and the consequences of land warfare will not easily be felt at sea.

Apart from limitations with respect to the scope of the concept of property, the prohibition to seize or destroy property under the Hague Regulations and the Fourth Geneva Convention is limited by an exception of military necessity. Article 23(g) HR and Article 53 GC IV allow the destruction of property if this is 'imperatively demanded by the necessities of war' or 'where such destruction is rendered absolutely necessary by

[845] Art 5:25 Civil Code.

[846] Art 5:27 Civil Code.

[847] Art 5:24 Civil Code.

[848] Generally on the ownership of water and land beneath surface waters, Van Dam, Mijnssen, Van Velten (Eds), *Mr C Asser's Handleiding tot de Beoefening van het Nederlands Burgerlijk Recht; Vol 3—Goederenrecht; Band II—Zakelijke Rechten*, No 96–7, 102–6.

[849] Compare Low and Hodgkinson who write that the argument that 'the climate, atmosphere, sea, and marine life are not property because they cannot be owned' is circular and that '[r]ather, the question should be answered by reviewing the rights which the law extends over an object in question. More specifically, if the law extends exclusive rights over an object, that object will often be described as property.' Low, Hodgkinson, *Compensation for Wartime Environmental Damage: Challenges to International Law After the Gulf War*, p 438.

[850] United Nations Convention on the Law of the Seas, signed on 10 Dec 1982, entered into force on 16 Nov 1994, UNTS, Vol 1833, No 31363.

[851] Similarly Simonds, who writes that the territorial sea certainly belongs to the coastal state and that coastal states have property rights over natural and mineral resources in the EEZ and the Continental Shelf. Simonds, *Conventional Warfare and Environmental Protection: A Proposal for International Legal Reform*, pp 183, 207; Low, Hodgkinson, *Compensation for Wartime Environmental Damage: Challenges to International Law After the Gulf War*, pp 439–41. Boelaert-Suominen believes that parts of the environment that 'do not "belong" to any of the parties involved would not be covered by the norm. This excludes migratory species to which a State does not retain exclusive property rights as well as natural resources in international areas.' Boelaert-Suominen, *International Environmental Law and Naval War; The Effect of Marine Safety and Pollution Conventions During International Armed Conflict*, p 51.

military operations.' In 'The Hostages Trial' of Wilhelm List and Others, the United States Military Tribunal at Nuremberg discussed the plea of military necessity by General Rendulic under whose command 'much physical destruction' had been carried out during the German retreat from Finnmark.[852] The orders were justified by reference to a 'strategically perilous situation arising out of the withdrawal from the war of Finland.'[853] Rendulic's army had been weakened because his best divisions had been called back to Germany and during their retreat from Finland they had been pursued by Russian troops. Afraid that the Russians would press further and that they would land by sea behind the German lines, Rendulic turned to a 'scorched earth' policy in Finnmark. Although in hindsight, these fears were not justified and that there was no military necessity for the destruction, the tribunal stated that 'we are obliged to judge the situation as it appeared to the defendant at the time' and since there was an existing possibility that the Russians would land, Rendulic could 'honestly conclude that urgent military necessity warranted the decision made' and could therefore not be held criminally liable for the destruction of property.[854]

Finally, the 1899 and 1907 Hague Regulations were considered to reflect customary international law by the International Military Tribunal at Nuremberg in 1946,[855] which means not only that Articles 23(g) and 55 HR are also binding on states that have not become party to both Conventions, but also that the general participation or *si omnes* clauses of the 1899 and 1907 Regulations[856] have lost their relevance. The Tribunal stated:

> The rules of land warfare expressed in the Convention undoubtedly represented an advance over existing international law at the time of their adoption. But (. . .) by 1939 these rules laid down in the Convention were recognized by

[852] Finnmark is the most northern province of Norway.

[853] United States Military Tribunal (Nuremberg), *Case No 47; The Hostages Trial; Trial of Wilhelm List and Others; 8th Jul, 1947–19th Feb, 1948; No (v) Rendulic,* in: The United Nations War Crimes Commission, *Law Reports of Trials of War Criminals; Vol VIII,* His Majesty's Stationary Office, London, 1949, p 45.

[854] United States Military Tribunal (Nuremberg), *Case No 47; The Hostages Trial; Trial of Wilhelm List and Others; 8th Jul, 1947–19th Feb, 1948; No (v) Rendulic,* in: The United Nations War Crimes Commission, *Law Reports of Trials of War Criminals; Vol VIII,* 1949, pp 68–9.

[855] Art 6(b) of the Charter of the International Military Tribunal at Nuremberg, referred to 'devastation' in general, not limited to property as such and not specified to anything in particular. The Article read: '*War crimes*: namely, violations of the laws or customary of war. Such violations shall include, but not be limited to (. . .) plunder of public or private property, wanton destruction of cities, towns or violates, or devastation not justified by military necessity.'

[856] Art 2 of the 1899 Hague Regulations stated that '[t]he provisions contained in the Regulations mentioned in Art 1 are only binding on the Contracting Powers, in case of war between two or more of them. These provisions shall cease to be binding from the time when, in a war between Contracting Powers, a non-Contracting Power joins one of the belligerents.' Art 2 of the 1907 Hague Regulations provided: 'The provisions contained in the Regulations referred to in Article 1, as well as in the present Convention, do not apply except between Contracting Powers, and then only if all the belligerents are parties to the Convention.'

all civilized nations, and were regarded as being declaratory of the laws and customs of war (. . .).[857]

3.2.3 Protection of Civilian Objects after 1977

Before 1977, civilian objects were primarily protected under the Hague Regulations and the Fourth Geneva Convention by prohibiting the unnecessary destruction of property during hostilities and during occupation. After 1977, explicit protection of civilian objects was provided by Additional Protocol I by the codification of the customary obligation to distinguish between military and civilian objects in Article 48 of Additional Protocol I and by the subsequent definitions of civilian and military objects. Article 48 states:

> In order to ensure respect for and protection of the civilian population and civilian objects, the Parties to the conflict shall at all times distinguish between the civilian population and combatants and between civilian objects and military objectives and accordingly shall direct their operations only against military objectives.

It was the first time the principle of discrimination and the customary obligation to distinguish between civilians and combatants and civilian and military objects was explicitly laid down in an international agreement. Earlier attempts to do so and adapt the laws of war to new technological developments had proved unsuccessful. In 1923 an international Commission of Jurists consisting of representatives of the United States, the United Kingdom, France, Italy, Japan and the Netherlands drafted a number of Rules on Air Warfare,[858] but this draft convention was never ratified. And in 1938, the International Law Association drafted a Convention for the Protection of Civilian Populations against New Engines of War,[859] but this draft treaty was never signed.

[857] International Military Tribunal (Nuremberg), *Judgments and Sentences; Oct 1, 1946*, American Journal of International Law, Vol 41, 1947, pp 248–9. Also in Dinstein, *The Conduct of Hostilities under the Law of International Armed Conflict*, p 10.

[858] 1923 Hague Rules of Aerial Warfare, in: Roberts, Guelff, *Documents on the Laws of War*, pp 141–53; Schindler, Toman (Eds), *The Laws of Armed Conflicts; A Collection of Conventions, Resolutions and Other Documents*, pp 208–17. Art 24(1) stated that '[a]erial bombardment is legitimate only when directed at a military objective, that is to say, an object of which the destruction or injury would constitute a distinct military advantage to the belligerent.'

[859] Draft Convention for the Protection of Civilian Populations Against New Engines of War, adopted by the ILA at its Fortieth Conference held at Amsterdam in 1938, in: Schindler, Toman (Eds), *The Laws of Armed Conflicts; A Collection of Conventions, Resolutions and Other Documents*, pp 223–9. Art 1 provided that '[t]he civilian population of a State shall not form the object of an act of war. The phrase "civilian population" within the meaning of this Convention shall include all those not enlisted in any branch of the combatant services nor for the time being employed or occupied in any belligerent establishment as defined in Article 2.'

Additional Protocol I was not only the first treaty to lay down the principle of distinction, its protection of the civilian objects and the civilian population is also most comprehensive. Article 52(1) generally states:

> Civilian objects shall not be the object of attack or reprisals. Civilian objects are all objects which are not military objectives as defined in paragraph 2.

Paragraph 2 states:

> Attacks shall be limited strictly to military objectives. In so far as objects are concerned, military objectives are limited to those objects which by their nature, location, purpose or use make an effective contribution to military action and whose total or partial destruction, capture or neutralization, in the circumstances ruling at the time, offers a definite military advantage.

Furthermore, Articles 57 and 58 of Chapter IV prescribe that care must be taken during hostilities to spare civilian objects which includes the taking of precautionary measures in order to avoid or minimise collateral damage.

Article 52(1) generally codifies the customary rule to distinguish between military and civilian objects, and although it was 'one of the most heavily debated provisions of the Additional Protocol',[860] the definition of military objects in paragraph 2 is nowadays generally considered to reflect customary international law. The definition reminds of Article 24(1) of the 1923 Hague Rules on Air Warfare[861] and has been repeated in Article 2(4) of the Second and in Article 1(3) of the Third Protocol to the 1981 Certain Conventional Weapons Convention, Article 1(f) of the 1999 Second Protocol to the Hague Cultural Property Convention,[862] and in paragraph 40 of the 1995 San Remo Manual on International Law Applicable to Armed Conflicts at Sea.[863] In 2000, the ICTY Committee established by the Prosecutor to review the 1999 NATO bombing campaign against Yugoslavia concluded that despite criticism:

> it provides the contemporary standard which must be used when attempting to determine the lawfulness of particular attacks. (. . .) The definition is, however, generally accepted as part of customary law.[864]

[860] Oeter, *Methods and Means of Combat*, in: D Fleck (Ed), *The Handbook of Humanitarian Law in Armed Conflicts*, p 156.

[861] Art 24(1) provides: 'Aerial bombardment is legitimate, only when directed at a military objective, that is to say, an object of which the destruction or injury would constitute a distinct military advantage to the belligerent.'

[862] Second Protocol to the Hague Convention of 1954 for the Protection of Cultural Property in the Event of Armed Conflict, opened for signature on 26 Mar 1999, entered into force on 9 Mar 2004, UNTS, Vol 2253, No 3511.

[863] Dinstein, *The Conduct of Hostilities under the Law of International Armed Conflict*, p 83.

[864] ICTY, *Final Report to the Prosecutor by the Committee Established to Review the NATO Bombing Campaign against the Federal Republic of Yugoslavia*, International Legal Materials, Vol 39, 2000, p 1269.

And in 2005, the ICRC concluded in its Study on Customary International Humanitarian Law that state practice had established this definition as a rule of customary law.[865]

In view of Article 52(2)'s definition of military objects, it seems possible to infer environmental protection from the obligation to distinguish between military and civilian objects. Because the environment as such does in principle not make 'an effective contribution to military action', elements of the natural environment may be regarded as a civilian object[866] and are therefore entitled to protection under Articles 52, 57, and 58 of Additional Protocol I.[867] This would, of course, only apply to those elements of the natural environment that are covered by Section I of Part IV, in accordance with Article 49(3), as has been explained before.[868]

Interestingly, this interpretation of Article 52 may either be supported or excluded by the context in which Article 52 is placed. Chapter III consists, in addition to Article 52, of four other Articles dealing with specific civilian objects, including the natural environment in Article 55. Article 55 prescribes specific care for the natural environment and prohibits the use of means and methods of warfare that cause widespread, long-term and severe damage to the environment thereby prejudicing the health and survival of the population. It is arguable therefore that Article 55 should be regarded as *lex specialis* with respect to the general obligation of Article 52,[869] although it

865 Henckaerts, Doswald-Beck (Eds), *Customary International Humanitarian Law; Vol I: Rules*, Rule 8, pp 29–30.

866 Similarly and very determined, Bothe, in: Bothe, *The Protection of the Environment in Times of Armed Conflict; Legal Rules, Uncertainty, Deficiencies, and Possible Developments*, p 55; Bothe, *Protection of the Environment in Times of Armed Conflict*, in: Al-Nauimi, Meese (Eds), *International Legal Issues Arising Under the United Nations Decade of International Law; Proceedings of the Qatar International Law Conference '94*, p 98. In the second contribution, Bothe also discussed two problems related to the application of this rule to environmental protection, namely the problem of balancing values as in the context of proportionality and the definition of military objects, which might include environmentally sensitive areas. Compare also Rogers' discussion of whether or not an area of land can be a military objective. Rogers, *Law on the Battlefield*, pp 68–9.

867 Donner and Heintschel von Heinegg strongly disagree, however. According to them, 'the natural environment can not [*sic*] be equated with civilian objects. Moreover, the term "object" necessarily refers to material things that can be seen or touched. The natural environment as the sum total of different and differing natural components and processes may not be characterized as such an object.' Heintschel von Heinegg, Donner, *New Developments in the Protection of the Natural Environment in Naval Armed Conflicts*, p 289.

868 Art 49(3) states: 'The provisions of this Section apply to any land, air or sea warfare which may affect the civilian population, individual civilians or civilian objects on land. They further apply to all attacks from the sea or from the air against objectives on land but do not otherwise affect the rules of international law applicable in armed conflict at sea or in the air.'

869 According to Kalshoven, it is 'evident from their headings, [that] these Articles [53–56] are a mixed bag, with only one feature in common: viz., that they single out for protection specified objects, or values, apparently considered to be of special importance in the context of the protection of the civilian population.' Kalshoven, *Reaffirmation and Development of International Humanitarian Law Applicable in Armed Conflicts: the Diplomatic Conference, Geneva, 1974–1977; Part II*, p 123. Similarly, Kalshoven, Zegveld, *Constraints on the Waging of War; An Introduction to International Humanitarian Law*, p 104.

is not certain whether it should set aside the general obligation.[870] If Article 55 sets aside Article 52, then Article 52 does not provide indirect protection to the environment for States Parties to Additional Protocol I; if Article 55 does not set aside Article 52, then it is possible to fall back on the general environmental protection of Article 52.[871]

On the one hand, Bothe seems to imply that the general obligation is not set aside by Article 55, when observing that 'the environment is protected as being part of the civilian world' and that neither Articles 55 nor Article 35(3):

> are meant to lower any standard of protection under general rules [of ius in bello]. Thus, Articles 35 and 55 prohibit causing damage to the environment even where the environment constitutes a military objective or where the damage to the environment may be considered as not being excessive in relation to the military advantage anticipated.[872]

Bothe seems to imply that Articles 35 and 55 only protect the environment when they can be considered military objectives.[873] When the environ-

[870] With respect to Art 56, Solf writes that 'even if the special protection is lost, the general protection of the Protocol and the rule of proportionality remain in effect.' Solf, *Protection of Civilians Against the Effects of Hostilities under Customary International Law and Under Protocol I*, p 134. Verwey does not interpret Art 52 in the light of Art 55, but rather Art 55 in the light of Art 52, in this context. Because Art 55 falls under ch III—Civilian Objects, the protection of the environment under Art 55 would cease to apply in case certain objects or elements of the environment would be identified as military objects. As has been observed earlier, this interpretation of Art 55 does not fully convince in view of the setting and structure of ch III of s I of Pt IV of Additional Protocol I and the text of Art 55. Verwey, *Observations on the Legal Protection of the Environment in Times of International Armed Conflict*, p 38; Verwey, *Protection of the Environment in Times of Armed Conflict: In Search of a New Legal Perspective*, p 13; Verwey, *Comment: Protection of the Environment in Times of Armed Conflict—Do We Need Additional Rules?*, in: Grunawalt, King, McClain, *Protection of the Environment during Armed Conflict*, p 562.

[871] According to the Commentary of the ILC on Art 55 of the Draft Arts on State Responsibility, '[i]t will depend on the special rule to establish the extent to which (. . .) more general rules (. . .) are displaced by that rule. In some cases it will be clear form the language of a treaty or other text that only the consequences specified are to flow. (. . .) In other cases, one aspect of the general law may be modified, leaving other aspects still applicable.' A/56/10, Draft Articles on Responsibility of States for Internationally Wrongful Acts, including Commentaries, adopted by the International Law Commission at its fifty-third session, Nov 2001; Yearbook of the International Law Commission, 2001; Vol II, Pt Two, forthcoming, p 357. Through <http://www.un.org/law/ilc/>. Also J Crawford, *The International Law Commission's Articles on State Responsibility; Introduction, Text and Commentaries*, Cambridge University Press, Cambridge, 2002, p 307.

[872] Bothe, *The Protection of the Environment in Times of Armed Conflict; Legal Rules, Uncertainty, Deficiencies, and Possible Developments*, pp 55–6. Similarly, Bothe, *War Crimes*, in: Cassese, Gaeta, Jones (Eds), *The Rome Statue of the International Criminal Court: A Commentary; Vol I*, p 401.

[873] Note, however, Verwey who seems to be of the opinion that once the environment can be identified as a military object it is not protected by Art 55 because of its position in a chapter dealing with 'Civilian Objects': 'Identifying affected parts, objects or assets of the environment as a military object or as an object of military significance would suffice to exclude the applicability of Article 55.' Verwey, *Protection of the Environment in Times of Armed Conflict: In Search of a New Legal Perspective*, p 13. Similarly, Verwey, *Observations on the Legal Protection of the Environment in Times of International Armed Conflict*, p 38; Verwey, *Comment: Protection of the Environment in Times of Armed Conflict—Do We Need Additional Rules?*, in: Grunawalt, King, McClain, *Protection of the Environment during Armed Conflict*, p 562.

ment is not used for military purposes or provides military advantages, then it falls under the general protection of Article 52.

Donner and Heintschel von Heinegg, on the other hand, believe that Article 55 does set aside the general obligation of Article 52 and dismiss the possibility that both rules would exist next to each other. Although they admit that:

> [p]robably the natural environment could be considered a civilian object that may not be interfered with unless the effects remain within the limits set by the rules on collateral damages,

they say that:

> [u]nfortunately, in view of the wording of Arts. 35 para. 3 and 55 AP I such a dynamic interpretation is not feasible.

According to them, both provisions are:

> confined to effects that are 'widespread, long-term and severe'. Methods and means of (. . .) warfare always have negative effects upon the environment. The States parties to AP I can, therefore, not be said to have agreed upon a general protection of the natural environment against negative effects of warfare.

Therefore, they write that the environment cannot be equated with civilian objects and would find it:

> difficult to explain why the drafters of AP I did not simply state that the term 'civilian object' also comprises the natural environment. Instead they agreed on two independent provisions that will protect it only against damages that are 'widespread, long-term and severe.'[874]

Unfortunately, the preparatory works do not provide much clarity in this respect,[875] but in view of the text of Article 52 and 55, and their position in Chapter III, it seems that the natural environment must be assumed to be a civilian object in the sense of Article 52. However, because the drafters believed it necessary to lay down a specific provision for the protection of the environment, it seems plausible that Article 55 does supplant and not supplement Article 52 in case of concurrent application. It does not appear from the text of Article 55 nor from the preparatory works that the drafters had in mind that one could fall back on Article 52 in case the restrictive conditions of Article 55 would not be met.

The drafters of the Statute of the International Criminal Court added an interesting point to the discussion whether or not the environment can in

[874] Heintschel von Heinegg, Donner, *New Developments in the Protection of the Natural Environment in Naval Armed Conflicts*, pp 288–9.

[875] The drafting history of Art 55 shows that the protection of the environment was more related to the protection of the civilian population than to civilian objects.

principle be regarded as a civilian object. In Article 8(2)(b)(iv) of the Rome Statute, the drafters listed as a war crime:

> [i]ntentionally launching an attack in the knowledge that such attack will cause incidental loss of life or injury to civilians or damage to civilian objects or widespread, long-term and severe damage to the natural environment which would be clearly excessive in relation to the concrete and direct overall military advantage anticipated.

This formulation clearly implies that the environment is not to be regarded as a civilian object, since it refers to civilian objects *or* the environment. Although the Statute as such does not affect the interpretation of Additional Protocol I, and although it is more likely that Article 8(2)(b)(iv) reflects a relatively new customary rule, this formulation is nevertheless authoritative and supports the claim that the environment should not be regarded as a civilian object.[876]

In addition to the natural environment in Article 55, Chapter III of Section I of Part IV, also specifically refers to cultural objects and places of worship—Article 53; objects that are indispensable to the survival of the civilian population—Article 54; and works and installations containing dangerous forces—Article 56, as civilian objects that need specific regulation. Especially the latter two provisions may unintentionally benefit the environment. Article 54(2) prohibits:

> to attack, destroy, remove or render useless objects indispensable to the survival of the civilian population, such as foodstuffs, agricultural areas for the production of foodstuffs, crops, livestock, drinking water installations and supplies and irrigation works, for the specific purpose of denying them for their sustenance value to the civilian population or to the adverse Party, whatever the motive, whether in order to starve out civilians, to cause them to move away, or for any other motive.

And Article 56(1) provides:

> Works or installations containing dangerous forces, namely dams, dykes and nuclear electrical generating stations, shall not be made the object of attack, even where these objects are military objectives, if such attack may cause the release of dangerous forces and consequent severe losses among the civilian population. (. . .).

[876] Bothe finds the link with civilian objects in Art 8(2)(b)(iv) unfortunate. As has been observed above, certain elements of the environment must be regarded as civilian objects and are ipso facto protected under the laws of war. However, the protection of civilian objects does not require that possible damage is widespread, long-term and severe. 'Thus, the combination of the two types of conditions makes sense only in two hypotheses: first, if the element of the environment has a military value of its own, secondly, to indicate a level or environmental damage which would in all cases be "excessive". But these hypotheses are not quite covered by the wording of subparagraph (b)(iv).' Bothe, *War Crimes*, in: Cassese, Gaeta, Jones (Eds), *The Rome Statue of the International Criminal Court: A Commentary; Vol I*, p 401.

Article 54 indirectly protects the environment,[877] since agricultural land, crops, and livestock may be regarded as elements of nature, despite being cultivated and despite the fact that they have turned into economical assets. And even if they would not be regarded as elements of the natural environment, their destruction, as well as the destruction of water installations and irrigation works may have detrimental consequences for the environment. After all, Article 54 has a historical link with the environment, since current Article 55, which prescribes care for the environment, was introduced in 1974 in relation with current Article 54.[878]

Article 56 is likely to provide even more substantial protection to the environment, since the dangerous forces that may be released by destroying dams, dykes, and nuclear power plants may not only result in severe losses among the civilian population, but are also likely to have harmful effects for the natural environment.[879] An amendment of a number of Arab states at the Diplomatic Conference in Geneva to include a prohibition to destroy 'oil rigs, petroleum storage facilities, and oil refineries' was generally defeated.[880]

Although the scope of protection is limited by three military exception clauses in paragraph 2, the protection provided may still be significant. If it had not been for the direct link with the civilian population, this Article might just as well been regarded as directly protecting the natural environment. This is evidenced among other things by a Resolution of a meeting of the ILA in Madrid on 4 September 1976, ie one year before conclusion of the Diplomatic Conference, and by a General Assembly Resolution in 1990. The ILA 'Resolution on the Protection of Water Resources and Water Installations in Times of Armed Conflict' prohibited the destruction of water installations 'when such destruction may involve . . . substantial damage to the basic ecological balance'. The General Assembly expressed in its Resolution on the Prohibition of Attacks on

[877] Similarly, Momtaz, *La Recours à l'Arme Nucléaire et la Protection de l'Environnement: l'Apport de la Cour Internationale de Justice,* in: Boisson de Chazournes, Sands (Eds), *International Law, the International Court of Justice and Nuclear Weapons,* p 370.

[878] Levie, *Protection of War Victims: Protocol 1 to the 1949 Geneva Conventions; Vol 3,* p 259. Czechoslovakia, the German Democratic Republic, and Hungary even proposed to add an environmental paragraph to the draft Article that dealt with objects that were indispensable to the survival of the civilian population. CDDH/III/64, 19 Mar 1974 (III, 221), in: Levie, *Protection of War Victims: Protocol 1 to the 1949 Geneva Conventions; Vol 3,* p 259.

[879] Similarly, Momtaz, *La Recours à l'Arme Nucléaire et la Protection de l'Environnement: l'Apport de la Cour Internationale de Justice,* in: Boisson de Chazournes, Sands (Eds), *International Law, the International Court of Justice and Nuclear Weapons,* pp 370–1.

[880] Kalshoven, *Reaffirmation and Development of International Humanitarian Law Applicable in Armed Conflicts: the Diplomatic Conference, Geneva, 1974–1977; Pt II,* p 136.

Nuclear Facilities[881] that such attacks 'could result in radioactive releases with grave consequences'.[882]

Finally, neither Article 54 nor Article 56 had customary equivalents before 1977,[883] and opinion is divided on the question whether both provisions have developed into rules of customary international law.[884]

3.2.4 Legal Appraisal

In view of the arguable *lex specialis—lex generalis* relationship between Articles 52 and 55, the practical value of indirect protection of the envir-

[881] A/Res/45/58J, adopted on 4 Dec 1990, by 141 to 1, with 11 abstentions; 'Prohibition of Attacks on Nuclear Facilities'.

[882] PC Szasz, *Environmental Destruction as a Method of Warfare; International Law Applicable to the Gulf War,* Disarmament, Vol 15, 1992, p 137.

[883] Dinstein, *The Conduct of Hostilities under the Law of International Armed Conflict,* pp 94, 132, 173; Greenwood, *Customary Law Status of the 1977 Geneva Protocols,* in: Delissen, Tanja (Eds), *Humanitarian Law of Armed Conflict; Challenges Ahead; Essays in Honour of Frits Kalshoven,* p 110; Oeter, *Methods and Means of Combat,* in: D Fleck (Ed), *The Handbook of Humanitarian Law in Armed Conflicts,* pp 191–2, 194; Solf, *Protection of Civilians Against the Effects of Hostilities under Customary International Law and Under Protocol I,* p 133; Solf, in: Bothe, Partsch, Solf, *New Rules for Victims of Armed Conflicts; Commentary on the Two 1977 Protocols Additional to the Geneva Conventions of 1949,* pp 278–9, 336. With respect to Art 54(1), the ICRC's 2005 Study on Customary International Humanitarian Law argues that the prohibition of starvation reflected customary international law. Most authors, however, refer to longstanding practice of starvation as a legitimate form of siege warfare. Henckaerts, Doswald-Beck (Eds), *Customary International Humanitarian Law; Vol I: Rules,* Rule 53, p 186. With respect to Art 54(5), it should be noted that the United States Military Tribunal at Nuremberg generally sanctioned scorched earth politics if it was reasonably warranted by urgent military necessity. United States Military Tribunal (Nuremberg), *Case No 47; The Hostages Trial; Trial of Wilhelm List and Others; 8th Jul, 1947–19th Feb, 1948; No (v) Rendulic,* in: The United Nations War Crimes Commission, *Law Reports of Trials of War Criminals; Vol VIII,* p 45. Art 54(5) only allows for scorched earth politics by 'any Party to the conflict in the defence of its national territory against invasion'.

[884] According to the ICRC, Art 54 and Art 56 do nowadays reflect customary international law. Customary Rule 54 prescribes: 'Attacking, destroying, removing or rendering useless objects indispensable to the survival of the civilian population are prohibited.' And Rule 42 prescribes: 'Particular care must be taken if works and installations containing dangerous forces, namely dams, dykes and nuclear electrical generating stations, and other installations located at or in their vicinity are attacked, in order to avoid the release of dangerous forces and consequent severe losses among the civilian population.' Henckaerts, Doswald-Beck (Eds), *Customary International Humanitarian Law; Vol I: Rules,* pp 139, 189. According to Solf in 1986, Art 54 is substantially new and 'is not yet customary international law.' Art 56, however, 'differs little from customary international law.' Solf, *Protection of Civilians Against the Effects of Hostilities under Customary International Law and Under Protocol I,* pp 133–4. In 1991, Greenwood writes that is arguable that both Arts 54 and 56 have become part of customary international law. Greenwood, *Customary Law Status of the 1977 Geneva Protocols,* in: Delissen, Tanja (Eds), *Humanitarian Law of Armed Conflict; Challenges Ahead; Essays in Honour of Frits Kalshoven,* p 110. Green writes in 2000 that Art 56 does not bind non-State Parties to Protocol I. Green, *The Contemporary Law of Armed Conflict,* p 158. And Dinstein, finally, believes in 2004 that both provisions were substantially new and do not yet reflect customary law. Dinstein, *The Conduct of Hostilities under the Law of International Armed Conflict,* pp 132, 173.

onment through the general protection of civilian objects does not seem to be significant. Furthermore, in view of the emergence of two customary rules of *ius in bello*, prohibiting wanton destruction of and excessive damage to the environment, it is likely that the indirect protection of the environment provided under customary law and the Hague Regulations through the protection of property and civilian objects in general has similarly lost most of its importance. Both new customary rules stem from the same principles of *ius in bello*, namely the principle of necessity and its sub-principle of proportionality, as the rules on the protection of property and civilian objects in general, and have a similar object and purpose. However, both new customary rules are specifically geared towards environmental protection, and it is therefore likely that the rules on indirect protection have been supplanted by these two new customary rules in accordance with the maxim *lex specialis derogat legi generali*.

3.3 The Law of Neutrality

In addition to the protection of civilian objects under *ius in bello*, also the law of neutrality may be taken to provide indirect protection to the environment during international armed conflict. Similar to the rules discussed above, the rationale behind the law of neutrality was never to protect the environment, but its terminology is sufficiently broad that it may be interpreted as including elements of the natural environment and the implementation of its rights and duties may nevertheless have a beneficial impact on the environment. The protection of the environment under the law of neutrality is therefore not direct but merely indirect.

The law of neutrality regulates the relationship between neutral states and belligerents,[885] ie between states that do not take 'part between two or more nations at war' and maintain 'a strict indifference as between the contending parties' and states 'which are actually in a state of war with each other, as well as their allies actively co-operating'.[886] The law of neutrality therefore presupposes the existence of a 'war' or, nowadays, of an international armed conflict, in view of common Article 2 of the four 1949 Geneva Conventions. Where the existence of a state of war depended on a declaration of war or the recognition of a state of war by both belligerents, and was therefore susceptible to abuse, the existence of an international armed conflict depends primarily on factual circumstances and just

[885] E Castrén, *The Present Law of War and Neutrality*, Suomalaisen Kirjallisuuden Seuran Kirjapainon Oy, Helsinki, 1954, p 422.

[886] Black (et al), *Black's Law Dictionary*, pp 106, 722.

requires the use of force[887] between states or between states and peoples exercising their right of self-determination.[888]

The concept of neutrality is one of the older concepts of public international law and 'emerged with the early development of international maritime law'.[889] After the Middle Ages, non-participating states increasingly pushed for and received protection against warring states through agreements, especially with respect to maritime commerce, and this practice found increasing recognition in the 18th and 19th century. Respect for neutral trading and the territorial integrity of neutral states became a means for limiting the consequences of war in a time when 'war was tolerated as a means of national policy'.[890]

Although it used to be common to declare neutrality before or as soon as war broke out, it is not legally necessary to do so. 'Neutrality automatically becomes effective at the outbreak of war between third States' and ends as soon as the war is ended or when the neutral state enters the war.[891] All a neutral state needs to do is refrain from the use of force against belligerents[892] so that it does not become a party to the conflict.

Despite claims to the contrary,[893] there is no status in-between belligerency and neutrality, such as 'non-belligerency' or 'qualified neutrality' which would allow a state to support one of the belligerents diplomatically or economically without participating in hostilities. The law of

[887] A non-international armed conflict requires 'protracted' armed violence, according to the ICTY. ICTY; Prosecutor v Dusko Tadic a/k/a 'Dule' (IT-94-1); Decision on the Defence Motion for Interlocutory Appeal on Jurisdiction, 2 Oct 1995, para 70, p 37, International Legal Materials, Vol 35, 1996, p 54, or at <http://www.un.org/icty/tadic/appeal/decision-e/51002.htm>. The United States regards the current struggle against international terrorism as a 'global war on terror' justifying measures under the laws of war that would normally be difficult to justify under the laws of peace. The general characterisation of this struggle as a 'global war', however, is denied by the ICRC and the Special Rapporteurs to the Commission on Human Rights on the situation of detainees at Guantánamo Bay. International Committee of the Red Cross, *The relevance of IHL in the context of terrorism*, Official Statement of 21 Jul 2005, s 1. Through: <http://www.icrc.org/>; E/CN.4/2006/120, Report of Special Rapporteurs to the Commission on Human Rights, of 27 Feb 2006; Economic, Social and Cultural Rights; Civil and Political Rights; The Situation of Detainees at Guantánamo Bay, para 21, p 9. See also the United States response by letter of 31 Jan 2006, addressed to the Office of the High Commissioner on Human Rights, in Annex II of the Report of the Special Rapporteurs, pp 43–4: 'The United States has made clear its position that it is engaged in a continuing armed conflict against Al Qaida, that the law of war applies to the conduct of that war and related detention operations (. . .).'

[888] See Art 1(4) of Additional Protocol I.

[889] Roberts, Guelff, *Documents on the Laws of War*, p 85.

[890] RL Bindschedler, *Neutrality, Concept and General Rules*, in: R Bernhardt (Ed), *Encyclopaedia of Public International Law; Vol Three; Jan Mayen to Pueblo Incident*, Elsevier, Amsterdam, 1997, pp 549–50.

[891] Bindschedler, *Neutrality, Concept and General Rules*, in: Bernhardt (Ed), *Encyclopaedia of Public International Law; Vol Three; Jan Mayen to Pueblo Incident*, p 549.

[892] Heintschel von Heinegg, Donner, *New Developments in the Protection of the Natural Environment in Naval Armed Conflicts*, p 296.

[893] Compare D Schindler, *Transformations in the Law of Neutrality Since 1945*, in: AJM Delissen, GJ Tanja (Eds), *Humanitarian Law of Armed Conflict; Challenges Ahead; Essays in Honour of Frits Kalshoven*, Martinus Nijhoff Publishers, Dordrecht, 1991, pp 371–7.

neutrality does not distinguish between economic, diplomatic or military support and regards any biased support of belligerents unlawful. Although diplomatic or economic support of one of the belligerents is not uncommon and may even be desirable, as in the case of the United States during World War II, it remains an internationally wrongful act entailing international responsibility.[894] This has not changed since 1945, although the Security Council may modify existing international obligations under the laws of neutrality by deciding to impose economic sanctions under Article 41 of the United Nations Charter against a state that has endangered international peace and security.[895] Decisions of the Security Council are binding under Article 25 of the Charter and in the event of a conflict between obligations under the Charter and the law of neutrality or other international legal obligations in general, the obligations under the Charter prevail.[896] In any case, there does not seem to be a legal duty for member states to assist states that have become the victim of aggression or to resort to countermeasures against aggressor states,[897] and the law of neutrality is therefore not incompatible with the system of collective security.[898]

[894] Bindschedler, *Neutrality, Concept and General Rules*, in: Bernhardt (Ed), *Encyclopaedia of Public International Law; Vol Three; Jan Mayen to Pueblo Incident*, pp 552–3. M Bothe, *Neutrality in Naval Warfare; What Is Left of Traditional International Law?*, in: AJM Delissen, GJ Tanja (Eds), *Humanitarian Law of Armed Conflict; Challenges Ahead; Essays in Honour of Frits Kalshoven*, Martinus Nijhoff Publishers, Dordrecht, 1991, pp 389–91; M Bothe, *The Law of Neutrality*, in: D Fleck (Ed), *The Handbook of Humanitarian Law in Armed Conflicts*, Oxford University Press, Oxford, 1995, p 485. Generally, Roberts, Guelff, *Documents on the Laws of War*, p 86.

[895] Neutral states do not escape responsibility for violations of the law of neutrality if the Security Council fails to designate one of the belligerents as aggressor. Each state has a duty to interpret the facts at their disposal in good faith and act accordingly. AJJ de Hoogh, *Comments*, in: HHG Post (Ed), *International Economic Law and Armed Conflict*, Martinus Nijhoff, Dordrecht, 1994, pp 43–6.

[896] Art 103 United Nations Charter.

[897] Also: De Hoogh, *Comments*, in: Post (Ed), *International Economic Law and Armed Conflict*, p 45. It should be noted, however, that according to Art 41(1) of the ILC's Draft Article on State Responsibility, 'States shall cooperate to bring to an end through lawful means any serious breach within the meaning of article 40.' Art 40 refers 'serious breaches' of obligations arising under peremptory norms of international law. In its Commentary, the ILC states that 'it is generally agreed that the prohibition of aggression is to be regarded as peremptory'. A/56/10, Draft Articles on Responsibility of States for Internationally Wrongful Acts, including Commentaries, adopted by the International Law Commission at its fifty-third session, Nov 2001; Yearbook of the International Law Commission, 2001; Vol II, Pt Two, forthcoming, p 283. Through <http://www.un.org/law/ilc/>. Also J Crawford, *The International Law Commission's Articles on State Responsibility; Introduction, Text and Commentaries*, Cambridge University Press, Cambridge, 2002, p 246. In the 1986 Nicaragua Case, however, the International Court of Justice only refers to frequent references to the prohibition on the use of force as a norm of *ius cogens*. Military and Paramilitary Activities in and against Nicaragua (Nicaragua v United States of America), Merits, Judgment, 27 Jun 1986, ICJ Reports 1986, p 14, para 190, pp 100–1. According to the ILC, it is uncertain whether present international law prescribes a duty to cooperate, and therefore Art 41(1) may reflect 'the progressive development of international law.' A/56/10, Draft Articles on Responsibility of States for Internationally Wrongful Acts, including Commentaries, p 287. Crawford, *The International Law Commission's Articles on State Responsibility; Introduction, Text and Commentaries*, p 249.

[898] Generally on the status of the law of neutrality in relation to the UN Charter: Bindschedler, *Neutrality, Concept and General Rules*, in: Bernhardt (Ed), *Encyclopaedia of Public*

The relationship between belligerents and neutral states is in principle governed by the law of peace, but the existence of an international armed conflict makes certain deviations necessary. Generally, neutrals must remain unbiased, deal with belligerents impartially and must prevent its territory from being used by any belligerent; belligerents must respect the territorial sovereignty of neutrals, not interfere with neutral trading and leave neutrals in peace. Therefore, and complementarily, belligerents have the right to make sure that neutrals observe their obligation to remain neutral and do not somehow support enemy states; neutrals have the right to demand respect for their sovereignty, have the right not to be adversely affected by the hostilities and the conflict in general, and the right to remain outside the war.[899] According to Dinstein, these rights and duties are based on two basic principles underlying the law of neutrality, namely 'non-participating in war and impartiality *vis-à-vis* the opposing belligerents.'[900]

In 1907 most of these general rights and duties were codified in two specific conventions on the rights and duties of neutral powers in case of war on land (Hague Convention V)[901] and in case of naval war (Hague Convention XIII),[902] and in 1928 the rules on neutrality in case of naval war were supplemented for participants of the Conference of American

International Law; Vol Three; Jan Mayen to Pueblo Incident, p 552; Bothe, *Neutrality in Naval Warfare; What Is Left of Traditional International Law?*, in: Delissen, Tanja (Eds), *Humanitarian Law of Armed Conflict; Challenges Ahead; Essays in Honour of Frits Kalshoven*, 391–7; Bothe, *The Law of Neutrality*, in: Fleck (Ed), *The Handbook of Humanitarian Law in Armed Conflicts*, pp 486–9; Bothe, Cassese, Kalshoven, Kiss, Salmon, Simmonds, *Protection of the Environment in Times of Armed Conflict*, pp 50–1; Heintschel von Heinegg, Donner, *New Developments in the Protection of the Natural Environment in Naval Armed Conflicts*, p 296; K Zemanek, *Neutrality in Land Warfare*, in: R Bernhardt (Ed), *Encyclopaedia of Public International Law; Vol Three; Jan Mayen to Pueblo Incident*, Elsevier, Amsterdam, 1997, pp 557–8. According to the International Court of Justice in the Nuclear Weapons Opinion upon the request of the General Assembly, 'the principle of neutrality (. . .) which is of a fundamental character' is applicable 'subject to the relevant provisions of the United Nations Charter'. Legality of the Threat or Use of Nuclear Weapons, Advisory Opinion, 8 Jul 1996, ICJ Reports 1996, para 89, p 261.

[899] Bindschedler, *Neutrality, Concept and General Rules*, in: Bernhardt (Ed), *Encyclopaedia of Public International Law; Vol Three; Jan Mayen to Pueblo Incident*, pp 551–2; Boelaert-Suominen, *International Environmental Law and Naval War; The Effect of Marine Safety and Pollution Conventions During International Armed Conflict*, pp 78–9; Bothe, *The Law of Neutrality*, in: Fleck (Ed), *The Handbook of Humanitarian Law in Armed Conflicts*, p 485; Bothe, Cassese, Kalshoven, Kiss, Salmon, Simmonds, *Protection of the Environment in Times of Armed Conflict*, pp 49–50; Castrén, *The Present Law of War and Neutrality*, pp 422–3; Dinstein, *Neutrality in Sea Warfare*, in: Bernhardt (Ed), *Encyclopaedia of Public International Law; Vol Three; Jan Mayen to Pueblo Incident*, pp 558–9; Zemanek, *Neutrality in Land Warfare*, in: Bernhardt (Ed), *Encyclopaedia of Public International Law; Vol Three; Jan Mayen to Pueblo Incident*, p 556.

[900] Y Dinstein, *Neutrality in Sea Warfare*, in: R Bernhardt (Ed), *Encyclopaedia of Public International Law; Vol Three; Jan Mayen to Pueblo Incident*, Elsevier, Amsterdam, 1997, p 558.

[901] Hague Convention (V) Respecting the Rights and Duties of Neutral Powers and Persons in Case of War on Land, signed on 18 Oct 1907, entered into force on 26 Jan 1910, AJIL, Vol 2, No 1/2, Supplement: Official Documents, 1908, p 117.

[902] Hague Convention (XIII) Concerning the Rights and Duties of Neutral Powers in Naval War, signed on 18 October 1907, entered into force on 26 January 1910, AJIL, Vol 2, No 1/2, Supplement: Official Documents, 1908, p 202.

States by the 1928 Havana Convention on Maritime Neutrality.[903] Also random provisions on neutrality were inserted in the 1899 and 1907 Hague Regulations, the non-binding 1923 Hague Rules on Air Warfare, the four 1949 Geneva Conventions and the 1977 Additional Protocol I to the Geneva Conventions, but there has not been any general restatement of the law of neutrality since the beginning of the 20th century.

Of these rights and duties of neutrals and belligerents, the respect for the territorial integrity of neutral powers is most interesting for the potential protection of the environment during international armed conflict. Article 1 of Hague Convention V with respect to land warfare states: 'The territory of neutral powers is inviolable.' Article 1 of Hague Convention XIII regarding naval warfare states:

> Belligerents are bound to respect the sovereign rights of neutral Powers and to abstain, in neutral territory or neutral waters, from any act which would, if knowingly permitted by any Power, constitute a violation of neutrality.

And Article 3 of the Havana Convention provides:

> Belligerent states are obligated to refrain from performing acts of war in neutral waters or other acts which may constitute on the part of the state that tolerates them, a violation of neutrality.

It seems that the drafters intended to prohibit incursions from and trespassing by belligerent armed forces and the carrying out of any activities that would benefit the trespasser and which would 'disadvantage, or are directed against, the other belligerent party.'[904] This appears from the wording and the context of these provisions. The territorial inviolability of neutral states in Article 1 of Hague Convention V, for example, is followed by two specific provisions that refer to trespassing. Article 2 forbids belligerents 'to move troops or convoys of either munitions of war or supplies across the territory of a neutral Power' and Article 3 forbids belligerents to establish communication equipment by belligerents on neutral territory or to use equipment for communication purposes that has been established by them before the war. Similarly, Article 1 of Hague Convention XIII is followed by two provisions dealing with hostile acts in neutral waters, including capture and search of ships.

The choice for the word 'inviolable', however, in Article 1 Hague Convention V allows for a wider interpretation than imagined by the

[903] Convention on Maritime Neutrality, signed on 20 Feb 1928, entered into force on 12 Jan 1931, AJIL, Vol 22, No 3, Supplement: Official Documents, 1928, p 151.

[904] Zemanek, *Neutrality in Land Warfare,* in: Bernhardt (Ed), *Encyclopaedia of Public International Law; Vol Three; Jan Mayen to Pueblo Incident,* pp 556–7. Also: Dissenting Opinion of Judge Shahabudeen, Legality of the Threat or Use of Nuclear Weapons, Advisory Opinion, 8 Jul 1996, ICJ Reports 1996, p 226, at p 387.

drafters.[905] In human rights instruments, for example, the term is used to denote a significant level of protection,[906] and semantically the term even seems to imply a level of protection against damage in general that verges on immunity. Firstly, 'inviolable' comes from the Latin *inviolabilis* and is related to the verb *violare* which means to harm, damage, violate. Secondly, the word 'inviolable' or 'inviolability' is defined by Collins Dictionary as that which 'must not or cannot be transgressed, dishonoured, or broken; to be kept sacred',[907] and by Black's Law Dictionary as: 'The attribute of being secured against violation. Safe from trespass or assault.'[908] Neither definition seems to limit the meaning of 'violable' to transgression or incursions by human beings as the drafters of Hague Convention V had in mind, nor do they seem to limit the meaning to *intentional* transgression, violation, trespassing or assault.

It is arguable, therefore, that, in principle, any physical damage caused by belligerents on the territory of neutral states entails a violation of this rule, whether the damage is intentional or collateral, and whether the impact is direct, or distant or close by.[909] Although this interpretation was strongly denied by the United States[910] and the United Kingdom[911] before

[905] According to Judge Shahabuddeen, Art 1 'has not been understood to guarantee neutral States absolute immunity from the effects of armed conflict'. However, the term 'inviolable' is not defined by Hague Convention V, 'nor does it say that the territory of a neutral State is violated only by belligerent incursion or bombardment.' The purpose of the drafters does not answer the question whether the territory of a neutral state is violated if the territory and its people are physically harmed by the use of nuclear weapons. Dissenting Opinion of Judge Shahabuddeen, Legality of the Threat or Use of Nuclear Weapons, Advisory Opinion, 8 Jul 1996, ICJ Reports 1996, p 226, at p 387.

[906] Art 4 of the African Charter of Human and Peoples' Rights, for example, provides: 'Human beings are inviolable. Every human being shall be entitled to respect for his life and the integrity of his person. No one may be arbitrarily deprived of this right.' African Charter on Human and Peoples' Rights, signed on 27 Jun 1981, entered into force 21 Oct 1986, UNTS, Vol 1520, No 26363.

[907] *Collins Dictionary*, p 808.

[908] Black, *Black's Law Dictionary*, p 573.

[909] Also: Bothe, *Protection of the Environment in Times of Armed Conflict*, in: Al-Nauimi, Meese (Eds), *International Legal Issues Arising Under the United Nations Decade of International Law; Proceedings of the Qatar International Law Conference '94*, p 101.

[910] According to the United States, 'the principle of neutrality is not a broad guarantee to neutral States of immunity from the effects of war, whether economic or environmental. Its purpose was to preclude military invasion or bombardment of neutral territory, and otherwise to define complementary rights and obligations of neutrals and belligerents. We are aware of no case in which a belligerent has been held responsible for collateral damage to neutral territory for lawful acts of war committed outside that territory.' Written Comments of the Government of the United States of America of 20 Jun 1995 (WHO), p 31; Written Statement of the Government of the United States of America of 20 Jun 1995 (GA), pp 31–2. Through <http://www.icj-cij.org/>.

[911] And the United Kingdom, stated before the Court: 'The principle that neutral territory is inviolable means that a belligerent may not, save in rare and clearly defined circumstances, actually conduct military operations on the territory of a neutral State. It has never meant that neutral States can expect to be subject to none of the effects of war. The whole purpose of the law of neutrality has always been to achieve a balance between the interests of the neutral State and the needs of the belligerents. The needs of a State force to fight for survival in the

the International Court of Justice in the Nuclear Weapons Opinions (GA and WHO), it is not improbable. It is not contradicted by the negotiating history of Article 1 Hague Convention V, which remains conspicuously silent on the scope of the provision,[912] and seems to be confirmed by the negotiating history of Article 1 of Hague Convention XIII,[913] by experts,[914] and in practice. After World War II, for example, the Allied Powers paid a considerable amount of compensation to Switzerland for damage caused on Swiss territory,[915] resulting either from bombing raids on German targets close to the border, or from misunderstandings regarding the geography on the part of the pilots.[916]

Surprisingly, the Allies did not only pay compensation for damage resulting from actions over or against neutral territory, such as crashed aircraft and the dropping of bombs and fuel tanks, but also for damage:

face of massive aggression must weigh very heavily in that balance.' CR 95/34, Oral Plea of the Government of the United Kingdom, of 15 Nov 1995 (WHO and GA), p 41. Through <http://www.icj-cij.org/>.

[912] Bothe, Cassese, Kalshoven, Kiss, Salmon, Simmonds, *Protection of the Environment in Times of Armed Conflict*, pp 55–6.

[913] Bothe, Cassese, Kalshoven, Kiss, Salmon, Simmonds, *Protection of the Environment in Times of Armed Conflict*, pp 57–9. According to Bothe et al the preparatory works 'make it clear that there was an awareness among the participants of certain broad principles underlying the text they were drafting, notably the principle that the sovereignty of the neutral State implies that its territory may not be affected by the military operations.'

[914] Bothe et al refer to the Harvard law School Research in International Law that published a Draft Convention on Rights and Duties of Neutral States in Naval and Aerial Warfare in 1939. Although 'there is little express authority' for a draft provisions that would prohibit activities by belligerents that would 'endanger life or property' in the territory of a neutral state, the 'Article seems to be sound in principle'. The Research Comment: 'A belligerent is, in principle, justified in engaging in hostile operations over the territory of its adversary. If, however, the result of such operations is to cause missiles to fall upon neutral territory, the belligerent may expose itself to neutral claims for damages. (. . .) The case is perhaps one for an international application of the doctrine of abus de droit, (. . .) in any particular factual situation it would remain a question for determination whether the belligerent had shown an improper disregard of the rights of the sovereign of the adjacent neutral territory.' Bothe, Cassese, Kalshoven, Kiss, Salmon, Simmonds, *Protection of the Environment in Times of Armed Conflict*, pp 60–1.

[915] The United States is supposed to have paid 62 million Swiss francs to Switzerland. Bothe, Cassese, Kalshoven, Kiss, Salmon, Simmonds, *Protection of the Environment in Times of Armed Conflict*, p 64. For other examples regarding compensation for damage to neutral states, see: Boelaert-Suominen, *International Environmental Law and Naval War; The Effect of Marine Safety and Pollution Conventions During International Armed Conflict*, pp 81–2; Bothe, Cassese, Kalshoven, Kiss, Salmon, Simmonds, *Protection of the Environment in Times of Armed Conflict*, p 65, fn 55. It is therefore surprising that the United States denied before the International Court of Justice that states had ever been held responsible for collateral damage to neutral territory from lawful acts outside that territory. Perhaps the payments to Switzerland were made *ex gratia*, ie voluntary without recognising liability or legal obligation. *Gratia* means kindness or benevolence. According to Black's Law Dictionary ex gratia is '[a] term applied to anything accorded as a favor; as distinguished from that which may be demanded *ex debito*, as a matter of right.' Black, *Black's Law Dictionary*, p 397.

[916] Bothe, *Protection of the Environment in Times of Armed Conflict*, in: Al-Nauimi, Meese (Eds), *International Legal Issues Arising Under the United Nations Decade of International Law; Proceedings of the Qatar International Law Conference '94*, p 101; Bothe, Cassese, Kalshoven, Kiss, Salmon, Simmonds, *Protection of the Environment in Times of Armed Conflict*, pp 62–5.

resulting from actions over belligerent territory but the effects of which were felt on the Swiss side of the boundary.[917]

These damages were paid for the destruction of property on the Swiss side of Lake Constanz after an attack on the German town Friedrichshafen. Interesting in this case is that the damage was not caused by bombs that missed their target, but by the shock-waves of the explosions.[918] According to Jaccard, a Swiss diplomat who was involved in the negotiations, the *locus acti* is 'irrelevant to the question of international responsibility for damages resulting from the act', as long as there is 'proximate cause (. . .) between the "Fernschäden" and the bombardments on non-Swiss territory.'[919] '*Fernschaden*' means distant damage and proximate cause requires that there is a direct connection between the bombardments and the damage on Swiss territory.[920]

By the same rationale, transboundary pollution resulting from the use of certain means or methods of warfare can also be regarded as a violation of the territorial inviolability of neutral states.[921] Clouds from burning oil wells, oil slicks, and the consequences of the use of weapons of mass destruction can be infinitely more damaging than shock-waves resulting from ordinary explosions and are usually collateral in nature and may occur at great distance from the *locus acti*. The fallout resulting from a nuclear explosion, for example, may cause significant damage to human health and the environment of neighbouring states and may even be felt around the globe. The special characteristics of nuclear weapons have been describe above, in Chapter II, and have been confirmed by the international community of states and by the International Court of Justice in the 1996 Nuclear Weapons Opinion (GA).[922]

[917] Bothe, Cassese, Kalshoven, Kiss, Salmon, Simmonds, *Protection of the Environment in Times of Armed Conflict*, pp 62, 65.

[918] Bothe, Cassese, Kalshoven, Kiss, Salmon, Simmonds, *Protection of the Environment in Times of Armed Conflict*, p 62.

[919] Quoted in: Bothe, Cassese, Kalshoven, Kiss, Salmon, Simmonds, *Protection of the Environment in Times of Armed Conflict*, pp 62–5. The argument resembles the subjective and objective territorial principles, based upon which a state may claim personal criminal jurisdiction over cross-border crimes committed by non-nationals. Malanczuk, *Akehurst's Modern Introduction to International Law*, pp 110–11; Shaw, *International Law*, pp 579–84.

[920] According to Black's Law Dictionary, proximate cause means primarily: 'That which, in a natural and continuous sequence, unbroken by any efficient intervening cause, produces injury, and without which the result would not have occurred.' Black, *Black's Law Dictionary*, p 852.

[921] Schmitt does not believe that the passage of pollutants into non-belligerent territory violates the territorial integrity of a neutral state. The principle of inviolability was based on physical intrusions whereas the principle of transboundary pollution is based on effect. Schmitt, *Green War: An Assessment of the Environmental Law of International Armed Conflict*, p 46.

[922] The International Court of Justice noted that the characteristics of nuclear weapons 'render [them] potentially catastrophic. The destructive power of nuclear weapons cannot be contained in either space or time. They have the potential to destroy all civilization and the entire ecosystem of the planet. The radiation released by a nuclear explosion would affect health, agriculture, natural resources and demography over a very wide area. Further, the

It is interesting to note, however, that in that case, there may be a difference between the standard of protection under the law of neutrality and the responsibility for transboundary pollution under the law of peace. As was observed above, the relationship between neutral states and belligerents is primarily governed by the law of peace subject only to a few modifications due to the existence of an international armed conflict. The inviolability of neutral territory under the law of neutrality seems to imply that any damage to neutral territory would entail an international wrongful act, whereas peacetime international law requires *serious* or *significant* damage from transboundary pollution for state responsibility. Even though Principle 21 of the Stockholm Declaration and Principle 2 of the Rio Declaration only refer to:

> the responsibility to ensure that activities within their jurisdiction or control do not cause damage to the environment of other States or of areas beyond the limits of national jurisdiction[923]

a damage threshold seems generally accepted.[924] In the 1938/1941 Trail Smelter Cases, the Arbitrators held:

> that under the principles of international law, (. . .), no State has the right to use or permit the use of its territory in such a manner as to cause injury by fumes in or to the territory of another or the properties or persons therein, when the case is of *serious consequence* and the injury is established by clear and convincing evidence (emphasis added).[925]

use of nuclear weapons would be a serious danger to future generations. Ionizing radiation has the potential to damage the future environment, food and marine ecosystem, and to cause genetic defects and illness in future generations.' Legality of the Threat or Use of Nuclear Weapons, Advisory Opinion, 8 Jul 1996, ICJ Reports 1996, para 35, pp 243–4.

923 Both principles reflect customary international law, according to the International Court of Justice in the Nuclear Weapons Opinion upon request of the General Assembly. Legality of the Threat or Use of Nuclear Weapons, Advisory Opinion, 8 Jul 1996, ICJ Reports 1996, para 29, pp 241–2. See also: Birnie, Boyle, *International Law & The Environment*, pp 104–37.

924 Also: Heintschel von Heinegg, Donner, *New Developments in the Protection of the Natural Environment in Naval Armed Conflicts*, p 302. Compare, however, the 1963 Partial Test Ban Treaty, which prohibits the carrying out of nuclear test explosions, in the atmosphere, including outer space, and under water, as well as 'in any other environment if such explosion causes radioactive debris to be present outside the territorial limits of the State under whose jurisdiction or control such explosion is conducted.' The Treaty apparently refers to underground explosions that cause transboundary pollution but does not seem to require any minimum damage. Treaty Banning Nuclear Weapon Tests in the Atmosphere, in Outer Space and Under Water, signed 5 Aug 1963, opened for signature on 8 Aug 1963, entered into force on 10 Oct 1963, UNTS, Vol 480, No 6964.

925 Trail Smelter Arbitration (US v Canada); 16 Apr 1938, 11 Mar 1941, in: H Lauterpacht (Ed), *Annual Digest and Reports of Public International Law Cases; Being a Selection from the Decisions of International and National Courts and Tribunals given during the Years 1938–1940*, (also published as International Law Reports, Vol 9), Butterworth & Co. (Publishers), London, 1942, Case No 104 (pp. 315–33), p 317.

And the 2001 Draft Articles on Prevention of Transboundary Harm from Hazardous Activities,[926] adopted by the ILC after some 20 years of preparation,[927] states in Article 1:

> The present Articles apply to activities not prohibited by international law which involve a risk of causing *significant* transboundary harm through their physical consequences (emphasis added).[928]

According to the International Law Commission, similar damage thresholds have not only been applied in practice, but have also been included in a number of conventions, legal instruments and domestic laws.[929]

Therefore, in case of less than significant or serious damage from transboundary pollution as a result of hostilities between belligerents, there seems to be a conflict between the law of neutrality and peacetime rules on transboundary pollution, the solution of which is not self-evident. Although the law regarding transboundary pollution is arguably newer than the law of neutrality protecting the territorial inviolability of neutral states, it is not likely that because of that fact the former will prevail over the latter. Both rules are fundamentally different in the sense that the law of neutrality becomes automatically effective with the outbreak of an international armed conflict and ipso facto belongs to the law of war, whereas modern rules on transboundary pollution are primarily intended to regulate international relations in times of peace and may only under certain circumstances and conditions continue to apply in times of war. This makes application of the Latin maxim *lex posterior derogat legi priori* in this case unlikely.

More plausible is the proposition that the law of neutrality takes precedence over peacetime rules on transboundary pollution based on the maxim *lex specialis derogat legi generali.* Although the law of neutrality is not humanitarian of character and does not contain rules on means and methods of warfare, the law of neutrality unmistakeably belongs to the law of war. According to the International Court of Justice, rules of *ius in*

[926] A/56/10, Draft Articles on Prevention of Transboundary Harm from Hazardous Activities; Report of the International Law Commission to the General Assembly on the work of its fifty-sixth session, Nov 2001. Through: <http://www.un.org/law/ilc/>.

[927] Compare the chronology at <http://www.un.org/law/ilc/texts/prevention/preventionfra.htm>.

[928] The term 'significant' must be understood as '*something more than "detectable" but need not be at the level of "serious" or "substantial"*'. Commentaries to the Draft Articles on Prevention of Transboundary Harm from Hazardous Activities, in: A/56/10, Report of the International Law Commission to the General Assembly on the work of its fifty-sixth session, Nov 2001, p 388. Through: <http://www.un.org/law/ilc/>.

[929] Commentaries to the Draft Articles on Prevention of Transboundary Harm from Hazardous Activities, in: A/56/10, Report of the International Law Commission to the General Assembly on the work of its fifty-sixth session, Nov 2001, p 388. Through: <http://www.un.org/law/ilc/>. Compare also the formulations that have been proposed by the ILC within the context of the 1997 UN Watercourses Convention. Birnie, Boyle, *International Law & The Environment*, pp 310–11.

bello must be seen as *leges speciales* in case of concurrent applicability with certain rules of *ius pacis*, the latter of which must be interpreted in the light of the former.[930] And according to Koskenniemi in his outline paper for the Study Group on Fragmentation of the International Law Commission:

> [i]t seems clear that, at least in the absence of evidence to the contrary, the laws of war must be regarded as *leges speciales* in relation to—and thus override—rules laying out the peacetime norms relating to the same subjects.[931]

Be that as it may, the issue is probably academic since no neutral state will likely complain over anything less than significant damage to the environment.

Finally, it is arguable that not only the environment on land is protected by the law of neutrality against damage resulting from hostile acts by belligerents, but also the environment at sea and in the air. Even though Hague Convention V is limited to the protection of neutral territory in case of war on land, it is not excluded that the concept of territory includes the territorial sea over which the coastal state exercises territorial jurisdiction,[932] nor is it impossible that the protection of neutral interests in general is extended under customary law to the neutral state's atmosphere and sea areas over which a neutral state has sovereign rights.[933] This would stem from the general principle of the law of neutrality as formulated by Bothe et al that 'a neutral state's sovereign rights as a non-participant must not be adversely affected by warlike acts of the belligerents.'[934]

The protection of the environment during international armed conflict under *ius in bello* is therefore diverse and based on a variety of rules. Firstly, the environment is directly protected under ENMOD, Additional Protocol I, the Incendiary Weapons Protocol, and the Rome Statute, as well

930 Legality of the Threat or Use of Nuclear Weapons, Advisory Opinion, 8 Jul 1996, ICJ Reports 1996, para 25, p 240; and to a lesser extent Legal Consequences of the Construction of a Wall in the Occupied Palestinian Territory, Advisory Opinion, 9 Jul 2004, ICJ Reports 2004, pp 41–2; Case Concerning Armed Activities on the Territory of the Congo (Democratic Republic of the Congo v Uganda), Merits, Judgment, 19 Dec 2005, ICJ Reports 2005, para 216, pp 69–70.

931 Koskenniemi, *Fragmentation of International Law*, Outline for Study Group, International Law Commission, 55th session, 2003, p 6. At: <http://www.un.org/law/ilc/sessions/55/55sess.htm>.

932 According to Heintschel von Heinegg and Donner, it is possible to have recourse to delimitation of coastal areas under the law of the sea, '[s]ince there is no definition in the law of neutrality as to the question of what constitutes *neutral territory*'. Heintschel von Heinegg, Donner, *New Developments in the Protection of the Natural Environment in Naval Armed Conflicts*, pp 296–7.

933 Compare also: Bothe, Cassese, Kalshoven, Kiss, Salmon, Simmonds, *Protection of the Environment in Times of Armed Conflict*, p 65. For the protection of the marine environment of neutral states and the marine environment in areas beyond national jurisdiction, see Heintschel von Heinegg, Donner, *New Developments in the Protection of the Natural Environment in Naval Armed Conflicts*, pp 296–308, respectively, pp 308–14.

934 Bothe, Cassese, Kalshoven, Kiss, Salmon, Simmonds, *Protection of the Environment in Times of Armed Conflict*, p 66.

as under three relatively new rules of customary international law that have arguably emerged in the 1990s. These are the obligation to show due regard for the environment during international armed conflict and the prohibitions of wanton destruction of and excessive collateral damage to the environment during international armed conflict. Secondly, it is arguable that the environment is indirectly protected under the law of neutrality as well as under various rules of conventional and customary international law that protect civilian objects during hostilities and belligerent occupation. It is likely, however, that the indirect protection of the environment through the protection of civilian objects has lost most of its importance after the arguable emergence of customary rules that directly protect the environment during international armed conflict in the 1990s.

IV

The Protection of the Environment During International Armed Conflict Under Ius ad Bellum

1—INTRODUCTION

THE PROTECTION OF the environment under *ius ad bellum* is not only subsidiary, but its protection is also indirect, since the rules on the use of force are neither primarily applicable during armed conflict, nor do they intend to protect the environment during armed conflict. Although its role in environmental protection may look far-fetched, and even a *contradictio in terminis* at first sight, environmental protection under *ius ad bellum* may be deduced from Resolution 687 of the Security Council in relation to the 1990–1991 Gulf War. By establishing Iraq's liability for environmental damage resulting from its invasion of Kuwait, the Security Council raises questions on the general relationship between *ius ad bellum* and *ius in bello*.

2—SECURITY COUNCIL RESOLUTION 687

2.1 Introduction

Both before and after the end of the 1990–1991 Gulf War, the Security Council adopted a number of resolutions in which it established the liability of Iraq for the damage it had caused by occupying Kuwait on 2 August 1990. Acting under chapter VII of the Charter, the Council reminded Iraq in Resolution 674 that it was liable:

> under international law for any loss, damage or injury arising in regard to Kuwait and third States and their nationals and corporations, as a result of the invasion and illegal occupation of Kuwait by Iraq.[1]

[1] S/RES/674 (1990), adopted on 29 Oct 1990, by 13 to 0, with 2 abstentions, on the situation between Iraq and Kuwait, para 8; S/RES/686 (1991), adopted on 2 Mar 1991, by 11 to 1, with 3 abstentions, on the situation between Iraq and Kuwait, para 2(b).

And in Resolution 687 of 3 April 1991, the Council reaffirmed in paragraph 16 that:

> Iraq, without prejudice to the debts and obligations of Iraq arising prior to 2 August 1990, which will be addressed through the normal mechanisms, is liable under international law for any direct loss, damage, *including environmental damage and the depletion of natural resources,* or injury to foreign Governments, nationals and corporations, as a result of Iraq's unlawful invasion and occupation of Kuwait (emphasis added).[2]

Both resolutions were adopted while 'bearing in mind [the Council's] objective of restoring international peace and security in the area'.[3] In accordance with paragraph 33 of Resolution 687, Iraq accepted, though under protest, the provisions of Resolution 687 by letter of 6 April 1991.[4]

2.2 The Scope of Iraq's Liability

Since the Security Council directly linked responsibility for environmental damage and the depletion of natural resources to Iraq's illegal use of force and its unlawful occupation of Kuwait, it is arguable that *ius ad bellum* not only protects international peace and security, but also indirectly protects the environment during international armed conflict.[5] After all, the damage to the natural environment and the depletion of natural resources either occurred or resulted from actions during an ongoing armed conflict and not just from the actual invasion of Kuwait on 2 August 1990. Furthermore, although the Security Council is a political organ and its decision of 3 April 1991 is addressed only to Iraq, the scope of Iraq's liability might deter future aggressor states to harm the environment and encourage them to keep environmental damage to a minimum.

Now, Iraq's liability for damage resulting from its breach of *ius ad bellum* and its subsequent occupation of Kuwait is not extraordinary under international law. After all, the responsibility of states for damage done to other

[2] S/RES/687 (1991), adopted on 3 Apr 1991, by 12 votes to 1, with 2 abstentions, on the situation between Iraq and Kuwait.

[3] S/RES/687 (1991), adopted on 3 Apr 1991, by 12 votes to 1, with 2 abstentions, on the situation between Iraq and Kuwait, preambular para 25. Similarly, S/RES/686 (1991), adopted on 2 Mar 1991, by 11 to 1, with 3 abstentions, on the situation between Iraq and Kuwait, para 2(b), preambular para 6.

[4] S/22456, 6 Apr 1991, Identical letters dated 6 Apr 1991 from the Permanent Representative of Iraq to the United Nations addressed respectively to the Secretary-General and the President of the Security Council.

[5] According to Low and Hodgkinson, '[t]he prohibition against the use of force in article 2(4) is capable of protecting any object, including the environment, which might be affected by the unlawful use of force. Article 2(4) is aimed at the protection of 'the territorial integrity or political independence of any State.' In other words, it protects state sovereignty which extends to protection of a state's people, property, and environment.' Low, Hodgkinson, *Compensation for Wartime Environmental Damage: Challenges to International Law After the Gulf War*, Virginia Journal of International Law, Vol 35, 1995, p 459.

states as a result of a breach of public international law and the corresponding obligation to make reparation is considered a fundamental principle of international law[6] and has long been recognised in international practice. In 1928, the Permanent Court of International Justice stated in the Chorzów Factory Case that:

> it is a principle of international law, and even a general conception of law, that any breach of an engagement involves an obligation to make reparation.[7]

And in 2001, after a laborious process, the ILC laid down 59 draft Articles on State Responsibility.[8] Draft Article 1 provides 'Every internationally wrongful act of a State entails the international responsibility of that State'; and Draft Article 31(1) provides: The responsible State is under an obligation to make full reparation for the injury caused by the internationally wrongful act.

What is noteworthy, however, is the scope of Iraq's liability under Resolution 687. Iraq is held liable for all:

> damage including environmental damage and the depletion of natural resources (. . .) as a result of Iraq's unlawful invasion and occupation of Kuwait.

Interpreted literally, this decision entails a form of strict liability for all environmental damage related to its invasion and occupation of Kuwait. Strict liability means '[l]iability without fault' and is usually only adopted by legislators or applied by courts in the context of product liability:

> in which [a] seller is liable for any and all defective or hazardous products which unduly threaten a consumer's personal safety.[9]

In this case, strict liability would mean that Iraq is liable for damage to the environment for which it normally could not be held responsible, and being liable without responsibility is exceptional under public international law.[10] Under paragraph 16 of Resolution 687, Iraq can be held

[6] According to Shaw, the responsibility of states flows from 'the nature of the international legal system', the concept of sovereignty and the corresponding legal equality of states. Shaw, *International Law*, Cambridge University Press, Cambridge, 2003, p 694.

[7] Case Concerning the Factory at Chorzów (Claim for Indemnity), 13 Sep 1928, Publications of the Permanent Court of International Justice, Collection of Judgments, Series A—No 17, AW Sijthoff's Publishing Company, 1928, p 29.

[8] A/56/10, Draft Articles on Responsibility of States for Internationally Wrongful Acts, including Commentaries, adopted by the International Law Commission at its fifty-third session, Nov 2001; Yearbook of the International Law Commission, 2001; Vol II, Part Two, forthcoming. Through <http://www.un.org/law/ilc/>. See also: J Crawford, *The International Law Commission's Articles on State Responsibility; Introduction, Text and Commentaries*, Cambridge University Press, Cambridge, 2002.

[9] Black (et al), *Black's Law Dictionary*, West Publishing, St Paul, MN, 1991, p 991.

[10] International liability for injurious consequences arising out of acts not prohibited by international law is currently only accepted by the International Law Commission and only in case of transboundary pollution. A/56/10, Draft Articles on Prevention of Transboundary Harm from Hazardous Activities; Report of the International Law Commission to the General Assembly on the work of its fifty-sixth session, Nov 2001. Through: <http://www.un.org/law/ilc/>.

liable for environmental damage resulting from actions that are not illegal under the law of armed conflict[11] and for damage resulting from actions by other belligerents and which therefore cannot be attributed to Iraq.[12]

Unfortunately, the preparatory works of Resolution 687 do not provide much clarity as far as the scope of Iraq's environmental liability is concerned. The resolutions preceding Resolution 687 did not refer to Iraq's liability for environmental damage and it is not clear when, why and on which basis the liability for environmental damage and the depletion of natural resources were included in the process that led to the adoption of paragraph 16 of Resolution 687. Furthermore, neither the original draft proposal,[13] nor the verbatim records,[14] provide much help. The draft proposal was almost literally adopted into Resolution 687 and the statements made during the session of the Security Council on 3 April 1991 do not give any indication as to the interpretation and scope of the environmental clause in paragraph 16. During this meeting, to which the Representatives of Kuwait and Iraq were also invited, most delegates confined themselves to generalities as far as Iraq's liability was concerned.[15] Only the delegates from Kuwait,[16] the Soviet Union[17] and the United Kingdom[18] referred to the ecological crisis as a result of burning oil wells and oil in the Persian Gulf, and only Cuba was critical of the scope of Iraq's responsibility.[19] The delegate of Iraq generally referred to the destruction caused by Coalition Forces in Iraq as well as their violations of international humanitarian law and reserved the right to request reparation.[20]

[11] Similarly Greenwood, *State Responsibility and Civil Liability for Environmental Damage Caused by Military Operations,* in: Grunawalt, King, McClain (Eds), *Protection of the Environment during Armed Conflict,* International Law Studies 1996, Vol 69, Naval War College, Newport, RI, 1996, p 403.

[12] See also SAJ Boelaert-Suominen, *Iraqi War Reparations and the Laws of War: a Discussion of the Current Work of the United Nations Compensation Commission with Specific Reference to Environmental Damage During Warfare,* Zeitschrift für öffentliches Recht, Vol 50, 1996, p 293. On the other hand, however, she believes that the Compensation Commission has 'the obligation to examine independently what the law is', since para 16 refers to Iraq's liability under international law. Boelaert-Suominen, *Iraqi War Reparations and the Laws of War: a Discussion of the Current Work of the United Nations Compensation Commission with Specific Reference to Environmental Damage During Warfare,* pp 270–1.

[13] S/22430, 2 Apr 1991, as corrected by S/22430/Corr.1, 3 Apr 1991, Draft Resolution from Belgium, France, Romania, United Kingdom of Great Britain and Northern Ireland, United States of America and Zaire.

[14] S/PV2981, 3 Apr 1991, Provisional Verbatim Records of the Two Thousand Nine Hundred and Eighty-First Meeting, on Wednesday, 3 Apr 1991.

[15] These were the delegates from Yemen, Zaire, the United States, France, the People's Republic of China, and Romania.

[16] S/PV2981, 3 Apr 1991, pp 13–17; 131–2.

[17] S/PV2981, 3 Apr 1991, p 103.

[18] S/PV2981, 3 Apr 1991, pp 114–15.

[19] S/PV2981, 3 Apr 1991, pp 68–70.

[20] S/PV2981, 3 Apr 1991, pp 23–32.

2.3 The United Nations Compensation Commission

Furthermore, the implementation of Iraq's liability under paragraph 16 of Resolution 687 by the United Nations Compensation Commission (UNCC), does not shed much light on the basis of the Council's decision to hold Iraq liable for environmental damage and the scope of its liability either. The UNCC was established in 1991 by Security Council Resolution 692,[21] in accordance with paragraph 18 of Resolution 687 in which the Council decided to:

> create a fund to pay compensation for claims that fall within paragraph 16 above and to establish a Commission that will administer the fund

and in accordance with recommendations from the Secretary-General.[22] The Commission is a subsidiary organ of the Security Council, governed by a Governing Council with similar membership as the Security Council,[23] and assisted by Commissioners being 'experts in fields such as finance, law, accountancy, insurance and environmental damage assessment' acting 'in their personal capacity'.

The Commission started its activities in 1991 and has almost completed its work at the end of 2005. In almost 14 years of work, the Commission has decided upon over 2.68 million claims claiming 354 billion US dollars in compensation. Of these claims, the Commission has approved almost 1.5 million of these claims, amounting to approximately 52.5 billion dollars, of which 19.2 billion dollars has been paid out.[24]

In order to work through these 2.68 million claims, the Governing Council divided the variety of claims into six categories and established panels to decide on each category.[25] The first two categories of claims dealt with by the Commission were established at the Governing Council's first session in the summer of 1991 and dealt with urgent claims of individuals 'who suffered personal losses as a result of the invasion and occupation of Kuwait'. These claims became known as Category A,

[21] S/RES/692 (1991), adopted on 20 May 1991, by 14 to 0, with 1 abstention, on the establishment of a United Nations Compensation Fund and a United Nations Compensation Commission.

[22] S/22559, 2 May 1991, Report of the Secretary-General Pursuant to Para 19 of Security Council Resolution 687 (1991).

[23] S/22559, 2 May 1991, Report of the Secretary-General Pursuant to Para 19 of Security Council Resolution 687 (1991), pp 2–3.

[24] At <http://www2.unog.ch/uncc/status.htm>.

[25] Categorisation had already been suggested by the Secretary-General. S/22559, 2 May 1991, Report of the Secretary-General Pursuant to Para 19 of Security Council Resolution 687 (1991), p 7.

B, C, and D claims.[26] Category E claims dealt with claims of 'corporations, other private legal entities and public-sector enterprises';[27] Category F claims dealt with claims of 'Governments and international organizations'.[28]

The Governing Council classified the claims for direct environmental damage and the depletion of natural resources under Category F4 which were therefore only available for Governments and international organisations. Damage to the environment and depletion of natural resources included:

> losses or expenses resulting from: (a) Abatement and prevention of environmental damage, including expenses directly relating to fighting oil fires and stemming the flow of oil in coastal and international waters; (b) Reasonable measures already taken to clean and restore the environment or future measures which can be documented as reasonably necessary to clean and restore the environment; (c) Reasonable monitoring and assessment of the environmental damage for the purposes of evaluating and abating the harm and restoring the environment; (d) Reasonable monitoring of public health and performing medical screenings for the purposes of investigation and combating increased health risks as a result of the environmental damage; and (e) Depletion of or damage to natural resources.[29]

The word 'includes' implies that compensable losses or expenses are not limited to these actions and must not be considered 'a limitative enumeration of such activities or events'.[30]

[26] Payments were available for persons who '(a) departed from Iraq of Kuwait during the period of 2 Aug 1990 to 2 Mar 1991; (b) suffered serious personal injury; or (c) whose spouse, child or parent died.' Claims under (a) became known as Category A claims; claims under (b) and (c) became known under Category B claims. Category C claims were all other personal losses, including business losses of up to 100,000 US Dollars. S/AC.26/1991/1, 2 Aug 1991; Criteria for Expedited Processing of Urgent Claims, paras 1 and 10–16. Category D claims were all other individual claims not covered under Categories A, B, and C. A/AC.26/1991/7/Rev1, 17 Mar 1992; Decision taken by the Governing Council of the United Nations Compensation Commission during its third session, at the 18th meeting, held on 28 Nov 1991, as revised at the 24th meeting held on 16 Mar 1992; Criteria for Additional Categories of Claims, paras 1–15. All decisions available through: <http://www.uncc.ch/>.

[27] A/AC.26/1991/7/Rev1, 17 Mar 1992; Decision taken by the Governing Council of the United Nations Compensation Commission during its third session, at the 18th meeting, held on 28 Nov 1991, as revised at the 24th meeting held on 16 Mar 1992; Criteria for Additional Categories of Claims, paras 16–29.

[28] A/AC.26/1991/7/Rev1, 17 Mar 1992; Decision taken by the Governing Council of the United Nations Compensation Commission during its third session, at the 18th meeting, held on 28 Nov 1991, as revised at the 24th meeting held on 16 Mar 1992; Criteria for Additional Categories of Claims, paras 30–42.

[29] A/AC.26/1991/7/Rev1, 17 Mar 1992; Decision taken by the Governing Council of the United Nations Compensation Commission during its third session, at the 18th meeting, held on 28 Nov 1991, as revised at the 24th meeting held on 16 Mar 1992; Criteria for Additional Categories of Claims, para 35.

[30] This has repeatedly been confirmed by the Panel of Commissioners that dealt with these claims, firstly, in: S/AC.26/2002/26, 3 Oct 2002; Report and Recommendations Made by the Panel of Commissioners Concerning the Second Instalment of 'F4' Claims, paras 22–3, p 9.

Furthermore, the condition for all damage categories that the damage and losses had to be the result of Iraq's unlawful invasion and occupation of Kuwait was further specified by the Governing Council as including damage resulting from:

> (a) military operations or threat of military action by either side during the period 2 August 1990 to 2 March 1991;31 (b) departure from or inability to leave Iraq or Kuwait (or a decision not to return) during that period; (c) actions by officials, employees or agents of the Government of Iraq or its controlled entities during that period in connection with the invasion or occupation; (d) the breakdown of civil order in Kuwait or Iraq during that period; or (e) hostage-taking or other illegal detention.[32]

It is thus interesting to note that, as was observed above, Iraq can indeed be held liable under (a) for damage resulting from military operations carried out by Coalition Forces.[33]

The UNCC received 168 F4 claims, worth almost 85 billion US Dollars. Of these 168 claims, 109 were awarded by the Governing Council in five installments, for an amount of over 5 billion dollars, which is over 6 per cent of the amount claimed.[34] The first instalment was decided upon on 22 June 2001;[35] the fifth and final instalment was issued on 30 June 2005.[36]

[31] It is peculiar that the Governing Council chose 2 Mar 1991 as its date of reference. On 2 Mar 1991 the Security Council adopted Resolution 686 in which it implied that hostilities had only been terminated temporarily when it decided in para 8 'to remain actively seized of the matter' 'in order to secure the rapid *establishment of a definitive end to the hostilities*' (emphasis added). According to para 33 of Security Council Resolution 687, '*a formal cease-fire* is effective between Iraq and Kuwait and the Member States cooperating with Kuwait in accordance with resolution 678 (1990)' only 'upon official notification by Iraq to the Secretary-General and to the Security Council of its acceptance of the provisions' of Resolution 687 (emphasis added). Iraq accepted the provisions of Resolution 687 by letter of 6 Apr 1991. S/22456, 6 Apr 1991, Identical letters dated 6 Apr 1991 from the Permanent Representative of Iraq to the United Nations addressed respectively to the Secretary-General and the President of the Security Council.

[32] S/AC.26/1991/1, 2 Aug 1991; Criteria for Expedited Processing of Urgent Claims, para 18 (Categories A, B, and C); A/AC.26/1991/7/Rev1, 17 Mar 1992; Decision taken by the Governing Council of the United Nations Compensation Commission during its third session, at the 18th meeting, held on 28 Nov 1991, as revised at the 24th meeting held on 16 Mar 1992; Criteria for Additional Categories of Claims, paras 6 (Category D), 21 (Category E), and 34 (Category F).

[33] Greenwood believes that as a matter of principle that 'an aggressor should not be held internationally responsible for unlawful conduct on the part of its adversaries, not least because that would actually be contrary to the objective of ensuring that State responsibility operated to ensure compliance with the law, rather than simply to provide compensation for the consequences of its violation.' Greenwood, *State Responsibility and Civil Liability for Environmental Damage Caused by Military Operations*, in: Grunawalt, King, McClain (Eds), *Protection of the Environment during Armed Conflict*, p 409.

[34] At <http://www2.unog.ch/uncc/status.htm>.

[35] A/AC.26/Dec.132 (2001), 21 Jun 2001; Decision concerning the first instalment of 'F4' claims taken by the Governing Council of the United Nations Compensation Commission at its 109th meeting, held on 21 Jun 2001 at Geneva; S/AC.26/2001/16, 22 Jun 2001; Report and Recommendations Made by the Panel of Commissioners Concerning the First Instalment of 'F4' Claims.

[36] A/AC.26/Dec.248 (2005), 30 Jun 2005; Decision concerning the fifth instalment of 'F4' claims taken by the Governing Council of the United Nations Compensation Commission at

Each report is a thankful source for environmental damage assessment but does not discuss the legal ins and outs of each claim. The reason for this is that the Commission was to act as a fact-finding organ, and not as:

> a court or an arbitral tribunal before which the parties appear; it is a political organ that performs an essentially fact-finding function of examining claims, verifying their validity, evaluating losses, assessing payments and resolving disputed claims. It is only in this last respect that a quasi-judicial function may be involved.[37]

This fact-finding function also appears from the Rules of Procedure as established by the Governing Council on 26 June 1992. Article 31 on 'Applicable Law' states:

> In considering the claims, Commissioners will apply Security Council resolution 687 (1991) and other relevant Security Council resolutions, the criteria established by the Governing Council for particular categories of claims, and any pertinent decisions of the Governing Council. In addition, where necessary, Commissioners shall apply other relevant rules of international law.

According to the Panel that dealt with environmental or F4 claims,[38] the latter sentence meant that:

its 146th meeting, on 30 Jun 2005; A/AC.26/2005/10, 30 Jun 2005; Report and Recommendations Made by the Panel of Commissioners Concerning the Fifth Instalment of 'F4' claims. The other decisions and reports were: A/AC.26/Dec.171 (2002), 3 Oct 2002; Decision concerning the second instalment of 'F4' claims taken by the Governing Council of the United Nations Compensation Commission at its 122nd meeting, held on 3 Oct 2002; A/AC.26/Dec.212 (2003), 18 Dec 2003; Decision concerning the third instalment of 'F4' claims taken by the Governing Council of the United Nations Compensation Commission at its 133rd meeting on 18 Dec 2003; A/AC.26/Dec.234 (2004), 9 Dec 2004; Decision concerning part one of the fourth instalment of 'F4' claims taken by the Governing Council of the United Nations Compensation Commission at its 141st meeting, on 9 Dec 2004; A/AC.26/Dec.235 (2004), 9 Dec 2004; Decision concerning part two of the fourth instalment of 'F4' claims taken by the Governing Council of the United Nations Compensation Commission at its 141st meeting, on 9 Dec 2004; S/AC.26/2002/26, 3 Oct 2002; Report and Recommendations Made by the Panel of Commissioners Concerning the Second Instalment of 'F4' Claims; S/AC.26/2003/31, 18 Dec 2003; Report and Recommendations Made by the Panel of Commissioners Concerning the Third Instalment of 'F4' Claims; S/AC.26/2004/16, 9 Dec 2004; Report and Recommendations Made by the Panel of Commissioners Concerning Part One of the Fourth Instalment of 'F4' Claims; S/AC.26/2004/17, 9 Dec 2004; Report and Recommendations Made by the Panel of Commissioners Concerning Part Two of the Fourth Instalment of 'F4' Claims.

[37] S/22559, 2 May 1991, Report of the Secretary-General Pursuant to Para 19 of Security Council Resolution 687 (1991), p 7. Compare, however, Boelaert-Suominen, who does believe that the Commission had an obligation to examine independently what the law was, since para 16 of Resolution 687 refers to Iraq's liability under international law. 'If the international law on liability is not as developed or clear as Resolution 687 misguidingly indicates, then one needs to put a question mark behind the tasks the Commission has been entrusted with: not merely those of an accountant, but in addition, those of a legislator and a judge.' Boelaert-Suominen, *Iraqi War Reparations and the Laws of War: a Discussion of the Current Work of the United Nations Compensation Commission with Specific Reference to Environmental Damage During Warfare*, pp 270–2.

[38] The F4 Panel of Commissioners consisted of Thomas A Mensah (Chairman), José R Allen and Peter H Sand. They were appointed by the Governing Council at its thirtieth session held from 14 to 16 Dec 1998. S/AC.26/2001/16, 22 Jun 2001; Report and

> recourse to 'other relevant rules of international law' is necessary where the Security Council resolutions and the decisions of the Governing Council do not provide sufficient guidance for the review of a particular claim.[39]

In practice, this meant that the Panel confined itself to applying Resolution 687 and Governing Council Decision 7, referred to above, and generally ignored other rules of public international law. For example, when Iraq argued before the Panel that it could not be held liable for environmental damage:

> unless it [reached] the 'threshold' that is generally accepted in international law for compensation in cases of state responsibility for transboundary environmental damage,

the Panel stated that 'the relevant decisions of the Governing Council [provided] sufficient guidance.'[40] And when Iraq similarly argued that it could not be held liable for damage to natural resources that did not have commercial value, since 'compensation in international law can only be paid for damage that is "financially assessable"', the Panel referred to its earlier statement and ruled that the primary applicable sources of law provided sufficient guidance. Furthermore, the Panel considered that its finding of liability for damage to environmental assets without commercial value was not 'inconsistent with any principle or rule of general international law.' There was no 'justification for the contention that general international law precludes compensation for pure environmental damage.'[41]

3—THE RELATIONSHIP BETWEEN *IUS AD BELLUM* AND *IUS IN BELLO*

3.1 Introduction

Still, the relationship between Iraq's liability for environmental damage under Resolution 687 and thus *ius ad bellum*, and its responsibility or lack of responsibility for environmental damage under *ius in bello* remains interesting. It is generally accepted that *ius ad bellum* and *ius in bello* are two distinct bodies of law entailing distinct responsibilities. This means, for example, that in principle the laws of war are equally binding on all

Recommendations Made by the Panel of Commissioners Concerning the First Instalment of 'F4' Claims, para 1, p 6.

[39] S/AC.26/2003/31, 18 Dec 2003; Report and Recommendations Made by the Panel of Commissioners Concerning the Third Instalment of 'F4' Claims, para 34, p 11.

[40] S/AC.26/2003/31, 18 Dec 2003; Report and Recommendations Made by the Panel of Commissioners Concerning the Third Instalment of 'F4' Claims, paras 33–5, p 11.

[41] A/AC.26/2005/10, 30 Jun 2005; Report and Recommendations Made by the Panel of Commissioners Concerning the Fifth Instalment of 'F4' claims, paras 44–58, pp 16–19.

belligerents irrespective of whether or not a belligerent has the right to wage war or use force under public international law.

3.2 The Distinction Between *Ius ad Bellum* and *Ius in Bello*

Although this distinction between *ius ad bellum* and *ius in bello* is nowadays considered 'absolute dogma'[42] as well as '[o]ne of the oldest and best established *axiomata* of international law',[43] it has not always been that way. During the Middle Ages, the use of force in international relations was determined by the *bellum iustum* or 'just war' doctrine, which did not in principle distinguish between the reasons for going to war and the actual conduct of hostilities. The focus of the just war doctrine was on the material causes for waging war,[44] which meant that 'war was not seen as a *de facto* situation to which the same set of rules applied in all cases.' This meant that:

> the rights and obligations of belligerents were unequal and depended exclusively on the causes which they claimed to be pursuing and on the material justness of those causes.

In principle:

> [a] belligerent without a just cause had no rights; he was simply a criminal who might be executed. Consequently, no legal restraints could be imposed on his behaviour.[45]

Despite the fact that Grotius was convinced that there were rules on the conduct of warfare that were common to all nations,[46] these rules were 'subordinate to the doctrine of just war.'[47]

The law of war as we know it today could only develop with the acceptance of war as a sovereign prerogative and consequently as a de facto situation. Only then could attention shift from the material causes for waging war to the rights and duties of belligerents and the conduct of

[42] L Doswald-Beck, *International Humanitarian Law and the Advisory Opinion of the International Court of Justice on the Legality of the Threat or Use of Nuclear Weapons*, International Review of the Red Cross, 1997, para 5.

[43] T Gill, *The Nuclear Weapons Advisory Opinion of the International Court of Justice and the Fundamental Distinction Between the Ius ad Bellum and the Ius in Bello*, Leiden Journal of International Law, Vol 12, 1999, p 614.

[44] Compare H Grotius, *De Iure Belli ac Pacis*, The Classics of International Law, Clarendon Press, Oxford, 1925, Book II, which focuses on the reasons for waging war.

[45] Kolb, *Origin of the twin terms jus ad bellum/jus in bello*, International Review of the Red Cross, 1997, para 1.

[46] Grotius, *De Iure Belli ac Pacis*, Book III, which focuses on the laws of war as derived from natural law.

[47] Kolb, *Origin of the twin terms jus ad bellum/jus in bello*, para 1.

hostilities. And only then could the law of war be recognised as an independent and distinct body of law applicable to all belligerents.[48]

Nowadays, equal application of *ius in bello* to all belligerents appears, among other things, from common Article 1 of the 1949 Geneva Conventions and the Preamble of Additional Protocol I to the Geneva Conventions of 1977. Common Article 1 provides: 'The High Contracting Parties undertake to respect and to ensure respect for the present Convention *in all circumstances*' (emphasis added). And in preambular paragraph 5 of Additional Protocol I, the High Contracting Parties reaffirm that:

> the provisions of the Geneva Conventions of 12 August 1949 and of this Protocol must be fully applied in all circumstances to all persons who are protected by those instruments, *without any adverse distinction based on the nature or origin of the armed conflict or on the causes espoused by or attributed to the Parties to the conflict* (emphasis added).[49]

After the renunciation of war in 1928,[50] and the prohibition of the use of force[51] and the criminalisation of wars of aggression in 1945,[52] equal application of *ius in bello* has come under pressure, however. Dinstein refers to two general arguments used against equal application. The first argument was taken up by the prosecution in the Nuremberg trial and rested on the contention that every military activity that was criminal in nature, such as killing of people and destruction of property, was only justified by the fact

[48] Kolb, *Origin of the twin terms jus ad bellum/jus in bello*, para 2.

[49] Compare also para 6 of the non-binding, yet authoritative 1994 San Remo Manual on International Law Applicable to Armed Conflicts at Sea, which provides: 'The rules set out in this document and any other rules of international humanitarian law shall apply equally to all parties to the conflict. The equal application of these rules to all parties to the conflict shall not be affected by the international responsibility that may have been incurred by any of them for the outbreak of the conflict.'

[50] Art I of the Pact of Paris, or Kellogg-Briand Pact; Treaty between the United States and Other Powers Providing for the Renunciation of War as an Instrument of National Policy, signed on 27 Aug 1928, entered into force on 24 Jul 1929, AJIL, Vol 22, No 4, Supplement: Official Documents, 1928, p 171.

[51] Art 2(4) Charter of the United Nations, United Nations Charter, signed on 26 Jun 1945, entered into force on 24 Oct 1945, AJIL, Vol 39, No 3, Supplement: Official Documents, 1945, p 190. See for extensive recent studies on Art 2(4): N Schrijver, *Article 2; Parae 4*, in: J-P Cot, A Pellet (Eds), *La Charte des Nations Unies; Commentaire article par article; Vol I*, Economica, Paris, 2005, and A Randelzhofer, *Article 2(4)*, in: B Simma (Ed), *The Charter of the United Nations; A Commentary*, Oxford University Press, Oxford, 2002.

[52] Art 6(a) of the Charter of the International Military Tribunal at Nuremberg, Agreement between the Government of the United States of America, the Provisional Government of the French Republic, the Government of the United Kingdom of Great Britain and Northern Ireland and the Government of the Union of Soviet Socialist Republics for the Prosecution and Punishment of the Major War Criminals of the European Axis, with annexed Charter of the International Military Tribunal, signed on 8 Aug 1945, entered into force on 8 Aug 1945, AJIL, Vol 39, No 4, Supplement: Official Documents, 1945, p 257. Compare also, Arts 5(1)(d) and 5(2) of the Rome Statute. Rome Statute of the International Criminal Court, opened for signature on 17 Jul 1998, entered into force 1 Jul 2002, UNTS, Vol 2187, No 38544.

that they are fighting a lawful war for legitimate reasons.[53] The second argument is related to the maxim *ex iniuria ius non oritur*, which means that you cannot benefit from rights that result from illegal activities.[54] Both arguments were rejected by the United States Military Tribunal at Nuremberg, by the Dutch post-World War II Special Court and Court of Cassation, and by the international community of states, as apparent from the 1949 Geneva Conventions and Protocol, both for practical and theoretical reasons.[55]

Despite general acceptance of the principle of equal application of *ius in bello* to all belligerents, both in treaty and in case-law, it has often been subject of research and a number of attempts have been made to limit its scope and to deviate from this standard. In 1939, the Harvard Research in International Law suggested, for example, with respect to equal application, to distinguish between rules on the conduct of hostilities and other rules of *ius in bello*.[56] In 1953, Lauterpacht proposed to let go of equal application after the end of hostilities with respect to title over property.[57] And in 1963, the *Institut de Droit International* or Institute of International Law decided to accept the principle of unequal treatment of belligerents in case the Security Council has labeled one of the parties as 'aggressor' or in case of collective action by United Nations forces based on a decision of the Security Council.[58]

[53] In the previous chapter, it has been put forward that the general justification for destruction during warfare and armed conflict lay in the concept of military necessity as formulated in the 1868 St Petersburg Declaration.

[54] Y Dinstein, *War, Aggression and Self-Defence*, Cambridge University Press, Cambridge, 2005, pp 156–7. Compare Greenwood's rebuttal of this argument by nuancing the concept of 'belligerent rights'. Although it is true that certain rules of *ius in bello* can be analysed that way, '[t]he purpose of the humanitarian rules which comprise the bulk of *ius in bello* is not to confer benefits upon the parties to a conflict but to protect individuals and to give expression to concepts of international public policy. Only property rights by a belligerent occupant and the law of neutrality confer legal rights, and must therefore be regarded as exceptions, according to Greenwood. Greenwood, *The relationship between ius ad bellum and ius in bello*, Review of International Studies, Vol 9, 1983, pp 227–30.

[55] Dinstein, *War, Aggression and Self-Defence*, pp 157–9; H Lauterpacht, *The Limits of the Operation of the Law of War*, The British Year Book of International Law, Vol 30, 1953, pp 211–24. Similarly, Greenwood, *The relationship between ius ad bellum and ius in bello*, p 226; Greenwood, *International Humanitarian Law (Laws of War); Revised Report for the Centennial Commemoration of the First Hague Peace Conference 1899*, London School of Economics and Political Science, London, 1999, pp 16–18.

[56] Arts 2–4 and 14 of the Draft Convention on Rights and Duties of States in Case of Aggression, American Journal of International Law, Vol 33, Supplement: Research in International Law, 1939. Dinstein, *War, Aggression and Self-Defence*, p 158.

[57] Lauterpacht, *The Limits of the Operation of the Law of War*, pp 233, 239; Dinstein, *War, Aggression and Self-Defence*, p 158. Compare also Greenwood's discussion of the arguments against equal application: Greenwood, *The relationship between ius ad bellum and ius in bello*, pp 226–30.

[58] Résolution I read: '*L'inégalité de traitement des parties durante bello est justifiée si le Conseil de Sécurité de l'O.N.U. a désigné l'une des parties comme agresseur et pourvu que cette inégalité de traitement ne dépasse pas les limites indiquées par les Résolutions suivantes.*' And Résolution II read: '*Sous réserve des stipulations des Résolutions qui suivent, l'inégalité de traitement est également justifiée quand il s'agit d'une action militaire des forces de l'O.N.U. opérant en vertu d'une décision du Conseil de Sécurité.*' JPA François; Institut de Droit International, *L'égalité d'application*

Moreover, and more recently, the International Court of Justice implicated in its 1996 Nuclear Weapons Advisory Opinion (GA) *ius ad bellum* in its discussion on whether or not the use of nuclear weapons would be legal under public international law. After concluding that:

> [i]n view of the unique characteristics of nuclear weapons, (. . .) the use of such weapons in fact seems scarcely reconcilable with respect for

the obligation to distinguish between military and civilian targets, and the prohibition of unnecessary suffering, the Court stated that yet, it did not have:

> sufficient elements to enable it to conclude with certainty that the use of nuclear weapons would necessarily be at variance with the principles and rules of law applicable in armed conflict in any circumstance.

Therefore, and considering the fundamental right of self-defence of states, it concluded that:

> in view of the present state of international law viewed as a whole (. . .) and of the elements of fact at its disposal, the Court is led to observe that it cannot reach a definitive conclusion as to the legality or illegality of the use of nuclear weapons by a State in an extreme circumstance of self-defence, in which its very survival would be at stake.[59]

Despite strong opposition, this conclusion was repeated in *dictum* 2E, which was adopted only by the President's casting vote.[60]

If the Court's judgment is to be understood as implying that any use of force, including the use of nuclear weapons, needs to comply with both *ius ad bellum* and *ius in bello* in order to be legal under public international law, then its statement is only comprehensive and in conformity with pre-existing doctrine.[61] The Court does seem to point in that direction within

des règles du droit de la guerre aux parties à un conflit armé (Quatrième Commission); 2. Rapport définitif, Annuaire de l'Institut de Droit International, Vol 50-I, 1963, Bâle, Editions juridiques et sociologiques SA, Basel, 1963, pp 111–27. Dinstein, *War, Aggression and Self-Defence*, pp 158–9. Similarly, Lauterpacht, *The Limits of the Operation of the Law of War*, pp 242–3.

[59] Legality of the Threat or Use of Nuclear Weapons, Advisory Opinion, 8 Jul 1996, ICJ Reports 1996, p 226, paras 95–7, pp 262–3.

[60] Judgment 2E reads: 'It follows from the above-mentioned requirements that the threat or use of nuclear weapons would generally be contrary to the rules of international law applicable in armed conflict, and in particular the principles and rules of humanitarian law; However, in view of the current state of international law, and of the elements of fact at its disposal, the Court cannot conclude definitively whether the threat or use of nuclear weapons would be lawful or unlawful in an extreme circumstance of self-defence, in which the very survival of the State would be at stake.' Legality of the Threat or Use of Nuclear Weapons, Advisory Opinion, 8 Jul 1996, ICJ Reports 1996, p 226, Judgment 2E, p 44.

[61] Similarly: C Greenwood, *Jus ad Bellum and Jus in Bello in the Nuclear Weapons Advisory Opinion*, in: L Boisson de Chazournes, P Sands (Eds), *International Law, the International Court of Justice and Nuclear Weapons*, Cambridge University Press, Cambridge, 1999, p 263. Compare also: Greenwood, *The relationship between ius ad bellum and ius in bello*, pp 229, 232–3. Greenwood refers, among other things, to the United States Military Tribunal in the United

the framework of its discussion of the threat or use of nuclear weapons in the light of the Charter of the United Nations.[62] The Court indicates that although the provisions on the use of force are applicable irrespective of the weapons used:

> a use of force that is proportionate under the law of self-defence, must, in order to be lawful also meet the requirements of the law applicable in armed conflict which comprise in particular the principles and rules of humanitarian law.[63]

Although it is possible that the customary requirement of proportionality under the law of self-defence makes it highly unlikely that nuclear weapons could be used under less than extreme circumstances, ie when the survival of the state is not at stake,[64] the Court's references to *ius ad bellum* in this context is certainly confusing and unfortunate, and has therefore been severely criticised in literature.[65] After all, the question as to the legality of illegality of the use of a particular weapon is pre-eminently a question of *ius in bello*, and has in principle nothing to do with the law on the use of force.

However, the Court does seem to suggest that an 'extreme circumstance of self-defence, in which the very survival of a State would be at stake' is an important and even determinative factor on whether or not

States v List which held that 'the entire German occupation of the Balkans was a violation of the *ius ad bellum*, so that everything which the occupying authorities did was contrary to international law, but when they exceeded the limits of an occupant's authority under the *ius in bello* they committed a double illegality.' United States Military Tribunal (Nuremberg), *Case No 47; The Hostages Trial; Trial of Wilhelm List and Others; 8th Jul, 1947–19th Feb, 1948*, in: The United Nations War Crimes Commission, *Law Reports of Trials of War Criminals; Vol VIII*, His Majesty's Stationary Office, London, 1949. According to Müllerson, the word 'generally' may indeed be understood as implying that the only exception possible for the use of nuclear weapons is in case of self-defence, but '[s]uch an interpretation (. . .) raises questions and it is not clear at all that the Court had this in mind.' R Müllerson, *On the Relationship between Jus ad Bellum and Jus in Bello in the General Assembly Advisory Opinion*, in: L Boisson de Chazournes, P Sands (Eds), *International Law, the International Court of Justice and Nuclear Weapons*, Cambridge University Press, Cambridge, 1999, p 269.

[62] Legality of the Threat or Use of Nuclear Weapons, Advisory Opinion, 8 Jul 1996, ICJ Reports 1996, p 226, paras 37–49, pp 244–7.

[63] Legality of the Threat or Use of Nuclear Weapons, Advisory Opinion, 8 Jul 1996, ICJ Reports 1996, p 226, para 42, p 245.

[64] According to Müllerson, an aggressor state 'has limited its right to survival', because it has committed an act of aggression. Müllerson, *On the Relationship between Jus ad Bellum and Jus in Bello in the General Assembly Advisory Opinion*, in: Boisson de Chazournes, Sands (Eds), *International Law, the International Court of Justice and Nuclear Weapons*, p 272.

[65] T Gill, *The Nuclear Weapons Advisory Opinion of the International Court of Justice and the Fundamental Distinction Between the Ius ad Bellum and the Ius in Bello*, Leiden Journal of International Law, Vol 12, 1999; WD Verwey, *De rechtmatigheid van kernwapens: het Hof in dilemma*, VN Forum, Vol 9, 1996; WD Verwey, *The International Court of Justice and the Legality of Nuclear Weapons: Some Observations*, in: K Wellens (Ed), *International Theory and Practice; Essays in Honour of Eric Suy*, Kluwer Law International, The Hague, 1998.

the use of nuclear weapons is lawful or not.[66] This interpretation is furthermore confirmed by Judge Fleischhauer, who writes in his Separate Opinion:

> To end the matter with the simple statement that recourse to nuclear weapons would be contrary to international law applicable in armed conflict, and in particular the principles and rules of humanitarian law, would have meant that the law applicable in armed conflict, and in particular the humanitarian law, was given precedence over the inherent right of individual or collective self-defence which every State possesses as a matter of sovereign equality and which is expressly preserved in Article 51 of the Charter. That would be so because if a State is the victim of an all out attack by another State, which threatens the very existence of the victimized State, recourse to the threat or use of nuclear weapons in individual (. . .) or collective (. . .) self-defence could be for the victimized State the last and only alternative to giving itself up and surrender. That situation would in particular exist if the attack is made by nuclear, bacteriological or chemical weapons. It is true that the right of self-defence as protected by Article 51 of the Charter is not weapon-specific (. . .). Nevertheless, the denial of the recourse to the threat or use of nuclear weapons as a legal option in any circumstance could amount to a denial of self-defence itself if such recourse was the last available means by way of which the victimized State could exercise its right under Article 51 of the Charter. A finding that amounted to such a denial therefore would not, in my view, have been a correct statement of the law; there is no rule in international law according to which one of the conflicting principles would prevail over the other. The fact that the attacking State itself would act in contravention of international law, would not alter the situation.[67]

If the existence of an 'extreme circumstance of self-defence, in which the very survival of a State would be at stake' is indeed considered a determinative factor on whether or not the use of nuclear weapons is lawful under public international law, then this would not only raise serious questions,[68] but it would also mean a deviation of the general rule that both *ius ad bellum* and *ius in bello* entail separate and independent responsibilities. Furthermore, this deviation could signal a renaissance of the *bellum iustum*

[66] Compare Greenwood, *Jus ad Bellum and Jus in Bello in the Nuclear Weapons Advisory Opinion*, in: Boisson de Chazournes, Sands (Eds), *International Law, the International Court of Justice and Nuclear Weapons*, p 263; Müllerson, *On the Relationship between Jus ad Bellum and Jus in Bello in the General Assembly Advisory Opinion*, in: Boisson de Chazournes, Sands (Eds), *International Law, the International Court of Justice and Nuclear Weapons*, pp 269–70.

[67] Separate Opinion of Judge Fleischhauer, Legality of the Threat or Use of Nuclear Weapons, Advisory Opinion, 8 Jul 1996, ICJ Reports 1996, p 226, para 3, at pp 306–7.

[68] Müllerson, *On the Relationship between Jus ad Bellum and Jus in Bello in the General Assembly Advisory Opinion*, in: Boisson de Chazournes, Sands (Eds), *International Law, the International Court of Justice and Nuclear Weapons*, pp 270–1.

doctrine,[69] though adapted to modern times, in which the reasons for going to war ultimately determine the lawfulness of any use of force under public international law.[70] Although undesirable,[71] this development is arguable in view of the limitation of the right to go to war before 1945 and the prohibition of the use of force since 1945.[72] The special and perhaps even peremptory status of the prohibition on the use of force under public international law,[73] and thus the special status of law on the use of force in general, might even warrant a reinterpretation of the distinction between *ius ad bellum* and *ius in bello*. After all, as was observed above, the law of war as we know it today and its equal application to belligerents could only develop with the acceptance of war as a sovereign right and consequently as a de facto situation.

3.3 The Financial Settlement of War Damages

If the distinction between *ius ad bellum* and *ius in bello* is indeed becoming blurred, then Security Council Resolution 687 is only illustrative of this development. However, there may be another, or additional justification for Iraq's liability for damage resulting from its invasion and subsequent occupation of Kuwait. Although the maxim *ex iniuria ius non oritur* has

[69] Greenwood comes to an exactly similar conclusion. Greenwood, *Jus ad Bellum and Jus in Bello in the Nuclear Weapons Advisory Opinion*, in: Boisson de Chazournes, Sands (Eds), *International Law, the International Court of Justice and Nuclear Weapons*, p 264. Greenwood writes: 'To allow the necessities of self-defence to override the principles of humanitarian law would put at risk all the progress in that law which has been made in the last hundred years or so and raise the spectre of a return to theories of the "just war" and the maxim embodied in the German proverb that *Kriegsraison geht vor Kriegsmanier* ('necessity in war overrules the manner of warfare').'

[70] Although, it is unlikely that in view of the status of *ius in bello* nowadays the reasons for going to war will ever determine the scope of a state's responsibilities under the rules of combat as was the case under the *bellum iustum* doctrine, but it cannot be excluded. Gill, for example, finds it 'perhaps most disturbing, (. . .) the way the Court introduces the notion that an extra-legal concept like 'the survival of the state' could override the rules and principles of the *jus in bello.*' Gill, *The Nuclear Weapons Advisory Opinion of the International Court of Justice and the Fundamental Distinction Between the Ius ad Bellum and the Ius in Bello*, p 623.

[71] An aggressor state would lose all interest in complying with the laws of war if it were held responsible for all use of force.

[72] Similarly, Lauterpacht, *The Limits of the Operation of the Law of War*, p 210.

[73] Compare Military and Paramilitary Activities in and against Nicaragua (Nicaragua v United States of America), Merits, Judgment, 27 Jun 1986, ICJ Reports 1986, p 14, para 190, pp 100–1. In a recent study, Schrijver acknowledges the peremptory status of the prohibition to use force, since the prohibition is widely accepted and recognised, and a very large majority of states accept the prohibition as peremptory. However, in view of the 'increasing number of new exceptions claimed by leading states', it is questionable 'how long the prohibition to use force still qualifies' as a norm of *ius cogens*. N Schrijver, *Challenges to the Prohibition to Use Force: Does the Straitjacket of Article 2(4) UN Charter Begin to Gall too Much?*, in: N Blokker, N Schrijver (Eds), *The Security Council and the Use of Force; Theory and Reality—A Need for Change?*, Martinus Nijhoff Publishers, Leiden, 2005, pp 39–43.

been rejected with respect to the scope of responsibilities on the conduct of hostilities, it may have relevance as to the financial settlement of war damage. According to Lauterpacht:

> [t]here is room in other spheres, not directly connected with the conduct of war, for giving effect to the principle that a State cannot acquire rights from its wrongful acts.[74]

> [W]hile international law sets no limit to the conditions of peace which the victor may exact from a defeated enemy, it has been customary not to compel the latter to pay compensation for damage arising out of operations connected with the lawful conduct of the war. That custom must henceforth be deemed to lack a juridical basis in the case of a war undertaken unlawfully.[75]

Compelling a state to pay compensation for war damages resulting from a war which had been started unlawfully as a general principle was foreshadowed by and had a precedent in the Treaty of Versailles,[76] Article 231 of which, read:

> The Allied and Associated Governments affirm and Germany accepts the responsibility of Germany and her allies for causing all the loss and damage to which the Allied and Associated Governments and their nationals have been subjected as a consequence of the war imposed upon them by the aggression of Germany and her allies.

Furthermore in Article 232, the Allied and Associated Governments recognise that Germany's resources are not adequate:

> after taking into account permanent diminution of such resources which will result from other provisions of the present Treaty, to make complete reparation for all such loss and damage.

Nevertheless:

> [t]he Allied and Associated Governments (. . .) require, and Germany undertakes, that she will make compensation for all damage done to the civilian population of the Allied and Associated Powers and to their property during the period of the belligerency of each as an Allied or Associated Power against Germany by such aggression by land, by sea and from the air, and in general all damage as defined in Annex 1 hereto.

For this purpose, the Contracting Parties established an 'Inter-Allied Commission, to be called the Reparation Commission' under Article 233, which was charged to consider the claims and to set the amount of the damage for which compensation was to be made.

[74] Lauterpacht, *The Limits of the Operation of the Law of War,* p 239.

[75] Lauterpacht, *The Limits of the Operation of the Law of War,* p 234.

[76] Covenant of the League of Nations or Peace Treaty of Versailles, signed on 28 Jun 1919, entered into force on 10 Jan 1920, AJIL, Vol 13, No 2, Supplement: Official Documents, 1919, p 128.

The similarity of Resolution 687 with the Treaty of Versailles is striking, not only as far as the scope of Germany's and Iraq's liability is concerned, but also with respect to the settlement of their liability through an international commission.[77] Although the circumstances were different in the beginning of the 20th century, and it is unlikely that wars of aggression were prohibited under international law in 1914, according to Lauterpacht:

> these provisions of the Treaty of Versailles must be regarded as having paved the way for the adoption of what seems the correct principle on the subject.[78]

Lauterpacht was apparently inspired by Fitzmaurice, who had made a similar, but more careful proposition in 1948. Fitzmaurice wrote that:

> [i]n the ordinary way, a State is not responsible for damage legitimately caused in the ordinary conduct of the war, but if a State is in the position of a wrongdoer in being at war at all, if it has gone to war in a manner involving a breach of international law and constituting an international crime, it might well be argued that it has legal responsibility for all the ensuing damage even if it would otherwise rank as damage legitimately caused in the normal conduct of operations. Of course, no State could in practice make good all such damage, and it is now well understood that the capacity of defeated belligerents to pay, or to make good damage is very limited. This, however, does not affect the question of responsibility; and the principle that States in the position of wrongdoers as a result of their aggression, are responsible for the ensuing damage, irrespective of any treaty provision, may well be a useful one to establish. The question of reparation will, however, always remain one which will have to be regulated by treaty, if only because it is necessary to provide specifically what payments are to be made, and what the method of payment is to be.[79]

The idea to hold aggressors liable for all war damage finds a strong precedent in the Treaty of Versailles and to a lesser extent in the peace treaties concluded after World War II,[80] and has also more recently found

[77] Similar to the Compensation Commission, the Reparation Commission was supposed to act as a fact-finding commission. Boelaert-Suominen writes that the Commission made it very clear that 'it [was] not concerned with inquiring whether the act for which Germany has accepted responsibility was legal or illegal, since it considered itself bound by the terms of the peace treaty that fixes Germany's obligation to pay.' Boelaert-Suominen, *Iraqi War Reparations and the Laws of War: a Discussion of the Current Work of the United Nations Compensation Commission with Specific Reference to Environmental Damage During Warfare*, p 307. Note, however, Gattini, who believes that it is incorrect from a 'historical and methodological standpoint' to evoke the Reparation Commission as a predecessor of the Compensation Commission. A Gattini, *The UN Compensation Commission: Old Rules, New Procedures on War Reparations*, European Journal of International Law, Vol 13, 2002, p 165.

[78] Lauterpacht, *The Limits of the Operation of the Law of War*, p 235.

[79] GG Fitzmaurice, *The Juridical Clauses of the Peace Treaties*, Recueil des Cours; Collected Courses of the Hague Academy of International Law Vol 73, 1948-II, Imprimeries Delmas, Bordeaux, 1950, pp 325–6.

[80] Lauterpacht, *The Limits of the Operation of the Law of War*, p 235.

adherents in literature.[81] Although the idea sounds appealing, it is unfortunate that none of the authors provide substantial evidence for the existence of this rule, and it is therefore uncertain whether such a general rule actually exists under public international law.

[81] These authors include Schwarzenberger, Low and Hodgkinson, Boelaert-Suominen, Greenwood and Gattini. Schwarzenberger wrote in 1968: 'However harsh—and, possibly, ill-advised—any particular solution may be, it derives its legal justification not only from the consent of the defeated State, but also from the victor's right, irrespective of any consent, to demand full reparation for the illegal resort of the defeated State to armed force. The victor need not even distinguish between legal and illegal acts of war of the vanquished. If the defeated State has broken its obligations under *jus ad bellum*, it cannot hide behind observance of *jus in bello*. Breaches of the laws and customs of war provide merely additional grounds for reparation.' Schwarzenberger, *International Law; As Applied by International Courts and Tribunals; Vol II; The Law of Armed Conflict*, Stevens & Sons, London, 1968, p 767. Referring to Schwarzenberger, Low and Hodgkinson wrote in 1995: 'Violations of *jus ad bellum* should be distinguished from violations of *jus in bello* because a party that violates *jus ad bellum* may be held responsible for all damages caused by such a war regardless of whether it acted lawfully in the context of *jus in bello*.' Low, Hodgkinson, *Compensation for Wartime Environmental Damage: Challenges to International Law After the Gulf War*, pp 412–13, 456. In 1996, Boelaert-Suominen concluded that 'general international law on compensation for war damage clearly establishes the principle that aggressor States are liable to pay reparation for damages resulting from breaches of the *ius ad bellum*. Reparations may cover damage to public and private property, loss of life and injuries to civilians and generally at least part of the war costs of the victorious State(s). However, the exact range of claims to be covered by the reparations regime, the amount of reparations and the modalities of implementation depend on the particular terms of the peace treaties.' Boelaert-Suominen, *Iraqi War Reparations and the Laws of War: a Discussion of the Current Work of the United Nations Compensation Commission with Specific Reference to Environmental Damage During Warfare*, p 308. In 1996, Greenwood wrote that although international claims on this basis had been rare 'a State is liable, in principle, to pay compensation for damage, including environmental damage, caused by an unlawful resort to force. That is so even if the act which was the immediate cause of the damage was not itself a violation of the laws of armed conflict. (. . .) State responsibility here flows from a breach not of the *jus in bello* but of the *jus ad bellum*.' Greenwood, *State Responsibility and Civil Liability for Environmental Damage Caused by Military Operations*, in: Grunawalt, King, McClain (Eds), *Protection of the Environment during Armed Conflict*, p 403 and similarly, pp 406–7. Three year later, he wrote: 'Since the aggressor's resort to force is unlawful, it incurs international responsibility for all the consequences of its use of force. It therefore has a duty to compensate not only those who have suffered loss as a result of the violations of the laws of war committed by its forces but also those injured by acts of the same forces which were not contrary to that law. In the latter case, the illegality which gives rise to the responsibility lies in the original wrongful resort to force. Moreover, since opposition to an illegal resort to force is an entirely foreseeable consequence of that unlawful act, the aggressor can also be held responsible for damage caused by lawful acts of war on the part of its opponents. This was the approach adopted in the aftermath of the Gulf conflict, when the Security Council reaffirmed, in resolution 687 (1991) that Iraq was "liable under international law for any direct loss, damage . . . or injury to foreign Governments, nationals or corporations as a result of its unlawful invasion and occupation of Kuwait".' Greenwood, *International Humanitarian Law (Laws of War); Revised Report for the Centennial Commemoration of the First Hague Peace Conference 1899*, p 19. And Gattini, finally, stated in 2002 that the starting point for the scope of Iraq's liability under Resolution 687 is 'the existence in contemporary international law of a norm which *post bellum* permits or even demands the liability of the aggressor state, charging it with an obligation to make good not only the entire amount of damage caused by itself, but also damage arising from the legitimate exercise of self-defence by the state that is the victim of the aggression.' Gattini, *The UN Compensation Commission: Old Rules, New Procedures on War Reparations*, p 173.

It is probably for a reason that Fitzmaurice wrote that:

> the principle that States in the position of wrongdoers as a result of their aggression, are responsible for the ensuing damage, irrespective of any treaty provision, may well be a useful one to establish,

thereby indicating that this principle was not *de lege lata* but *de lege ferenda*. Furthermore, Fitzmaurice pointed out that '[t]he question of reparation will (. . .) always remain one which will have to be regulated by treaty'.[82] After all, sovereignty entails legal equality of states which also means that one state cannot impose its will upon another state, or *par in parem non habet imperium*.[83] Indeed, the liability of the Axis Powers after both World Wars was based on treaties to which Germany and the other states had consented to be bound, rather than on a general principle or rule of public international law, and:

> [i]t is [therefore] easy to see why the Security Council devoted special attention to getting Iraq's formal consent on the cease-fire conditions.[84]

3.4 Converging Responsibilities under *Ius ad Bellum* and *Ius in Bello*

Ius ad bellum and *ius in bello* are nevertheless strongly related. Greenwood concluded in 1983, that both categories of rules are 'closer today than they have been for over two centuries' and while they operated 'at different stages' in the past, 'they now apply simultaneously'. Still:

> they remain distinct branches of international law, not merely for historical reasons, but because they are logically independent of each other, operate in different ways, with different degrees of precision and different sanctions. They are separate but complementary systems of rules, which are capable of being studied and applied separately but which must both be considered in evaluating the legality of a state's use of force.[85]

[82] Compare also Boelaert-Suominen: 'However, the exact range of claims to be covered by the reparations regime, the amount of reparations and the modalities of implementation depend on the particular terms of the peace treaties.' Boelaert-Suominen, *Iraqi War Reparations and the Laws of War: a Discussion of the Current Work of the United Nations Compensation Commission with Specific Reference to Environmental Damage During Warfare*, p 308.

[83] In translation: an equal does not have power over an equal.

[84] Boelaert-Suominen, *Iraqi War Reparations and the Laws of War: a Discussion of the Current Work of the United Nations Compensation Commission with Specific Reference to Environmental Damage During Warfare*, p 309. S/22456, 6 Apr 1991, Identical letters dated 6 Apr 1991 from the Permanent Representative of Iraq to the United Nations addressed respectively to the Secretary-General and the President of the Security Council.

[85] Greenwood, *The relationship between ius ad bellum and ius in bello*, pp 232–3. Compare Boelaert-Suominen's discussion on the relationship between *ius ad bellum* and *ius in bello*. She distinguishes between two schools of thought. The first school claims that both sets of rules apply simultaneously under the UN Charter. The second school believes that 'punishment for the use of force in contravention of *ius ad bellum*, regardless of its legality under the *ius in bello*, inevitably leads to an erosion of the *ius in bello*.' Boelaert-Suominen, *Iraqi War Reparations and the Laws of War: a Discussion of the Current Work of the United Nations Compensation Commission with Specific Reference to Environmental Damage During Warfare*, pp 298–302.

Both sets of rules indeed seem to operate at different levels and in different ways. *Ius in bello* primarily regulates the conduct of hostilities and the protection of victims of armed conflict; its character is largely humanitarian and its beneficiaries are mostly human individuals. *Ius ad bellum*, on the other hand, regulates the maintenance and restoration of international peace and security, is primarily intended to regulate the behavior of states[86] and therefore seems to operate more at macro level.

Although both sets of rules seem to operate at different levels, they do not operate completely independently of each other and it is possible therefore that responsibilities under both sets of rules overlap. This simultaneous applicability of both *ius ad bellum* and *ius in bello* must be clearly distinguished from parallel and simultaneous application of different sets of rules under national law. In a national legal system, for example, it is possible that a particular case is judged both under criminal and under civil law, which means that someone who is suspected of a certain crime may be found not guilty within the framework of criminal proceedings, but can nevertheless be found liable for civil damages in a civil lawsuit. This is possible not only because both criminal law and civil law operate independently and have different objects and purposes, but also because the responsibilities under both sets of rules are owed to different actors or different subjects of law. The responsibilities of individuals under criminal law are owed towards the community or society as a whole and criminal proceedings are therefore instigated by public prosecutors representing the state or the people. The responsibilities of individuals under civil law, on the other hand, are principally owed towards other private individuals and civil lawsuits consequently feature two or more private parties.

This is different under public international law as far as *ius ad bellum* and *ius in bello* are concerned. Although both sets of rules operate at different levels, have a different object and purpose and even have different beneficiaries, the obligations under both sets of rules are in principle owed by one state to another, which means that under the law of state responsibility, in principle only states will be able to claim compensation for war damages.[87]

Converging of responsibilities under *ius ad bellum* and *ius in bello* may occur in two situations. Firstly, states exercising their right of self-defence need to comply with the general principles of necessity and

[86] The individual criminal responsibility for the crime of aggression under *ius ad bellum* is exceptional.

[87] N Quénivet, *The right to claim compensation for violations of international humanitarian law: The German judgment on the Varvarin bridge*, Bofaxe No 267E, 27 Dec 2003. Through: <http://www.ruhr-uni-bochum.de/ifhv/publications/bofaxe/>.

proportionality[88] under *ius ad bellum* in their overall conduct of hostilities.[89] And secondly, aggressor states that have violated *ius ad bellum* may be liable to pay compensation for war damages both under *ius ad bellum* and *ius in bello.*

This overlap could be problematic in case a state incurs responsibility under *ius ad bellum* but further acts completely in accordance with *ius in bello.* In the first situation, it is likely that a defending state which takes measures that are unnecessary or disproportionate under the law of self-defence remains internationally responsible under *ius ad bellum* despite observing the laws of war.[90] This follows from the object and purpose of both requirements to keep the overall level of force and the scope of the conflict to a minimum.[91] Therefore, a state that uses force in self-defence and which takes measures that have a damaging effect on the environ-

[88] Compare para 4 of the 1994 San Remo Manual which reads: 'The principles of necessity and proportionality apply equally to armed conflict at sea and require that the conduct of hostilities by a State should not exceed the degree and kind of force, not otherwise prohibited by the law of armed conflict, required to repel an armed attack against it and to restore its security.' Doswald-Beck, *International Humanitarian Law and the Advisory Opinion of the International Court of Justice on the Legality of the Threat or Use of Nuclear Weapons,* s 5. Greenwood, *The relationship between ius ad bellum and ius in bello,* pp 223–4; Greenwood, *Jus ad Bellum and Jus in Bello in the Nuclear Weapons Advisory Opinion,* in: Boisson de Chazournes, Sands (Eds), *International Law, the International Court of Justice and Nuclear Weapons,* pp 258–9; Greenwood, *International Humanitarian Law (Laws of War); Revised Report for the Centennial Commemoration of the First Hague Peace Conference 1899,* pp 23–5.

[89] Military and Paramilitary Activities in and against Nicaragua (Nicaragua v United States of America), Merits, Judgment, 27 Jun 1986, ICJ Reports 1986, p 14, para 194, p 103; Legality of the Threat or Use of Nuclear Weapons, Advisory Opinion, 8 Jul 1996, ICJ Reports 1996, p 226, para 41, p 240; Case Concerning Oil Platforms (Islamic Republic of Iran v United States of America), Merits, Judgment, 6 Nov 2003, ICJ Reports 2003, paras 43, 74, 76, pp 24, 35, 37; Case Concerning Armed Activities on the Territory of the Congo (Democratic Republic of the Congo v Uganda), Merits, Judgment, 19 Dec 2005, ICJICJ Reports 2005, para 147, p 53.

[90] Compare Greenwood, *The relationship between ius ad bellum and ius in bello,* pp 223–5, who refers to examples from the Falklands War and the Arab-Israeli conflict. Gardam distinguishes between the application of necessity and proportionality during armed conflict: 'Proportionality, unlike necessity, remains relevant throughout the conflict.' Gardam, *Necessity and Proportionality in Jus ad Bellum and Jus in Bello,* in: Boisson de Chazournes, Sands (Eds), *International Law, the International Court of Justice and Nuclear Weapons,* p 280.

[91] According to Gardam, '[c]urrent international law represents the view of states that the overall evil of war always outbalances the good except in cases of self-defence. This process of balance is continued in the legal requirements of necessity and of proportionality for a legitimate exercise of the right of self-defence.' Gardam, *Necessity and Proportionality in Jus ad Bellum and Jus in Bello,* in: Boisson de Chazournes, Sands (Eds), *International Law, the International Court of Justice and Nuclear Weapons,* p 277. Compare also Greenwood, *The relationship between ius ad bellum and ius in bello,* p 223; Greenwood, *Jus ad Bellum and Jus in Bello in the Nuclear Weapons Advisory Opinion,* in: Boisson de Chazournes, Sands (Eds), *International Law, the International Court of Justice and Nuclear Weapons,* pp 258–9. In case of a declaration of war, 'the range of measures which may be employed in self-defence becomes more extensive'. '[A] declaration of war will usually suggest that the conflict is on a more extensive scale since, in modern times, a declaration of war has come to be regarded as a statement of an intention to fight a total rather than a limited conflict.' Greenwood, *The relationship between ius ad bellum and ius in bello,* p 224.

ment, but which are not in violation of *ius in bello* may still be held internationally responsible if the operation in total is not in conformity with the principles of necessity and proportionality under the law of self-defence.

In the second situation, however, the outcome is less obvious. On the one hand, it is arguable that an aggressor state should pay compensation for all material damage inflicted upon another state, even if its acts are in conformity with *ius in bello*. If not, it could get away with a violation of *ius ad bellum* without paying compensation for damage resulting from hostilities. This would be another indication that the distinction between *ius ad bellum* and *ius in bello* is becoming blurred or in any case less strict than always assumed.

On the other hand, it is arguable that an aggressor state should not have to pay compensation for material damage committed within the framework of lawful operations under the laws of war. This would be in conformity with the historical dichotomy between both sets of rules and the object and purpose of *ius in bello*, which assumes the existence of an armed conflict, irrespective of its cause, as well as with the general principle of law that the loss rests where it falls.[92] If an aggressor state would still have to pay compensation for material damage even when it observes the law of armed conflict, it might lose all economic incentives to observe the laws of war.[93] This does not mean that an aggressor state would not have to pay any compensation at all. It could, for example, be held liable for all economical damage resulting from the probable collapse of a victim state's economy, which could be substantial. Fortunately, this second situation is strictly hypothetical and not likely to occur in practice.[94]

[92] Compare, eg, the relationship between *ius in bello* and *ius pacis*. In an outline paper for a Study Group of the International Law Commission on the Fragmentation of International Law, Koskenniemi concluded that '[a] general type of *lex specialis*, constituting an exception to legal normality are the laws of war. It seems that, at least in the absence of evidence to the contrary, the laws of war must be regarded as *leges speciales* in relation to—and thus override—rules laying out the peace-time norms relating to the same subjects.' In the 1996 Nuclear Weapons Opinion (GA) and the 2004 Wall Opinion, the International Court of Justice stated that in case of simultaneous application of both human rights law and international humanitarian law, the former must be interpreted as *lex generalis*, in the light of the latter. Koskenniemi's outline paper as well as the two advisory opinions have been referred to above, and will be discussed more elaborately in Ch V. M Koskenniemi, *Fragmentation of International Law*, Outline for Study Group, International Law Commission, 55th session, 2003, p 6. At: <http://www.un.org/law/ilc/sessions/55/55sess.htm>. Legality of the Threat or Use of Nuclear Weapons, Advisory Opinion, 8 Jul 1996, ICJ Reports 1996, para 25, p 240; Legal Consequences of the Construction of a Wall in the Occupied Palestinian Territory, Advisory Opinion, 9 Jul 2004, ICJ Reports 2004, pp 41–2. According to Koskenniemi, the European Court of Human Rights adopted a similar approach in the 1974 Neumann case. Koskenniemi, *Fragmentation of International Law*, Outline for Study Group, International Law Commission, 55th session, 2003, p 4.

[93] Other incentives arguably include humanitarian concerns, fear of reprisals, and fear of individual criminal responsibility.

[94] Besides, these issues are usually dealt with within the framework of a treaty.

It will certainly be interesting to see how the Eritrea-Ethiopia Claims Commission will determine the scope of Eritrea's liability for its violation of the *ius ad bellum* on 12 May 1998 and its subsequent occupation of territory then under administration of Ethiopia, as recently established on 19 December 2005.[95] The fact that the Commission dealt with claims under *ius in bello* and *ius ad bellum* separately could indicate that the scope of Eritrea's liability under *ius ad bellum* does not extend to damage resulting from the actual conduct of hostilities.

Furthermore, there is also a chance that the International Court of Justice will rule on the scope of a state's liability for violating *ius ad bellum* and *ius in bello*. In the case between the Democratic Republic of Congo (DRC) and Uganda, the Court established the international responsibility of Uganda both under *ius ad bellum* and *ius in bello*, and considered that it would determine the 'nature, form and amount of the reparation due' to the DRC, 'in a subsequent phase of the proceedings' in case the Parties would not be able to reach an agreement.[96]

In any case, the scope of Iraq's liability for all damage resulting from its invasion and occupation of Kuwait under Resolution 687 should be regarded as exceptional and only justified by the powers and responsibility of the Security Council for the maintenance or restoration of international peace and security.[97] From an environmental perspective, however, Resolution 687 must be welcomed and should certainly bear repetition.[98] After all, the scope of Iraq's liability by reference to Iraq's breach of *ius ad bellum* is arguably much wider than its responsibility would have been under *ius in bello*, and Resolution 687's reference to the environment and the subsequent work of the UNCC have done more for the environment than any other written or unwritten rule on the protec-

[95] Partial Award; *Jus ad Bellum*; Ethiopia's Claims 1–8; between The Federal Republic of Ethiopia and the State of Eritrea; Eritrea Ethiopia Claims Commission; The Hague, Dec 19, 2005. Through: <http://www.pca-cpa.org>.

[96] Case Concerning Armed Activities on the Territory of the Congo (Democratic Republic of the Congo v Uganda), Merits, Judgment, 19 Dec 2005, ICJICJ Reports 2005, para 260, p 82.

[97] See, for a discussion of the powers of the Security Council to establish a Compensation Commission and to decide on issues of liability and compensation: Low, Hodgkinson, *Compensation for Wartime Environmental Damage: Challenges to International Law After the Gulf War*, pp 467–79.

[98] Greenwood refers to the practical advantages for claimants: Greenwood, *State Responsibility and Civil Liability for Environmental Damage Caused by Military Operations*, in: Grunawalt, King, McClain (Eds), *Protection of the Environment during Armed Conflict*, p 407. See also Low, Hodgkinson, *Compensation for Wartime Environmental Damage: Challenges to International Law After the Gulf War*, p 467. Low and Hodgkinson believe that despite the advantages, the precedential value of Resolution 687 is limited 'because of its legal basis and its characterization as a peace treaty.' Low, Hodgkinson, *Compensation for Wartime Environmental Damage: Challenges to International Law After the Gulf War*, p 477–9. See also Bunker on the limits to the precedential value of this construction: AL Bunker, *Protection of the Environment During Armed Conflict: One Gulf, Two Wars*, Review of European Community and international environmental law, Vol 13, 2004, p 209.

tion of the environment during international armed conflict may have done instead. If this Resolution is any indication on how the Security Council will deal with aggressor states in the future, it may not only be a stronger deterrent[99] than other rules of public international law, but it may also function as a safety net that could solve some of the deficiencies of the protection of the environment under *ius in bello*.

[99] Similarly Greenwood, *State Responsibility and Civil Liability for Environmental Damage Caused by Military Operations*, in: Grunawalt, King, McClain (Eds), *Protection of the Environment during Armed Conflict*, p 412.

V

The Protection of the Environment During International Armed Conflict Under Ius Pacis

1—INTRODUCTION

THE PROTECTION OF the environment during international armed conflict under *ius pacis* is based on the potential application of peacetime norms of international environmental law in times of international armed conflict. Therefore, and similar to the protection of the environment under *ius ad bellum*, the protection of the environment under *ius pacis* is only of subsidiary importance. To the extent that peacetime international environmental law does apply in times of international armed conflict, however, its protection is direct, since the object and purpose of international environmental law is the protection and safeguarding of the environment for present and future generations.

Before discussing the level of the protection of the environment under *ius pacis* (section 2.3), however, it may be useful to spend a few words on the general relationship between *ius pacis* and *ius in bello* first (section 2.1), illustrated by the applicability of international human rights law during international armed conflict (section 2.2), as recognised by the International Court of Justice in the 1996 Nuclear Weapons Opinion (GA) as well as in the 2004 Wall Opinion.

2—THE RELATIONSHIP BETWEEN *IUS PACIS* AND *IUS IN BELLO*

2.1 General

Although it has been argued in previous times that war is a sociological phenomenon that falls outside the realm of law, this point of view has never been accepted as a legal premise and international practice has shown 'that war does not mean the total disruption of all legal bonds between States.'[1]

[1] J Delbrück, *War, Effects on Treaties*, in: R Bernhardt (Ed), *Encyclopaedia of Public International Law; Vol Four; Quirin, Ex Parte to Zones of Peace*, Elsevier, Amsterdam, 2000, p 1368.

The development and application of the laws of war by itself constitutes evidence of the functioning of public international law in times of armed conflict, and so does the practice of concluding armistice agreements between belligerents, and agreements for the exchange of prisoners.[2] The scope of applicable peacetime norms of international law during international armed conflict, however, is still uncertain and the subject of discussion.

It is important, first of all, to distinguish clearly between the legal relationship between belligerents *inter se* and between belligerents and non-belligerents. The latter relationship will in principle only be affected by the law of neutrality, which means that, in principle, both belligerents and non-belligerents in their mutual relations will have to observe their international obligations under *ius pacis*.[3] The former relationship, on the other hand, may severely be affected by the outbreak of hostilities and will thus be the focus of attention.

Secondly, it is important to distinguish between the applicability of treaties and customary international law during international armed conflict. Most attention in legal doctrine has been given to the effects of hostilities on the former, while little has been written with respect to the effects of hostilities on the latter. However, since general customary international law is in principle binding on all states, it seems appropriate to compare its applicability during international armed conflict to the applicability of multilateral treaties. As will be shown further below, the applicability of multilateral treaties between belligerents depends on its categorisation.

As to the applicability of peacetime treaties during international armed conflict amongst belligerents, the customary law of treaties has always been rather inconclusive, and it is therefore unfortunate that the drafters of the 1969 Vienna Convention on the Law of Treaties decided not to include rules on the effect of hostilities on treaties in the Convention. Article 73 of the Convention dealing with 'Cases of State succession, State responsibility and outbreak of hostilities' provides:

> The provisions of the present Convention shall not prejudge any question that may arise in regard to a treaty from (. . .) the outbreak of hostilities between States.

In 1963, the International Law Commission (ILC) found that this topic 'could not conveniently be dealt with' since it would:

[2] Compare AD McNair, *The Law of Treaties*, Clarendon Press, Oxford, 1961, pp 696–7.

[3] McNair, *The Law of Treaties*, p 728. McNair writes that only under exceptional circumstances 'an implied condition may be found to exist (. . .) which excludes or modifies the operation of such a treaty during the war.' See also A/CN.4/552, First Report on the Effects of Armed Conflicts on Treaties, by Mr Ian Brownlie, Special Rapporteur, of 21 Apr 2005; International Law Commission, fifty-seventh session, Geneva, 2 May–3 Jun and 4 Jul–5 Aug 2005, Draft Art 3, p 10. At: <http://www.un.org/law/ilc/sessions/57/57sess.htm>.

> inevitably involve a consideration of the effect of the provisions of the Charter concerning the threat or use of force upon the legality of the recourse to the particular hostilities in question.[4]

And in 1966, it justified its exclusion of this topic by considering that:

> in the international law of today the outbreak of hostilities between States must be considered as an entirely abnormal condition, and that the rule governing its legal consequences should not be regarded as forming part of the general rules of international law applicable in the normal relations between States. (. . .) accordingly, the Commission concluded that it was justified in considering the case of an outbreak of hostilities between parties to a treaty to be wholly outside the scope of the general law of treaties to be codified in the present articles; and that no account should be taken of that case or any mention made of it in the draft articles.[5]

The fact that the Vienna Convention does not specifically deal with this topic does not mean ipso facto that the Convention may not otherwise be relevant. First of all, peremptory norms of general international law, also known as *ius cogens*, remain applicable at all times, including times of international armed conflict. This follows from the imperative nature of these norms, as laid down in Articles 53 and 64 of the Convention. And secondly, states parties have the right to invoke the general rules of treaty law on termination and suspension of treaties under the Convention and customary international law, including rules on supervening impossibility of performance (Article 61), and fundamental change of circumstances (Article 62).[6]

As far as the effect of international armed conflict on treaties among belligerents is concerned, Delbrück distinguished three theories. The first and the oldest theory stipulates that, subject to a few exceptions, in principle all treaty relations are terminated between belligerent states.[7] The second

[4] A/5509, Report of the Commission to the General Assembly; Report of the International Law Commission covering the work of its fifteenth session, 6 May–12 Jul 1963; Yearbook of the International Law Commission, 1963; Vol II, United Nations, New York, 1964, p 189, para 14.

[5] A/6309/Rev1, Reports of the Commission to the General Assembly; Part II; Report of the International Law Commission on the work of its eighteenth session, Geneva, 4 May–19 Jul 1966, in: Yearbook of the International Law Commission 1966; Vol II, United Nations, New York, 1967, pp 267–7,

[6] See also A/CN.4/552, First Report on the Effects of Armed Conflicts on Treaties, by Mr Ian Brownlie, Special Rapporteur, Draft Art 13.

[7] Delbrück, *War, Effects on Treaties*, in: Bernhardt (Ed), *Encyclopaedia of Public International Law; Vol Four; Quirin, Ex Parte to Zones of Peace*, 1369. Also McNair, who provides a number of historical examples of the application of this theory, McNair, *The Law of Treaties*, pp 698–702; A/CN.4/550, The effect of armed conflict on treaties: an examination of practice and doctrine; Memorandum by the Secretariat, 1 Feb 2005; International Law Commission, fifty-seventh session, Geneva, 2 May–3 Jun 2005 and 4 Jul–5 Aug 2005, pp 12–13; and Brownlie: 'War is the polar opposite of peace and involves a complete rupture of relations, and a return to anarchy. It follows that all treaties are annulled without exception. The right of abrogation arises from the occurrence of war regardless of the original intention of the parties'. A/CN.4/552, First Report on the Effects of Armed Conflicts on Treaties, by Mr Ian Brownlie, Special Rapporteur, of 21 Apr 2005; International Law Commission, fifty-seventh session, Geneva, 2 May–3 Jun and 4 Jul–5 Aug 2005. At: <http://www.un.org/law/ilc/sessions/57/57sess.htm>, p 4.

theory assumes the exact opposite and prescribes that in principle all treaties remain valid in times of international armed conflict and that termination of treaties is the exception rather than the rule.[8] According to Delbrück, neither theory has ever been accepted in international practice and therefore a third and more pragmatic theory was developed in the course of the 20th century. This theory was based on the recognition that there is no general rule on the effects of war on treaties, and has therefore adopted a more pragmatic approach balancing the interests of both the belligerents and the international community of states as a whole.[9] War does not ipso facto terminate or suspend treaties, and suspension or termination depends on the classic but difficult to determine criteria of intention of the parties as reflected in the text of the treaty, or the object and purpose of the treaty in question.[10]

This more pragmatic approach became necessary in view of developments in international relations. Firstly, the nature of international armed conflict has changed since 1945 from large-scale war and occupation to more low-profile armed activities, not only because of the increasing costs of international armed conflict, but also because of the prohibition of the use of force in international relations under the United Nations Charter. And secondly, globalisation has led to an interdependent world, not only among states, but also among private individuals and private corporations, and interests involved in the maintenance of international legal relations are significant.

Nowadays, it seems that the current legal situation reflects a combination of the pragmatic approach with the second theory. This appears from the expert writings of, for example, McNair in 1961,[11] as well as from

[8] Delbrück, *War, Effects on Treaties*, in: Bernhardt (Ed), *Encyclopaedia of Public International Law; Vol Four; Quirin, Ex Parte to Zones of Peace*, 1369. Also A/CN.4/550, The effect of armed conflict on treaties: an examination of practice and doctrine; Memorandum by the Secretariat, p 13. Brownlie refers with respect to this theory to the argument that since 1919 the right to go to war and the right to use force in international relations has been limited and subsequently prohibited and that therefore 'the use of force should not be recognized as a general solvent of treaty obligations.' A/CN.4/552, First Report on the Effects of Armed Conflicts on Treaties, by Mr Ian Brownlie, Special Rapporteur, p 5.

[9] Delbrück, *War, Effects on Treaties*, in: Bernhardt (Ed), *Encyclopaedia of Public International Law; Vol Four; Quirin, Ex Parte to Zones of Peace*, p 1369. Brownlie refers to two separate rationales, namely the compatibility of the treaty with the state of hostilities and the intention of the parties at the time of conclusion. A/CN.4/552, First Report on the Effects of Armed Conflicts on Treaties, by Mr Ian Brownlie, Special Rapporteur, p 5. Also McNair referred in 1961 to the writings of Sir Cecil Hurst, who had submitted in 1921–1922 that 'the element on which must depend an answer to the question whether or not a particular treaty is or is not abrogated by the outbreak of war between the parties, is to be found in *the intention of the parties at the time when they concluded the treaty*, rather than in the nature of the treaty which they concludEd' (emphasis added). Quoted in: McNair, *The Law of Treaties*, p 698.

[10] A/CN.4/550, The effect of armed conflict on treaties: an examination of practice and doctrine; Memorandum by the Secretariat, pp 1, 9–12, 13–14.

[11] AD McNair, *The Law of Treaties*, Clarendon Press, Oxford, 1961.

studies published by the authoritative *Institut de Droit International* in 1985,[12] the Secretariat of the United Nations in 2005,[13] and the ILC in 2005.[14]

According to McNair, 'war does not *per se* put an end to pre-war treaty obligations in existence between opposing belligerents' and the essence of the modern view lay in:

> the need of discriminating between different categories of treaties for the purpose of ascertaining the effect of the outbreak of war upon them.[15]

Therefore, he distinguished nine categories, two categories of which were ipso facto abrogated by the outbreak of war, and one ipso facto suspended. The two treaty categories that were automatically abrogated, according to McNair, were the so-called 'political treaties', such as 'treaties of mutual friendship, or alliance, disarmament, neutrality, [and] non-aggression', and, in principle, commercial treaties;[16] the category of treaties which would be suspended as a matter of principle were extradition treaties.[17] The other six treaty categories would remain in force despite the outbreak of hostilities, either because they were specifically intended to apply during international armed conflict, or because they were accepted as remaining applicable. These were: treaties on the laws of war, treaties declaring, creating, or regulating permanent rights or a permanent regime or status,[18] capitulations, multilateral treaties constituting

[12] *Institut de Droit International*, Session of Helsinki–1985, *The Effects of Armed Conflicts on Treaties* (Fifth Commission, Rapporteur: Mr Bent Broms), through: <http://www.idi-iil.org/>.

[13] A/CN.4/550, The effect of armed conflict on treaties: an examination of practice and doctrine; Memorandum by the Secretariat, 1 Feb 2005; International Law Commission, fifty-seventh session, Geneva, 2 May–3 Jun 2005 and 4 Jul–5 Aug 2005.

[14] A/CN.4/552, First Report on the Effects of Armed Conflicts on Treaties, by Mr Ian Brownlie, Special Rapporteur, of 21 Apr 2005; International Law Commission, fifty-seventh session, Geneva, 2 May–3 Jun and 4 Jul–5 Aug 2005. At: <http://www.un.org/law/ilc/sessions/57/57sess.htm>.

[15] McNair, *The Law of Treaties*, pp 697, 703.

[16] McNair, *The Law of Treaties*, pp 703, 718–19. Similarly as far as political treaties are concerned: Delbrück, *War, Effects on Treaties*, in: Bernhardt (Ed), *Encyclopaedia of Public International Law; Vol Four; Quirin, Ex Parte to Zones of Peace*, p 1371.

[17] McNair, *The Law of Treaties*, pp 716–18. Delbrück refers mainly to multilateral treaties which may be suspended in full or in part in case of armed conflict.

[18] International regimes are 'treaty-based settlements which are intended, by defining the status of a certain area, to form part of the international order' in order to 'stabilize controversial political situations (. . .) or to secure the common use of the area in question'. International regimes are usually based on a treaty between states or states and intergovernmental organisations; reflect a general interest; and 'endows the area with a general status *erga omnes*.' Examples of international regimes include the treaties laying down the permanent neutrality of Switzerland, the demilitarised status of Antarctica and the Aaland Islands, the use of international rivers, canals, straits, oceans and outer space. E Klein, *International Régimes*, in: R Bernhardt (Ed), *Encyclopedia of Public International Law; Vol Two; East African Community to Italy-United States Air Transport Arbitration (1965)*, North-Holland Publishing Company, Amsterdam, 1995, pp 1354–6.

an international regime, multilateral treaties creating international unions, and multilateral law-making treaties.[19]

In 1985, the *Institut de Droit International* adopted 11 articles in its Helsinki Resolution on 'The Effects of Armed Conflicts on Treaties',[20] considering that armed conflicts continued to erupt in violation of the prohibition to use force under international law and considering:

> that the practice of States with regard to the effects of armed conflicts on treaties to which they are parties is not uniform and that it is therefore appropriate to affirm certain principles of international law on this problem.[21]

As their point of departure, the *Institut* submitted in Article 2 that:

> [t]he outbreak of an armed conflict does not *ipso facto* terminate or suspend the operation of treaties in force between the parties to the armed conflict.

This is subsequently repeated in Article 5 with respect to the relationship between belligerents and non-belligerents, and with respect to multilateral treaties. Furthermore, those treaties are applicable during armed conflict which become operative in accordance with their own provisions and which must be regarded operative by reason of their nature (Article 3), 'treaty provision relating to the protection of the human person' (Article 4), and treaties establishing international organisations (Article 6).

Twenty years later, the Secretariat took a different approach in its 2005 study on The Effect of Armed conflict on Treaties, which was written after the ILC had added this topic to its long-term program in 2000 and had included it in its current program of work in 2004.[22] After an extensive analysis of international state practice and doctrine, it distinguished, similar to McNair, a number of treaty categories that were either susceptible or not susceptible to termination or suspension. These categories are then divided into four separate groups, namely: treaties with a very high likelihood of applicability, treaties with a moderately high likelihood of applicability, treaties with a varied or emerging likelihood of applicability, and treaties with a low likelihood of applicability. The first group included

[19] McNair, *The Law of Treaties*, pp 703–23. See also Delbrück who distinguishes 4 categories of treaties that are not affected by war, namely treaties on the laws of war; treaties creating an international régime or status; treaties on private international law and treaties regulating private interests, whose implementation is not incompatible with the existence of an armed conflict; and treaties between belligerents and non-belligerents. Delbrück, *War, Effects on Treaties*, in: Bernhardt (Ed), *Encyclopaedia of Public International Law; Vol Four; Quirin, Ex Parte to Zones of Peace*, p 1370.

[20] *Institut de Droit International*, Session of Helsinki–1985, *The Effects of Armed Conflicts on Treaties* (Fifth Commission, Rapporteur: Mr Bent Broms), through: <http://www.idi-iil.org/>.

[21] *Institut de Droit International*, Session of Helsinki–1985, *The Effects of Armed Conflicts on Treaties*, preambular paras 2 and 3.

[22] The latter decision was endorsed by the General Assembly on 2 Dec 2004. A/Res/59/41, adopted without a vote on 2 Dec 2004; Report of the International Law Commission on the work of its fifty-sixth session, operative para 5.

treaties on the laws of war, treaties with an express applicability clause, treaties regulating a permanent regime or status, treaties containing peremptory norms of international law, human rights treaties, intergovernmental debt treaties and diplomatic conventions. The second group included reciprocal inheritance treaties and multilateral law-making treaties. The third group included international transport agreements, environmental treaties, extradition treaties, border-crossing treaties, treaties of friendship, commerce and navigation,[23] intellectual property treaties, and penal transfer treaties. And the fourth group included treaties with express non-applicability provisions and treaties whose implementation are incompatible with armed conflict.[24] In addition, the Memorandum contains substantive discussions on a number of other topics, including effect of the size of the conflict, in light of the effect of World War II on treaties;[25] the effect of enforcement operations under chapter VII of the Charter;[26] and the effect of domestic hostilities on the applicability of treaties.[27]

Brownlie adopts an approach similar to the resolution of the *Institut de Droit International* in his 2005 report, in which he drafted 14 articles with commentaries for further discussion by the ILC. In Draft article 3, he follows the *Institut* by laying down the basic assumption that:

> [t]he outbreak of an armed conflict does not ipso facto terminate or suspend the operation of treaties as: (a) Between the parties to the armed conflict; (b) Between one or more parties to the armed conflict and a third State.[28]

And subsequently, according to Brownlie, the:

> indicia of susceptibility to termination or suspension or treaties in case of an armed conflict is determined in accordance with the intention of the parties at the time the treaty was concluded.[29]

[23] Compare, eg, the central role of the 1955 Treaty of Amity, Economic Relations and Consular Rights between the United States and Iran in the Case Concerning Oil Platforms (Islamic Republic of Iran v United States of America), Merits, Judgment, 6 Nov 2003, ICJICJ Reports 2003.

[24] A/CN.4/550, The effect of armed conflict on treaties: an examination of practice and doctrine; Memorandum by the Secretariat, pp 2, 14–48. An example of a treaty which is not applicable during armed conflict is the Chicago Convention on International Civil Aviation; an example of a treaty which is not compatible with armed conflict is a treaty of alliance.

[25] A/CN.4/550, The effect of armed conflict on treaties: an examination of practice and doctrine; Memorandum by the Secretariat, pp 48–51.

[26] A/CN.4/550, The effect of armed conflict on treaties: an examination of practice and doctrine; Memorandum by the Secretariat, pp 79–80.

[27] A/CN.4/550, The effect of armed conflict on treaties: an examination of practice and doctrine; Memorandum by the Secretariat, pp 80–2.

[28] A/CN.4/552, First Report on the Effects of Armed Conflicts on Treaties, by Mr Ian Brownlie, Special Rapporteur, Draft Art 3, p 10.

[29] A/CN.4/552, First Report on the Effects of Armed Conflicts on Treaties, by Mr Ian Brownlie, Special Rapporteur, Draft Art 4(1), p 11.

Although Brownlie admits that there are still many uncertainties, he believes that reliance on the intention of the contracting parties is justified by considerations of policy.[30] This way, the topic remains within the framework of the law of treaties; it 'conduces to the individualization of situations and avoid the imposition of "one fits all" solutions'; and it is 'effectively an application of the principle of *pacta sunt servanda*'.[31]

In addition, Draft article 7(1) provides that:

> [i]n the case of treaties the object and purpose of which involve the necessary implication that they continue in operation during an armed conflict, the incidence of an armed conflict will not as such inhibit their operation.

Brownlie then lists in paragraph 2 eleven categories of treaties that have this specific character, including treaties relating to the protection of the environment.[32] Brownlie admits that strictly spoken Draft article 7 is superfluous in view of Draft articles 3 and 4 and in view of the general applicability of the criterion of intention, but he found that the identification of categories of treaties not susceptible of termination during armed conflict was so common in literature that he had to follow suit. The categories listed in paragraph 2 are largely based on the examples given in literature and are included for the sake of discussion by the Commission.[33]

It appears from these studies, first of all, that there is general agreement on the basic assumption that armed conflict does not ipso facto terminate treaty relations between belligerents. And secondly, it appears that a number of treaty categories are singled out because they are presumed to remain applicable during armed conflict. These are, in addition to treaties that are explicitly intended to apply during armed conflict, treaties establishing intergovernmental organisations, treaties establishing permanent regimes, law-making treaties, diplomatic conventions, treaties containing peremptory norms of international law, and treaties protecting funda-

[30] A/CN.4/552, First Report on the Effects of Armed Conflicts on Treaties, by Mr Ian Brownlie, Special Rapporteur, Comment to Draft Art 4, pp 11–15.

[31] A/CN.4/552, First Report on the Effects of Armed Conflicts on Treaties, by Mr Ian Brownlie, Special Rapporteur, Comment to Draft Art 4, p 15.

[32] The other categories are: '(a) Treaties expressly applicable in case of an armed conflict; (b) Treaties declaring, creating, or regulating permanent rights or a permanent regime or status; (c) Treaties of friendship, commerce and navigation and analogous agreements concerning private rights; (d) Treaties for the protection of human rights; (. . .) (f) Treaties relating to international watercourses and related installations and facilities; (g) Multilateral law-making treaties; (h) Treaties relating to the settlement of disputes between States by peaceful means, including resort to conciliation, mediation, arbitration and the International Court of Justice; (i) Obligations arising under multilateral conventions relating to commercial arbitration and the enforcement of awards; (j) Treaties relating to diplomatic relations; (k) Treaties relating to consular relations.'

[33] A/CN.4/552, First Report on the Effects of Armed Conflicts on Treaties, by Mr Ian Brownlie, Special Rapporteur, Comment to Draft Art 7, pp 20–1.

mental human rights.[34] It seems therefore that, apart from the first category, the common denominator of the other categories is the common interest of the international community of states, either because these treaties have a constitutional character, or because their provisions are considered to be of fundamental importance.

Before discussing the relationship between international environmental law and *ius in bello,* it may be worthwhile to spend a few words on the relationship between international human rights law and *ius in bello,* or international humanitarian law.[35] This relationship may serve as a clarifying example and frame of reference. Not lastly, because the International Court of Justice dealt with this relationship in 1996, in 2004, and in 2005.[36]

2.2 The Relationship between Human Rights Law and *Ius in Bello*

The relationship between human rights law and *ius in bello,* or international humanitarian law, is not easy to assess, as both branches of law aim to protect the individual, but do so under different circumstances. Human rights law protects individuals primarily in times of peace, whereas international humanitarian law regulates the protection of individuals in times of armed conflict.[37] This seems to indicate that there is a horizontal and independent relationship between both fields of law, something that both Detter and Provost underline. Detter prefers 'to retain a horizontal distinction, rather than to introduce a new, hierarchical one' in the sense of a *lex generalis—lex specialis* relationship,[38] and Provost writes that both fields constitute 'two wholly independent systems'.[39]

Because of their independent status and different scope of application, however, overlap is almost inevitable. International humanitarian law becomes applicable according to common Article 2 of the 1949 Geneva Conventions, in:

[34] The continuing applicability of multilateral law-making treaties seems to be related to the fact that in principle the relationship between belligerents and non-belligerents is not affected by the outbreak of hostilities.

[35] As has been explained in Ch III, s 1.5, the terms *ius in bello,* laws of war, law of armed conflict, and international humanitarian law are nowadays used interchangeably.

[36] Legality of the Threat or Use of Nuclear Weapons, Advisory Opinion, 8 Jul 1996, ICJ Reports 1996, para 25, p 240; and to a lesser extent Legal Consequences of the Construction of a Wall in the Occupied Palestinian Territory, Advisory Opinion, 9 Jul 2004, ICJ Reports 2004, pp 41–2; Case Concerning Armed Activities on the Territory of the Congo (Democratic Republic of the Congo v Uganda), Merits, Judgment, 19 Dec 2005, ICJ Reports 2005, para 216, pp 69–70.

[37] Dinstein also refers to the fact that the beneficiaries of most human rights regulations are human beings, whereas those of the law of international armed conflict are most often states. Dinstein, *The Conduct of Hostilities under the Law of International Armed Conflict,* Cambridge University Press, Cambridge, 2004, pp 20–2.

[38] Detter, *The Law of War,* Cambridge University Press, Cambridge, 2000, p 161.

[39] R Provost, *International Human Rights and Humanitarian Law,* Cambridge University Press, Cambridge, 2002, p 274.

> all cases of declared war or of any other armed conflict which may arise between two or more of the High Contracting Parties, even if the state of war is not recognized by one of them[,]

and:

> in all cases of partial or total occupation of the territory of a High Contracting Party, even if the said occupation meets with no armed resistance.[40]

Before 1949, international conventions on the laws of war were silent on the conditions necessary for their applicability, but they were generally believed to become only applicable in times of war.[41] This meant, since 1907, either a formal declaration of war,[42] or recognition of a state of war by both sides, and was therefore susceptible to abuse.[43] In order to remedy this, common Article 2 relies primarily on factual circumstances for the applicability of the Geneva Conventions, both with respect to the existence of an 'armed conflict' and with respect to the occupation of territory.[44]

[40] Compare also Art 1(3) and 1(4) of 1977 Additional Protocol I and Art 1(1) Additional Protocol II.

[41] JS Pictet (Ed), *The Geneva Conventions of 12 Aug 1949; Commentary; Vol I—Geneva Convention for the Amelioration of the Condition of the Wounded and Sick in Armed Forces in the Field*, ICRC, Geneva, 1952, p 28.

[42] Art 1 of Hague Convention (III) Relative to the Opening of Hostilities, signed on 18 Oct 1907, entered into force on 26 Jan 1910, AJIL, Vol 2, No 1/2, Supplement: Official Documents, 1908, p 85, states: 'The Contracting Powers recognize that hostilities between themselves must not commence without previous and explicit warning, in the form either of a declaration of war, giving reasons, or of an ultimatum with conditional declaration of war.' The convention was adopted after the 1904–1905 war between Japan and Russia had commenced without a formal declaration of war. Schindler, Toman (Eds), *The Laws of Armed Conflicts; A Collection of Conventions, Resolutions and Other Documents*, Martinus Nijhoff Publishers, Dordrecht, 1988, p 57. According to Dinstein, Hague Convention III cannot be considered to reflect customary international law. Before 1907, most wars started without a declaration of war. Y Dinstein, *War, Aggression and Self-Defence*, Cambridge University Press, Cambridge, 2005, p 32. Also: Detter, *The Law of War*, pp 10–11.

[43] Pictet (Ed), *The Geneva Conventions of 12 Aug 1949; Commentary; Vol I—Geneva Convention for the Amelioration of the Condition of the Wounded and Sick in Armed Forces in the Field*, p 28. Greenwood writes that recognition of a state of war by one state was sufficient for the creation of a state of war, but Pictet notes that non-recognition of a state of war by one side, for whatever reason, could lead to contesting of the applicability of the laws of war in general. Greenwood, *Scope of Application of Humanitarian Law*, in: Fleck (Ed), *The Handbook of Humanitarian Law in Armed Conflicts*, Oxford University Press, Oxford, 1995, p 39. See also Detter on the intention of belligerents and the subjective 'state of war' doctrine. Detter, *The Law of War*, pp 11–12.

[44] The phrase 'even if the state of war is not recognized by one of them' is considered to be a drafting error by Detter and Greenwood, because it would open the possibility of non-recognition in case both parties do not recognise the state of war. It should read 'even if the state of war is not recognized by both or either of them'. Detter, *The Law of War*, p 14; Greenwood, *Scope of Application of Humanitarian Law*, in: Fleck (Ed), *The Handbook of Humanitarian Law in Armed Conflicts*, p 41. In any case, non-recognition by both parties would be covered by the factual criterion of the existence of an 'armed conflict'.

The legal use of the term 'war' has nowadays become rare,[45] and has almost completely been superseded by the term 'armed conflict'.[46] The meaning of the term remains ambiguous, however. Where '[o]ne may argue almost endlessly about the legal definition of "war" ',[47] the concept of 'armed conflict' was deliberately left undefined in order to keep the term purely factual and prevent legal disputes on the interpretation of a definition.[48] According to the International Committee of the Red Cross (ICRC) Commentary, 'armed conflict' is believed to start with the simple 'opening of hostilities' and to include '[a]ny difference (. . .) leading to the intervention of armed forces'.[49] Although this seems straightforward, opinion is divided on the required intensity-level of violence necessary to trigger the applicability of the conventions. The Commentary of the ICRC on the Geneva Conventions says that it does not matter how long a conflict lasts or how many casualties occur;[50] and Greenwood recalls an incident in the 1980s in which a United States fighter was shot down over Syria, after which the United States claimed that this amounted to an armed conflict and that therefore the pilot was entitled to prisoner-of-war status.[51]

This interpretation was accepted by the Appeals Chamber of the International Criminal Tribunal for the Former Yugoslavia in one of the Tadic Decisions. It said:

[45] Dinstein, *War, Aggression and Self-Defence*, pp 31–3; Greenwood, *Scope of Application of Humanitarian Law*, in: Fleck (Ed), *The Handbook of Humanitarian Law in Armed Conflicts*, pp 39, 41, 43–4. Dinstein mentions some of the reasons for states to refrain from a declaration of war. These are both pragmatic and psychological. Pragmatic, because a declaration of war would automatically activate the laws of neutrality both internationally and domestically. Psychological, because of the criminalisation of wars of aggression.

[46] Dinstein calls this 'war in a material sense' as opposed to war in a 'technical sense'. The reason for this distinction lies in his use of Oppenheim's comprehensive concept of 'war' as a starting-point for his own definition of 'war' and for further discussion. Dinstein, *War, Aggression and Self-Defence*, pp 3–34. Also Detter on the possible differences in meaning between the terms 'war' and 'armed conflict'. Detter, *The Law of War*, pp 17–20.

[47] Pictet (Ed), *The Geneva Conventions of 12 Aug 1949; Commentary; Vol I—Geneva Convention for the Amelioration of the Condition of the Wounded and Sick in Armed Forces in the Field*, p 32.

[48] C Greenwood, *Scope of Application of Humanitarian Law*, in: D Fleck (Ed), *The Handbook of Humanitarian Law in Armed Conflicts*, Oxford University Press, Oxford, 1995, p 42.

[49] Pictet (Ed), *The Geneva Conventions of 12 Aug 1949; Commentary; Vol I—Geneva Convention for the Amelioration of the Condition of the Wounded and Sick in Armed Forces in the Field*, p 32.

[50] 'The respect due to human personality is not measured by the number of victims.' Pictet (Ed), *The Geneva Conventions of 12 Aug 1949; Commentary; Vol I—Geneva Convention*, p 32. Compare also the ICRC's Commentary to Additional Protocol I which provides that '[n]either the duration of the conflict, nor its intensity, play a role: the law must be applied to the fullest extent required by the situation of the persons and the objects protected by it.' Y Sandoz, C Swinaraski, B Zimmerman (Eds), *Commentary on the Additional Protocols; of 8 Jun 1977 to the Geneva Conventions of 12 Aug 1949*, ICRC, Martinus Nijhoff Publishers, Geneva, 1987, p 40. The Commentary is also available through <http://www.icrc.org/>.

[51] Greenwood, *Scope of Application of Humanitarian Law*, in: Fleck (Ed), *The Handbook of Humanitarian Law in Armed Conflicts*, p 40.

> [W]e find that an armed conflict exists whenever there is a resort to armed force between States (. . .). International humanitarian law applies from the initiation of such armed conflicts and extends beyond the cessation of hostilities until a general conclusion of peace is reached; or, in the case of internal conflicts, a peaceful settlement is achieved. Until that moment, international humanitarian law continues to apply in the whole territory under the control of a party, whether or not actual combat takes place there.[52]

Apparently, any resort to armed force between states constitutes an international armed conflict.[53]

Human rights law, on the other hand, does not depend on factual circumstances such as the existence of peace or the absence of an armed conflict for its applicability. When human rights law has entered into force, it remains in force indefinitely, even in times of international armed conflict. Generally speaking, that is, because its formal scope of application may be geographically limited,[54] and under certain exceptional circumstances, human rights law may be derogated from when the supreme interests of a state must prevail over the interests of individuals.

Article 4(1) of the International Covenant on Civil and Political Rights (hereinafter ICCPR or the Covenant),[55] for example, allows States Parties to derogate from some of their obligations under the Convention in times of public emergency that threaten the life of the nation. It is generally agreed that public emergencies may include armed conflict,[56] which means that when a state is involved in an armed conflict of whatever nature, it may derogate from obligations under the Covenant.

[52] International Criminal Tribunal for the Former Yugoslavia; Prosecutor v Dusko Tadic a/k/a 'Dule' (IT-94-1); Decision on the Defence Motion for Interlocutory Appeal on Jurisdiction, 2 Oct 1995, para 70, p 37, International Legal Materials, Vol 35, 1996, p 54, or at <http://www.un.org/icty/tadic/appeal/decision-e/51002.htm>. A non-international armed conflict, however, requires 'protracted armed violence between governmental authorities and organized armed groups or between such groups within a State', according to the Tribunal.

[53] Mostly, however, states have been reluctant to regard incidents with a limited level of violence as armed conflicts. Greenwood, *Scope of Application of Humanitarian Law,* in: Fleck (Ed), *The Handbook of Humanitarian Law in Armed Conflicts,* p 42.

[54] The applicability of the European Convention for Protection of Human Rights and Fundamental Freedoms, for example, is limited in Art 1 to the 'jurisdiction' of the Contracting Parties; the applicability of the International Covenant on Civil and Political Rights is limited in Art 2 to the 'territory' and the 'jurisdiction' of the States Parties ('Each State Party to the present Covenant undertakes to respect and to ensure to all individuals within its territory and subject to its jurisdiction the rights recognized in the present Covenant (. . .).' Under customary international law, however, the scope of protection of human rights may not be geographically limited.

[55] International Covenant on Civil and Political Rights, opened for signature on 19 Dec 1966, entered into force on 23 Mar 1976, UNTS, Vol 999, No 14668. The Convention was prepared by the Commission on Human Rights together with the International Covenant on Economic, Social and Cultural Rights, and an Optional Protocol to the International Covenant on Civil and Political Rights, transmitted to the General Assembly by the Economic and Social Council by Resolution 545 B (XVIII) of 29 Jul 1954, and adopted by the Assembly by Resolution 2200A (XXI), adopted unanimously on 16 Dec 1966.

[56] Dinstein, *The Conduct of Hostilities under the Law of International Armed Conflict,* pp 22–3.

However, a second criterion needs to be fulfilled before derogation is actually allowed. In addition to the existence of a public emergency, derogation of obligations by States Parties under the Covenant is dependent on the severity of the situation. Article 4(1) states that derogation is only permitted in time of a public emergency which threatens the life of the nation, but only 'to the extent strictly required by the exigencies of the situation.' This criterion raises a threshold and requires a proportionality test. If derogation is not necessary in view of the circumstances, the rights and duties under the Covenant remain in force, even in times of a public emergency arising from an international armed conflict.

In any case, and irrespective of the existence of a public emergency which threatens the life of the nation, derogation is excluded under Article 4(2) with respect to a number of specific human rights, including the right to life, and the prohibitions of torture and slavery. Therefore, these provisions remain in force for States Parties under all circumstances, including times of international armed conflict.

Because the applicability of both branches of law are triggered by different criteria, three different kinds of situations are therefore imaginable: inapplicability of either system, exclusive applicability of either system, and concurrent applicability of both systems.[57] Inapplicability of either system arises when, on the one hand, a particular situation does not warrant applicability of international humanitarian law because there is no armed conflict, and, on the other hand, human rights law is not applicable because that particular situation is nevertheless so serious that derogation from derogable human rights prescriptions is justified and proportional.

Exclusive applicability of either system is possible, under two sets of circumstances. Firstly, human rights law is exclusively applicable, when there is no armed conflict on the one hand, and there is no possibility to derogate from human rights provisions on the other hand. Secondly, and conversely, international humanitarian law is exclusively applicable, when there is an armed conflict on the one hand, and circumstances that justify proportional derogation from derogable human rights provisions, on the other hand.

Concurrent applicability of both human rights law and international humanitarian law requires an armed conflict on the one hand, and on the other hand either the absence of circumstances that would justify derogation of derogable human rights law. This third possibility, is most interesting, since it raises the question of the exact relationship between both branches. An answer was provided by the International Court of Justice in

[57] The International Court of Justice only distinguished between exclusive applicability of either human rights or international humanitarian law and concurrent application of both branches of international law. Legal Consequences of the Construction of a Wall in the Occupied Palestinian Territory, Advisory Opinion, 9 Jul 2004, ICJ Reports 2004, para 106, pp 41–2.

its 1996 Nuclear Weapons Opinion (GA) in relation to the right to life as laid down in Article 6 of the Covenant, which provides that '[e]very human being has the inherent right to life' and that '[n]o one shall be arbitrarily deprived of his life'. Article 6 is non-derogable, according to Article 4(2), which ipso facto implies concurrent application of human rights law and international humanitarian law in times of armed conflict in this particular case. As to the question how both Article 6 and international humanitarian law interact, the Court concludes:

> The test of what is an arbitrary deprivation of life (. . .) then falls to be determined by the applicable *lex specialis*, namely, the law applicable in armed conflict which is designed to regulate the conduct of hostilities. Thus whether a particular loss of life, through the use of a certain weapon in warfare, is to be considered an arbitrary deprivation of life contrary to Article 6 of the Covenant, can only be decided by reference to the law applicable in armed conflict and not deduced from the terms of the Covenant itself.[58]

This seems to indicate that as soon as a human rights provision and a rule of international humanitarian law are applicable at the same time, the latter takes precedence over the former based on the general principle of law or maxim *lex specialis derogat legi generali*,[59] although not based on a pure conflict of rules.[60] In this case, precedence would mean that the human rights provision must be interpreted in light of international humanitarian law.

Unfortunately, the International Court of Justice did not further elaborate upon this relationship in its 2004 Wall Opinion and in the 2005 case between the Democratic Republic of Congo and Uganda. Although the Court confirmed in both cases the *lex specialis–lex generalis* relationship between international humanitarian and human rights law,[61] it merely identified and interpreted the applicable rules without discussing their mutual relationship.[62]

[58] Legality of the Threat or Use of Nuclear Weapons, Advisory Opinion, 8 Jul 1996, ICJ Reports 1996, para 25, p 240.

[59] Although the maxim *lex specialis derogat legi generali* is one of the general rules of conflict and stems from classic Roman law, it cannot be found in this specific form. The Roman lawyer Papinianus however, described the rule as follows: '*In toto iure generi per speciem derogatur*' (D. 50,17,80) and it is found in similar words in canon law in Liber Sextus 5,13,34. Generally on the *lex specialis* principle, see: M Koskenniemi, *Fragmentation of International Law*, Outline for Study Group, International Law Commission, 55th session, 2003. At: <http://www.un.org/law/ilc/sessions/55/55sess.htm>. Koskenniemi refers in this context to an early application of the principle by Grotius in his *De Iure Belli ac Pacis*.

[60] Compare Koskenniemi, *Fragmentation of International Law*, p 4.

[61] Legal Consequences of the Construction of a Wall in the Occupied Palestinian Territory, Advisory Opinion, 9 Jul 2004, ICJ Reports 2004, paras 105–6, pp 41–2; Case Concerning Armed Activities on the Territory of the Congo (Democratic Republic of the Congo v Uganda), Merits, Judgment, 19 Dec 2005, ICJ Reports 2005, para 216, pp 69–70.

[62] Legal Consequences of the Construction of a Wall in the Occupied Palestinian Territory, Advisory Opinion, 9 Jul 2004, ICJ Reports 2004, paras 123–37, pp 47–55; Case Concerning Armed Activities on the Territory of the Congo (Democratic Republic of the Congo v Uganda), Merits, Judgment, 19 Dec 2005, ICJ Reports 2005, paras 219–21, p 71.

Finally, the continued application of human rights law during armed conflict could have an intriguing and interesting consequence. Since the Court established that non-derogable human rights remain applicable during armed conflict but must be interpreted in light of international humanitarian law, national courts or international human rights courts could be involved in the interpretation of international humanitarian law through their application of international human rights law. It is rather difficult to find redress for violations of the laws of war in general,[63] and this way, national and international courts can be involved as an additional and relatively powerful enforcement mechanism for international humanitarian law.

2.3 The Relationship between International Environmental Law and *Ius in Bello*

2.3.1 *Introduction*

With respect to the relationship between peacetime International Environmental Law and *ius in bello*, it is important to distinguish between the impact of International Environmental Law in the relationship between belligerents and between belligerents and non-belligerents. The former will be dealt with in section 2.3.2; the latter will be dealt with in section 2.3.3.

2.3.2 *Belligerent vs Belligerent*

Contrary to international human rights law, rules of international environmental law are not generally considered to remain applicable among belligerents during international armed conflict. As a matter of fact, neither McNair, nor the *Institut de Droit International* mention international environmental law in their studies on the effects of war or international armed conflict on treaties,[64] and the recent studies by the UN Secretariat and Brownlie only make tentative references to the possibility of their continued applicability. The Memorandum of the Secretariat categorises treaties on international environmental law as treaties of the third category with a 'varied or emerging likelihood of applicability'. And Brownlie lists international environmental treaties in his Draft article 7(2) as one of

[63] Compare Quénivet and her discussion of the decision of 10 Dec 2003 of a German civil court sitting in Bonn. N Quénivet, *The right to claim compensation for violations of international humanitarian law: The German judgment on the Varvarin bridge*, Bofaxe No 267E, 27 Dec 2003. Through: <http://www.ruhr-uni-bochum.de/ifhv/publications/bofaxe/>.

[64] Their silence is not surprising in view of the relatively young history of international environmental law.

the eleven treaty categories whose object and purpose presume application during armed conflict.

Both however admit that their applicability is not yet generally accepted. The Secretariat concludes that although the topic has received significant attention in literature[65] and an increasing number of commentators have argued that peacetime environmental treaties remain applicable during international armed conflict, states are still divided.[66] And Brownlie explained that he had added environmental treaties to Draft article 7(2) because he believed that 'the Commission should be asked to examine the candidature of this category of treaties.' Nevertheless, Brownlie did find some evidence in the Nuclear Weapons Opinion (GA) for the 'presumption that environmental treaties apply in case of armed conflict'.[67]

This current lack of agreement also appears from statements made by states in the Sixth Committee of the General Assembly in 1991 and 1992 and before the International Court of Justice within the framework of the two Advisory Opinions on the legality of the use of nuclear weapons (WHO and GA). In the Sixth Committee, only Iran and the Netherlands, the latter speaking on behalf of the European Community, referred to the relationship between international environmental law and the laws of war, and both expressed doubts as to its applicability during international armed conflict. Iran stated that:

> [t]here was no universally accepted rule concerning the application of international law on the protection of the environment to belligerent parties,[68]

but thought it would be a good idea if the United Nations:

> elaborated a provision to the effect that the norms governing the protection of the environment were neither suspended nor terminated in time of war.[69]

And the Netherlands submitted that:

> [i]t would also be necessary to examine the relationship between international environmental law and humanitarian law, which seemed to be developing

[65] According to the Memorandum of the Secretariat, '[r]ecent scholarly consideration of the applicability of peacetime environmental treaties during armed conflict has spawned the most significant discussion of the effect of armed conflict on treaties since the Second World War. (. . .) Whatever the cause, the effect of armed conflict on international environmental law has received more modern attention than the effect of armed conflict on any other kind of treaty, and marks the most significant development in the topic since the 1985 study by the Institut de droit international.' A/CN.4/550, The effect of armed conflict on treaties: an examination of practice and doctrine; Memorandum by the Secretariat, p 35.

[66] A/CN.4/550, The effect of armed conflict on treaties: an examination of practice and doctrine; Memorandum by the Secretariat, pp 35–40.

[67] A/CN.4/552, First Report on the Effects of Armed Conflicts on Treaties, by Mr Ian Brownlie, Special Rapporteur, pp 29–30.

[68] A/C.6/46/SR.18, Summary Record of the 18th meeting of the Sixth Committee of the General Assembly on 22 Oct 1991, p 7, para 31.

[69] A/C.6/46/SR.18, Summary Record of the 18th meeting of the Sixth Committee of the General Assembly on 22 Oct 1991, p 8, para 33.

along rather independent lines, even though the development of environmental law had consequences for the interpretation of rules concerning the protection of the civilian population.[70]

Also before the International Court of Justice, opinions were divided on this particular question. Although quite a few states made references to international environmental law, the importance of the protection of the environment, and the damage that nuclear explosions would inflict on the environment,[71] only few states argued that peacetime norms of international environmental law indirectly applied during international armed conflict by reference to the so-called principle of 'environmental security' or 'environmental safety',[72] and only one state—the Solomon Islands—claimed that international environmental law continued to bind belligerents during international armed conflict. France,[73] the United Kingdom,[74] and the United States,[75] on the other hand, adamantly denied this, referring to the intention of the contracting parties and the scope and nature of the environmental agreements and customary rules involved.

Therefore, it does not seem likely that peacetime rules of international law must be presumed to remain applicable during international armed conflict as such. This conclusion may also be drawn from the Nuclear Weapons Opinion (GA), where the Court states that:

> the issue is not whether the treaties relating to the protection of the environment are or are not applicable during an armed conflict, but rather whether the obligations stemming from these treaties were intended to be obligations of total restraint during military conflict. The Court does not consider that the treaties in question could have intended to deprive a State of the exercise of its right of self-defence under international law because of its obligations to protect the environment.[76]

[70] A/C.6/46/SR.20, Summary Record of the 20th meeting of the Sixth Committee of the General Assembly on 24 Oct 1991, p 2, para 3.

[71] These were Australia, Egypt, India, Iran, Marshall Islands, Mexico, Moldova, Nauru, The Netherlands, North Korea, The Philippines, Samoa, The Solomon Islands, Sri Lanka, Qatar, Ukraine, and Zimbabwe.

[72] These were India, Iran, Malaysia, and Nauru.

[73] CR 95/24, Oral Plea of the Governments of the Republic of France, of 2 Nov 1995, on the Legality of the Use by a State of Nuclear Weapons in Armed Conflict and on the Legality of the Threat or Use of Nuclear Weapons, pp 21–2. Through: <http://www.icj-cij.org/>.

[74] Written Comments of the Government of the United Kingdom on other Written Statements of 16 Jun 1995 (WHO), pp 68–71, paras 3.109–3.116; Written Statement of the Government of the United Kingdom of 16 Jun 1995 (GA), pp 68–71, paras 3.109–3.116; CR 95/34, Oral Plea of the Governments of the United Kingdom, of 15 Nov 1995 (WHO and GA), pp 42–3. Through: <http://www.icj-cij.org/>.

[75] Written Comments of the Government of the United States of America of 20 Jun 1995 (WHO), pp 10–19; Written Statement of the Government of the United States of America of 20 Jun 1995 (GA), pp 34–42; CR 95/34, Oral Plea of the Government of the United States of America, of 15 Nov 1995 (WHO and GA), pp 64–6. Through: <http://www.icj-cij.org/>.

[76] Legality of the Threat or Use of Nuclear Weapons, Advisory Opinion, 8 Jul 1996, ICJ Reports 1996, p 226, at p 242, para 30.

Apparently, the Court did not want to accept full-fledged applicability of international environmental law similar to the applicability of international human rights law.[77]

Although international environmental law is thus not likely to remain applicable as such, individual treaties or rules of international environmental law may very well remain applicable because they are either embodied in one of the categories that are presumed to remain applicable during international armed conflict, or because they are analogous to these treaty categories. In addition to treaties that explicitly provide for their applicability during international armed conflict, these are most likely treaties establishing intergovernmental organisations, treaties establishing permanent regimes, law-making treaties, diplomatic conventions, treaties containing peremptory norms of international law, and treaties protecting fundamental human rights. Of these categories, the last two have sometimes been referred to as involving substantive environmental rights and obligations, which would then ipso facto remain applicable during international armed conflict.

Firstly, it has been argued that international human rights law includes a right to a healthy environment. This would appear, for example, from Article 12 of the 1966 International Covenant on Economic, Social and Cultural Rights,[78] from the 1972 Stockholm Declaration and the 1992 Rio Declaration, and has also been included in a number of other international treaties and agreements.[79] Article 12 of the Covenant provides:

> The State Parties to the present Covenant recognize the right of everyone to the enjoyment of the highest attainable standard of physical and mental health.

To achieve 'the full realization of this right', States Parties must take measures including those necessary for '[t]he improvement of all aspects of environmental and industrial hygiene.' Principle 1 of the Stockholm Declaration states:

[77] This non-applicability of principles of environmental law may also be deduced from the Court's 2005 Judgment in the case between the Democratic Republic of Congo and Uganda. In this case, the Court found 'that it cannot uphold the contention of the DRC that Uganda violated the principle of the DRC's sovereignty over its natural resources'. Although the Court recognised the importance and the customary nature of the principle, it stated that the General Assembly Resolutions in which it was expressed did not suggest it was applicable 'to the specific situation of looting, pillage and exploitation of certain natural resources by members of the army of a State military intervening in another State'. Case Concerning Armed Activities on the Territory of the Congo (Democratic Republic of the Congo v Uganda), Merits, Judgment, 19 Dec 2005, ICJ Reports 2005, para 244, p 77.

[78] International Covenant on Economic, Social and Cultural Rights, opened for signature on 19 Dec 1966, entered into force on 3 Jan 1966, UNTS, Vol 993, No 14531.

[79] Birnie, Boyle, *International Law & The Environment*, Oxford University Press, Oxford, 2002, p 252; Shaw, *International Law*, Cambridge University Press, Cambridge, 2003, pp 756–8; S Vöneky, *A New Shield for the Environment: Peacetime Treaties as Legal Restraints of Wartime Damage*, Review of European Community and international environmental law, Vol 9, 2000, p 23, fn 39.

Man has the fundamental right to freedom, equality and adequate conditions of life, in an environment of a quality that permits a life of dignity and well-being, and he bears a solemn responsibility to protect and improve the environment for present and future generations.

And Principle 1 of the Rio Declaration stipulates:

Human beings are at the centre of concerns for sustainable development. They are entitled to a healthy and productive life in harmony with nature.

Although the above provisions use the terms 'right' and 'entitlement', it is doubtful whether they can be regarded as a full-fledged right, let alone a fundamental human right. Article 12 recognizes the right of individuals to enjoy the 'highest attainable standard of mental and physical health' for the realisation of which states need to take measures to improve environmental hygiene. The Stockholm Declaration merely refers to a number of fundamental rights to be enjoyed 'in an environment of a quality that permits a life of dignity and well-being', and stipulates that man has the responsibility to protect the environment for future generations. And the Rio Declaration only refers to an entitlement rather than a right to a healthy life in harmony with nature, which is not only less strong,[80] but refers also only indirectly to the environment. Like most of the so-called 'second generation' human rights, ie economic, social and cultural rights, most norms are hortatory by nature and encourage states to provide favorable conditions for their inhabitants 'to develop equal to their full potential.'[81] Nevertheless, there is certainly a relationship between international human rights law and international environmental law, and there are certainly indications that the human and natural environment are being incorporated into human rights law,[82] but it is probably too early and too

[80] For the distinction between full-fledged subjective rights and other conditional rights and entitlements, see: WD Verwey, *The Preferential Status of Developing Countries in International Trade Law after the Uruguay Round,* in: E Denters, N Schrijver (Eds), *Reflections on International Law from the Low Countries; in Honour of Paul de Waart,* Martinus Nijhoff Publishers, The Hague, 1998, pp 48–67.

[81] Birnie, Boyle, *International Law & The Environment*, p 253.

[82] Birnie, Boyle, *International Law & The Environment*, pp 252–97; Kiss, Shelton, *International Environmental Law*, pp 661–717; P Sands, *Principles of international environmental law; Vol I; Frameworks, standards and implementation,* Cambridge University Press, Cambridge, 2003, pp 291–307. Shaw refers to the final report on Human Rights and the Environment, delivered in 1994 to the UN Sub-Commission on Prevention of Discrimination and Protection of Minorities which included a set of draft principles on the subject. And the *Institut de Droit International* adopted at its 1997 meeting in Strasbourg a resolution on the Environment, Art 2 of which read: 'Every human being has the right to live in a healthy environment.' *Institut de Droit International,* Session of Strasbourg–1997, *Environment* (Eighth Commission, Rapporteur: Mr Luigi Ferrari Bravo), through: <http://www.idi-iil.org/>. Shaw, *International Law,* pp 757–8. Vöneky refers to Kälin who wrote as Special Rapporteur to the Commission on Human Rights that 'the deliberate causing of large-scale environmental damage which severely affects the health of a considerable proportion of the population concerned, or creates risks for the health of future generations, amounts to a serious violation of the right to the enjoyment of the highest attainable standard of health as embodied in art. 12 of the

far-fetched to consider that rules of international environmental law remain applicable during international armed conflict, because of their connection with international human rights law.

Secondly, it has been argued that the conventional and customary prohibition to cause massive pollution to the environment constitutes a peremptory norm of general international law, or *ius cogens*. Evidence for this contention was found in Article 19 of the 1976 Draft Articles on State Responsibility,[83] in which the ILC introduced the concept of 'international crimes' upon recommendation of Special Rapporteur Ago.[84] In view of its object and purpose, the concept of international crimes was related to the concepts of *ius cogens* and obligations *erga omnes*,[85] and was defined by the Commission as:

> [a]n internationally wrongful act which results from the breach by a State of an international obligation so essential for the protection of fundamental interests of the international community that its breach is recognized as a crime by that community as a whole.[86]

According to the ILC, international crimes included breaches or violations of the prohibition of aggression, the right of self-determination, fundamental human rights, as well as:

> a serious breach of an international obligation of essential importance for the safeguarding and preservation of the human environment, such as those prohibiting massive pollution of the atmosphere or of the seas.[87]

This latter category was included by the Commission at a time when international environmental law was only in a developmental phase. After all, the United Nations Conference on the Human Environment in Stockholm had only taken place four years earlier. Still, in view of the

International Covenant on Economic, Social and Cultural Rights.' Vöneky, *A New Shield for the Environment: Peacetime Treaties as Legal Restraints of Wartime Damage*, p 24.

[83] A/31/10, Report of the International Law Commission on the work of its twenty-eighth session, 3 May–23 Jul 1976; Yearbook of the International Law Commission, 1976; Vol II, Pt Two; Report of the Commission to the General Assembly on the work of its twenty-eighth session, United Nations, New York, 1977.

[84] A/CN.4/291, Fifth report on State responsibility, by Mr Roberto Ago, Special Rapporteur; The internationally wrongful act of the State, source of international responsibility (continued); Yearbook of the International Law Commission, 1976; Vol II, Pt One; Documents of the twenty-eighth session (excluding the report of the Commission to the General Assembly), United Nations, New York, 1977.

[85] Art 53 Vienna Convention on the Law of Treaties; Case Concerning the Barcelona Traction, Light and Power Company, Limited (Belgium v Spain), Judgment of 5 Feb 1970, ICJ Reports, 1970, paras 33 and 34, pp 32–3,. See also AJJ de Hoogh, *Obligations Erga Omnes and International Crimes; A Theoretical Inquiry into the Implementation and Enforcement of the International Responsibility of States*, Kluwer Law International, The Hague, 1996, pp 44–70.

[86] Draft Art 19(2) of the 1976 Draft Articles on State Responsibility.

[87] Draft Art 19(3)(a)–(d) of the 1976 Draft Articles on State Responsibility.

results of the 1972 Conference and in view of the negotiation of a convention on the prohibition of environmental modification techniques for military purposes, the ILC believed that it seemed undeniable that:

> the existing rules of general international law on the subject and those which will of necessity be added to them in the future [were] bound to be regarded to a great extent as 'peremptory' rules by the international community as a whole.

Furthermore:

> [i]t seemed equally undeniable that the obligations flowing from these rules are intended to safeguard interests so vital to the international community that a serious breach of these obligations cannot fail to be seen by all members of the community as an internationally wrongful act of a particularly serious character, as an 'international crime'.[88]

Apparently, the members of the ILC were not of the opinion that obligations for the safeguarding of the environment and the prohibition of massive pollution of the atmosphere and the oceans already constituted peremptory norms of international law. They were only 'bound to be regarded' as such and their incorporation into Draft Article 19 must be valued in light of the spirit of the time. The Commission's prediction never materialised, however, and in 2001, it decided to drop Article 19 and the concept of 'international crimes' from its final draft, because of strong controversy among its members.[89] Thus, peremptory norms of international environmental law do not yet appear to have come into existence,[90] which means that also on this basis the continued applicability of international law during international armed conflict cannot be presumed.[91]

In addition, it has also been argued that peacetime international environmental treaties remain applicable because they are sufficiently similar to the above-mentioned treaty categories that are commonly held applicable

[88] A/31/10, Report of the International Law Commission on the work of its twenty-eighth session, 3 May–23 Jul 1976; Yearbook of the International Law Commission, 1976; Vol II, Pt Two; Report of the Commission to the General Assembly on the work of its twenty-eighth session, Commentary to Art 19, p 109.

[89] Crawford, *The International Law Commission's Articles on State Responsibility; Introduction, Text and Commentaries*, Cambridge University Press, Cambridge, 2002, pp 35–8.

[90] See the commentaries of the ILC to Arts 26 (para 5) and 50 (paras 3–6) of the 2001 Draft Articles on State Responsibility. A/56/10, Draft Articles on Responsibility of States for Internationally Wrongful Acts, including Commentaries, adopted by the International Law Commission at its fifty-third session, Nov 2001; Yearbook of the International Law Commission, 2001; Vol II, Pt Two, forthcoming, pp 208, 283–4. Through <http://www.un.org/law/ilc/>. Also J Crawford, *The International Law Commission's Articles on State Responsibility; Introduction, Text and Commentaries*, pp 188, 245–7.

[91] Compare, however, Vöneky who believes with a number of other writers that 'today there seem to be good reasons to hold the view that at least the prohibition of massive pollution of the environment is a peremptory norm of international law and an obligation with effect *erga omnes*.' Vöneky, *A New Shield for the Environment: Peacetime Treaties as Legal Restraints of Wartime Damage*, p 24; S Vöneky, *Peacetime Environmental Law As a Basis of State Responsibility for Environmental Damage Caused by War*, in: JE Austin, CE Bruch (Eds), *The Environmental Consequences of War*, Cambridge University Press, Cambridge, 2000, p 203.

during international armed conflict. Vöneky argues that a number of environmental treaties remain applicable because they have similarities with treaties establishing objective regimes,[92] or because they protect common goods in the interest of the state community as a whole, similar to human rights treaties.[93] Under the former group, Vöneky lists Part XI and XII of the 1982 United Nations Convention on the Law of the Seas,[94] dealing with the seabed and ocean floor outside national jurisdiction and the protection of the marine environment, as well as the 1959 Antarctica Treaty[95] and a number of other conventions related to Antarctica.[96] Under the latter group, Vöneky lists a number of universal treaties, including the 1992 United Nations Framework Convention on Climate Change,[97] the 1992 Convention on Biological Diversity,[98] the 1985 Vienna Convention for the Protection of the Ozone Layer,[99] and the World Heritage Convention,[100] as well as a

[92] Vöneky, *A New Shield for the Environment: Peacetime Treaties as Legal Restraints of Wartime Damage*, pp 25–7; Vöneky, *Peacetime Environmental Law As a Basis of State Responsibility for Environmental Damage Caused by War*, in: Austin, Bruch (Eds), *The Environmental Consequences of War*, pp 204–10.

[93] Vöneky, *A New Shield for the Environment: Peacetime Treaties as Legal Restraints of Wartime Damage*, pp 27–30; Vöneky, *Peacetime Environmental Law As a Basis of State Responsibility for Environmental Damage Caused by War*, in: Austin, Bruch (Eds), *The Environmental Consequences of War*, pp 210–17.

[94] United Nations Convention on the Law of the Sea, signed on 10 Dec 1982, entered into force on 16 Nov 1994, UNTS, Vol 1833, No 31363.

[95] The Antarctic Treaty, signed on 1 Dec 1959, entered into force on 23 Jun 1961, UNTS, Vol 402, No 5778. See also Protocol on Environmental Protection to the Antarctic Treaty, together with Schedule and Annexes, opened for signature on 4 Oct 1991, enters into force upon ratification, ILM, Vol 30, 1991, p 1461.

[96] Vöneky, *A New Shield for the Environment: Peacetime Treaties as Legal Restraints of Wartime Damage*, p 27, fn 83. Art I of the Antarctica Treaty already establishes that 'Antarctica shall be used for peaceful purposes only' and that '[t]here shall be prohibited, inter alia, any measures of a military nature, such as the establishment of military bases and fortifications, the carrying out of military maneuvers, as well as the testing of any types of weapons.'

[97] United Nations Framework Convention on Climate Change, opened for signature on 4 Jun 1992, entered into force on 21 Mar 1994, UNTS, Vol 1771, No 30822. See also Kyoto Protocol to the United Nations Framework Convention on Climate Change, opened for signature on 16 Mar 1998, entered into force 16 Feb 2005, ILM, Vol 37, 1998, p 32.

[98] Convention on Biological Diversity, opened for signature on 5 Jun 1992, entered into force on 29 Dec 1993, UNTS, Vol 1760, No 30619.

[99] Convention for the Protection of the Ozone Layer, opened for signature on 22 Mar 1985, entered into force on 22 Sep 1988, UNTS, Vol 1513, No 26164. See also Montreal Protocol on Substances that Deplete the Ozone Layer, opened for signature on 16 Sep 1987, entered into force on 1 Jan 1989, as amended in London (27–29 Jun 1990), Nairobi (19–21 Jun 1991) and Copenhagen (23–24 Nov 1992), UNTS, Vol 1522, No 26369. Protocol to the 1985 Vienna Convention for the Protection of the Ozone Layer, opened for signature on 22 Mar 1985, entered into force on 22 Sep 1988, UNTS, Vol 1513, No 26164.

[100] Convention Concerning the Protection of the World Cultural and Natural Heritage, signed on 23 Nov 1972, entered into force on 17 Dec 1975, UNTS, Vol 1037, No 15511. She also referred to the Convention on Wetlands of International Importance especially as Waterfowl Habitat, opened for signature 2 Feb 1971, entered into force 21 Dec 1975, UNTS, Vol 996, No 14583; Convention on the Conservation of Migratory Species of Wild Animals, opened for signature on 23 Jun 1979, entered into force on 1 Nov 1983, UNTS, Vol 1651, No 28395; Convention on International Trade in Endangered Species of Wild Fauna and Flora, opened for signature on 3 Mar 1973, entered into force on 1 Jul 1975, UNTS, Vol 993, No 14537.

number of regional treaties.[101] Treaties that intend to protect shared natural resources only remain applicable:

> if they are aimed at protecting an environmental good in the common interest of the state community as a whole.[102]

Although appealing and well-argued, Vöneky's thesis results only in indirect environmental protection, since it is merely based on an analogy with other treaty categories which are agreed to remain applicable during international armed conflict. Furthermore, the analogy approach seems also unnecessary since a similar and more direct result can be achieved, by reference to the principle that the legal relationship between belligerents and non-belligerents is in principle not affected by the outbreak of hostilities.

It is generally agreed that the relationship between *ius pacis* and *ius in bello* is based on the principle that hostilities do not ipso facto terminate peacetime legal relations between belligerents. With respect to treaties, it depends on the intention of the contracting parties as reflected in the text of the treaty and the compatibility of the treaty's object and purpose whether or not it remains applicable during international armed conflict; with respect to customary law, which is in principle binding on all states, and which must always be observed towards non-belligerents, its applicability between belligerents seems to depend on its compatibility with the existence of an international armed conflict.

There are undoubtedly rules of international environmental law whose object and purpose are compatible with the existence of an international armed conflict, but the intention criterion is more problematic. Most treaties remain silent on their applicability during hostilities,[103] despite the fact that most environmental treaties were concluded after 1977. This implies that the drafters of these treaties were aware of the environmental protection provisions under Additional Protocol I and the 1977 Convention on the Prohibition of Military or Any Other Hostile Use of Environmental Modification Techniques (ENMOD) and they may have been of the opinion that references in peacetime instruments were either unnecessary, irrelevant, or undesirable. It does not seem likely that

[101] Vöneky refers, for instance, to the 1979 Convention on the Conservation of European Wildlife and Natural Habitats and the 1968 African Convention on the Conservation of Nature and Natural Resources. Vöneky, *A New Shield for the Environment: Peacetime Treaties as Legal Restraints of Wartime Damage*, pp 28–9.

[102] Vöneky, *A New Shield for the Environment: Peacetime Treaties as Legal Restraints of Wartime Damage*, p 29.

[103] Only few treaties expressly provide that they remain applicable during armed conflict, and only few treaties expressly exclude application during armed conflict. The 1954 Convention for the Prevention of Pollution of the Sea by Oil provides in Art XIX(1): 'In case of war or other hostilities, a Contracting Government which considers that it is affected, whether as a belligerent or as a neutral, may suspend the operation of the whole or any part of the present Convention in respect of all or any of its territories.'

the lack of references should be interpreted as intending these provisions to remain applicable at all times, including international armed conflict.

Be that as it may, even if rules of international environmental law would remain applicable during international armed conflict, either because their object and purpose is compatible with the existence of an international armed conflict, or because the drafters somehow intended them to remain applicable, then it is still doubtful whether their effect would be significant. It is most likely that the rules of *ius in bello* that directly protect the environment during international armed conflict would prevail over these peacetime norms of international environmental law, by reference to the maxim *lex specialis derogat legi generali.* This would appear from the more specific character of the laws of war and the fact that general rules of international environmental law are primarily intended to protect the environment during peace time.[104] Furthermore, if even non-derogable human rights law must yield to international humanitarian law, as has been discussed above, then it is unlikely that the impact and protection of peacetime international environmental law is much stronger.

Even though the International Court of Justice stated in its Nuclear Weapons Opinion (GA) that:

> the issue is not whether the treaties relating to the protection of the environment are or are not applicable during an armed conflict,[105]

it did come to a similar conclusion. According to the Court, the issue with respect to international environmental law was:

[104] Compare, e.g., the finding of the International Court of Justice in the 2005 case between the Democratic Republic of Congo (DRC) and Uganda. Upon the contention of the DRC that Uganda had violated the principle of the DRC's sovereignty over natural resources, as expressed in various General Assembly Resolutions, the Court stated: 'While recognizing the importance of this principle, which is a principle of customary international law, the Court notes that there is nothing in these General Assembly resolutions which suggests that they are applicable to the specific situation of looting, pillage and exploitation of certain natural resources by members of the army of a State militarily intervening in another State'. Case Concerning Armed Activities on the Territory of the Congo (Democratic Republic of the Congo v Uganda), Merits, Judgment, 19 Dec 2005, ICJICJ Reports 2005, para 244, p 77. Although this statement could be interpreted as implying that the principle is in principle not applicable during armed conflict, it could also mean that the principle is not applicable under these specific circumstances because it is set aside by more specific rules of *ius in bello.* Vöneky on the other hand writes that '[t]he claim that the law of armed conflict as *lex specialis* generally supersedes peacetime environmental law is (. . .) not convincing.' According to her, 'there is no *opinio iuris* that the applicability of peacetime environmental treaties during armed conflict is excluded.' Vöneky, *A New Shield for the Environment: Peacetime Treaties as Legal Restraints of Wartime Damage,* p 25. Also Vöneky, *Peacetime Environmental Law As a Basis of State Responsibility for Environmental Damage Caused by War,* in: Austin, Bruch (Eds), *The Environmental Consequences of War,* pp 217–18.

[105] Legality of the Threat or Use of Nuclear Weapons, Advisory Opinion, 8 Jul 1996, ICJ Reports 1996, p 226, at p 242, para 30.

> rather whether the obligations stemming from these treaties were intended to be obligations of total restraint during military conflict.

The Court did not believe:

> that the treaties in question could have intended to deprive a State of the exercise of its right of self-defence under international law because of its obligations to protect the environment. Nonetheless, States must take environmental considerations into account when assessing what is necessary and proportionate in the pursuit of legitimate military objectives. Respect for the environment is one of the elements that go to assessing whether an action is in conformity with the principles of necessity and proportionality.[106]

In other words, peacetime rules of international environmental law must be interpreted in light of principles of *ius ad bellum* and *ius in bello*, which is similar to the relationship between international human rights law and international humanitarian law as established by the Court in the Nuclear Weapons Opinion (GA) and the Wall Opinion,[107] and similar to the relationship between *ius ad bellum* and *ius in bello*, as has been established above. Therefore, the impact of general international environmental law on the relationship between belligerents does not seem to be considerable.

2.3.3 Belligerent vs Non-Belligerent

Although the impact of general international law among belligerents does not seem to be considerable, its impact on the relationship between belligerents and non-belligerents seems to be substantial. As has been observed above, the legal relationship between belligerents and non-belligerents will only be affected by the law of neutrality, which means that, in principle, both belligerents and non-belligerents will have to observe their international obligations under *ius pacis*. And since most peacetime rules of international environmental law are multilateral in character, a belligerent state will always have to take these rules into consideration and be aware of its responsibilities towards non-belligerents.[108] Especially those rules that intend to protect and preserve common goods and which contain obligations to all other contracting parties and

[106] Legality of the Threat or Use of Nuclear Weapons, Advisory Opinion, 8 Jul 1996, ICJ Reports 1996, p 226, at p 242, para 30.

[107] Legality of the Threat or Use of Nuclear Weapons, Advisory Opinion, 8 Jul 1996, ICJ Reports 1996, para 25, p 240; Legal Consequences of the Construction of a Wall in the Occupied Palestinian Territory, Advisory Opinion, 9 Jul 2004, ICJ Reports 2004, pp 41–2.

[108] Note, however, that the impact of these multilateral obligations under customary and conventional law is proportionally limited by the number of belligerents. Thus, in case of a world war, the impact of these rules is much less significant than in case of an armed conflict between two states.

even towards the international community of states as a whole,[109] may significantly limit a belligerent's freedom of action. For example, under customary international law, states are held responsible for damage to the territory of other states that results from activities that take place under their jurisdiction, and consequently they are obliged to prevent transboundary pollution.[110] And under conventional law, states have various obligations to prevent atmospheric pollution[111] and damage to the marine

[109] According to Art 1 of the 2005 Resolution on 'Obligations *Erga Omnes* in International Law' of the *Institut de Droit International*, these are all obligations *erga omnes*. Art 1 provides: 'For the purposes of the present articles, an obligation erga omnes is: (a) an obligation under general international law that a State owes in any given case to the international community, in view of its common values and its concern for compliance, so that a breach of that obligation enables all States to take action; or (b) an obligation under a multilateral treaty that a State party to the treaty owes in any given case to all the other States parties to the same treaty, in view of their common values and concern for compliance, so that a breach of that obligation enables all these States to take action.' The *Institut* also agreed in the Resolution's Preamble that 'obligations relating to the environment of common spaces' are examples of obligations that 'bind all subjects of international law for the purposes of maintaining the fundamental values of the international community'. *Institut de Droit International*, Session of Krakow–2005, *Obligations Erga Omnes in International Law*, (Fifth Commission, Rapporteur: M Giorgio Gaja), through: <http://www.idi-iil.org/>. Cassese refers in this context to so-called 'community obligations' which have the following unique features: (i) 'they are obligations protecting fundamental values (such as peace, human rights, self-determination of peoples, protection of the environment)'; (ii) 'they are obligations *erga omnes*, that is towards all the member States of the international community (or, in the case of multilateral treaties, all the other contracting States); (iii) they are linked to correlative rights of each state, or contracting state; (iv) this right may be exercised by each individual state even if it is not materially or morally injured by the violation; (v) the right is exercised is exercised on behalf of the entire international community of states 'to safeguard fundamental values of this community'. Cassese, *International Law*, Oxford University Press, Oxford, 2001, pp 15–17.

[110] This obligation was first recognised by the 1938–1941 Trail Smelter Arbitration and is reflected in Principle 21 of the 1972 Stockholm Declaration, Principle 2 of the 1992 Rio Declaration and the 2001 Draft Articles on Prevention of Transboundary Harm from Hazardous Activities. Trail Smelter Arbitration (US v Canada); 16 Apr 1938, 11 Mar 1941, in: H Lauterpacht (Ed), *Annual Digest and Reports of Public International Law Cases; Being a Selection from the Decisions of International and National Courts and Tribunals given during the Years 1938–1940*, (also published as International Law Reports, Vol 9, Butterworth & Co. (Publishers), London, 1942, Case No 104 (pp. 315–33); A/CONF.48/14/Rev1, Report of the United Nations Conference on the Human Environment, Stockholm, 5–16 Jun 1972, Declaration of the United Nations Conference on the Human Environment, United Nations, New York, 1973; A/CONF.151/26/Rev.l (Vol I), Report of the United Nations Conference on Environment and Development, Rio de Janeiro, 3–14 Jun 1992, Vol I, Resolutions Adopted by the Conference; Resolution 1, Adoption of Texts on Environment and Development; Annex I, Rio Declaration on Environment and Development, United Nations, New York, 1993; A/56/10, Draft Articles on Prevention of Transboundary Harm from Hazardous Activities; Report of the International Law Commission to the General Assembly on the work of its fifty-sixth session, Nov 2001. Through: <http://www.un.org/law/ilc/>.

[111] This has been laid down, eg, in the 1979 Geneva Convention on Long-Range Transboundary Air Pollution, and its eight additional protocols of 1984, 1985, 1988, 1991, 1994, 1998 (2), and 1999. Convention on Long-Range Transboundary Air Pollution, signed on 13 Nov 1979, entered into force on 16 Mar 1983, UNTS, Vol 1302, No 21623.

environment;[112] as well as obligations to protect the ozone layer,[113] flora and fauna,[114] and the world's natural heritage.[115]

Therefore, if a belligerent state chose to use means and methods of warfare which would damage the environment in such a way that it would violate its obligations under these general rules of international environmental law, it would in principle incur international responsibility.[116] Only in cases of transboundary pollution is it likely that the obligation of belligerents to respect the inviolability of neutral states under the law of neutrality prevails as *lex specialis* over obligations under peacetime international environmental law, but this obligation seems even more restrictive than those under general international environmental law. As has been explained above, general international environmental law requires 'serious' or 'significant' damage from transboundary pollution for an international wrongful act, whereas the territorial inviolability of neutral states under the law of neutrality does not stipulate any damage threshold and seems to imply almost absolute immunity from transboundary harm. Although both the Stockholm and the Rio Declaration only refer to the:

> responsibility to ensure that activities within their jurisdiction or control do not cause damage to the environment of other States or of areas beyond the limits of national jurisdiction,[117]

[112] This has been regulated, eg, by the International Convention for the Prevention of Pollution from Ships, adopted on 2 Nov 1973, and modified by Protocol, adopted on 17 Feb 1978, entered into force on 2 Oct 1983, UNTS, Vol 1340, No 22484; and the 1982 United Nations Convention on the Law of the Sea, signed on 10 Dec 1982, entered into force on 16 Nov 1994, UNTS, Vol 1833, No 31363.

[113] The protection of the ozone layer has been dealt with, eg, by the 1985 Vienna Convention on the Protection of the Ozone Layer and its 1987 Montreal Protocol. Convention for the Protection of the Ozone Layer, opened for signature on 22 Mar 1985, entered into force on 22 Sep 1988, UNTS, Vol 1513, No 26164; Montreal Protocol on Substances that Deplete the Ozone Layer, opened for signature on 16 Sep 1987, entered into force on 1 Jan 1989, as amended in London (27–29 Jun 1990), Nairobi (19–21 Jun 1991) and Copenhagen (23–24 Nov 1992), UNTS, Vol 1522, No 26369. Protocol to the 1985 Vienna Convention for the Protection of the Ozone Layer, opened for signature on 22 Mar 1985, entered into force on 22 Sep 1988, UNTS, Vol 1513, No 26164.

[114] The protection of flora and fauna is reflected in a large number of specific conventions as well as in the 1992 Convention on Biological Diversity, opened for signature on 5 Jun 1992, entered into force on 29 Dec 1993, UNTS, Vol 1760, No 30619.

[115] Convention Concerning the Protection of the World Cultural and Natural Heritage, signed on 23 Nov 1972, entered into force on 17 Dec 1975, UNTS, Vol 1037, No 15511.

[116] For the invocation of the responsibility of a state by injured states (individually or collectively) or by states with a legal interest, see Arts 42 and 48 of the Draft Articles on State Responsibility.

[117] Principle 21 of the Stockholm Declaration and Principle 2 of the Rio Declaration. Both principles reflect customary international law, according to the International Court of Justice in the Nuclear Weapons Advisory Opinion. Legality of the Threat or Use of Nuclear Weapons, Advisory Opinion, 8 Jul 1996, ICJ Reports 1996, para 29, pp 241–2.

the 1938/1941 Trail Smelter Cases required 'serious consequences'[118] and the 2001 ILC Draft Articles on Prevention of Transboundary Harm from Hazardous Activities refer to 'significant harm'.[119]

A belligerent state could only escape international responsibility under general international environmental law, if it can temporarily suspend its obligations towards other contracting parties under a treaty to which it is a party, in conformity with the law of treaties, or if it can show the existence of so-called 'circumstances precluding wrongfulness' under the law of state responsibility.[120] The former is possible, for example, in case of a supervening impossibility of performance or a fundamental change of circumstances.[121] The latter is possible if the belligerent state is using force in self-defence, or if it can show *force majeure*, distress, or necessity.[122]

According to Article 61 of the Vienna Convention on the Law of Treaties, a supervening impossibility of performance can only be invoked in case of a 'permanent disappearance or destruction of an object indispensable for the execution of the treaty' and may not be invoked if the impossibility is the result of a breach of other obligations under international law. And, according to Article 62 of the Vienna Convention, a fundamental change of circumstances may only be invoked if the change was not foreseen, and:

> (a) the existence of those circumstances constituted an essential basis of the consent of the parties to be bound by the treaty; and (b) the effect of the change is radically to transform the extent of obligations still to be performed under the treaty.

[118] Trail Smelter Arbitration (US v Canada); 16 Apr 1938, 11 Mar 1941, in: H Lauterpacht (Ed), *Annual Digest and Reports of Public International Law Cases; Being a Selection from the Decisions of International and National Courts and Tribunals given during the Years 1938–1940*, (also published as International Law Reports, Vol 9), Butterworth & Co (Publishers), London, 1942, Case No 104 (pp. 315–33), p 317.

[119] Art 1 of the Draft Articles on Prevention of Transboundary Harm from Hazardous Activities, in: A/56/10, Draft Articles on Prevention of Transboundary Harm from Hazardous Activities; Report of the International Law Commission to the General Assembly on the work of its fifty-sixth session, Nov 2001. Through: <http://www.un.org/law/ilc/>.

[120] Similarly Vöneky, *A New Shield for the Environment: Peacetime Treaties as Legal Restraints of Wartime Damage*, pp 30–2; Vöneky, *Peacetime Environmental Law As a Basis of State Responsibility for Environmental Damage Caused by War*, in: Austin, Bruch (Eds), *The Environmental Consequences of War*, pp 218–23.

[121] Other reasons for suspending or terminating treaties under the Vienna Convention on the Law of Treaties are consent of the parties (Arts 54–59), material breach (Art 60), and the emergence of new peremptory rules of general international law (Art 64). Termination or suspension of a multilateral treaty as a consequence of a prior breach of the treaty by one of the belligerents under Art 60(2)(c) does not seem likely in this context since the treaty should be of such a character that 'a material breach of its provisions by one party radically changes the position of every party with respect to the further performance of its obligations under the treaty.' This radical change is unlikely in the case of environmental protection treaties.

[122] The other circumstances precluding wrongfulness under the Draft Articles on State Responsibility are consent (Art 20), and countermeasures in respect of an internationally wrongful act (Art 22).

Article 62 may not be invoked by a state who is responsible for the fundamental change of circumstances if that change is the result of a breach of international obligations. Both articles are nowadays considered to reflect customary international law.[123]

Generally, the wrongfulness of breaches of international law can be precluded according the Draft Articles on State Responsibility, if a state can prove *force majeure* (Article 23), which is:

> the occurrence of an irresistible force or of an unforeseen event, beyond the control of the State, making it materially impossible in the circumstances to perform the obligation;

distress (Article 24), if the 'author' of the wrongful act faces a life-threatening situation; or necessity (Article 25), if the act is the only way 'to safeguard an essential interest against a grave and imminent peril; and does not seriously impair' essential interests of other states or 'of the international community as a whole'.[124] *Force majeure*, distress, or necessity do not preclude wrongfulness if the state invoking them has itself caused or at least contributed to the emergency situation.

Finally, according to Article 21 of the Draft Articles:

> [t]he wrongfulness of an act of a State is precluded if the act constitutes a lawful measure of self-defence taken in conformity with the Charter of the United Nations.

According to the ILC, lawful self-defence does not only preclude the wrongfulness of the use of force under public international law, but may also justify non-performance of other obligations 'provided that such non-performance is related to the breach of that provision.'[125] This would not be possible with respect to rules of *ius in bello* or human rights law, but might very well include international environmental law. This also seems to be the conclusion of the International Court of Justice in the Nuclear Weapons Opinion (GA). In the above-quoted passage in which the Court says that the issue is not whether or not peacetime rules of international environmental law remain applicable during international armed conflict, but whether or not 'the obligations stemming from these treaties were

[123] Gabčíkovo-Nagymaros Project (Hungary/Slovakia), Judgment, 25 Sep 1997, ICJ Reports 1997, para 46, p 38.

[124] Compare, however, Bothe, who writes that 'the existence of an armed conflict does not constitute a state of necessity in this sense.' M Bothe, *Protection of the Environment in Times of Armed Conflict*, in: N Al-Nauimi, R Meese (Eds), *International Legal Issues Arising Under the United Nations Decade of International Law; Proceedings of the Qatar International Law Conference '94*, Martinus Nijhoff Publishers, The Hague, 1995, pp 101–2.

[125] A/56/10, Draft Articles on Responsibility of States for Internationally Wrongful Acts, including Commentaries, adopted by the International Law Commission at its fifty-third session, Nov 2001; Yearbook of the International Law Commission, 2001; Vol II, Part Two, forthcoming, p 178. Through <http://www.un.org/law/ilc/>. Also Crawford, *The International Law Commission's Articles on State Responsibility; Introduction, Text and Commentaries*, p 166.

intended to be obligations of total restraint during military conflict.' The Court then continues by stating that it is impossible that these rules could have been intended to restrict a state's right to use force in self-defence 'because of its obligations to protect the environment.' Rather:

> States must take environmental considerations into account when assessing what is necessary and proportionate in the pursuit of legitimate military objectives. Respect for the environment is one of the elements that go to assessing whether an action is in conformity with the principles of necessity and proportionality.[126]

It seems therefore that the possibility to escape international responsibility for breaches of rules of general international environmental law during international armed conflict is only open to states that have become the victim of an armed attack.[127] Only states using force in self-defence comply with the requirement that the non-performance of their obligations under conventional and customary environmental law is not the result of their own behavior. Aggressor states thus bear full responsibility towards other contracting parties that are not involved in the conflict, or the community of states as a whole, for breaches of general international environmental law and are precluded from suspending their obligations under multilateral treaties and invoking circumstances precluding wrongfulness.

[126] Legality of the Threat or Use of Nuclear Weapons, Advisory Opinion, 8 Jul 1996, ICJ Reports 1996, p 226, at p 242, para 30.

[127] Please note that this leaves unaffected the obligation of the state using force in self-defence, ie as a belligerent state, to observe its obligations under the law of neutrality. The obligation to observe the territorial inviolability of a neutral state would therefore make the possibility to invoke self-defence as a circumstance precluding wrongfulness moot in case of transboundary pollution.

Appraisal and Conclusions

1—INTRODUCTION

THIS STUDY IS intended to determine whether or not the use of any kind of nuclear weapon would violate existing norms of public international law relating to the protection and safeguarding of the environment during international armed conflict. After discussing various aspects of nuclear weapons and their effects in Part I, and after establishing the legal framework of environmental protection during international armed conflict in Part II, it should be possible to assess under which circumstances this might be the case (section 2), and to draw a final conclusion (section 3).

2—APPRAISAL

2.1 Introduction

An appraisal of the (il)legality of the use of nuclear weapons under public international law from the perspective of the protection of the environment during international armed conflict consists of two parts. First, it has to be established which of the rules discussed in Part II may be applicable to the use of nuclear weapons (section 2.2). Subsequently, it is assessed which of these rules are most relevant in view of the effects discussed in Part I (section 2.3).

2.2 Applicability

Before assessing under which circumstances a state would violate its obligations under the rules of public international law discussed in Part II of this thesis, it is necessary to determine whether the rules in question are applicable to the use of nuclear weapons during international armed conflict. This applicability seems beyond dispute with respect to the general provisions of *ius ad bellum* and *ius pacis* since they are not weapon-specific. The applicability of the relevant rules under *ius in bello* to the use of nuclear weapons, however, is less obvious.

Firstly, the 1977 Convention on the Prohibition of Military or Any Other Hostile Use of Environmental Modification Techniques (ENMOD) specifically prohibits the use of environmental modification techniques and does not refer to the use of nuclear weapons or any other weaponry in general. Only when nuclear weapons would be used to manipulate natural processes, for example to cause tsunamis or earthquakes—as explained in the Convention's Understanding Relating to Article II—would their use would come within the scope of the Convention. It is important, however, to realise that under such circumstances, it would be the actual use of environmental modification techniques, and not the use of nuclear weapons as such that would constitute a violation of Article I ENMOD.

Secondly, it has been claimed that Additional Protocol I is not applicable to the use of nuclear weapons or to weapons of mass destruction in general, since they were supposedly excluded from the scope of the negotiations held in Geneva between 1974 and 1977. When the International Committee for the Red Cross (ICRC) introduced its Draft Protocols in 1973 that would form the basis for negotiation at the Diplomatic Conference, it stipulated:

> Problems relating to atomic, bacteriological and chemical warfare are subjects of international agreements or negotiations by governments, and in submitting these draft Additional Protocols the ICRC does not intend to broach those problems. It should be borne in mind that the Red Cross as a whole, at several International Red Cross Conferences, has clearly made known its condemnation of weapons of mass destruction and has urged governments to reach agreements for the banning of their use.[1]

This interpretation is supported by a number of States Parties to Additional Protocol I and has also been argued before the International Court of Justice. Among the current 164 States Parties to the Protocol, eight states specifically declared, upon ratification, that it was their understanding that Additional Protocol I only applied to conventional weapons, without prejudice to other rules of public international law applicable to other types of weapons,[2] and one state expressed its uncertainty as to the applicability of Additional Protocol I to the use of nuclear weapons.[3] Before the International Court of Justice, the non-applicability of the new rules of Additional Protocol I to the use of nuclear weapons was argued by the

[1] International Committee of the Red Cross, *Draft Additional Protocols to the Geneva Conventions of Aug 12, 1949; Commentary*, ICRC, Geneva, 1973, p 2.

[2] These states were Belgium, Canada, France, Germany, Italy, the Netherlands, Spain, and the United Kingdom. Reservations through: <http://www.icrc.org/ihl.nsf>.

[3] Reservation/Declaration from the Republic of Ireland upon ratification on 19 May 1999. Through: <http://www.icrc.org/ihl.nsf>.

United Kingdom,[4] the United States,[5] France,[6] the Russian Federation,[7] and the Netherlands;[8] while New Zealand implied that this might be the case.[9] Of these six states, the United States is not a State Party to the Protocol, while the United Kingdom and France were not yet Parties to the Protocol at the time they were pleading before the Court.

On the other hand, India stated at the Diplomatic Conference upon adoption of Article 35 that it had joined the consensus because it believed that Article 35 applied to all categories of weapons, including nuclear weapons and other weapons of mass destruction.[10] And before the International Court of Justice, Mexico,[11] Egypt,[12] the Solomon Islands,[13] the Marshall Islands,[14] Nauru,[15] Malaysia,[16] and Samoa[17] claimed that the

[4] Written Statement of the Government of the United Kingdom of 16 Jun 1995 (GA), paras 3.45–3.55, pp 40–6; Written Statement of the Government of the United Kingdom (WHO), pp 64–5, 82; Written Comments of the Government of the United Kingdom on other Written Statements of 16 Jun 1995 (WHO), paras 3.10–3.13 and 3.45–3.55, pp 25–7, 40–6; CR 95/34, Oral Plea of the Government of the United Kingdom, of 15 Nov 1995 (WHO and GA), pp 36–7.

[5] Written Statement of the Government of the United States of America of 20 Jun 1995 (GA), pp 25–8; Written Statement of the Government of the United States of America of 10 Jun 1994 (WHO), pp 28–9; Written Comments of the Government of the United States of America on the Submissions of Other States of 20 Jun 1995, pp 23–31; CR 95/34, Oral Plea of the Government of the United States, of 15 Nov 1995 (WHO and GA), pp 73–5.

[6] Written Statement of the Government of Republic of France of 20 Jun 1995 (GA), para 21, pp 31–4; Written Statement of the Government of Republic of France 20 Jun 1994 (WHO), pp 26–7; CR 95/24, Oral Plea of the Government of France, of 2 Nov 1995 (WHO and GA), p 23.

[7] Written Statement and Comments of the Government of the Russian Federation of 19 Jun 1995 (WHO), pp 10–11; CR 95/29, Oral Plea of the Government of the Russian Federation, of 10 Nov 1995 (WHO and GA), pp 44–5.

[8] Written Statement of the Government of the Netherlands of 16 Jun 1995 (GA), para 23, p 8; Written Statement of the Government of the Netherlands (WHO), para 30, p 10.

[9] Written Statement of the Government of New Zealand of 20 Jun 1995 (GA), para 97, p 22.

[10] CDDH/SR.39, Annex; VI, 113; Plenary Meeting of 25 may 1977, in: HS Levie, *Protection of War Victims: Protocol 1 to the 1949 Geneva Conventions; Vol 2*, Oceana Publications, Dobbs Ferry, NY, 1980, p 279.

[11] Written Statement of the Government of Mexico of 19 Jun 1995 (GA), para 74, p 12.

[12] Written Comments of the Government of Egypt on Other Written Statements of Sep 1995 (GA), pp 19–21; CR 95/23, Oral Plea of the Government of Egypt, of 1 Nov 1995 (WHO and GA), pp 35–6.

[13] Written Statement of the Government of the Solomon Islands of 10 Jun 1994 (WHO), paras 3.5, 3.11–3.24, 3.90–3.91, pp 26, 29–36, 72–4; Written Comments or Further Written Observations of the Government of the Solomon Islands of 20 Jun 1995 (WHO), pp 48–9; Written Statement of the Government of the Solomon Islands of 19 Jun 1995 (GA), paras 3.18–3.19, 3.22–3.35, 3.99, 3.102, pp 29–30, 31–8, 73–4, 75; Written Comments or Further Written Observations of the Government of the Solomon Islands of 20 Sep 1995 (GA), pp 6–7; CR 95/32, Oral Plea of the Government of the Solomon Islands, of 14 Nov 1995 (WHO and GA), p 60.

[14] CR 95/32, Oral Plea of the Government of the Marshall Islands, of 14 Nov 1995 (WHO and GA), pp 34–5.

[15] Written Statement of the Government of Nauru of Sep 1994 (WHO), Memorial I, pp 51–2; Memorial III, pp 21–2; Written Comments or Response of the Government of Nauru on Submissions of Other States of 15 Jun 1995 (WHO), Memorial II, pp 18–19.

[16] Written Comments of the Government of Malaysia of 19 Jun 1995 (WHO), pp 18–19.

[17] CR 95/31, Oral Plea of the Government of Samoa, of 13 Nov 1995 (WHO and GA), p 46.

Protocol did apply to the use of nuclear weapons because of a lack of consensus during the Diplomatic Conference; because of the evolution of international humanitarian law since 1977; because declarations cannot modify the scope of the Protocol's obligations; and / or because such reservations would be against the object and purpose of the convention. Of these seven states, the Marshall Islands, Nauru, and Malaysia were and are still not Parties to the Protocol.[18]

Since it is generally agreed that the general customary rules of the laws of war do apply to the use of nuclear weapons, including those that are reflected in Additional Protocol I,[19] the applicability of Additional Protocol I is of fundamental importance for the purposes of the present study. The protection of the environment during international armed conflict was established as a new norm in 1977, and since it is unlikely that Articles 35(3) and 55 have developed into general rules of customary international law, the relevance of both norms to the legality of the use of nuclear weapons depends on the applicability of the Protocol.

The claim that Additional Protocol I is not applicable to the use of nuclear weapons is based on the ICRC's introduction to its Draft Protocols in which it stated that it did not intend to 'broach' the problems relating atomic, chemical and bacteriological warfare. According to the ICRC, these 'problems were subjects of other international agreements or negotiations by governments', and it is very likely that the ICRC did not want to initiate these topics for discussion,[20] because of experiences from the past. In 1956, the ICRC had drafted specific Rules for the Limitation of the Dangers Incurred by the Civilian Population in Time of War,[21] Article 14(1) of which provided:

> Without prejudice to the present or future prohibition of certain specific weapons, the use is prohibited of weapons whose harmful effects—resulting in particular from the dissemination of incendiary, chemical, bacteriological, radioactive or other agents—could spread to an unforeseen degree or escape,

[18] Neither the Marshall Islands nor Nauru have military forces of their own. The defence of the former falls under the responsibility of the United States; the defence of the latter falls under the responsibility of Australia.

[19] Compare, eg, the statements made before the International Court of Justice by the United Kingdom and the United States of America. Compare also Resolution XXVIII of the XXth International Conference of the Red Cross in Vienna in 1965 in which the Conference declared that 'all Governments and other authorities responsible for action in armed conflicts should confirm at least to the following principles: (. . .) that the general principles of the Law of War apply to nuclear and similar weapons'. D Schindler, J Toman (Eds), *The Laws of Armed Conflicts; A Collection of Conventions, Resolutions and Other Documents*, Martinus Nijhoff Publishers, Dordrecht, 1988, pp 259–60.

[20] According to *Collins Dictionary*, 'to broach' means primarily 'to initiate (a topic) for discussion'. *Collins Dictionary*, HarperCollins Publishers, Glasgow, 1998, p 201.

[21] Draft Rules for the Limitation of the Dangers Incurred by the Civilian Population in Time of War, International Committee of the Red Cross, 1956, in: Schindler, Toman (Eds), *The Laws of Armed Conflicts; A Collection of Conventions, Resolutions and Other Documents*, pp 251–7.

> either in space or in time, from the control of those who employ them, thus endangering the civilian population.

Article 14(1) unmistakably referred to the use of nuclear weapons and because it was believed by various governments to entail a condemnation of nuclear weapons, 'there was no concrete sequel to the ICRC draft.'[22]

In view of these experiences, it was obvious that discussing nuclear weapons and other weapons of mass destruction would likely endanger the success of the Diplomatic Conference. Discussing conventional weapons, on the other hand, was considered less risky. In the same Introduction to its Draft Protocols, the ICRC wrote:

> With regard to the 'conventional' weapons which cause unnecessary suffering or strike indiscriminately civilian population and combatants alike, the ICRC, at the request of the second session of the Conference of Government Experts, undertook a study to describe such weapons and their effects. A report thereon will be made available to all governments and institutions which may be interested and if necessary the ICRC is prepared to continue its research in this field which could lead, for example, to the convening of a special meeting of government experts in order to study the problem.[23]

As explained in Chapter III, section 2.2.4, the Diplomatic Conference established an Ad Hoc Committee on Conventional Weapons as well as a specific Conference of Experts which met twice in Lucerne and Lugano between 1974 and 1977, but was unable to reach agreement. Therefore, the Diplomatic Conference recommended that a specific diplomatic conference should be convened under the auspices of the United Nations,[24] which was eventually convened in 1979 and 1980 and which drafted the Certain Conventional Weapons Convention with annexed Protocols.

From the discussions during the Diplomatic Conference and the final result of the Conventional Weapons Conference, it appears that conventional weapons were either discussed in order to prohibit their use, or, if that turned out to be impossible, to set specific parameters for their use during armed conflict. If nuclear weapons and other weapons of mass destruction had been 'broached' at the Diplomatic Conference, it is likely

[22] Y Sandoz, C Swinaraski, B Zimmerman (Eds), *Commentary on the Additional Protocols; of 8 Jun 1977 to the Geneva Conventions of 12 Aug 1949*, International Committee of the Red Cross, Martinus Nijhoff Publishers, Geneva, 1987, para 1841. The Commentary is also available through <http://www.icrc.org/>.

[23] International Committee of the Red Cross, *Draft Additional Protocols to the Geneva Conventions of Aug 12, 1949; Commentary*, p 2. Discouraged by the discussions preceding the Diplomatic Conference, however, the ICRC had refrained from including specific proposals in its draft Protocols.

[24] Diplomatic Conference on the Reaffirmation and Development of International Humanitarian Law Applicable in Armed Conflicts; Resolution 22; adopted on 9 Jun 1977; follow-up regarding prohibition or restriction of use of certain conventional weapons. International Committee of the Red Cross, *Protocols Additional to the Geneva Conventions of 12 Aug 1949*, ICRC, Geneva, 1996.

that similar attempts would have been made to prohibit or at least to regulate their use, and it is therefore not surprising that the ICRC and the negotiating states decided to keep these items off the agenda.

Specific regulation of nuclear weapons was not only considered undesirable during the heydays of the Cold War, but the major Powers also preferred to discuss problems relating to weapons of mass destruction in general within the framework of the Committees preceding the Conference on Disarmament in Geneva.[25] The ICRC did not want to prejudice these negotiations and stated that '[p]roblems relating to atomic, bacteriological and chemical warfare are subjects of international agreements or negotiations by governments'. Apparently, it was believed that it was more appropriate to approach the regulation of weapons of mass destruction from an arms control and disarmament perspective focusing primarily on the possession of these weapons in times of peace—*ius pacis*—rather than on their use during armed conflict—*ius in bello*. Nuclear disarmament had been on the international agenda since 1946,[26] resulting, among other things, in the 1963 Partial Test Ban Treaty, the 1968 Non-Proliferation Treaty, and the 1996 Comprehensive Nuclear-Test-Ban Treaty.[27] And chemical and biological weapons had been on the disarmament agenda since 1968, culminating in the 1972 Biological Weapons Convention and, after cumbersome negotiations, the 1993 Chemical Weapons Convention.[28] The latter Convention also prohibits the use of chemical weapons and can therefore be characterised both as a disarmament and a *ius-in-bello* instrument.

In view of these circumstances, it is difficult to see why a number of states interpret the ICRC's introductory note as indicating that Additional Protocol I does not apply to nuclear weapons. The ICRC merely indicated that it had no intention to interfere with the delicate arms control and disarmament negotiations held in other fora, and that it would not pursue specific regulation of nuclear weapons or other weapons of mass destruc-

[25] The Conference on Disarmament was preceded by the Ten-Nation Disarmament Committee (1959–1960), the Eighteen-Nation Committee on Disarmament (1961–1969), the Conference of the Committee on Disarmament (1969–1978), and the Committee on Disarmament (1979–1983).

[26] In its very first resolution, the United Nations General Assembly had established an Atomic Energy Commission which was supposed to make proposals, among other things, 'for the elimination from national armaments of atomic weapons and of all other major weapons adaptable to mass destruction'. A/Res/1 (I), adopted unanimously on 24 Jan 1946, on the establishment of a commission to deal with the problems raised by the discovery of atomic energy.

[27] The Comprehensive Nuclear-Test-Ban Treaty, together with Annexes and Protocol, opened for signature on 24 Sep 1996, has not entered into force yet, ILM, Vol 35, 1996, p 1439.

[28] Even the 1925 Geneva Protocol for the Prohibition of the use in War of Asphyxiating, Poisonous or Other Gases, and of Bacteriological Methods of Warfare was negotiated within the framework of a disarmament treaty, since it was a protocol to the 1925 Convention for the Supervision of the International trade in Arms and Ammunition and in Implements of War that never entered into force.

tion during the Diplomatic Conference on the Reaffirmation and Development of International Humanitarian Law. The fact that some states actually believed that none of the treaty rules they were negotiating were in principle applicable to the use of nuclear weapons does not alter the Protocol's scope of application. The text of the Protocol is of general character, does not refer to any specific weapon or weapon category, and must therefore be presumed to be applicable to any type of weapon.

This conclusion seems to be confirmed by the International Court of Justice in the Nuclear Weapons Opinion (GA). Although it stated that there was not:

> any need for the Court to elaborate on the question of the applicability of Additional Protocol I of 1977 to nuclear weapons,

it did:

> observe that while, at the Diplomatic Conference of 1974–1977, there was no substantive debate on the nuclear issue and no specific solution concerning this question was put forward, Additional Protocol I in no way replaced the general customary rules applicable to all means and methods of combat including nuclear weapons. In particular, the Court recalls that all States are bound by those rules in Additional Protocol I which, when adopted, were merely the expression of the pre-existing customary law, such as the Martens Clause, reaffirmed in the first article of Additional Protocol I. The fact that certain types of weapons were not specifically dealt with by the 1974–1977 Conference does not permit the drawing of any legal conclusions relating to the substantive issues which the use of such weapons would raise.[29]

This last remark, in combination with its references to Articles 35(3) and 55 earlier in the Advisory Opinion,[30] seems to imply that the Court did not sympathise with the argument that nuclear weapons were excluded from the Protocol's scope of application.

Although eight states declared upon ratification that they believed that the rules introduced by Additional Protocol I were not applicable to nuclear weapons, without prejudice to other rules of international humanitarian law, including the nuclear-weapon states France and the United Kingdom, which declarations should be interpreted as reservations, they do not seem to be compatible with the object and purpose of Additional Protocol I, and they are therefore not allowed under the law of treaties.[31] The object and purpose of Additional Protocol I includes among other things the alleviation of the consequences of war and the protection of the victims of armed conflict and it would therefore be unacceptable that the

[29] Legality of the Threat or Use of Nuclear Weapons, Advisory Opinion, 8 Jul 1996, ICJ Reports 1996, p 226, para 84, p 259.

[30] Legality of the Threat or Use of Nuclear Weapons, Advisory Opinion, 8 Jul 1996, ICJ Reports 1996, p 226, para 31, p 242.

[31] Compare Art 19(c) of the Vienna Convention on the Law of Treaties.

use of the most destructive weapon ever invented would be excluded from the scope of the provisions of the Protocol.

Thirdly, the Incendiary Weapons Protocol does not seem to be applicable to the use of nuclear weapons. The Protocol prohibits the use of incendiary weapons, which weapon is defined in Article 1(1) as:

> any weapon or munition which is primarily designed to set fire to objects or to cause burn injury to persons through the action of flame, heat, or combination thereof, produced by a chemical reaction of a substance delivered on the target. (a) Incendiary weapons can take the form of, for example, flame throwers, fougasses, shells, rockets, grenades, mines, bombs and other containers of incendiary substances. (b) Incendiary weapons do not include: (i) Munitions which may have incidental incendiary effects, such as illuminants, tracers, smoke or signalling systems; (ii) Munitions designed to combine penetration, blast or fragmentation effects with an additional incendiary effect, such as armour-piercing projectiles, fragmentation shells, explosive bombs and similar combined-effects munitions in which the incendiary effect is not specifically designed to cause burn injury to persons, but to be used against military objectives, such as armoured vehicles, aircraft and installations or facilities.

Apart from the fact that the Incendiary Weapons Protocol is annexed to the 1981 Certain Conventional Weapons Convention, which would ipso facto render application to nuclear weapons problematic,[32] also the definition embodied in Article 1(1) seems to exclude nuclear weapons. Although the incendiary effects of nuclear weapons are substantial, amounting to approximately 35 per cent of the explosive energy in the case of fission weapons and 38 per cent in the case of fusion weapons, the primary effect of a nuclear explosion is the shock wave, which comprises approximately 50 per cenet of the explosive energy of fission weapons and approximately 54 per cent of fusion weapons. And even though the output of a nuclear explosion in the form of thermal radiation increases at higher altitudes at the expense of blast energy,[33] Article 1(1) requires that the flame or heat is 'produced by a chemical reaction of a substance delivered on the target'. The flash and heat produced by the a nuclear explosion is produced by a nuclear reaction.

Fourthly, the Rome Statute establishes individual criminal responsibility for genocide, crimes against humanity, war crimes, and aggression, and does therefore in principle not regulate state behavior. However, it is possible that the use of nuclear weapons which leads to widespread, long-term and severe damage to the environment and which is clearly excessive

[32] Conventional weapons were defined by the Conventional Armaments Commission in the late 1940s, as all armaments 'except atomic weapons and weapons of mass destruction [*sic*]'. Resolution of the Commission for Conventional Armaments, 12 Aug 1948, on the definition of armaments, para 1. Through: <http://www.yale.edu/lawweb/avalon/avalon.htm>.

[33] Together heat and blast always account for 85% of the total energy output of fission weapons and 92% of fusion weapons.

in relation to the concrete and direct overall military advantage anticipated may entail individual criminal responsibility under Article 8(2)(b)(iv) of the Statute, and arguably state responsibility under a relatively new rule of customary international law.

Fifthly, it is likely that the three relatively new customary rules of public international law that have arguably emerged in the course of the 1990s (a duty of care for the environment during international armed conflict, a prohibition of wanton destruction of the environment during international armed conflict, and a prohibition of excessive collateral damage to the environment during international armed conflict), as discussed in Chapter III, section 2.3.3, are applicable to the use of nuclear weapons. Each of these rules is of a general character, and the evidence found to support their existence does not refer to specific weapon categories.

And sixthly, the Hague Regulations and the rules on neutrality discussed in Chapter III, section 3, which could provide indirect protection to the environment during international armed conflict also apply to the use of nuclear weapons. They are not weapon-specific and were concluded long before the first use of nuclear weapons. This proposition has been accepted by nuclear weapon states[34] and by the International Court of Justice. According to the Court, it follows from 'the intrinsically humanitarian character of the legal principles in question' that they:

> [permeate] the entire law of armed conflict and [apply] to all forms of warfare and to all kinds of weapons, those of the past, those of the present and those of the future.[35]

However, in view of the emergence of the customary prohibition of wanton destruction of the environment and the prohibition of excessive damage to the environment, it is likely that the indirect protection of the environment through the protection of property and civilian objects under the Hague Regulations and customary law has lost most of its significance. As has been explained in Chapter III, both rules prevail over the rules providing indirect protection as *leges speciales*.

[34] Written Statement of the Government of the United Kingdom of 16 Jun 1995 (GA), paras 3.45–3.55, pp 40–6; Written Comments of the Government of the United Kingdom on other Written Statements of 16 Jun 1995 (WHO), paras 3.45–3.55, pp 40–6; CR 95/34, Oral Plea of the Government of the United Kingdom, of 15 Nov 1995 (WHO and GA), pp 36–7; Written Statement of the Government of the United States of America of 20 Jun 1995 (GA), pp 25–8; Written Statement of the Government of the United States of America of 10 Jun 1994 (WHO), pp 28–9; Written Comments of the Government of the United States of America on the Submissions of Other States of 20 Jun 1995, pp 23–31; CR 95/34, Oral Plea of the Government of the United States, of 15 Nov 1995 (WHO and GA), pp 73–5; Written Statement and Comments of the Government of the Russian Federation of 19 Jun 1995 (WHO), pp 10–11; CR 95/29, Oral Plea of the Government of the Russian Federation, of 10 Nov 1995 (WHO and GA), pp 44–5. See also: Written Statement of the Government of New Zealand of 20 Jun 1995 (GA), para 97, p 22.

[35] Legality of the Threat or Use of Nuclear Weapons, Advisory Opinion, 8 Jul 1996, ICJ Reports 1996, p 226, para 86, p 259.

2.3 Assessment

2.3.1 Introduction

Having established which of the rules discussed in Part II are in fact applicable to the use of nuclear weapons, it is possible to assess which rules will be most relevant in this context, and which rules may provide optimal protection. Since the actual effects and consequences of the use of nuclear weapons depend on a large number of circumstances, it is difficult to draw specific conclusions regarding the legality of the use of nuclear weapons in general. These circumstances include: the type of weapon involved and its configuration; the weapon's explosive power and its explosive yield; the height of detonation and the type of burst; the target aimed at and its military significance; the surroundings of the target, eg desert, tropical rain forest, or open sea, and the sensitivity of the surrounding biosphere; the season; and the weather and climate conditions at the time of the explosion.

In accordance with Part II, this assessment will first focus on the primary protection of the environment under *ius in bello* (section 2.3.2), and subsequently on the subsidiary protection of the environment under *ius ad bellum* (section 2.3.3) and *ius pacis* (section 2.3.4).

2.3.2 Protection under Ius in Bello

Having established that Additional Protocol I, the three customary rules of public international law, the Hague Regulations, and the rules concerning neutrality are in principle applicable to the use of nuclear weapons, it must be determined under which circumstances their use may entail a violation of rules that protect the environment during international armed conflict. It seems appropriate to evaluate first those rules that directly protect the environment during international armed conflict, starting with the three new rules of customary international law that have arguably emerged in the course of the 1990s.

Firstly, it is unlikely that the use of nuclear weapons would ever violate the customary prohibition of wanton destruction of the environment that is not justified by military necessity. Although a nuclear explosion may cause significant damage to the environment, it is not likely that any nuclear-weapon state would reasonably deploy its ultimate and most expensive weaponry without military necessity and for the sole purpose of destroying or polluting the natural environment. All nuclear-weapon states have taken great pains to manufacture nuclear weapons, and every use of nuclear weapons nowadays involves a considerable risk of retaliation and escalation. Therefore their employment is only to be expected under exceptional circumstances.[36]

[36] Compare, eg, Joint Chiefs of Staff, *Doctrine for Joint Nuclear Operations*, Joint Publication 3–12, Final Coordination (2), 15 Mar 2005, through: <http://www.globalsecurity.org/>.

Secondly, it is not impossible that under certain circumstances the use of nuclear weapons during international armed conflict will entail a violation of the customary prohibition to cause excessive collateral damage to the environment. And if the environmental damage is widespread, long-term and severe, the person responsible for the decision to launch the nuclear strike in question may even be held individually criminally responsible under the Rome Statute.

The average nuclear weapon is not only considerably more powerful than any conventional weapon in terms of blast and thermal radiation, but it also releases nuclear radiation, which makes it unique and distinguishes it from other weapon categories. Blast and heat may entail immediate and significant damage to the military target as well as to the surrounding area in the direct vicinity of the target. Nuclear radiation may entail damage through contamination of large areas causing death not only among people, but also among plants and animals, at large distances from ground zero and long after the attack. As has been explained in Chapter II, contamination as a result of residual radiation is most likely in case of surface bursts, ie nuclear explosions during which the fireball touches the surface, low air bursts that suck up large quantities of surface material into the radioactive cloud, and shallow underground bursts, in which the fireball actually breaks through the surface.[37] Contamination as a result of initial radiation is most likely in case of low-yield explosions, and particularly Enhanced Radiation Weapons or neutron bombs. Only high altitude air bursts and deep sub-surface bursts will not cause significant environmental damage resulting from nuclear radiation.

Although both effects may cause extensive collateral damage to the environment, the answer to the question whether or not the damage is in fact excessive must be determined by reference to the actual military advantage anticipated.[38] If a military object is very valuable for military purposes and poses a significant threat to the security of the state, then its

[37] The critical height for local fallout to occur is, according to the WHO Report, given by the formula $H=55\ W^{0.4}$, where H is the altitude in meters, and W the yield in kilotons. World Health Organization; Report of the WHO Management Group on Follow-up of resolution WHA36.28: 'The Role of Physicians and Other Health Workers in the Preservation and Promotion of Peace . . .', *Effects of Nuclear War on Health and Health Services*, World Health Organization, Geneva, 1987, p 48.

[38] Compare, eg, Y Dinstein, *The Conduct of Hostilities under the Law of International Armed Conflict*, Cambridge University Press, Cambridge, 2004, pp 120–1. Compare also Art 51(5)(b) of Additional Protocol I which defines indiscriminate attacks as attacks 'which may be expected to cause incidental loss of civilian life, injury to civilians, damage to civilian objects, or a combination thereof, which would be excessive in relation to the concrete and direct military advantage anticipated'; as well as Art 8(2)(b)(iv) of the Rome Statute which establishes as a war crime: 'Internationally launching an attack in the knowledge that such attack will cause incidental loss of life or injury to civilians or damage to civilian objects or widespread, long-term and severe damage to the natural environment which would be clearly excessive in relation to the concrete and direct overall military advantage anticipated'.

destruction may justify considerable collateral damage. And vice versa, if a military object is not very valuable for military purposes and if it is not very important for the war effort, then its destruction does not seem to justify serious collateral damage. The prohibition of excessive collateral damage always entails a balancing of values, and application of this test therefore depends entirely on the circumstances of each specific case.

For example, a nuclear strike against a hardened target on or under the surface will likely require a surface burst, a low air burst or even a shallow underground burst to destroy it, which means significant environmental damage both to the geosphere, the atmosphere, and the biosphere.[39] Despite the fact that most nuclear powers nowadays possess very sophisticated and very accurate delivery vehicles which allow for lower yield warheads, the area that will be affected will in any case be considerable. Blast and thermal radiation will completely destroy a large area directly surrounding the target, which may take years to recover;[40] and nuclear radiation will severely contaminate an area which may extend far beyond ground-zero, and which may not be safe for human habitation for a long time.

The harmful effects of radioactive fallout manifest themselves in flora and fauna primarily after inhalation, absorption or ingestion. Inhalation may occur when particles are still airborne, or after the aerosols have settled on the ground but have been re-suspended by wind or physical activity. Absorption and ingestion are only likely after a longer period of time when the particles have landed on the ground by gravitation or precipitation. The former may occur after particles have sunk into the groundwater; the latter may occur accidentally when people or animals eat plants or vegetables that contain loose particles, or after particles have entered the food chain.[41] It subsequently depends on the radioactive

[39] Compare AH Westing, *Weapons of Mass Destruction and the Environment*, Stockholm International Peace Research Institute, Taylor & Francis, London, 1977, pp 15–22.

[40] An 18 kt air burst will blow down most trees within an area of 565 ha and kill most vertebrates within an area of 43 ha by blast; and ignite most (dry) vegetation within an area of 1170 ha and kill most vertebrates by thermal radiation within an area of 1570 ha. An 18 kt surface burst will blow down most trees within an area of 362 ha and kill most vertebrates within an area of 24 ha by blast; and ignite most (dry) vegetation within an area of 749 ha and kill most vertebrates by thermal radiation within an area of 1000 ha. 1 ha equals 10,000 square meters. Westing, *Weapons of Mass Destruction and the Environment*, pp 16–17, Tables 1.12 and 1.13. Compare also, as far as recovery is concerned, the slopes and direct surroundings of Mount St Helens in the State of Washington in the United States, which still looks like a moonscape 26 years after the volcano erupted on 18 May 1980. At: <http://www.fs.fEdus/gpnf/mshnvm/>.

[41] Compare, eg the International Atomic Energy Agency's (IAEA) Report on Depleted Uranium (DU),which is a rest product after uranium enrichment and which consists largely of U-238. DU is used by a number of states for military purposes as tank armor or as armor penetration ammunition. International Atomic Energy Agency, *Features: Depleted Uranium*, paras 12 and 13. At: <http://www.iaea.org/NewsCenter/Features/DU/du_qaa.shtml>.

element involved to what extent bio-accumulation occurs in plants and animals and how it is transported in the food chain.[42]

However, this kind of damage to the environment may be justified in case the target poses a significant threat and its destruction entails a distinct military advantage. This may be the case, for instance, if the target is a hardened nuclear missile silo, a nuclear missile platform (including submarines and battleships), or the enemy's underground military headquarters. But this kind of damage may not be justified if the target is an ordinary fortified structure, a munitions depot, a factory, or simply part of the enemy lines.

Thirdly, it is not unlikely that any use of nuclear weapons might be contrary to the customary obligation to show due regard for the environment during international armed conflict. The potential environmental damage resulting from a nuclear strike warrants a thorough investigation into the possible effectiveness of employing alternative weapons; into the long-term impact of radioactive contamination;[43] and into the risk of escalation.

Nowadays, most nuclear-weapon states possess highly sophisticated weapons that can hit targets over long distances with high accuracy or a very small Circular Error Probable (CEP), which is 'defined as the radius of the circle, with the target at its center within which the missile has a 50 per cent probability of landing'.[44] Nuclear weapons may therefore not always be necessary to destroy a military objective.

Furthermore, there is little information about the long-term impact of radioactivity on flora and fauna. Firstly, the initial damage to the biosphere after a nuclear strike may affect the stability of the ecosystem in the region for a number of reasons.[45] And secondly, each species has a different radio-sensitivity[46] and since bio-accumulation of radioactive elements will eventually occur, there may be adverse effects on the environment in the future. The Chernobyl Forum Expert Group 'Environment' did observe genetic defects in plants in animals in the zone surrounding the Chernobyl reactor, but it is uncertain whether the anomalies have 'any

[42] Compare eg the behavior of uranium, for which bio-accumulation is not very high; which is not effectively transported in the food chain; and 98% of which leaves the body after ingestion through faeces. International Atomic Energy Agency, *Features: Depleted Uranium*, paras 2, 9, 12, 14.

[43] Similarly K Hulme, *War Torn Environment: Interpreting the Legal Threshold*, Martinus Nijhoff Publishers, Leiden, 2004, pp 80–8.

[44] J Rotblat, *Nuclear Radiation in Warfare*, Stockholm International Peace Research Institute, Taylor & Francis, London, 1981, p 19. Similarly: United Nations Organization; UN Department of Disarmament Affairs; Report of the Secretary-General, *Nuclear Weapons: A Comprehensive Study*, United Nations Publication, New York, NY, 1991, p 30.

[45] Westing, *Weapons of Mass Destruction and the Environment*, pp 21–2.

[46] J Rotblat, *Nuclear Radiation in Warfare*, Stockholm International Peace Research Institute, Taylor & Francis, London, 1981, pp 100–2.

detrimental biological significance'.[47] Therefore, it recommended in its 2005 Study on the environmental consequences of the 1986 Chernobyl disaster that:

> the long-term impact of radiation on plant and animal populations should be further investigated in the exclusion zone of the Chernobyl accident.

And:

> [i]n particular multigenerational studies of the recently identified radiobiological phenomena of genome instability and of the radiation effect on the genetic structure of plant and animal populations might bring fundamentally new scientific information.[48]

And finally, escalation after an initial nuclear strike is almost unavoidable in case of international armed conflict between nuclear-weapon states; and even in the unlikely event that a multiple nuclear exchange would be carried out without violating the humanitarian law of armed conflict, the effects of multiple nuclear explosions on the environment would be devastating. Firstly, the direct environmental consequences because of blast, heat, and radiation will go beyond imagination; secondly, multiple nuclear explosions in the stratosphere may cause serious depletion of the ozone layer which protects all living creatures from carcinogenic ultraviolet radiation; and thirdly, there is a distinct possibility that the resulting fires will inject so much dust and black smoke into the atmosphere that it may cause a so-called 'nuclear winter'. Although this hypothesis has been criticised, it is generally agreed that a nuclear war entails a high risk of global environmental disruption, climate change, and devastating consequences for flora and fauna.

Fourthly, it is possible that under certain circumstances, the use of nuclear weapons by States Parties to Additional Protocol I would violate Articles 35(3) and 55 of Additional Protocol I. As has been explained above, Additional Protocol I is most likely applicable to the use of nuclear weapons, including its new provisions. Both Articles prohibit the use of means and methods of warfare that are intended or expected to result in widespread, long-term and severe damage to the environment which is usually interpreted in literature as referring to decades and not intended to prohibit the damage resulting from hostilities in northern France during World War I. This interpretation of the damage threshold is based on statements made during the Diplomatic Conference.

[47] Chernobyl Forum, *Environmental Consequences of the Chernobyl Accident and Their Remediation: Twenty Years of Experience*, Report of the UN Chernobyl Forum Expert Group 'Environment' (EGE), Aug 2005, pp 209, 203–5; Chernobyl Forum, *Chernobyl's Legacy: Health, Environmental and Socio-Economic Impacts; and Recommendations to the Governments of Belarus, the Russian Federation and Ukraine*, Sep 2005, p 23. Through: <http://www.iaea.org/>.

[48] Chernobyl Forum, *Environmental Consequences of the Chernobyl Accident and Their Remediation: Twenty Years of Experience*, p 209.

If the damage must indeed be measured in terms of decades and if the damage must indeed be more severe and more widespread than the kind of damage inflicted upon the environment in northern France during World War I, then it is uncertain whether the use of any single nuclear weapon will be contrary to Articles 35(3) and 55. Although both blast and heat will cause significant damage on the ground in case of air bursts, surface bursts and shallow underground bursts,[49] it is the radioactive contamination resulting from both initial and residual radiation that will distinguish the consequences of a nuclear explosion from the extensive conventional battlefield damage in northern France. Contamination resulting from initial radiation is possible in case of low-yield explosions[50] and most likely in case of Enhanced Radiation Weapons, but the area affected will be relatively small and in the vicinity of ground-zero. Contamination resulting from residual radiation—local or intermediate/global fallout—is most likely in case of surface bursts, low air bursts and shallow sub-surface bursts and may have a significant impact on large areas far beyond ground-zero.

As has been explained in Chapter II, local fallout generally comes down within 24 hours after the explosion in a cigar-shaped pattern, downwind from ground-zero. This local or early fallout is most damaging, since it contains between 40 and 70 per cent of the total radioactivity, and may be of such intensity that certain areas will be severely affected and even remain unfit for human habitation for decades. This appeared, for example, after nuclear testing at Bikini Atoll in the Marshall Islands,[51] and at the Semipalatinsk area in north-eastern Kazakhstan;[52] and after the explosion at

[49] Westing, *Weapons of Mass Destruction and the Environment*, pp 16–17, Tables 1.12 and 1.13.

[50] As has been explained in Ch II, initial nuclear radiation is relatively dominant in comparison with blast and heat, in case of low-yield explosions.

[51] After 16 tests in a time-span of 12 years at Bikini Atoll, including the 15 Mt Bravo test with a military configuration of the first hydrogen bomb in 1954, the islands were still considered generally unsafe for habitation in 1998 by the IAEA ie 40 years after the last test. The conclusion of the IAEA was based on the presumption that the local population would almost entirely consume locally produced food, and since substantial amounts of radioactive elements had entered the food chain around Bikini Atoll, this would lead to an annual dose that was considered too high by IAEA safety standards. P Stegnar, *Review at Bikini Atoll; Assessing Radiological Conditions at Bikini Atoll and the Prospects for Resettlement*, IAEA Bulletin, Vol 40(4), 1998, pp 15–17. Currently, part of the Atoll has been rehabilitated. See: <http://www.bikiniatoll.com/> and the Marshall Islands Program of the United States Department of Energy, through: <http://www.eHdoe.gov/>.

[52] In 1998, the IAEA recommended that access should be restricted to the Semipalatinsk test site in Kazakhstan since there was too little money for cleaning, and the annual dose that resettled people would receive would be too high. After 460 nuclear tests, both in the atmosphere and underground, in the course of 40 years, researchers found some places with residual radioactivity where surface tests had been carried out or where radioactive material was vented into the atmosphere after underground tests. P Stegnar, T Wrixon, *Semipalatinsk Revisited; Radiological Evaluation of the Former Nuclear Test Site*, IAEA Bulletin, Vol 40(4), 1998, pp 12–14.

the nuclear power plant in Chernobyl.[53] IAEA researchers did not find much residual radioactivity at French test sites in French Polynesia at Mururoa and Fangataufa Atoll, where 178 nuclear tests had been conducted, both underground and in the atmosphere, between 1966 and 1996.[54]

Investigations seem to indicate, however, that apart from increased mortality during the first few months, both flora and fauna generally recovered within years after contamination as a result of reproduction and immigration. For example, both the United States Strategic Bombing Survey and the British Mission to Japan investigated the effects of both nuclear explosions over Hiroshima and Nagasaki and concluded that neither explosion had had significant environmental effects.[55] And in 2005, the Chernobyl Forum found that the area directly surrounding ground-zero, which is still closed for human activity, had actually become 'a unique sanctuary for biodiversity.'[56]

Therefore, although the consequences of radioactivity may be felt decades after contamination by human beings if they remain or settle in a contaminated area, the environment in general and the biosphere in particular do not necessarily have to suffer for such a long time. As has been observed earlier, different species have different radio-sensitivities and humans appear to be more sensitive to nuclear radiation than birds or trees: generally speaking 'the higher the species on the evolutionary scale the greater the sensitivity'.[57] On the other hand, uncertainty exists as far as adverse effects in the long-term are concerned, both resulting from instability of the ecosystem,[58] and from the genetic defects that were found after Chernobyl,[59] and environmental monitoring therefore remains

[53] The Chernobyl disaster in 1986 caused fallout over an area of more than 200,000 square kilometers and caused significant contamination within 100 kilometers of ground-zero. Both flora and fauna suffered increased mortality and adverse effects in hot spots up to 30 kilometers from the explosion but generally recovered within a few years after the explosion although a few places still remain uninhabitable and inaccessible for human beings in 2005, according to the Chernobyl Forum.

[54] E Gail de Planque, *The Mururoa Study; International Study of the Radiological Situation at the Atolls of Mururoa and Fangataufa*, IAEA Bulletin, Vol 40(4), 1998, pp 21–3.

[55] The British stated that 'in spite of stories to the contrary, plant life was flourishing in both cities.' British Mission to Japan, *The Effects of the Atomic Bombs at Hiroshima and Nagasaki*, Report of the British Mission to Japan, His Majesty's Stationery Office, London, 1946, p 15.

[56] Chernobyl Forum, *Chernobyl's Legacy: Health, Environmental and Socio-Economic Impacts; and Recommendations to the Governments of Belarus, the Russian Federation and Ukraine*, Sep 2005, pp 24, 15–24, 39–46; Chernobyl Forum, *Environmental Consequences of the Chernobyl Accident and Their Remediation: Twenty Years of Experience*, Report of the UN Chernobyl Forum Expert Group 'Environment' (EGE), Aug 2005, pp 194–209. Through: <http://www.iaea.org/>.

[57] Rotblat, *Nuclear Radiation in Warfare*, pp 100–2. See also: Chernobyl Forum, *Environmental Consequences of the Chernobyl Accident and Their Remediation: Twenty Years of Experience*, pp 191–4.

[58] Westing, *Weapons of Mass Destruction and the Environment*, pp 21–2.

[59] Chernobyl Forum, *Environmental Consequences of the Chernobyl Accident and Their Remediation: Twenty Years of Experience*, pp 209, 203–5; Chernobyl Forum, *Chernobyl's Legacy: Health, Environmental and Socio-Economic Impacts; and Recommendations to the Governments of Belarus, the Russian Federation and Ukraine*, p 23.

necessary.[60] However, since these effects are not yet known or predictable, they do not yet fall within the terms of Articles 35(3) and 55. Both provisions require that the damage to the environment is either intended or to be expected.

Particles that do not come down as local fallout may remain in the atmosphere for months or even years if an explosion is so large that the radioactive cloud reaches the stratosphere, which starts at an altitude of 12 km. Such particles will eventually come down as intermediate or global fallout by means of precipitation which means that wet regions will receive more fallout than dry regions. Although nuclear explosions may therefore cause long-term atmospheric pollution, the particles are relatively harmless as long as they remain airborne, and may have lost most of their activity by the time they are deposited on the ground.

It is therefore prima facie uncertain whether the use of any nuclear weapon will conflict with Articles 35(3) and 55 if the triple standard must be interpreted in terms of decades and qualified as more severe than extensive conventional battlefield damage. Even the reference to the prohibition of the use of means and methods that damage the natural environment 'and thereby prejudice the health or survival of the population' in the second sentence of Article 55(1) seems of no avail since it is just illustrative of the general duty of care 'to protect the natural environment against widespread, long-term and severe damage' in the first sentence of this Article.

If, however, the triple standard of Articles 35(3) and 55 is not interpreted in terms of decades, but in accordance with current convictions and current appreciation of the environment, then it is very likely that under certain circumstances the use of nuclear weapons will be contrary to both provisions. The damage to the immediate surroundings of ground-zero by blast and heat may be widespread, long-term, and severe; and contamination of the environment will often not only be widespread, but may also last for a number of years and cause increased mortality as well as genetic defects.

Fifthly, the use of nuclear weapons will likely also conflict with general rules of *ius in bello* that indirectly protect the environment. However, in view of the decreased importance of the conventional and customary rules that provide indirect protection to the environment during international armed conflict through the protection of property and civilian objects, it may suffice to note that the protection provided would have been similar to the protection provided by the customary prohibition of wanton destruction of and excessive damage to the environment. It seems plausible that the only difference between both sets of rules is that the indirect

[60] Chernobyl Forum, *Environmental Consequences of the Chernobyl Accident and Their Remediation: Twenty Years of Experience*, p 209.

protection of civilian objects was limited to land warfare and the direct protection under both relatively new customary rules also extends to naval and aerial warfare.

As far as the law of neutrality is concerned, it seems almost unavoidable that the use of nuclear weapons will violate the territorial inviolability of neutral states as prohibited in Article 1 of Hague Convention V in case of war on land. Only the use of nuclear weapons within the context of naval warfare or aerial warfare are excluded from the scope of the Convention, and only the effects of a deep underground burst may not be felt in the territory of neutral states.[61] In all other cases, it is probable that the physical effects of blast and heat will be felt within the territory of a neutral state, if the explosion is close enough to the border; that the Electromagnetic Pulse will cause material damage in neutral states; and that some of the fallout will somehow come down in the territory of a neutral state. This fallout does not have to be significant, but the term inviolability in Article 1 seems to imply a level of protection that verges on immunity.

2.3.3 *Protection under* Ius ad Bellum

In addition to the primary protection of the environment during international armed conflict under *ius in bello*, the subsidiary protection of the environment during international armed conflict under *ius ad bellum* could have additional value. The law on the use of force is not weapon-specific and may therefore under circumstances apply to the use of nuclear weapons.

On the one hand, states resorting to armed force in self-defence must comply with the principles of necessity and proportionality under *ius ad bellum* in their overall conduct of operations. This means that a defending state may still be held liable under *ius ad bellum* for damage to the environment if its operations are considered unnecessary or disproportionate in relation to repelling an attack, even if its acts are in conformity with, or at least not prohibited by, rules of *ius in bello*.

On the other hand, an aggressor state may similarly be held liable under *ius ad bellum* for damage caused to the environment during hostilities, even if its acts do not constitute violations of *ius in bello*. This is arguable in view of the separate responsibilities under both sets of rules,[62] and by

[61] Even an underground burst may cause transboundary pollution, however, which was foreseen in Art 1 of the 1963 Partial Test Ban Treaty. In addition to the obligation 'not to carry out any nuclear weapon test explosion, or any other nuclear explosion, at any place under its jurisdiction or control: (a) in the atmosphere; beyond its limits, including outer space; or under water, including territorial waters or high seas', Art 1(b) also prohibits nuclear testing 'in any other environment if such explosion causes radioactive debris to be present outside the territorial limits of the State under whose jurisdiction or control such explosion is conducted.'

[62] The scope of responsibilities under each set of rules is still uncertain, however. It will be interesting to see how the Eritrea-Ethiopia Claims Commission will determine the scope of Eritrea's liability for its violation of *ius ad bellum* in 1998, after settling damages for violations of *ius in bello* in earlier decisions.

reference to Security Council Resolution 687, despite the fact that the scope of Iraq's liability after the 1990–1991 Gulf War has been interpreted exceptionally wide. It has even been argued that aggressor states must be held financially responsible for all damages inflicted during international armed conflict, which would be another indication that the dichotomy between *ius ad bellum* and *ius in bello* should no longer be interpreted as strictly as it used to be.

2.3.4 *Protection under* Ius Pacis

Also the subsidiary protection of the environment during international armed conflict under *ius pacis*, finally, may turn out to be substantial and may considerably contribute to limiting a state's options to use nuclear weapons during hostilities. Although peacetime international environmental law does not seem to have much impact on the relationship between belligerents inter se, it remains fully applicable in the relationship between belligerents and non-belligerents. This means that a belligerent will have to observe all its international obligations under treaty and customary law towards non-belligerents; and that it will be internationally responsible for violations of rules of international environmental law if it is either unlawful to suspend or terminate relevant treaty obligations, or if it is unable to invoke circumstances precluding wrongfulness. As explained in Chapter V, the possibility to escape international responsibility for breaches of international environmental law during international armed conflict only seems to be available to states that have become the victim of an armed attack, and does not seem to be available for aggressor states.

Most international treaties on international environmental law are multilateral in character and it is therefore not unlikely that the environmental consequences arising from the use of nuclear weapons will conflict with a nuclear-weapon states' treaty obligations to protect the marine environment, the ozone layer and the biosphere. Furthermore, under customary international law it is prohibited to cause transboundary pollution that causes serious or significant damage within the territory of another state, and since only under rare circumstances, a nuclear explosion will not cause nuclear fallout, it is highly probably that the use of nuclear weapons will conflict with this rule. Although it is likely that the obligation to respect the territorial inviolability of neutral states in case of land warfare will in most cases prevail as *lex specialis* over the general obligation to prevent serious transboundary pollution, the differences in standard are most probably merely academic and will not provide major difficulties in practice.

3—CONCLUSIONS

All in all, there are quite a few rules that protect the environment during international armed conflict and which have to be taken into consideration by states considering deployment of nuclear weapons. Although the ultimate legality of the use of nuclear weapons under this set of rules depends on a large number of variables, it seems that the following rules may be the ones most relevant in case of the most likely employment of nuclear weapons, ie surface bursts, shallow underground bursts, and low air bursts.

Among the rules of *ius in bello* providing for direct protection, it is most likely that the customary prohibition to use means and methods of warfare that cause excessive damage to the environment and the customary obligation to observe a duty of care or show due regard will probably provide the best protection and the strongest impediments to the potential use of nuclear weapons. The usefulness in this connection of Articles 35(3) and 55 Additional Protocol I depends on the interpretation of their triple standard, and the outcome of studies reporting on the long-term consequences of genetic modifications in plants and animals found in the neighborhood of Chernobyl, and on the gathering of more knowledge regarding the consequences of instabilities inflicted upon local ecosystems after a nuclear detonation. If the damage threshold is interpreted more in conformity with current notions of environmental protection, and/or it turns out that instabilities in ecosystems and genetic anomalies have further-reaching consequences for the environment in general, then both provisions can be considered as providing strong additional protection of the environment for States Parties to Additional Protocol I.

Furthermore, both the territorial inviolability of neutral states under the law of neutrality (*ius in bello*) and rules of international environmental law under the law of peace (*ius pacis*) may provide significant additional protection. First of all, almost all kinds of nuclear explosions will cause transboundary pollution through radioactive fallout, the only possible exceptions being deep underground bursts and low-yield high altitude bursts. And secondly, the effects of all other kinds of nuclear explosions may have serious consequences for the environment, including the atmosphere, the geosphere, and the biosphere, and may therefore conflict with other rules of peacetime international environmental law, both conventional and customary.

And finally, under certain circumstances, the environmental consequences resulting from the use of nuclear weapons may conflict with certain requirements under *ius ad bellum*, or may entail international liability to pay financial compensation for illegal use of force under public international law. The former proposition may arise in case of use of force in self-defence which is either unnecessary or disproportionate; the latter proposition could arise if the scope of an aggressor state's liability for violation of the prohibition of the use of force extends to all damage resulting from hostilities.

The protection of the environment during international armed conflict may not be perfect and may be surrounded by uncertainty, but the law seems nevertheless reasonably adequate. As with all rules of public international law, its effectiveness depends on proper implementation, in particular 'where matters of high policy are concerned'.[63] The environment is priceless and timeless and always in dire need of protection, especially from the most destructive weapon ever invented. We do not only owe that to ourselves, but also to our children, to their children, and to all future generations.

[63] I Brownlie, *Some Legal Aspects of the Use of Nuclear Weapons*, International and Comparative Law Quarterly, Vol 14, 1965.

Annexes

A. INTERNATIONAL TREATIES AND AGREEMENTS

1864

Geneva Convention for the Amelioration of the Condition of the Wounded in Armies in the Field, signed on 22 August 1864, entered into force on 22 June 1865, AJIL, Vol 1, No 2, Supplement: Official Documents, 1907, p 90.

1868

St Petersburg Declaration Renouncing the Use, in Time of War, of Explosive Projectiles Under 400 Grammes Weight, signed on 11 December 1868, entered into force on 11 December 1868, AJIL, Vol 1, No 2, Supplement: Official Documents, 1907, p 95.

1874

Final Protocol of the Brussels Conference, with the Project of an International Declaration concerning the Laws and Customs of War, signed on 27 August 1874, never entered into force, AJIL, Vol 1, No 2, Supplement: Official Documents, 1907, p 96.

1899

Hague Convention (II) with respect to the Laws and Customs of War on Land, with annexed Regulations, signed on 29 July 1899, entered into force on 4 September 1900, AJIL, Vol 1, No 2, Supplement: Official Documents, 1907, p 129.

Hague Convention (III), for the Adaptation to Maritime War of the Principles of the Geneva Convention of 22 August 1864, signed on 29 July 1899, entered into force on 4 September 1900, AJIL, Vol 1, No 2, Supplement: Official Documents, 1907, p 159.

Hague Declaration (IV, 1) to Prohibit for the Term of Five Years the Launching of Projectiles and Explosives from Balloons, and Other

Methods of a Similar Nature, signed on 29 July 1899, entered into force on 4 September 1900, D Schindler, J Toman (Eds), *The Laws of Armed Conflicts; A Collection of Conventions, Resolutions and Other Documents,* Martinus Nijhoff Publishers, Dordrecht, 1988, p 201.

Hague Declaration (IV, 2) on the Use of Projectiles the Object of Which is the Diffusion of Asphyxiating or Deleterious Gases, signed on 29 July 1899, entered into force on 4 September 1900, D Schindler, J Toman (Eds), *The Laws of Armed Conflicts; A Collection of Conventions, Resolutions and Other Documents,* Martinus Nijhoff Publishers, Dordrecht, 1988, p 105.

Hague Declaration (IV, 3) on the Use of Bullets Which Expand or Flatten Easily in the Human Body, signed on 29 July 1899, entered into force 4 September 1900, D Schindler, J Toman (Eds), *The Laws of Armed Conflicts; A Collection of Conventions, Resolutions and Other Documents,* Martinus Nijhoff Publishers, Dordrecht, 1988, p 109.

1906

Geneva Convention Amelioration of the Condition of the Wounded in the Field, signed on 6 July 1906, entered into force on 9 August 1907, AJIL, Vol 1, No 2, Supplement: Official Documents, 1907, p 201.

1907

Hague Convention (III) Relative to the Opening of Hostilities, signed on 18 October 1907, entered into force on 26 January 1910, AJIL, Vol 2, No 1/2, Supplement: Official Documents, 1908, p 85.

Hague Convention (IV) Respecting the Laws and Customs of War on Land, with annexed Regulations, signed on 18 October 1907, entered into force on 26 January 1910, AJIL, Vol 2, No 1/2, Supplement: Official Documents, 1908, p 90.

Hague Convention (V) Respecting the Rights and Duties of Neutral Powers and Persons in Case of War on Land, signed on 18 October 1907, entered into force on 26 January 1910, AJIL, Vol 2, No 1/2, Supplement: Official Documents, 1908, p 117.

Hague Convention (VIII) Relative to the Laying of Automatic Submarine Contact Mines, signed on 18 October 1907, entered into force on 26 January 1910, AJIL, Vol 2, No 1/2, Supplement: Official Documents, 1908, p 138.

Hague Convention (IX) Concerning Bombardment by Naval Forces in Time of War, signed on 18 October 1907, entered into force on 26 January 1910, AJIL, Vol 2, No 1/2, Supplement: Official Documents, 1908, p 146.

Hague Convention (X) for the Adaptation to Maritime Warfare of the Principles of the Geneva Convention, signed on 18 October 1907, entered into force on 26 January 1910, AJIL, Vol 2, No 1/2, Supplement: Official Documents, 1908, p 153.

Hague Convention (XIII) Concerning the Rights and Duties of Neutral Powers in Naval War, signed on 18 October 1907, entered into force on 26 January 1910, AJIL, Vol 2, No 1/2, Supplement: Official Documents, 1908, p 202.

Hague Declaration (XIV) Prohibiting the Discharge of Projectiles and Explosives from Balloons, signed on 18 October 1907, entered into force on 27 November 1909, AJIL, Vol 2, No 1/2, Supplement: Official Documents, 1908, p 216.

1919

Covenant of the League of Nations or Peace Treaty of Versailles, signed on 28 June 1919, entered into force on 10 January 1920, AJIL, Vol 13, No 2, Supplement: Official Documents, 1919, p 128.

1925

Geneva Protocol for the Prohibition of the use in War of Asphyxiating, Poisonous or Other Gases, and of Bacteriological Methods of Warfare, signed 17 June 1925, entered into force on 8 February 1928, AJIL, Vol 25, No 2, Supplement: Official Documents, 1931, p 94.

1928

Convention on Maritime Neutrality, signed on 20 February 1928, entered into force on 12 January 1931, AJIL, Vol 22, No 3, Supplement: Official Documents, 1928, p 151.

Treaty between the United States and Other Powers Providing for the Renunciation of War as an Instrument of National Policy, signed on 27 August 1928, entered into force on 24 July 1929, AJIL, Vol 22, No 4, Supplement: Official Documents, 1928, p 171.

1929

Geneva Convention for the Amelioration of the Condition of the Wounded in the Field, signed on 27 July 1929, entered into force on 19 June 1931, AJIL, Vol 27, No 2, Supplement: Official Documents, 1933, p 43.

Geneva Convention relative to the Treatment of Prisoners of War, signed on 27 July 1929, entered into force on 19 June 1931, AJIL, Vol 27, No 2, Supplement: Official Documents, 1933, p 59.

1943

Quebec Agreement between the United States and the United Kingdom, signed and entered into force on 19 August 1943 At: <http://www.atomicarchive.com/Docs/ManhattanProject/Quebec.shtml>.

1945

United Nations Charter, signed on 26 June 1945, entered into force on 24 October 1945, AJIL, Vol 39, No 3, Supplement: Official Documents, 1945, p 190.

Statute of the International Court of Justice, signed on 26 June 1945, entered into force on 24 October 1945, AJIL, Vol 39, No 3, Supplement: Official Documents, 1945, p 215.

Agreement between the Government of the United States of America, the Provisional Government of the French Republic, the Government of the United Kingdom of Great Britain and Northern Ireland and the Government of the Union of Soviet Socialist Republics for the Prosecution and Punishment of the Major War Criminals of the European Axis, with annexed Charter of the International Military Tribunal, signed on 8 August 1945, entered into force on 8 August 1945, AJIL, Vol 39, No 4, Supplement: Official Documents, 1945, p 257.

1946

Charter of the International Military Tribunal for the Far East, established by special proclamation of General MacArthur as the Supreme Commander in the Far East for the Allied Powers on 19 January 1946, at: <http://www.yale.edu/lawweb/avalon/imtfech.htm>.

1947

Trusteeship Agreement for the Former Japanese Mandated Islands; Between the United States and the United Nations Security Council; Approved by the Security Council on 2 April 1947, UNTS, Vol 8, No 123.

1948

Constitution of the World Health Organization, signed on 22 July 1946, entered into force on 7 April 1948, UNTS, Vol 14, No 221.

Treaty between Belgium, France, Luxembourg, the Netherlands, and the United Kingdom of Great Britain and Northern Ireland for Collaboration in Economic, Social and Cultural Matters and for Collective Self-Defense, signed on 17 March 1948, entered into force on 25 August 1948, UNTS, Vol 19, No 304.

Convention on the Prevention and Punishment of the Crime of Genocide, opened for signature on 9 December 1948, entered into force on 12 January 1951, UNTS, Vol 78, No 1021.

1949

Geneva Convention (I) for the Amelioration of the Condition of the Wounded and Sick in Armed Forces in the Field, signed on 12 August 1949, entered into force on 21 October 1950, UNTS, Vol 75, No 970.

Geneva Convention (II) for the Amelioration of the Condition of Wounded, Sick and Shipwrecked Members of Armed Forces at Sea, signed on 12 August 1949, entered into force on 21 October 1950, UNTS, Vol 75, No 971.

Geneva Convention (III) relative to the Treatment of Prisoners of War, signed on 12 August 1949, entered into force on 21 October 1950, UNTS, Vol 75, No 972.

Geneva Convention (IV) relative to the Protection of Civilian Persons in Time of War, signed on 12 August 1949, entered into force on 21 October 1950, UNTS, Vol 75, No 973.

1954

Convention for the Protection of Cultural Property in the Event of Armed Conflict, signed on 14 May 1954, entered into force on 7 August 1956, UNTS, Vol 249, No 3511.

Protocol No III (with annexes) on the Control of Armaments to the Treaty between Belgium, France, Luxembourg, the Netherlands, and the United Kingdom of Great Britain and Northern Ireland for Collaboration in Economic, Social and Cultural Matters and for Collective Self-Defence, signed on 23 October 1954, entered into force on 6 May 1955, UNTS, Vol 211, No 304.

1955

Exchange of Notes Constituting an Agreement Relating to the Settlement of Japanese Claims for Personal and Property Damages Resulting from Nuclear Tests in the Marshall Islands in 1954, Tokyo 4 January 1955, UNTS, Vol 237, No 3346.

1956

Statute of the International Atomic Energy Agency, signed on 26 October 1956, entered into force on 29 July 1957, UNTS, Vol 276, No 3988.

1958

Agreement between the United States and the United Kingdom for Co-operation on the Uses of Atomic Energy for Mutual Defense Purposes, signed on 3 July 1958, entered into force on 4 August 1958, UNTS, Vol 326, No 4707.

1959

The Antarctic Treaty, signed on 1 December 1959, entered into force on 23 June 1961, UNTS, Vol 402, No 5778.

1963

Treaty Banning Nuclear Weapon Tests in the Atmosphere, in Outer Space and Under Water, signed 5 August 1963, opened for signature on 8 August 1963, entered into force on 10 October 1963, UNTS, Vol 480, No 6964.

1966

International Covenant on Civil and Political Rights, opened for signature on 19 December 1966, entered into force on 23 March 1976, UNTS, Vol 999, No 14668.

International Covenant on Economic, Social and Cultural Rights, opened for signature on 19 December 1966, entered into force on 3 January 1966, UNTS, Vol 993, No 14531.

1967

Treaty for the Prohibition of Nuclear Weapons in Latin America (Tlatelolco Treaty), together with Protocols, signed and opened for signature on 14 February 1967, entered into force on 22 April 1968, UNTS, Vol 634, No 9068.

1968

Treaty on the Non-Proliferation of Nuclear Weapons, opened for signature on 1 July 1968, entered into force 5 March 1970, UNTS, Vol 729, No 10485.

1969

Vienna Convention on the Law of Treaties, signed on 23 May 1969, entered into force on 27 January 1980, UNTS, Vol 1155, No 18232.

1971

The Convention on Wetlands of International Importance especially as Waterfowl Habitat, opened for signature 2 February 1971, entered into force 21 December 1975, UNTS, Vol 996, No 14583.

1972

Convention on the Prohibition of the Development, Production and Stockpiling of Bacteriological (Biological) and Toxic Weapons and on Their Destruction, opened for signature on 10 April 1972, entered into force on 26 March 1975, UNTS, Vol 1015, No 14860.

Interim Agreement between the United States of America and the Union of Soviet Socialist Republics on Certain Measures with respect to the Limitation of Strategic Offensive Arms, together with Protocol and Associated Documents, signed on 26 May 1972, entered into force on 3 October, 1972, UNTS, Vol 944, No 13445.

Convention Concerning the Protection of the World Cultural and Natural Heritage, signed on 23 November 1972, entered into force on 17 December 1975, UNTS, Vol 1037, No 15511.

1973

Convention on International Trade in Endangered Species of Wild Fauna and Flora, opened for signature on 3 March 1973, entered into force on 1 July 1975, UNTS, Vol 993, No 14537.

International Convention for the Prevention of Pollution from Ships, adopted on 2 November 1973, and modified by Protocol, adopted on 17 February 1978, entered into force on 2 October 1983, UNTS, Vol 1340, No 22484.

1977

Convention on the Prohibition of Military or any Other Hostile Use of Environmental Modification Techniques, opened for signature on 18 May 1977, entered into force on, 5 October 1978, UNTS, Vol 1108, No 17119.

Protocol Additional to the Geneva Conventions of 12 August 1949, and Relating to the Protection of Victims of International Armed Conflicts, opened for signature on 12 December 1977, entered into force on 7 December 1978, UNTS, Vol 1125, No 17512.

Protocol Additional to the Geneva Conventions of 12 August 1949, and Relating to the Protection of Victims of Non-International Armed

Conflicts, opened for signature on 12 December 1977, entered into force on 7 December 1978, UNTS, Vol 1125, No 17513.

1979

Convention on Long-Range Transboundary Air Pollution, signed on 13 November 1979, entered into force on 16 March 1983, UNTS, Vol 1302, No 21623.

Treaty between the United States of America and the Union of Soviet Socialist Republics on the Limitation of Strategic Offensive Arms, together with Protocol, Memorandum of Understanding, Joint Statement, and Associated Documents (SALT, also referred to as SALT II), signed on 18 June 1979, never entered into force, CD/28 of 27 June 1979 and CD/29 of 2 July 1979.

Convention on the Conservation of Migratory Species of Wild Animals, opened for signature on 23 June 1979, entered into force on 1 November 1983, UNTS, Vol 1651, No 28395.

1981

Convention on Prohibitions or Restrictions on the Use of Certain Conventional Weapons Which May be Deemed To Be Excessively Injurious or To Have Indiscriminate Effects and Protocols, opened for signature on 10 April 1981, entered into force on 2 December 1983, UNTS, Vol 1342, No 22495.

Protocol on Prohibitions or Restrictions on the Use of Incendiary Weapons (Protocol III) to the Convention on Prohibitions or Restrictions on the Use of Certain Conventional Weapons Which May be Deemed To Be Excessively Injurious or To Have Indiscriminate Effects, opened for signature on 10 April 1981, entered into force on 2 December 1983, UNTS, Vol 1342, No 22495.

African Charter on Human and Peoples' Rights, signed on 27 June 1981, entered into force 21 October 1986, UNTS, Vol 1520, No 26363.

1982

United Nations Convention on the Law of the Sea, signed on 10 December 1982, entered into force on 16 November 1994, UNTS, Vol 1833, No 31363.

1985

Convention for the Protection of the Ozone Layer, opened for signature on 22 March 1985, entered into force on 22 September 1988, UNTS, Vol 1513, No 26164.

South Pacific Nuclear Free Zone Treaty (*sic*) (Rarotonga Treaty), together with Annexes and Protocols, signed and opened for signature on 6 August 1985, entered into force on 11 December 1986, UNTS, Vol 1445, No 24592.

1987

Montreal Protocol on Substances that Deplete the Ozone Layer, opened for signature on 16 September 1987, entered into force on 1 January 1989, as amended in London (27–29 June 1990), Nairobi (19–21 June 1991) and Copenhagen (23–24 November 1992), UNTS, Vol 1522, No 26369 Protocol to the 1985 Vienna Convention for the Protection of the Ozone Layer, opened for signature on 22 March 1985, entered into force on 22 September 1988, UNTS, Vol 1513, No 26164.

Treaty between the United States of America and the Union of Soviet Socialist Republics on the Elimination of Their Intermediate-Range and Shorter-Range Missiles, together with Protocols, Memorandum of Understanding, and Associated Documents (INF), signed on 8 December 1987, entered into force on 1 June 1988, UNTS, Vol 1657, No 28521.

1991

Treaty between the United States of America and the Union of Soviet Socialist Republics on the Reduction and Limitation of Strategic Offensive Arms, together with Annexes, Protocols, Memorandum of Understanding, and Associated Documents (START I), signed on 31 July 1991, entered into force 5 December 1994, CD/1192 of 5 April 1993.

Protocol on Environmental Protection to the Antarctic Treaty, together with Schedule and Annexes, opened for signature on 4 October 1991, enters into force upon ratification, ILM, Vol 30, 1991, p 1461.

1992

United Nations Framework Convention on Climate Change, opened for signature on 4 June 1992, entered into force on 21 March 1994, UNTS, Vol 1771, No 30822.

Convention on Biological Diversity, opened for signature on 5 June 1992, entered into force on 29 December 1993, UNTS, Vol 1760, No 30619.

1993

Treaty between the United States of America and the Russian Federation on Further Reduction and Limitation of Strategic Offensive Arms, together with Protocols, Memorandum of Understanding, and Associated Documents (START II), signed on 3 January 1993, has not entered into force yet, CD/1194 of 5 April 1993.

Convention on the Prohibition of the Development, Production, Stockpiling and Use of Chemical Weapons and on Their Destruction, together with Annexes, opened for signature on 13 January 1993, entered into force on 29 April 1997, UNTS, Vol 1975, No 33757.

1995

Protocol on Blinding Laser Weapons (Protocol IV) to the Convention on Prohibitions or Restrictions on the Use of Certain Conventional Weapons Which May be Deemed To Be Excessively Injurious or To Have Indiscriminate Effects, opened for signature on 13 October 1995, entered into force on 30 July 1998, UNTS, Vol 2024, No 22495.

Treaty on the Southeast Asia Nuclear Weapon-Free Zone (*sic*) (Bangkok Treaty), together with Annex and Protocol, signed and opened for signature on 15 December 1995, entered into force on 27 March 1997, UNTS, Vol 1981, No 33873.

1996

African Nuclear-Weapon-Free Treaty (*sic*) (Pelindaba Treaty), together with Annexes and Protocols, signed and opened for signature on 11 April 1996, has not entered into force yet, ILM, Vol 35, 1996, p 698.

Amended Protocol on Prohibitions or Restrictions on the Use of Mines, Booby-Traps and Other Devices (Amended Protocol II) to the Convention on Prohibitions or Restrictions on the Use of Certain Conventional Weapons Which May be Deemed To Be Excessively Injurious or To Have Indiscriminate Effects, opened for signature on 3 May 1996, entered into force on 3 December 1998, UNTS, Vol 2048, No 22495.

The Comprehensive Nuclear-Test-Ban Treaty, together with Annexes and Protocol, opened for signature on 24 September 1996, has not entered into force yet, ILM, Vol 35, 1996, p 1439.

1997

Convention on the Prohibition of the Use, Stockpiling, Production and Transfer of Anti-Personnel Mines and on Their Destruction, signed on 18 September 1997, entered into force on 1 March 1999, UNTS, Vol 2056, No 35597.

1998

Kyoto Protocol to the United Nations Framework Convention on Climate Change, opened for signature on 16 March 1998, entered into force 16 February 2005, ILM, Vol 37, 1998, p 32.

Statute of the International Criminal Court, opened for signature on 17 July 1998, entered into force on 1 July 2002, UNTS, Vol 2187, No 38544.

1999

Second Protocol to the Hague Convention of 1954 for the Protection of Cultural Property in the Event of Armed Conflict, opened for signature on 26 March 1999, entered into force on 9 March 2004, UNTS, Vol 2253, No 3511.

2001

Amendment to the Convention on Prohibitions or Restrictions on the Use of Certain Conventional Weapons Which May Be Deemed To Be Excessively Injurious or To Have Indiscriminate Effects, signed on 21 December 2001, entered into force on 18 May 2004, UNTS, Vol 2260, No 22495.

2002

Agreement between the United Nations and the Government of Sierra Leone on the Establishment of the Special Court for Sierra Leone, with annexed Statute, signed on 16 January 2002, entered into force on 12 April 2002, UNTS, Vol 2178, No 38342.

Treaty between the United States of America and the Russian Federation on Strategic Offensive Reductions, signed 24 May 2002, has not entered into force yet, ILM, Vol 41, 2002, p 799.

2003

Agreement between The United Nations and The Royal Government of Cambodia Concerning The Prosecution Under Cambodian Law Of Crimes Committed During The Period Of Democratic Kampuchea, signed on 6 June 2003, entered into force on 20 October 2004, A/Res/57/228B, adopted without a vote on 22 May 2003, on the Khmer Rouge Trials.

Protocol on Explosive Remnants of War (Protocol V) to the Convention on Prohibitions or Restrictions on the Use of Certain Conventional Weapons Which May be Deemed To Be Excessively Injurious or To Have Indiscriminate Effects, opened for signature on 28 November 2003, entered into force on 12 November 2006, CCW/MSP/2003/2.

2005

Protocol Additional to the Geneva Conventions of 12 August 1949, and Relating to the Adoption of an Additional Distinctive Emblem (Additional Protocol III), opened for signature on 8 December 2005, entered into force on 14 January 2007, at <http://www.icrc.org/ihl.nsf/>.

B. UNITED NATIONS DOCUMENTS

General Assembly

Resolutions

A/Res/1 (I), adopted unanimously on 24 January 1946, on the establishment of a commission to deal with the problems raised by the discovery of atomic energy.

A/Res/95 (I), adopted unanimously on 11 December 1946; affirmation of the principles of international law recognized by the Charter of the Nürnberg Tribunal.

A/Res/124 (II) adopted unanimously on 15 November 1947, on the agreement between the United Nations and the World Health Organization.

A/Res/174 (II), adopted on 21 November 1947, by 44 to 0, with 6 abstentions; establishment of an international law commission.

A/Res/177 (II), adopted on 21 November 1947, by 42 to 1, with 8 abstentions; formulation of the principles recognized in the Charter of the Nürnberg Tribunal and in the judgment of the Tribunal.

A/Res/260A (III), adopted on 9 December 1948, by 56 to 0; prevention and punishment of the crime of genocide; Annex: Convention on the Prevention and Punishment of the Crime of Genocide.

A/Res/260B (III), adopted on 9 December 1948, by 46 to 6, with 3 abstentions; study by the International Law Commission of the Question of an International Criminal Jurisdiction.

A/Res/489 (V), adopted on 12 December 1950, by 42 to 7, with 5 abstentions; international criminal jurisdiction

A/Res/502 (VI), adopted on 11 January 1952, by 42 to 5, with 7 abstentions, on regulation, limitation, and balanced reduction of all armed forces and all armaments; international control of atomic energy.

A/Res/897 (IX), adopted on 4 December 1954, by 54 to 0, with 3 abstentions; Draft Code of Offences against the Peace and Security of Mankind.

A/Res/898 (IX), adopted on 14 December 1954, by 34 to 0, with 7 abstentions; international criminal jurisdiction.

A/Res/1378 (XIV) adopted unanimously on 20 November 1959, on general and complete disarmament.

A/Res/1514 (XV), adopted on 14 December 1960, by 89 to 0, with 9 abstentions; declaration on the granting of independence to colonial countries and peoples.

A/Res/1541 (XV), adopted on 15 December 1960, by 69 to 2, with 21 abstentions; principles which should guide Members in determining whether or not an obligation exists to transmit the information called for under Article 73(e) of the Charter.

A/Res/1653 (XVI), adopted on 24 November 1961, by 55 to 20, with 26 abstentions; declaration on the prohibition of the use of nuclear and thermo-nuclear weapons.

A/Res/2200A (XXI), adopted unanimously on 16 December 1966, on the International Covenant on Economic, Social and Cultural Rights, International Covenant on Civil and Political Rights and Optional Protocol to the International Covenant on Civil and Political Rights; Annex: International Covenant on Economic, Social and Cultural Rights; International Covenant on Civil and Political Rights; Optional Protocol to the International Covenant on Civil and Political Rights.

A/Res/2444 (XXIII), adopted unanimously on 19 December 1968, on the respect for human rights in armed conflicts.

A/Res/2625 (XXV), adopted without a vote on 24 October 1970; Declaration on Principles of International Law concerning Friendly Relations and Co-operation among States in accordance with the Charter of the United Nations.

A/Res/2994 (XXVII), adopted on 15 December 1972, by 112 to 0, with 10 abstentions; United Nations Conference on the Human Environment.

A/Res/3264 (XXIX), adopted on 9 December 1974, by 126 to 0, with 5 abstentions, on the prohibition of action to influence the environment and climate for military and other purposes incompatible with the maintenance of international security, human well-being and health; Annex Draft Convention on the Prohibition of Action to Influence the Environment and Climate for Military and Other Purposes Incompatible with the Maintenance of International Security, Human Well-Being and Health.

A/Res/3475 (XXX), adopted without a vote on 11 December 1975, on the prohibition of action to influence the environment and climate for military and other hostile purposes, which are incompatible with the maintenance of international security, human well-being and health.

A/Res/31/72, adopted on 10 December 1976, by 96 to 8, with 30 abstentions, on the Convention on the Prohibition of Military or any Other Hostile Use of Environmental Modification Techniques; Annex: Convention on the Prohibition of Military or Any Other Hostile Use of Environmental Modification Techniques.

A/Res/32/44, adopted by consensus on 8 December 1977, on respect for human rights in armed conflict.

A/Res/32/152, adopted on 19 December 1977, by 115 to 0, with 21 abstentions, on incendiary and other specific conventional weapons which may be the subject of prohibitions or restrictions of use for humanitarian reasons.

A/Res/35/153, adopted without a vote on 12 December 1980, on the United Nations Conference on Prohibitions or Restrictions of Use of Certain conventional Weapons Which May Be Deemed to Be Excessively Injurious or to Have Indiscriminate Effects.

A/Res/36/106, adopted on 10 December 1981, by 129 to 0, with 17 abstentions; Draft Code of Offences against the Peace and Security of Mankind.

A/Res/37/7, adopted on 28 October 1982, by 111 to 1, with 18 abstentions; World Charter for Nature; Annex: World Charter for Nature

A/Res/42/187, adopted without a vote on 11 December 1987; Report of the World Commission on Environment and Development.

A/Res/44/228, adopted without a vote on 22 December 1989; United Nations Conference on Environment and Development.

A/Res/45/58J, adopted on 4 December 1990, by 141 to 1, with 11 abstentions; 'Prohibition of Attacks on Nuclear Facilities'.

A/Res/47/33, adopted without a vote on 25 November 1992; Report of the International Law Commission on the work of its 44th session.

A/Res/47/37, adopted without a vote on 25 November 1992, on the protection of the environment in times of armed conflict.

A/Res/47/190, adopted without a vote on 22 December 1992; Report of the United Nations Conference on Environment and Development.

A/Res/49/50, adopted without a vote on 9 December 1994, on the United Nations Decade of International Law.

A/Res/49/53, adopted without a vote on 9 December 1994; establishment of an international criminal court.

A/Res/49/75 K, adopted on 15 December 1994, by 78 to 43, with 38 abstentions, request for an advisory opinion from the International Court of Justice on the legality of the threat of use of nuclear weapons.

A/Res/50/46, adopted by consensus on 11 December 1995; establishment of an international criminal court.

A/Res/51/45 M, adopted on 10 December 1996, by 115 to 22, with 32 abstentions; follow-up to the Advisory Opinion of the International Court of Justice on the Legality of Nuclear Weapons.

A/Res/51/207, adopted without a vote on 17 December 1996; establishment of an international court.

A/Res/52/38 O, adopted on 9 December 1997, by 116 to 26, with 24 abstentions; follow-up to the Advisory Opinion of the International Court of Justice on the Legality of Nuclear Weapons.

A/Res/53/77 W, adopted on 4 December 1998, by 123 to 25, with 25 abstentions; follow-up to the Advisory Opinion of the International Court of Justice on the Legality of Nuclear Weapons.

A/Res/54/54 Q, adopted on 1 December 1999, by 114 to 28, with 22 abstentions; follow-up to the Advisory Opinion of the International Court of Justice on the Legality of Nuclear Weapons.

A/Res/55/2, adopted without a vote on 8 September 2000; Millennium Declaration.

A/Res/55/33 X, adopted on 20 November 2000, by 119 to 28, with 22 abstentions; follow-up to the Advisory Opinion of the International Court of Justice on the Legality of Nuclear Weapons.

A/Res/56/4, adopted without a vote on 5 November 2001; Observance of the International Day for Preventing the Exploitation of the Environment in War and Armed Conflict.

A/Res/56/24 S, adopted on 29 November 2001, by 111 to 29, with 21 abstentions: follow-up to the Advisory Opinion of the International Court of Justice on the Legality of Nuclear Weapons.

A/Res/57/228B, adopted without a vote on 22 May 2003, on the Khmer Rouge Trials.

A/Res/57/253, adopted without a vote on 21 February 2003; World Summit on Sustainable Development.

A/Res/59/41, adopted without a vote on 2 December 2004; Report of the International Law Commission on the work of its fifty-sixth session.

Other Documents and Reports

A/2645, Report of the 1953 Committee on International Criminal Jurisdiction; 27 July–20 August 1953; General Assembly Official Records: Ninth Session, Supplement No 12, United Nations, New York, 1954.

A/5509, Report of the Commission to the General Assembly; Report of the International Law Commission covering the work of its fifteenth session, 6 May–12 July 1963; Yearbook of the International Law Commission, 1963; Vol II, United Nations, New York, 1964.

A/6309/Rev1, Reports of the Commission to the General Assembly; Part II; Report of the International Law Commission on the work of its eighteenth session, Geneva, 4 May–19 July 1966, in: Yearbook of the International Law Commission 1966; Vol II, United Nations, New York, 1967.

A/31/10, Report of the International Law Commission on the work of its twenty-eighth session, 3 May–23 July 1976; Yearbook of the International Law Commission, 1976; Volume II, Part Two; Report of the Commission to the General Assembly on the work of its twenty-eighth session, United Nations, New York, 1977.

A/31/27, Report of the Conference of the Committee on Disarmament; Volume I, United Nations, New York.

A/31/27, Report of the Conference of the Committee on Disarmament; Volume II, United Nations, New York.

A/42/427, Report of the World Commission on Environment and Development, of 4 August 1987.

A/46/10, Report of the International Law Commission to the General Assembly on the work of its forty-third session, 29 April to 19 July 1991; Yearbook of the International Law Commission, 1994; Vol II, Part Two, United Nations, Geneva, 1994.

A/46/141, 8 July 1991, Request for the inclusion of an additional item in the provisional agenda of the forth-sixth session; Exploitation of the Environment as a Weapon in Times of Armed Conflict and the Taking of Practical Measures to Prevent Such Exploitation; Annex: Explanatory Memorandum.

A/48/269, Report of the Secretary-General to the General Assembly on the Protection of the Environment in the Environment in Times of Armed Conflict, of 29 July 1993.

A/49/10, Report of the International Law Commission to the General Assembly on the work of its forty-sixth session, 2 May to 22 July 1994; Yearbook of the International Law Commission, 1994; Vol II, Part Two,

United Nations, Geneva, 1996 Also through <http://www.un.org/law/ilc/>.

A/49/323, Report of the Secretary-General on the United Nations Decade of International Law, of 19 August 1994.

A/51/10, Report of the International Law Commission to the General Assembly on the work of its forty-eighth session (6 May–26 July 1996); Yearbook of the International Law Commission, 1996; Vol II, Part II, United Nations, Geneva, 1998 Also through <http://www.un.org/law/ilc/>.

A/56/10, Draft Articles on Responsibility of States for Internationally Wrongful Acts, including Commentaries, adopted by the International Law Commission at its fifty-third session, November 2001; Yearbook of the International Law Commission, 2001; Volume II, Part Two, forthcoming Through <http://www.un.org/law/ilc/>.

A/56/10, Draft Articles on Prevention of Transboundary Harm from Hazardous Activities; Report of the International Law Commission to the General Assembly on the work of its fifty-sixth session, November 2001 Through: <http://www.un.org/law/ilc/>.

A/CN4/15, Question of International Criminal Jurisdiction; Report by Ricardo J Alfaro, Special Rapporteur, 3 March 1950; Yearbook of the International Law Commission, 1950; Volume II, United Nations, New York, 1957.

A/CN4/16, Article 24 of the Statute of the International Law Commission; Ways and means for making the evidence of customary international law more readily available; Working Paper by Manley O Hudson, Special Rapporteur, 3 March 1950; Yearbook of the International Law Commission, 1950; Volume II, United Nations, New York, 1957 Also through: <http://www.un.org/law/ilc/>.

A/CN4/34; Report of the International Law Commission on its Second Session, 5 June to 29 July 1950, Official Records of the General Assembly, Fifth session, Supplement No 12 (A/1316), Yearbook of the International Law Commission, 1950; Volume II, United Nations, New York, 1957 Also through: <http://www.un.org/law/ilc/>.

A/CN4/291, Fifth report on State responsibility, by Mr Roberto Ago, Special Rapporteur; The internationally wrongful act of the State, source of international responsibility (continued); Yearbook of the International Law Commission, 1976; Volume II, Part One; Documents of the twenty-eighth session (excluding the report of the Commission to the General Assembly), United Nations, New York, 1977.

A/CN4/SR40, Summary record of the 40th meeting; Ways and means for making the evidence of customary international law more readily available, Yearbook of the International Law Commission, 1950; Vol I Also through: <http://www.un.org/law/ilc/>.

A/CN4/SERA/1996, Yearbook of the International Law Commission, 1996; Vol I; Summary records of the meetings of the forty-eighth session 6 May–26 July 1996, United Nations, Geneva, 1998.

A/CN4/L644, Report of the Study Group on Fragmentation of International Law: Difficulties arising from the Diversification and Expansion of International Law, of 18 July 2003; International Law Commission, fifty-fifth session, Geneva, 5 May–6 June 2003 and 7 July–8 August 2003 At: http://www.un.org/law/ilc/sessions/55/55sess.htm.

A/CN.4/550, The effect of armed conflict on treaties: an examination of practice and doctrine; Memorandum by the Secretariat, 1 February 2005; International Law Commission, fifty-seventh session, Geneva, 2 May–3 June 2005 and 4 July–5 August 2005.

A/CN.4/552, First Report on the Effects of Armed Conflicts on Treaties, by Mr Ian Brownlie, Special Rapporteur, of 21 April 2005; International Law Commission, fifty-seventh session, Geneva, 2 May–3 June and 4 July–5 August 2005 At: < http://wwwunorg/law/ilc/sessions/57/57sesshtm>.

A/C1/52/7, Letter dated 31 October 1997 from the Chargé d'affaires ai of the Permanent Mission of Costa Rica to the United Nations addressed to the Secretary-General; circulated by the United Nations Secretary-General on 17 November 1997.

A/C.6/46/SR.18, Summary Record of the 18th meeting of the Sixth Committee of the General Assembly on 22 October 1991.

A/C.6/46/SR.19, Summary Record of the 19th meeting of the Sixth Committee of the General Assembly on 23 October 1991.

A/C.6/46/SR.20, Summary Record of the 20th meeting of the Sixth Committee of the General Assembly on 24 October 1991.

A/C.6.46/SR.43, Summary Record of the 43rd meeting of the Sixth Committee of the General Assembly on 25 November 1991.

A/C.6/46/L.13, Draft Decision proposed by the Chairman of the 6th Committee of the General Assembly of 21 November 1991.

A/C.6/47/L.2, Draft Resolution on the Protection of the Environment during Armed Conflict.

A/C.6/47/SR.8, Summary Record of the 8th meeting of the Sixth Committee of the General Assembly on 1 October 1992.

A/C.6/47/SR.9, Summary Record of the 9th meeting of the Sixth Committee of the General Assembly on 6 October 1992.

A/C.6/47/SR.19, Summary Record of the 19th meeting of the Sixth Committee of the General Assembly on 23 October 1992.

A/CONF.48/14/Rev.1, Report of the United Nations Conference on the Human Environment, Stockholm, 5–16 June 1972, Declaration of the United Nations Conference on the Human Environment, United Nations, New York, 1973.

A/CONF.151/26/Rev.l (Vol I), Report of the United Nations Conference on Environment and Development, Rio de Janeiro, 3–14 June 1992, Volume I, Resolutions Adopted by the Conference; Resolution 1, Adoption of Texts on Environment and Development; Annex I, Rio Declaration on Environment and Development, United Nations, New York, 1993.

A/CONF.151/26/Rev.l (Vol I), Report of the United Nations Conference on Environment and Development, Rio de Janeiro, 3–14 June 1992, Volume I, Resolutions Adopted by the Conference; Resolution 1, Adoption of Texts on Environment and Development; Annex II, Agenda 21, United Nations, New York, 1993.

A/CONF.199/20, Report of the World Summit on Sustainable Development, Johannesburg, South Africa, 26 August–4 September 2002, Resolution 1; Annex: Johannesburg Declaration on Sustainable Development United Nations, New York, 2002.

Security Council

Resolutions

S/RES/18 (1947), adopted on 13 February 1947, by 10 to 0, with 1 abstention; implementation of General Assembly Resolutions on the principles governing the general regulation and reduction of armaments and information on armed forces.

S/RES/21 (1947), adopted unanimously on 2 April 1947; on the Trusteeship of Strategic Areas; Trusteeship Agreement for the Trust Territory of the Pacific Islands.

S/RES/540 (1983), adopted on 31 October 1983, by 12 to 0, with 3 abstentions, on the situation between Iraq and the Islamic Republic of Iran.

S/RES/674 (1990), adopted on 29 October 1990, by 13 to 0, with 2 abstentions, on the situation between Iraq and Kuwait.

S/RES/686 (1991), adopted on 2 March 1991, by 11 to 1, with 3 abstentions, on the situation between Iraq and Kuwait.

S/RES/687 (1991), adopted on 3 April 1991, by 12 to 1, with 2 abstentions, on the situation between Iraq and Kuwait.

S/RES/692 (1991), adopted on 20 May 1991, by 14 to 0, with 1 abstention, on the establishment of a United Nations Compensation Fund and a United Nations Compensation Commission.

S/RES/808 (1993), adopted unanimously on 22 February 1993, on the establishment of an international criminal Tribunal for the Former Yugoslavia.

S/RES/827 (1993), adopted unanimously on 25 May 1993, on the establishment of an international tribunal for the Former Yugoslavia.

S/RES/955 (1994), adopted on 8 November 1994, by 13 to 0, with 1 abstention, on the establishment of an international tribunal for Rwanda and the adoption of the statute of the tribunal.

S/RES/1246, adopted unanimously on 11 June 1999, on the establishment of a United Nations Mission in East Timor.

S/RES/1272 (1999), adopted unanimously on 25 October 1999, on the establishment of the United Nations Transitional Authority in East Timor.

S/RES/1503 (2003), adopted unanimously on 28 August 2003, on the International Criminal Tribunal for the former Yugoslavia and International Criminal Tribunal for Rwanda.

Economic and Social Council

Reports

E/CN.4/2006/120, Report of Special Rapporteurs to the Commission on Human Rights, of 27 February 2006; Economic, Social and Cultural Rights; Civil and Political Rights; The Situation of Detainees at Guantánamo Bay.

Secretariat

Regulations

ST/SGB/1997/1, 28 May 1997, Secretary-General's Bulletin, on procedures for the promulgation of administrative issuances.

ST/SGB/1999/13, 6 August 1999, Secretary-General's Bulletin, on the observance by United Nations forces of international humanitarian law.

Reports

United Nations Organization; UN Department of Disarmament Affairs; Report of the Secretary-General, *Nuclear Weapons: A Comprehensive Study*, United Nations Publication, New York, NY, 1991.

United Nations Organization; UN Department of Disarmament Affairs; Report of the Secretary-General, *Study on the Climatic and Other Global Effects of Nuclear War*, United Nations Publication, New York, NY, 1989.

International Court of Justice

Written Statements and Comments

Written Statements and Written Comments in both Nuclear Weapons Opinions, through: <http://www.icj-cij.org/>.

Oral Pleadings

CR 95/22, Oral Pleas of the Representative of the World Health Organization and of the Government of Australia, of 30 October 1995, on the Legality of the Use by a State of Nuclear Weapons in Armed Conflict and on the Legality of the Threat or Use of Nuclear Weapons, through: <http://www.icj-cij.org/>.

CR 95/23, Oral Pleas of the Governments of the Arab Republic of Egypt and the Republic of France, of 1 November 1995, on the Legality of the Use by a State of Nuclear Weapons in Armed Conflict and on the Legality of the Threat or Use of Nuclear Weapons, through: <http://www.icj-cij.org/>.

CR 95/24, Oral Pleas of the Governments of the Republic of France and the Federal Republic of Germany, of 2 November 1995, on the Legality of the Use by a State of Nuclear Weapons in Armed Conflict and on the Legality of the Threat or Use of Nuclear Weapons, through: through: <http://www.icj-cij.org/>.

CR 95/25, Oral Pleas of the Governments of Indonesia and Mexico, of 3 November 1995, on the Legality of the Use by a State of Nuclear Weapons in Armed Conflict and on the Legality of the Threat or Use of Nuclear Weapons, through: through: <http://www.icj-cij.org/>.

CR 95/26, Oral Pleas of the Governments of the Islamic Republic of Iran and Italy, of 6 November 1995, on the Legality of the Use by a State of Nuclear Weapons in Armed Conflict and on the Legality of the Threat or Use of Nuclear Weapons, through: through: <http://www.icj-cij.org/>.

CR 95/27, Oral Pleas of the Governments of Japan and Malaysia, of 7 November 1995, on the Legality of the Use by a State of Nuclear Weapons in Armed Conflict and on the Legality of the Threat or Use of Nuclear Weapons, through: through: <http://www.icj-cij.org/>.

CR 95/28, Oral Pleas of the Governments of new Zealand and the Philippines, of 9 November 1995, on the Legality of the Use by a State of Nuclear Weapons in Armed Conflict and on the Legality of the Threat or Use of Nuclear Weapons, through: through: <http://www.icj-cij.org/>.

CR 95/29, Oral Pleas of the Governments of Qatar and the Russian Federation, of 10 November 1995, on the Legality of the Use by a State of Nuclear Weapons in Armed Conflict and on the Legality of the Threat or Use of Nuclear Weapons, through: through: <http://www.icj-cij.org/>.

CR 95/31, Oral Pleas of the Governments of San Marino and Samoa, of 13 November 1995, on the Legality of the Use by a State of Nuclear Weapons in Armed Conflict and on the Legality of the Threat or Use of Nuclear Weapons, through: through: <http://www.icj-cij.org/>.

CR 95/32, Oral Pleas of the Governments of the Marshall Islands and the Solomon Islands, of 14 November 1995, through: through: <http://www.icj-cij.org/>.

CR 95/33, Oral Pleas of the Government of Costa Rica, of 14 November 1995, on the Legality of the Use by a State of Nuclear Weapons in Armed Conflict and on the Legality of the Threat or Use of Nuclear Weapons, through: through: <http://www.icj-cij.org/>.

CR 95/34, Oral Pleas of the Governments of the United Kingdom and the United States of America, of 15 November 1995, on the Legality of the Use by a State of Nuclear Weapons in Armed Conflict and on the Legality of the Threat or Use of Nuclear Weapons, through: through: <http://www.icj-cij.org/>.

CR 95/35, Oral Plea of the Government of Zimbabwe, of 15 November 1995, on the Legality of the Use by a State of Nuclear Weapons in Armed Conflict and on the Legality of the Threat or Use of Nuclear Weapons, through: through: <http://www.icj-cij.org/>.

Other Documents

S/22430, 2 April 1991, as corrected by S/22430/Corr.1, 3 April 1991, Draft Resolution from Belgium, France, Romania, United Kingdom of Great Britain and Northern Ireland, United States of America and Zaire.

S/22456, 6 April 1991, Identical letters dated 6 April 1991 from the Permanent Representative of Iraq to the United Nations addressed respectively to the Secretary-General and the President of the Security Council.

S/22559, 2 May 1991, Report of the Secretary-General Pursuant to Paragraph 19 of Security Council Resolution 687 (1991).

S/25704, 3 May 1993, Report of the Secretary-General Pursuant to Paragraph 2 of Security Council Resolution 808 (1993), on the Statute of an International Criminal Tribunal For the Former Yugoslavia.

S/PV.2981, 3 April 1991, Provisional Verbatim Records of the Two Thousand Nine Hundred and Eighty-First Meeting, on Wednesday, 3 April 1991.

S/AC.26/1991/1, 2 August 1991; Criteria for Expedited Processing of Urgent Claims.

A/AC.26/1991/7/Rev.1, 17 March 1992; Decision taken by the Governing Council of the United Nations Compensation Commission during its third session, at the 18th meeting, held on 28 November 1991, as revised at the 24th meeting held on 16 March 1992; Criteria for Additional Categories of Claims.

S/AC.26/2001/16, 22 June 2001; Report and Recommendations Made by the Panel of Commissioners Concerning the First Instalment of 'F4' Claims.

S/AC.26/2002/26, 3 October 2002; Report and Recommendations Made by the Panel of Commissioners Concerning the Second Instalment of 'F4' Claims.

S/AC.26/2003/31, 18 December 2003; Report and Recommendations Made by the Panel of Commissioners Concerning the Third Instalment of 'F4' Claims.

S/AC.26/2004/16, 9 December 2004; Report and Recommendations Made by the Panel of Commissioners Concerning Part One of the Fourth Instalment of 'F4' Claims.

S/AC.26/2004/17, 9 December 2004; Report and Recommendations Made by the Panel of Commissioners Concerning Part Two of the Fourth Instalment of 'F4' Claims.

A/AC.26/2005/10, 30 June 2005; Report and Recommendations Made by the Panel of Commissioners Concerning the Fifth Instalment of 'F4' claims.

A/AC.26/Dec.132 (2001), 21 June 2001; Decision concerning the first instalment of 'F4' claims taken by the Governing Council of the United Nations Compensation Commission at its 109th meeting, held on 21 June 2001 at Geneva.

A/AC.26/Dec.171 (2002), 3 October 2002; Decision concerning the second instalment of 'F4' claims taken by the Governing Council of the United Nations Compensation Commission at its 122nd meeting, held on 3 October 2002.

A/AC.26/Dec.212 (2003), 18 December 2003; Decision concerning the third instalment of 'F4' claims taken by the Governing Council of the United Nations Compensation Commission at its 133rd meeting on 18 December 2003.

A/AC.26/Dec.234 (2004), 9 December 2004; Decision concerning part one of the fourth instalment of 'F4' claims taken by the Governing Council of the United Nations Compensation Commission at its 141st meeting, on 9 December 2004.

A/AC.26/Dec.235 (2004), 9 December 2004; Decision concerning part two of the fourth instalment of 'F4' claims taken by the Governing Council of the United Nations Compensation Commission at its 141st meeting, on 9 December 2004.

A/AC.26/Dec.248 (2005), 30 June 2005; Decision concerning the fifth instalment of 'F4' claims taken by the Governing Council of the United Nations Compensation Commission at its 146th meeting, on 30 June 2005.

Resolution of the Commission for Conventional Armaments, 12 August 1948, on the definition of armaments.

UNTAET/Reg/2000/15, of 6 June 2000, on the Establishment of Panels with Exclusive Jurisdiction over Serious Criminal Offences.

C. JUDICIAL DECISIONS

1927

The Case of the SS 'Lotus', 7 September 1927, Publications of the Permanent Court of International Justice, Collection of Judgments, Series A—No 10, AW Sijthoff's Publishing Company, 1927.

1928

The Island of Palmas (or Miangas), April 4, 1928, Arbitral Award; rendered by Max Huber, Arbitrator, American Journal of International Law, Vol 22, 1928, p 867.

Case Concerning the Factory at Chorzów (Claim for Indemnity), 13 September 1928, Publications of the Permanent Court of International Justice, Collection of Judgments, Series A—No 17, AW Sijthoff's Publishing Company, 1928.

1938–1941

Trail Smelter Arbitration (US v Canada); 16 April 1938, 11 March 1941, in: H Lauterpacht (Ed), Annual Digest and Reports of Public International Law Cases; Being a Selection from the Decisions of International and National Courts and Tribunals given during the Years 1938–1940, (also published as International Law Reports, Vol 9, Butterworth & Co (Publishers), London, 1942, Case No 104 (pp 315–33).

1946

International Military Tribunal (Nuremberg), *Judgments and Sentences; October 1, 1946*, American Journal of International Law, Vol 41, 1947.

1947–1948

United States Military Tribunal (Nuremberg), Case No 47; The Hostages Trial; Trial of Wilhelm List and Others; 8th July, 1947–19th February, 1948, in: The United Nations War Crimes Commission, Law Reports of Trials of War Criminals; Volume VIII, His Majesty's Stationary Office, London, 1949.

1963

District Court of Tokyo, Japan, on 7 December 1963; Ryuchi Shimoda *et al* v The State, in: E Lauterpacht (Ed), International Law Reports, Vol 32, Butterworths, London, 1966.

1969

North Sea Continental Shelf, Judgment, ICJ Reports 1969, p 3.

1970

Case Concerning the Barcelona Traction, Light and Power Company, Limited (Belgium v Spain), Judgment of 5 February 1970, ICJ Reports, 1970, p 3.

1977

Texaco Overseas Petroleum Company and California Asiatic Oil Company v The Government of the Libyan Arab Republic; Dupuy, Sole Arbitrator; Arbitral Award on the Merits, 19 January 1977, in: H Lauterpacht (Ed), *International Law* Reports, Volume 53, Grotius Publications Limited, Groningen, Cambridge, 1979.

1986

Military and Paramilitary Activities in and against Nicaragua (Nicaragua v United States of America), Merits, Judgment, 27 June 1986, ICJ Reports 1986, p 14.

1995

International Criminal Tribunal for the Former Yugoslavia; Prosecutor v Dusko Tadic a/k/a 'Dule' (IT-94-1); Decision on the Defence Motion for Interlocutory Appeal on Jurisdiction, 2 October 1995, International Legal Materials, Vol 35, 1996, p 32, or at http://www.un.org/icty/tadic/appeal/decision-e/51002.htm.

1996

Legality of the Use by a State of Nuclear Weapons in Armed Conflict, Advisory Opinion, 8 July 1996, ICJ Reports 1996, p 66.

Legality of the Threat or Use of Nuclear Weapons, Advisory Opinion, 8 July 1996, ICJ Reports 1996, p 226.

1997

Gabčíkovo-Nagymaros Project (Hungary/Slovakia), Judgment, 25 September 1997, ICJ Reports 1997, p 7.

2002

Case Concerning Sovereignty over Pulau Ligitan and Pulau Sipadan (Indonesia/Malaysia), Merits, Judgment, 17 December 2002, ICJ Reports 2002, p 625.

2003

Case Concerning Oil Platforms (Islamic Republic of Iran v United States of America), Merits, Judgment, 6 November 2003, ICJ Reports 2003.

2004

Legal Consequences of the Construction of a Wall in the Occupied Palestinian Territory, Advisory Opinion, 9 July 2004, ICJ Reports 2004.

2005

Case Concerning Armed Activities on the Territory of the Congo (Democratic Republic of the Congo v Uganda), Merits, Judgment, 19 December 2005, ICJ Reports 2005.

Partial Award; *Jus ad Bellum*; Ethiopia's Claims 1–8; between The Federal Republic of Ethiopia and the State of Eritrea; Eritrea Ethiopia Claims Commission; The Hague, December 19, 2005 Through: <http://www.pca-cpa.org>.

D. MILITARY MANUALS AND HANDBOOKS

The United States of America

JB Berger III, D Grimes, ET Jensen and others (Eds), *Operational Law Handbook (2004)*, International and Operational Law Department, The Judge Advocate General's Legal Center and School, Charlottesville, VA, 2004 Through: https://www.jagcnet.army.mil/.

FM 27-10, *The Law of Land Warfare*, Department of the Army, Washington, DC, 1956, as changed in 1976 Also through: http://www.afsc.army.mil/.

NWP 1-14M, *The Commander's Handbook on the Law of Naval Operations*, Department of the Navy, Norfolk, VA, 1995 Also through: http://www.nwc.navy.mil/.

AR Thomas, JC Duncan (Eds), *Annotated Supplement to The Commander's Handbook on the Law of Naval Operations*, International Law Studies 1999, Volume 73, Naval War College, Newport, RI, 1999.

Air Force Pamphlet 110–31, *International Law—The Conduct of Armed Conflict and Air Operations*, Department of the Air Force, Washington, DC, 1976.

Air Force Pamphlet 110–34, *Commander's Handbook on the Law of Armed Conflict*, Department of the Air Force, Washington, DC, 1980.

TL Strand, MW Goldman and others (Eds), *The Military Commander and the Law*, Air Force Judge Advocate General School, Maxwell, AL, 2004 Through: http://milcom.jag.af.mil/.

Law of War Handbook, Center for Law and Military Operations (CLAMO), Charlottesville, VA, 2005 Through: https://www.jagcnet.army.mil/.

TS Tudor, JK Walker, NS Richards and others (Eds), *Air Force Operations and the Law; A Guide for Air and Space Forces*, United States Air Force; Judge Advocate General's Department; International and Operations Law Division, Air Force Pentagon, Washington, DC, 2002.

The United Kingdom of Great Britain and Northern Ireland

UK Ministry of Defence, *The Manual of the Law of Armed Conflict*, Oxford University Press, Oxford, 2004.

The Federal Republic of Germany

ZDv 15/2, *Humanitäres Völkerrecht in bewaffneten Konflikten*, Bundesministerium der Verteidigung, Bonn, 1991 Or DSK AV207320065, *Humanitäres Völkerrecht in bewaffneten Konflikten—Handbuch*, Bundesministerium der Verteidigung—Verwaltung und Recht II 3, Bonn, 1992.

The Netherlands

VS 27-412, *Humanitair Oorlogsrecht*, internal publication, Koninklijke Landmacht, Ministerie van Defensie, Den Haag, January 2005.

Model Manuals

Oxford Manual on the Law of War on Land, drafted by the Institut de Droit Internationale, in: D Schindler, J Toman (Eds), *The Laws of Armed Conflicts; A Collection of Conventions, Resolutions and Other Documents*, Martinus Nijhoff Publishers, Dordrecht, 1988, pp 35–48.

APV Rogers, P Malherbe, *Fight it Right; Model Manual on the Law of Armed Conflict for Armed Forces*, International Committee of the Red Cross, ICRC, Geneva, 1999.

E. BIBLIOGRAPHY

A

B Abijola, *Protection of the Environment in Times of Armed Conflict*, in: N Al-Nauimi, R Meese (Eds), *International Legal Issues Arising Under the United Nations Decade of International Law; Proceedings of the Qatar International Law Conference '94*, Martinus Nijhoff Publishers, The Hague, 1995.

G Abi-Saab, *The 1977 Additional Protocols and General International Law: Some Preliminary Reflexions*, in: AJM Delissen, GJ Tanja (Eds), *Humanitarian Law of Armed Conflict; Challenges Ahead; Essays in Honour of Frits Kalshoven*, Martinus Nijhoff Publishers, Dordrecht, 1991.

F Ahlheid, H Bremer, S Kemper, P Rijke, T van de Vliet, *Res Loquitur Ipsa; Cicero's pleidooi voor Titus Annius Milo en de retorische traditie*, Hermaion, Emmeloord, 1994.

GH Aldrich, *Prospects for United States Ratification of Additional Protocol I to the 1949 Geneva Conventions*, American Journal of International Law, Vol 85, 1991.

—— *Why the United States of America Should Ratify Additional Protocol I*, in: AJM Delissen, GJ Tanja (Eds), *Humanitarian Law of Armed Conflict; Challenges Ahead; Essays in Honour of Frits Kalshoven*, Martinus Nijhoff Publishers, Dordrecht, 1991.

HH Almond, Jr, *Waldemar Solf (1913–1987)*, American Journal of International Law, Vol 82, 1988.

H von Arx, T Marauhn, *Nuclear Tests*, in: R Bernhardt (Ed), *Encyclopaedia of Public International Law; Volume Three; Jan Mayen to Pueblo Incident*, Elsevier, Amsterdam, 1997.

TMC Asser Instituut, *Elementair Internationaal Recht 2005*, TMC Asser Press, Den Haag.

A Aust, *Modern Treaty Law and Practice*, Cambridge University Press, Cambridge, 2000.

B

L Badash, *Introduction*, in: L Badash, JO Hirschfelder, HP Broida (Eds), *Reminiscences of Los Alamos 1943–1945*, D Reidel Publishing Company, Dordrecht, 1980.

—— *Scientists and the Development of Nuclear Weapons; From Fission to the Limited Test Ban Treaty 1939–1963*, Humanities Press International, Inc, Atlantic Highlands, NJ, 1995.

B Baker, *Legal Protections for the Environment in Times of Armed Conflict*, Virginia Journal of International Law, Vol 33, 1993.

Balkan Task Force; United Nations Environment Program / United Nations Center for Human Settlements, *The Kosovo Conflict: Consequences for the Environment & Human Settlements*, UNEP / UNCHS, Nairobi, 1999.

DP Barash, *Introduction to Peace Studies*, Wadsworth Publishing Company, Belmont, CA, 1991.

B Baruch, United States Representative to the Atomic Energy Commission of the United Nations, *Control of Atomic Energy; United States Plan*, delivered at the opening session of the Commission, June 14, 1946, American Association for the United Nations, Inc, New York, NY, 1946.

PAJ van den Berg, *The Politics of European Codification; A History of the Unification of Law in France, Prussia, the Austrian Monarchy and the Netherlands*, Europa Law Publishing, Groningen, 2006.

BJ Bernstein, *The Atomic Bombings Reconsidered*, Foreign Affairs, Vol 74, 1995.

G Best, *The Restraint of War in Historical and Philosophical Perspective*, in: AJM Delissen, GJ Tanja (Eds), *Humanitarian Law of Armed Conflict; Challenges Ahead; Essays in Honour of Frits Kalshoven*, Martinus Nijhoff Publishers, Dordrecht, 1991.

H Bethe, *The Road from Los Alamos*, The American Institute of Physics, New York, NY, 1991.

RL Bindschedler, *Neutrality, Concept and General Rules*, in: R Bernhardt (Ed), *Encyclopaedia of Public International Law; Volume Three; Jan Mayen to Pueblo Incident*, Elsevier, Amsterdam, 1997.

P Birnie, A Boyle, *International Law & The Environment*, Oxford University Press, Oxford, 2002.

HC Black (*et al*), *Black's Law Dictionary*, West Publishing, St Paul, MN, 1991.

H Blix, *Arms Control Treaties Aimed at Reducing the Military Impact on the Environment*, in: J Makarczyk (Ed), *Essays in International Law in Honour of Judge Manfred Lachs*, Martinus Nijhoff Publishers, The Hague, 1984.

—— *Means and Methods of Combat*, in: United Nations Educational, Scientific and Cultural Organization, *International Dimensions of Humanitarian Law*, Martinus Nijhoff Publishers, Dordrecht, 1988.

D Bodansky, *Legal Regulation of the Effects of Military Activity on the Environment*, Environmental Research of the Federal Ministry of the Environment, Nature Conservation and Nuclear Safety; Research Report 201 18 103; UBA—FB 000499—On Behalf of the Federal Environmental Agency, Erich Schmidt Verlag, Berlin, 2003.

SAJ Boelaert-Suominen, *Iraqi War Reparations and the Laws of War: a Discussion of the Current Work of the United Nations Compensation Commission with Specific Reference to Environmental Damage During Warfare*, Zeitschrift für öffentliches Recht, Vol 50, 1996.

—— *International Environmental Law and Naval War; The Effect of Marine Safety and Pollution Conventions During International Armed Conflict*, Newport Paper Number Fifteen, Naval War College Press, Newport, RI, 2000 Also through: <http://www.nwc.navy.mil/press/>.

L Boisson de Chazournes, P Sands (Eds), *International Law, the International Court of Justice and Nuclear Weapons*, Cambridge University Press, Cambridge, 1999.

M Bothe, *Commentary–1977 Geneva Protocol I Additional to the Geneva Conventions of 12 August 1949, and Relating to the protection of Victims of International Armed Conflicts*, in: N Ronzitti (Ed), *The Law of Naval Warfare; A Collection of Agreements and Documents with Commentaries*, Martinus Nijhoff Publishers, Dordrecht, 1988.

—— *Neutrality in Naval Warfare; What Is Left of Traditional International Law.*, in: AJM Delissen, GJ Tanja (Eds), *Humanitarian Law of Armed Conflict; Challenges*

Ahead; Essays in Honour of Frits Kalshoven, Martinus Nijhoff Publishers, Dordrecht, 1991.

—— *The Protection of the Environment in Times of Armed Conflict; Legal Rules, Uncertainty, Deficiencies, and Possible Developments*, German Yearbook of International Law, Vol 34, 1991.

—— *Environmental Destruction as a Method of Warfare; Do We Need New Law.*, Disarmament, Vol 15, 1992.

—— *Protection of the Environment in Times of Armed Conflict*, in: N Al-Nauimi, R Meese (Eds), *International Legal Issues Arising Under the United Nations Decade of International Law; Proceedings of the Qatar International Law Conference '94*, Martinus Nijhoff Publishers, The Hague, 1995.

—— *The Law of Neutrality*, in: D Fleck (Ed), *The Handbook of Humanitarian Law in Armed Conflicts*, Oxford University Press, Oxford, 1995.

—— *Criminal Responsibility for Environmental Damage in Times of Armed Conflict*, in: RJ Grunawalt, JE King, RS McClain (Eds), *Protection of the Environment during Armed Conflict*, International Law Studies 1996, Vol 69, Naval War College, Newport, RI, 1996.

—— *War and Environment*, in: R Bernhardt (Ed), *Encyclopaedia of Public International Law; Volume Four; Quirin, Ex Parte to Zones of Peace*, Elsevier, Amsterdam, 2000.

—— *War Crimes*, in: A Cassese, P Gaeta, JRWD Jones (Eds), *The Rome Statue of the International Criminal Court: A Commentary; Volume I*, Oxford University Press, Oxford, 2002.

M Bothe, KJ Partsch, WA Solf, *New Rules for Victims of Armed Conflicts; Commentary on the Two 1977 Protocols Additional to the Geneva Conventions of 1949*, Martinus Nijhoff Publishers, The Hague, 1982.

M Bothe, A Cassese, F Kalshoven, A Kiss, J Salmon, KR Simmonds, *Protection of the Environment in Times of Armed Conflict*, Report prepared upon request of the European Commission, SJ/110/85, Brussels, 1985.

A Bouvier, *Protection of the Natural Environment in Time of Armed Conflict*, International Review of the Red Cross, 1991.

H Briezeveld, L Mathot, *Scoop; Natuurkunde voor de Bovenbouw 5/6 VWO*, Wolters-Noordhoff, Groningen, 1991.

British Medical Association; Report of the British Medical Association's Board of Science and Education, *The Medical Effects of Nuclear War*, John Wiley & Sons, Chichester, 1983.

British Mission to Japan, *The Effects of the Atomic Bombs at Hiroshima and Nagasaki*, Report of the British Mission to Japan, His Majesty's Stationery Office, London, 1946.

I Brownlie, *Some Legal Aspects of the Use of Nuclear Weapons*, International and Comparative Law Quarterly, Vol 14, 1965.

—— *Principles of Public International Law*, Oxford University Press, Oxford, 2003.

T Buergenthal, HG Maier, *Public International Law; In a Nutshell*, West Publishing, St Paul, MN, 1990.

AL Bunker, *Protection of the Environment During Armed Conflict: One Gulf, Two Wars*, Review of European Community and international environmental law, Vol 13, 2004.

C

A Cassese, *International Law*, Oxford University Press, Oxford, 2001.

—— *Crimes against Humanity*, in: A Cassese, P Gaeta, JRWD Jones (Eds), *The Rome Statue of the International Criminal Court: A Commentary; Volume I*, Oxford University Press, Oxford, 2002.

—— *From Nuremberg to Rome: International Military Tribunals to the International Criminal Court*, in: A Cassese, P Gaeta, JRWD Jones (Eds), *The Rome Statue of the International Criminal Court: A Commentary; Volume I*, Oxford University Press, Oxford, 2002.

E Castrén, *The Present Law of War and Neutrality*, Suomalaisen Kirjallisuuden Seuran Kirjapainon Oy, Helsinki, 1954.

Chernobyl Forum, *Chernobyl's Legacy: Health, Environmental and Socio-Economic Impacts; and Recommendations to the Governments of Belarus, the Russian Federation and Ukraine*, September 2005; through: <http://wwwiaeaorg/>.

Chernobyl Forum, *Environmental Consequences of the Chernobyl Accident and Their Remediation: Twenty Years of Experience*, Report of the UN Chernobyl Forum Expert Group 'Environment' (EGE), August 2005; through: <http://wwwiaeaorg/>.

TB Cochran, WM Arkin, MM Hoenig, *Nuclear Weapons Databook; Volume I, US Nuclear Forces and Capabilities*, Ballinger Publishing Company, Cambridge, MA, 1984.

E Cody, *Chinese Rainmakers Competing for Clouds; Widespread Drought Leads to Regional Rivalries*, The Washington Post, 2 August 2004.

Collins Cobuild English Dictionary, HarperCollins Publishers, Glasgow, 1995.

Collins Dictionary, HarperCollins Publishers, Glasgow, 1998.

Committee for the Compilation of Materials on Damage Cause by the Atomic Bombs in Hiroshima and Nagasaki, *The Impact of the A-Bomb; Hiroshima and Nagasaki, 1945–85*, Iwanami Shoten, Tokyo, 1985.

Congress of the United States; Office of Technology Assessment, *The Effects of Nuclear War*, Allanheld, Osmun & Co Publishers, Inc, Montclair, NJ, 1980 Also published as M Riordan (Ed), *The Day after Midnight; The Effects of Nuclear War*, Cheshire Books, Palo Alto, CA, 1982.

J Crawford, *The International Law Commission's Articles on State Responsibility; Introduction, Text and Commentaries*, Cambridge University Press, Cambridge, 2002.

D

AW Dahl, *Environmental Destruction as a Method of Warfare; Environmental Destruction in War*, Disarmament, Vol 15, 1992.

CC van Dam, FHJ Mijnssen, AA van Velten (Eds), *Mr C Asser's Handleiding tot de Beoefening van het Nederlands Burgerlijk Recht; Volume 3—Goederenrecht; Band II—Zakelijke Rechten*, veertiende druk, Kluwer, Deventer, 2002.

J Dean, *The INF Treaty Negotiations*, in: Stockholm International Peace Research Institute, *SIPRI Yearbook 1988; World Armaments and Disarmament*, Oxford University Press, 1988.

G den Dekker, *The Law of Arms Control; International Supervision and Enforcement*, Martinus Nijhoff Publishers, The Hague, 2001.

J Delbrück, *War, Effects on Treaties*, in: R Bernhardt (Ed), *Encyclopaedia of Public International Law; Volume Four; Quirin, Ex Parte to Zones of Peace*, Elsevier, Amsterdam, 2000.

D van Delft, *Alles voor de Duitse bom*, NRC Handelsblad, 9–10 februari 2002.

—— *Broodje bom*, NRC Handelsblad, 19–20 maart 2005.

AJM Delissen, GJ Tanja (Eds), *Humanitarian Law of Armed Conflict; Challenges Ahead; Essays in Honour of Frits Kalshoven*, Martinus Nijhoff Publishers, Dordrecht, 1991.

R Desgagné, *The Prevention of Environmental Damage in Time of Armed Conflict: Proportionality and Precautionary Measures*, in: H Fischer, A McDonald (Eds), *Yearbook of International Humanitarian Law; Volume 3; 2000*, TMC Asser Press, The Hague, 2002.

I Detter, *The Law of War*, Cambridge University Press, Cambridge, 2000.

Y Dinstein, *Military Necessity*, in: R Bernhardt (Ed), *Encyclopaedia of Public International Law; Volume Three; Jan Mayen to Pueblo Incident*, Elsevier, Amsterdam, 1997.

—— *Neutrality in Sea Warfare*, in: R Bernhardt (Ed), *Encyclopaedia of Public International Law; Volume Three; Jan Mayen to Pueblo Incident*, Elsevier, Amsterdam, 1997.

—— *Protection of the Environment in International Armed Conflict*, in: JA Frowein, R Wolfrum (Eds), *Max Planck Yearbook of United Nations Law*, Vol 5, 2001, Kluwer Law International, The Hague, 2001

—— *War, Aggression and Self-Defence*, Cambridge University Press, Cambridge, 2001.

—— *The Conduct of Hostilities under the Law of International Armed Conflict*, Cambridge University Press, Cambridge, 2004.

M Dixon, *Textbook on International Law*, Blackstone Press, London, 2000.

K Dörmann, *Elements of War Crimes under the Rome Statute of the International Criminal Court; Sources and Commentary*, International Committee of the Red Cross, Cambridge University Press, Cambridge, 2004.

L Doswald-Beck, *International Humanitarian Law and the Advisory Opinion of the International Court of Justice on the Legality of the Threat or Use of Nuclear Weapons*, International Review of the Red Cross, 1997.

MA Drumbl, *Waging War against the World: the Need to Move from War Crimes to Environmental Crimes*, in: JE Austin, CE Bruch (Eds), *The Environmental Consequences of War*, Cambridge University Press, Cambridge, 2000.

MD Dupuis, JQ Heywood, MYF Sarko, *The Sixth Annual American Red Cross—Washington College of Law Conference on International Humanitarian Law: A Workshop on Customary International Law and the 1977 Protocols Additional to the 1949 Geneva Conventions*, American University Journal of International Law & Policy (currently American University International Law Review), Vol 2, 1987.

TN Dupuy, GM Hammerman (Eds), *A Documentary History of Arms Control and Disarmament*, TN Dupuy Associates, Dunn Loring, VA, 1973.

E

PR Ehrlich, J Harte, MA Harwell, PH Raven, C Sagan, GM Woodwell, J Berry, ES Ayensu, AH Ehrlich, T Eisner, SJ Gould, HD Grover, R Herrera, RM May, E Mayr, CP McKay, HA Mooney, N Myers, D Pimentel, JM Teal, *Long-Term Biological Consequences of Nuclear War*, Science, Vol 222, 1983.

J Engels, *Een cruciale wandeling*, Trouw, 3 januari 2002.

F

R Falk, *The Inadequacy of the Existing Legal Approach to Environmental Protection in Wartime*, in: JE Austin, CE Bruch (Eds), *The Environmental Consequences of War*, Cambridge University Press, Cambridge, 2000.

R Ferm, *Appendix 12B; Nuclear Explosions, 1945–98*, in: Stockholm International Peace Research Institute, *SIPRI Yearbook 1999; Armaments, Disarmament and International Security*, Oxford University Press, Oxford, 1999.

GG Fitzmaurice, *The Juridical Clauses of the Peace Treaties*, Recueil des Cours; Collected Courses of the Hague Academy of International Law Vol 73, 1948-II, Imprimeries Delmas, Bordeaux, 1950.

M Fitzmaurice, *The Practical Working of the Law of Treaties*, in: MD Evans, *International Law*, Oxford University Press, Oxford, 2003.

D Fleck, *Topical Approaches towards Developing the Laws of Armed Conflict at Sea*, in: AJM Delissen, GJ Tanja (Eds), *Humanitarian Law of Armed Conflict; Challenges Ahead; Essays in Honour of Frits Kalshoven*, Martinus Nijhoff Publishers, Dordrecht, 1991.

D Fleck (Ed), *The Handbook of Humanitarian Law in Armed Conflicts*, Oxford University Press, Oxford, 1995.

JPA François; Institut de Droit International, *L'égalité d'application des règles du droit de la guerre aux parties à un conflit armé (Quatrième Commission); 2 Rapport définitif*, Annuaire de l'Institut de Droit International, Vol 50-I, 1963, Bâle, Editions juridiques et sociologiques SA, Basel, 1963.

JA Frowein, *Potsdam Agreements on Germany (1945)*, in: R Bernhardt (Ed), *Encyclopaedia of Public International Law; Volume Three; Jan Mayen to Pueblo Incident*, Elsevier, Amsterdam, 1997.

G

E Gail de Planque, *The Mururoa Study; International Study of the Radiological Situation at the Atolls of Mururoa and Fangataufa*, IAEA Bulletin, Vol 40(4), 1998.

J Gardam, *Necessity and Proportionality in Jus ad Bellum and Jus in Bello*, in: L Boisson de Chazournes, P Sands (Eds), *International Law, the International Court of Justice and Nuclear Weapons*, Cambridge University Press, Cambridge, 1999

H-P Gasser, *For Better Protection of the Natural Environment in Armed Conflict: A Proposal for Action*, The American Journal of International Law, Vol 89, 1995.

—— *Guidelines for Military Manuals and Instructions on the Protection of the Environment in Times of Armed Conflict*, International Review of the Red Cross, 1996.

A Gattini, *The UN Compensation Commission: Old Rules, New Procedures on War Reparations*, European Journal of International Law, Vol 13, 2002.

G Geerts, T den Boon (*et al*) (Eds), *Van Dale; Groot Woordenboek der Nederlandse Taal*, Van Dale Lexicografie, Utrecht, 1999.

T Gill, *The Nuclear Weapons Advisory Opinion of the International Court of Justice and the Fundamental Distinction Between the Ius ad Bellum and the Ius in Bello*, Leiden Journal of International Law, Vol 12, 1999.

S Glasstone, PJ Dolan (Eds), *The Effects of Nuclear Weapons*, US Department of Defense and the US Department of Energy, Washington, DC, 1977.

J Goldblat, *Legal Protection of the Environment against the Effects of Military Activities*, Bulletin of Peace Proposals, Vol 22, 1991.

—— *Arms Control; The New Guide to Negotiations and Agreements*, International Peace Research Institute, Oslo; Stockholm International Peace Research Institute; SAGE Publications, London, 2002.

CS Grace, *Nuclear Weapons; Principles, Effects and Survivability*, Brassey's, London, 1994.

LC Green, *The Environment and the Law of Conventional Warfare*, The Canadian Yearbook of International Law, Vol 29, 1991.

LC Green, *What One May Do in Combat—Then and Now*, in: AJM Delissen, GJ Tanja (Eds), *Humanitarian Law of Armed Conflict; Challenges Ahead; Essays in Honour of Frits Kalshoven*, Martinus Nijhoff Publishers, Dordrecht, 1991.

—— *The Contemporary Law of Armed Conflict*, Manchester University Press, Manchester, 2000.

C Greenwood, *The relationship between ius ad bellum and ius in bello*, Review of International Studies, Vol 9, 1983.

—— *The Twilight of the Law of Belligerent Reprisals*, Netherlands Yearbook of International Law, Vol 20, 1989.

—— *Customary Law Status of the 1977 Geneva Protocols*, in: AJM Delissen, GJ Tanja (Eds), *Humanitarian Law of Armed Conflict; Challenges Ahead; Essays in Honour of Frits Kalshoven*, Martinus Nijhoff Publishers, Dordrecht, 1991.

—— *Historical Development and Legal Basis*, in: D Fleck (Ed), *The Handbook of Humanitarian Law in Armed Conflicts*, Oxford University Press, Oxford, 1995.

—— *Scope of Application of Humanitarian Law*, in: D Fleck (Ed), *The Handbook of Humanitarian Law in Armed Conflicts*, Oxford University Press, Oxford, 1995.

—— *State Responsibility and Civil Liability for Environmental Damage Caused by Military Operations*, in: RJ Grunawalt, JE King, RS McClain (Eds), *Protection of the Environment during Armed Conflict*, International Law Studies 1996, Vol 69, Naval War College, Newport, RI, 1996.

—— *International Humanitarian Law (Laws of War); Revised Report for the Centennial Commemoration of the First Hague Peace Conference 1899*, London School of Economics and Political Science, London, 1999.

—— *Jus ad bellum and Jus in Bello in the Nuclear Weapons Advisory Opinion*, in: L Boisson de Chazournes, P Sands (Eds), *International Law, the International Court of Justice and Nuclear Weapons*, Cambridge University Press, Cambridge, 1999.

H Grotius, *De Iure Belli ac Pacis*, The Classics of International Law, Clarendon Press, Oxford, 1925.

AJ Grotto, *Nuclear Bunker Busters and Article VI of the Non-Proliferation Treaty*, ASIL Insights, February 2005.

LG Groves, *Now It Can Be Told; The Story of the Manhattan Project*, Andre Deutsch Publishers, London, 1963.

P Guggenheim, *L'origine de la notion de l'«opinio juris sive necessitatis» comme deuxième élément de la coutume dans l'histoire du droit des gens*, in: H Accioly (*et al*), *Hommage d'une Génération de Juristes au Président Basdevant*, Éditions A Pedone, Paris, 1960.

S Gupta, *Iraq's Environmental Warfare in the Persian Gulf*, Georgetown International Environmental Law Review, Vol 6, 1993.

LD Guruswamy, BR Hendricks, *International Environmental Law in a Nutshell*, West Publishing, St Paul, MN, 1997.

H

DJ Harris, *Cases and Materials on International Law*, Sweet & Maxwell, London, 2004.

GJF van Hegelsom, *Comments*, in: IF Dekker, HHG Post (Eds), *The Gulf War of 1980–1988*, Martinus Nijhoff Publishers, Dordrecht, 1992.

W Heintschel von Heinegg, *The Law of Armed Conflict at Sea*, in: D Fleck (Ed), *The Handbook of Humanitarian Law in Armed Conflicts*, Oxford University Press, Oxford, 1995.

W Heintschel von Heinegg, M Donner, *New Developments in the Protection of the Natural Environment in Naval Armed Conflicts*, German Yearbook of International Law, Vol 37, 1994.

J-M Henckaerts, *International Legal Mechanisms for Determining Liability for Environmental Damage under International Humanitarian Law*, in: JE Austin, CE Bruch (Eds), *The Environmental Consequences of War*, Cambridge University Press, Cambridge, 2000.

—— *Towards Better Protection for the Environment in Armed Conflict: Recent Developments in International Humanitarian Law*, Review of European Community and international environmental law, Vol 9, 2000.

—— *Study on customary international law: A contribution to the understanding and respect for the rule of law in armed conflict*, International Review of the Red Cross, Vol 87, 2005.

J-M Henckaerts, L Doswald-Beck (Eds), *Customary International Humanitarian Law; Volume I: Rules*, International Committee of the Red Cross, Cambridge University Press, Cambridge, 2005.

—— *Customary International Humanitarian Law; Volume II: Practice; Part 1*, International Committee of the Red Cross, Cambridge University Press, Cambridge, 2005.

LJ van den Herik, *The Contribution of the Rwanda Tribunal to the Development of International Law*, Martinus Nijhoff Publishers, Leiden, 2005.

K Herndl, *The Lotus*, in: R Bernhardt (Ed), *Encyclopaedia of Public International Law; Volume Three; Jan Mayen to Pueblo Incident*, Elsevier, Amsterdam, 1997.

Herodotus, *Het verslag van mijn onderzoek*, Vertaling HL van Dolen, SUN, Nijmegen, 2000.

FAF von der Heydte, *Air Warfare*, in: R Bernhardt (Ed), *Encyclopaedia of Public International Law; Volume One; Aalands Islands to Dumbarton Oaks Conference (1944)*, North-Holland Publishing Company, Amsterdam, 1992.

EMH Hirsch Ballin, *Nucleaire Wapens in het Internationale Recht*, Ars Aequi, Vol 46, 1997.

JO Hirschfelder, *Scientific-Technological Miracle at Los Alamos*, in: L Badash, JO Hirschfelder, HP Broida (Eds), *Reminiscences of Los Alamos 1943–1945*, D Reidel Publishing Company, Dordrecht, 1980.

PE Hodgson, *Nuclear Physics in Peace and War*, Hawthorn Books Publishers, New York, NY, 1963.

D Holdstock, L Waterston, *Nuclear weapons, a continuing threat to health*, The Lancet, Vol 355, 2000.

AJJ de Hoogh, *Comments*, in: HHG Post (Ed), *International Economic Law and Armed Conflict*, Martinus Nijhoff, Dordrecht, 1994.

—— *Obligations Erga Omnes and International Crimes; A Theoretical Inquiry into the Implementation and Enforcement of the International Responsibility of States*, Kluwer Law International, The Hague, 1996.
—— *Commentary*, in: A Klip, G Sluiter (Eds), *Annotated Leading Cases of International Criminal Tribunals; Volume VII: The International Criminal Tribunal for the Former Yugoslavia 2001*, Intersentia, Antwerp, 2005.
K Hulme, *War Torn Environment: Interpreting the Legal Threshold*, Martinus Nijhoff Publishers, Leiden, 2004.

I

M Imaizumi (*et al*), *Radiation Dose-Response Relationships for Thyroid Nodules and Autoimmune Thyroid Diseases in Hiroshima and Nagasaki Atomic Bomb Survivors 55–58 Years After Radiation Exposure*, Journal of the American Medical Association, Vol 295, 2006, No 9, 1 March 2006.
International Atomic Energy Agency, *Features: Depleted Uranium* At: <http://www.iaea.org/NewsCenter/Features/DU/du_qaa.shtml>.
International Committee of the Red Cross, *Draft Additional Protocols to the Geneva Conventions of August 12, 1949; Commentary*, ICRC, Geneva, 1973.
International Council of Scientific Unions; Scientific Committee on Problems of the Environment 28; AB Pittock, TP Ackerman, PJ Crutzen, MC MacCracken, CS Shapiro, RP Turco, *Environmental Consequences of Nuclear War; Volume I: Physical and Atmospheric Effects*, John Wiley & Sons, Chichester, 1986.
International Council of Scientific Unions; Scientific Committee on Problems of the Environment 28; MA Harwell, TC Hutchinson (Eds), *Environmental Consequences of Nuclear War; Volume II: Ecological and Agricultural Effects*, John Wiley & Sons, Chichester, 1985.
International Criminal Tribunal for the Former Yugoslavia (ICTY), *Final Report to the Prosecutor by the Committee Established to Review the NATO Bombing Campaign against the Federal Republic of Yugoslavia*, International Legal Materials, Vol 39, 2000.

J

Flavius Josephus, *De Oude Geschiedenis van de Joden (Antiquitates Judaicae)*, Vertaling FJAM Meijer, MA Wes, Ambo, Amsterdam, 2005.
L Juda, *Negotiating a treaty on environmental modification warfare: the convention on environmental warfare and its impact upon arms control negotiations*, International Organization, Vol 32, 1978.
R Jungk, *Brighter than a Thousand Suns*, Grove Press, Inc, New York, NY, 1958.

K

F Kalshoven, *Belligerent Reprisals*, AW Sijthoff, Leiden, 1971.
—— *The Conference of Government Experts on the Use of Certain Conventional Weapons, Lucerne, 24 September–18 October 1974*, Netherlands Yearbook of International Law, Vol 6, 1975.
—— *The Conference of Government Experts on the Use of Certain Conventional Weapons, Second Session, Lugano, 28 January–26 February 1976*, Netherlands Yearbook of International Law, Vol 7, 1976.

F Kalshoven, *Reaffirmation and Development of International Humanitarian Law Applicable in Armed Conflicts: The Diplomatic Conference, Geneva, 1974–1977; Part I*, Netherlands Yearbook of International Law, Vol 8, 1977.

—— *Reaffirmation and Development of International Humanitarian Law Applicable in Armed Conflicts: the Diplomatic Conference, Geneva, 1974–1977; Part II*, Netherlands Yearbook of International Law, Vol 9, 1978.

—— *Arms, Armaments and International Law*, Recueil des Cours; Collected Courses of the Hague Academy of International Law, Vol 191, 1985-II, Martinus Nijhoff Publishers, Dordrecht, 1986.

—— *Prohibitions or restrictions on the use of methods and means of warfare*, in: IF Dekker, HHG Post (Eds), *The Gulf War of 1980–1988*, Martinus Nijhoff Publishers, Dordrecht, 1992.

—— *War, Laws of*, in: R Bernhardt (Ed), *Encyclopaedia of Public International Law; Volume Four; Quirin, Ex Parte to Zones of Peace*, Elsevier, Amsterdam, 2000.

F Kalshoven, L Zegveld, *Constraints on the Waging of War; An Introduction to International Humanitarian Law*, International Committee of the Red Cross, Geneva, 2001.

SN Kile, *Nuclear arms control and non-proliferation*, in: Stockholm International Peace Research Institute, *SIPRI Yearbook 2005; Armaments, Disarmament and International Security*, Oxford University Press, Oxford, 2005.

SN Kile, HM Kristensen, *Appendix 12A World nuclear forces 2005*, in: Stockholm International Peace Research Institute, *SIPRI Yearbook 2005; Armaments, Disarmament and International Security*, Oxford University Press, Oxford, 2005.

DG Kimball, *Nuclear Bunker-Buster (As We Know It) is Dead*, though: <http://www.armscontrol.org/>.

RJB King, *Cancer Biology*, Pearson Education, Harlow, 2000.

A Kirchner, *Environmental Protection in Time of Armed Conflict*, European Environmental Law Review, 2000.

A Kiss, D Shelton, *International Environmental Law*, Transnational Publishers, Ardsley, NY, 2000.

GB Kistiakowsky, *Reminiscences of Wartime Los Alamos*, in: L Badash, JO Hirschfelder, HP Broida (Eds), *Reminiscences of Los Alamos 1943–1945*, D Reidel Publishing Company, Dordrecht, 1980.

E Klein, *International Régimes*, in: R Bernhardt (Ed), *Encyclopedia of Public International Law; Volume Two; East African Community to Italy-United States Air Transport Arbitration (1965)*, North-Holland Publishing Company, Amsterdam, 1995.

K Knip, *Mininukes*, NRC Handelsblad, 31 mei–1 juni 2003.

R Kolb, *Origin of the twin terms jus ad bellum/jus in bello*, International Review of the Red Cross, 1997.

P Kooijmans, *De Kernwapens en het Volkenrecht*, AR Staatkunde, Vol 80, 1980.

M Koskenniemi, *Fragmentation of International Law*, Outline for Study Group, International Law Commission, 55th session, 2003 At: <http://www.un.org/law/ilc/sessions/55/55sess.htm>.

DS Kothari (*et al*), *Nuclear Explosions and Their Effects*, The Publications Division, Ministry of Information and Broadcasting, New Delhi, 1958.

H Krane, *Introductory Nuclear Physics*, John Wiley & Sons, New York, NY, 1988.

L

H Lauterpacht, *The Limits of the Operation of the Law of War*, The British Year Book of International Law, Vol 30, 1953.

The Lawyers Committee on Nuclear Policy, *Statement on the Illegality of Nuclear Weapons*, Nederlands Juristenblad, Vol 59, 1984.

R Lemkin, *Axis Rule in Occupied Europe; Laws of Occupation—Analysis of Government—Proposals for Redress*, Carnegie Endowment for International Peace, Washington, DC, 1944.

HS Levie, *Protection of War Victims: Protocol 1 to the 1949 Geneva Conventions; Volume 2*, Oceana Publications, Dobbs Ferry, NY, 1980.

—— *Protection of War Victims: Protocol 1 to the 1949 Geneva Conventions; Volume 3*, Oceana Publications, Dobbs Ferry, NY, 1980.

L Lijnzaad, GJ Tanja, *Protection of the Environment in Times of Armed Conflict: The Iraq-Kuwait War*, Netherlands International Law Review, Vol 40, 1993.

L Low, D Hodgkinson, *Compensation for Wartime Environmental Damage: Challenges to International Law After the Gulf War*, Virginia Journal of International Law, Vol 35, 1995

M

P Macalister-Smith, *Western European Union*, in: R Bernhardt (Ed), *Encyclopaedia of Public International Law; Volume Four; Quirin, Ex Parte to Zones of Peace*, Elsevier, Amsterdam, 2000.

KJ Madders, *Neutrality in Air Warfare*, in: R Bernhardt (Ed), *Encyclopaedia of Public International Law; Volume Three; Jan Mayen to Pueblo Incident*, Elsevier, Amsterdam, 1997.

P Malanczuk, *Akehurst's Modern Introduction to International Law*, Routledge, London, 1997.

JH Manley, *A New Laboratory Is Born*, in: L Badash, JO Hirschfelder, HP Broida (Eds), *Reminiscences of Los Alamos 1943–1945*, D Reidel Publishing Company, Dordrecht, 1980.

T Marauhn, *Environmental Damage in Times of Armed Conflict—not 'really' a Matter of Criminal Responsibility.*, International Review of the Red Cross, 2000.

E Margolis, *The Hydrogen Bomb Experiments and International Law*, The Yale Law Journal, Vol 64, 1955.

A McDonald, *The International Legality of Depleted Uranium Weapons*, Background paper for presentation on 'The International legal ramifications of the use of DU weapons', Symposium on The Health Impact of Deplete Uranium Munitions, held at the New York Academy of Medicine, 14 June 2003, through <http://www.nuclearpolicy.org/DUSymposium.html>.

AD McNair, *The Law of Treaties*, Clarendon Press, Oxford, 1961.

LW McNaught, *Nuclear Weapons and Their Effects*, Brassey's Defence Publishers, London, 1984.

JH McNeill, *Protection of the Environment in Times of Armed Conflict: Environmental Protection in Military Practice*, Hague Yearbook of International Law, Vol 6, 1993.

EL Meyrowitz, *The Prohibition of Nuclear Weapons: The Relevance of International Law*, Transnational Publishers, Dobbs Ferry, NY, 1990.

FHJ Mijnssen, P de Haan (Eds), *Mr C Asser's Handleiding tot de Beoefening van het Nederlands Burgerlijk Recht; Volume 3—Goederenrecht; Band I—Algemeen Goederenrecht*, veertiende druk, WEJ Tjeenk Willink, Deventer, 2001.

AS Miller, M Feinrider (Eds), *Nuclear Weapons and Law*, Greenwood Press, Westport, CT, 1984.

G Molier, *De (on)rechtmatigheid van humanitaire interventie; Respect voor staatssoevereiniteit versus bescherming van mensenrechten.*, Boom Juridische uitgevers, Den Haag, 2003.

D Momtaz, *La Recours à l'Arme Nucléaire et la Protection de l'Environnement: l'Apport de la Cour Internationale de Justice*, in: L Boisson de Chazournes, P Sands (Eds), *International Law, the International Court of Justice and Nuclear Weapons*, Cambridge University Press, Cambridge, 1999.

V Morris, *Protection of the Environment in Wartime: The United Nations General Assembly Considers the Need for a New Convention*, International Lawyer, Vol 27, 1993.

E Mourlon-Druol, *Smaller, but smarter. The Robust Nuclear Earth Penetrator (RNEP), the Bush administration and the second nuclear age*, Bofaxe No 257E, 25 August 2003 Through: <http://www.ruhr-uni-bochum.de/ifhv/publications/bofaxe/>.

R Müllerson, *On the Relationship between Jus ad Bellum and Jus in Bello in the General Assembly Advisory Opinion*, in: L Boisson de Chazournes, P Sands (Eds), *International Law, the International Court of Justice and Nuclear Weapons*, Cambridge University Press, Cambridge, 1999.

N

VP Nanda, D Krieger, *Nuclear Weapons and the World Court*, Transnational Publishers, Ardsley, NY, 1998.

FA Nelissen, *Scheepswrakken en wrakke schepen; Een volkenrechtelijke beschouwing vanuit milieu-perspectief*, TMC Asser Instituut, Den Haag, 1997.

JL Nogee, *Soviet Policy Towards International Control of Atomic Energy*, University of Notre Dame Press, Notre Dame, IN, 1961.

A Nollkaemper, *De dialectiek tussen individuele en collectieve aansprakelijkheid in het volkenrecht*, Inaugural lecture, Vossiuspers AUP, Amsterdam, 2000.

RS Norris, WM Arkin, *NRDC Nuclear Notebook; Known Nuclear Tests Worldwide, 1945–98*, Bulletin of the Atomic Scientists, Vol 54(6), 1998.

—— *Appendix 8A; Tables of Nuclear Forces*, in: Stockholm International Peace Research Institute, *SIPRI Yearbook 2000; Armaments, Disarmament and International Security*, Oxford University Press, Oxford, 2000.

O

S Oeter, *Methods and Means of Combat*, in: D Fleck (Ed), *The Handbook of Humanitarian Law in Armed Conflicts*, Oxford University Press, Oxford, 1995.

T Ohkita, J Rotblat, *Biological Effects of Nuclear War; Acute Effects of Radiation; The LD-50 Value*, in: World Health Organization; Report of the WHO Management Group on Follow-up of resolution WHA3628: 'The Role of Physicians and Other Health Workers in the Preservation and Promotion of Peace . . .', *Effects of Nuclear War on Health and Health Services*, World Health Organization, Geneva, 1987.

JR Oppenheimer, *The New Weapon: The turn of the Screw*, in: D Masters, K Way (Eds), *One World or None: A Report to the Public on the Full Meaning of the Atomic Bomb*, McGraw-Hill, New York, 1946.

P

KJ Partsch, *Armed Conflict, Fundamental Rules*, in: R Bernhardt (Ed), *Encyclopedia of Public International Law; Volume Two; East African Community to Italy-United States Air Transport Arbitration (1965)*, North-Holland Publishing Company, Amsterdam, 1995.

—— *Humanitarian Law and Armed Conflict*, in: R Bernhardt (Ed), *Encyclopedia of Public International Law; Volume Two; East African Community to Italy-United States Air Transport Arbitration (1965)*, North-Holland Publishing Company, Amsterdam, 1995.

—— *Armed Conflict*, in: R Bernhardt (Ed), *Encyclopedia of Public International Law; Volume One; Aalands Islands to Dumbarton Oaks Conference (1944)*, North-Holland Publishing Company, Amsterdam, 1992.

D Pfirter, *Article 8(2)(b)(iv)—Excessive Incidental Death, Injury or Damage*, in: RS Lee (Ed), *The International Criminal Court; Elements of Crimes and Rules of Procedure and Evidence*, Transnational Publishers, Ardsley, NY, 2001.

JS Pictet (Ed), *The Geneva Conventions of 12 August 1949; Commentary; Volume I—Geneva Convention for the Amelioration of the Condition of the Wounded and Sick in Armed Forces in the Field*, International Committee of the Red Cross, Geneva, 1952.

G Plant (Ed), *Environmental Protection and the Law of War; A 'Fifth Geneva' Convention on the Protection of the Environment in Time of Armed Conflict*, Belhaven Press, London, 1992.

HHG Post, *Some Curiosities in the Sources of the Law of Armed Conflict Conceived in a General International Legal Perspective*, Netherlands Yearbook of International Law, Vol 25, 1994.

—— *The Role of State Practice in the Formation of Customary International Humanitarian Law*, in: IF Dekker, HHG Post (Eds), *On the Foundations and Sources of International Law*, TMC Asser Press, The Hague, 2003.

—— *War Crimes in Air Warfare*, in: N Ronzitti, G Venturini (Eds), *The Law of Air Warfare—Contemporary Issues*, Eleven International Publishing, Utrecht, 2006.

S Power, *A Problem from Hell; America and the Age of Genocide*, Perennial, New York, NY, 2003.

R Provost, *International Human Rights and Humanitarian Law*, Cambridge University Press, Cambridge, 2002.

Q

N Quénivet, *The right to claim compensation for violations of international humanitarian law: The German judgment on the Varvarin bridge*, Bofaxe No 267E, 27 December 2003 Through: <http://www.ruhr-uni-bochum.de/ifhv/publications/bofaxe/>.

JP Quinn, RT Evans, MJ Boock, *United States Navy Development of Operation-Environmental Doctrine*, in: JE Austin, CE Bruch (Eds), *The Environmental Consequences of War*, Cambridge University Press, Cambridge, 2000.

R

A Randelzhofer, *Article 2(4)*, in: B Simma (Ed), *The Charter of the United Nations; A Commentary*, Oxford University Press, Oxford, 2002.

E Rauch, *The Protocol Additional to the Geneva Conventions for the Protection of Victims of International Armed Conflicts and the United Nations Convention on the Law of the Sea: Repercussions on the Law of Naval Warfare; Report to the Committee for the Protection of Human Life in Armed Conflict of the International Society for Military Law and Law of War*, Duncker & Humblot, Berlin, 1984.

D Rauschning, *Nuclear Warfare and Weapons*, in: R Bernhardt (Ed), *Encyclopaedia of Public International Law; Volume Three; Jan Mayen to Pueblo Incident*, Elsevier, Amsterdam, 1997.

H-K Ress, *Nuclear Energy, Peaceful Uses*, in: R Bernhardt (Ed), *Encyclopaedia of Public International Law; Volume Three; Jan Mayen to Pueblo Incident*, Elsevier, Amsterdam, 1997.

R Rhodes, *The Making of the Atomic Bomb*, Simon and Schuster, New York, NY, 1986.

LN Ridenour, *There is no Defense*, in: D Masters, K Way (Eds), *One World or None: A Report to the Public on the Full Meaning of the Atomic Bomb*, McGraw-Hill, New York, 1946.

A Roberts, *Environmental Issues in International Armed Conflict: The Experience of the 1991 Gulf War*, in: RJ Grunawalt, JE King, RS McClain (Eds), *Protection of the Environment during Armed Conflict*, International Law Studies 1996, Vol 69, Naval War College, Newport, RI, 1996

—— *The Law of War and Environmental Damage*, in: JE Austin, CE Bruch (Eds), *The Environmental Consequences of War*, Cambridge University Press, Cambridge, 2000.

A Roberts, R Guelff, *Documents on the Laws of War*, Oxford University Press, Oxford, 2000.

APV Rogers, *Law on the Battlefield*, Manchester University Press, Manchester, 2004.

APV Rogers, P Malherbe, *Fight it Right; Model Manual on the Law of Armed Conflict for Armed Forces*, International Committee of the Red Cross, ICRC, Geneva, 1999.

BVA Röling, *International Law in an Expanded World*, Djambatan, Amsterdam, 1960.

—— *Inleiding tot de wetenschap van oorlog en vrede*, Van Gorcum, Assen, 1968.

—— *Volkenrecht en Vrede*, Kluwer, Deventer, 1985.

—— *The Concept of Security and the Function of National Armed Power*, in: A Cassese (Ed), *The Current Legal Regulation of the Use of Force*, Martinus Nijhoff Publishers, Dordrecht, 1986.

BVA Röling, O Sukovic, *The Law of War and Dubious Weapons*, Stockholm International Peace Research Institute, Almqvist & Wiksell International, Stockholm, 1976.

BVA Röling, CF Rüter, *The Tokyo Judgment; The International Military Tribunal for the Far East (IMTFE) 29 April 1946–12 November 1948; Volume I*, University Press Amsterdam, Amsterdam 1977.

J Rotblat, *Nuclear Radiation in Warfare*, Stockholm International Peace Research Institute, Taylor & Francis, London, 1981.

—— *Leaving the bomb project*, Bulletin of the Atomic Scientists, August 1985.

The Royal Society of Canada; Report of the Committee on the Environmental Consequences of Nuclear War, *Nuclear Winter and Associated Effects; A Canadian Appraisal of the Environmental Impact of Nuclear War*, The Royal Society of Canada, Ottawa, Ontario, 1985.

S

Y Sandoz, C Swinaraski, B Zimmerman (Eds), *Commentary on the Additional Protocols; of 8 June 1977 to the Geneva Conventions of 12 August 1949*, International Committee of the Red Cross, Martinus Nijhoff Publishers, Geneva, 1987 The Commentary is also available through <http://www.icrc.org/>.

P Sands, *Principles of international environmental law; Volume I; Frameworks, standards and implementation*, Cambridge University Press, Cambridge, 2003.

BK Schafer, *The Relationship between the International Laws of Armed Conflict and Environmental Protection: The Need to Reevaluate what Types of Conduct are Permissible during Hostilities*, California Western International Law Journal, Vol 19, 1989.

D Schindler, *Transformations in the Law of Neutrality Since 1945*, in: AJM Delissen, GJ Tanja (Eds), *Humanitarian Law of Armed Conflict; Challenges Ahead; Essays in Honour of Frits Kalshoven*, Martinus Nijhoff Publishers, Dordrecht, 1991.

D Schindler, J Toman (Eds), *The Laws of Armed Conflicts; A Collection of Conventions, Resolutions and Other Documents*, Martinus Nijhoff Publishers, Dordrecht, 1988.

MN Schmitt, *Green War: An Assessment of the Environmental Law of International Armed Conflict*, Yale Journal of International Law, Vol 22, 1997.

—— *Humanitarian Law and the Environment*, Denver Journal of International Law and Policy, Vol 28, 2000.

—— *War and the Environment: Fault Lines in the Prescriptive Landscape*, in: JE Austin, CE Bruch (Eds), *The Environmental Consequences of War*, Cambridge University Press, Cambridge, 2000.

N Schrijver, *Sovereignty over Natural Resources: Balancing Rights and Duties in an Interdependent World*, Doctoral Thesis, University of Groningen, 1995.

—— *Sovereignty over Natural Resources: Balancing Rights and Duties*, Cambridge University Press, Cambridge, 1997.

—— *Article 2; Paragraphe 4*, in: J-P Cot, A Pellet (Eds), *La Charte des Nations Unies; Commentaire article par article; Vol I*, Economica, Paris, 2005.

—— *Challenges to the Prohibition to Use Force: Does the Straitjacket of Article 2(4) UN Charter Begin to Gall too Much.*, in: N Blokker, N Schrijver (Eds), *The Security Council and the Use of Force; Theory and Reality—A Need for Change.*, Martinus Nijhoff Publishers, Leiden, 2005.

G Schwarzenberger, *The Legality of Nuclear Weapons*, Stevens & Sons, London, 1958.

—— *International Law; As Applied by International Courts and Tribunals; Volume II; The Law of Armed Conflict*, Stevens & Sons, London, 1968.

GT Seaborg, *A Chemist in the White House; From the Manhattan Project to the End of the Cold War*, The American Chemical Society, Washington, DC, 1998.

F Seitz, H Bethe, *How Close is the Danger*, in: D Masters, K Way (Eds), *One World or None: A Report to the Public on the Full Meaning of the Atomic Bomb*, McGraw-Hill, New York, 1946.

R Serber, *The Los Alamos Primer; The First Lectures on How to Build an Atomic Bomb*, University of California Press, Berkeley, 1992.

MN Shaw, *International Law*, Cambridge University Press, Cambridge, 2003.

SN Simonds, *Conventional Warfare and Environmental Protection: A Proposal for International Legal Reform*, Stanford Journal of International Law, Vol 29, 1992.

JN Singh, *Nuclear or Thermonuclear World War; Any Legal Justification.*, Harnam Publications, New Delhi, 1982.

N Singh, E McWhinney, *Nuclear Weapons and Contemporary International Law*, Martinus Nijhoff Publishers, Dordrecht, 1989.

HD Smyth, *Atomic Energy; A General Account of the Development of Methods of Using Atomic Energy for Military Purposes under the Auspices of the United States Government 1940–1945*, US Government Printing Office, Washington, DC; His Majesty's Stationary Office, London, 1945.

AD Sofaer, *The Rationale for the United States Decision*, The American Journal of International Law, Vol 82, 1988.

WA Solf, *Protection of Civilians Against the Effects of Hostilities under Customary International Law and Under Protocol I*, American University Journal of International Law & Policy, Vol 1, 1986.

H Spieker, *Völkergewohnheitsrechtlicher Schutz der Natürlichen Umwelt im internationalen bewaffneten Konflikt; Waffenwirkung und Umwelt I*, Universitätsverlag Brockmeyer, Bochum, 1992.

P Stegnar, *Review at Bikini Atoll; Assessing Radiological Conditions at Bikini Atoll and the Prospects for Resettlement*, IAEA Bulletin, Vol 40(4), 1998.

P Stegnar, T Wrixon, *Semipalatinsk Revisited; Radiological Evaluation of the Former Nuclear Test Site*, IAEA Bulletin, Vol 40(4), 1998.

CD Stone, *The Environment in Wartime: An Overview*, in: JE Austin, CE Bruch (Eds), *The Environmental Consequences of War*, Cambridge University Press, Cambridge, 2000.

L Strikwerda, *Inleiding tot het Nederlandse internationaal privaatrecht*, Wolters-Noordhoff, Groningen, 1997.

PC Szasz, *Study of and Proposals for Improvements to Existing Legal Instruments Relating to the Environment and Armed Conflicts*, draft article 21 June 1991; Conference on the use of the environment as a tool of conventional warfare, Ottawa, 1991, not published.

—— *Environmental Destruction as a Method of Warfare; International Law Applicable to the Gulf War*, Disarmament, Vol 15, 1992.

T

RG Tarasofsky, *Legal Protection of the Environment during International Armed Conflict*, Netherlands Yearbook of International Law, Vol 24, 1993.

H Thirlway, *The Sources of International Law*, in: MD Evans, *International Law*, Oxford University Press, Oxford, 2003.

C Tomuschat, *Crimes Against the Environment*, Environmental Policy & Law, Vol 26, 1996.

O Triffterer (Ed), *Commentary on the Rome Statute of the International Criminal Court; Observers' Notes, Article by Article*, Nomos Verlagsgesellschaft, Baden-Baden, 1999.

A Tucker, J Gleisner, *Crucible Despair: The Effects of Nuclear War*, The Menard Press, London, 1982.

RP Turco, OB Toon, TP Ackerman, JP Pollack, C Sagan, *Nuclear Winter: Global Consequences of Multiple Nuclear Explosions*, Science, Volume 222, 1983.

U

United Nations Organization; UN Department of Disarmament Affairs; Report of the Secretary-General, *Nuclear Weapons: A Comprehensive Study*, United Nations Publication, New York, NY, 1991.

United Nations Organization; UN Department of Disarmament Affairs; Report of the Secretary-General, *Study on the Climatic and Other Global Effects of Nuclear War*, United Nations Publication, New York, NY, 1989.

United Nations Scientific Committee on the Effects of Atomic Radiation, *UNSCEAR 2001 Report; Annex Hereditary effects of radiation*, through: <http://www.unscear.org/>.

United Nations War Crimes Commission, *History of the United Nations War Crimes Commission and the Development of the Laws of War*, His Majesty's Stationary Office, London, 1948.

United States Arms Control and Disarmament Agency, *Arms control and Disarmament Agreements; Texts and Histories of the Negotiations*, US Government Printing Office, Washington, DC, 1996.

United States Department of Defense, *Conduct of the Persian Gulf War; Final Report to Congress; Pursuant to Title V of the Persian Gulf Conflict Supplemental Authorization and Personnel Benefits Act of 1991 (Public Law 102–25)*, US Government Printing Office, Washington, DC, 1992 Also published as United States Department of Defense, *Report to Congress on the Conduct of the Persian Gulf War—Appendix on the Role of the law of War*, in: International Legal Materials, Vol 31, 1992.

United States Strategic Bombing Survey, *The Effects of the Atomic bombs on Hiroshima and Nagasaki*, Chairman's Office, 30 June 1946; United States Government Printing Office, Washington, DC, 1946.

V

WD Verwey, *Chemical Warfare in Vietnam: Legal or Illegal.*, Netherlands International Law Review, Vol 18, 1971.

—— *Riot Control Agents and Herbicides in War; Their Humanitarian, Toxicological, Ecological, Military, Polemological, and Legal Aspects*, AW Sijthoff, Leyden, 1977.

—— *Bert VA Röling; 1906–1985*, TMC Asser Instituut, The Hague, 1985.

—— *Humanitarian Intervention under International Law*, Netherlands International Law Review, Vol 32, 1985.

—— *Observations on the Legal Protection of the Environment in Times of International Armed Conflict*, Hague Yearbook of International Law, Vol 7, 1994.

—— *Protection of the Environment in Times of Armed Conflict: In Search of a New Legal Perspective*, Leiden Journal of International Law, Vol 8, 1995.

—— *Comment: Protection of the Environment in Times of Armed Conflict—Do We Need Additional Rules.*, in: RJ Grunawalt, JE King, RS McClain (Eds), *Protection of the Environment during Armed Conflict*, International Law Studies 1996, Vol 69, Naval War College, Newport, RI, 1996.

WD Verwey, *De rechtmatigheid van kernwapens: het Hof in dilemma*, VN Forum, Vol 9, 1996.

——*The International Court of Justice and the Legality of Nuclear Weapons: Some Observations*, in: K Wellens (Ed), *International Theory and Practice; Essays in Honour of Eric Suy*, Kluwer Law International, The Hague, 1998.

—— *The Preferential Status of Developing Countries in International Trade Law after the Uruguay Round*, in: E Denters, N Schrijver (Eds), *Reflections on International Law from the Low Countries; in Honour of Paul de Waart*, Martinus Nijhoff Publishers, The Hague, 1998.

EW Vierdag, *The Time of the 'Conclusion' of a Multilateral Treaty: Article 30 of the Vienna Convention on the Law of Treaties and Related Provisions*, British Year Book of International Law, Vol 59, 1988.

S Vöneky, *A New Shield for the Environment: Peacetime Treaties as Legal Restraints of Wartime Damage*, Review of European Community and international environmental law, Vol 9, 2000.

—— *Peacetime Environmental Law As a Basis of State Responsibility for Environmental Damage Caused by War*, in: JE Austin, CE Bruch (Eds), *The Environmental Consequences of War*, Cambridge University Press, Cambridge, 2000.

—— *Die Fortgeltung des Umweltvölkerrechts in internationalen bewaffneten Konflikten*, Springer, Berlin, 2001.

W

AH Westing, *Weapons of Mass Destruction and the Environment*, Stockholm International Peace Research Institute, Taylor & Francis, London, 1977.

—— *Proposal for an International Treaty for Protection Against Nuclear Devastation*, Bulletin of Peace Proposals, Vol 20, 1989.

—— *In Furtherance of Environmental Guidelines for Armed Forces during Peace and War*, in: JE Austin, CE Bruch (Eds), *The Environmental Consequences of War*, Cambridge University Press, Cambridge, 2000.

EP Wigner, *Roots of the Atomic Age*, in: D Masters, K Way (Eds), *One World or None: A Report to the Public on the Full Meaning of the Atomic Bomb*, McGraw-Hill, New York, 1946.

JCM Willems, *Juridische Aspecten van Kernwapens*, Nederlands Juristenblad, Vol 59, 1984.

World Health Organization; Report of the WHO Management Group on Follow-up of resolution WHA3628: 'The Role of Physicians and Other Health Workers in the Preservation and Promotion of Peace . . .', *Effects of Nuclear War on Health and Health Services*, World Health Organization, Geneva, 1987.

N Wühler, *United Nations Compensation Commission*, in: R Bernhardt (Ed), *Encyclopaedia of Public International Law; Volume Four; Quirin, Ex Parte to Zones of Peace*, Elsevier, Amsterdam, 2000.

Y

G Young, *The New Power*, in: D Masters, K Way (Eds), *One World or None: A Report to the Public on the Full Meaning of the Atomic Bomb*, McGraw-Hill, New York, 1946.

Z

K Zemanek, *Neutrality in Land Warfare,* in: R Bernhardt (Ed), *Encyclopaedia of Public International Law; Volume Three; Jan Mayen to Pueblo Incident,* Elsevier, Amsterdam, 1997.

MC Zwanenburg, *Accountability under International Humanitarian Law for United Nations and North Atlantic Treaty Organization Peace Support Operations,* Doctoral Thesis, University of Leiden, EM Meijers Instituut, Leiden, 2004.

—— *Accountability of Peace Support Operations,* Martinus Nijhoff Publishers, Leiden. 2005.

Index